PENGUIN BOOKS

THE BRAHMA PURANA VOLUME 2

Bibek Debroy is a renowned economist, scholar and translator. He has worked in universities, research institutes, the industry and for the government. He has widely published books, papers and articles on economics. As a translator, he is best known for his magnificent rendition of the Mahabharata in ten volumes, the three-volume translation of the Valmiki Ramayana and additionally the *Harivamsha*, published to wide acclaim by Penguin Classics. He is also the author of *Sarama and Her Children*, which splices his interest in Hinduism with his love for dogs.

PRAISE FOR *THE MAHABHARATA*

'The modernization of language is visible, it's easier on the mind, through expressions that are somewhat familiar. The detailing of the story is intact, the varying tempo maintained, with no deviations from the original. The short introduction reflects a brilliant mind. For those who passionately love the Mahabharata and want to explore it to its depths, Debroy's translation offers great promise . . .'—*Hindustan Times*

'[Debroy] has really carved out a niche for himself in crafting and presenting a translation of the Mahabharata . . . The book takes us on a great journey with admirable ease'—*Indian Express*

'The first thing that appeals to one is the simplicity with which Debroy has been able to express himself and infuse the right kind of meanings . . . Considering that Sanskrit is not the simplest of languages to translate a text from, Debroy exhibits his deep understanding and appreciation of the medium'—*The Hindu*

'Debroy's lucid and nuanced retelling of the original makes the masterpiece even more enjoyably accessible'—*Open*

'The quality of translation is excellent. The lucid language makes it a pleasure to read the various sto⋯⋯⋯⋯⋯⋯⋯⋯⋯⋯⋯⋯

'Extremely well-organized, and⋯⋯⋯⋯⋯⋯⋯⋯⋯⋯tion, plot summaries and notes. Th⋯⋯⋯⋯⋯⋯⋯⋯well thought-out layout which mak⋯⋯⋯⋯⋯⋯⋯*iew*

'The dispassionate vision [Debroy] brings to this endeavour will surely earn him merit in the three worlds'—*Mail Today*

'Debroy's is not the only English translation available in the market, but where he scores and others fail is that his is the closest rendering of the original text in modern English without unduly complicating the readers' understanding of the epic'—*Business Standard*

'The brilliance of Ved Vyasa comes through, ably translated by Bibek Debroy'—*Hindustan Times*

PRAISE FOR *THE VALMIKI RAMAYANA*

'It is a delight to read Bibek Debroy's translation of the Valmiki Ramayana. It's like Lord Ram has blessed Dr Debroy, and through him, blessed us with another vehicle to read His immortal story'—Amish Tripathi

'Bibek Debroy's translation of the Ramayana is easy to navigate . . . It is an effort for which Debroy deserves unqualified praise'—*Business Standard*

'A nuanced translation of a beloved epic . . . There is much to recommend this three volume set that can renew our interest in the Ramayana, surely one of the greatest stories ever told'—*Indian Express*

PRAISE FOR *THE BHAGAVATA* PURANA

'An exhaustive but accessible translation of a crucial mythological text' —*Indian Express*

'The beauty of recounting these stories lies in the manner in which the cosmic significance and the temporal implications are intermingled. Debroy's easy translation makes that experience even more sublime'—*Business Standard*

'The Puranas are 18 volumes with more than four lakh shlokas, and all in Sanskrit—the language of our ancestors and the sages, which only a few can speak and read today and only a handful have the mastery to translate. Bibek Debroy is one such master translator, who wears the twin title of economist and Sanskrit scholar, doing equal justice to both'—*Outlook*

THE BRAHMA PURANA
Volume 2

Translated *by* Bibek Debroy

PENGUIN BOOKS

An imprint of Penguin Random House

PENGUIN BOOKS

USA | Canada | UK | Ireland | Australia
New Zealand | India | South Africa | China | Singapore

Penguin Books is part of the Penguin Random House group of companies
whose addresses can be found at global.penguinrandomhouse.com

Published by Penguin Random House India Pvt. Ltd
4th Floor, Capital Tower 1, MG Road,
Gurugram 122 002, Haryana, India

| Penguin
Random House
India

First published in Penguin Books by Penguin Random House India 2021

Translation copyright © Bibek Debroy 2021

All rights reserved

10 9 8 7 6 5 4 3 2

ISBN 9780143454908

Typeset in Sabon by Manipal Technologies Limited, Manipal

Printed at Repro India Limited

www.penguin.co.in

MIX
Paper from
responsible sources
FSC® C047271

For Shaifalika Panda and Subhrakant Panda

Contents

Acknowledgements

The corpus of the Puranas is huge—in scope, coverage and size. The Mahabharata is believed to contain 100,000 *shloka*s. The Critical Edition of the Mahabharata, edited and published by the Bhandarkar Oriental Research Institute (Pune), doesn't contain quite that many. But no matter, this gives us some idea of the size. To comprehend what 100,000 shlokas mean in a standard word count, the ten-volume unabridged translation I did of the Mahabharata amounts to a staggering 2.5 million words. After composing the Mahabharata, Krishna Dvaipayana Vedavyasa composed the eighteen *mahapurana*s, or major Puranas. So the belief goes. Collectively, these eighteen Puranas amount to 400,000 *shloka*s, translating into a disconcerting and daunting number of 10 million words.

After translating the Bhagavadgita, the Mahabharata, the Harivamsha (160,000 words) and the Valmiki Ramayana (500,000 words), it was but natural to turn one's attention towards translating the Puranas. (All these translations have been, and will be, published by Penguin India.) As the most popular and most read Purana, the Bhagavata Purana chose itself as the first to be translated (3 volumes, 500,000 words). The Markandeya Purana, another popular Purana (1 volume, 175,000 words) came next. That these translations were well-received was encouragement along the intimidating journey of translating the remaining Puranas and I am indebted to the reviewers of these various translations, including those of the Bhagavata Purana and the Markandeya Purana.

Which Purana should one choose next to translate? This journey of translation has been marked by several coincidences. While still in the process of choosing, I happened to visit Pushkara for the first time in my life. Temples to Brahma are rare. Among Brahma's temples, the most important is the one in Pushkara. As I gazed at Brahma's image, at his *kamandalu* and *akshamala*, the decision made itself. It had to be the Brahma Purana. The eighteen Maha-Puranas, as the introduction explains, are sometimes individually identified with Brahma, Vishnu and Shiva. The Bhagavata Purana is a Purana identified with Vishnu. The Markandeya Purana, though identified with Brahma, is partly about Devi, and hence, by extrapolation, identified with Shiva. One should accordingly choose Brahma Purana, often described as the first Purana, though the present text is clearly not the original Brahma Purana. Average familiarity with the Brahma Purana might not be as great as with the Bhagavata Purana or the Markandeya Purana, but there was no denying the Brahma Purana's importance. Hence, this translation in two volumes, running into 390,000 words. The coincidence did not end there. I had completed the actual translation and was going to start on the Introduction. In the interim, I happened to visit Rajamahendravaram (Rajamahendrapuram or Rajahmundry if you prefer) for the first time in my life. From Pushkara Ghat, I looked on at the wide expanse of the Godavari and watched the *arati* to Goutami. I visited the Koti Lingeshvara temple. The places described in the Goutami *mahatmya* section seemed to come alive, from Tryambakeshvara to Antaravedi, from the Sahya range to the confluence with the ocean.

The journey of translation hasn't been an intimidating one only for me. Penguin India must also have thought about it several times, before going ahead with the Purana translations. Most people have some idea about the Ramayana and the Mahabharata. But the Puranas are typically rendered in such dumbed-down versions that the market has to be created. However, Penguin India also believed in the Purana Project, which still stretches into some interminable horizon in the future, almost two decades down the line. For both author and publisher, this is a long-term commitment. But Bhagavata Purana, Markandeya Purana and Brahma Purana have been done.

With the publication schedule inevitably disrupted because of the COVID pandemic, Vishnu Purana comes next, followed by Shiva Purana. I am indebted to Penguin India. In particular, Meru Gokhale, Ambar Sahil Chatterjee, Tarini Uppal and Rea Mukherjee have been exceptionally patient, persevering and encouraging. But for them, the Purana Project might not have taken off. I also thank the copy editors. These Purana translations have been brought alive by the wonderful cover designs and illustrations, and I thank the illustrators and the designers.

Ever since this translation journey started in 2006, my wife, Suparna Banerjee Debroy, has been a constant source of support, ensuring the conducive and propitious environment for the work to continue unimpeded. Part II has a dialogue between Agni and Atreyi. Agni tells Atreyi, 'At first, you were a *patni*. Then, for sustaining, you became a *bharya*. To give birth, you became *jaya*. Through your own qualities, you became *kalatra*.' The vocabulary of Sanskrit is immensely rich. There are multiple synonyms for every word, each with a slightly different nuance. This is also true of the word 'wife'—*patni*, *bharya*, *jaya* and *kalatra* are instances. Suparna has been all these and more. In every Purana text, I have been struck by the importance given to a wife, in her different roles and in the case of the Bhagavata Purana and the Markandeya Purana, I have quoted verses. The Brahma Purana is no different. सर्वमेतत्सुखार्थं हि वाञ्छन्ति मनुजाः किल। सुखमूला हि दाराश्च तस्मात्तं त्वं समाचर। 1.121.25 'Men desire wives for every kind of happiness. A wife is the source of happiness. Therefore, act in that way.' मम धर्मस्य जननी मम देहस्य चेश्वरी। धर्मार्थकाममोक्षाणां सैव नित्यं सहायिनी। तुष्टे हसन्ती रूष्टे च मम दुःखंमार्जनी। 2.10.30-31. 'She is the mother of my *dharma*. She is the mistress of my body. She is always my aide in the pursuit of *dharma*, *artha*, *kama* and *moksha*. When I am content, she laughs. When I am angry, she wipes away my misery.' One should note that this is said by a male pigeon about his wife. पुंसः सर्वेषु कार्येषु भार्यैवेह सहायिनी। स्वल्पानामपि कार्याणां नहीं सिद्धिस्तया विना। 2.59.60 'In every task undertaken by a man, the wife is an aide. Without her, there is no success in even the slightest of tasks.' The translation work is not a slight task and without her as an aide and support, it wouldn't have happened.

The Brahma Purana is rich in geography and it brought alive for me the region in, and around Odisha, a state I am especially fond of. Shaifalika Panda and Subhrakant Panda have told us stories about Odisha and have also invited us there. This is an opportunity to tell our dear friends some stories about Odisha, by dedicating this book to a warm and generous couple.

Bibek Debroy
August 2021

Introduction

The word Purana means old, ancient. The Puranas are old texts, usually referred to in conjunction with *Itihasa* (the Ramayana and the Mahabharata).[1] Whether *Itihasa* originally meant only the Mahabharata, with the Ramayana being added to that expression later, is a proposition on which there has been some discussion. But that's not relevant for our purposes. In the Chandogya Upanishad, there is an instance of the sage Narada approaching the sage Sanatkumara for instruction. Asked about what he already knows, Narada says he knows *Itihasa* and Purana, the Fifth Veda.[2] In other words, *Itihasa*–Purana possessed an elevated status. This by no means implies that the word Purana, as used in these two Upanishads and other texts too, is to be understood in the sense of the word being applied to a set of texts known as the Puranas today. The Valmiki Ramayana is believed to have been composed by Valmiki and the Mahabharata by Krishna Dvaipayana Vedavyasa. After composing the Mahabharata, Krishna Dvaipayana Vedavyasa is believed to have composed the Puranas. The use of the word composed immediately indicates that *Itihasa*–Purana are 'smriti' texts, with a human origin. They are not 'shruti' texts, with a divine origin. Composition does not mean these texts were rendered into writing. Instead, there was a process of oral transmission,

[1] For example, *shloka*s 2.4.10, 4.1.2 and 4.5.11 of the Brihadaranyaka Upanishad use the two expressions together.
[2] Chandogya Upanishad, 7.1.2.

with inevitable noise in the transmission and distribution process. Writing came much later.

Pargiter's book on the Puranas is still one of the best introductions to this corpus.[3] To explain the composition and transmission process, one can do no better than to quote him. 'The Vayu and Padma Puranas tell us how ancient genealogies, tales and ballads were preserved, namely, by the *suta*s,[4] and they describe the *suta*'s duty . . . The Vayu, Brahmanda and Visnu give an account on how the original Purana came into existence. Those three Puranas say: Krishna Dvaipayana divided the single Veda into four and arranged them, and so was called Vyasa. He entrusted them to his four disciples, one to each, namely Paila, Vaisampayana, Jaimini and Sumantu. Then with tales, anecdotes, songs and lore that had come down from the ages, he compiled a Purana, and taught it and the *Itihasa* to his fifth disciple, the suta Romaharsana or Lomaharsana . . . After that he composed the Mahabharata. The epic itself implies that the Purana preceded it . . . As explained above, the *suta*s had from remote times preserved the genealogies of gods, rishis and kings, and traditions and ballads about celebrated men, that is, exactly the material—tales, songs and ancient lore—out of which the Purana was constructed. Whether or not Vyasa composed the original Purana or superintended its compilation, is immaterial for the present purpose. After the original Purana was composed, by Vyasa as is said, his disciple Romaharsana taught it to his son Ugrasravas and Ugrasravas the sauti appears as the reciter in some of the present Puranas; and the sutas still retained the right to recite it for their livelihood. But, as stated above, Romaharsana taught it to his six disciples, at least five of whom were brahmans. It thus passed into the hands of the brahmans, and their appropriation and development of it increased in the course of time, as the Purana grew into many Puranas, as Sanskrit learning became peculiarly the province of the brahmans, and as new and frankly sectarian Puranas were composed.' Pargiter cited reasons for his belief that

---

[3] *Ancient Indian Historical Tradition*, F. E. Pargiter, Oxford University Press, London, 1922.

[4] *Suta*s were bards, minstrels, raconteurs.

the Mahabharata was composed before the original Purana, though that runs contrary to the popular perception about the Mahabharata having been composed before the Puranas. That popular and linear perception is too simplistic, since texts evolved in parallel, not necessarily sequentially.

In popular perception, Krishna Dvaipayana Vedavyasa composed the Mahabharata. He then composed the Puranas. Alternatively, he composed an original core Purana text, which has been lost, and others embellished it through additions. The adjective 'Purana', meaning old account or old text, became a proper noun, signifying a specific text. To be classified as a Purana, it has to possess five attributes—*pancha lakshmana*. That is, five topics must be discussed—*sarga*, *pratisarga*, *vamsha*, *manvantara* and *vamshanucharita*. The clearest statement of this is in the Matsya Purana. Unlike the Ramayana and the Mahabharata, there is no Critical Edition of the Puranas.[5] Therefore, citing chapter and verse from a Purana text is somewhat more difficult, since verse, if not chapter, may vary from text to text. With that caveat, the relevant *shloka* (verse) should be in the fifty-third chapter of the Matysa Purana. *Sarga* means the original or primary creation. The converse of *sarga* is universal destruction, or *pralaya*. That period of *sarga* lasts for one of Brahma's days, known as *kalpa*. When Brahma sleeps, during his night, there is universal destruction.

In measuring time, there is the notion of a *yuga* (era) and there are four *yuga*—*satya yuga* (also known as *krita yuga*), *treta yuga*, *dvapara yuga* and *kali yuga*. *Satya yuga* lasts for 4,000 years, *treta yuga* for 3,000 years, *dvapara yuga* for 2,000 years and *kali yuga* for 1,000 years. However, all these are not human years. The gods have a different timescale and these are the years of the gods. As one progressively moves from *satya yuga* to *kali yuga*, virtue (*dharma*) declines. But at the end of *kali yuga*, the cycle begins afresh, with *satya yuga*. An entire cycle, from *satya yuga* to *kali yuga*, is known

[5] The Critical Edition of the Valmiki Ramayana was brought out by the Baroda Oriental Institute, now part of the Maharaja Sayajirao University of Baroda. The Critical Edition of the Mahabharata was brought out by the Bhandarkar Oriental Research Institute, Pune.

as a *mahayuga* (great era). However, a *mahayuga* is not just 10,000 years. There is further complication. At the beginning and the end of every *yuga*, there are some additional years. These additional years are 400 for *satya yuga*, 300 for *treta yuga*, 200 for *dvapara yuga* and 100 for *kali yuga*. A *mahayuga* thus, has 12,000 years, adding years both at the beginning and at the end. 1,000 *mahayuga* make up one *kalpa* (eon), a single day for Brahma. A *kalpa* is also divided into fourteen *manvantara*s, a *manvantara* being a period during which a Manu presides and rules over creation. Therefore, there are 71.4 *mahayuga* in a *manvantara*. Our present *kalpa* is known as the Shveta Varaha Kalpa. Within that, six Manus have come and gone. Their names are (1) Svyambhuva Manu, (2) Svarochisha Manu, (3) Uttama Manu, (4) Tapasa Manu, (5) Raivata Manu and (6) Chakshusha Manu. The present Manu is known as Vaivasvata Manu. Vivasvat, also written as Vivasvan, is the name of Surya, the sun-god. Vaivasvata Manu has that name because he is Surya's son. Not only do Manus change from one *manvantara* to another. So do the gods, the ruler of the gods and the seven great sages, known as the *saptarshi*s (seven rishis). Indra is a title of the ruler of the gods. It is not a proper name. The present Indra is Purandara. However, in a different *manvantara*, someone else will hold the title. In the present seventh *manvantara*, known as Vaivasvata *manvantara*, there will also be 71.4 *mahayuga*. We are in the twenty-eighth of these. Since a different Vedavyasa performs that task of classifying and collating the Vedas in every *mahayuga*, Krishna Dvaipayana Vedavyasa is the twenty-eighth in that series. Just so that it is clear, Vedavyasa isn't a proper name. It is a title conferred on someone who collates and classifies the Vedas. There have been twenty-seven who have held the title of Vedavyasa before him and he is the twenty-eighth. His proper name is Krishna Dvaipayana, Krishna because he was dark and Dvaipayana because he was born on an island (*dvipa*). This gives us an idea of what the topic of *manvantara* is about. This still leaves *pratisarga*, *vamsha* and *vamshanucharita*. The two famous dynasties/lineages were the solar dynasty (*survya vamsha*) and lunar dynasty (*chandra vamsha*) and all the famous kings belonged to one or the other of these two dynasties. *Vamshanucharita* is about these lineages and the conduct of these kings. There were the gods and sages (*rishis*) too, not always born through a process of physical procreation. Their lineages are described under the heading of *vamsha*. Finally, within that cycle of primary creation and destruction, there are smaller and secondary cycles of creation and destruction. That's the domain of *pratisarga*. In greater or lesser degree, all the Puranas cover these five topics, some more than the others. The Purana which strictly adheres to this five-topic classification is the Vishnu Purana.

There are Puranas and Puranas. Some are known as Sthala Puranas, describing the greatness and sanctity of a specific geographical place. Some are known as Upa-Puranas, minor Puranas. The listing of Upa-Puranas has regional variations and there is no country-wide consensus about the list of Upa-Puranas, though it is often accepted there are eighteen. The Puranas we have in mind are known as Maha-Puranas, major Puranas. Henceforth, when we use the word Puranas, we mean Maha-Puranas. There is consensus that there are eighteen Maha-Puranas, though it is not obvious that this number of eighteen existed right from the beginning. The names are mentioned in several of these texts, including a *shloka* that follows the *shloka* cited from the Matsya Purana. Thus, the eighteen Puranas are (1) Agni (15,400); (2) Bhagavata (18,000); (3) Brahma (10,000); (4) Brahmanda (12,000); (5) Brahmavaivarta (18,000); (6) Garuda (19,000); (7) Kurma (17,000); (8) Linga (11,000); (9) Markandeya (9,000); (10) Matsya (14,000); (11) Narada (25,000); (12) Padma (55,000); (13) Shiva (24,000); (14) Skanda (81,100); (15) Vamana (10,000); (16) Varaha (24,000); (17) Vayu (24,000); and (18) Vishnu (23,000). A few additional points about this list. First, the Harivamsha is sometimes loosely described as a Purana, but strictly speaking, it is not a Purana. It is more like an addendum to the Mahabharata. Second, Bhavishya (14,500) is sometimes mentioned, with Vayu excised from the list. However, the Vayu Purana exhibits many more Purana characteristics than the Bhavishya Purana does. There are references to a Bhavishya Purana that existed, but that may not necessarily be the Bhavishya Purana as we know it today. That's true of some other Puranas too. Texts have been completely restructured hundreds of years later. Third, it is not just a question of Bhavishya Purana and Vayu Purana. In the lists given in some

Puranas, Vayu is part of the eighteen, but Agni is knocked out. In some others, Narasimha and Vayu are included, but Brahmanda and Garuda are knocked out. Fourth, when a list is given, the order also indicates some notion of priority or importance. Since that varies from text to text, our listing is simply alphabetical, according to the English alphabet. The text of the Brahma Purana has no such listing of Puranas. But in the last chapter of Part I, Chapter 1(138), which praises the Purana, it describes itself as the first Purana, Adi Purana. Indeed, the Brahma Purana is described as Adi Purana in several other Purana texts too, underlining its importance.

The numbers within brackets indicate the number of *shloka*s each of these Puranas has, or is believed to have. The range is from 10,000 in Brahma to a mammoth 81,100 in Skanda. The aggregate is a colossal 409,500 *shloka*s. To convey a rough idea of the orders of magnitude, the Mahabharata has, or is believed to have, 100,000 *shloka*s. It's a bit difficult to convert a *shloka* into word counts in English, especially because Sanskrit words have a slightly different structure. However, as a very crude approximation, one *shloka* is roughly twenty words. Thus, 100,000 *shloka*s become 2 million words and 400,000 *shloka*s, four times the size of the Mahabharata, amounts to 8 million words. There is a reason for using the expression 'is believed to have', as opposed to 'has'. Rendering into writing is of later vintage, the initial process was one of oral transmission. In the process, many texts have been lost, or are retained in imperfect condition. This is true of texts in general and is also specifically true of *Itihasa* and Puranas. The Critical Edition of the Mahabharata, mentioned earlier, no longer possesses 100,000 *shloka*s. Including the Harivamsha, there are around 80,000 *shloka*s. The Critical Edition of the Mahabharata has of course deliberately excised some *shloka*s. For the Puranas, there is no counterpart of Critical Editions. However, whichever edition of the Puranas one chooses, the number of *shloka*s in that specific Purana will be smaller than the numbers given above. Either those many *shloka*s did not originally exist, or they have been lost. This is the right place to mention that a reading of the Puranas assumes a basic degree of familiarity with the Valmiki Ramayana and the Mahabharata, more the latter than the former. Without that familiarity, one will often fail to appreciate the context completely. More than passing familiarity with the Bhagavad Gita, strictly speaking a part of the Mahabharata, helps.[6]

Other than the five attributes, the Puranas have a considerable amount of information on geography and even geological changes (changes in courses of river) and astronomy. Therefore, those five attributes shouldn't suggest the Puranas have nothing more. They do, and they have therefore been described as encyclopedias. Bharatavarsha is vast and heterogeneous and each Purana may very well have originated in one particular part of the country. Accordingly, within that broad compass of an overall geographical description, the extent of geographical information varies from Purana to Purana. Some are more familiar with one part of the country than with another. For example, for the Brahma Purana, Part I has extensive descriptions of the Utkala region, while Part II has the same for the region of Dandkaranya, through which the Godavari flows. Though not explicitly mentioned in the five attributes, the Puranas are also about pursuing *dharma, artha, kama* and *moksha*, the four objectives of human existence, and about the four *varna*s and the four *ashrama*s. The general understanding and practice of *dharma* is based much more on the Puranas than on the *Veda*s. Culture, notions of law, rituals, architecture and iconography are based on the Puranas. There is beautiful poetry too.

Perhaps one should mention that there are two ways these eighteen Puranas are classified. The trinity has Brahma as the creator, Vishnu as the preserver and Shiva as the destroyer. Therefore, Puranas where creation themes feature prominently are identified with Brahma (Brahma, Brahmanda, Brahmavaivarta, Markandeya). Puranas where Vishnu features prominently are identified as Vaishnava Puranas (Bhagavata, Garuda, Kurma, Matysa, Narada, Padma, Vamana, Varaha, Vishnu). Puranas where

---

[6] The Bhagavad Gita translation was published in 2006 and reprinted in 2019, the translation of the Critical Edition of the Mahabharata in 10 volumes between 2010 and 2014 (with a box set in 2015) and the translation of the Critical Edition of the Valmiki Ramayana in 2017. The translations are by Bibek Debroy, and in each case, the publisher is Penguin.

Shiva features prominently are identified as Shaiva Puranas (Agni, Linga, Shiva, Skanda, Vayu). While there is a grain of truth in this, Brahma, Vishnu and Shiva are all important and all three feature in every Purana. Therefore, beyond the relative superiority of Vishnu vis-à-vis Shiva, the taxonomy probably doesn't serve much purpose. The Brahma Purana is so named because it was originally recounted by Brahma, with subsequent transmissions by Vedavyasa and Lomaharshana, Vedavyasa's disciple. The second classification is even more tenuous and is based on the three *guna*s of *sattva* (purity), *rajas* (passion) and *tamas* (ignorance). For example, the Uttara Khanda of the Padma Purana has a few *shloka*s along these lines, recited by Shiva to Parvati. With a caveat similar to the one mentioned earlier, this should be in the 236th chapter of Uttara Khanda. According to this, the Puranas characterized by *sattva* are Bhagavata, Garuda, Narada, Padma, Varaha and Vishnu. Those characterized by *rajas* are Bhavishya, Brahma, Brahmanda, Brahmavaivarta, Markandeya and Vamana, Those characterized by *tamas* are Agni, Kurma, Linga, Matysa, Skanda and Shiva.

Within a specific Purana text, there are earlier sections, as well as later ones. That makes it difficult to date a Purana, except as a range. Across Purana texts, there are older Puranas, as well as later ones. Extremely speculatively, the dating will be something like the following. (1) Agni (800–1100 CE); (2) Bhagavata (500–1000 CE); (3) Brahma (700–1500 CE); (4) Brahmanda (400–600 CE); (5) Brahmavaivarta (700–1500 CE); (6) Garuda (800–1100 CE); (7) Kurma (600–900 CE); (8) Linga (500–1000 CE); (9) Markandeya (250–700 CE); (10) Matsya (200–500 CE); (11) Narada (900–1600 CE); (12) Padma (400–1600 CE); (13) Shiva (1000–1400 CE); (14) Skanda (600–1200 CE); (15) Vamana (450–900 CE); (16) Varaha (1000–1200 CE); (17) Vayu (350–550 CE); (18) Vishnu (300 BCE to 450 CE); and (19) Bhavishya (500–1900 CE). Reiterating once again that there is no great precision in these ranges, by this reckoning, the Vishnu Purana is the oldest and some parts of the Bhavishya Purana are as recent as the nineteenth century.

As mentioned earlier, there is no Critical Edition for the Puranas. Therefore, one has to choose a Sanskrit text one is going to translate from. If one is going to translate all the Puranas, it is preferable, though not essential, that one opts for a common source for all the Purana texts. The common source for the Brahma Purana, and all the Purana translations, is the one brought out by Nag Publishers, with funding from the Ministry of Human Resource Development.[7] To the best of my knowledge, other than this translation, there is only one unabridged translation of the Brahma Purana in English.[8] Though this translation was undertaken by a board of scholars, a discerning reader, who compares the two translations, will find that we have differed from this earlier translation in interpreting some verses and words.

For some Puranas, the range of possible dates of composition, as indicated above, is narrow. Agni, Brahmanda, Garuda, Kurma, Matsya, Varaha, Vayu and Vishnu are examples. The range is however extremely wide for Brahma Purana, from 700 to 1500 CE. There clearly was an original Brahma Purana, large chunks of which have been lost. In other words, the present Brahma Purana might not be the same as the original Brahma Purana, which has been lost.

R.C. Hazra's dissertation is still one of the best introductions to the Purana corpus, for all the Puranas, not just the Brahma Purana.[9] 'It is a general belief that the present Brahma Purana is the original one, the peculiarity being that it has suffered through additions and losses. This belief is at the base of almost all statements that have been made so long by scholars about its date and authoritativeness. From an examination of the Puranas and the Smriti-Nibandhas, however, it has been found that the present Brahma Purana is not the original one but is merely an Upa Purana of the same title and that it was known as such even as later as in the sixteenth century A.D, if not later. Almost all the Nibandha-writers have profusely drawn upon the 'Brahma Purana' or 'Brahma' which

---

[7] *The Brahmamahapuranam*, Nag Publishers, Delhi, 1985.

[8] The Brahma Purana, Parts I to IV, translated by a board of scholars, Motilal Banarsidass Publishers, Delhi, 1985 to 1986.

[9] *Studies in the Puranic Records on Hindu Rites and Customs*, R. C. Hazra, University of Dacca, 1940. This has since been reprinted several times, by different publishers.

was therefore, one of the most authoritative works in the whole range of Puranic literature. But, curiously enough, not a single of the numerous quotations made is traceable in the present Brahma Purana. The apocryphal Brahma Purana, with its borrowed and non-borrowed chapters, does not seem to have been composed, or rather compiled, earlier than the beginning of the tenth century AD. Had it been composed earlier, it should have been drawn upon, or at least referred to, by the Nibandha-writers earlier than the middle of the thirteenth century. The determination of the date of composition of the chapters of Purusottamaksetra-mahatmya is rather difficult. They could not possibly have been written earlier than the end of the ninth century AD because there is mention of the Siva-temple at the side of the Markandeya Lake. This temple was built in 820 AD by Kundala-kesarin, king of Orissa. Again, the expensive stone temple, which mythical king Indradyumna is said to have built at Purusottama-ksetra, may be identical with that built by Ananta-varman Codaganga (Saka 998–1069), one of the eastern Ganga kings of Orissa. We cannot, however, put much stress on this supposition because it is not known definitely that there was no Vishnu-temple at Puri before the time of Ananta-varman Codaganga . . . It is extremely difficult to prove that the Sun-temple mentioned by the Brahma Purana is the same as that built between 1240 and 1251 AD by Narasimhadeva I of the Ganga dynasty of Orissa. It is therefore highly probable that there was already an ancient Sun-temple at Konarka before 1240 AD, and Narasimhadeva I either built another which has superseded the ancient temple in its fame and glory or rebuilt the ancient one which can be expected to have been in a dilapidated condition.'

Stated simply, there are sections on Purushottama *kshetra* and Jagannatha, underlining the lower end of the range of 1500 CE. There are references to Indradyumna and Konarka, the present temple having been built around 1250 CE, though an earlier temple might have existed at the same site. However, there are also sections that are of earlier vintage. There is the question of the relative superiority of Shiva and Surya, vis-à-vis Vishnu. For example, the Brahma Purana has 108 of Surya's names. There are chapters that are verbatim reproductions of sections from the Mahabharata, Hari

Vamsha and other Puranas, but there are also sections on Surya that are new. One should not deduce that the Brahma Purana copied from these texts, since these various texts might have had a common origin. The sections on Utkala read like a Sthala Purana, not deserving of the status of a Maha-Purana. To compound matters, there is the Goutami Mahatmya section, about the greatness of the river Goutami or Godavari. This too, has the attribute of a Sthala Purana and is different in nature from the rest of the Brahma Purana. Should it at all have been included in a translation of the Brahma Purana? We have decided to include it, because it is part of the Brahma Purana text published by Nag Publishers. It was also included in the Brahma Purana translation undertaken earlier by the board of scholars. Accordingly, we have labelled the main Brahma Purana text as Part I of the text and the Goutami Mahatmya section as Part II of the text. As mentioned earlier, the Brahma Purana text is believed to possess 10,000 *shloka*s. Part I, the main portion of the text, has 9,137 *shloka*s, fairly close to the cited number of 10,000. Part II has 4,681 *shloka*s, with an aggregate of 13,818 *shloka*s for the entire text. There are 138 chapters in Part I and 105 in Part II, a total of 243 chapters for the entire text. In numbering the chapters, the first number refers to the part and the second number (within brackets) refers to the number of the chapter within that part. Thus, Chapter 2(35) means the thirty-fifth chapter from Part II. While parts of the Brahma Purana were composed by those familiar with the region of Utkala and Dandakaranya, Chapter 1(23) reveals some familiarity with other parts of the country too.

In the translations of the Bhagavad Gita, the Mahabharata, the Hari Vamsha, the Valmiki Ramayana, the Bhagavata Purana and the Markandeya Purana,[10] we followed the principle of not using diacritical marks. The use of diacritical marks (effectively the international alphabet of Sanskrit transliteration) makes the pronunciation and rendering more accurate, but also tends to put off readers who are less academically inclined. Since diacritical marks are not being used, there is a challenge of rendering Sanskrit

[10] *The Bhagavata* Purana, Volumes 1-3, Penguin Books, 2018. *The Markandeya* Purana, Penguin Books, 2019.

names in English. Sanskrit is a phonetic language and we have used that principle as a basis. Applied consistently, this means that words are rendered in ways that may seem unfamiliar. Hence, Gautama will appear as Goutama here. This is true of proper names, and, in a few rare cases, of geographical names. The absence of diacritical marks causes some minor problems. How does one distinguish Vasudeva Krishna from Krishna's father, Vasudeva? Often, the context will make the difference clear. If not, we have written the son as Vaasudeva and the father as Vasudeva. In translating, the attempt has been to provide a word for word translation, so that if one were to hold up the Sanskrit text, there would be a perfect match. In the process, the English is not as smooth as it might have been, deliberately so.

The intention is also to offer a translation, not an interpretation. That sounds like a simple principle to adopt and, for the most part, is easy to follow. However, there is a thin dividing line between translation and interpretation. In some instances, it is impossible to translate without bringing in a little bit of interpretation. Inevitably, interpretation is subjective. We have tried to minimize the problem by (a) reducing interpretation; (b) relegating interpretation to footnotes; and (c) when there are alternative interpretations, pointing this out to the reader through those footnotes.

But all said and done, there is no substitute to reading these texts in the original Sanskrit. To the average person, the name of the Brahma Purana may not be as familiar as that of the Bhagavata Purana or the Markandeya Purana, but it is an important Purana. Therefore, it is worth reading and translating.

Part I of Brahma Purana

Chapter 1(113) (Virtuous practices)

Vyasa said, 'In this way, a householder must properly worship the gods and the ancestors with *havya* and *kavya*.[1] Guests, relatives, servants, all other beings like animals, birds, ants, mendicants who seek alms and travelers who come to the house must be offered food. O *brahmanas*! This is good conduct for

---

[1] Oblations respectively offered to gods and ancestors.

virtuous householders. If one transgresses *nitya* and *naimmitaka* rites,[2] one commits a sin.'

The sages asked, 'O *brahmanas*! You have spoken about *nitya* and *naimittika* rites. The tasks undertaken by a man are of three types—*nitya*, *naimittika* and *kamya*. O sage! We wish to hear about *sadachara*.[3] Please tell us. What are these, enabling a man to obtain happiness in this world and in the next one?'

Vyasa replied, 'A householder must always examine his conduct. A man devoid of good conduct does not obtain benefit in this world or in the next one. Sacrifices, donations and austerities do not bring benefit to a man who transgresses the norms of *sadachara*. A person with good conduct obtains a long lifespan like that of Brahma. Tasks that have *dharma* and *sadachara* should be the signs of conduct. O *brahmanas*! I will tell you about the nature of good conduct. One must follow these with single-minded attention. A person who is a householder must seek to attain the three objectives.[4] Thereby, a householder obtains success in this world and also obtains success in the world hereafter. A person who knows himself should use one-fourth of what he possesses for the world hereafter.[5] He should use half to sustain himself and for *nitya* and *naimittika* rites. The remaining quarter should be used to increase the original wealth. O *brahmanas*! If he acts in this way, the *artha* becomes successful. To counter sins, a learned person must indulge in acts of *dharma*. Such tasks undertaken for the next world also bring success in this world. Depending on what one desires, conduct to accomplish the three objectives are of two contrary types—those that are desirable and those that are perverse. Since they are linked to each other, one must think about each of these. O supreme among *brahmanas*! Understand the ones that are perverse in nature. *Artha* that is pursued for *dharma* is good, but *artha* that is not used for *dharma*

---

[2] *Nitya* rites are those that are regularly performed, *naimittika* rites those undertaken for a special reason or occasion. *Kamya* rites are those undertaken to accomplish a desire.

[3] Good behaviour.

[4] Of *dharma*, *artha* and *kama*.

[5] Spend one-fourth of the wealth on *dharma*.

causes suffering to one's own self.[6] Similarly, *dharma* is of two types and *kama* is also of two types. One must get up at the time of brahma *muhurta*[7] and think about *dharma* and *artha*. After getting up, one must perform one's ablutions. One must control oneself and bathe and purify oneself. This is the time of the morning *sandhya*, when the *nakshatra*s are still in the western horizon.[8] As is proper, he should worship them, along with the sun. He should drink water or take food only after this. He must avoid lies, excessive talk and false and harsh words. O *brahmanas*! He must avoid wicked texts and the service of those who are wicked. He must always control himself and offer oblations in the morning and in the evening. At the time of sunrise and sunset, he must not look at the sun. Some tasks must be performed in the forenoon—cleaning the hair while looking at a mirror, brushing the teeth and washing the mouth and offering oblations to the gods. Urine and excrement must not be released in habitations within villages, *tirtha*s,[9] fields, along roads and in pastures and pens of cows. One should not look at another person's wife when she is naked or at one's own excrement. One should not see, touch or converse with a woman who is going through her period. One should not release urine or excrement in water or indulge in sexual intercourse inside water. One should not stand on urine, excrement, hair, ashes, or the sharp edges of swords. A wise person will not stand on husk, burning coal, bits of ropes and garments that are strewn along the path or are lying on the ground. A householder should eat only after he has worshipped the gods, the ancestors, humans and other creatures according to his wealth.

[6] To make the meaning clear, we have taken some liberties with the text here.

[7] A *muhurta* is a period of 48 minutes. Brahma *muhurta* is named after Brahma and is an auspicious time just before dawn, regarded as the last *muhurta* of the night. The precise hour depends on the time when the sun rises.

[8] *Sandhya* is the intervening period between day and night. The morning *sandhya* is dawn, the evening *sandhya* is dusk. Midday is also referred to as *sandhya*. A *nakshatra* is an asterism. It is usually a star, but can also be a collection of stars.

[9] A *tirtha* is a sacred place of pilgrimage, where there is water.

Purifying himself after rinsing his mouth and maintaining silence, a man must eat his food while seated facing the east or the north. He must always place his hands on his knees. Except when the food is tainted, a learned person will not point out defects in the food. He should avoid the direct use of salt and should not eat leftover food.[10] A self-controlled man will not pass urine or excrement while he is standing or walking. He will never eat anything that has been touched by *ucchishta*. If he has eaten anything that is *ucchishta*, he will avoid studying then. He will not willfully look at the sun, the moon or the *nakshatra*s. If a seat, a bed or a vessel is broken, he must not use it. A person must stand up and offer his *guru* his own seat. An intelligent person will always converse kindly with them.[11] He must always follow them and not act against them. Clad in a single garment, one should not eat or worship the gods. O *brahmanas*! Without a fire, an intelligent person will not offer oblations. A man must never bathe or sleep naked. When he scratches his head, he must not use both of his hands together. Without examining it and without any reason, a learned person does not wash his head. After the head has been washed, he must not allow oil to touch any of his limbs. One must avoid studying on any of the days when studying is prohibited. One must never show disrespect to *brahmanas*, the fire, cows or the sun. During the day, urine and excrement must be released while facing the north. During the night, it should be the south. However, at a time when there is some impediment, they can be released as one wishes. One should not speak about any wicked deed a *guru* may have done. When he is angry, one should placate him. One should not listen to those who slander him. The right of path should be given to *brahmanas*, the king, those who are miserable and afflicted, to those who are superior in learning, pregnant women, to those who are suffering from disease, those who are greater, the deaf, mute and blind and to those who are intoxicated or mad. A learned person must perform *pradakshina*[12]

---

[10] *Ucchishta*, stale or leftover food.

[11] People like a *guru*. *Guru* means a preceptor, as well as a senior.

[12] *Pradakshina* is an act of circumambulation. But it is more specific in the sense that the person/object being circumambulated must always be to one's right.

of a temple, a tree in a chaitya,[13] a crossroads where four roads meet and a *guru* who is superior in learning. One should not wear footwear, garments or garlands worn by another.

'On the eighth, fourteenth or fifteenth lunar day or on auspicious days, one should not smear the limbs with oil. On these days, one must also avoid intercourse with a woman. A wise person will never sit with his legs or feet extended. One should not fling one's legs around nor should one rub one leg against another leg. He should avoid the use of harsh words to revile and pierce the inner organs of a *pumshchali*,[14] a child or a fallen person who has performed a misdeed. A discriminating person should never be insolent, proud or harsh. He should not laugh at or revile those who are stupid, mad, distressed, malformed, suffering from delusion, lacking a limb, or a poor person. He should not impose punishment on anyone else. Nor, for the sake of instruction, should he punish a son or a disciple. When he is about to sit, a wise person will not drag the seat towards him with a foot. He should not prepare *samyava*,[15] *krisara*[16] or flesh for himself. In the morning and in the evening, he should eat only after the guests have been honoured. Without speaking, he must clean his teeth with his face towards the east or the north. O *brahmanas*! Forbidden wood must never be used for cleaning the teeth. A man must not sleep with his head facing the north or the west. One should sleep with the head facing the south or the east.[17] One should not bathe in water that smells nor should one bathe at night. Bathing at night is permissible only on days when there is an eclipse. After bathing, one should not use one's hands or a piece of

---

[13] The word *chaitya* has several meanings—sacrificial shed, temple, altar, sanctuary and a tree that grows along the road.

[14] A *pumshchali* is a loose woman, in a specific sense. *Svairini*s are loose women who have sex with anyone they want, but only with those from the same *varna*. *Kamini*s are loose women who have sex with anyone they want, irrespective of *varna*. *Pumshchali*s have no sense of discrimination and are almost like harlots.

[15] Made out of wheat flour, sugar, ghee and milk.

[16] *Krisara* is a dish made out of sesamum and grain.

[17] The text uses the respective expressions Agastya's direction and Purandara's direction.

cloth to wipe the water from the body. After bathing, one should not
get rid of the water by shaking one's head or shaking one's garment.
Unless he has bathed, a learned person will never apply unguents
on his body. He should not wear a red garment, a black garment,
or a garment that is multicoloured. Garments or ornaments must
not be contrary to the rules. A damaged or torn garment must never
be used. One should not eat food that has hair or lice in it, food
that has been trodden upon or food that a dog has looked at. One
should avoid meat licked by a dog, meat where the essence has been
tainted, the flesh from the back and flesh cooked in vain.[18] A man
should not use salt directly. O *brahmanas*! Food that has been left
for a long time, food that is dry or is tainted in any other way must
be avoided. O supreme *brahmanas*! However, derived products
of cakes, vegetables, sugarcane and milk and derived products of
meat need not be avoided even if they have been left for a very
long time. One should not sleep between sunrise and sunset. A man
must not sleep after a bath. He should not sleep when his mind is
distracted. He should not sleep when seated. When he sits down, or
when he lies down, he must not make a sound. A man must not eat
without giving a share to those who are looking. According to the
injunctions, he must eat after he has bathed in the morning and in
the evening. A learned man will not have intercourse with another
person's wife. If a man has intercourse with another man's wife, his
good merits from sacrifices and civic works are destroyed. In this
world, there is nothing that is as destructive of a man's lifespan as
having intercourse with another person's wife. After properly and
reverentially performing *achamana*,[19] one should perform the rites
for the gods, the fire and the ancestors and greet the *guru*. The act
of taking food must be done only after this. The water used for
achamana must be without foam, without a smell and without dirt.
The rinsing must be done with the head facing the north or the east.
For cleaning oneself,[20] five kinds of earth must be avoided—earth
from inside a water body, from the habitation, from a termite-hill,

[18] Without the intention of offering it at a sacrifice.
[19] Ablutions, the rinsing of the mouth.
[20] After passing stool.

from a rat-hole and leftover earth from an earlier act of cleaning. After cleaning oneself, the hands and the feet must be cleaned attentively. Seated, with his knees next to each other, a man must sip water three or four times. He must touch his limbs and his head with the water twice. With these rites, he purifies himself properly with water. After sneezing, spitting or wearing a garment, a learned person must rinse his mouth. After sneezing, spitting, passing wind or passing excrement, he must do this. When he touches something that should not be touched, he must perform *achamana*, look at the sun and touch his right ear to the extent he can. He must follow this in the due order. If one act in the order is missing, he should proceed with the next one. It is said that if a preceding act is missing, one should proceed with the subsequent one. One should not gnash one's teeth, nor should one strike one's own body. At the time of the two *sandhya*s, one should not sleep, study or eat. One should not indulge in sexual intercourse or depart at the time of *sandhya*. In the afternoon, one should faithfully offer oblations to the ancestors. This is also true of washing the head or performing rites for the gods and the ancestors. Shaving must be done while facing the north or the east. Even when she has been born in a good lineage, a woman who is diseased, without a limb or malformed in a limb must be avoided. The girl one marries should not be related on the father's side for seven generations and on the mother's side for five generations. It is necessary to avoid all jealousy and protect the wife. Sleep and sexual intercourse during the day must be avoided. Acts that cause torment to others and affliction to creatures must always be shunned. During the four days when a woman goes through her period, all the *varna*s must avoid association with her. If the birth of a daughter is to be avoided, one must avoid intercourse on the fifth night and indulge in it on the sixth night. Even nights are the best. Boys are born through intercourse on even nights and girls through intercourse on odd nights. Intercourse on festive days[21] gives birth to a son who is against *dharma*. Intercourse in the evening gives birth to a eunuch. When shaving, a discriminating person will avoid a desolate spot. One should never listen to what insolent people say.

[21] *Parva* days, when intercourse is to be avoided.

An excellent seat should never be affectionately offered to a person who is not excellent. O *brahmanas*! A wise person has a bath after shaving, after intercourse with a woman, after vomiting and after visiting a cremation ground. O *brahmanas*! The gods, the Vedas, *brahmanas*, virtuous and great-souled ones, preceptors, women who are faithful to their husbands, those who perform sacrifices and ascetics must not be criticized. Nor should one laugh at them. One should wear white garments and adorn oneself with white flowers. One must always be clad in what is auspicious, never in something that is inauspicious. A learned person must never associate with, or contract a friendship with, a person who is insolent, mad, foolish, proud, wicked in conduct, those who are defiled because of age and class, those who spend excessively, men who are enemies, those who are unskilled in their work, those who are censured, those who associate with rogues, those who are without money, men who are addicted to arguing and those who are debased in any other way. One should stand up and greet well-wishers, those who have been initiated, the king, *snataka*s[22] and the father-in-law when they visit the house, using words of welcome. O *brahmanas*! One should offer them proper hospitality according to one's means. When they have stayed for more than a year and they return to their own residences, they must be honoured in the proper way.'

'After having honoured them in the due order, he must worship the fire, progressively rendering oblations into it. The first offering must be given to Brahma, the second to Prajapati, the third to the divinities in the house, the fourth to Kashyapa and the last to Anumati.[23] This is the way offerings must be made in the house. I have already described to you the recommended *nitya* rituals. O *brahmanas*! Hear about how offerings must be made to the Vishvadevas. In separate regions, there must be separate offerings for the divinities. Three offerings must be made to Parjanya, the

---

[22] A *snataka* is a student who has finished studying and is ready to embark on the next phase of life. The word *snataka* is derived from *snana* (the act of taking a bath), ritually performed before anything auspicious is undertaken.

[23] Anumati is the personified form of the fifteenth lunar *tithi*.

earth and the water-pot.[24] After this, an offering will be given to Vayu and beginning with the east, each cardinal direction must progressively be given offerings. Progressive offerings are rendered to Brahma, the sky, the sun, the Vishvadevas and all the creatures in the universe. Purifying oneself, offerings are given to Usha[25] and the lord of creatures[26] in the northern direction. Uttering '*svadha cha namah*', offerings to the ancestors are given in the southern direction.[27] Using his right hand, he will then follow the rituals, take the remaining bit of food and water and offer it in the north-western direction to Vayu, uttering, 'To Yakshma.'[28] Thereafter, he will prostrate himself before the gods and the *brahmanas*. For *achamana*, brahma-*tirtha* is the line at the base of the right thumb.[29] The region between the right thumb and the right index finger is said to be *pitri-tirtha*. With the exception of the *nandimukha* ritual, this is used to offer water to the ancestors.[30] The tips of the fingers are known as *deva-tirtha* and are used for rites connected with the gods. The base of the little finger is known as *kaya-tirtha* and is used for rites connected with Prajapati. The rites for the gods and the ancestors must always be performed with these *tirtha*s and an inappropriate *tirtha* must never be used. Brahma-*tirtha* is best for *achamana* and *pitri-tirtha* must always be used for the ancestors. *Deva-tirtha* must be used for the gods and *kaya-tirtha* must be used for rites connected with Prajapati. During the *nandimukha* ritual, a wise person will use *kaya-tirtha* to perform the *pinda* and water rites. Everything connected with Prajapati must be through *kaya-tirtha*.

[24] We have translated *manika* as water-pot. The word also means jewel.

[25] The personified form of dawn.

[26] Shiva, the word used is *bhutapati*.

[27] 'Svadha! I bow down to you too.' *Svadha* is an exclamation made when offering oblations to the ancestors. *Svaha* is an exclamation made when offering oblations to the gods.

[28] Loosely, the sense is that 'let disease be kept away'.

[29] These *tirtha*s are parts of the hand, sacred to specific divinities.

[30] Nandimukhas are a special class of ancestors and the *nandimukha* rite is for them.

'A discriminating person must not hold water and fire at the same time. In front of *guru*s, gods, ancestors and *brahmanas*, he will not stretch out his legs. He glances towards[31] a cow that is suckling her calf. He should not drink water from the cup of his palms. The rites of purification, whether the transgression is major or minor, must be undertaken at the right time. An intelligent person will not delay the rite of purification. One should not use one's mouth to blow into a fire. O *brahmanas*! One should not reside in a region that does not have four things—a person who lends money, a physician, a learned brahmana and a river full of water. A wise person will always reside in a place where there is a powerful king who is devoted to *dharma* and has control over his servants. How can there be happiness when the king is wicked? There is happiness from residing in a place where self-controlled citizens always follow law and the people are devoid of jealousy and are tranquil. A discriminating person should live in a kingdom where the farmers are generally strong and not excessively proud, where there is no dearth of crops and medicinal herbs. O *brahmanas*! One should never live in a place where three kinds of people exist—those who are always eager to conquer, those who are always addicted to festivities and those who are former enemies. A learned person will always reside with companions who are good in conduct. O *brahmanas*! For the sake of your welfare, I have described all this to you.'

'I will next tell you about food and about how it is to be taken. Stale rice, even if it has been kept for a long time, can be eaten as long as it is soaked in oil. Products of wheat, barley and milk, when kept for a long time can be eaten without being soaked in oil. The meat of hares, tortoises, lizards, porcupines and fish with scales can be eaten. However, the meat of domesticated pigs and domesticated hens should not be eaten. There is no taint from eating meat that is leftover after the offerings to the gods and ancestors or at *shraddha* ceremonies in accordance with the wishes of *brahmanas*, once it has been purified,[32] or meat that is for medication. Conch shells, stones,

---

[31] Meaning, he should not call the cow at that time.
[32] By sprinkling water over it.

gold, silver, ropes, garments, vegetables, roots, fruits, wickerwork baskets, leather objects, jewel-encrusted garments, coral, pearls and vessels and spoons are also best cleaned with water. Iron is cleaned with water, stone through rubbing and oily vessels with warm water. Winnowing baskets, deer skin, mortars, pestles and heaps of garments are cleaned by sprinkling water over the collection. All kinds of bark are properly cleaned with water and earth. Objects made of wool or hair are cleaned with *kalka* paste[33] and then with the oil of sesamum seeds. There must always be purification and cleansing. Thus, a cotton garment is always purified with water and ashes. Objects made of ivory, bones or horn are purified through paring. An earthen vessel is purified when it is baked again. Something obtained as alms, an object fashioned through the hand of an artisan, an article traded and a woman's mouth are pure. Something brought along a road, an object that is unknown, something that has been cleaned by a retinue of servants, something that has been praised earlier, something that is long past, an object that has passed through many hands, a light object, something that has many children inside it, something for which aged people have made efforts, a store of coal when the required task is over and the two breasts of a woman are pure. Odourless water that has a flow is said to be pure. The ground is purified over time and when cattle roam over it. A dwelling-house is purified by smearing,[34] scraping, sprinkling and sweeping. Something tainted with hair, worms or flies, or smelt by cattle, is purified with earth, water and ashes. Objects made of *udumbara*[35] wood are cleaned with acid, those made of tin through a caustic solution, those of copper with water and ashes and through repeated washing. Something with a bad smell is purified by using earth and water to remove the bad smell. Other objects are thus purified when their bad complexion and bad odour has been removed. Meat dropped by a *chandala*[36] or a

---

[33] A paste made out the sediment of oily substances.
[34] With cow dung.
[35] The fig tree.
[36] One usually equates *chandala* with shudra, but there were eight different types of shudras, though the listing varies. For instance, *vyadha*

predatory creature is pure. Oil that has spilt on the road is pure. Water that satisfies a cow is pure. Dust particles, a fire, a horse, a cow, a shadow, rays,[37] the wind, the earth and a drop of water do not get polluted even if they come into contact with something vile like a fly. The mouth of a goat or the mouth of a horse is pure, but this is not true of the mouth of a calf when its mother is still suckling it. A fruit brought down by a bird is pure. Like an object that is traded, a seat, a bed, a vehicle, the bank of a river and grass are pure because the rays of the sun and the moon fall on them and the air passes over them. After travelling on the road, bathing, eating, drinking and other tasks, one must change one's garment and perform *achamana*. If one comes into contact with a bad road, mud and water or an object made of brick or clay, nothing need be done. They are purified by the wind. If a large quantity of rice has been tainted, a bit from the top should be thrown away. The remainder is purified by sprinkling some earth and water on it. If one eats something that should not be eaten, whether voluntarily or involuntarily, to atone for this sin, one should fast for three nights. If a person touches a woman who is going through her period, a woman who has touched her, a woman who has just delivered, an outcaste or one who has borne a dead body, he must purify himself by having a bath. If a brahmana touches a human bone that has fat in it, he is purified by bathing. However, if he touches a human bone without fat, he should perform *achamana*, touch a cow and look at the sun. A wise person will never walk over blood or spit or leap over an obstacle. Leftovers, urine, excrement and water used to wash the feet must be cast away outside the house. One should not bathe in another person's water without taking up five *pinda*s of clay from there. One should bathe in natural ponds,[38] the Ganga and rivers and lakes. A wise person will not remain in gardens and similar places at the wrong time. One should not converse with those who are hated by people or with women who do not have

---

(hunter), *vyalagrahi* (those who eat snakes), *vagatita* (one with whom one does not speak), *chandala* (*brahmana* mother, shudra father) and so on.

[37] Referring to the sun or the moon.

[38] Literally, those dug by the gods.

brave sons. One should not touch or have a conversation with those who criticize the gods, the ancestors, the sacred texts, sacrifices and *sanyasi*s. If one happens to touch or converse with them, one should purify oneself by looking at the sun. A wise person who looks at a woman going through her period, an abandoned dead body that has been cast away, a person who is against *dharma*, a woman who has just delivered, a eunuch, a naked person, an outcast, a person who carries dead bodies or an adulterer, should purify himself in the same way. When a person who knows about *dharma* touches a mendicant who should not be fed, a heretic, a cat, an ass, a cock, a person who has fallen down, a *chandala* or a person who carries a dead body, a woman during her period or a village pig, he is purified by taking a bath. This must also be done if a person touches a woman who has just delivered, a man who is tainted and polluted in this way, a person who does not perform the daily *nitya* tasks in his home, a person who has been abandoned by *brahmanas*, or a worst among men who lives on sin. The *nitya* rites must never suffer. I will tell you about the only occasions when they need not be performed. In the case of birth and death, a brahmana can refrain from donations and offering oblations for ten days. A *kshatriya* can refrain from *nitya* rites for twelve days, a *vaishya* for fifteen days and a shudra for a month. Thereafter, as instructed, one should engage in one's own tasks. The dead body must be cremated outside the house by people who belong to the same *gotra*. After this, water is offered to the departed spirit on the first, third, seventh or ninth day.[39] On the fourth day, the ashes and bones[40] are collected by people who belong to the same *gotra*. After they have undertaken the task of collection, it is recommended that their upper bodies be touched. After the collection, all the rites should be performed by those who are from the same *gotra*. On the day of death, only *sapinda*s are allowed to touch each other.[41] When death is caused

[39] Depending respectively on the *varna*.

[40] *Asthi*, those left after cremation.

[41] There is a long list of those who are *sapinda*s, such as, in the absence of a son, a daughter, a daughter's son, a father, a mother, a brother, a brother's son and so on. There is another such list of *sahodaka*s.

by a weapon, hanging by a rope, fire or poison, the same method must be followed. When death occurs because of an act of *praya*,[42] when the person dies when he is in some other country or when the dead person is a child, the period of impurity lasts for one day, though some say impurity lasts for three days. If a *sapinda* dies after another *sapinda*'s death, the period of impurity is reckoned from the day on which the first *sapinda* died. The daily purification rites mentioned earlier, must be performed. These are also the recommended norms for a birth, to be followed after delivery by *sapinda*s and *sahodaka*s. When a son is born, a father must have a bath wearing the clothes he was wearing at the time of birth. If after the birth of the first son, another son is born, the period of impurity is reckoned from the day of the first birth. After ten, twelve, fifteen days and a month,[43] all the *varna*s should perform their respective recommended rites. Thereafter, for the departed spirit, an *ekoddishta*[44] ceremony must be performed. As gifts to *brahmanas*, learned people give whatever is cherished in the world and whatever is loved in the house. Desiring one's undecaying prosperity, in the name of the departed spirits, one should give all that possesses qualities. When those days are over, one touches water, a mount or a weapon. Each *varna* undertakes the proper completion of the rites. If one observes all the rites recommended and purifies oneself, one obtains prosperity in this world and in the next world. If one studies the three Vedas every day, one becomes learned. Having accumulated riches according to *dharma*, one must make efforts to undertake sacrifices. O *brahmanas*! One must act so that one is not condemned. One must unhesitatingly do whatever need not be kept a secret from great people. O *brahmanas*! If a householder acts in this way, he obtains *dharma*, *artha* and *kama* in this world and all that is auspicious in the world hereafter. This is the secret to increasing the lifespan, prosperity and intelligence. This is sacred and destroys all sins. This is auspicious and ensures prosperity, nourishment and freedom from disease. It ensures fame and deeds

---

[42] Act of giving up one's life by fasting to death.
[43] As is obvious, the duration depends on the *varna*.
[44] A monthly rite continued for one year.

and increases the strength and energy of men. O supreme among sages! It ensures the excellent objective of heaven and men must always observe it, whether they are *brahmanas*, *kshatriyas*, *vaishyas* or shudras. Those who desire their benefit must carefully get to know everything about this. Having learnt it, a person must undertake it at the right time. He will then be freed from all sins and attain greatness in heaven. O excellent *brahmanas*! You have been told about the essence of all essences. This is the *dharma* mentioned in the *shruti* and *smriti* texts. O *brahmanas*! This must never be revealed to non-believers, those who are evil in intelligence, those who are insolent or foolish and those who indulge excessively in false debates.'

Chapter 1(114) (The tasks of *varnas* and *ashramas*)

The sages said, 'O *brahmanas*! We wish to hear about the specific dharma for different *varnas*. O noble brahmana! Please tell us about the dharma for the four *ashramas*.'[45]

Vyasa replied, 'Listen attentively. In due order, I will tell you about the *dharma* for *brahmanas*, *kshatriyas*, *vaishyas* and shudras and the *dharma* for the *varnas*. A brahmana must always practice compassion, donations, austerities, sacrifices to the gods and self-studying. He must always observe the water-rites and maintain the sacrificial fire. O *brahmanas*! For the sake of subsistence, he will perform sacrifices for others. He will teach *brahmanas*. In the case of sacrifices, he will consciously accept donations. O *brahmanas*! He must always do what ensures benefit for everyone and never cause harm to anyone. Friendliness towards all creatures is the greatest wealth for a brahmana. O *brahmanas*! His intelligence must be such that he regards a cow and someone else's jewel

---

[45] The four stages (*ashramas*) of life are *brahmacharya* (celibate student stage), *garhasthya* (householder), *vanaprastha* (retiring to the forest) and *sannyasa* (stage of renunciation).

as equal. O *brahmanas*! When he has intercourse with his wife just after her period is over, that is praised. A *kshatriya* will give *brahmanas* whatever they wish for. O *brahmanas*! He must study and perform different kinds of sacrifices. He must earn his living through weapons. Protecting the earth is the best means of subsistence for him. Protection of the earth has been thought of first. Lords of the earth have become successful in their objectives by protecting the earth. When there is a king, sacrifices and other rites are protected. The task of a king is to punish the wicked and protect the virtuous. That is the way he establishes the *varna*s and attains the desired worlds. O supreme sages! Brahma, the grandfather of the worlds, gave *vaishya*s animal husbandry, trade and agriculture as a means of subsistence. Studying, sacrifices and donations are also praised as *dharma* for them, as is the performance of *nitya*, *naimittika* and other rites. A shudra's tasks derive from the sustenance of *dvija*s.[46] Therefore, he must give them whatever riches he earns through sale and purchase or artisanship, in the form of donations. A shudra must also perform all the rites for the ancestors and *paka-yajna*.[47] O supreme *brahmanas*! The following are said to be general qualities of all the *varna*s—receiving gifts for the sustainment of servants and others, approaching one's own wife at the time of her period, compassion towards all creatures, forbearance, lack of pride, truthfulness, the easy observance of purity and everything auspicious, amiable speech, friendliness, lack of desire, lack of miserliness and lack of jealousy. These are the general characteristics of all the *ashrama*s. O *brahmanas*! Secondary *dharma* and qualities also exist for *brahmanas* and others. When there is a calamity, a brahmana can follow the tasks indicated for a *kshatriya* or a *vaishya*. In times of a calamity,

---

[46] *Dvija* is sometimes used as a synonym for *brahmana*. But it actually means a person who has had two births, the first the physical birth and the second the symbolic birth at the time of the sacred thread ceremony. Thus, as is the case here, *dvija* also means the first three *varna*s.

[47] This has been interpreted as the recommended modes for cooking food offered at sacrifices. However, *paka-yajna* also means a simple sacrifice undertaken at home and that seems to be a better meaning.

a *kshatriya*[48] can follow the tasks indicated for a *vaishya* or a shudra and a *vaishya* can follow the tasks indicated for a shudra. O *brahmanas*! If he is incapable, he can give up either. However, even in the case of a calamity, one must not mix up the two kinds of tasks.[49] O *brahmanas*! I have, thus described to you the *dharma* of the *varnas*.

'I will now properly tell you about the *dharma* of the *ashramas*. Listen, after the sacred thread ceremony[50] has been performed, a boy must study the Vedas. O *brahmanas*! He will reside in his *guru*'s house, controlling himself and practicing *brahmacharya*. His task there is to practice purity in conduct and serve his preceptor. He must observe the vows and turn his mind towards receiving the Vedas. O *brahmanas*! He must control himself and worship the sun and the fire at the time of both the *sandhya*s. He must stand up and greet the preceptor. When the preceptor stands, he will stand. When the preceptor walks, he will walk. When the preceptor is seated, he will be seated below him. O best among *brahmanas*! A disciple must avoid anything that is against the preceptor. He will stand in front of him and with a single-minded attention study the Vedas recited by him.[51] When he is permitted by his preceptor, he will eat the food received as alms. He will bathe in the water in which his teacher[52] has bathed. He must be ready to collect kindling and water at dawn. After having received the Vedas he is entitled to receive, a wise person will take leave from his *guru* and having taken his leave, will enter the stage of *garhasthya*. Following the norms, he will obtain a wife and earn riches through his own tasks. O *brahmanas*! According to his own capacity, he must perform all the tasks indicated for a householder. He must worship the ancestors,

---

[48] The word used is *rajanya*, meaning royalty. But this means *kshatriya*.

[49] That is, a *kshatriya* must not simultaneously follow the tasks of both a *vaishya* and a shudra.

[50] Known as *upanayana*.

[51] The preceptor.

[52] We have deliberately used the word teacher, as opposed to preceptor (*guru*). Here, the text uses the word *acharya*. Unless used synonymously, in the hierarchy of teachers, *upadhyaya* is inferior to *acharya* and *acharya* is inferior to *guru*. The word for disciple/student is *shishya*.

perform sacrifices to the gods, offer food to the guests, honour the
sages by studying and have offspring to honour Prajapati. Through
his offerings he will honour creatures and through his true words,
the entire world. In this way, through his own clean deeds, a man
obtains the worlds. There are those who follow *brahmacharya* and
travel around while sustaining themselves on what is obtained as
alms. They depend on the householder. Therefore, the stage of
garhasthya is the best. O *brahmanas*! There are *brahmanas* who
roam around the earth, disseminating the Vedas, bathing in *tirtha*s
and visiting different places on earth. They have no fixed abode.
When they are hungry in the evening, it is the householder who
always offers them food and shelter. Therefore, it is said that they
depend on the householder. A householder must welcome them
with gifts and pleasant words. When they come to his house,
he must offer them a bed, a seat and food. When a guest who
has arrived at a house goes away dissatisfied, he leaves his bad
deeds with the householder and takes away the householder's
good deeds. For a householder, the following are never praised—
disrespect to others, egotism, insolence, slander, causing harm and
harsh words. If a householder properly follows the supreme norms
that have been indicated, he is freed from every kind of bondage
and attains excellent worlds. O *brahmanas*! When a householder
is ripe and has completed all the tasks meant for a householder,
he leaves for the forest. He can entrust the care of his wife with
his sons, or take her with him. He survives on leaves, roots and
fruits. He does not cut his hair or shave his beard and his hair is
matted. O *brahmanas*! Like a sage, he lies down on the ground
and can be a guest at anyone's house. His upper garment must
be made of hide, *kasha* grass or *kusha* grass. O supreme among
brahmanas! It is recommended that he should bathe thrice a day.
For him, the following are praised—worshipping the gods, offering
oblations honouring all those who visit him, begging for alms and
performing sacrifices. It is recommended that he smear his limbs
with oil obtained from the forest. O Indras among *brahmanas*!
A sage who is in *vanaprastha* must always tolerate extreme heat
and cold. Those are his austerities. Like a fire, it burns down his
taints and he attains the eternal worlds. The learned have spoken

of the fourth *ashrama* as that of the *bhikshu*.[53] O excellent ones! I will speak about it. Understand its nature. O supreme among *brahmanas*! He must give up all attachment towards his sons, wives and objects. He will proceed to the fourth *ashrama* only when he has given up all envy. O supreme *brahmanas*! He will not undertake any task indicated for the three *varnas*. He will be friendly towards all creatures and treat all of them as his friends. In his thoughts, words and deeds, he will never cause injury to creatures born from the womb, from the egg and so on. He will give up all sense of attachment. He will stay in a village for one night and in a city for five nights.[54] He will not exhibit affection or hatred for inferior species. For the sake of sustaining his life, he should visit houses and ask for alms, but only when the coal is not burning and when the incumbents have not eaten.[55] He will not be distressed when nothing is obtained. Nor will he be delighted when something is obtained. He will always abhor gains that are extremely sought after. Such extremely sought-after gains bind down a sage. Casting aside, *kama*, *krodha*, *darpa*, *lobha*, *moha* and the other taints, he will free himself from the sense of 'mine'.[56] As he roams around the earth, he will grant all creatures freedom from fear. When he is freed from everything connected with the body, he will never suffer from fear. He will perform the *agnihotra* sacrifice from within his own body, using his own mouth to offer oblations to the fire that is within his body. A brahmana will use what he has obtained through begging to offer oblations to the fire that is in his consciousness. When he is in the *ashrama* of *moksha*, his resolution and intelligence must be to purify himself in this way. Like a fire without kindling, such *dvijas*[57] are serene and go to Brahma's world.'

[53] Literally, a mendicant who begs. This is *sannyasa*.

[54] So that there is no attachment towards a home.

[55] When the cooking is over and there is still food in the house.

[56] The six vices are *kama* (desire), *krodha* (anger), *lobha* (avarice), *moha* (delusion), *mada* (arrogance) and *matsarya* (jealousy). *Darpa* is a synonym for *mada*.

[57] Meaning the first three *varnas*, not just *brahmanas*.

Chapter 1(115) (Transition between *varna*s)

The sages said, 'O immensely fortunate one! You know everything and are engaged in the welfare of all creatures. O sage! There is nothing that you do not know, of the past, the present and the future. Through what *karma* does one obtain a destination as an inferior *varna* and how does one attain the status of a superior *varna*? O immensely intelligent one! Please tell us this.' Through what karma does a shudra obtain the status of a brahmana? We wish to hear how a brahmana becomes a shudra.'

Vyasa replied, 'The beautiful summit of the Himalayas is decorated with many kinds of minerals. There are many kinds of trees and creepers and varied wonders. The three-eyed Mahadeva, the destroyer of Tripura,[58] resides there. The goddess, the daughter of the king of the mountains,[59] bowed down before the lord of the gods. O *brahmanas*! In ancient times, the one with the beautiful eyes asked him this question. O supreme among sages! I will tell you about this. Listen.'

Uma said, 'O illustrious one! O destroyer of Bhaga's eyes and Pusha's teeth![60] O one who destroyed Daksha's sacrifice! O three-eyed one! I have a great doubt. In ancient times, the illustrious Svayambhu[61] created the four *varna*s. How and through what *karma* does a *vaishya* become a shudra? Through the practice of what *dharma* does the reverse progression happen?[62] Through what karma is a brahmana born as a shudra? O lord! Through what karma does a *kshatriya* become a shudra? O god! O Bhutapati![63] I have a doubt about this. Please tell me. Through what kind of nature can the three *varna*s become *brahmanas*?'

---

[58] Shiva destroyed a city of the demons known as Tripura.

[59] Uma, Shiva's consort, was the daughter of the Himalayas.

[60] At the time of Daksha's sacrifice, Shiva gouged out Bhaga's eyes and knocked down Pusha's teeth.

[61] Brahma.

[62] *Pratiloma*, the upward progression, a shudra becoming a *vaishya*.

[63] Lord of beings, Shiva's name.

Maheshvara replied, 'O goddess! The status of becoming a brahmana is difficult to obtain. It is my view that *brahmanas* are naturally auspicious, while *kshatriya*s, *vaishya*s and shudras are naturally not auspicious. Through wicked deeds of *karma*, *brahmanas* are dislodged from their position. Though they have obtained the status of the best *varna*, they are flung down from there. If a *kshatriya* or a *vaishya* follows the *dharma* of a brahmana and earns his living through what is specified for a brahmana, he obtains the status of a brahmana. If a brahmana gives up what is meant for him and follows the *dharma* of a *kshatriya*, he is dislodged from the status of being a brahmana and is born as a *kshatriya*. The status of being a brahmana is extremely difficult to obtain. However, having attained it, out of avarice or confusion, if a brahmana undertakes the tasks of a *vaishya*, the brahmana becomes a *vaishya*. That is also how a *vaishya* becomes a shudra. A brahmana who is dislodged from his own *dharma* becomes a shudra. A person who has been ousted from his own *varna* goes to hell. A person who has been dislodged from Brahma's world is born as a shudra. O immensely fortunate one! A *kshatriya* or a *vaishya* who deviates from his own *dharma* and *karma* and follows the *karma* of a shudra is dislodged from his own *varna* and is born as one whose *varna* is mixed. Such a brahmana, *kshatriya* or *vaishya* can also become a shudra. A shudra engaged in his own *dharma*, one who is pure and conversant with *jnana* and *vijnana*[64] and knowledgeable about *dharma*, one who is devoted to *dharma*, obtains the fruits of that *dharma*. O goddess! In this connection, the *brahman* has also been spoken about. Those who desire success in the pursuit of *dharma* must be devoted to adhyatma.[65] O goddess! The food cooked by an *ugra*[66] is condemned. Food cooked collectively or at the time of birth or death, is also condemned. When the cooking of food is announced publicly or when that food has been cooked by a shudra, that too must never be taken. O goddess! Gods and great-souled

---

[64] *Jnana* is knowledge gleaned from the sacred texts and the *guru*, *vijnana* is that obtained through inward reflection.

[65] Beyond the *atman*, that is, the metaphysical.

[66] Someone with a *kshatriya* father and a shudra mother.

ones always condemn food cooked by a shudra. It is my view that
what has emanated from the grandfather's mouth is sufficient
proof. If a brahmana dies with the remnants of food cooked by a
shudra in his stomach or offers oblations to the fire or performs
sacrifices with such food,[67] he obtains the status of being a shudra.
Because of the leftovers of food cooked by a shudra, such a
brahmana is expelled from the status of being a brahmana and
becomes a shudra. There is no need to reflect on this. If a brahmana
dies with the remnants of food cooked by any *varna* in his stomach,
that brahmana attains the status of the *varna* by whose food he has
sustained himself. The status of being a brahmana brings happiness
and is extremely different to obtain. Having obtained it, if a person
shows it disrespect by eating food that should not be eaten, he falls
down from the status of being a brahmana. A drunkard, one who
kills a brahmana, a thief, a robber, one who breaks his vows, an
impure person, one who does not study, a wicked person, a greedy
person, one who performs wicked deeds, a deceiver, one who does
not observe vows, one who is the husband of a *vrishala* lady,[68] a
pimp, a person who sells *soma* and a person who serves those who
should not be served—such a brahmana falls down from the status
of being a brahmana. One who has intercourse with his preceptor's
wife, one who hates his preceptor, one who loves reviling his
preceptor and one who hates *brahmanas*—such a brahmana falls
down from the status of being a brahmana. O goddess! By
performing the following auspicious deeds, a shudra becomes a
brahmana and a *vaishya* becomes a *kshatriya*. A shudra becomes a
vaishya by properly undertaking all the tasks recommended for a
shudra, offering hospitality to everyone and eating the left over
food, carefully attending to and serving the superior *varna*s, showing
respect to those who are superior, always remaining established on
the virtuous path, always worshiping gods and *dvijas*, observing the
vow of offering hospitality to everyone, attentively having

---

[67] We have translated this literally. But this may mean offering oblations
to the digestive fire.

[68] *Vrishala* is a synonym for shudra, though it has some specific
meanings too.

intercourse with his wife at the time of her period, being restrained in diet, being skilled, by searching for virtuous people and not eating meat in vain.[69] A *vaishya* becomes a brahmana by being truthful in speech, by being free from *ahamkara*, by being bereft of the opposite pair of sentiments, by being accomplished in conciliation, by always performing sacrifices, by studying, by being extremely pure, by being controlled, by doing good deeds towards *brahmanas*, by not being envious of any of the *varna*s, by following the vows of a householder, by eating twice a day, by eating leftovers, by following a restrained diet, by being without desire, by not speaking about himself, by performing *agnihotra* sacrifices, by following the rites and offering oblations into the fire, by being hospitable to all guests and eating leftover food and by maintaining the three fires.[70] A pure *vaishya* who deserves to be born in a *kshatriya* lineage is a true *vaishya*. If a *vaishya* remains clean since birth, he is born as a *kshatriya*. If he is consecrated, clean and devotes himself to the vows, he becomes a brahmana. He performs sacrifices with copious quantities of *dakshina*. If he studies and always resorts to the three fires, he goes to heaven. A *kshatriya* must follow *dharma* and protect the subjects. His hand must always be wet.[71] Pure in his discrimination, he must always distinguish the true from the false. To obtain success in the pursuit of *dharma*, *artha* and *kama*, he must use his staff of *dharma* to burn down.[72] He must be controlled in his tasks and take a share of one-sixth.[73] He must not be addicted to carnal intercourse and must be readily accomplished in *artha*. He must have *dharma* in his soul and must always approach his wife at the time of her period. He must be controlled and must always fast. He must be pure and engaged in self-studying. He must always sleep inside his house and not outside its boundaries. With a happy mind,

---

[69] That is, without first offering the meat in a sacrifice.

[70] *Ahavaniya, garhapatya* and *dakshinatya* (the fire that burns in a southern direction).

[71] He must be generous. One touches water before any act, such as that of giving donations. In that sense, the hand remains wet.

[72] To burn down his sins.

[73] As taxes.

he must always be hospitable and pursue the three objectives.[74] He must always tell shudras who desire food, 'It has been cooked.' He should not glance at anything with selfish eyes of desire. He must gather everything required for gods and ancestors. In his house, he must worship them, even if that has to be done through begging. Following the norms, he must offer oblations and perform *agnihotra* twice a day. For the welfare of cattle and *brahmanas,* he must advance into battle and even be killed. If he purifies himself through *mantra*s to the three fires, he becomes a brahmana. He becomes full of *jnana* and *vijnana*. He cleanses himself and becomes accomplished in the Vedas. Through his own deeds, a *vaishya* who has *dharma* in his soul becomes a *kshatriya*. O goddess! These are the fruits of deeds for those who are born in different classes. By cleansing himself, even a shudra can become a brahmana. In that way, if a brahmana deviates from cleaning himself and from clean food, he loses his state of being a brahmana and becomes a shudra. O goddess! If a shudra is pure in soul and conquers his senses and if he is pure in his deeds, he becomes a brahmana. Brahma has himself said this. If a shudra is engaged in his own tasks and purifies himself, he becomes a brahmana. Know that this is my view. Birth, sacraments, learning and offspring cannot be the reason for someone being a brahmana. Good conduct alone is the reason. In this world, those who are *brahmanas* are characterized by good conduct. If he is established by good conduct, even a shudra becomes a brahmana. O one with the beautiful hips! It is my view that a brahmana is one in whom the essence of the *brahman* exists. If the *nirguna*[75] and sparkling *brahman* exists, that person is a brahmana. O goddess! Such unblemished people indicate what should be done in different states. Brahma, the creator of subjects and the one who bestows boons, has himself said this. The brahmana is like a giant field that is roaming around on its feet. O beautiful one! If anyone sows seeds in this field, that act of agriculture yields fruits after death. If a person wants to be content, he must always think of adhering to the virtuous path. His conduct should be characterized by adhering to

---

[74] *Dharma, artha* and *kama.*
[75] Devoid of *guna*s.

the brahmana's path. A person who is a householder should study the *samhita* texts[76] at home. He must always be engaged in studying but should never resort to teaching for earning his living. Such a brahmana is always established in the virtuous path. He offers oblations into the fire and studies and is fit to be merged into the *brahman*. O goddess! Having obtained the status of being a brahmana, one must always seek to protect it. O one with the beautiful smiles! He must engage in his tasks and receive gifts from worthy donors. I have thus told you the secret about how a shudra can become a brahmana and about how a brahmana can be dislodged from *dharma* and become a shudra.'

Chapter 1(116) (Virtuous Conduct)

Uma asked, 'O illustrious one! O lord of all beings! O one who is worshipped by the gods and the *asuras*! O god! O lord! I have a doubt about *dharma* and *adharma* for men. Please tell me. An embodied being is always bound by three bonds of thoughts, words and deeds. How is he freed from this? O god! Through what good conduct, deeds and good qualities, do men go to heaven?'

Maheshvara replied, 'O goddess! O one who knows the true purport of *dharma*! O Uma! O one who is always devoted to *dharma*! This question is beneficial to all beings and increases their intelligence. Listen. Those who are engaged in true *dharma* are serene and show no external signs. Their doubts have been dispelled and they are not bound by notions of *dharma* or impediments to *dharma*. They know the truth about creation and destruction. They know everything and their vision is impartial. They are devoid of attachment. Such men are freed from the bondage of *karma*. In thoughts, words and deeds, they do not cause harm to anyone. They are not immersed in anything and *karma* does not bind them down. They refrain from causing injury to life. They are good in conduct and full of compassion. They are impartial towards those

[76] Any arranged collection of texts, the word is applied to various texts.

who hate them and love them. They are controlled and are freed from the bondage of *karma*. They are compassionate towards all creatures. They are trusted by all creatures. The conduct of such men is free from violence and they go to heaven. They are always free from any sense about what belongs to them and what belongs to others. They never associate with the wives of others. Such men enjoy wealth that has been obtained through *dharma* and go to heaven. They are devoted to their own wives and approach them at the time of their period. They refrain from the pleasure that comes from vulgar carnal pursuits. Such men go to heaven. They refrain from theft and are always satisfied with their own riches. They earn a living through their own fortune. Such men go to heaven. Men with good conduct cover their eyes when they look at the wives of others. They are virtuous in their conduct and they conquer their senses. Such men go to heaven. In this way, men must always follow the path determined by the gods. Learned men must always follow a path that is untarnished. A learned man must always follow a path that does not unnecessarily harm others. This is a path marked by donations, rites and austerities, with good conduct, purity and compassion. This path, and no other, must be followed by those who desire to go to heaven.'

Uma said, 'O god! O Bhutapati! O unblemished one! Tell me about speech that binds people and that which frees them.'

Maheshvara replied, 'Men who do not resort to the *adharma* of uttering a lie, for their own sake or for others, go to heaven. Men who do utter a falsehood for the sake of subsistence, *dharma* or addiction to *kama*, go to heaven. Men who do not say what is not true, go to heaven. Men who go to heaven speak soft, sweet and welcoming words, clearly articulated and devoid of sin. Virtuous men who do not speak harsh, acerbic, cruel words and those who do not slander go to heaven. Those who do not slander their friends or speak so as to hurt others are men who go to heaven. Men who avoid harsh words that are full of malice towards others, those who are tranquil and impartial towards all creatures, go to heaven. Men who do not deceive or speak excessively, those who are not adversarial and are always amiable in speech, go to heaven. Their words are not spoken out of rage and do not pierce the heart.

Men who are peaceful and not angry go to heaven. O goddess! Through such speech, men always serve the cause of *dharma*. These are auspicious qualities of the truth. Learned men must always avoid lies.'

Uma said, 'O immensely fortunate one! O god of the gods! O wielder of the Pinaka![77] What kind of thoughts always bind down a man? Please tell me.'

Maheshvara replied, 'O fortunate one! Men whose thoughts are always full of *dharma* go to heaven. I will describe this. Listen. O one with the auspicious face! When a man's thoughts lead him astray and when his inner being leads him astray, he is bound. Listen. When he sees another person's possession kept in a desolate spot in the forest, but a man's thoughts do not turn towards seizing them, he goes to heaven. There are men who are never delighted when another person's possessions are left in a desolate spot in the village or in the house. They go to heaven. In that way, there are men whose thoughts are not overwhelmed by desire. They do not wish to seize the unprotected wives of others. Such men go to heaven. There are men whose thoughts regard friends and enemies equally. They are friendly towards whom they meet. Such men go to heaven. Men who go to heaven are learned, compassionate, pure, devoted to the truth and satisfied with their own riches. They are without any sense of enmity and their minds are naturally prone towards friendliness. They are compassionate towards all creatures. Such men go to heaven. There are learned men who perform rites. They are forgiving and love their well-wishers. They always know about *dharma* and *adharma*. Such men go to heaven. O goddess! There are men who do not wish to accumulate the fruits of auspicious or inauspicious deeds. They go to heaven. When their fortunes are on the ascendance, there are men who are always devoted to gods and *brahmanas*, avoiding those who are wicked. They go to heaven. O goddess! I have described the fruits of auspicious deeds and the path followed by those who go to heaven. What else do you want to hear?'

[77] A *pinaka* is both a trident and a bow. In particular, *Pinaka* means Shiva's bow. Shiva is known as Pinaki. He wields both a bow and a trident.

Uma said, 'O Maheshvara! I have a great doubt about mortals. You are accomplished. Therefore, you should explain it to me now. O lord! Through what deeds does a man obtain a long lifespan? O lord of the gods! Through what austerities does he obtain a great lifespan? Through what deeds does a man obtain a short lifespan on earth? O god! O unblemished one! You should tell me about perverse deeds. Some have good fortune, others suffer from ill fortune. Some are born in noble lineages, others are born in inferior lineages. Some men are ugly to behold, as if they are made of wood. There are other men who are handsome to behold. Some are limited in wisdom, others become learned. Some are extremely wise, others lack in *jnana* and *vijnana*. Some speak little, others are very eloquent. O god! This is the way men appear. You should explain this to me.'

Maheshvara replied, 'O goddess! I will tell you about the fruits of *karma*. All men on earth reap the fruits of their own deeds. There may be a man who is an Indra among *yogis*. Nevertheless, he always raises his staff to destroy life. There may be a man who always raises his weapons to kill various categories of beings. He is cruel towards all creatures and always causes anxiety. He is even merciless towards worms and insects that seek refuge. O goddess! Such a man always goes to hell. On the other hand, there may be one who has *dharma* in his soul. He is born in his own form.[78] Those who are violent go to hell. Those who are non-violent go to heaven. In that terrible hell, a man suffers from pain and hardships. If he manages to pass through that hell in some fashion, he is born as human, but has a brief lifespan. O goddess! If a person performs wicked and violent deeds that injures all beings, he is born with a brief lifespan. O goddess! There are men who perform auspicious deeds that avoid injury to life. They do not hurl their weapons or use their staffs. They do not cause violence. They do not strike or kill, or approve of killing. They are affectionate towards all creatures and look upon others as their own self. O goddess! Such men always deserve divinity. They are happy and always enjoy bliss and objects of pleasure. They are good in conduct and follow the

[78] He is reborn as human.

path of good *karma*. When they are born in the world of humans, they have a long lifespan. This is because they are free of causing violence to life. This is what Brahma has said.'

Chapter 1(117) (Attaining Heaven)

Uma asked, 'Through what kind of conduct does a man attain heaven? What should be his behaviour and *karma*? What is the nature of his donations?'

Maheshvara replied, 'O goddess! The following kind of man goes to the world of the gods. He is generous and shows honour to *brahmanas*. The immensely intelligent one donates food, cooked food and drinks to those who are miserable, afflicted and distressed. He constructs places to rest like assembly halls, wells and lakes. He is pure and controls himself, performing *nitya* and other rites. He is a man who with an extremely serene mind and always donates seats, couches, vehicles, homes, jewels, riches, different kinds of grains, excellent fields and women. O goddess! Such a man is born in the world of the gods. There, he enjoys excellent objects of pleasure for an extremely long period of time. Along with the *apsaras*, he amuses himself in Nandana and other places. O wife of Mahesha! O goddess! When he is dislodged from heaven, he is born in an extremely fortunate lineage and is worshipped by men. He enjoys wealth and grain. With all the qualities that characterize desire, he is happy. He enjoys a lot and performs great deeds. The man is wealthy. O goddess! Among beings, such men are extremely fortunate. They are generous. Earlier, Brahma has said that everyone finds them handsome to behold. O goddess! On the other hand, there are *brahmanas* who are miserly and do not give to others. They are limited in intelligence and do not give food, even when they possess it. Their tongues are full of greed. Therefore, those who seek, the distressed, the blind, the miserable, mendicants and guests, return dissatisfied. They never give wealth, garments and objects of pleasure, gold, cattle or cooked food. They should not be greedy, but are greedy. There are non-believers who do not give. O goddess!

Since their intelligence is perverse, such men go to hell. After the passage of time, they are born as humans. However, because they are limited in intelligence, they are born in a family that does not possess a great deal of wealth. They suffer from hunger and thirst and people treat them as outcasts. Their hopes to obtain objects of pleasure are not met and they spend their lives in *adharma*. These men are born in families with limited fortune and are addicted to trifling objects of pleasure. O goddess! Through this kind of *karma*, men are born as those who are limited in wealth. There are others who are always insolent, proud in their behaviour towards others. They are limited in intelligence and do not offer a seat or stool to those who deserve one. Since they suffer in intelligence, they do not yield passage to those who deserve to be given right of way. They do not offer *arghya*[79] and food to those who should be worshipped and honoured according to the rites. Suffering in intelligence, they do not offer *padya* and *achamaniya*.[80] They do not greet their revered *guru*s with loving and welcoming words. Because their arrogance increases, they are full of avarice. They disrespect those who are elders and who should be honoured. O goddess! All men who are of this type go to hell. After several years, when such men pass through hell, they take birth in condemned lineages like *shvapaka*s and *pulkasa*s.[81] These condemned lineages lack in intelligence. Having been born in such lineages, they do not show respect to seniors and elders. O goddess! But there are men who go to heaven—those who are not insolent and proud, those who worship gods and guests, those who are worshipped and revered by the worlds, those who speak sweet words, those who are pleasant in all their deeds, those who are engaged in what is agreeable with all creatures, those who are pleasant of face and do not hate, those who always speak soft and gentle words, those who welcome everyone, those who do not

---

[79] A gift given to a guest to show respect.

[80] Respectively, water to wash the feet and rinse the mouth.

[81] *Shvapaka*s are sometimes equated with *chandala*s. *Shva* means dog and *paka* means to cook. Thus, *shvapaka* means someone who cooks dogs (eats dogs) or cooks for dogs (lives with dogs). A *pulkasa* (equivalently *pukkasa*) is the son of a *nishada* father and a shudra mother.

cause injury to creatures, those who perform all the rites properly, those who do not sit down without performing worship, those who always grant the right of way to those to whom the path should be yielded, those who always worship their *gurus* and those who welcome revered guests and others who arrive. When they are born as humans, this is in special lineages. Having been born, they enjoy extensive objects of pleasure and possess all the jewels. They worship those who should be worshipped and follow *dharma*. They are revered by all creatures and worshipped by all the worlds. A man always reaps the fruits of the deeds he has himself performed. I have described the *dharma* Vidhatri[82] has himself spoken about. O beautiful one! There are those whose conduct and behaviour is such that they go to hell—those whose conduct is terrible, those who cause fear to all creatures, those who use hands, feet, ropes, rods and stones to stupefy and oppress beings, those who are limited in wisdom and violently cause agitation and those who attack creatures and always cause anxiety amongst people. After the due progress of time, they become humans. They are born among worst families, in lineages that suffer from many impediments. Through his own deeds, such a man reaps the fruits of an inferior lineage that is hated by people. O goddess! Among men and relatives and kin, this should be known. There are also men who look towards all beings with compassion. Their vision is friendly and they behave like fathers towards them. They conquer their senses and are without any sense of enmity. They do not agitate or kill beings and are full of compassion. They control their hands and feet and earn trust among all creatures. They do not use ropes, rods, stones and weapons to agitate creatures. Such a man always performs auspicious deeds. With such conduct and behaviour, he is born in heaven. Such a man easily enjoys happiness and is always without anxiety. O goddess! This is the path of the virtuous and there are no impediments along it.'

Uma said, 'One can see men who are full of great enthusiasm and skill. They possess *jnana* and *vijnana*. They are wise and know about *artha*. O god! There are others who are suffer in wisdom

[82] Brahma.

and are devoid of *jnana* and *vijnana*. Through what kind of *karma* does a man become wise? O Virupaksha![83] Why does a man suffer in wisdom? O supreme among those who uphold every kind of *dharma*! Please dispel my doubt about this. O god! Some are born blind. Others suffer from ailments. Some men are seen to be eunuchs. Please tell me the reason for this.'

Maheshvara replied, '*Brahmanas* who are learned in the Vedas, those who know about success in *dharma*, those who always ask about what is good and what is bad and those who avoid inauspicious deeds and practice auspicious ones—such people always obtain happiness in this world and go to heaven. When they are born as humans, they are intelligent. They are born as those who are fortunate. They are learned and devoted to sacrifices. They do not look at the wives of others with wicked eyes. If a person's nature is evil like that, he is born blind. If a man looks at a naked woman with a vile mind, because of his wicked deed, he is born as the one who suffers from ailments. If a man is so foolish that he performs the wicked act of having intercourse with someone he shouldn't, he is limited in his wisdom and is born as a eunuch. Men who tie up animals, violate their preceptor's bed and indulge in indiscriminate intercourse are born as eunuchs.'

Uma asked, 'O supreme among gods! What kind of a deed is honoured and what is condemned? How does a man obtain what is beneficial?'

Maheshvara replied, 'If a man constantly searches for the beneficial path and asks *brahmanas*, if he searches for *dharma* and the qualities, he obtains heaven. O goddess! If he is born as a human, he becomes a person who controls himself. He is born intelligent and wise, with a strong memory. O goddess! This is the *dharma* of the virtuous which brings prosperity. It is the path one should traverse along. For the welfare of men, I have always spoken about it.'

Uma said, 'There are men who are limited in intelligence. They revile *dharma*. They do not wish to approach *brahmanas* who are learned in the Vedas. Some men observe vows. They are devoted

---

[83] Virupaksha, meaning with malformed eyes, is Shiva's name.

and exercise self-control. There are others who are without vows. They deviate from rituals. There are others who are like *rakshasas*. But there are those who perform sacrifices. There are others who are free of delusion. What is the *karma* that leads to this? Please tell me.'

Maheshvara replied, 'For this world, the *agama* texts[84] have already laid down the parameters of *dharma*. Having followed the authority laid down in these, there are men who are seen to be firm in their vows. However, there are those who are confounded by confusion. They speak of what is *adharma* as *dharma*. They are without vows and destroy the ordinances. They are said to be brahma-*rakshasas*.[85] After the passage of time, because they make efforts, they become humans. But they become the worst among men, who do not offer oblations or exclaim *vashatkara*.[86] O goddess! For the sake of dispelling all your doubts, I have thus described the ocean of *dharma* to you and what is good and bad for men.'

Chapter 1(118) (Maheshvara tells the sages about Vishnu)

Vyasa said, 'O *brahmanas*! Having heard the words that her husband had spoken, the mother of the universe was astounded and extremely happy. The best among sages were also near Tripurari.[87] In connection with visiting the *tirthas*, those *brahmanas* had gone to that mountain. They worshipped the divinity with the trident in his hand and prostrated themselves before him. For the welfare of the worlds, they asked him about their doubt.'

The sages said, 'O Trilochana![88] O destroyer of Daksha's sacrifice! We bow down before you. O Jagannatha![89] We are

---

[84] *Agamas* are texts other than the *Vedas*, such as the *tantra* texts.

[85] A *brahmana* who becomes a *rakshasa*.

[86] An exclamation made at the time of offering oblations.

[87] The enemy of Tripura, Shiva's name.

[88] The three-eyed one, Shiva.

[89] The lord of the universe, being used for Shiva, though it is also used for Vishnu.

asking you about a doubt that exists in our hearts. This *samsara*[90] is extremely terrible. It is fearful and makes the hair of the body stand up. Men who are limited in intelligence wander around for a very long time. Through what means can they be freed from the bondage of birth and *samsara*? We have great curiosity about this. Please tell us.'

Maheshvara replied, 'Men are bound in the noose of their *karma* and they suffer miseries. O *brahmanas*! I do not see any means other than the supreme Vasudeva. Those who properly worship the one who holds the conch shell, the *chakra* and the mace in their thoughts, words and deeds reach the supreme destination. Trying like an animal, what is the point of remaining alive in this world if the consciousness is not inclined towards Vasudeva, who pervades the universe?'

The sages said, 'O wielder of Pinaka! O one who destroyed Bhaga's eyes! O one who is revered by all the worlds! O Shankara! We wish to hear about Vasudeva's greatness.'

Maheshvara replied, 'Hari, the eternal being, is superior to the grandfather. Krishna's golden radiance is like that of the sun rising in a sky without clouds. He possesses ten arms and is greatly energetic. He is the destroyer of the enemies of the gods. Hrishikesha has the *shrivatsa* mark on his chest and is the leader of all the gods. Brahma originated from his stomach and I originated from his head. The stellar bodies were born from the hair on his head. The gods and *asura*s were born from his body hair. The *rishi*s and the eternal worlds emerged from his body. He himself resides in Brahma. He resides in all the gods. The lord of the three worlds is the one who created the entire earth. He is the one who destroys all beings, mobile and immobile. He is supreme among gods. The scorcher of enemies is himself the protector of the gods. He knows everything. He has created everything. He goes everywhere. His face is in every direction. There is no being in the three worlds who is superior to him. He is eternal. He is immensely fortunate. He is known as Govinda. He is the one who kills all the kings in a battle. He is the one who bestows honours. To accomplish the tasks of the gods, he

---

[90] The cycle of life.

assumes a human form. Without Trivikrama's[91] power, the large number of gods have no strength. Without their leader, they cannot undertake the tasks of the gods in this world. He is the leader of all creatures. He is revered by all creatures. Every task, superior and inferior, is done by the protector of the gods. He is identical with the *brahman*. He is the constant refuge of *brahmarshi*s. Brahma resides in his navel and I reside in his body. All the gods happily reside in his body. The god, Pundarikaksha[92] has Shri[93] in his stomach. He resides with Shri. He has the Sharnga bow,[94] the *chakra* and a sword as weapons. The enemy of all the *naga*s[95] is on his standard. He possesses excellence, good conduct, purity, self-control, valour, bravery, a handsome body, capacity to ascend, energy, uprightness, prosperity, lack of violence, beauty and strength. He possesses all kinds of divine weapons that are extraordinary to behold. He possesses the *maya* of yoga.[96] He possesses one thousand eyes. He possesses malformed eyes. He is extremely generous. He uses his words to praise those who are friendly. He loves his relatives and kin. He is forgiving and does not speak about himself. He is the divinity who bestows the *brahman*. He destroys the fear of those who are afflicted by fear. He enhances the delight of his friends. He is the refuge of all creatures. He is engaged in protecting those who are distressed. He possesses learning and wealth. All creatures bow down to him. He performs good deeds for those who seek refuge with him. He generates fear among enemies. He knows about good policy. He follows good policy. He knows about the *brahman*. He has conquered his senses.

'For the existence of the gods, the one with supreme intelligence, the great-souled Govinda, will be born in Manu's lineage. This is the auspicious line purified by *dharma*, descended from Prajapati Manu. Manu will have a son named Amsha and Amsha's son

[91] Trivikrama, the one with the three strides, is Vishnu's name, a reference to the *vamana avatara*.

[92] Vishnu's name, the one with eyes like lotuses.

[93] The goddess of wealth and prosperity, Lakshmi.

[94] Bow made out of horn, used by Vishnu.

[95] Garuda, the enemy of all the *naga*s (serpents).

[96] Known as *yogamaya*, the power of illusion.

will be Antardhama. Antaradhama's son will be the unblemished Prajapati,[97] Havirdhama. O *brahmanas*! Havirdhama's son will be Prachinabarhi. Prachinabarhi will have ten sons, Prachetas as the foremost. Daksha Prajapati will be born as the son of Prachetas. Aditya will be born through Dakshayani.[98] Aditya's son will be Manu.[99] Ila and Sudyumna will be born in Manu's lineage. Pururava will be born from Budha.[100] Ayus will be Pururava's son. Nahusha will be the son of Ayus and Yayati will be the son of Nahusha. The immensely strong Yadu will be Yayati's son and Yadu's son will be Kroshta. Kroshta will have a great son named Vrijinivan. Vrijinivan's son will be the unvanquished Ushangu.[101] Ushangu will have a brave son, Chitraratha. Ushangu will also have a younger son, known by the name of Shura. O supreme among *brahmanas*! This lineage will be famous for its valour, conduct, character, qualities, performance of sacrifices and purity. Shura, supreme among *kshatriyas*, will be immensely valiant and immensely famous. He will extend his lineage and bestow honours. His son will be Vasudeva, famous by the name of Anakadundubhi. His son will be four-armed Vasudeva.[102] He will donate. He will show respect to *brahmanas*. He will have the *brahman* in him. He will love *brahmanas*. Having defeated King Jarasandha, Yadava[103] will free all the kings who will be imprisoned inside a cave in a mountain. The valiant one will become an excellent jewel among all the kings. Throughout earth, his valour will be unimpeded.

---

[97] The title of Prajapati is applied to anyone who is a creator of beings.

[98] Dakshayani means Daksha's daughter, Aditi, married to the sage Kashyapa. Aditya, the sun-god, is the son of Kashyapa and Aditi.

[99] In the line of Manus, this is Vaivasvata Manu, the son of Vivasvat, the sun-god.

[100] Pururava is the first king of the lunar dynasty (*chandra vamsha*). He is the son of Ila, which is Sudyumna's feminine form.

[101] The word 'son' has to be interpreted in a broad sense, since some generations are often missed in the telling. For instance, there were two Chitrarathas and two Shuras in the line and this concise telling treats them as identical.

[102] The son is Vaasudeva and the father is Vasudeva.

[103] Descended from Yadu, meaning Krishna.

Through his valour, the prosperous one will be the king over all the kings. The brave lord will subdue all of them and reside in Dvaraka. Having conquered the ones with evil desires, he will protect the goddess earth. Along with excellent *brahmanas* who deserve to be worshipped, you should approach him. He is like the eternal *brahman* and should be duly worshipped. Anyone who desires to see me or Brahma the grandfather should see the powerful and illustrious Vasudeva. When he is seen, I am also seen. There is no need to reflect on this. O stores of austerities! Know that Vasudeva is the grandfather. If Pundarikaksha is pleased with a person, the large number of gods with Brahma leading are also pleased with him. If a man in this world seeks refuge with Keshava, he obtains deeds, fame and heaven. He becomes one who himself follows *dharma* and indicates the contours of *dharma* for others. A person who knows about *dharma* should always worship Achyuta, the lord of the gods. When the lord is worshipped, *dharma* is always present. The immensely energetic divinity desires to do what is good for subjects. It is for the sake of *dharma* that the tiger among men has created crores of rishis. Having been created by Brahma, Sanatkumara and the others[104] who dwell in Mount Gandhamadana, performing austerities. O bulls among *brahmanas*! Therefore, the eloquent one, who knows about *dharma*, must be bowed down to. When he is worshipped, he returns the worship. When he is honoured, he returns the honour. When he is constantly seen, he shows himself. When one seeks refuge with him, he offers refuge. O supreme among *brahmanas*! When the divinity is constantly venerated, he shows veneration. Therefore, supreme austerities are in worshipping Vishnu. He is the great and original god and worshipping him always characterizes the virtuous. In the world, the eternal one is always worshipped by the gods. If one follows him and seeks refuge with him, one accordingly obtains freedom from fear. In thought, words and deeds, *brahmanas* must always bow down to him. If one takes care, Devaki's son will certainly be seen. O excellent sages! I have thus described the path to you. When the lord of all the

---

[104] Sanaka, Sananda, Sanatana and Sanatkumara are sons born through Brahma's mental powers.

gods is seen, all the supreme gods will be seen. The grandfather of the worlds and I always bow down to the lord of the universe, the divinity who is the great Varaha. There is no doubt that all three[105] will be seen in him. We, all the gods, reside in his body. His elder brother has the complexion of a collection of white mountains. The one who holds up the earth[106] will be famous as Bala, the wielder of the plough. The lord is Ananta and his three hoods will be seen. Despite his strength and valour, Suparna,[107] Kashyapa's son, was unable to see the ends of the supreme-souled divinity. Filled with great joy, he wanders around as Shesha. Encircling the earth, he resides inside that serpent. He is Ananta Vishnu, the one who holds the earth. The one who is Rama is Achyuta Hrishikesha, the one who holds the entire earth. Those two tigers among men are divine in their valour. The wielder of the *chakra* and the plough deserve to be seen and deserve to be honoured. O stores of austerities! It is through his favour that I have spoken about this sacred account to you. You must make efforts to worship the best among the Yadus.'

Chapter 1(119) (Vishnu's devotees)

The sages asked, 'How wonderful is Krishna's account. We have heard this extraordinary account. It is sacred and destroys all sins. It is blessed and destroys *samsara*. O great sage! There are men who are devoted to worshipping Vasudeva. After devotedly worshipping Vasudeva in the proper way, where do they go? O great sage! Do they go to heaven or obtain *moksha*? O best among sages! Or is it the case that they obtain both the fruits? O one who knows everything! Our hearts have a doubt on this account and you should dispel it. O supreme among sages! Other than you, there is no one in this world who is capable of dispelling this doubt.'

---

[105] Brahma, Vishnu and Shiva.

[106] Balarama is a manifestation of Shesha/Ananta, who holds up the earth.

[107] Meaning Garuda.

Vyasa replied, 'This is praiseworthy. O best among sages! What you have spoken about is noble and praiseworthy. Listen progressively to what brings happiness to Vishnu's devotees. O *brahmanas*! As soon as men are consecrated into worshipping Krishna, they obtain *moksha*. What needs to be said about those who constantly worship Achyuta? O supreme sages! Heaven or *moksha* are not difficult for them to obtain. Vishnu's devotees can obtain other objects of desire that are extremely difficult to obtain, but they do not hanker for them. O tigers among sages! After ascending a mountain of jewels, a man can take away whichever jewel he wants. In that way, whatever one wishes for can be obtained from Krishna. He is like a *kalpavriksha*,[108] instantly yielding any fruit one desires. O *brahmanas*! A man can take whatever he cherishes from Krishna. If one faithfully worships Vasudeva, the preceptor of the worlds, in the proper way, a man obtains the fruits of *dharma*, *artha*, *kama* and *moksha*. With a pure heart, if a man worships Jagannatha, he obtains objects of desire that are extremely difficult for the gods to obtain. If one constantly worships the undecaying Vasudeva with devotion, there is nothing in the three worlds that is difficult to obtain. In this world, men who constantly worship Hari are blessed. He is the divinity who destroys all sins and bestows all the fruits that one desires. *Brahmanas*, *kshatriyas*, *vaishyas*, women, shudras and *antyajas*[109] who worship the best among gods obtain the supreme destination. O sages! O unblemished ones! Therefore, hear what you have asked me about. I will briefly tell you about the destinations obtained by those great-souled ones. They give up this human body which is temporary and is the abode of ailments. It is characterized by old age and death and is like a bubble in the water. It has flesh and blood and is associated with the stench of urine and excrement. It consists of pillars made out of bones, fat, sinews, skin and arteries. On *vimana*s which can travel as they will, have the complexion of the rising sun and are decorated with nets of bells, to the sound of divine *gandharva*s singing and praised by

---

[108] A tree that bestows whatever one wishes for.
[109] *Antyaja*s are those who belong to lower classes, such as *chandala*s. They live just outside habitations.

*gandharva*s and ornamented *apsara*s, they go to separate abodes of the guardians of the worlds. They enjoy those separate worlds which are decorated with different objects of pleasure for the duration of a *manvantara*. After this, they go to a world in the firmament that bestows every kind of happiness. O *brahmanas*! For ten *manvantara*s, they enjoy excellent objects of pleasure there. O *brahmanas*! Thereafter, Vishnu's devotees go to the world of the *gandharva*s. They enjoy those agreeable objects of pleasure for a period that is equal to twenty *manvantara*s. After this, they are worshipped and they go to Aditya's world. For thirty *manvantara*s, they enjoy objects of pleasure that are superior to those enjoyed by the gods. O *brahmanas*! Thereafter, they go to Chandra's world which brings bliss. Devoid of old age and death, they enjoy the auspicious qualities of objects of pleasure for a duration that is equal to forty *manvantara*s. O best among sages! On ornamented *vimana*s, they next go to the world of the *nakshatra*s, ornamented with all the qualities. They enjoy the desired objects of pleasure for fifty *manvantara*s. O *brahmanas*! After this, they go to the world of the gods, which is extremely difficult to obtain. O *brahmanas*! For the duration of sixty *manvantara*s, they enjoy many kinds of objects of pleasure that are extremely difficult to obtain. They also obtain the eight *siddhi*s.[110] Next, they are worshipped by the gods and they go to Shakra's world.[111] They enjoy themselves with superior and inferior divine objects of pleasure for a period that is equal to seventy *manvantara*s and this enhances their mental delight. From there, they go to Prajapati's supreme world where they enjoy all the desired objects of pleasure with all the wished for qualities. With every kind of happiness, they spend a duration of eighty *manvantara*s there. O *brahmanas*! After this, devotees of Vishnu go to the grandfather's world. They happily sport there for ninety

---

[110] *Yoga* leads to eight major *siddhi*s or powers. These are *anima* (becoming as small as one desires), *mahima* (as large as one desires), *laghima* (as light as one wants), *garima* (as heavy as one wants), *prapti* (obtaining what one wants), *prakamya* (travelling where one wants), *vashitvam* (powers to control creatures) and *ishitvam* (obtaining divine powers).

[111] Shakra is another name for Indra.

manvantaras. When they again return to this world, they are born in the families of supreme *brahmanas*. O *brahmanas*! They are born as *yogis* who know the purport of the Vedas and the sacred texts. In this way, they enjoy all the desired objects of pleasure in all the worlds. Having returned here, they again progressively ascend upwards. O supreme *brahmanas*! They enjoy the desired objects of pleasure for one hundred years and then go to a different world. When they have progressively completed ten births, they proceed from Brahma's world to Hari Vishnu's divine world. Having gone there, they enjoy all the undecaying objects of pleasure with all the qualities for one hundred *manvantaras*. They do not experience birth or death. O supreme *Brahmanas*! After this, they go to Varaha's world. They became gigantic in size and immensely strong. They possess divine bodies and wear earrings. O Indras among *Brahmanas*! Assuming four-armed forms, they sport there for ten thousand crore years. O excellent *Brahmanas*! They possess that eternal state where they are worshipped by all the gods. O *Brahmanas*! From there, those persevering ones go to Narasimha's abode. They happily sport there for ten thousand crore years. When this is over, they go to Vishnu's city, frequented by the *siddhas*. They happily sport there for ten thousand years. O *Brahmanas*! Then, those excellent *sadhakas*[112] go to Brahma's world again. They remain there for a very long time, for many hundreds of crores of years. Thereafter, those lords among *sadhakas* go to Narayana's city. They enjoy diverse objects of pleasure for one hundred million crores of years. Thereafter, those supreme *sadhakas* go to Aniruddha's city. They have divine forms and are immensely strong, praised by the gods and the *asuras*. Vishnu's devotees remain there for fourteen thousand crore years. They do not suffer from old age or death. Without any anxiety, they next go to Pradyumna's city. O *Brahmanas*! They remain there for three hundred thousand crores of years. They can travel wherever they want. They are happy, full of strength and power. Thereafter, the *yogis* go to the place where Samkarshana is the lord. They reside there for a very long time, enjoying thousands of objects of

---

[112] A *sadhaka* is someone who is aspiring for success, or has accomplished it.

pleasure. They then enter Vasudeva, who is unblemished and has no form and no name. Freed from old age and death, they enter the supreme truth. Having gone there, there is no doubt that they attain emancipation. In this way, those learned ones progressively obtain emancipation. O tigers among sages! Engaged in worshipping Vasudeva, they are freed.'

Chapter 1(120) (The *chandala* and the *brahma-rakshasa*)

Vyasa said, 'There is no doubt that a man who controls himself and fasts on *ekadashi*[113] in either *paksha* goes to Vishnu's supreme abode. He must follow the norms and bathe properly. He must conquer his senses and wear washed garments. He must control himself well and following the norms, worship Vishnu properly. He must use flowers, fragrances, lamps, incense, *naivedya*[114] and different kinds of gifts. He must perform *japa*,[115] offer oblations and donate *dakshina*. He must chant many kinds of stotrams and use pleasant singing and musical instruments. He must prostrate himself like a rod and exclaim excellent sounds of 'Victory'. Worshipping in this way, he must remain awake during the night. Devoted to Vishnu, he must chant Vishnu's songs and accounts.'

The sages asked, 'O great sage! What are the fruits obtained from remaining awake during the night and singing Vishnu's songs? We have great curiosity and wish to hear about this. Please tell us.'

Vyasa replied, 'O tigers among sages! Listen. I will duly tell you about the fruits that are mentioned from remaining awake during the night and singing Vishnu's songs. The city named Avanti is famous on earth. Holding a conch shell, a *chakra* and a mace, the illustrious Vishnu is there. On the outskirts of that city, there was a *chandala* who was accomplished in singing. Earning riches

---

[113] The eleventh lunar day.
[114] Offering of food.
[115] Silent chanting.

through legitimate means, he was engaged in nurturing his servants. The *chandala* was devoted to Vishnu and was firm in observing the monthly vows. When *ekadashi* arrived, he fasted and sang. The songs were praises of Vishnu and to express the sentiments, used notes like *gandhara, shadaja, naishada, panchama* and *dhaivata*.[116] He stayed awake during the night and sang these chants to Vishnu. On the morning of *dvadashi*,[117] he prostrated himself before the lord and returned home. O supreme among *brahmanas*! He ate after feeding his nephews, daughters, sons-in-law and family members. In this way, he resided there for many years, pleasing Vishnu through many kinds of wonderful songs. On one occasion in the month of Chaitra,[118] when *ekadashi* of *krishna paksha* approached, he went to an excellent forest to serve Vishnu. Full of great devotion, he started to collect wild flowers. On the banks of the Kshipra, in that great forest, he reached the foot of a *vibhitaka*[119] tree. On seeing that he was without a protector, a *rakshasa* seized him so as to devour him. The *chandala* told him, "You should not devour me today. O fortunate one! You can eat me tomorrow in the morning. I give you my word that I will return. O *rakshasa*! I have a great task to be performed today. Therefore, please release me. I pledge truthfully that I will return tomorrow and you can eat me then. To serve Vishnu, I have to remain awake during the night. O *rakshasa*! You should not create an impediment in my observance of the vow." The *rakshasa* replied, "O Matanga![120] I have not eaten for ten days and I have obtained you today. I will not free you. I am suffering from great hunger and I will eat you." Hearing the words of the one who roamed in the night,[121] Matanga spoke to him in soft words, assuring him that he was firm and truthful in his words.'

---

[116] This is usually stated as *shadaja, rishabha, gandhara, madhyama, panchama, dhaivata* and *nishada*, that is, *sa-re-ga-ma-pa-dha-ni*.

[117] The twelfth lunar day.

[118] March–April.

[119] A kind of myrobalan.

[120] *Matanga* is a synonym for *chandala*.

[121] *Rakshasa*s wander around in the night and are known as *nishachara*s.

Matanga said, 'O brahma-*rakshasa*! Listen to me. Everything in the universe has a foundation in truth. I truthfully pledge to you that I will return. The sun, the moon, the fire, the wind, the earth, the firmament, the water, the mind, night and day and the two *sandhya*s know everything that a man does. The sins of having intercourse with someone else's wife, stealing objects that belong to another person, killing a brahmana, drinking, violating a preceptor's bed, being the husband of a woman who is barren, being the husband of a *vrishala* lady, subsisting on offerings made to an image, eating fish and flesh, eating the meat of a pig, eating the meat of a tortoise, eating flesh in vain,[122] eating flesh from the back, killing a friend, being ungrateful, being the husband of a widow, the pollution due to child-birth, being cruel in deeds, being a miser, leaving guests unsatisfied, having intercourse on *amavasya*, *shashthi*, *ashtami* or *chaturdashi*[123] during *krishna paksha* or *shukla paksha*, being a brahmana who has intercourse with his wife during her period, having intercourse with a woman just after performing *shraddha*,[124] eating without having had a bath, eating filth, having intercourse with a friend's wife, indulging in back-biting, being addicted to confusion and insolence, destroying honey, going back on a word given to a brahmana, lying about a daughter, lying about cows and mules, killing a woman or a child, uttering a falsehood, being harsh towards gods, Vedas, *brahmanas*, kings, sons, friends and virtuous women, lying or being wicked in conduct towards a *guru*, committing arson, setting fire to a forest, being a sinful householder, killing a cow, being the worst among *brahmanas*, not marrying before the younger brother has got married, getting married before the elder brother has got married, receiving from, or giving to such people[125] and killing a fetus—if I do not fulfil my pledge, let all these sins descend on me. O *rakshasa*! What is the need to speak a

---

[122] Without offering it in sacrifice first.

[123] Respectively, the night of the new moon, the sixth lunar day, the eighth lunar day and the fourteenth lunar day.

[124] A funeral ceremony.

[125] The elder brother who has not married before his younger brother, or the younger brother who has got married before his elder brother.

lot? I give you my pledge. Listen to a pledge that is so terrible that it is difficult to utter it. There are sins from earning a living through one's daughter, lying under oath, bearing false witness, performing a sacrifice for a person who does not deserve to sacrifice, being an eunuch, being the worst listener, resorting to *sannyasa* and then becoming a householder and being a *brahmachari* who succumbs to desire. If I do not return to your presence, let me be tainted with all these sins.'

Vyasa continued, 'Hearing Matanga's words, the brahma-*rakshasa* was astounded. He said, "Go and be truthful to your pledge." Thus, addressed by the *kunapasha*, the *shvapacha* gathered flowers.[126] Having gathered them, he went to Vishnu's temple. He gave them to a brahmana, who washed them with water and using these to worship Vishnu, went to his own house. O stores of austerities! Matanga fasted throughout the night, remaining awake. He sat down on the ground outside[127] and sang. When night turned into dawn, he praised the god and prostrated himself before him. True to his pledge, he left for the place where the *rakshasa* was. As he was proceeding along the road, a man asked him, "O fortunate one! Where are you going?" When he told him everything, he said, "The body is the means for achieving *dharma*, *artha*, *kama* and *moksha*. An intelligent person should make great efforts to protect the body. If a man remains alive, he obtains *dharma*, *artha*, happiness and *moksha* as the ultimate destination. By remaining alive, one obtains fame. In this world, who remembers a dead person?" Hearing these words, Matanga replied in words that were full of meaning. Matanga said, "O fortunate one! I am going because I regard truth as most important. I have made a pledge." He said again, "You are foolish in your intelligence. O virtuous one! Have you not heard the words spoken by Manu?[128] There are five kinds of lies that are not

---

[126] *Shvapacha* is one who is an outcaste. Literally, one who eats dogs, or eats with dogs. This is thus a synonym for *chandala*. *Kunapa* is a dead body and Kunapasha (one who eats dead bodies) is an indirect way of referring to the brahma-*rakshasa*.

[127] Outside the temple.

[128] This is a reference to *Manu Samhita*, for example, 8.11.

sins—for the sake of protecting cows, women and *brahmanas* ; lies in connection with marriages; for the sake of well-wishers; when life is in danger; and when all the riches are liable to be destroyed. The words of *dharma* about not indulging in falsehood do not apply in the case of women, at the time of marriage, when there are enemies, when one is liable to be deceived, when wealth can be destroyed or when the person is himself liable to be destroyed." Hearing his words, Matanga replied, "O fortunate one! Do not say this. Truth is revered in the worlds. Every happiness that exists in the universe is obtained through truth. It is because of truth that the sun heats. It is because of truth that water has juices. It is because of truth that fire burns. It is because of truth that the wind blows. *Dharma*, *artha*, *kama* and *moksha* are extremely difficult to obtain. However, they are generated through truth. Therefore, the truth must not be discarded. Truth is the supreme *brahman*. Truth is the best among sacrifices. Heaven is gained through truth. Therefore, truth must not be abandoned." Saying this, Matanga ignored that excellent man. He went to the place where the brahma-*rakshasa*, the destroyer of beings was. The brahma-*rakshasa* saw that the *chandala* was approaching and his eyes dilated in wonder. He shook his head and spoke. The brahma-*rakshasa* said, "This is praiseworthy. O immensely fortunate one! This is to be lauded. You are truthful to your words. Since you have the attributes of truth, I do not think that you are a *matanga*. Because of your deeds, I think that you are a pure brahmana who cannot decay. O foremost among fortunate ones! O refuge of *dharma*! Tell me something. During the night, what did you do in Vishnu's temple? Please tell me." Matanga replied, "Listen to what I did during the night in Vishnu's temple. I will tell you the truth. I lowered my head and remained below Vishnu's temple. I remained awake during the night, chanting Vishnu's songs." The brahma-*rakshasa* asked him, "How long have you observed this vow of faithfully remaining awake in Vishnu's temple? Please tell me." He smiled and said, "O *rakshasa*! I have done this for twenty years. I remain awake every month, during *ekadashi*." Hearing Matanga's words, the brahma-*rakshasa* spoke. The brahma-*rakshasa* said, "You should do exactly what I am asking you to do. O virtuous one! Give me the benefits of remaining awake for a single night. If you do that, I will free you. I will not free you otherwise. O immensely fortunate one! I pledge three times." Saying this, he stopped. Matanga replied, "O roamer in the night! I have surrendered myself to you. What is the need to speak? As you will eat me up." The *rakshasa* again said, "Give me the benefit of remaining awake for two *yamas*[129] and the benefit of singing. You should show me this much of compassion." Matanga told the *rakshasa*, "Why are you speaking in this incoherent way? As you will eat me up. I will not give you the benefit of remaining awake during the night." Hearing Matanga's words, the brahma-*rakshasa* spoke to him again. The brahma-*rakshasa* said, "Which extremely evil-minded person will look at you with a view to harm you or make you suffer? You are protected by your deeds of *dharma*. A virtuous person should exhibit compassion towards a foolish person who is distressed and confounded by material objects, suffering from terrible sins and hell's afflictions. O immensely fortunate one! That is the reason you should show me compassion and give me the benefit of remaining awake during the night. Give me the benefit of one *yama* and go to your own residence." At this, the *chandala* again said, "I will not go to my own residence. How can I possibly give you the benefit of remaining awake even for a single *yama*?" At this, the brahma-*rakshasa* smiled and spoke to the *chandala*. The brahma-*rakshasa* said, "When night is over, you find delight in activities like singing songs. Give me those and save me from this sin." Addressed in this way, Matanga spoke to him.

Matanga asked, 'What is the perverse deed that you committed earlier? Because of that taint, you have been born as a brahma-*rakshasa*.' Hearing Matanga's words, the brahma-*rakshasa* remembered what he had himself done and tormented with grief, replied. The brahma-*rakshasa* said, 'Hear who I used to be earlier and what I had done. Because of that I have been born in the wicked womb of a *rakshasa* lady. Earlier I was a brahmana, known by the name of Somasharma. I was the son of Devasharma. He was devoted to studying and performed sacrifices. There was a certain

---

[129] A *yama* is a period of three hours and two *yamas* are six hours. Night consists of three *yamas*.

yajamana[130] who had been prohibited from using the sacred thread or *mantra*s. Engaged in that king's tasks, I performed the rites near the sacrificial post. Confused and overcome by greed, I was the priest who kindled the fire for the sacrifice. When that was over, in my folly and insolence, I started a large sacrifice that would last for twelve days. While that was going on, I suffered from a pain in my stomach. Though ten days had passed, the sacrifice had not yet been completed. When oblations were being given to Virupaksha,[131] it was the moment that is associated with *rakshasa*s. I died at that time and because of the taint, was born as a brahma-*rakshasa*. There was a person for whom the sacred thread and the sound of *mantra*s had been prohibited. In my folly and ignorance about sacrifices, I had performed a sacrifice for one who was not entitled to perform a sacrifice. Because of that perverse deed, I became a brahma-*rakshasa*. I have thus been submerged in this great ocean of sin. Save me. At least give me the benefit of the last song you sing while you remain awake during the night.' The *chandala* told him, 'If you refrain from taking life, I will give you the benefit of the last song. When he agreed to this, Matanga invoked the fruits of remaining awake and singing a song for half a *muhurta*[132] and gave those to him. Having obtained the fruits of that song, the brahma-*rakshasa* bowed down to Matanga. He cheerfully went to the supreme *tirtha* of Prithudaka.[133] O *brahmanas*! He made up his mind to fast there and give up his life. As a result of the powers of Prithudaka, enhanced by the fruits of the song, he was released from his state as a *rakshasa* and obtained Brahma's world, which is extremely difficult to obtain. He resided there for ten thousand years without any fear. When this was over, he was born as a controlled brahmana who retained his memory. O *brahmanas*! I will tell you about his conduct later.'

---

[130] A person who employs priests to perform sacrifices.

[131] Shiva.

[132] A *muhurta* is a period of 48 minutes and in a 24-hour period, there are 30 *muhurta*s.

[133] Prithudaka is named after King Prithu. It is believed that Vishvamitra became a *brahmarshi* in the Sarasvati temple there. This is identified as Pehowa in Karnal district.

'Listen to my words. I will tell you the rest of Matanga's story. When the *rakshasa* left, the intelligent one who was in control of himself went to his residence. Since he remembered what he had been told, he became pure and non-attached. He left his wife in the care of his sons and started to roam around the earth. He started with Kokamukha and went to see Skanda.[134] Having seen Skanda, he went to Dharachakra and performed *pradakshina* there. He then went to the supreme mountain of Vindhya, with a large number of lofty peaks. O *Brahmanas*! He went to the *tirtha* of Papapramochana. The one born in a *chandala* family bathed in the place that cleanses sins. Freed from his sins, he remembered many of his former births. In an earlier birth, he had been a mendicant, controlled in his mind, speech and body. He was intelligent and accomplished in the Vedas and the *Vedanga*s.[135] Once, thieves were taking cows away from a city. Since the alms were polluted by the dust, the mendicant discarded them. Because of the taint of that *adharma*, he was born in the womb of a *chandala* lady. Having bathed in Papapramochana, he died on the banks of the Narmada. O *brahmanas*! He was born as a supreme brahmana in Varanasi but was stupid. He dwelt there for thirty years. There was a *siddha* man[136] who possessed the powers of *yoga* and *maya* but was disfigured. Roaming around, he arrived there. On seeing him, he laughed and spoke to him. "O *siddha*! Are you well? Where have you come from?" Thus addressed, the *siddha* thought that he had been recognized. The revered one replied, "I have come from the world of heaven." The foolish person asked the *siddha*, "In heaven, do you know the supreme *apsara* Urvashi? She was born from Narayana's thighs." The *siddha* replied, "I know Urvashi, the supreme ornament in heaven. She was born from a virtuous person

[134] Kokamukha *tirtha* was probably in Nepal and Skanda means a temple to Skanda/Kumara/Kartikeya.

[135] *Vedanga* means a branch of the *Veda*s and these were six kinds of learning that were essential to understand the *Veda*s—*shiksha* (phonetics), *kalpa* (rituals), *vyakarana* (grammar), *nirukta* (etymology), *chhanda* (metre) and *jyotisha* (astronomy).

[136] A *siddha* is someone who has obtained success. The *siddha* had disguised himself to hide his powers.

and holds the whisk for Shakra." The brahmana had no sense of
what was right and told the *siddha*, "O friend! Lovingly, will you
carry my message to Urvashi? Please tell her what I have said and
tell me what she says in reply." When the *siddha* agreed to this, the
brahmana was filled with joy. The *siddha* went to the abode of the
gods, on the slopes of Meru. He met Urvashi and told her what the
brahmana had said. She told the supreme *siddha*, "Please tell the
brahmana, I do not know who the lord of Kashi is. I know that you
have been told the truth but my memory hasn't retained it." Saying
this, she left. After a long period of time, the *siddha* again went
to Varanasi and met that foolish person again. On seeing him, he
asked, "What did the lady who was born from the thighs tell you?"
The *siddha* replied, "Urvashi herself told me that she does not
know." Hearing the siddha's words, a smile played on his lips and
he again said, "Please tell Urvashi, 'How can you possibly know?'"
Agreeing to do this, the *siddha* went to heaven. He saw Urvashi
emerging from Shakra's residence. When the supreme *siddha* told
her, she told the *siddha*, "Let the supreme brahmana undertake
some rituals. O *siddha*! Through those rituals I will know who he
is, not otherwise." He went to the foolish brahmana and told him
what Urvashi had said. He told the *siddha*, "I will observe a supreme
rite. O *siddha*! In front of you, I am taking this pledge about the
ritual. I tell you truthfully that from today, I will not eat *saktu*."[137]
Thus addressed, the *siddha* went to heaven and met Urvashi. He
told her, "He has said that from today, he will never eat *saktu*."
Urvashi told the *siddha*, "Now I know what he is like. From the
ritual he has chosen, it is evident that he is foolish and should be
laughed at." Saying this, Narayana's daughter[138] quickly went to
her own residence. As he willed, the *siddha* wandered around on
earth. Urvashi, supreme among beautiful ones, went to the city of
Varanasi. The one with the divine body had a bath in the waters
of Matsyodari.[139] O sages! The foolish one also went to bathe in

---

[137] Pounded ground meal, colloquially known as *sattu*.

[138] Urvashi was born from Narayana's thighs.

[139] The stream known as Matsyodari has now been reduced to a lake
known as Macchodari, in Varanasi.

River Matsyodari. When he went there, he saw Urvashi having a bath. When he saw her, Manmatha[140] caused great agitation in him. From his gestures and attempts, Urvashi realized that this was the foolish person himself. Knowing that he was the foolish person the *siddha* had spoken about, she smiled and spoke to him. Urvashi said, "O immensely fortunate one! Quickly tell me what you desire from me. Trust me. I will do whatever you ask me to do." The foolish brahmana replied, "O one with the beautiful smiles! Save me by giving yourself to me." Urvashi told the brahmana, "I am observing some rituals now. Remain here for a while and wait for my return." When the brahmana said he would remain there, she went off to heaven. When she returned after only a month, the divine lady saw that the brahmana had become emaciated. Without any food, he had remained on the banks of the river. Seeing that he was firm in his resolution, she assumed the form of an old lady. On the banks of the river, she made a mixture of *saktu*, sugar, honey and *ghee*. She went to River Matsyodari and bathed there. The one with the beautiful eyes sat down on the ground and summoned the brahmana with these meaningful words. Urvashi said, "O brahmana! For the sake of good fortune, I have observed a great vow. O brahmana! I am giving you this for the completion of the vow. Please accept it." He said, "Coated in sugar, what are you giving me? O virtuous one! O fortunate one! My throat is suffering from hunger. Please tell me." She told him, "O brahmana! This is *saktu*, mixed with ground sugar. Without any delay, accept this and save your life." Hearing this, he remembered. Though he was suffering from hunger, he replied, "O fortunate one! I have taken a vow and cannot accept this. In front of the noble *siddha*, I said that I would not take *saktu*. Urvashi will get to know. Please give it to someone else." She said, "O fortunate one! You made that vow about *saktu* mixed in wood. This has not been mixed in wood. Eat it. You are suffering from hunger." The brahmana replied, "I did not qualify it in any way. O fortunate one! I took a general vow." She told him, "O brahmana! Do not eat it. Accept it and go home. Your family members will eat it." He replied, "O one

<hr />

[140] The god of love.

with the excellent teeth! I will not go home now. The beautiful
one surpasses everyone in the three worlds in qualities.[141] Madana
afflicted me and I sought her. When she left, she assured me and
told me to remain here for a while. I agreed to do that. O fortunate
one! It has only been a month since she left and I have stayed here.
O one who is firm in vows! I am devoted to the truth and wish to
unite with her." Hearing his words, she assumed her own excellent
form. Her smile was full of deep sentiments. Urvashi spoke to the
brahmana. Urvashi said, "O brahmana! This is wonderful. Your
resolution has been firm and you have been truthful to your vow.
Wishing to see me, you have followed it without any deceit. O
brahmana! I am Urvashi and I have come here to test you. Tested,
your resolution has been seen to be firm. You are a *rishi*, truthful
in your austerities. Go to the region of the boar, famous by the
name of Rupatirtha. O Indra among *brahmanas*! You will achieve
success there and obtain me." O *brahmanas*! Saying this, Urvashi
leapt up into the sky and departed.'

The brahmana, devoted to the truth and austerities, went to
Rupatirtha. Filled with serenity, he observed pure vows and rituals
there. When he gave up his body, he went to the excellent world
of the *gandharvas*. There, he enjoyed the appropriate objects of
pleasure for one hundred *manvantaras*. After this, he was born in
an excellent lineage as a king, devoted to delighting his subjects.
He performed many kinds of sacrifices at which excellent *dakshina*
was distributed. Handing over the kingdom to his sons, he again
went to the region of the boar. He died in Rupatirtha and went
to Shakra's world. There, he enjoyed objects of pleasure for one
hundred manvantaras. Dislodged from there, he was born in the
excellent city of Pratishthana as Pururava, Budha's son. O stores
of austerities! He then united with Urvashi. In this way, in earlier
times, there was a brahmana who followed truth and austerities
in the place known as Rupatirtha. If one worships and pleases
Vishnu, one can obtain objects of pleasure and emancipation even
in this life.

[141] Referring to Urvashi.

Chapter 1(121) (On *maya*)

The sages said, 'We have heard the benefits of singing to Krishna while one remains awake during the night. That is how the *chandala* obtained the supreme destination. O immensely intelligent one! Please tell us about developing devotion towards Vishnu. We now wish to hear about austerities and deeds that ensure this.'

Vyasa replied, 'O tigers among sages! Listen. I will tell you about it in the proper order, about how a man derives great fruits through devotion towards Krishna. This *samsara* is extremely terrible and brings great fear to all beings. It is full of hundreds of miseries and causes great grief to men. They have to be born thousands of times as inferior species. O *brahmanas*! It is only sometimes that one obtains birth in a human body. Having become human, it is rare to be a brahmana. Having become a brahmana, it is rare to have discrimination. From a sense of discrimination, one develops intelligence about *dharma*. Intelligence brings supreme benefit. However, across successive births, until a man has not destroyed his accumulated sins, devotion towards Vasudeva, who pervades the universe, is not generated. O *brahmanas*! I will tell you how devotion towards Krishna comes about. In thoughts, words and deeds, there may be devotion towards other gods. O supreme among *brahmanas*! When there is single-minded devotion in the inner core, he performs sacrifices to them. O *brahmanas*! He controls himself and is devoted to Agni.[142] When the fire-god is satisfied, devotion towards Bhaskara[143] results. O *brahmanas*! Then, he constantly worships Aditya. When Bhaskara is pleased, devotion towards Shankara results. He then makes efforts and follows the norms to worship Shambhu.[144] When Trilochana is satisfied, devotion towards Keshava results. He worships the undecaying Jagannatha, known as Vasudeva. O supreme among *brahmanas*! It is then that he obtains objects of pleasure and emancipation.'

[142] The fire-god.

[143] The sun-god. Another name for Bhaskara is Aditya.

[144] Both Shankara and Shambhu are Shiva's names, as is Trilochana, meaning the three-eyed one.

The sages said, 'O great sage! Men who are not devoted to Vishnu are seen. O brahmana! What is the reason for them not worshipping Vishnu?'

Vyasa replied, 'O supreme among sages! Two kinds of creation are known in this world. Earlier, Svayambhu[145] created *asura*s and gods. When one obtains a divine nature, Achyuta is worshipped. When a man obtains an *asura* nature, he reviles Hari. The *vijnana* of those worst among men is destroyed by Vishnu's *maya*. O *brahmanas*! Unable to obtain Hari, they head towards an inferior destination. His deep *maya* is incomprehensible to gods and *asura*s. This causes great delusion among men and those who have not cleaned their souls find it impossible to cross.'

The sages said, 'We wish to understand Vishnu's *maya* which is so very difficult to cross. O one who knows about *dharma*! We have great curiosity. You should tell us about it.'

Vyasa replied, 'That *maya* drags the worlds. It is like a dream, like magic. With the exception of Keshava himself, who is capable of understanding Hari's *maya*? Because of that *maya*, great mortification affected the conduct of a brahmana and Narada. O *brahmanas*! Listen to my words. Earlier, in a city, there used to be a prosperous king known as Agnidhra. His son, Kamadamana, was pure and found delight in *dharma*. His conduct was forgiving and he was engaged in serving his father. He was accomplished in delighting the subjects and he made efforts to learn the *shruti* texts and the sacred texts.[146] His father made attempts to get him married, but he did not desire it. His father asked him, "Why don't you want to have a wife? Men desire wives for every kind of happiness. A wife is the source of happiness. Therefore, act in that way." He heard his father's words and out of respect for him, remained silent. O *brahmanas*! However, every once in a while, his father continued to urge him. At this, he told his father, "O father! This does not

---

[145] The self-creating one, Brahma.

[146] The *shruti* texts, such as the *Veda*s, *Brahmana*s, *Aranyaka*s and *Upanishad*s are in the nature of revelation and do not have human authors. *Smriti* texts have human authors.

suit my name.[147] It is evident that I should follow the vow of being devoted to Vishnu, seeking refuge in him." His father told him, "O son! You should not act in this way. This is not *dharma*. No learned man will act in this way. O son! Act in accordance with my words. I am your father and master. Do not immediately immerse my lineage in the destruction of hell."[148] Hearing his father's words, the self-controlled son remembered an ancient account about the wonder that was *samsara*. He cheerfully replied to his father.'

The son said, 'O father! Listen to my words. They are full of truth and reason. O king! One should act in accordance with one's name. That is the way of the truth. I have been through thousands of births with hundreds of occasions of old age and death. I have been united with many wives and have been separated from all of them. I have obtained hundreds of states—grass, shrubs, creepers, plants, reptiles, wild animals, birds, domesticated animals, women, men and so on. I have repeatedly become a *gana*, *kinnara*, *gandharva*, *vidyadhara*, giant *uraga*, *yaksha*, *guhyaka*, *rakshasa*, *danava*, *apsara* and god.[149] O father! Thousands of times, I have become creatures that live in rivers. I have been through many creations and many destructions. O father! I have been through many births as a man, a god, a *gandharva*, a giant *uraga*, a *vidyadhara*, a bird and a *kinnara*. In a lineage, I was born as a *maharshi*, given to great austerities. My devotion to Janardana, the protector of the world who killed Madhu,[150] was unwavering. I devotedly followed many kinds of vows and fasting and satisfied the one who wields the *chakra* and mace as weapons. Satisfied, the great-souled Vishnu arrived before me, astride the king of the birds. He wished to bestow a boon on me. In a loud voice, he told me, 'O brahmana! Ask for the boon you wish. I will give it to you.' I told the lord Hari, 'O Keshava! If you are satisfied with me, I will ask for a boon. O Janardana! I wish to know about your supreme *maya*.' At this, Madhu and Kaitabha's

---

[147] Kamadamana means someone who has conquered desire.

[148] Without a son, one is destined for the hell named *put*.

[149] *Gana* (companion of Shiva), *kinnara/kimpurusha*, *vidyadhara*, *uraga/naga* and *guhyaka* (companion of Kubera) are semi-divine species.

[150] Vishnu killed two demons named Madhu and Kaitabha.

enemy replied, 'O brahmana! What will you do with my *maya*? I
will bestow *dharma*, *artha* and *kama* on you. I will give you the best
of sons and freedom from disease. Thereupon, I again spoke to
Murari.[151] 'I wish to conquer *dharma* and *artha*. I wish to know
about your *maya*. O lotus-eyed one! Show that to me now.' The
excellent Nrisimha,[152] Shri's lord, the lord Vishnu, addressed me in
these words. 'No one knows my *maya* and no one will ever know it.
O brahmana! Earlier, there was a *devarshi* known as Narada. He
was Brahma's son and was full of devotion towards me. Earlier, full
of faith, he satisfied me with his devotion. I went to him to confer a
boon on him and he asked for the boon that you have asked for.
Though I tried to restrain him because of his excessive folly, he
asked for the boon that you have asked for. At this, I told him, 'O
Narada! Immerse yourself in water. Once you are so submerged,
you will know my *maya*.' Accordingly, Narada submerged himself
in the water and turned into Sushila, the daughter of the king of
Kashi. When she attained youth, he[153] bestowed her on Charudharma,
the excellent son of the king of Vidarbha. United with Sudharma,[154]
the *maharshi* enjoyed unmatched desire. When his father went to
heaven, the kingdom passed onto him and the powerful one happily
protected the kingdom of Vidarbha, surrounded by many sons and
grandsons. Thereafter, there was a great battle between King
Sudharma and the king of Kashi. In that battle, the king of Vidarbha
and the king of Kashi were both destroyed along with their sons and
grandsons. Sushila got to know that her father had been killed along
with his sons and that her husband had also been killed, along with
his sons and grandsons. Sushila emerged from the city and went to
the field of battle. She saw the great carnage in her father's army
and her husband's army there. Miserable, she lamented for a very
long time. Afflicted by grief, she went to her mother. She collected

[151] Murari means Mura's enemy. Since Vishnu killed a demon named
Mura, he is known as Murari.

[152] Nrisimha is the same as Narasimha, Vishnu's half-man half-lion
avatara.

[153] The king of Kashi.

[154] Charudharma and Sudharma have the same meaning.

the remains of her brothers, sons, brothers' sons, grandsons, husband and father and went to the great cremation ground where she lit a large funeral pyre. She kindled the fire herself and when the fire was blazing, Sushila rushed forth and entered the fire, exclaiming, 'Alas, son! Alas, son!' She once again turned into the sage Narada and the fire turned into sparkling crystal. He emerged from the full lake and saw Keshava, supreme among gods, in front of him. He was four-armed and held a conch shell, mace and sword in his hands. He laughed and spoke to *devarshi* Narada. 'O *maharshi*! Who is your son? Tell me. O one whose intelligence has been destroyed! Who are you grieving over?' Narada stood there, ashamed, and I spoke to him again. 'O Narada! My *maya* is like this, full of misery. The one who is seated on the lotus,[155] the great Indra and Rudra are incapable of understanding it. It will be extremely difficult for you to understand it.' Hearing my words, the great *maharshi* replied, 'O Vishnu! Grant me devotion. O lord! At whatever time I remember you, may I always be able to see you. O Achyuta! This is a place where afflicted by grief, I climbed into the funeral pyre. Let it be a *tirtha* that destroys all sins. O Keshava! Along with the one who is seated on the lotus, may you always be present here.' O brahmana! I told Narada, 'Your funeral pyre will be the *tirtha* of Sitoda. As Vishnu, I will always be present here and Maheshvara will remain towards the north. When Virinchi's mouth utters harsh words, the three-eyed one will sever it.[156] To free the skull, he will come to this *tirtha* of yours. When the destroyer of Tripura bathes in this *tirtha*, the skull will fall down on the ground. Therefore, this *tirtha* will be famous on earth by the name of Kapalamochana.[157] From that time, the one who rides on the clouds[158] has not left that supreme and extremely sacred *tirtha*, to

[155] Brahma.

[156] Virinchi is Brahma. There are different stories about why Shiva severed Brahma's fifth head. The severed head stuck to Shiva's hand.

[157] Kapalamochana means the place where the skull (*kapala*) was released (*mochana*). There are various Kapalamochana tirthas, but this one is probably the temple in Varanasi.

[158] Indra.

free himself from the sin of killing a brahmana.[159] O brahmana! As long as the slayer of the enemy of the immortals does not leave that *kshetra*, the foremost *kshetra* will continue to bestow great merits. The gods refer to the *tirtha* as Vimukta and praise it as a place that bestows undecaying merits. Even if a man commits great sins, if he enters it, he becomes pure and clean. If he thinks of me, the illustrious one, through my favours, he becomes pure and obtains emancipation. In another birth, he may become what is known as a *rudra-pishacha*[160] and experience miseries. After many years, he will be freed from his sins and take birth in the house of a brahmana. When he becomes pure and is in control of himself, at the time of his death, for his welfare, Rudra will recite the *taraka mantra* to him.[161] After telling Narada, the noble brahmana all this, I went to my own abode in the ocean of milk. The brahmana *rishi* went to heaven and was worshipped by the king of the *gandharva*s. All this has been said to make you understand. My *maya* is incapable of being understood. If you wish to understand it, trust me and enter this water. You will understand.' Thus, Hari made the brahmana understand. To understand the meaning of *yoga*, he immersed himself in the water. O father! The brahmana immersed himself in the water in Kokamukha and became a maiden in a *chandala*'s house. She was beautiful and possessed good conduct and qualities. When she attained youth, she was married to the son of a *chandala*. He was named Subahu and he was devoid of beauty. She did not like her husband, although he was attached to her. She gave birth to two sons who were blind. After this, she gave birth to a daughter who was deaf. Her husband was poor. Therefore, every day, she used to go to the river and cry miserably. On one occasion, she took her pot with her and entered the water to have a bath. She instantly regained her form as a brahmana, good in conduct and devoted to

---

[159] This is a reference to Indra killing Vritra. The consequent sin refused to leave him.

[160] A *pishacha* is a demon who eats flesh, *rudra* means terrible.

[161] For those who die in Varanasi, at the time of death, Shiva chants the *taraka mantra*. *Taraka mantra* means the *mantra* that enables one to cross over. Different versions are given of *taraka mantra*.

the rites of *yoga*. When she did not return for a long time, to search
for her, her husband went to the extremely sacred river. He saw the
water-pot on the bank, but could not see her. Extremely miserable,
he started to cry loudly. The two blind sons and the deaf daughter
also came there. On seeing that their father was crying miserably,
they too started to weep, suffering from grief. He asked some
brahmanas who were on the banks of the river. 'Did you see a
woman come here for water?' They replied, 'We saw her come here
for water and enter, but we did not see her emerge again from the
water. We know only this much.' Hearing these extremely terrible
words, tears started to flow from his eyes and he wept in grief.
Seeing him, his sons and daughter weep, I also became afflicted by
grief. O lord of the earth![162] My sorrow made me remember that I
was the *chandala* lady. O king! I spoke to the *matanga*. 'Why are
you crying? O foolish one! You are not going to get her back
through your weeping. This lamentation is useless.' He told me,
'These sons are blind and the daughter is deaf. O brahmana! They
are grieving. How can I comfort them and rear them now?' Saying
this, along with his sons and daughter, he started to shriek and cry.
The more the *shvapaka* cried, the more I felt compassion for him. I
restrained the afflicted person and told him about the account of my
birth. Miserable and suffering, along with his sons and daughter, he
entered Kokamukha. As soon as the *matanga* entered the water,
because of the power of the *tirtha*, he was cleansed on his sins. O
father! While I looked on, he ascended a *vimana* that was like the
moon and went to heaven. When he entered the water and died,
that misery caused great delusion in me. O noble king! I entered the
extremely sacred waters of Kokamukha and went to heaven. I was
born in a *vaishya* lineage and suffered from pain. However, because
of the favours of that supreme *tirtha*, I remembered my previous
birth. My mind was greatly detached. Controlling my speech and
mind, I went to Kokamukha. Resorting to a vow, I dried up my
body and went to heaven. O father! When I was dislodged from
there, I was born in your house. But because of Hari's favours, I
remembered my former births. Having worshipped the divinity

---

[162] Kamadamana is relating all this to his father, King Agnidhra.

Murari in Kokamukha, I have given up all desire for the auspicious and the inauspicious.' Saying this, he prostrated himself before his father and went to the foremost *tirtha* of Kokamukha. The bull among men worshipped Vishnu in the form of Varaha and obtained success. Thus, Kamadamana gave up his body which was full of taints in the greatly sacred and supreme *tirtha* of Kokamukha. Along with his sons and grandsons,[163] he went to heaven in a *vimana* that resembled the sun. I have thus spoken about the supreme lord's *maya*. Even the gods find it impossible to think about it. O *brahmanas*! It resembles a dream, or magic. Using this, Murari confounds the universe.

Chapter 1(122) (*kali yuga*)

The sages said, 'O Vyasa! We have heard what you have told us about the manifestation of Vishnu's sacred *maya*, which is so very difficult to understand. O great sage! We wish to hear from you about the withdrawal of everything at the end of the *kalpa*, known as the great *pralaya*.'[164]

Vyasa replied, 'O best among sages! Hear about the annihilation at the end of a *kalpa*, when *prakrita pralaya* occurs.[165] A human month is a day for the ancestors and a human year is a day for the residents of heaven. O supreme *brahmanas*! One thousand *mahayuga* amount to one of Brahma's days. The four *yuga* are *krita*, *treta*, *dvapara* and *kali*. Twelve thousand years of the gods are said to amount to this.[166] The four *yuga* are similar to each other

---

[163] Since he did not marry, this leaves an unexplained inconsistency.

[164] *Kalpa* is one of Brahma's days, the time for creation. When Brahma's night starts, there is a great destruction (*pralaya*).

[165] *Prakrita pralaya* will be explained in Chapter 1(124).

[166] This leaves a lot of things unsaid. A *mahayuga* is a cycle of *krita*, *treta*, *dvapara* and *kali*. *Krita* has 4,000 divine years, *treta* has 3000 divine years, *dvapara* has 2000 divine years and *kali* has 1000 divine years. There are 400 additional years at either end of *krita*, 300 at either end of *treta*, 200 at either end of *dvapara* and 100 at either end of *kali*. This amounts to

in form. O sages! *Krita yuga* is said to be the first and *kali* is the last. In the first *krita yuga*, Brahma carried out his creation. In that way, annihilation occurs at the end of the last *kali yuga*.'

The sages said, 'O illustrious one! You should explain to us the nature of *kali yuga* in detail. O illustrious one! That is when the four feet of *dharma* decline.'[167]

Vyasa replied, 'O *brahmanas*! O unblemished ones! You have asked me about the nature of *kali yuga*. This has great detail. I will tell you briefly. Understand. In *kali yuga*, the conduct of men is not based on *varna*s and *ashrama*s. The rituals of *Sama*, *Rig* and *Yajur Veda* are not carried out. Marriages in *kali yuga* do not follow *dharma*, disciples do not seek out preceptors. The sons do not follow *dharma*, the progressive rituals about the sacrificial fire do not exist. In *kali yuga*, the strongest person becomes the lord of everyone regardless of the lineage in which he has been born. A man subsists by accepting a maiden from all *varna*s.[168] In *kali yuga*, a brahmana is initiated through any possible method. O Indras among *brahmanas*! In *kali yuga*, anything is regarded as a means of atonement. O *brahmanas*! In *kali yuga*, anything is said and everything is accepted as a sacred text. In *kali yuga*, everyone is a god and everything is an *ashrama*. In *kali yuga*, one fasts, makes efforts and donates wealth as one pleases and that is regarded as dharma. In *kali yuga*, men become intoxicated with even a little bit of wealth. The beauty of women is decided on the basis of their hair. Since gold, jewels, gems and garments deteriorate in *kali yuga*, women can only dress their hair. If they lack in riches, women abandon their husbands. In *kali yuga*, only the rich become the husbands of women. Anyone who donates a lot becomes the lord of men and nobility of lineage is decided on the basis of such lordship. Accumulated riches are exhausted in building a house. When riches are exhausted, the mind turns towards earning money.

12,000 divine years for a *mahayuga* and there are 1,000 *mahayuga* in one of Brahma's days.

[167] Dharma has four feet in *krita*, three in *treta*, two in *dvapara* and one in *kali*. Each *yuga* loses a foot.

[168] Irrespective of *varna*.

Without money, there are no objects of pleasure in *kali yuga*. In *kali yuga*, women love intercourse and become *svairinis*.[169] They desire men who have earned wealth through illegitimate means. O *brahmanas*! Even if he is asked by a well-wisher, no man will tolerate something that harms his own selfish end, even if it is to the extent of one-quarter of a *pana*.[170] In *kali yuga*, the mind of a brahmana will always be full of virility. Cows will be honoured only as long as they yield milk. There will often be a drought and subjects will suffer on account of hunger. Therefore, all of them will constantly look up towards the sky.[171] Like ascetics, men will subsist on roots, leaves and fruits for food. Extremely miserable because it does not rain, they will kill themselves. They will always suffer from famine and hardships and will be unable to master these. In *kali yuga*, the happiness of men will suffer and they will be distracted. They will eat without having a bath. They will not worship the fire, gods or guests. When *kali yuga* arrives, *pinda* will not be given and water-rites will not be performed. In *kali yuga*, women will be greedy and short in stature. They will want to eat a lot. They will be unfortunate but will have many children. Women will use both their hands to scratch their heads. They will ignore the instructions of their seniors and husbands and will go out uncovered. They will be angry and devoted to nourishing themselves. They will not clean their bodies. In *kali yuga*, women will speak harsh and false words. They will be wicked in conduct and will always desire those who are wicked in conduct. The women of the family will be attracted towards men who are evil in conduct. Those who are prohibited and those who are without vows will study the Vedas. Householders will not offer oblations into the fire and will not offer appropriate donations. Those who reside in forests will eat what villagers should eat. Mendicants will be driven by bonds of affection towards their

---

[169] *Svairinis* are loose women who have sex with anyone they want, but only with those from the same *varna*. *Kaminis* are loose women who have sex with anyone they want, irrespective of *varna*. *Pumshchalis* have no sense of discrimination are almost like harlots.

[170] A *pana* is a small coin.

[171] For rain.

sons. Kings will no longer protect. Instead, they will use interest and taxes to take away. When *kali yuga* arrives, they will take away the wealth of people. Anyone who possesses superior horses, chariots and elephants will become a king. In *kali yuga*, anyone who is weak will be a servant to everyone. *Vaishya*s will abandon their own means of subsistence, agriculture and trade and take to the means of livelihood for shudras. They will earn a living through artisanship. Shudras will observe the vow of begging for alms. The worst among men will exhibit signs of renunciation. Those who have not gone through *samskara*s will indulge in heretical activities. People will greatly suffer from famine and taxes. Miserable, they will migrate to regions where wheat and barley exist. The path indicated in the Vedas will decay and people will become heretics. As *adharma* increases, the lifespan of people will decline. People will torment themselves with austerities that are not sanctioned by the sacred texts. Because of the sins of men and kings, infants will die young. In *kali yuga*, when they are five, six or seven years old, girls will give birth to children and the fathers will be eight, nine or ten years old. The hair will turn grey at the age of twelve years. In *kali yuga*, no one will live till the age of twenty years. In *kali yuga*, men will be limited in wisdom. They will bear false signs and will be wicked inside. They will, therefore, be destroyed within a brief span of time. Whenever there are signs of heretics increasing in importance, the learned recognize that *kali yuga* is increasing. Whenever the path of the Vedas followed by the virtuous tends to suffer, the learned infer that *kali yuga* is increasing in importance. O *brahmanas*! Whenever men who follow *dharma* tend to suffer, the learned infer that *kali yuga* is increasing its influence. Whenever sacrifices to the lord Purushottama, the lord of sacrifices, are not undertaken, that should be taken as a sign of *kali yuga*'s strength increasing. Whenever there is no pleasure in discussing the Vedas and there is attraction towards heretical doctrines, the wise and the learned infer that *kali yuga* is increasing in importance. O *brahmanas*! In *kali yuga*, Vishnu, the lord of the universe, the lord who has created everything, is not worshipped. Men are overwhelmed by heretics and are verbose in exclaiming, "What use are gods? What use are *brahmanas* and the Vedas? What is the point of purifying one's

birth with water?" Parjanya[172] rains little and therefore the yield of
crops is limited. O *brahmanas*! When *kali yuga* arrives, fruits have
limited substance. Garments extend only up to the knees. All trees
are generally like the *shami* tree.[173] In *kali yuga*, all the *varna*s are
generally like shudras. Grain is generally as small as an atom.[174]
Milk is obtained from goats. When *kali yuga* arrives, unguents
are only made out of *oushira* grass.[175] In *kali yuga*, men generally
regard fathers-in-law and mothers-in-law as the seniors. O supreme
among sages! Brothers-in-law and the wife's relatives are regarded
as well-wishers. Men who follow their father-in-law say, "Whose
mother? Whose father? A man is the result of his own *karma*." In
thoughts, words and deeds, they are repeatedly overwhelmed by
taints. Therefore, limited in intelligence, men commit sins every
day. O *brahmanas*! They are without truth, without purification
and without modesty. Therefore, in *kali yuga*, everything is a source
of misery. There is no studying and no *vashatkara*. There are no
exclamations of *svadha* and *svaha*. A brahmana becomes rare in
this world. Supreme and excellent good merits, which required
austerities in *krita yuga*, can be achieved in a short span of time.'[176]

The sages asked, 'At what time does a limited amount of *dharma*
yield great fruits? You should tell us in detail. We wish to hear.'

Vyasa replied, 'O *brahmanas*! *Kali yuga* is blessed, since only
a little bit of effort yields great fruits. Women and shudras become
blessed. Listen. O *brahmanas*! The fruits of *brahmacharya* and *japa*
take ten years in *krita yuga*, but are achieved through six months
in *treta* and one month in *dvapara*. It is said that a virtuous man
achieves this through one day and night in *kali yuga*. Fruits were
obtained through *dhyana* in *krita*, performing sacrifices in *treta* and
worshipping in *dvapara*. Those are obtained by chanting Keshava's
name in *kali yuga*. With a little bit of effort, a man achieves the
best of *dharma* in *kali yuga* and becomes knowledgeable about

---

[172] The god of rain.
[173] Meaning, they are as thorny as the *shami* (silk-cotton) tree.
[174] *Anu* has been translated as atom.
[175] A fragrant grass.
[176] In *kali yuga*, even limited efforts yield great results.

dharma. That is the reason I am satisfied with *kali yuga*. Earlier, *dvija*s followed supreme vows and grasped the Vedas. They followed the norms and performed sacrifices with wealth obtained through *dharma*. However, fruitless talk, pointless food and taking themselves to be *dvija*s led to their downfall, along with those of the mendicants. The tasks were imperfectly completed and this led to every object being tainted. O *brahmanas*! They ate and drank what they wished and this led to them not gaining anything. This was true of every attempt they made for the world hereafter. In this world, they suffered great hardships even though they humbly undertook sacrifices. However, shudras served *dvija*s and were engaged in *paka-yajna*, thereby conquering their own worlds. Hence, shudras are more blessed. O tigers among sages! They did not suffer from any sins regarding what should be eaten and what should not be eaten. There were no virtuous rules for them. Thus, such men were engaged in their own *dharma* and always earned riches without any conflict. O supreme among *brahmanas*! There are great hardships in following the rules on who one should donate to, how one should follow the norms and perform sacrifices and how wealth should be earned. It is very difficult to comprehend the mystery of what is a virtuous rule for men. O supreme among *brahmanas*! Hence, through their own efforts, these other men progressively conquered their own worlds, those of Prajapati and others. O *brahmanas*! By serving her husband in thoughts, words and deeds, a woman also obtains these regions and worlds. Unlike a man, she obtains them without a great deal of effort. For the third time, I am stating that women are virtuous. O *brahmanas*! I have thus told you what you came here for. Clearly ask whatever you want and I will tell you. With a little bit of effort, a great deal of *dharma* is achieved in *kali yuga*. Using their own qualities like water, men can wash off every kind of sin. O supreme sages! Shudras achieve this by being devoted to serving *dvija*s and women easily obtain this by serving their husbands. That is the reason it is my view that these three are the most blessed.[177] In *krita* and others, *dvija*s had to make a great

---

[177] Two are shudras and women. The third seems to be those who make a little bit of effort in *kali yuga*.

deal of effort to achieve *dharma*. But, through a few austerities, men can obtain success.[178] O supreme among sages! Those who follow *dharma* at the end of a *yuga*[179] are blessed. I have told you what you desired and also what was not asked. O ones who know about *dharma*! O *brahmanas*! What else should be done?

Chapter 1(123) (*Kali yuga* continued)

The sages said, 'O brahmana! We do not know whether the age that causes hardship[180] is imminent. The decay and end of *dvapara yuga* has arrived. We have come to you with a thirst for knowing about the *dharma* that is appropriate for this time. We will happily undertake whatever few deeds ensure supreme *dharma*. However, we are also scared and anxious that the end of the *mahayuga* will arrive. O one who knows about *dharma*! You should tell us about the signs of *dharma* being destroyed.'

Vyasa replied, 'Kings will take away their shares of taxes, but will not protect. The influence of the end of the *mahayuga* will be such that they will only be engaged in protecting themselves. Those who are not *kshatriya*s will become kings. *Brahmanas* will resort to means of subsistence meant for shudras. At the end of the *mahayuga*, shudras will practice the conduct of *brahmanas*. At the end of a *mahayuga*, learned *brahmanas*, *kandaprishtha*s and those who do not perform rites or offer oblations will eat while seated in the same row.[181] Men will not be polished in conduct. They will be addicted to *artha* and will love liquor and flesh. At the end of the *mahayuga*, the worst among men will approach the wives of their friends. Thieves will conduct themselves as kings.

---

[178] In *kali yuga*.
[179] The end of a *mahayuga*.
[180] *Kali yuga*.
[181] While eating, they should be seated in different rows (*pankti*). A *kandaprishtha* is a *brahmana* who earns a living by making arrows, or is the husband of a courtesan.

Kings will practice theft. When the *mahayuga* comes to an end,
servants will take away food without being asked to do so. Wealth
will be something to boast about. The conduct of the virtuous will
no longer be honoured. At the end of the mahayuga, those who
have fallen down will not be condemned. Men will have noses
missing. They will be disfigured and their hair will be disheveled.
Women who have not attained the age of sixteen years will give
birth. At the end of the *mahayuga*, habitations will have shops for
selling food. Crossroads will have shops for selling cattle. There
will be shops for women to dress their hair. Everyone will speak
about the *brahman* and *brahmanas* will follow the Vajasaneya
texts.[182] *Brahmanas* who speak will be *antyavasina* and will be
like shudras.[183] Their teeth will be white. They will be victorious
in debates. Their heads will be shaved and they be dressed in
ochre garments. Earning a living through deceitful intelligence,
shudras will speak about *dharma*. When the *mahayuga* is about
to come to an end, there will be plenty of predatory creatures and
cows will diminish in number. With the suffering of the virtuous,
knowledge will come to an end. Those who should dwell in the
extremities will live in the middle. Those who should dwell in
the middle will live in the extremities. At the time of the end of
the *mahayuga*, the subjects will be without shame and everything
will be destroyed. The best of *brahmanas* will sell the fruits of
austerities and sacrifices. At the end of the *mahayuga*, the seasons
will turn adverse. In *kali yuga*, bulls that are not one year old will
be yoked to the plough. When the *mahayuga* decays, Parjanya's
showers will become erratic. Anyone who is born in a noble
lineage will be capable of becoming a protector. In that way, at
the end of the *mahayuga*, all the subjects will become inferior.
When the *mahayuga* comes to an end, men will not follow dharma
and sons will not give what is due to their fathers. The land will
mostly turn barren and the roads will be infested with thieves.
At the end of the *mahayuga*, everyone will engage in trade. The

---

[182] The *Vajasaneya Samhita* of the *Yajur Veda*.
[183] Those who speak about *dharma*. *Antyavasina* means one who lives
towards the extremities of a habitation. This is, thus, a synonym for *antyaja*.

sons will divide what they have received as inheritance from their
father. Overcome by avarice, they will act against each other and
make efforts to take away from the others. At the end of the
mahayuga, beauty of form and jewels will diminish. Therefore,
women will only dress their hair. For a householder, sexual
intercourse will lack potency. When the end of the *mahayuga*
arrives, no one will be loved as much as one's own wife. There
will be many women who are wicked in conduct. Their beauty
will be futile because there will be few men and many women.
That is a sign of the end of the *mahayuga*. There will be many
people who are beggars and they will not give to each other.
They will decay and face destruction because of kings, thieves,
fire and punishment. The crops will not yield fruit. Young men
will behave like those who are aged. At the end of the *mahayuga*,
people will be happy when they are wicked in conduct. During
the monsoon, harsh winds will blow close to the ground and will
shower down stones. At the end of the *mahayuga*, doubts will be
raised about the world hereafter. Like *vaishya*s, king will earn
subsistence through wealth and grain. As the *yuga* progressively
move on, there will be no relatives. Contracts and pledges will
no longer be seen to have any validity. As the *mahayuga* starts to
decay, debts will no longer be humbly honoured. Happiness will
bear no fruits. But anger among men will be fruitful. At the end of
the *mahayuga*, goats will be reared for the sake of milk. Sacrifices
will be performed without following the sacred texts. Men who
pride themselves on being learned will not be able to cite any
proof. There is no doubt that there will be no one to speak about
the sacred texts. Everyone will know everyone and no one will
serve the elders. When the end of the *mahayuga* arrives, there will
be no one who is wise. The *dvija*s will not undertake tasks on the
basis of the conjunctions of the *nakshatra*s. When the end of the
yuga arrives, kings will generally be thieves. Bastards, deceivers
and drunkards will speak about the *brahman*. When the end of
the *mahayuga* arrives, the best among *brahmanas* will officiate
at horse sacrifices performed by those who should not perform
sacrifices and eat food that should not be eaten. When the end of
the *mahayuga* arrives, *brahmanas* will thirst after wealth. Since

they will not study, they will only know how to utter "*Bhoh*".[184] Fastened with grass, women will wear a single conch shell around their necks. The *nakshatra*s will be faded and the ten directions will turn perverse. When the end of the *mahayuga* arrives, the tinge of *sandhya* will turn ashen. Sons will dispatch fathers to perform their own tasks and daughters-in-law will send their mothers-in-law. In that last *yuga*, men and women will live like this. They will eat without offering oblations into the fire. *Brahmanas* will not offer oblations into the fire. Without giving alms and offering sacrifices, men will themselves eat. Deceiving husbands who are asleep, women will go to others. This is despite the husbands not being diseased, not being jealous and not lacking in beauty and enterprise. When the end of the *mahayuga* arrives, no one will be grateful for a good turn that is done.'

The sages asked, 'When *dharma* is suspended and men suffer from taxes, which regions will they reside in? What will they eat? How will they amuse themselves? What will be their tasks? What will be their wishes? What will be their stature? What will be their span of life? After what duration of time will *krita yuga* arrive again?'

Vyasa replied, 'When *dharma* loses its qualities, the subjects fall down from above. When good conduct suffers, so do their lifespans. When the lifespan suffers, strength declines. The decline in strength leads to pallor. Pallor leads to their suffering from ailments and this suffering from ailments leads to non-attachment and this non-attachment contributes to self-understanding. Self-understanding brings about an inclination towards *dharma*. When this supreme objective is reached, they attain *krita yuga*. Some are goaded into the good conduct of *dharma*, others remain in a medium state. Some will only be curious and ponder, 'What is the *dharma* of good conduct?' Some will decide that the true proof is only through direct perception and inference. There are other people who will say that nothing can ever be proved. Some will thus be non-believers and contribute to the impairment of *dharma*. There will be foolish men

---

[184] 'Bhoh' is difficult to translate. It is a bit like 'Hey'. The intention is to state that they will not know anything more than this exclamation.

and *Brahmanas* will pride themselves on their learning. Since they
will only have faith in what is instantaneous, they will be deprived
of the *jnana* of the sacred texts. With their *jnana* disappearing,
men will become insolent. In this way, *dharma* will be destroyed.
However, there will still be superior ones who will be respected.
They will act in accordance with what is auspicious and be devoted
to donating. When people eat everything, when they think they can
protect themselves, when they are without compassion and without
shame, that is a sign of *kali yuga*.[185] During the time of *kali yuga*,
when devotion towards *jnana* has been destroyed, even people who
have not been through *samskara* can obtain success with a little bit
of effort. O *brahmanas*! When people from inferior *varna*s resort to
the eternal conduct of *brahmanas*, that is a sign of *kali yuga*. When
the *mahayuga* declines, there will be great battles, heavy rains, strong
winds and scorching heat. That is a sign of *kali yuga*. When the
end of the *mahayuga* presents itself, disfigured *rakshasa*s who learn
through their ears[186] will become kings and enjoy the earth. There
will be no studying and no exclamations of *vashatkara*. There will
be evil and insolent leaders. In the form of *brahmanas*, predatory
creatures will eat everything. Vows will be fruitless. People will
be foolish and attached to *artha*. They will be inferior and their
garments will be inferior. The conduct of business will be perverse.
They will be dislodged from eternal *dharma*. They will steal the
jewels of others and force themselves on the wives of others. They
will be full of desire and evil-souled. They will indulge in frauds and
be reckless. However, because of such powers everywhere among
people, there will be many unthinking sages in many different kinds
of forms. When *kali yuga* arrives, the foremost people will be those
who are good with words. They will be worshipped by all men.
There will be thieves who steal crops, others who steal garments.
There will be those who steal food, others who steal baskets. There
will be thieves who steal from thieves. There will be killers who
kill killers. When thieves destroy thieves, peace will descend. The
period will be without substance and full of agitation. There will

---

[185] The text uses the word *kashaya*, meaning *kali yuga*.
[186] The will rule through hearsay, without verifying the facts.

be no rites and rituals. Suffering from the burden of taxes, men will resort to the forest. The rites of sacrifices will cease. *Rakshasa*s, predatory creatures, insects, rats and snakes will make men suffer. But even when the *mahayuga* decays, there will be superior men in some spots. They will enjoy peace, food, freedom from disease and support from relatives. They will protect themselves from being robbed by thieves and will be like laden boats. In different spots, they will exist in groups. In general, people will be dislodged from their own countries, along with their relatives and will lack in substance. When time decays, this is what will happen to all men. Out of fear, all of them will come together. Suffering from hunger, such men will take their sons and will cross River Koushiki.[187] Men will seek refuge in Anga, Vanga, Kalinga, Kashmira and Koshala and the valleys of Mount Rishikanta. They will reside everywhere on the slopes of the Himalayas and the shores of the salty ocean. They will attire themselves in many kinds of decaying leaves, bark and hides that they make themselves. When the *mahayuga* decays, they will reside there. Along with *mleccha*s,[188] men will inhabit the forests. The earth will not be empty, but nor will it have new forests. Kings will be protectors and also those who do not protect. Men will subsist on deer, fish, birds, carnivorous beasts, snakes, insects, honey, vegetables, fruits and roots. They will live like sages and attire themselves in decayed leaves, bark and hides that they make themselves and subsist on fruits. They will not be able to extract oil from oilseeds, but will injure themselves with the wooden stakes.[189] They will always rear goats, sheep, donkeys and camels. They will resort to the banks of rivers and use dams to stop the flow of the waters. They will trade with each other and buy and sell cooked food.[190] They will be covered with hair everywhere on the body. They will have many wives but no sons. They will be devoid of lineage and good conduct. Men will be like this, without any sense of

[187] Koshi in Bihar.
[188] Those who do not speak Sanskrit, barbarians.
[189] Used for the extraction.
[190] According to the injunctions, cooked food should not be bought and sold.

dharma. The inferior subjects will follow a *dharma* that is inferior. The lifespan of mortals will at most be thirty years. They will be weak and attached to material objects. They will be overwhelmed by old age and misery. At that time, there will be disease and the senses will suffer. The lifespan will be reduced further because of the violence that they cause to each other. Though they will love the sight of virtuous people, they will themselves need to be tended to. However, because of uncertainty about the nature of conduct, they will praise the truth. When nothing is gained through desire, they will follow *dharma*. Afflicted by the decay of their own side, they will cleanse themselves. They will practice serving, donations, truth and protecting life. In this way, benefit will be obtained and one-fourth of *dharma* will be regained. When the qualities change and this has been gained, they will see that this is *dharma* and ask, 'What is this tasty thing?' Just as there was progressive decay, there will be progressive expansion. When *dharma* is duly accepted, there will be *krita yuga* again. The good conduct of *krita yuga* is said to subsequently decay during *kali yuga*. This is just like the moon becoming pale in complexion, as a result of the progression of time. In *kali yuga*, it is as if the moon is shrouded in darkness. However, in krita yuga, the moon emerges from darkness. But the learned know that the supreme meaning of the *brahman* is in the purport of the Vedas. Something that is indeterminate and unknown is regarded as something to be given away.[191] Rites are said to be austerities and it is austerities that ensure steadfastness. Qualities are obtained by refraining from deeds, but qualities are also obtained by resorting to pure deeds. From one *yuga* to another *yuga*, on seeing men who follow the dictates of the time and the place, *rishi*s have pronounced benedictions over them. From one *yuga* to another *yuga*, sacred and auspicious benedictions are obtained by those who follow *dharma*, *artha* and *kama* and rites to the gods. The *yuga* circle around for a long time, depending on their nature and conduct, as determined by the creator. In this world of the living, rise and fall also circle around, neither remaining for more than an instant.'

---

[191] That is, regarded as valueless. Unless comprehended, the true value of *dharma* is also not realized.

Chapter 1(124) (*naimittika* destruction)

Vyasa said, 'It has been held that there are three kinds of withdrawals of all living creatures—*naimittika*, *prakritika*[192] and *atyantika*. When everything is withdrawn into the *brahman* at the end of a *kalpa*, that is *naimittika*. *Atyantika* is the one that leads to *moksha* and *prakrita* amounts to two *parardhas*.'

The sages said, 'O illustrious one! Tell us what has been said about the duration of a *parardha*, since doubling it one obtains a *prakrita* withdrawal.'

Vyasa replied, 'O *brahmanas*! Each number is counted as ten times the number that succeeds it.[193] Thus, *parardha* is at the eighteenth place.[194] O *brahmanas*! When a *parardha* is double, *prakrita laya* takes place.[195] In that destruction, everything manifest is withdrawn into the unmanifest, the original cause. The basic measurement of time for humans is *nimesha*.[196] Fifteen *nimesha*s make up one *kashtha* and thirty *kashtha*s make up one *kala*. Fifteen *kala*s make up one *nadika*. In a vessel that is six and a half *pala*s[197] in weight, with sides measuring four *angula*s, a hole that is four *angula*s in length is made and a golden wire four *angula*s long and one *masha* in weight is inserted into it. The time taken for this to be submerged in water is one *nadika*. O supreme *brahmanas*! In Magadha, the measurement is for water to pass through a *prastha*.[198] Two *nadika*s make up one *muhurta*. Thirty

---

[192] The same as *prakrita pralaya*.

[193] In Sanskrit, the higher number is written to the right. Therefore, literally, each number is ten times the number that precedes it. But we have changed it, so that there is no confusion.

[194] 1 followed by seventeen zeros.

[195] *Laya/pralaya* means destruction.

[196] The twinkling of an eye.

[197] A *pala* is a measure of weight, but its stated weighted varies across sources. 30 grams is a rough indication. *Angula* is the length of a finger. *Masha* is just short of one gram. This entire shloka is very cryptic and impossible to understand. Therefore, we have expanded the translation, so as to make the meaning clear.

[198] A *prastha* is thirty-two *pala*s. Instead of six and a half *pala*s, the vessel has a weight of thirty-two *pala*s.

*muhurta*s make up a day and night.[199] There are thirty days in a
month. Twelve months make up a year and this is equivalent to a day
and night in heaven. Three hundred and sixty human years amount to
one year for the gods. Twelve thousand divine years amount to a set of
the four *yuga*.[200] One thousand *mahayuga* amount to one of Brahma's
days. O supreme *brahmanas*! This is a *kalpa* and within this, there
are fourteen Manus. O *brahmanas*! At the end of this, Brahma's
naimittika laya occurs. O Indras among *brahmanas*! Its nature is
terrible. Listen to my words. I will tell you about *prakrita laya* later.
At the end of one thousand *mahayuga*, the earth is almost destroyed.
For one hundred years, a terrible drought occurs. O best among sages!
Almost every being on earth that has limited energy and substance
suffers a great deal and is destroyed. The illustrious and undecaying
Krishna assumes the form of Rudra. He makes all the subjects headed
for destruction a part of his own self. O supreme sages! The illustrious
Vishnu is stationed in the form of the sun, with seven rays and drinks
up all the water. O *brahmanas*! After having drunk up all the water
of the creatures and beings, he dries up the entire surface of the earth.
The oceans, the rivers, the mountains, the springs in the mountains
and all the water in the nether regions is conveyed to destruction.
There is a lack of water. Having drunk up the water, seven suns each
with one thousand rays are generated. Those seven suns heat from
above and below. O *brahmanas*! They scorch the three worlds and
the seven nether regions.[201] The blazing and resplendent suns scorch
the three worlds. No liquid is left in the mountains, trees and oceans.
O *brahmanas*! Everywhere in the three worlds, the trees and water are
scorched. The earth assumes the form of the back of a tortoise. Hara
Rudra, the destroyer of the creation of beings, assumes the form of the
fire of destruction. Using the breath of the serpent Shesha, he burns
the nether regions from below. The great blaze scorches all the nether
regions and reaching the earth, burns down everything on the surface
of the earth. There are terrible garlands of fire in *bhuvarloka* and

[199] Therefore, a *muhurta* is 48 minutes and a *nadika* is 24 minutes.
[200] That is, a *mahayuga*.
[201] The seven nether regions are Atala, Vitala, Nitala, Sutala, Talatala,
Rasatala and Patala.

svarloka.[202] Giant storms swirl around. All the three worlds come to resemble a frying pan. Surrounded by whirling flames, all the residents of these two worlds lose their strength. O *brahmanas*! Suffering from the heat, they seek refuge in Maharloka. But there too, the subjects are scorched by the great heat. Surrounded by this grief, seeking to save themselves, they go to Janaloka. O supreme among sages! Having scorched the entire universe in his form of Rudra, from the breath that is expelled from his mouth, Janardana creates clouds. They resemble elephants born in excellent lineages and there is thunder tinged with lightning. These dense and terrible *samvartaka* clouds[203] cover the sky. Some are like masses of collyrium, others are like Kumuda.[204] Some clouds have the complexion of smoke, other clouds are yellow. Some have the complexion of turmeric, others have the complexion of the juice of lac. Some are like lapis lazuli, others are like blue sapphire. Some are like the conch shell or the moon. Others are like *jati* and *kunda* flowers.[205] Some are like the *indragopa* insect,[206] others have the complexion of red arsenic. Some have the complexion of lotus petals, other clouds rise up atop other clouds. Some have the forms of excellent cities, others are like mountains. Some clouds have the complexion of the turrets of mansions, others have the complexion of barren ground. They are gigantic in form and with their loud roars, they fill up the firmament. O *brahmanas*! Extremely dense, they shower down and pacify that extremely terrible fire that has spread everywhere in the three worlds. When the fire has been extinguished, the clouds shower down for more than one hundred years. O supreme sages! They shower and flood the entire universe. O *brahmanas*! The torrential downpour floods and deluges *bhuloka* and *bhuvarloka*, and above this, *svarloka*. The worlds are enveloped in darkness and everything mobile and immobile is destroyed. The giant clouds shower down for more than one hundred years.

---

[202] *Bhuloka* is earth, *svarloka* is heaven and *bhuvarloka* is the space between the two.

[203] Clouds of destruction.

[204] The name of a gigantic elephant that guards the southern direction.

[205] Both are types of white jasmine.

[206] A reddish insect, sometimes identified with a firefly.

Chapter 1(125) (*Prakritika* destruction)

Vyasa said, 'O supreme among sages! The water approaches the place of the *saptarshis*[207] and everything in the three worlds becomes a single ocean of water. O *brahmanas*! After more than one hundred years have passed, the wind generated from Vishnu's breathing dispels those clouds. The unthinkable and illustrious creator of all beings has all the beings in him. He is the origin, but is without a beginning. He drinks up all the wind in the firmament. The lord lies down on that single ocean of water, resting on Shesha. Hari is the creator of everything. Assuming the form of the *brahman*, the illustrious one lies down. Sanaka and the other *siddha*s who have gone to Janaloka praise him. Those who desire *moksha* and have gone to Brahmaloka think about him. In his own divine *maya*, he lies down in *yoganidra*.[208] The supreme lord, known as Vasudeva, thinks about himself. O Indras among *brahmanas*! This withdrawal is known as *naimittika*. This is because Hari, in his form of the *brahman*, lies down as *nimitta*.[209] When the one who is the *atman* of everything is awake, the universe moves. When Achyuta lies down in his bed of *maya*, everything shuts down. One thousand *mahayuga* are one day for the one who originated from the lotus.[210] When the entire universe is reduced to a single ocean of water, it is said to be night for him. When he wakes up at the end of the night, Aja[211] creates again. As has been told to you earlier, it is Vishnu who assumes the form of Brahma to do all this. O *brahmanas*! This *pralaya*, the withdrawal at the end of a *kalpa*, is known as *naimittika*.[212] I have told you about this. Hear about *prakrita pralaya* next. O Brahmanas! Through lack of rain and fire, everything in the nether regions and in all the worlds is completely destroyed. Mahat and the other specific transformations

---

[207] The Great Dipper, part of Ursa Majoris.

[208] Asleep, immersed in *yoga*.

[209] Thus the expression *naimittika*, *nimitta* means cause.

[210] Brahma.

[211] The one without birth, Brahma.

[212] This is secondary destruction, at the end of one of Brahma's days. *Prakrita pralaya* occurs when Brahma's lifespan is over.

are destroyed. This withdrawal is brought about when Krishna so desires it. First, water devours smell and the other attributes of the earth. When smell is taken away, the earth is ready for destruction. When the subtle attribute of smell vanishes, the earth merges into water. The forceful water is everywhere and emits a loud roar. It fills everything, exists everywhere and roams around. Everywhere, Lokaloka[213] is enveloped in waves of water. The attribute of water is drunk up by fire. When taste, the attribute of water, is destroyed, the water is severely scorched and is also destroyed. With taste, the attribute of water, destroyed, water merges into fire. The energy of fire surrounds water from every direction. That fire pervades every direction and water is withdrawn. Fire gradually fills up everything in the universe. The rays are everywhere, above, below and diagonal. Form is the subtle attribute of fire, giving it luster, but fire is drunk up by wind. When that is destroyed, everything is filled up by wind. The subtle attribute of fire is form and fire loses its form. When fire has been pacified, the great wind starts to blow. The entire world is without light, since all that energy is inside the wind. It is withdrawn inside the wind, which was its origin. The wind blows in the ten directions, above, below and diagonal. Space devours touch, the subtle attribute of wind. Wind is pacified and space remains, without any cover. It has no form, taste, touch or smell and is without any embodied form. It is not manifest, but fills everything. Everything is enveloped by space with its subtle attribute of sound. The attribute of sound is next devoured by *ahamkara*.[214] The senses exist simultaneously with *ahamkara*. However, since *ahamkara* is based on pride,[215] it is said that *ahamkara* has a *tamas* characteristic. *Mahabuddhi*,[216] with its sense of discrimination, devours *ahamkara*. This great space exists inside and outside the universe. In this way, *Mahabuddhi* and the

---

[213] The mountain that separates the region illuminated by the sun from the region not illuminated by the sun.

[214] The text uses the word *bhutadi* (origin of the elements), meaning *ahamkara*.

[215] *Abhimana*.

[216] The great intelligence.

seven *prakriti*s are progressively drawn into each other.[217] Everything
is enveloped in darkness and merges into the cosmic egg, which is
in the water. The seven *dvipa*s, ending in the oceans and the seven
worlds, along with the mountains, are surrounded by water, which is
drunk up by fire. Fire merges into wind and wind, finds its destruction
in space. Space is devoured by *ahamkara* and *ahamkara* is devoured
by Mahat.[218] O *brahmanas*! Prakriti devours Mahat and everything
else. O supreme among *brahmanas*! Prakriti is that in which all the
gunas[219] are in balance. Nothing is excessive or deficient. Prakriti
is said to be the cause. Pradhana[220] is the supreme cause beyond
this. Prakriti is sometimes manifest and sometimes unmanifest. O
brahmanas! The manifest part of Prakriti merges into the unmanifest
part. After this, there is a single pure *akshara*[221] that pervades
everything. O Indra among *brahmanas*! A portion of the *paramatman*
exists within all beings. When everything is destroyed, all conceptions
of names and categories are also destroyed. What exists is known as
the *paramatman*. This knowledge about the *paramatman* is *jnana*.
This is the *brahman*, the supreme abode. This is the *paramatman*, the
supreme lord. This is Vishnu, who exists everywhere. On obtaining
him, no one returns. I have told you that Prakriti has both a manifest
part and an unmanifest part. Both Purusha and Prakriti merge into the
paramatman. The *paramatman* is the supreme lord, the foundation
of everything. In the Vedas and Vedanta, he is chanted about, using
the name of Vishnu. There are two kinds of rites in the Vedas—with
nivritti and *pravritti*.[222] In both of these, Purusha is worshipped.
He is the embodied form of the sacrifice. Using the paths of the *Rig
Veda*, the *Yajur Veda* and the *Sama Veda*, he is worshipped through

[217] This is the essence of *samkhya* philosophy and the seven *prakriti*s
presumably mean the five elements, the mind and *ahamkara*. This use of
the word *prakriti* is not to be confused with the subsequent Prakriti.

[218] Mahat is another word for Mahabuddhi.

[219] *Sattva*, *rajas* and *tamas*.

[220] Purusha, also referred to in these sections as the unmanifest part of
Prakriti.

[221] The one without destruction, the *paramatman*.

[222] *Nivritti* is detachment from fruits and renunciation of action.
Pravritti is action with a desire for the fruits.

pravritti. He is the lord of the sacrifice. He is Purusha. He is the being in the sacrifice. He is Purushottama. He is also worshipped through the path of *jnana*. His *atman* is *jnana*. He is the embodiment of *jnana*. When this path of *yoga* and *nivritti* is used, Vishnu confers the fruits of emancipation. There are things that are spoken about through *hrasva*, *dirgha* and *pluta* vowels and there are things that are beyond speech.[223] The undecaying Vishnu is all of these. He is manifest and he is unmanifest. He is the undecaying Purusha. He is the *paramatman*. He is the *atman* of the universe. Hari assumes the form of the universe. It is into him that the manifest and unmanifest forms of Prakriti merge. O *brahmanas*! Purusha also merges into the undifferentiated *atman*. O *brahmanas*! I have spoken to you about a period of time that lasts for two *parardha*s. O Indras among *brahmanas*! When Prakriti is manifest, this is spoken about as the Lord Vishnu's day. O stores of austerities! When Prakriti merges into Purusha, that duration of time is his night. However, for the *paramatman*, there is no real night or day. For the lord, such expressions are only used to articulate matters. O tigers among sages! I have, thus, spoken to you about *prakrita laya*.'

Chapter 1(126) (*Atyantika* destruction)

Vyasa said, 'O *brahmanas*! After learning about the three kinds of suffering, *adhyatymika* and the others,[224] a learned man obtains *jnana*, develops non-attachment and proceeds to *atyantika* destruction. There are two kinds of *adhyatmika* suffering, physical and mental. The physical suffering can be of many types. Listen. Pain in the head, cold, fever, rheumatism, fistula, enlargement of the spleen, piles, swelling, asthma, nausea, disease of the eyes, diarrhea, leprosy, those that are described as diseases of the limbs and many

[223] *Hrasva* or short vowels are pronounced over one *matra* (a prosodial or syllabic instant), *dirgha* or long vowels over two *matra*s and *pluta* or elongated vowels over three *matra*s.

[224] Relating to *adhidaivika* (destiny), *adhibhoutika* (nature) and *adhyatmika* (one's own nature).

others—these result from the body. You should now hear about
mental torment. O best among *brahmanas*! There are many kinds of
torments of the mind—desire, anger, fear, hatred, greed, confusion,
grief, sorrow, jealousy, dishonour, envy and malice. O supreme
among sages! These are the different kinds of ailments. Men suffer
from *adhibhoutika* suffering on account of animals, birds, other
men, *pishacha*s, *uraga*s, *rakshasa*s and reptiles. O foremost among
supreme *brahmanas*! *Adhidaivika* sufferings are said to be because
of cold, heat, wind, rain, water and lightning. O supreme among
sages! Due to conception, birth, old age, ignorance, death and hell,
there are thousands of different kinds of hardships. In the womb,
the delicate being is surrounded by a lot of excrement. Engulfed in
this, its back, neck and joints in the bones are broken. The mother
eats food that is excessively pungent, bitter, sharp, hot and salty and
makes it suffer. Confined in this way, it suffers a lot of pain. It is
not the lord of its own self and cannot stretch or contract its limbs.
Lying down in the great mire of urine and excrement, it suffers in
every possible way. It is breathless, but is conscious and remembers
hundreds of births. Because of the bondage of its own karma, it
suffers from this great misery in the womb. When the infant is born,
its face is smeared with urine, blood, excrement and semen. The
joints in its body suffer from the wind known as *prajapatya*. When
it is born, those strong winds make it face downwards. Suffering,
it emerges from the mother's womb with a great deal of difficulty.
When it is touched by the wind outside, it suffers from a great loss
of consciousness. O supreme among sages! When it is born, all its
vijnana is destroyed. Its limbs seem to be pierced by thorns. It seems
to be sliced with saws. It falls down on the ground, like an insect
from a wound full of pus. It isn't capable of scratching itself or
turning around. Someone else is its master. It is only through the
desires of others that it can drink milk and obtain food. When it
lies down on a dirty bed, it is bitten by insects and gnats. Though
it is bitten by them, it is incapable of repulsing them. There are
many kinds of hardship at the time of birth and there are other
kinds of miseries after birth. When he becomes a child, he faces
adhibhoutika suffering. Enveloped by the darkness of ignorance,
a man is foolish inside. He does not know, "Where have I come

from? Who am I? Where will I go? What is my *atman*? Why am I
fettered in these bonds? What is the reason? Or is there no reason?
What should be done? What should not be done? What should be
spoken? What should not be spoken? What is *dharma*? What is
adharma? What constitutes it and how? What is duty? What is not
duty? What is good? What is bad?" In this way, he is foolish like
an animal because of the great power of ignorance. Addicted to the
penis and the stomach, men suffer from pain. Ignorance is due to the
sentiment of *tamas*. O *brahmanas*! Though there is an inclination to
undertake tasks because of ignorance about what should be done,
karma suffers. *Maharshi*s have said that when *karma* suffers, one
goes to hell. Therefore, those who are ignorant suffer pain in this
world and in the world hereafter. A man's body is devastated by old
age and the body turns flaccid. The teeth decay and are dislodged.
The sinews and nerves are covered by wrinkles. The pupils are fixed
towards the sky. Hair sticks out of the nostrils. The body trembles.
All the creature's bones stick out. The joints of the bones in the
back are bent. Since the digestive fire no longer functions, he eats
little. He can only move a little. He can move, rise, lie down, sit or
exert himself with a great deal of effort. Sight and hearing weakens.
He exudes saliva that smears his face. Unable to control anything,
he looks forward to dying. He is incapable of feeling anything that
happens at that moment. He cannot remember anything. He has to
make tremendous efforts to speak even a little. Because of problems
with breathing, he remains awake at night. When he is aged, others
have to make him get up or lie down. He is dishonoured by his
own servants, sons and wives. All purity becomes lax, but he still
retains his desire for sporting and eating. His family members laugh
at him and his relatives no longer feel any attachment towards
him. He feels and remembers everything that he has done in his
youth as if they have been done in some other birth. Tormented,
he heaves deep sighs. These are the miseries he suffers in old age.
Now hear about the miseries he faces at the time of death. His neck,
hands and legs become loose. The man keeps trembling. Because
of these miseries, he sighs repeatedly. He repeatedly tries to find
strength in his knowledge. Extremely anxious because of a sense
of ownership, he wonders, "What will happen to my gold, grain,

sons, wives, servants and home?" Major ailments strike at his inner organs like terrible saws. Like the terrible destroyer, the joints in his bones clutch at his inner organs. The pupils of his eyes roll and he repeatedly flings his hand and feet around. His throat and palate turn dry and he cries out in distress. The *udana* breath makes him suffer and chokes his throat. He is enveloped in great heat and he is afflicted by hunger and thirst. He leaves the body with great difficulty and is oppressed by Yama's servants. With great difficulty, he assumes another body in which he undergoes pain. Men face many other terrible sufferings at the time of death. When men die, they go to *naraka*. Hear about this. Yama's servants seize him with nooses and strike him with sticks. The sight of Yama is terrible. The path that takes one to Yama is also terrible. O supreme *brahmanas*! It is strewn with terrible mire, sand, fires, machines and weapons. All of these cause[225] great pain. Saws and black crucibles are used to make men suffer. They are struck with battle-axes. They are buried in pits in the ground. They are impaled on spikes and forced to enter the mouths of tigers. Vultures devour them and they are fed to wolves. They are boiled in oil and smeared with corrosive mud. They are hurled down from above and catapults are used to fling them away. Because of the sins, there are many kinds of hardships in hell. O *brahmanas*! The number of miseries in *naraka* cannot be counted. O best among *brahmanas*! It is not that miseries are faced only in hell. Because of the fear of falling down, there is no respite in heaven either. He is conceived in a womb again and takes birth as a man again. He finds himself in a womb again. Having been born, he dies again. Sometimes, he dies as soon as he is born. Sometimes, he dies during childhood or youth. O *brahmanas*! Anything that men find pleasing has the seed of misery. It is this seed that gives rise to the tree of unhappiness. Men endeavour to find a lot of happiness in wives, sons, friends, homes, fields, wealth and other things. However, these bring unhappiness. Tormented by the grief of *samsara*, the senses are scorched. Without the tree that yields emancipation, how can men possibly obtain happiness?

[225] The hells.

'The learned say that the three kinds of misery make one suffer in the womb at the time of birth and old age. Though they may be seen to exhibit the signs of delight, they actually cause misery. It is held that the only medication is *atyantika* destruction into the illustrious one. Therefore, a learned man must make efforts to achieve this. O supreme *brahmanas*! The means of obtaining him are said to be *jnana* and *karma. Jnana* is said to be of two types—from the *agama* texts and from discrimination.[226] The *agama* texts are full of *shabda*-brahma. *Para*-brahma is achieved through discrimination.[227] Ignorance is like blinding darkness, the *jnana* that results from the sense of discrimination is like a lamp. O *brahmanas*! *Jnana* that results from a sense of discrimination is like the sun. O supreme sages! Manu has spoken about the meaning of the Vedas. That should be remembered. In this connection, I will state it. Listen to my words. There are two brahmans that should be known, *shabda*-brahma and *para*-brahma. If one is conversant with *shabda*-brahma, one achieves *para*-brahma. The *Atharva Veda* has said that both kinds of learning must be understood. The achievement of *para*-brahma is without decay. *Rig Veda* and the others lead to the other one. Those who desire emancipation should comprehend the supreme refuge of the *brahman*. He is not manifest. He is without old age. He cannot be thought of. He is without birth. He is without decay. He cannot be indicated. He has no form. He has no hands or feet. He is not associated with anything else. He is the worthy one. He goes everywhere. He is eternal. He is the cause behind the origin of beings. Everything that deserves to be pervaded is pervaded by him. The learned ones look on him that way. He is the one who is spoken about in the words of the sacred texts. He is subtle. He is Vishnu's supreme destination. He is creation and destruction. He is the one who knows about the creation and destruction of beings. He is their refuge. He is knowledge. He is ignorance. He is spoken of as the illustrious one. He is the one

---

[226] *Viveka.*

[227] *Shabda*-brahma is the ritualistic elements of the *Veda*s, the *karmakanda. Para*-brahma is the *paramatman.*

who possesses unlimited learning, power, strength, lordship, vigor
and energy. He is devoid of any inferior qualities. He is spoken
of as Bhagavan. The *paramatman* resides in all beings. As the
atman who resides in all beings, he is Vasudeva. When asked by
the *maharshi*s earlier, this is what Prajapati[228] said. In truth, the
number of names by which Vasudeva is known is infinite. When
he resides inside all beings and is the creator and arranger of the
universe, he is the Lord Vasudeva. Though he assumes the natures,
*guna*s and taints of all beings, he is beyond all *guna*s.[229] Since
he is beyond all coverings, but envelopes the entire world, he is
Akhilatman.[230] He possesses all the auspicious qualities. With a
little bit of his powers, he creates all the categories of beings. To
bring about the success of everything in the universe, depending
on his wishes, he assumes different forms. There are no limits to
his great energy, strength and prosperity. Through his own energy
and powers, he is a reservoir of every kind of quality. He is greater
than the greatest. He is the lord of all those who are supreme.
When one reaches him, there is no hardship. In his individual and
collective forms, he is Ishvara.[231] He is not manifest. He manifests
himself in his own forms. He is the lord of everything. His eyes are
everywhere. He knows everything. He possesses all the powers.
He is known as Parameshvara.[232] He is without any taints. He
is pure and supreme. He sparkles in his single form. He can be
comprehended, one can see him and one can go to him through
jnana. Everything else that is spoken about is ignorance.'

Chapter 1(127) (The practice of *yoga*)

---

[228] Brahma.
[229] He is both Saguna and Nirguna.
[230] The *atman* of everything.
[231] The lord.
[232] The supreme lord.

The sages said, 'Please tell us about *yoga* now. When one comes into contact with miseries, it is the medication. When we understand it, we will be united with the undecaying Purushottama.'

Suta said, 'Hearing their words, Krishna Dvaipayana Vyasa, the *yogi*, supreme among all those who know about *yoga*, was greatly delighted. He spoke.'

Vyasa said, 'O *brahmanas*! I will tell you about *yoga*. It destroys worldly existence. Listen. By practising it, a *yogi* obtains *moksha*, which is so very difficult to obtain. He must devotedly worship his *guru* and hear about the texts on *yoga*. He must become accomplished in *itihasa*, Puranas and the *Veda*s. An intelligent person must understand about the diet that causes harm to *yoga*, about the time and the place. Having understood everything, he must practise *yoga*. He must be without the opposite pairs of sentiments[233] and without possessions. He must subsist on *saktu*, *yavagu*, *takra*, roots, fruits, milk, barley and bits of oilcake.[234] Such a diet helps obtain success in yoga. One must never practise *yoga* when the mind is unhappy, when one is excited, when one is exhausted, when one is hungry, when the opposite pairs of sentiments exist, when it is cold, when it is hot, where there is too much of wind, where there is sound, near water, inside a cattle-pen that is dilapidated, at crossroads, in a place frequented by reptiles, in a cremation ground, on the banks of a river, near a fire, in a *chaitya*,[235] in a place where there is a termite-hill, where there is reason for fear, near a well, or where there is a heap of dry leaves. These places must be avoided. If, because of folly, one practises *yoga* in spots that are described to be impediments, I will tell you about the taints that result—deafness, stupidity, loss of memory, dumbness, blindness and fever. These result immediately and give rise to ignorance. Therefore, a person who knows about *yoga* must make every effort to protect himself against these, since it is the body which ensures success in achieving *dharma*, *artha*, *kama* and *moksha*. It must be practised in

---

[233] Heat and cold, happiness and unhappiness and so on.

[234] *Yavagu* is gruel made from any grain (including barley) and *takra* is buttermilk.

[235] The word *chaitya* has several meanings—sacrificial shed, temple, altar, sanctuary and a tree that grows along the road.

an *ashrama*, in a desolate spot, in a secret place, where there is no sound, where there is no fear, near a tree, in an empty house, in a pure and beautiful place, where one is alone and in a temple. One must control oneself and practise it in the first or last *yama* of the night.[236] It can also be practised in the forenoon or at midday. He must be restrained in diet and must conquer his senses. Immobile, he must seat himself on a beautiful and comfortable seat facing the east. It should not be too high or too low. He must be without desire, must be truthful and pure. He must not sleep too much. He must conquer his anger and be engaged in the welfare of all beings. He must withstand the opposite pair of sentiments. He must persevere. He must hold his body, head and legs steady. He must place both of his hands on his navel. He must be calm and be seated in *padmasana*.[237] He must fix his eyes on the tip of his nose. He must control his speech and practise *pranayama*.[238] The sage must withdraw his senses and his mind and fix them in the heart. Immobile and covering his mouth, he must continuously chant *pranava*.[239] He must use *rajas* to control *tamas* and use *sattva* to control *rajas*. He must close his eyes and remain steady, withdrawn, peaceful and serene. Purshottama, the one who bestows emancipation, is omnipresent. The unblemished one resides inside the cavity of his heart, which is like a lotus. In this way, the *yogi* will always be united with the unsullied one. He must first fix the senses of perception, the organs of action and the elements in the *kshetrajna*.[240] After this, a person who knows about *yoga* will unite the *kshetrajna* with the *paramatman*. That supreme destination has the characteristic of being like one hundredth the size of the tip of a strand of hair.[241] Immersed in *dhyana*, a *yogi* will use the lamp of his mind to see this. Like a tortoise draws in its limbs, a person who knows about *yoga* will withdraw his senses. When the objects of the senses are discarded and the mind is unwaveringly fixed in the *paramatman*,

[236] 9 p.m. to midnight, or 3.00 a.m. to 6.00 a.m.

[237] The lotus posture.

[238] The control of the breath of life (*prana*).

[239] *Pranava* means to chant 'Oum'. Covering the mouth means that he should not say anything else.

[240] *Kshetrajna* means the *atman*.

[241] It is small and subtle.

it is evident that success in *yoga* will be achieved. Detached from material objects, the consciousness merges into the supreme *brahman*. The supreme destination of *yoga*, one of *samadhi*, is then achieved.[242] At that time, the *yogi*'s consciousness is detached from every kind of *karma*. Immersed in bliss, he achieves *nirvana*.[243] Beyond the three states, this is known as *turiya*.[244] This is Purushottama. When a *yogi* uses the strength of *yoga* to achieve this, there is no doubt that he is liberated. He does not desire any of the objects of desire. He is always beautiful to behold. His intelligence always transcends everything. The *yogi* cannot but be freed. A person who knows about *yoga* does not serve the senses. He is not attached to anything. Through the constant practise of *yoga*, there is no doubt that he will be freed. *Yoga* is not achieved through *padmasana* or by glancing at the tip of the nose. The union of the mind and the senses[245] is spoken of as *yoga*. O best among sages! I have, thus, spoken to you about *yoga*. It bestows emancipation. It leads to emancipation from *samsara*. What else do you wish to hear?'

Lomaharshana continued, 'Listening to Vyasa's words, they worshipped him and praised and applauded his words. They got ready to ask him again.'

Chapter 1(128) (*Samkhya* and *Yoga*)

The sages said, 'O sage! The words have emerged like *amrita* from the ocean of your mouth. O best among *brahmanas*! We do not see any end to the satisfaction that is generated from drinking it. O sage! Therefore, tell us in detail about *yoga*. It

---

[242] *Yoga* has eight elements—*yama* (restraint), *niyama* (rituals), *asana* (posture), *pranayama* (breathing), *pratyahara* (withdrawal), *dharana* (retention), *dhyana* (meditation) and *samadhi* (liberation). That's the reason the expression *ashtanga* (eight-formed) *yoga* is used.

[243] The state of emancipation, when everything is extinguished.

[244] A living being has four states—waking, dreaming, sleeping and *turiya*. *Turiya* is the fourth state, when one perceives union between the human soul *atman* and the *brahman*.

[245] With the *atman*.

bestows emancipation. O best among bipeds! We also desire to hear
about *samkhya*. O brahmana! There may be a learned brahmana
who is wise. He performs sacrifices and is known as being wise. He
does not suffer from jealousy and is devoted to the *dharma* of the
truth. How does he attain the *brahman*? Is this achieved through
austerities, *brahmacharya*, renouncing everything, intelligence,
samkhya or *yoga*? This is what we are asking you. Please tell us.
Through what method does a man achieve the fixation of the mind
and the senses? You should explain the truth about this to us.'

Vyasa replied, 'This is never achieved without *jnana* and
austerities. This is never achieved without controlling the senses.
Success is never achieved without renouncing everything. Earlier,
all the great elements were created by Svayambhu. These are also
embedded in the bodies of all living beings. The body results from
the element that is the earth. Everything viscous results from the
element that is the water. The eyes are said to result from the
element that is the fire. *Prana* and *apana* find their foundation in
the element of the wind.[246] The cavities in the body result from the
element of space. Vishnu exists in the stride, Shakra in strength,
Agni in the stomach in the form of the desire to eat, the divinities
of the directions in the ears and Sarasvati in the tongue, in the form
of speech. The two ears, the two eyes, the tongue and the nose as
the fifth—these are said to be the gates used to accomplish success
in reception. Sound, touch, form, taste and smell as the fifth—these
are always known as the objects of the senses, distinct from the
senses. Like a helpless snake that has no poison, the senses are
always connected with the mind. Connected with the mind, the
atman is always present inside the heart of the being. The mind is
the lord of all the senses. The *atman* of a being controls or releases
the mind. The following are always present in the body of a living
and embodied being—the senses, the objects of the senses, innate
nature, consciousness, the mind, *prana* and *apana*. There is no
refuge for *sattva* in this. Anything for which the word *guna* is used,

---

[246] *Prana* draws breath into the body, *apana* exhales it. *Vyana*
distributes it through the body and *samana* assimilates it. *Udana* gives rise
to sound. These are the five forms of the breath of life.

has no consciousness. Energy creates the living being, but never the *guna*s. The body consists of seventeen and is surrounded by sixteen attributes.[247] O *brahmanas*! The learned use the mind to see the *paramatman* in the *jivatman*.[248] It cannot be perceived through the eyes or through any of the senses. Illuminated by the mind, the great *atman* manifests itself. It is devoid of sound, touch, form, taste or smell. It doesn't possess a body and is bereft of the senses. However, it can be perceived inside the body. It is greatly revered, but is not manifested in the bodies of all mortals. If a person sees it, after death, he is fit to merge into the *brahman*. The wise looks equally upto a brahmana who is learned and humble, a cow, an elephant, a dog and a *shvapaka*.[249] It exists in all beings, mobile and fixed. The great *atman* resides in everything. When a person sees his *atman* in all beings and all beings in his *atman*, he is one for whom the *atman* in the being merges with the *brahman*.[250] A person understands his *atman* to the extent that he sees his *atman* in the *paramatman*. If a person always knows this, he is thought to be fit for immortality. A person who sees his *atman* in all creatures is engaged in the welfare of all beings. Seeking the destination along this path, even the gods are confused and stumble. The movement of birds in the sky or that of birds in the water cannot be discerned. Like that, the progress of those who possess *jnana* can also not be discerned. Using the *paramatman* in the *jivatman*, time cooks all beings. But no one knows when time is itself cooked. It[251] is not above or below. Nor is it located diagonally. Nor can anyone ever grasp it in the middle. All the worlds are located in it and nothing is outside it. Even if an arrow is properly released from the string

[247] This is left unexplained. The sixteen attributes should be the five senses of perception, the five organs of action, the five elements and the mind. Adding the *jivatman*, one gets seventeen.

[248] Respectively, the universal soul and the soul in a creature. The text uses the word *atman* for both. We have expanded it, so that the meaning is clear.

[249] This is identical with *Bhagavad Gita* 5.18.

[250] The first part of this shloka occurs in many other places, including the *Ashtavakra Gita* and *Anushasana Parva* of the *Mahabharata*.

[251] The *paramatman*.

of a bow and if one possesses the speed of thought, one will never be able to reach the end of that ultimate cause. There is nothing more subtle than that. There is nothing grosser than that. It has hands and feet everywhere, its eyes, heads and mouths are in every direction. Its eyes are everywhere. It exists, enveloping everything in the world.[252] It is smaller than the smallest. It is greater than the greatest. It certainly exists inside all beings, but it cannot be perceived. The *atman* has two kinds of expressions—the perishable and the imperishable. The perishable is in all beings and the divine and imperishable part is immortal. Hamsa creates a city with nine gates and always controls it.[253] In this way, it exists in all beings, mobile and immobile. Those who know about the supreme say that it possesses the attribute of the swan because it can separate the undecaying essence from the accumulation that is the bodies of men. However, what is known as Hamsa is also perishable. The deeper one is imperishable.[254] A person who knows this gives up his *prana* and birth and obtains what is imperishable.

'O *brahmanas*! I have accurately told you the truth about what you asked me. I have described to you the *jnana* behind *samkhya*. O *brahmanas*! I will next tell you how *yoga* is undertaken. This amounts to bringing the mind, the intelligence and the senses together, for the pervasive *jnana* about the *atman*. This is supreme knowledge. This can be understood by those who are tranquil and self-controlled, devoted to knowledge about the *adhyatma*.[255] The intelligence of these people is such that they take delight in the *atman* and in performing pure deeds. The wise know that there are five taints in the path of *yoga*—desire, anger, avarice, fear and slumber as the fifth. Anger is defeated through mental self-control, desire by discarding such thoughts. A persevering person must

---

[252] This is identical to *Bhagavad Gita* 13.13.

[253] Hamsa (a swan) is used as a term for the *atman*. A swan is believed to have discrimination. From a mixture of milk and water, it can drink up the water. The body is the city with the nine gates (two eyes, two ears, two nostrils, the mouth, the anus and the genital organ).

[254] The *shloka*s are cryptic. The meaning seems to be that the *jivatman* (Hamsa) is perishable because it eventually merges into the *paramatman*.

[255] Transcendental knowledge about the *paramatman*.

destroy slumber by focusing on *sattva*. Fortitude protects against the penis and the stomach. The eyes guard against the action of the hands and the feet. The mind guards against the eyes and the ears, deeds guard against the mind and speech. One conquers fear by not being distracted, insolence is conquered by associating with those who are wise. In this way, with constant attention, one conquers the taints in the path of *yoga*. A person must always bow down to *brahmanas*, the fire and gods. One must avoid insolent and violent speech and practice what is pleasant to the mind. The seed of the *brahman*'s energy is everywhere in the universe and he sees this in mobile and immobile objects, that which is manifest and that which is not manifest. Meditation, studying, donations, truth, modesty, uprightness, forgiveness, purity, purification of the *atman* and conquest of the senses—through these, energy increases and wicked inclinations are curbed. He must be impartial towards all beings and towards what has been obtained and what has not been obtained. He must cleanse his *atman*, control his diet, conquer his senses and become energetic. Having subjugated desire and anger, he will serve the supreme *brahman*. He will single-mindedly control his mind and senses. At the beginning of the night and at the end of the night, he will fix the *jivatman* in the *paramatman*. A being has five senses. Even if one of them is moistened like water flowing from the foot of a mountain, the wisdom is drained away. A killer of fish takes away turtles. Like that, the mind must first be restrained. A person who knows about *yoga* next restrains the ears, the eyes, the tongue and the nose. He restrains them and fixes them in his mind. After that, he restrains all the resolutions in his mind and fixes them in his *atman*. The five senses and the mind are fixed in heart. In this way, with the mind as the sixth, they are fixed in the *atman*. He is pleased with these having been fixed and the *brahman* manifests itself. Like a flame without smoke, it is as radiant as the sun. He sees the *paramatman* in his *atman*, dazzling like lightning or the fire. Everything is seen in it and it is seen to pervade everything. Learned *brahmanas* see the great *atman* in this way. They are the ones who possess fortitude and are immensely wise, engaged in the welfare of all beings. Firm in one's vows, one must thus practice for a limited period. He must be seated in a desolate spot, seeking similarity with the imperishable one. He must use *yoga* to control confusion, the whirlwind of errors, extraordinary sensations about hearing, seeing and touch, the wind that seems to be too hot or too cold and understanding about evil portents.[256] Through equanimity, he can ignore them and withdraw from them. The *yogi* will control himself like a sage and not reveal himself to the three worlds. He must practise *yoga* on the summit of a mountain, in a *chaitya* or under a tree. Like vessels stored in a room, he must control all his senses. He must single-mindedly think of what is permanent and use *yoga* to control the mind. The mind is fickle, but these are the means whereby one is capable of restraining it. He must practice in this way and not waver. Single-minded, he must seek to make a residence in an empty house. In his words, thoughts and deeds, he must avoid the excessive crossing of norms. Impartial, he must be restrained in diet, impartial towards what has been obtained and what has not been obtained. He will be indifferent towards being congratulated or honoured. He must be indifferent towards both the auspicious and the inauspicious. He will not be delighted when something has been obtained, nor think about something that has not been obtained. He will follow the *dharma* of the wind and be impartial towards all creatures. Secure in this way, a virtuous person will be impartial towards everything, everywhere. Within six months, he will approach *shabda*-brahma. He will see what is beyond all pain and grief and be impartial towards a lump of earth or iron and gold. On seeing that others are suffering or confused, he will not desist from the path. Even a person from an inferior *varna,* or a woman who desires dharma, obtains the supreme destination along this path. O *brahmanas*! He is ancient and without birth. He is without decay. He is eternal. He is beyond the perception of the senses. He is the imperceptible Parameshthi. On being united with him, the learned obtain a destination from which there is no return.'

---

[256] That is, he should not get distracted by such extraordinary powers.

Chapter 1(129) (*Samkhya* and *Yoga* continued)

The sages said, 'The words of the Vedas say—undertake tasks and renounce them.[257] What destination is obtained by those who follow knowledge? What destination is obtained by those who undertake tasks? O illustrious one! We wish to hear about these two. Please tell us. There seems to be a contradiction between these since they are inconsistent with each other.'

Vyasa replied, 'O tigers among sages! Listen. I will briefly tell you what you have asked me about. I will tell you about both tasks and knowledge and about what is perishable and what is imperishable. I will tell you about the destination obtained by those who follow knowledge and the destination obtained by those who undertake tasks. O *brahmanas*! Listen now. The answer is deep and complex. *Dharma* exists. There are those who say it does not exist. This is similar to equating *dharma* with a *yaksha*, if something like a *yaksha* at all exists. The Vedas are established on two paths—the characteristic of one kind of *dharma* is *pravritti*, while that of the other is said to be *nivritti*. Tasks bind a being, knowledge frees him. Therefore, mendicants who know about the supreme do not engage in tasks. As a result of *karma*, after death, one is born again, in an embodied form with the sixteen attributes.[258] Knowledge leads to the eternal and unmanifest, the imperishable *atman*. Therefore, men who are limited in their understanding praise *karma*. As a result, they serve the pleasure obtained through a net of bodies. There are those who possess supreme intelligence about *dharma*. They are accomplished in their vision and do not praise *karma*. A person who drinks from a river does not praise a well. Through *karma*, one obtains the fruits of happiness and unhappiness, of birth and death. Through knowledge, one obtains such a destination once one reaches it, one does not grieve. When one has gone there, one is not born. When one has gone there, one does not die. When one has

---

[257] Though the word used is 'and', the sense is of two alternative paths, of *pravritti* and *nivritti*.

[258] The sixteen mentioned earlier.

gone there, one does not decay. When one has gone there, one does
not increase. The supreme *brahman* is there. It is unmanifest, fixed
and certain. It does not have transformations. It has no extensions.
It is immortal and a person who knows about *yoga* goes there. In
thoughts and deeds, one is not obstructed by the opposite pairs of
sentiments there. One is impartial and friendly towards everyone.
One is engaged in the welfare of all living beings. O *brahmanas*!
There is a being that is full of knowledge and there is another being
that is full of *karma*. O *brahmanas*! This is like the subtle touch of
the moon, as opposed to the *kalas* it is based on.[259] The *rishi*s have
spoken and sung about this in detail. This is like a strand in a wheel
in the sky. One is incapable of seeing it, or speaking about it. O
brahmanas! In the embodied form, there are eleven transformations
or digits within it.[260] Know that these are the results of *karma* and
gunas. Like the moon in the sky, there is an intelligent divinity that
resides within this. Know this to be the eternal *kshetrajna*. One can
always comprehend this through *yoga*. Know that the *gunas* of a
jivatman are *sattva*, *rajas* and *tamas*. But know that the *gunas* of the
jivatman are those of the *paramatman*. It is said that the attribute of
a living being is consciousness and that this attribute of a living being
makes it exert itself. Those who know about what is superior to the
kshetra[261] have thought of the seven worlds.[262] The transformation
of Prakriti is known as *kshetrajna*. No one knows it and it does not
know anyone. It performs tasks through the senses, with the mind
as the sixth. This is like a well-trained charioteer, using excellent
horses to firmly control the chariot. The objects of the senses are
superior to the senses. The mind is superior to the objects of the
senses. Intelligence is superior to the mind and the great *atman* is
superior to intelligence.[263] The unmanifest is superior to the great

[259] As the moon goes through waxing and waning, there are sixteen
kalas (digits).

[260] This probably means the five senses of perception, the five organs of
action and the mind.

[261] *Kshetra* is the physical body.

[262] Bhuloka, Bhuvarloka, Svarloka, Maharloka, Satyaloka, Tapoloka
and Janaloka.

[263] This is similar to Bhagavad Gita 3.42, though not identical.

atman. The immortal is superior to the unmanifest. What is superior to the immortal? That is the supreme and ultimate destination. In all beings, the *atman* is hidden and is not seen. It can only be discerned by those who are focused in their intelligence, those who can see what is more subtle than the subtle. Using his intelligence, he will make his senses and mind merge into the inner *atman*. He will not think a lot and will not use his senses to think about the objects of the senses. Using his knowledge, he will force the mind to be engaged in supreme *dhyana*. He will be serene in his *atman* and no one will control him. He will then proceed to the supreme destination. If the *atman* comes under the control of any of the senses and if memory is fickle, a mortal person submits his *atman* to death. Discarding all resolution, the consciousness must be submerged in *sattva*. If the consciousness is merged in *sattva*, one does not suffer from decay and death. With a cheerful consciousness, a mendicant casts aside all that is auspicious and all that is inauspicious. With his joyful *atman* immersed in the *paramatman*, he enjoys infinite bliss. The sign of this joy is like a happy dream. It is like a blazing lamp that does not flicker from the wind. Thus, in the first part of the night or towards the end of the night, one should unite the *jivatman* with the *paramatman*. He must restrain his diet and cleanse his soul. He will then see the *paramatman* in his own *atman*. This is the secret of all the Vedas. This is the unmatched freedom from all ailments. This visualization of the *atman*, from the sacred texts must be passed on to one's son. This is what has been spoken about in the texts about *dharma* and the texts about truth. After churning those for ten thousand years, this *amrita* has been extracted. This is like producing butter from curds, or fire from kindling. In that way, for the sake of emancipation, the learned have extracted this *jnana*. This sacred knowledge must be spoken about to *snatakas*[264] and sons. It must not be imparted to ascetics who are not tranquil and controlled. Nor must it be imparted to those who are learned in the Vedas or those who are not followers. It must not be given to those who are not jealous and not upright, or those who have

---

[264] A *snataka* is an individual who has completed the *brahmacharya* stage of studying and is ready to enter the next stage of life.

no sense of direction. It must not be given to those who are prone
to arguing or to those who indulge in slander. It must be imparted
to a serene ascetic who praises it, one who is praiseworthy. This
secret *dharma* must be spoken about to beloved sons, disciples
and followers, never to anyone else. Even if the earth, with its full
complement of jewels is donated, a man who knows what is good
for him takes this truth to be superior. This superhuman knowledge
of *adhyatma* has a deep meaning. This has been seen by *maharshi*s
and has been chanted about in Vedanta. O excellent ones! I have
told you whatever you have asked me about, about what is in my
mind and about the doubts in your hearts. All of you have heard
this. What shall I tell you about next?'

The sages said, 'Please tell us about *adhyatma* again, in detail.
O illustrious one! O excellent *rishi*! Let us understand *adhyatma*.'

Vyasa replied, 'O *brahmanas*! I will tell you what a man reads
about *adhyatma* and about the explanations. Understand. The
great elements are earth, water, fire, wind and space. The one who
created these elements is inside all beings.'

The sages said, 'Space and the others have no embodied form
and no one can see them. How does one describe their existence in
bodies? What are the qualities of the senses? How does one observe
them?'

Vyasa replied, 'I will describe this as it has been described.
Listen attentively to the truth, exactly as it is. The three attributes of
space are sound, the ears and the void. The three attributes of wind
are *prana*, movement and touch. The three attributes of fire are said
to be form, the eye and the digestive process. The three attributes of
water are taste, the tongue and sweat. The three attributes of earth
are smell, the nose and the body. This is described as the category
of senses that evolved from the five elements. Touch is the attribute
of wind, taste is the attribute of water, form is the attribute of fire,
sound is the attribute of space and smell is said to be the attribute
of earth. The mind, intelligence and innate nature are attributes that
have their own origins. They do not follow the other attributes.
It is held that they are superior to the other attributes. A turtle
extends and withdraws its limbs. Like that, a person with superior
intelligence restrains the aggregate of the senses. If a person acts in a

way that he sees above, diagonally and below his feet, this indicates that he possesses supreme intelligence. The *guna*s lead intelligence. However, intelligence leads the senses. The mind is the sixth. If intelligence does not exist, how can all the *guna*s exist? A man has five senses and the mind is said to be the sixth. Intelligence is said to be the seventh. Know that *kshetrajna* is the eighth. The eye sees, the mind doubts. Intelligence studies this, while the *kshetrajna* is said to be only a witness. *Sattva*, *rajas* and *tamas* have their own origins. These *guna*s are noticed to equally exist in all beings. When one discerns the *atman* and is happy and serene, this means one is united with *sattva*. When it is noticed that a person is tormented in his body or mind, this displays the functioning of *rajas*. When one is filled with a terrible confusion that cannot be discussed or understood, it is caused by *tamas*. Joy, delight, bliss, self-dependence and mental stability—these are said to be the qualities of *sattva*. Arrogance, false speech, greed, confusion and lack of forgiveness—when these signs exist, that has been caused by *rajas*. Confusion, being distracted, languor, slumber, lack of understanding and a tendency to somehow remain alive—these are known to be the qualities of *tamas*. There are three kinds of urges behind action. The mind leads to sentiments, intelligence determines and the heart considers what is pleasant. The objects of the senses are superior to the senses. The mind is superior to the objects of the senses. Intelligence is superior to the mind. The *atman* is said to be superior to intelligence.[265] Since intelligence leads the *atman*, the comprehension of the *atman* depends on intelligence. When it leads to perverse sentiments, it adversely affects the mind. The senses are separate. It is intelligence that causes perversion. At the time of hearing, it acts like the ear. At the time of touching, it acts like the skin. At the time of seeing, it acts like the eye. At the time of tasting, it acts like the tongue. At the time of smelling, it acts like the nose. It is intelligence that causes the perversion. In those that are referred to as senses, it is intelligence that is established in them. Intelligence exists in a man and it is intelligence that causes sentiments. Sometimes, one obtains happiness. Sometimes, one grieves. It is never actually happy,

---

[265] As mentioned earlier, this is similar to Bhagavad Gita 3.42.

unhappy or confused. It itself causes those sentiments and acts like a leader in engineering those three sentiments.[266] This is like the ocean, the lord of rivers, rushing towards the great shore-line and causing waves. Whatever intelligence wishes for is followed by the mind. However, it is cited as existing independently. All the senses are collectively gathered in intelligence. All of them have evolved in the due order. When the intelligence is undivided, the mind follows this. When *rajas* starts to function, it can overcome *sattva*. Know that these three inclinations[267] pursue their objectives like the spokes in the wheel of a chariot follow the rim. One must use the senses with supreme intelligence and ignite the mind. One can choose to be indifferent or one can direct them towards appropriate ends. If one understands this as innate nature, one is not confused. One does not grieve, nor is one delighted. One is always devoid of envy. The senses follow desire and cannot perceive the *atman*. Since they function in many ways, a person whose soul isn't cleansed cannot control them. The mind is like reins, used to restrain them properly. The resplendent *atman* then manifests itself like a form illuminated by a lamp. When darkness is dispelled, all creatures are brought to light. This is the way one should think about it. An aquatic bird is not touched by the water it roams around in. Like that, a *yogi*'s free *atman* is not smeared by the taints of the *guna*s. If one accomplishes wisdom in this way, there is no taint from association with material objects. Even one is not attached to anything, how can one be contaminated? Such a person casts aside his former *karma* and finds delight in the great *atman*. He sees his *atman* in all beings. Sometimes, because of contact with the *guna*s, he is born again and comes into contact with the *guna*s. The *guna*s do not know the *atman*, but the *atman* knows the *guna*s. Understanding the functioning of the *guna*s, he should see how they act. A man must perceive the difference between *satva* and *kshetrajna*. One of them creates the *guna*s, the other does not create the *guna*s.[268] They are separate in nature, even though they are naturally connected to

---

[266] Joy, misery and confusion.

[267] *Sattva*, *rajas* and *tamas*.

[268] *Kshetrajna* and *sattva*.

each other. This is like rock and gold existing together,[269] a gnat and *udumbura*[270] being together, or a blade of *munja* grass and the grass. They exist separately, though they exist together and seem to be dependent on each other.'

Chapter 1(130) (*Samkhya* and *Yoga* continued)

Vyasa said, 'Sattva creates the *guna*s and *kshetrajna* presides over them. When all the *guna*s act, *kshetrajna* is like an indifferent master. They have their individual natures and it creates all these *guna*s, just as a weaver creates the strands in its web. *Pravritti* cannot be discerned. Therefore, one cannot withdraw from *pravritti*. Some hold this view. Others hold the view that one can follow *nivritti*. One must use one's intelligence to study these views and come to a conclusion. There may be a great doubt on this matter. The *atman* has no birth or death. After comprehending this, a man must amuse himself accordingly. He must never be angry or delighted. He must always be without envy. Using his intelligence, he must always steadily ponder about this in his heart. All happiness and reason to grieve are temporary. Therefore, he must sever all doubts. Having been dislodged on earth, a man will then cross it the way he crosses a full river, even if he is immersed in the water. O *brahmanas*! A learned person is not tormented. A person who knows the truth behaves as if he is walking on solid ground. He only thinks about the *atman* and *jnana* about the *atman*. A man understands the creation of beings, how they emerge and where they go. Having examined it properly, he obtains what is auspicious and excellent. This is the objective behind the birth of *dvija*s, especially *brahmanas*, *jnana* and affection towards the *atman*, which is the ultimate refuge. Having understood this, one becomes a *buddha*?[271] What other sign can there be of becoming a *buddha*? After learning this, learned men become

---

[269] In mineral form.
[270] The cluster fig tree, a gnat is attracted to its fruit.
[271] A *buddha* is an awakened and enlightened person.

emancipated and accomplish their objective. Those who are not learned face a great fear in the world hereafter, but a learned person faces no such fear. A learned person attains the eternal destination and there is nothing superior to that. Unable to see the gods, or the mother of the worlds, a man grieves. But an accomplished person who has understood both what has been done and what has not been done, does not sorrow. If a person undertakes tasks without being attached, all his former *karma* is burnt away. When he undertakes tasks in this world, that is caused by both the auspicious and the inauspicious that he has formerly done.'

The sages said, 'Please tell us about the special *dharma* that is superior to all other kinds of *dharma* and better than everything that exists.'

Vyasa replied, 'I will tell you about the ancient *dharma*, praised by the *rishi*s. This is superior to every other kind of *dharma*. O supreme sages! Listen. The senses cause agitation and spread in every direction. Like a father controlling his sons during childhood, one must use one's intelligence to control them. The greatest austerity is concentrating the mind and the senses. This is superior to every other kind of *dharma*. This is spoken of as supreme *dharma*. Using knowledge, one must control them, with the mind as the sixth. A person must be content in his own *atman* and must not think many kinds of thought. When the cows return from grazing, they are kept in their own abodes. Like that, one should see the eternal *paramatman* in one's own *atman*. The great *atman* is in all *atman*s and is like a smoke without fire. Learned *brahmanas* see this great *atman*. This is like a great tree with many branches and flowers and fruit. If one does not know the *atman*,[272] where is the question of the flowers or the fruit? If one does not know the *atman*, how can one ask—where will I go and where have I come from? There is the other one[273] that exists in one's inner core and witnesses everything. When the mind is illuminated with the lamp of knowledge, one sees the *paramatman* in one's *jivatman*. O *brahmanas*! When you see the *atman* in this way, you will develop non-attachment. Like snakes

[272] Which is like the great tree.
[273] The *jivatman*.

shedding their skin, you will be freed of all sins. With this supreme intelligence, you will be devoid of anxiety and will be free from unpleasant thoughts. This world is like a terrible river with currents everywhere. The five senses are crocodiles. The resolutions in the mind are like the banks. Avarice and confusion are the grass that covers the banks. Desire and anger are reptiles. Truth is like *tirtha*s and falsehood is like eddies. In this excellent river, anger forms the mud. It originates in the unmanifest and flows swiftly, full of desire and anger. Using intelligence, one can cross the river. However, those who have not cleansed their souls find it impossible to cross. It flows into the ocean that is *samsara*, with the womb as a nether region that is impossible to traverse. This starts with a person's birth and becomes difficult to cross because there are many tongues.[274] A persevering and learned person, accomplished in wisdom, can cross it. When one crosses it, one is freed from everything. A person becomes pure and his soul is cleansed. Using that excellent intelligence, he is fit to merge into the *brahman*. He overcomes every kind of hardship. He is serene and his soul is cleansed. When he looks at all manner of beings again, he is not angered, nor is he pleased. His mind does not turn towards violence. He sees the origin and destruction of all beings. The learned think that this is the best kind of *dharma*. Sages, truthful in speech and upholders of *dharma*, have held this to be the best kind of *dharma*. O *brahmanas*! The *atman* pervades everything. This is what should be instructed to one's sons. For their welfare, it should be revealed to those who are controlled and those who are followers. This great *jnana* about the *atman* is secret and is most mysterious. I have told you about it. One's sparkling *jivatman* is a witness to all this. The *brahman* is not masculine, feminine or neuter. It does not experience joy or misery. It has the past, present and future inside it. On knowing this, a man or a woman does not have to return to earth again. There are many kinds of views which state different things. O *brahmanas*! I have told you what is true, not what is not true. If the son possesses the qualities, out of compassion and affection towards that virtuous

---

[274] Which preach and talk about different things.

son and to ensure his benefit, one should tell the son what I have told you.'

The sages said, 'The grandfather has spoken about the methods through which one can attain emancipation and the methods through which one cannot. O sage! We wish to hear about the proper methods.'

Vyasa replied, 'O immensely wise ones! We must subject this to skilled scrutiny. O unblemished ones! One must always examine all the different methods. Intelligence is used to fashion a pot, but intelligence is not the cause of the pot. In that way, there are different methods to achieve *dharma*. But these other methods have not caused *dharma*. The path that leads to the eastern ocean does not lead to the western ocean. There is only one path to liberation. O unblemished ones! Hear about it from me. Forgiveness must be used to overcome anger. By discarding all resolution, one overcomes desire. By resorting to *sattva*, a persevering person must destroy slumber. A learned person must protect the body against fear and being distracted. Through fortitude, one must control wishes, hatred and desire. Through the practice of *jnana*, a person who knows the truth will conquer slumber and audacity. The *yogi* will conquer ailments by only eating after the food eaten earlier has been digested. A person who has seen the truth will use contentment to conquer greed towards material objects and confusion. Compassion and indifference must be used to conquer what is *adharma*. He must use what he has got to conquer desire and must conquer his capacity by avoiding attachment. A learned person will conquer attachment by recognizing that these are temporary. He will conquer hunger through *yoga*. He will use compassion and see his *atman* in all *atman*s. He will use satisfaction to conquer thirst. To conquer lassitude, he will wake up early. He will use determination to conquer debates. He will conquer excessive speech through silence and use bravery to conquer fear. Using the insight of *jnana*, he will use his intelligence to conquer his speech and mind. Knowledge about the great *atman* will be used to sever everything. What exists in his inner core can be used to sever everything. A tranquil person who is pure in his deeds will understand this. Those who are wise know that there are five taints in the pursuit of *yoga* and these must be destroyed—desire, anger, avarice, fear and dreaming as the fifth. Through serving the practice of *yoga*, one casts all these aside. Meditation, studying, donations, truth, modest, uprightness, forgiveness, purity in conduct and purification and control of the senses—these increase energy and destroy sins. All resolutions are accomplished and *vijnana* starts to function. A person who is restrained in diet and has conquered his senses, cleanses his sins and becomes energetic. Having subjugated desire and anger, he achieves the destination of the *brahman*. This is beyond foolishness and attachment, devoid of desire and anger. This is a state where there is no distress, no boasting and no anxiety. This is the sparkling, pure and contented path towards *moksha*. Speech and the mind are controlled and as one wishes, a state without decay can be achieved.'

Chapter 1(131) (Practice of *yoga*)

The sages said, 'O brahmana! You should tell us the specific characteristics of *samkhya* and *yoga*. O one who knows about *dharma*! O supreme among sages! You know everything.'

Vyasa replied, 'Those who know about *samkhya* praise *samkhya*, those who know about *yoga* praise *yoga*. They will give reasons to establish why their own view is superior. O supreme among sages! How can something that does not believe in the lord confer emancipation? Citing this reason, there are learned ones who rightly say that *yoga* is superior. There are also *brahmanas* who cite proper reasons about *samkhya*'s superiority. If one knows about the destination of everything and is not attached to material objects, only then can he be liberated, once he casts aside his body, not otherwise. Citing this, immensely wise ones say that *samkhya* shows the path to *moksha*. These are beneficial words, rationale in favour of the respective sides, and worthy of being accepted. You are revered by virtuous people and should accept the view that is superior. The reasons in favour of *yoga* are directly perceived, the determination of *samkhya* is based on the sacred texts. O supreme *brahmanas*! Both of these views are based on the truth. Sages who are revered by virtuous people know about both views. If something is practised in accordance with the sacred texts, it conveys the person to the supreme destination. O unblemished ones! They are identical in what they say about purity and compassion towards beings. They are equal in what they say about vows. But they are not identical in their *darshana*.'[275]

The sages said, 'O great sage! For this world, they are identical in vows, purity and compassion. O supreme among *brahmanas*! How are they not identical in their *darshana*? Please tell us.'

Vyasa replied, 'Those who practise yoga can only suffer from five defects—attachment, confusion, affection, desire and anger. Just as fish cut through a large net and reach the water again, those who practice yoga can destroy their sins and obtain the desired destination. This is like a powerful deer escaping the snare and reaching an unrestricted path, free of all bondage. O *brahmanas*! The bonds that result from avarice and the other things are powerful. Severing them, a person who practises *yoga* proceeds along a sparkling and unrestricted path. O *brahmanas*! They are firm and do not waver, destroying all snares. Without the strength of *yoga*, how can one not have doubts? O Indras among *brahmanas*! O *brahmanas*! This is like a weak person getting caught in a snare. O unblemished ones! It is extremely rare for a person without *yoga* to escape from the bonds. O scorcher of enemies! This is like weak birds getting ensnared in a trap. They cannot escape from the calamity. It is only the strong who can free themselves. O *brahmanas*! Those who practice *yoga* are bound in the bondage that results from *karma*. The weak are destroyed, but the strong free themselves. O *brahmanas*! A small fire is weak and can be pacified. It is said that the strength of yoga pacifies it even when it is fed with a large quantity of kindling. O *brahmanas*! Fanned by the wind, the fire may also become stronger and swiftly burn down everything on earth. A *yogi* who possesses *jnana* about the truth is extremely strong and blazes in his energy. He is like the sun which dries up everything in the universe at the time of

---

[275] *Darshana* is more than a school of philosophical thought, since it also includes insight about *adhyatma*.

universal destruction. O *brahmanas*! A weak man is borne away by the force of the current. Like that, a weak *yogi* is borne away by material objects. An elephant can withstand that same current. Having obtained the strength of *yoga*, material objects cannot make one deviate. Those who possess the strength of *yoga* subjugate everything through *yoga*. They become like Prajapati Manu, the lord of all the great elements. O *brahmanas*! Because of the great energy of *yoga*, they are not subjugated by anything—Yama, the angry Destroyer, or powerful and valiant Death. O supreme *brahmanas*! There are many thousands of *jivatman*s. Through the strength of yoga, one can enter all of them and wander around the earth. Having obtained material objects, one can again practice fierce austerities. O *brahmanas*! Like the sun casts aside all qualities of energy, one can again fling them aside. O supreme sages! To obtain the best strength from *yoga*, one should unhesitatingly seek refuge with Vishnu. All strength is in him and he has the power to bestow emancipation. O supreme *brahmanas*! I have spoken about the strength of *yoga*. O *brahmanas*! As an example, let me again tell you about what is subtle. O *brahmanas*! One must fix one's *atman* in the act of *dharana*. O supreme among sages! Hear about the subtle examples. An archer who is not distracted controls himself and strikes the target. Like that, there is no doubt that a person who practices *yoga* properly attains *moksha*. A man whose mind is unwaveringly full of concentration can control his mind and ascend a flight of stairs with a vessel full of oil. In that way, if a person does not waver at all from *yoga*, his *atman* will be freed. If he frees himself from blemishes, he will see his *atman*, like the sun in a mirror. O Indras among *brahmanas*! The helmsman of a ship concentrates and swiftly conveys the ship across the great ocean. In that way, a person who knows about *yoga* uses *yoga* to control his *atman*. O *brahmanas*! When he gives up his body, he obtains a destination that is extremely difficult to attain. O *brahmanas*! A charioteer controls himself and uses well-trained horses to quickly convey a bull among archers to the desired destination. O *brahmanas*! In that way, a *yogi* immerses himself in *dharana*. Like a released arrow that strikes the target, he swiftly obtains the supreme objective. He unwaveringly uses his *jivatman* to enter the *paramatman* and remain there. This is like fish destroying a net and obtaining a destination that does not suffer from decay. An infinitely valiant *yogi* engaged in the great vow must concentrate in the following spots—the navel, the head, the stomach, the heart, the chest, the sides, the eyes, the ears and the nose. O supreme among *brahmanas*! In this way, he properly unites his *jivatman* with the subtle *paramatman*. Using this excellent *yoga* unwaveringly, he swiftly destroys what is known as *karma*, both auspicious and inauspicious. If he so desires, he is liberated.'

The sages asked, 'O excellent one! Through what kind of food does a *yogi* conquer and obtain strength? You should tell us about this.'

Vyasa replied, 'O excellent *brahmanas*! If he eats barley for a long period of time and eats once a day, a *yogi* purifies his soul and obtains strength.[276] For fortnights, months and many diverse seasons, he should roam around and dwell in caves. He should drink milk mixed with water. Thereby, a *yogi* obtains strength. O supreme among sages! Without a break, he should constantly fast for a month. In this way, a *yogi* purifies his soul properly and obtains strength. He must conquer desire, anger, cold, heat, rains, fear, sorrow, slumber, harshness, material objects and hatred. O *brahmanas*! These are seen to be terrible and extremely difficult to conquer. O excellent sages! Touch, sleep and lethargy are also difficult to conquer. But when this is done, the great and subtle *paramatman* blazes in one's *jivatman*. One is devoid of attachment and becomes immensely wise. Meditation and studying become the wealth. Even for learned *brahmanas*, this path is held to be difficult. O excellent sages! Just as only a few can pass through a terrible forest filled with snakes and reptiles, only a few can comfortably and quickly travel along this path. Without water and covered with thorns, the traveler finds it difficult to traverse. In general, it is dense with trees. In some places, the trees have been burnt down by forest fires. The path is infested with thieves and it is difficult to travel comfortably. In that way, only a few *brahmanas* can travel

---

[276] There is an additional *shloka* that is not included as part of the main text. Hence, we have not translated it. This talks about eating bits of grain and oilcakes and avoidance of oily substances.

along the path of *yoga*. It is held that a person with many taints cannot travel along this path comfortably. O supreme *brahmanas*! It is as sharp as a razor's edge. This *dharana* of *yoga* cannot be traversed by a person who has not cleansed his soul. O *brahmanas*! A boat without a helmsman does not convey men to an auspicious destination. O *brahmanas*! Like that, *dharana* is difficult to follow. If one follows the principles and remains established in the *dharana* of *yoga*, one triumphs over death, birth and misery and is characterized by happiness. This has been described in many sacred texts and many sages have followed it. This path of *yoga* has been recommended for those who are *dvijas*. O Indras among sages! This is immersed in the *brahman* and has been approved by Brahma, Isha, Vishnu, the one who bestows boons, Bhava, the great-souled Dharma and Brahma's great-souled sons.[277] Progressively, the *yogi* passes through the hardship of *tamas*, the extremely great *rajas*, the pure *sattva* and supreme Prakriti. He obtains *siddhi*s, the goddess who is Varuna's wife,[278] all kinds of energy and extremely great fortitude. He obtains the status of the lord of the stars,[279] the sky that is sparkling in nature, the Vishvadevas, the gods, the *uragas*, the ancestors, all the mountains, the terrible oceans, all the rivers, trees, serpents, Sadhyas, large numbers of *yaksha*s, the directions, the *gandharva*s, the *siddha*s, men and women. The *yogi* soon enters the great *atman* and is emancipated. O best of *brahmanas*! This account is auspicious and even the extremely energetic gods find it to be attractive. Through *yoga*, all mortals can swiftly experience Narayana.'

Chapter 1(132) (Principles of *samkhya*)

The sages said, 'O Indra among *brahmanas*! You have properly described the practices along the path of *yoga*. This is revered

---

[277] Brahma's sons are Sanaka, Sananda, Sanatana and Sanatkumara. Both Isha and Bhava must mean Shiva, so there is repetition.

[278] Varuni, the goddess of liquor.

[279] The moon.

by the virtuous and you have rightly described it to your disciples
with a view by ensuring their welfare. Please tell us now about the
practice of *dharma* along the path of *samkhya*. All the knowledge
in the three worlds is known to you.'

Vyasa replied, 'O sages! Listen. These principles of *samkhya*
have been laid down by ancient mendicants who knew about the
atman, Lord Kapila and others. O excellent sages! Some confusion
can be seen along this path. But it has many qualities and no defects.
O *brahmanas*! Through *jnana* about *samkhya*, men can conquer
taints associated with material objects, which are so very difficult
to conquer. O *brahmanas*! One can obtain and know about all
the material objects possessed by *pishacha*s, *uraga*s, *gandharva*s,
ancestors, those who roam around as inferior species, Suparna,[280]
the Maruts, the *maharshi*s, the *rajarshi*s, the *asura*s, the Vishvadevas,
the *devarshi*s and also the supreme objectives of *yoga*. One is
enveloped by these objects and also those in Brahma's dominion.
People understand the truth about lifespans and the supreme nature
of time. O excellent sages! They understand the duration of supreme
bliss and the duration of the misery those addicted to material objects
descend into. O *brahmanas*! They understand about downfall into
inferior species and hell. O *brahmanas*! They also understand the
qualities and taints associated with heaven. They understand about
the qualities and taints associated with the Vedas, as practised by
those who follow the Vedas. They understand the qualities and
taints associated with the path of *jnana yoga*. O *brahmanas*! They
also understand the qualities and taints associated with knowledge
of *samkhya*. One understands the ten qualities of *sattva*, the nine
qualities of *rajas*, the eight qualities of *tamas*, the seven qualities of
buddhi and the six qualities of the sky.[281] One also understands the
three qualities of the great *tamas*, the two qualities of *rajas* and the
single quality of *sattva*. Following the path, one understands the
truth about non-appearance and destruction. Possessing *jnana* and
vijnana, one can use these as instruments to cleanse one's soul. One

---

[280] Garuda.

[281] Since *samkhya* texts differ, it is difficult to enumerate which qualities
are intended in these numbers.

obtains the auspicious end of *moksha* and after that, the subtlety of the sky. Form is associated with the eye and the attribute of smell is associated with the nose. Sound is received through the ears and the attribute of taste through the tongue. Touch is associated with the skin and the wind is experienced through this. Confusion is associated with *tamas* and avarice is dependent on confusion. Vishnu is in the stride, Shakra in strength and Anala[282] is associated with the stomach. The goddess[283] is associated with water and water depends on energy. Energy is associated with wind and wind depends on space. Space is associated with the earth and *tamas* is dependent on Mahat. *Rajas* is associated with *sattva* and *sattva* is associated with the *atman*. The *atman* is associated with the lord, the divinity Narayana. The divinity is associated with *moksha* and *moksha* is not associated with anything. One understands that *sattva guna* is surrounded by the sixteen physical qualities.[284] One understands that innate nature and cognition depend on the body. The *atman* is in the middle and no sin is associated with it. O Indras among *brahmanas*! For those desiring material pleasures, there is a second aspect to be known. All the senses and the objects of the senses are based on the *atman*. Through the former sacred texts, one should know that *moksha* is extremely difficult to obtain. One must also first understand about the power of the wind and the truth about *prana*, *apana*, *samana*, *vyana* and *udana*. Each of these is divided into seven flows and each of the seven is again divided into seven. O *brahmanas*! One should know about Prajapati, *rishi*s, the many excellent creations, *saptarshi*s, many *rajarshi*s who were scorchers of enemies, *surarshi*s,[285] Maruts, other *brahmarshi*s who resembled the sun and those who witnessed prosperity over a long period of time. O *brahmanas*! One will hear about a great number of beings who came about their destruction. One will know the destination of auspicious words and those who should be worshipped by evil-doers.

---

[282] Agni.

[283] Earth.

[284] Five senses of perception, five organs of action, five elements and the mind.

[285] Synonym for *devarshi*s.

One will understand the hardships of those who descend into Vaitarani and Yama's world. One will understand about the inauspicious movements of diverse kinds of species. O *brahmanas*! One will understand about the inauspicious residence in the womb, feeding on blood and water, in a place that is full of phlegm, urine and excrement and has a foul stench; about the mixing of semen and blood and the origin of marrow and sinews; about the hundreds of veins in the city with the nine gates;[286] and for one's own welfare, one will understand about the various kinds of *yoga*. O excellent sages! One will understand the despicable *tamas* conduct of creatures and about beautiful ones with *sattva*, who nevertheless have falsehood in their *atman*s. There are great ones who know about the *atman* and *samkhya*, but nevertheless perform condemned acts. One understands evil portents and the moon's energy. One witnesses the progressive downfall of stars and *nakshatra*s. O *brahmanas*! One understands the miserable separation of couples and witnesses the inauspicious act of beings feeding on one another. One understands the confusion of childhood and the inauspicious aspect of the body. Even among those who possess *sattva*, there are some who confront anger and confusion. Among thousands of men, only one turns his mind towards *moksha*. The former sacred texts of *vijnana* have said that *moksha* is extremely difficult to obtain. O *brahmanas*! One also understands the oppression due to material objects, how one attaches a lot of respect towards what has not been obtained, but is indifferent towards what has been obtained. One understands the auspicious end of beings who had shattered their bodies and given up their lives. O *brahmanas*! One understands the misery faced by those who possess *sattva*, since they have to reside in the families of beings. They tolerate this and wait for death. One understands the destinations obtained by those who kill *brahmanas* and the extremely terrible end faced by those who fall down. One understands the inauspicious ends of those who are addicted to drinking liquor, of evil-souled *brahmanas* and of those who are attached to the wives of their preceptors. O excellent *brahmanas*! One properly understands how men behave well towards their mothers and how they treat

---

[286] The body is the city with nine gates.

all beings like divinities. Using this *jnana*, one understands the destinations obtained by those who perform inauspicious deeds. One understands the separate destinations obtained by those who become inferior species. One understands the wonderful arguments in the Vedas and the progression of the seasons. One witnesses the passing of years, months, seasons and days. One directly perceives the waxing and waning of the moon. One also witnesses the ebb and flow of tides in the oceans. One also witnesses the decline and increase in wealth. In particular, one witnesses the periods that join the *yuga*. One properly understands the truth about the incapacity brought on by the ego. One understands all of one's own taints, all of which are established within one's own self. One understands the inauspicious taints that arise out of one's own body.'

The sages asked, 'O one who knows about the *brahman*! What taints do you see in connection with portents? We have a doubt about this. You should completely explain this mystery to us.'

Vyasa replied, 'O excellent sages! Listen. Those who know about Kapila's path of *samkhya* speak about five taints that are seen in the bodies of all embodied creatures—desire, anger, fear, slumber and breathing as the fifth. Anger is severed through forgiveness, desire by abandoning all resolution, slumber by resorting to *sattva* and fear by not becoming distracted. O *brahmanas*! Defects in breathing are destroyed by being restrained in diet. One uses hundreds of good qualities to understand about good qualities and hundreds of taints to understand about taints. One uses hundreds of reasons to understand about reasons and hundreds of wonderful things to understand the truth about wonderful things. The world is like foam in water. It has been created through hundreds of kinds of Vishnu's *maya*. It resembles a painting and is as futile as substance inside a hollow reed. One sees that it is being whirled around in *tamas*. It resembles bubbles during the monsoon. Though it seems to be pleasant, it generally brings destruction. Transcending the destruction, there is great fear. Like an elephant that is incapacitated in mud, one is submerged in *rajas* and *tamas*. O *brahmanas*! Therefore, those who are immensely wise in *samkhya* cast aside all affection on account of offspring. O *brahmanas*! Using *samkhya*, one comprehends the great *jnana* that pervades everything. O

excellent ones! Using the weapon of *jnana* about the *atman* and the
staff of austerities, one severs the inauspicious odours associated
with *rajas* and *tamas*, the auspicious odours associated with *sattva*
and touch and other things that are dependent on the body. Using
wisdom, one crosses over the terrible water of miseries with great
pools of thoughts and grief, extremely terrible ailments and death,
giant serpents in the form of great fear, the turtles of *tamas* and the
fish of *rajas*. O excellent *brahmanas*! Affection is like mud, old age
is like rough ground, touch is like an island, *karma* is the depths and
truth represents the banks on which learned ones who observe vows
stand. Violence is the swift and forceful current, filled with many
kinds of tastes, and the many kinds of pleasure are great jewels.
However, there is the wind of grief and fever. There are giant eddies
of grief and thirst. Fierce ailments are like a giant storm of dust. O
excellent *brahmanas*! The joints in the bones are stairs that lead
down to unite with phlegm. Donations resemble a store of pearls.
The terrible flow of blood is like coral. Loud roars are heard in
the form of laughter and screams. Many kinds of ignorance make
this very difficult to cross. The dirt accumulating from drops of
tears are the brine, resulting from union and attachment. When
one takes birth in this world, one obtains sons and relatives as
habitations. Non-violence and truth set the boundaries. Union with
the breath of life constitutes the waves. For all beings, this is like an
ocean of milk and excellent followers are the milk. This ocean of
misery has a subterranean fire[287] and *moksha* is a destination that is
extremely difficult to obtain. Using *jnana yoga*, accomplished and
unblemished mendicants cross this. After crossing many difficult
births, they enter the sparkling sky. On seeing them arrive there,
the sun bears them along on its rays. O *brahmanas*! As they spread
through that region, the rays enter them like the fibres in a lotus.
Those unblemished ones are borne along and received by the
wind. Those stores of austerities have overcome attachment and
are successful, endowed with energy. O *brahmanas*! The wind is
subtle, cool, fragrant and pleasant to the touch. O Indras among

---

[287] The text uses the word *vadava*. The subterranean fire is known as
vadava (mare), because it is in the form of a mare's head.

brahmanas! They proceed to the auspicious and supreme worlds of the seven Maruts.[288] They are then borne along to a supreme destination in the sky. The sky bears them to a supreme destination in the world of *rajas*. O Indras among *brahmanas*! *Rajas* bears them to a supreme destination in the world of *sattva*. *Sattva*, pure in soul, bears them to the supreme and auspicious Narayana. The lord, pure in soul himself bears them to the *paramatman*. Having attained the *paramatman*, they lose their taints and are always unblemished. O *brahmanas*! They are fit to become immortal and do not return. O *brahmanas*! Shedding the opposite pairs of sentiments, those great-souled ones obtain the supreme destination. They are full of truth and uprightness and possess compassion towards all beings.'

The sages asked, 'They obtain the excellent spot of the illustrious one and are firm in their vows. Till their death and rebirth, do they amuse themselves there? What is the truth about that region? You should tell us accurately. O excellent one! With your exception, there is no other man who is worthy of being asked this question. It would be a great taint of *moksha* if others, *rishi*s who are successful and supreme mendicants who possess *vijnana*, also go there.[289] O brahmana! We can see the supreme *dharma* that is characterized by *pravritti*. However, if a person is immersed in supreme *jnana*, does he have to undergo misery after that?'

Vyasa replied, 'O best among sages! You have stated your question properly and have asked about your doubt. O excellent sages! The learned are also confused about this question. Listen to my words about the supreme truth concerning this. This reflects the supreme intelligence of great-souled ones like Kapila. O *brahmanas*! The senses of an embodied being understand what is in its own body. There are organs of action and senses of perception. Through these, the *jivatman* understands what is subtle.[290] Without the *jivatman*, there is no doubt that wicked deeds bring about

---

[288] The Maruts, the wind-gods, are sometimes listed as seven and sometimes as forty-nine.

[289] The question seems to imply, what is special about *samkhya*?

[290] We have expanded these sentences a bit, to make the meaning clear.

destruction, like waves being destroyed in the ocean. When the embodied being is asleep or eager, along with the senses, the subtle *jivatman* wanders around, like the wind that goes everywhere. O unblemished ones! It duly sees everything. It touches everything and remembers. O *brahmanas*! It understands everything that had happened earlier. The senses are no longer masters. Like snakes that have lost their poison, they are properly restricted to their own respective spots. All the senses are in their respective spots. The subtle *jivatman* acknowledges their movements. However, when it moves around there is no doubt. O excellent ones! It comprehends all the *gunas*—*sattva guna, rajas guna* and *tamas guna*. O ones who know everything! It understands the attributes of the mind, the attributes of space, the attributes of the wind, the attributes that result from affection, the attributes of water and the attributes of the earth. O *brahmanas* O supreme *brahmanas*! It understands all the attributes in the *kshetra*. The *kshetrajna*, the *jivatman*, roams around amidst good and bad *karma*. O *brahmanas*! For the great-souled one, the senses are like disciples. They transcend Prakriti and reach the pure and subtle refuge, the great-souled Narayana, who has no transformation and is greater than the greatest. Freed of all sins, they enter him and no longer suffer from any decay. O excellent ones! The *paramatman* does not possess any *gunas*. O *brahmanas*! The senses and the mind approach the supreme one, like disciples approaching the *guru* at the right time for instructions. Within a short period of time, it is possible to obtain the traits of serenity. O Indras among *brahmanas*! In this way, using *samkhya* and *yoga*, those who desire *moksha* can obtain emancipation. O *brahmanas*! Using *samkhya*, immensely wise ones obtain the ultimate destination. O Indras among *brahmanas*! There is no knowledge which is equal to this *jnana*. You should have no doubt on this account. It is held that *samkhya* represents supreme *jnana*. Earlier, it has been stated that the eternal *brahman* is everlasting and without decay. It has no beginning, no middle and no end. It does not suffer from the opposite pairs of sentiments. It is the eternal doer. Those who are serene in their souls speak of it as the eternal and pre-eminent one. All acts of creation and destruction flow from there. In the sacred texts, the *maharshi*s have praised it in this way. All *brahmanas*,

Vedas and people who are conversant with the *Sama Veda* speak of him as the supreme one, the divinity Ananta, the supreme Achyuta, the one who is devoted to *brahmanas*. O *brahmanas*! Those who know about the *guna*s speak of him in this way and worship him. Those who follow *yoga* are supremely united with him and so are those who follow *samkhya*, infinite in their vision. O Indras among *brahmanas*! He has no embodied form. The sacred texts say that *samkhya* is his embodied form. O excellent sages! He should be known through many signs. O excellent *brahmanas*! There are two kinds of beings on earth. They are known as mobile and immobile and the mobile ones are superior. O *brahmanas*! *Jnana* is greater than the greatest. O Indras among sages! Everything that has been instructed in the Vedas, *samkhya* and *yoga* and in the different Puranas has originated in *samkhya*. O great Indras among sages! Everything great that has been instructed in *itihasa*, the meanings of the sacred texts, all special instruction and all the *jnana* in the worlds has been spoken about in *samkhya*. O *brahmanas*! All that has been instructed about supreme strength and *jnana*, everything that has been said about *moksha* and subtle austerities, has been laid down in *samkhya*. Those who follow *samkhya* always overcome their hardships and always happily obtain what is beneficial. Bearing those principles in mind, they become successful in their objectives. When they fall down again, this is in the homes of *brahmanas*. When they cast aside their bodies, the followers of *samkhya* and *yoga* obtain *moksha* or become residents of heaven. O brhmanas! Between the two, people are more interested in *samkhya*. It is extremely valuable and virtuous people on earth follow it. For them, no birth is seen as inferior species. Nor is there a downward movement and residence in regions meant for evil-doers. *Brahmanas* and sages who are not devoted to it never become the best. *Samkhya* is extensive, supreme, ancient and sparkling. It is like a large ocean that has no end. Great-souled sages who follow *samkhya* render everything to the immeasurable Narayana, the one who holds up everything. I have thus spoken about the supreme truth, about the ancient Narayana who is everywhere in the universe. At the time of creation, he is the one who creates. At the time of annihilation, he is again the one who destroys.'

Chapter 1(133) (Conversation between Vasishtha and Karala-Janaka)

The sages asked, 'What is said to be *akshara*,[291] so that one does not return from it again? O great sage! We wish to ask you about the distinction between *akshara* and *kshara*. O best among sages! O bull among sages! We wish to understand the truth. You are spoken about as the best among those who possess knowledge. You are accomplished in the Vedas. You are best among immensely fortunate *rishi*s and great-souled mendicants. O immensely wise one! We desire to hear the truth about everything. We are not satisfied at hearing about this supreme *amrita*.'

Vyasa replied, 'In this connection, I will describe to you an ancient account, about a conversation between Vasishtha and Karala-Janaka.[292] Vasishtha, best among *rishi*s, possessed a form like that of the sun. When he was seated, King Janaka asked him about the *jnana* that would bring supreme benefit. He asked him about the *paramatman*, about what would ensure benefit and about the destination and determination of *adhyatma*. When Maitra-Varuni[293] was seated, he joined his hands in salutation and honoured him. In ancient times, King Karala-Janaka asked the supreme *rishi* in words that were well articulated, humble, sweet and devoid of arguments. Janaka said, "O illustrious one! I wish to hear about the supreme and eternal *brahman*, on obtaining whom learned ones do not return. What is that which is spoken of as *kshara*, into which the universe is itself destroyed? What it said to be *akshara*, auspicious, beneficial and without any taint?"'

Vasishtha said, 'O lord of the earth! Listen to how this universe is destroyed, where it is destroyed initially and how long it takes. Know that twelve thousand years constitute a *mahayuga* and four such taken one thousand times are said to make up a *kalpa*, one

---

[291] *Akshara*, means imperishable, without decay. *Kshara* means perishable, with decay.

[292] King Karala belonged to the Janaka lineage.

[293] Vasishtha's name.

of Brahma's days.[294] O king! Understand that Brahma's night is of the same duration. When he wakes up, he undertakes his infinite tasks of creation. Though he is without form, the universe is his embodied form. O excellent king! Svayambhu Shambhu is the foundation and origin and I will tell you about him. He is Ishana and he is resplendent and without decay. *Anima, laghima* and *prapti* are in him.[295] The extremities of his hands and feet extend in all the directions. His eyes, head and mouths are everywhere. His ears are everywhere in the world and he is stationed enveloping everything. This illustrious Hiranyagarbha[296] is said to be *buddhi*. In the texts of *yoga*, he is known as Mahat and Virinchi. He is addressed by many different names in the sacred texts of *samkhya*. He has many different forms and he is the *atman* of the universe. He is known as Ekakshara.[297] All the three worlds are held up by him and he pervades them with his *atman*. He is also known as Bahurupa and Vishvarupa.[298] Through transformations, he creates himself from his own *atman*. Pradhana is an extremely great city created from the union.[299] The great energy of *ahamkara* is revered be Prajapati. The manifest[300] is created from the unmanifest and this

---

[294] A *mahayuga* consists of a cycle of *satya yuga, treta yuga, dvapara yuga* and *kali yuga*, made up of twelve thousand years of the gods. 1000 *mahayuga* make up one *kalpa*, one of Brahma's days. We have amended the text to make it conform to the standard usage. Probably because of typos, the text causes confusion. The word *kalpa* is used for a *mahayuga* and four hundred *kalpa*s are equated with one of Brahma's days.

[295] *Yoga* leads to eight major *siddhi*s or powers. These are *anima* (becoming as small as one desires), *mahima* (as large as one desires), *laghima* (as light as one wants), *garima* (as heavy as one wants), *prapti* (obtaining what one wants), *prakamya* (travelling where one wants), *vashitvam* (powers to control creatures) and *ishitvam* (obtaining divine powers).

[296] Equated with Ishana.

[297] Literally, the single one and the one without decay.

[298] Respectively, the one with many forms and the one with the universe as his form.

[299] Of the elements.

[300] Hiranyagarbha.

is said to be *vidya-sarga*.[301] Mahat and *ahamkara* represent *avidya-sarga*.[302] Mobile and immobile were also created from the single one. Those who have thought about and know the purport of the *shruti* and *smriti* texts, have said that *vidya* and *avidya* are known in this way.[303] O king! Know that the elements are created from *ahamkara* as the third.[304] O king! Know that the fourth creation resulting from *ahamkara*, is *vaikrita*. This consists of wind, light, space, water and earth and their attributes of sound, touch, form, taste and scent. There is no doubt that these ten categories were created simultaneously. O Indra among kings! Know that there is a fifth kind of creation, known as *bhoutika-sarga*. These are the ears, the skin, the eyes, the tongue, the nose as the fifth, speech, the two hands, the two feet, the anus and the genitals. These are the senses of knowledge and the organs of action. O king! They were created at the same time as the mind. It is the truth that these twenty four exist in all forms.[305] A brahmana who knows and has seen the truth about this does not sorrow. The excellent three worlds are produced in this way. O best among men! In this ocean which is like hell, this must always be known. O son![306] In everything that is *kshara*, *yaksha*s, demons, *gandharva*s, *kinnara*s, giant *uraga*s, *charana*s, *pishacha*s, *devarshi*s, travelers in the night,[307] gnats, insects, mosquitoes, filthy worms, rats, dogs, *shvapaka*s, *aineya*s,[308] *chandala*s, *pulkasa*s, elephants, horses, mules, tigers, wolves, cattle and in everything that has form in the water, on earth and in the

---

[301] The creation of knowledge.

[302] The creation of ignorance.

[303] This is a terse *shloka* and the meaning isn't obvious. The sense seems to be something like the following. While there was knowledge initially, ego and consciousness cloud it and lead to ignorance.

[304] The first being Hiranyagarbha and the second being *ahamkara*. This third creation of the elements is known as *bhuta-sarga*.

[305] The 5 senses, the 5 objects of the senses, the 5 organs of action, the 5 elements, mind, intelligence, ego and consciousness.

[306] The word used is *tata*. While this means son, it is used for anyone who is younger or junior.

[307] *Rakshasa*s.

[308] Black antelopes.

sky, it[309] exists. We have heard that everything that possesses a body dies on one or another day. However, the *atman* that is in beings is *akshara*. It is said that it is *akshara*, though the universe is *kshara*. The universe is full of confusion. It is manifest, but has originated from the unmanifest. The *akshara* is great and eternal and is always delinked from the *kshara*. O great king! I have told you what leads to no return. However, there is also a twenty fifth. This is eternal and goes by the name of *tattva*. The learned ones who know the truth call it *tattva* because it depends on *sattva*.[310] Everything that is manifest and has form is based on the unmanifest which has no form. Those twenty four are manifest. However, the twenty fifth has no form. It exists in the heart of all beings and its form is established in one's own *atman*. Consciousness and lack of consciousness always exists in all bodies that have form. But it has no form. Following the *dharma* of creation and destruction, it creates and it destroys. It is *nirguna*. However, because it has the signs of the *guna*s, it can always be perceived. In this way, the great-souled and intelligent one ensures crores of creations and destructions, but does not think that it identifies with any of these. In the womb, it is united with *tamas*, *sattva* and *rajas*. Though it possesses an understanding, it resides with those who do not have intelligence. Therefore, it thinks, "I am not someone else." "I am this one." It follows the *guna*s. Having been enveloped by *tamas*, it has many kinds of sentiments that are *tamas* in nature. In that way, *rajas* and *sattva* lead to the sentiments of *rajas* and *sattva*. There are the three complexions of white, red and black.[311] Know that Prakriti gets associated with all these forms. *Tamas* conveys to hell and *rajas* to the status of humanity. With *sattva*, one enjoys happiness and goes to the world of the gods. If one indulges in wicked deeds beyond this world, one obtains birth as inferior species. With both good and bad deeds, one becomes human. With only good deeds, one becomes a god. The learned ones say this about *moksha* and the unmanifest. This is the twenty-fifth and it functions on the basis of *jnana*.'

---

[309] The *atman*.

[310] *Tattva* means the true state, identified with the *paramatman*.

[311] Respectively associated with *sattva*, *rajas* and *tamas*.

Chapter 1(134) (Conversation between Vasishtha and Karala-Janaka continued)

'Vasishtha said, 'Because it moves from a state of understanding to a state of lack of intelligence, it rushes from one physical body to thousands of bodies. This includes birth as inferior species. Sometimes, it obtains the status of a god because of the qualities of austerities and *yoga*. From the status of humanity, it goes to heaven. From heaven, it obtains the status of humanity. From humanity it sinks into a residence in hell. This is like an insect weaving a sheath around itself[312] using thread as strands. In that way, the qualities are always like threads woven around the *atman*. Though it should be beyond opposite sentiments, it is thus that creatures succumb to opposite sentiments. Because of this, headaches, eye-diseases, toothaches, throat problems, dropsy, hemorrhoids, diseases like enlargement of glands, cholera, white leprosy, leprosy, *agnidaha*,[313] *sidhma*,[314] epilepsy and many other kinds of opposites are naturally seen in bodies. It sees itself to be afflicted by these and other ailments and identifies with the bodies. Because of arrogance, a man performs many kinds of good deeds. He attires himself in a single garment or undertakes *chaturvas*.[315] He always lies down on the ground. He lies down like a frog or seats himself in *virasana*.[316] After *virasana*, he lies down under the sky. Or he lies down on bricks and stones or on round boulders and stones. He lies down on ashes or bare stones. Or he smears himself and lies down on the ground. He sleeps in places meant for heroes, in mud and on stakes. Searching for many kinds of fruits, he futilely uses these different kinds of beds. He lies down in gardens or threshing floors. Or he wears silk and the skin of black antelopes. He attires himself in hemp or hair, or is dressed in tiger-skin, lion-skin, woven silk, garments made out of leaves and

---

[312] A cocoon.

[313] Disease treated by thermal cauterization.

[314] Spots. There were 18 kinds of leprosy and this is one of those.

[315] Different kinds of austerities are being described. *Chaturvas* is a vow of eating once in four days.

[316] Literally, posture of a hero. A seated position used by ascetics.

garments made out of bark. He wears those woven by insects and torn rags. Dressed in many other kinds of attire, he thinks himself to be intelligent. There are many kinds of food and many kinds of jewels. He sometimes eats once a day or on alternate nights. Alternatively, he eats at every fourth hour, sixth hour or eighth hour. Sometimes, he eats once every six days or eight days. He fasts for a month or eats only roots and fruits. He subsists on air or water, or only eats oilcakes, curds and cow dung. He drinks only cow's urine and eats flowers of the *kasha* tree.[317] He eats moss or only subsists on other things. He subsists on leaves that have fallen down or a fruit that has fallen down. In a desire for obtaining success, he undergoes many other kinds of hardship. There are many types and many kinds of chandrayana.[318] There are different kinds of *dharma* and *adharma* indicated for the *ashrama*s. A person may follow this or something else. He may follow diverse heretical doctrines. He may reside in the desolate shadows of mountains, or near springs. He may resort to many kinds of forests or desolate banks of rivers. There are desolate groves and large caves in mountains. There are many kinds of rituals and diverse types of austerities. There are different kinds of sacrifices and diverse forms of knowledge. There are the paths of merchants and those of *brahmana*s, *kshatriyas*, *vaishya*s and shudras. There are many kinds of donations, indicated for the miserable, the blind and the helpless. Instigated by the different *guna*s, *sattva*, *rajas* and *tamas*, he thinks he is pursuing *dharma*, *artha* and *kama*. With these influencing his *atman*, he engages in all these virtuous tasks. He performs rites to the sounds of *svadha*, *vashat* and *svaha*. He officiates at sacrifices, teaches, gives donations, receives, performs sacrifices, studies and does many other things. For birth, death, disputes, causing death and everything connected with the good and the bad, it has been said that this is the eternal path. But it is the Goddess Prakriti who

[317] *Kasha* is a kind of grass.
[318] A *chandrayana* is fasting determined by the moon's progress. For example, during *krishna paksha*, the food taken is diminished by one mouthful per day and during *shukla paksha*, it is increased by one mouthful per day.

actually does everything. At the time of the fear of the great destruction, at the end of the day,[319] all those qualities are withdrawn, like the sun withdrawing its net of rays at the time of setting. In this way, she[320] can be thought of as repeatedly sporting with everything. Depending on the *atman*, there are many kinds of qualities that bring pleasure to the heart. But this is the way the *dharma* of creation and destruction works. There are rituals along the path of rituals. Those who are attached to the three qualities follow those three qualities. Driven by those, a person follows rituals along a path of rituals. He[321] has a sense of ownership and it is that which binds him down. O lord! It is because of ignorance that he thinks that all these can be transcended through the path of rituals and refraining from them. Everything is blinded by Prakriti. In many ways, everything is pervaded by *rajas* and *tamas*. "I always suffer from the opposite pair of sentiments, but I will transcend them. They originate in me. At the time of destruction, they merge into me. Therefore, all of these must be transcended." O lord of men! Since the intelligence is partial, the *atman* thinks in this way. "These objects of pleasure will be enjoyed by me. I will enjoy the fruits of good and bad deeds in the world and then go to the world of the gods. It is my task to ensure happiness and through these good deeds, happiness will be mine. I will obtain happiness till the end of this life and also ensure it when I am born and born again. But because of what I do, till the end of my life, I may also confront misery. There is great misery for humans and the prospect of submerging in hell. From hell, it will take a long period of time before I become human again. From humanity, I may obtain divinity. From divinity, I may again obtain humanity. From humanity, I may also progressively have to descend into hell." Those who always think in this way are those whose *atmans* are covered by a sense of "mine" and they always circle around there. At the end of death, they have to go through millions of births. If a person acts in this way with a desire for good and bad fruits in mind, he obtains

---

[319] Brahma's day.
[320] Prakriti.
[321] The *atman*.

the fruit of having to assume a body in the three worlds. But it is actually Prakriti who performs the tasks, with good and bad fruits. Prakriti can go anywhere in the three worlds and enjoy the fruits. Inferior species, humanity and the world of the gods—all those three regions should be known as belonging to Prakriti. Prakriti has no signs. But she is said to possess signs in this world. In that way, Purusha is also thought of as possessing signs. Prakriti is without signs or taints, but she enters inside something[322] that possesses signs. Therefore, instated in a body that has life, one thinks this is the work of the *atman*. The ear and the other senses and the five organs of action become associated with the *guna*s and this brings attachment to the *guna*s. Because of the senses, the *atman* thinks, "I am the one who is acting." Though it has no wounds, it takes itself to be wounded. It is without signs, but thinks it possesses signs. It is beyond time, but thinks itself to be subject to time. It is beyond truth, but thinks itself to be truth. It is immortal, but thinks itself to be mortal. It is without death, but thinks that it dies. It is motionless, but thinks itself to possess motion. It is without a field,[323] but thinks itself to possess a field. It is without attachment, but thinks that it possesses attachment. It is devoid of principles, but thinks that it is the principle. It is beyond creation, but thinks itself to be created. It is without decay, but the intelligence is such that it takes itself to be perishable. Though understanding exists, because of association with those who do not possess understanding, it goes through thousands of crores of births that lead to downfall. It goes through thousands of births, ending in death, as inferior species, as human, and in the world of the gods. Like the encasement of the moon, it waxes and wanes thousands of times. Though understanding exists, because of perverse intelligence, it destroys itself. It is read that the moon always has *kala*s[324]. Fifteen of these seem to increase and decrease, but sixteen are always there. Only the ignorant think in

[322] The body.
[323] The body.
[324] The moon's diameter is divided into sixteen *kala*s. The moon waxes and wanes by one *kala* each day and the sixteenth one is the one that remains on the night of the new moon.

this way, not the intelligent. O king! Like the moon, the sixteenth is always subtle and sustained.[325] It is not united with anything, not even the gods. Nor is it used up. O supreme among kings! If the sense of 'mine' is destroyed, it is born again. Since Prakriti possesses three *guna*s, it also has three *guna*s.'

Chapter 1(135) (Conversation between Vasishtha and Karala-Janaka continued)

Janaka said, 'The relationship between *kshara* and *akshara* is desired. It is said that it is like the relationship between a woman and a man. Without a man, a woman can never conceive. Without a woman, a man can also not create a form.[326] They have a relationship with each other and depend on the qualities of each other. That is the way forms are created among all kinds of beings. For the sake of desire, they have intercourse with each other at the right season and resort to each other's qualities. That is the way forms result. Let me tell you about these signs. There are qualities for a man and there are qualities for a mother. O brahmana! We know that bones, sinews and marrow come from the father. We have heard that skin, flesh and blood comes from the mother. O best among *brahmana*s! This is what has been read in the sacred texts of the Vedas. Since it has been laid down in the Vedas and one reads about it in the sacred texts, it can be taken as proof. The proofs of the Vedas and the sacred texts represent eternal proof. This is the eternal relationship between Prakriti and Purusha. O illustrious one! But nothing has been said about the *dharma* of *moksha*. Or are these signs to be determined thereafter? Please tell me the truth about this. You are always present in front of me. I desire emancipation. I desire that

---

[325] The 5 senses, the 5 organs of action, mind, intelligence, ego, ignorance and Prakriti (or consciousness influenced by Prakriti) are probably the 15 which are modified. Pure consciousness (not influenced by Prakriti) is the 16th.

[326] Have offspring.

which grants freedom from ailments. It[327] cannot be vanquished. It is without decay. It is eternal and is beyond the senses. It is the ultimate lord.'

Vasishtha replied, 'What you have said about the proofs of the Vedas and the sacred texts is indeed true and you have accepted the truth. O lord of men! O one who knows the truth! But though you have accepted both those types of books, the Vedas and the sacred texts, you must grasp the truth that is there in those books. If a person is eager to accept books like the Vedas and the sacred texts, but does not know the truth about the purport of those books, then his acceptance is fruitless. A person who does not understand the purport of those books only bears a burden. If a person does not understand the truth about the purport of a book, then his study of that book is fruitless. If a person like me is asked about the purport of a book, he should explain what he has grasped by studying the truth carefully. If a person is gross in his intelligence and cannot explain the meaning of a book, then it is evident that his knowledge is limited and he cannot speak about its meaning. A man who does not know the truth in the texts should not explain them. If he does this out of greed or pride, he is a sinner and will descend into hell. There are gaps in his understanding of the texts and he does not expound the truth. A person who has not cleansed his soul does not know the purport or the truth. O Indra among kings! Therefore, listen to what has been instructed by the great-souled ones who know about *samkhya* and *yoga*. What is seen by those who practice *yoga* is exactly that which is followed by those who practice *samkhya*. A person who sees that *samkhya* and *yoga* are identical is intelligent. O son![328] Skin, flesh, fat, bile, marrow and sinews— these belong to the senses and you have spoken to me about them. Objects result from objects and senses from the senses. Like seeds from seeds, bodies originate from bodies. The *atman* is beyond senses, without seed and without objects. How can that great-souled one, who possesses no *guna*s, give rise to *guna*s? Qualities result from qualities and are destroyed into them. These *guna*s are born

---

[327] The *atman*.
[328] The word used is *tata*.

from Prakriti and merge into it. Skin, flesh, blood, fat, bile, marrow, bones and sinews—know that these eight are created from the semen and Prakriti. Male and non-male—these three[329] genders are said to result from Prakriti. This is spoken of as Vayu, Puman and Rasa.[330] Prakriti has no gender. But her offspring obtain gender and form. For example, flowers and fruits have form, though they result from what is formless. It is inferred that gender is obtained in this way. O son! It is the twenty-fifth one who determines the gender of the *atman*.[331] He is without beginning and without end. He is infinite. He is alone and witnesses everything. It is because of the pride of the *guna*s that he is said to possess *guna*s. How can there be *guna*s in something that is without *guna*s? However, *guna*s must result from *guna*s. People who have insight about the *guna*s know this. When one identifies with Prakriti's *guna*s, one thinks that one possesses *guna*s and perceives differences in the *guna*s. A person who knows about all the schools of *samkhya* and *yoga* has the intelligence to speak about the supreme. Such immensely wise ones are intelligent and have abandoned ignorance. Those who are ignorant speak of a manifest Ishvara who possesses his own *guna*s. Ishvara is always established as someone who is devoid of *guna*s. Those who are accomplished in *samkhya* and *yoga* understand about the supreme. They know about a twenty fifth who is beyond Prakriti's qualities. Those who know about the unmanifest can overcome the fear of birth. Those who know go there, just as the intelligent ones do.[332]

---

[329] Non-male includes female and neuter.

[330] It is difficult to make sense of this sentence. Vayu was born from the breath of Purusha, so perhaps Vayu stands for the breath of life. Rasa means semen. This leaves Puman. If Vayu and Rasa have been understood correctly, Puman might mean the physical body.

[331] Five senses of perception, five organs of action, five gross elements, five subtle elements, intelligence, mind and *ahamkara* and Prakriti account for twenty-four. Purusha is the twenty-fifth.

[332] This is expressed in a convoluted way. Intelligent ones know about Vishnu. Those who know are those who know about the unmanifest. But since Vishnu and the unmanifest one are identical, the two destinations are also identical. Intelligent is an expression being applied to the practitioners of *samkhya*, while those who know is a label that is being applied to the practitioners of *yoga*.

O scorcher of enemies! These are the indications that have been properly instructed, though the paths of those who are intelligent and those who know are separate. They respectively speak about the signs of what is *kshara* and what is *akshara*. There is a single one who is *akshara* and everything else is said to be *kshara*. When a person has studied the twenty five attributes properly, he realizes that all kinds of *darshana* lead to the single one and many kinds of *darshana* are irrelevant. There is a truth that is over and above individual indications. In the twenty-five categories, the learned speak of this as the truth. The supreme truth is said to be what is beyond the twenty-five. There are categories and there is conduct according to the categories. While this is true, the eternal truth is above this and the categories and conduct should be discarded.'

Janaka said, 'O supreme among *brahmanas*! You have spoken about the characteristics of the many and the one.[333] But I still detect some doubt about the signs of the two. O unblemished one! This is comprehended by both those are knowledgeable and those who are ignorant.[334] However, because my intelligence is gross, I still have some doubt about the truth of this. You have spoken about the causes behind that which is *kshara* and that which is *akshara*. O unblemished one! However, because my intelligence is fickle, I have forgotten about all of that. That is the reason I wish to know how one can be seen in many. How does a knowledgeable or ignorant person comprehend the truth about this? O illustrious one! Tell me, completely and separately, what *samkhya* and *yoga* say on knowledge and ignorance and on the *akshara* and the *kshara*.'

Vasishtha replied, 'I will tell you what you have asked me about. O great king! Hear separately from me about the practice of *yoga*. For *yogi*s who practice *yoga*, meditation is the supreme strength. Those who possess knowledge say that there are two kinds of meditation— concentration of the mind and *pranayama*. *Pranayama* possesses qualities, while concentration of the mind is without qualities.[335]

---

[333] The many is destructible and the one is indestructible.

[334] That the *atman* is one.

[335] *Pranayama* is performed while chanting *mantra*s, but concentration of the mind doesn't require *mantra*s.

O lord of men! With the exception of two times, passing urine and
releasing excrement, or eating, at all other times, the mind should
be devoted to this. A sage uses his mind to withdraw from the senses
and the objects of the senses and should engage in the twenty-two
and the supreme twenty-four.[336] The intelligent person uses these
to direct the *jivatman* to the *paramatman*. Learned ones have said
that this should not be practiced when one is standing or walking.
It has been heard that the *paramatman* must always be known. It
has been determined that this is for someone whose mind has been
delinked from objects and not for others. He must be free from all
attachments. He must be restrained in diet and conquer the senses.
During the early and later part of the night, the mind must be fixed
in the heart. O lord of Mithila! All the senses must be stilled by the
mind. The mind must be stilled with intelligence. Having done this,
one should be as motionless as stone. He must be as motionless as
a pillar. Like a piece of wood, he must not move. When learned
ones who know about the techniques are like this, they are said to
be united in *yoga*. He does not hear. He does not inhale. He does
not taste. He does not see anything. He does not know any touch
and there is no resolution in his mind. He does not pay attention to
anything or understand anything. He is like a piece of wood. The
learned say that such a person is then united with Prakriti. One is
seen to blaze like a lamp in a place where there is no wind. There are
no other signs. Such a person ascends upwards and doesn't descend
into inferior species. Then he sees what is to be seen. Having seen,
he does not speak. O son! People like us say that the heart of the
knower and what is to be known, the *atman*, have become one.
He is like a smokeless fire with the seven flames.[337] He is like the
sun with its rays. He is like the fiery lightning in the sky. He sees
the *paramatman* in his own self. Great-souled and persevering and
learned *brahmanas* see it in this way. This is the *brahman*, who has
no origin. This is immortality that exists in the *atman*. It is said that

---

[336] The twenty-four have been mentioned earlier. In *pranayama*, there
are different methods of breathing and controlling *prana*, with a list that
runs into around fifty. Clearly, twenty-two of these are being singled out.

[337] A fire has seven flames.

this is more subtle than what is most subtle and greater than what is greatest. Though it is inside all beings, it is certain that it cannot be seen. The creator of the world can be seen through the wealth of intelligence and the lamp of the mind. O son! It is the greatness that is beyond darkness. It is located beyond darkness. Those who know about the truth of the Vedas say that it is the dispeller of darkness. It is sparkling. It is the revered one. It is without attributes. It has the characteristic of being without traits. *Yogis* say that this is *yoga*. What other signs of *yoga* can there be? This is the way they see the supreme and undecaying one in their own *atman*s. I have thus told you the truth about the *darshana* of *yoga*.'

'I will now tell you about the knowledge of *samkhya* and about its enumeration. Those who know about Prakriti say that the unmanifest Prakriti is the supreme. O supreme among kings! From this, the second entity, known as Mahat, is generated. We have heard that the third entity, *ahamkara*, results from Mahat. Those who have the insight of *samkhya* say that the five elements are created from *ahamkara*. These eight are Prakriti.[338] There are sixteen transformations of these. In particular, there are the five senses and the five organs of action. Learned ones who know about *samkhya* say that this is the truth. They know about the ordinances of *samkhya* and are always established along the path of *samkhya*. Whatever is generated from the cause, is also destroyed within it. As they have been created from inside it, they are destroyed in reverse order. They are created in the proper order, but are destroyed in the reverse order.[339] O supreme among kings! The qualities are always like waves in an ocean and are dissolved in the qualities. This is the way the creation and destruction of Prakriti also takes place. When there is destruction, the single one[340] alone remains and many are subsequently created from it. O Indra among kings! This is what has been determined by those who have reflected on it and this

[338] The five elements, *ahamkara*, Mahat and the original Prakriti.

[339] That is, *ahamkara* is created after Mahat, but is destroyed before Mahat.

[340] In this context, Purusha.

is what should be known. It is evident that the presider[341] is not manifest. It is both one and many and so is the case with Prakriti. There is a single one at the time of destruction and many at the time of creation. Prakriti generates from its womb and the *atman* makes it many.[342] The great-souled one is established over the twenty-five that constitute the *kshetra*.[343] O Indra among kings! That is the reason the best among ascetics say that it[344] is the presider. We have heard that it is the presider and it presides over the field.[345] Because it knows the *kshetra*, the unmanifest one is known as *kshetrajna*. Since the unmanifest one lay down in earlier times, it is spoken of as Purusha.[346] Those that are known as *kshetra* and *kshetrajna* are distinct. While *kshetra* is also not manifest, it becomes discernible because of the twenty-fifth. Knowledge and the object of knowledge are said to be distinct. Knowledge is not manifest, but becomes known because of the twenty-fifth. The *kshetra* is not manifest and neither are the truth and Ishvara. The lack of Ishvara isn't the truth. Truth is known because of the twenty-fifth. These are the principles of *samkhya* philosophy and there is no enumeration beyond this. *Samkhya* only describes the action of Prakriti. The enumeration can be twenty-four or forty. One can enumerate one thousand such categories. However, the twenty-fifth is beyond all these. It is said that if a person has got to know the twenty-fifth, he is the one who knows. A person who knows this, realizes that it is the *atman* alone that exists. I have properly spoken to you about the true nature of *samkhya darshana*. A person who knows this, obtains tranquility. Prakriti is manifest to such a person as something that is directly seen. It is the one with qualities and there is also the entity without qualities. When they no longer exist separately for a person, he does

[341] Purusha.

[342] Purusha makes Prakriti many.

[343] Prakriti is the *kshetra* (field) and the great-souled one is the *brahman*.

[344] The *brahman*.

[345] The field or *kshetra* is Prakriti and the one who knows about the field, *kshetrajna*, is the *brahman*.

[346] The word *pura* means earlier, ancient, in the beginning. Hence, Purusha means the original or primeval one.

not have to return again. A person who understands the relationship between these two unmanifest entities is no longer *kshara*. It is held that such a person's vision is perfect. But there are also those who do not see properly and do not see everything as one. O scorcher of enemies! They do not reach the unmanifest and have to return again and again. Such *brahmanas* have not understood everything about the infinite. They are born in manifest forms and are under the subjugation of the manifest. Everything that is manifest results from the unmanifest and the twenty-fifth. A person who knows this does not suffer from any fear.'

Chapter 1(136) (Conversation between Vasishtha and Karala-Janaka continued)

Vasishtha continued, 'O supreme among kings! I have spoken to you about the *darshana* of *samkhya*. Now listen to me as I describe knowledge and ignorance to you progressively. The manifest, which is subject to the *dharma* of creation and destruction, is said to be ignorance. Twenty principles, subject to creation and destruction, are said to represent both *vidya* and *avidya*.[347] Listen in due course to the relationship between them. This has been described as knowledge. O son! *Rishi*s who have the insight of *samkhya* have laid this down. Among the senses and the organs of action, the senses are said to represent knowledge. Among the senses, it is said that intelligence represents knowledge. The learned ones have said that the mind is superior to the senses and represents knowledge. Compared to the mind, the five elements are said to represent knowledge. There is no doubt that *ahamkara* is superior to the five elements. O lord of men! Compared to *ahamkara*, intelligence represents knowledge. Compared to intelligence, the unmanifest Prakriti, expressive of the truth about the supreme lord, is knowledge. O best among men! Among the

[347] Respectively, knowledge and ignorance. The twenty principles are ten senses (perception and action) and the ten elements (gross and subtle).

different kinds of knowledge that are to be known, the ordinances
are said to be the supreme. The unmanifest and twenty-fifth is
said to be the supreme form of knowledge. Among everything that
can be known, this is said to be the supreme kind of knowledge.
The twenty-fifth is the object of knowledge and knowledge about
this is said to be unmanifest. A person who knows about the
twenty-fifth knows about what is unmanifest. I have told you the
difference between knowledge and ignorance. I will now tell you
what has been said about the destructible and the indestructible.
Listen. Both[348] have been said to be perishable and imperishable.
I will tell you the reasons that have been cited in support of this
on the basis of what is known. There is the view that both are
imperishable and both are without a beginning and without an
end. Therefore, both are supreme. Those who have thought about
knowledge have said that both are truly nothing but principles.
Though it leads to the principles of creation and destruction, the
unmanifest[349] is said to be imperishable. It is through its qualities
that it repeatedly creates. Mahat and the other qualities are
respectively generated. It is said that the twenty-fifth presides over
the *kshetra*. The unmanifest that is the twenty-fifth withdraws from
the net of qualities and the qualities merge into it. The qualities
merge into its quality and the single one that remains is Prakriti.
Kshetrajna then merges into *kshetra*.[350] Prakriti, characterized by
its qualities, then goes towards destruction. With the qualities
withdrawn, we have heard that Prakriti becomes *nirguna*. In this
way, *kshetrajna*'s knowledge of *kshetra* is also destroyed. Prakriti
is then devoid of qualities like the *paramatman*. He[351] realizes
that just like himself, Prakriti is devoid of qualities. Discarding
Prakriti, he then becomes pure. The intelligent one realizes himself
to be distinct.[352] O Indra among kings! When he gives up that

---

[348] The *jivatman* and Prakriti.

[349] Prakriti.

[350] Purusha into Prakriti.

[351] Purusha.

[352] Distinct from Prakriti. Succeeding *shloka*s suggest that this is a
description of a *yogi* in meditation.

combination, he exists separately and Prakriti is also seen to be distinct from that combination. When he no longer desires Prakriti and that net of *gunas*, he can behold the supreme. Having seen the supreme, he is free from all anxiety. "What have I done? I have been like a person overtaken by destiny. Because of my ignorance, I have been like a fish entangled in a net. Because of my delusion, I have moved from one body to another body. My conduct has been like that of an ignorant fish, moving from one body of water to another body of water and thinking in its ignorance that the water is everything. In that fashion, because of my ignorance, I have not known my own *atman*. Shame on my intelligence that I have been repeatedly submerged. Because of my confusion, I have followed the course from one body to another body. This[353] is alone my friend when I face destruction. I am capable of being united with it. I am just as it is. I see myself as equal to it. I am like it. It is without blemish. I can see that I am just like it. I have been ignorant and deluded. Because of ignorance and delusion, I have been properly entangled. Though without attachments, I have spent a long period of time being attached. For a long period of time, I have been controlled by others, but did not realize it. There are different kinds of states, high, medium and low.[354] How can I be like that? How can I dwell with *maya*[355] as an equal? Because of my ignorance, I went to her earlier. I will steady myself now. I will not dwell with her and be deceived for a long period of time. I am without transformations. However, I have been deceived by the one who possesses transformations.[356] That is not her crime. It is my crime. It is because of my sentiments that I became attached and withdrew from what had presented itself.[357] That is the reason I assumed many forms and moved from one body to another body. Despite being one without a body, I have assumed

[353] The *brahman*.

[354] Referring to states of birth—high being gods, medium being humans and low being inferior species.

[355] Prakriti.

[356] Prakriti.

[357] The *brahman*.

the form of a body and have been assailed because of that sense of ownership. Prakriti has accordingly conveyed me into those wombs. I am without a form. Thanks to the sense of ownership, what acts have I performed in those forms? She is in those wombs and destroys sense and consciousness. I do not possess any sense of ownership. But goaded by *ahamkara*, I have been equated with her and have performed acts. She divided my *atman* into many parts and repeatedly engaged me. However, now my intelligence is such that I have no sense of ownership and no *ahamkara*. I have acted so as to discard the sense of ownership and have always removed a sense of *ahamkara* from myself. Having escaped from all that, I have resorted to what is beneficial. I will go to that tranquility and not be united with what is without consciousness. That kind of union is beneficial. I have no similarity with her." He, thus, realizes the supreme relationship with the twenty-fifth. He abandons what is *kshara* and not beneficial and is conveyed to the *akshara*. This is unmanifest. But because of the nature of becoming manifest, one without *guna*s is vested with *guna*s. O one from Mithila! Having seen the original one who is *nirguna*, he becomes like it. I have spoken to you about the indications of what is *akshara* and *kshara*, according to the knowledge that I have obtained and according to what the sacred texts have instructed. I will now again tell you about what I have heard. Listen. This is knowledge that is sparkling, without any doubt, extremely pure and subtle. I have told you what the sacred texts of both *samkhya* and *yoga* instruct. This has been stated in the sacred texts of *samkhya* and *darshana* of *yoga*. O lord of the forests! This knowledge of *samkhya* can awaken people and for the welfare of disciples, this has been clearly enunciated. Learned people say that those sacred texts are extensive. In texts of *yoga*, rebirth is placed at the forefront. O lord of men! Those who follow *samkhya* do not see the truth about a supreme twenty-fifth. What they regard as supreme has already been accurately described.[358] Those who

---

[358] *Samkhya* philosophy does not believe in a personal god and this simply states that.

cite indications from *yoga* speak about the truth of awakening, knowledge, that which is to be known and the one who knows.[359]

Chapter 1(137) (Conversation between Vasishtha and Karala-Janaka concluded)

Vasishtha continued, 'Hear about awakening and the unmanifest one, from whom the store of *guna*s is created. He sustains these *guna*s and creates and withdraws them. O lord of men! For the sake of sport, Aja[360] divides his own self into many parts and collects them again. The one who can understand this action[361] does not understand. Because he is capable of understanding the one who is not manifest, he is spoken of as *budhyamana*.[362] Nevertheless, he cannot understand the one who is not manifest, whether it is with *guna*s or without *guna*s. Therefore, rare is the case when he is awakened. The learned texts have said that whenever *budhyamana* gets to know the unmanifest and twenty-fifth one, he becomes united with it. That is the reason the one who is not manifest is spoken of as ignorant.[363] *Budhyamana* is spoken of as being both unmanifest and ignorant. Nothing with life can comprehend the great-souled and twenty-fifth. The twenty-sixth is sparkling, immeasurable and eternal and it can understand.[364] It can always understand the twenty-fourth and the twenty-fifth. The immensely

[359] The one who knows is the *jivatman* and the one who is to be known is the *paramatman* or *brahman*. *Yoga* talks of both.

[360] The *brahman*. Aja means without birth. Throughout this chapter, the *shloka*s are very difficult to understand and several liberties have been taken.

[361] The *jivatman*.

[362] *Budhyamana* means the one who comprehends and is being used for the *jivatman*, which can understand the nature of the *paramatman*.

[363] This seems to be a reference to the *jivatman*, but can mean Prakriti too.

[364] The *jivatman* seems to be the twenty-fourth, Prakriti the twenty-fifth and the *paramatman* the twenty-sixth.

radiant one[365] follows her nature, vis-à-vis both what is seen and is not seen. O son! Those who truly understand can not only see the twenty-fourth and the twenty-fifth, but also the unmanifest *brahman*. When a person knows the *atman*, he thinks himself to be it.[366] He uses that insight to look at Prakriti and the unmanifest. With that pure and unsullied knowledge, he comprehends the supreme. O tiger among kings! He is then established in knowledge about the twenty-sixth. He then casts aside the unmanifest[367], which is subject to the *dharma* of creation and destruction. Though because of consciousness, Prakriti is invested with *guna*s, he knows the one without *guna*s. Having seen the unmanifest, he is only full of *dharma*. Having approached the whole, he is freed and obtains the *atman*. This is spoken of as the truth. It is beyond the truth. It is immortal and without decay. O king! By hearing about it, one gets to comprehend the truth. The learned ones talk about twenty-five principles. O son! A person who knows about the truth is not immersed in *samsara*. The swift freeing from principles is a sign of intelligence. A wise person knows himself to be the twenty-sixth. However, though awakened by the intelligent twenty-sixth, there is still ignorance. The sacred texts of *samkhya* have spoken about the signs of this. When one is united with consciousness and the twenty-fifth,[368] because of that consciousness, one does not comprehend the sense of unity. O lord of Mithila! O lord of men! Because of the rules of attachment, one is not awakened. However, when one is awakened and loses attachment, one realizes unity. Without any sense of attachment, a learned person approaches the twenty-sixth. Abandoning the unmanifest,[369] the lord obtains the understanding. With knowledge about the twenty-sixth awakened, he realizes that the twenty-four are valueless. O unblemished one! It is in this way that *budhyamana* gains understanding. As indicated in the sacred texts, I have spoken to you about the true nature of understanding.

---

[365] Prakriti.
[366] Thinks that the *jivatman* is no different from the *paramatman*.
[367] Prakriti.
[368] Prakriti.
[369] Prakriti.

One must understand the difference between the gnat and the fig,[370] the fish and the water and this and that.[371] That is the way a person must approach the one and the many. When one is full *jnana* and *vijnana*, this is said to be *moksha*. This twenty-fifth resides in bodies and when one has understanding about the unmanifest, this is said to be *moksha*. It has been determined that this is the only method for emancipation and there is no other. Because it[372] dwells in the body, it conveys the impression of being different. By uniting with purity, one becomes pure. An intelligent person does not unite with what is impure. O bull among men! If a person's intelligence turns towards this *dharma*, he becomes free. By following the *dharma* of detachment, the *atman* becomes free. By uniting with the *dharma* of emancipation, one becomes emancipated. By striving for emancipation, one unites with emancipation. By performing pure deeds, one becomes pure and extremely intelligent. By uniting with the unblemished *atman*, one's own *atman* becomes unblemished.[373] By uniting with the absolute, one obtains the absolute in one's *atman*. By uniting with the one who is free, one uses that freedom to obtain freedom. O great king! I have told you the truth. I have accurately described the exact truth to you. This is about the immortal, pure and original *brahman*. Accept the purport of this. O king! You can pass on this supreme knowledge to a person who does not follow the Vedas, as long as that person is free of malice. But he must seek this knowledge, which leads to an awakening. As long as he bows down and follows instructions, you can pass this on, for the sake of his awakening. However, it should not be passed on to a person who has falsehood in his soul, or is deceitful, impotent, or fraudulent in his intelligence. Nor must the knowledge be given to learned men who are jealous. It must be imparted to disciples. Listen to the ones to whom it can be given. A person who is faithful, possesses qualities, one who always abstains from censuring others, one who performs pure *yoga* for the sake of knowledge, a forgiving

---

[370] Gnats are found inside ripe figs.
[371] The *jivatman* and the *paramatman*.
[372] The *jivatman*.
[373] Respectively, the *paramatman* and the *jivatman*.

person who is full of compassion, one who can discriminate about good conduct, a person who loves the rituals, one who is extremely learned and does not engage in quarrels, a person who is humble in attire and one has no selfish motives—these are the people to whom it can be given. It is said that this pure and supreme knowledge of the *brahman* should not be given to those who are devoid of these qualities. Those who know about *dharma* have said that no benefits accrue from giving it to undeserving people. If a person does not observe the vows, it should not be given to him, even if one obtains the earth, full of riches, in exchange. O Indra among men! But there is no doubt that this supreme knowledge can be communicated to a person who has conquered his senses. O Karala! Having heard about the supreme *brahman* now, you should not have the slightest reason for fear. I have spoken about the pure and the supreme, the dispeller of sorrow, the one who is without a beginning, a middle and an end. This is fathomless and without birth and death. It is auspicious and frees from disease and fear. Having understood it, abandon all your delusion now. Know that this is the true nature of knowledge. O lord of men! In ancient times, I gratified the eternal Hiranyagarbha and obtained it from him. I made efforts to please the one who is fierce in his energy. Having obtained knowledge about the supreme *brahman*, I have now passed it on to you. O Indra among men! Asked by you, I have now told you exactly what I learned. O Indra among men! This is what I obtained from Brahma. This is great knowledge, the ancient wisdom about *moksha*.'

Vyasa said, 'O best among sages! I have told you what Vasishtha, the best among sages, said in ancient times. I have spoken to you about the twenty-fifth, the supreme *brahman* from whom, one does not return. If one does not comprehend this supreme and undecaying knowledge, one has to return again. But if one comprehends the truth, there is no decay and no death. O *brahmanas*! I heard about this supreme and beneficial knowledge from the *devarshi*[374] and have recounted it to you. O *dvijas*! The great-souled Vasishtha obtained it from Hiranyagarbha. Narada obtained it from Vasishtha, tiger among *rishis*. I got to know about

[374] Narada.

the great and eternal from Narada. O best among sages! Do not grieve. You have heard about this supreme objective. A person who knows about the *kshara* and the *akshara* has no reason to fear. A person who does not know about it has reason to fear. Because of ignorance and foolishness in the soul, a person has to repeatedly return and assume bodies. After death, he is born thousands of times and dies again. He is sometimes in the world of the gods, but is also born as inferior species. If he is freed from that, he is immersed in an ocean of ignorance. That ocean of ignorance is terrible. It is said to be unmanifest and fathomless. O *brahmanas*! Day after day, beings are submerged in it. But you have crossed that eternal, unmanifest and fathomless ocean of ignorance. O *brahmanas*! Therefore, you have been freed from *rajas* and from *tamas*. O best among sages! I have, thus, described the supreme essence of all essences. I have spoken about supreme *moksha*. Knowing this, one does not return. This must never be given to those who are non-believers or those who are without faith. O *brahmanas*! It must not be given to those who are evil in intelligence or those who turn away from devotion.'

Chapter 1(138) (Praise of the Purana)

Lomasharshana said, 'O *brahmanas*! In ancient times, the sage Vyasa recited the Purana in a melodious tone. His words were full of substance and were free of the eighteen defects.[375] The Purana had no blemishes and was pure and complete, containing the gist of many sacred texts. It was pure in character and adorned with *samkhya* and *yoga*. It stated *purvapaksha*[376] and arrived at a firm

---

[375] This could be a reference to *nyaya*. But *nyaya* only has sixteen categories (*padarthas*). But there were eighteen kinds of learning—four Vedas, six Vedangas, *mimasa*, *nyaya*, *dharmashastra*, Puranas, *arthashastra*, *ayurveda*, *dhanurveda* and *gandharva vidya*. So defect might mean not knowing about these. Defects listed for rhetoric also do not amount to eighteen in number.

[376] In debating, one first stated the views of the opponent, known as *purvapaksha*. This was then rebutted to arrive at a final conclusion.

conclusion. As is proper, the immensely intelligent one made them hear it and stopped. The best among sages heard the first Purana, known as Brahma Purana. It was in conformity with the Vedas and yields all the fruits one wishes for. They became happy and extremely delighted. They were repeatedly astounded. They praised the sage, Krishna Dvaipayana Vyasa.'

The sages said, 'O best among sages! This is wonderful. This Purana is in conformity with the *shruti* texts. It is supreme and bestows all the desired fruits. It destroys every kind of sin. It has colourful lines and syllables. You have recited it and we have heard. O lord! There is nothing in the three worlds not known to you. O immensely fortunate one! Like Brihaspati among the gods, you know everything. O immensely wise one! O one immersed in the *brahman*! O great sage! We bow down before you. You have expressed the meaning of the Vedas in Bharata.[377] O great sage! Who is capable of describing all your qualities? You have studied the four Vedas, the *Vedanga*s and *vyakarana*.[378] Thereafter, you composed the sacred text of Bharata. You are full of knowledge. We bow down before you. O Vyasa! We bow down before you. O one who is extensive in intelligence! O one with eyes like the large petals of a blossoming lotus! Bharata is like a lamp full of oil, kindled by you for the sake of knowledge. There are those who are blinded by ignorance, whirled around because of their perverse vision. Using the torch of knowledge, you have opened their eyes.'

Lomaharshana continued, 'Having said this, they worshipped Vyasa and he honoured them back. Successful in their objective, they returned to where they had come from, their own hermitages. O best among sages! In that way, I have described the eternal Purana to you. It is extremely sacred and destroys every kind of sin. O supreme *brahmanas*! You asked me questions. Through Vyasa's favours, I have answered all of them. This should be heard by householders, mendicants and *brahmachari*s. It bestows wealth and happiness on men and destroys every kind of sin. *Brahmanas* who are devoted to the *brahman* and other self-controlled *brahmanas* must hear it.

[377] That is, Mahabharata.
[378] Grammar.

All those who desire their own benefit must make great efforts to hear it properly. A brahmana will obtain learning, a *kshatriya* will be victorious in battle, a *vaishya* will get inexhaustible riches and a shudra will obtain happiness. If a man purifies himself and thinking about something he desires, listens to it, there is no doubt that the man will obtain whatever he wishes for. This is Vaishnava Purana and destroys every kind of sin. It is special among all sacred texts and accomplishes the objectives of human existence. I have recited the Purana which is in conformity with the Vedas. If one listens to it, heaps of sins and taints are destroyed. If a man listens to it, he obtains the fruits that are obtained by fasting in Prayaga, Pushkara, Kurukshetra and Arbuda. O *brahmanas*! If a person listens to this extremely sacred account even once, he obtains the fruits obtained by performing *agnihotra*, with excellent oblations for a year. A man obtains fruits by bathing in the waters of the Yamuna on *dvadashi* in the month of Proshthapada,[379] or by seeing Hari in Mathura. O *brahmanas*! If a person focuses his mind on Keshava, concentrates and recites this Purana properly, those same fruits are obtained. If a man reads it or hears it, he obtains fruits that are the same as the fruits a man obtains by seeing Shri. This Purana is in conformity with the Vedas. If a person constantly reads it or hears it, after death, he goes to Hari's abode. A brahmana who controls himself and always makes others hear it on *ekadashi* and *dvadashi* and on auspicious days, goes to Vishnu's world. O *brahmanas*! This is blessed. It confers fame, a long lifespan and happiness and extends deeds. It bestows strength and nourishment. It dispels nightmares. This is the best of accounts. If a person controls himself well and faithfully recites it at the time of the three *sandhya*s, he obtains everything that he desires. A diseased person is freed of disease. A person who has been bound is freed of his bonds. A person who is afraid loses his fear. A person suffering from a hardship is freed of the hardship. A person remembers his past lives and obtains learning. He obtains sons, intelligence, animals and fortitude. A man obtains *dharma*, *artha*, *kama* and *moksha*. If a man controls his mind and reads it, there is no doubt that he obtains everything that he wishes for.

[379] Bhadra.

This bestows heaven and emancipation. If a man purifies himself and constantly listens to it with devotion in his mind, prostrating himself before Vishnu, the preceptor of the worlds and the bestower of boons, he obtains happiness. Cleansed of sins, he enjoys divine bliss in heaven. After that, he is freed from Prakriti's *guna*s and obtains an extremely sparkling destination with Hari. Therefore, excellent *brahmanas* who are devoted to their own dharma and desire to proceed along the path of liberation, controlled bulls among *kshatriya*s who always desire what is good for themselves, *vaishya*s who have been born in pure lineages and shudras who are devoted to *dharma* must always listen to this excellent account. It bestows many fruits—*dharma*, *artha* and *moksha*. O best among men! May your minds always turn towards *dharma*. In the world hereafter, that alone is the friend. Even if a person is accomplished, the power of *artha* and women have no stability. A man obtains a kingdom through *dharma*. It is through *dharma* that a man goes to heaven. A man obtains a long lifespan, deeds, austerities, *dharma* and *moksha* through the practice of *dharma*. *Dharma* is a mother and a father. In the world hereafter, *dharma* is a friend. *Dharma* is the saviour and bestows *moksha*. There is nothing other than *dharma*. This Purana is in conformity with the Vedas and is the greatest secret. It should not be revealed to those who are evil in intelligence, especially not to non-believers. I have recounted this supreme Purana. It destroys sin and extends *dharma*. O sages! You have heard this supreme secret. Now grant me permission to leave.'

This ends Part I of Brahma Purana.

Part II (Goutami Mahatmya)

Chapter 2(1): 33 shlokas
Chapter 2(2): 44 shlokas
Chapter 2(3): 36 shlokas
Chapter 2(4): 68 shlokas
Chapter 2(5): 88 shlokas
Chapter 2(6): 50 shlokas
Chapter 2(7): 40 shlokas
Chapter 2(8): 77 shlokas
Chapter 2(9): 22 shlokas
Chapter 2(10): 94 shlokas
Chapter 2(11): 22 shlokas
Chapter 2(12): 16 shlokas
Chapter 2(13): 30 shlokas
Chapter 2(14): 20 shlokas
Chapter 2(15): 24 shlokas
Chapter 2(16): 71 shlokas
Chapter 2(17): 26 shlokas
Chapter 2(18): 49 shlokas
Chapter 2(19): 47 shlokas
Chapter 2(20): 36 shlokas
Chapter 2(21): 13 shlokas
Chapter 2(22): 49 shlokas
Chapter 2(23): 28 shlokas
Chapter 2(24): 50 shlokas
Chapter 2(25): 32 shlokas
Chapter 2(26): 27 shlokas

Chapter 2(27): 33 shlokas
Chapter 2(28): 22 shlokas
Chapter 2(29): 12 shlokas
Chapter 2(30): 33 shlokas
Chapter 2(31): 20 shlokas
Chapter 2(32): 11 shlokas
Chapter 2(33): 12 shlokas
Chapter 2(34): 92 shlokas
Chapter 2(35): 31 shlokas
Chapter 2(36): 58 shlokas
Chapter 2(37): 88 shlokas
Chapter 2(38): 131 shlokas
Chapter 2(39): 58 shlokas
Chapter 2(40): 230 shlokas
Chapter 2(41): 86 shlokas
Chapter 2(42): 28 shlokas
Chapter 2(43): 23 shlokas
Chapter 2(44): 25 shlokas
Chapter 2(45): 20 shlokas
Chapter 2(46): 25 shlokas
Chapter 2(47): 20 shlokas
Chapter 2(48): 33 shlokas
Chapter 2(49): 20 shlokas
Chapter 2(50): 18 shlokas
Chapter 2(51): 26 shlokas
Chapter 2(52): 105 shlokas

Chapter 2(1) (Description of *tirtha*s)

The sages said, 'Having heard in detail about the *tirtha*s, we are not satisfied. Please tell us about the secret once again, in detail, about the greatness of the *tirtha*s and about the *tirtha* that is best among them all.'

Brahma replied, 'O best among *brahmanas*! Earlier, Narada asked me exactly the same question and I made great efforts to tell him.'

Narada said, 'O origin of the universe! O lord of the universe! I have heard from you that visiting the *tirtha*s is superior to austerities, sacrifices and donations. O lord of the gods! Which are the different *tirtha*s and what fruits are obtained from visiting them? Which is always the best among all the *tirtha*s?'

Brahma replied,[380] 'O tigers among sages! There are four kinds of *tirtha*s—those of gods, *asura*s, *rishi*s and men. These are famous in the three worlds of heaven, earth and the nether regions and are visited by the gods. In every way, the *tirtha*s of *rishi*s are better than the *tirtha*s of men. The *tirtha*s of *asura*s bring greater benefits than the *tirtha*s of *rishi*s. O son![381] In every way, the *tirtha*s of gods are better than the *tirtha*s of *asura*s. Those created by Brahma, Vishnu and Mahesha are spoken of as the *tirtha*s of the gods. No one knows of anything superior than those created by these three. In the three worlds, there are *tirtha*s that are spoken of as belonging to mortals.[382] Among these, those in Jambu-dvipa are said to be the best in qualities. Among the *tirtha*s in Jambu-dvipa, the sacred texts state that the ones in Bharatavarsha are famous. Within Bharata, Dandakaranya[383] is the best among all *tirtha*s. O son! It is spoken of as a *tirtha* that is a *karma bhumi*.[384] All the *tirtha*s that I spoke to you about are there. I will briefly describe their names to you. Listen. Depending on whether they are for gods, *asura*s or humans, there are differences between them. There are six rivers between the Himalayas and the Vindhyas and they are divine in origin. O brahmana! There are also six rivers, divine in origin, between the Vindhyas and the southern ocean. These twelve rivers are described as the most important. Since Bharata confers a great deal of merit, it is worshipped. The gods also speak of this *varsha*[385] as *karma*

---

[380] This is Brahma replying to Narada.
[381] Narada was Brahma's son.
[382] Those for humans.
[383] The forest (*aranya*) known as Dandaka.
[384] Region where *karma* is performed and its fruits enjoyed.
[385] Continent.

bhumi. The *tirtha*s of *rishi*s and the others[386] were created by the gods. Worshipping there, one obtains benefit, emancipation and prosperity. One obtains fruits for one's own self, or fame. O Narada! The *tirtha*s created by men are known as human *tirtha*s. O excellent sage! In this way, there are four different kinds of *tirtha*s. No one knows about these differences. O Narada! Therefore, you should hear about this. There are many who are heard to speak of themselves as learned. However, which person, meritorious in deeds, will hear or speak about his own qualities?'

Narada said, 'I wish to hear the truth about their nature and differences. Hearing about this, one is eternally freed from all sins. O Brahma! In the first *krita yuga*, there is no method other than that of frequenting the *tirtha*s. Through a little bit of effort, one obtains the desired objectives. O Dhatri![387] As a speaker, there is no one who is your equal. As one who knows, there is no one who is your equal. You originated from the lotus in Vishnu's navel. You were the first to be born.'

Brahma replied, 'The six rivers to the south of the Vindhyas are said to be Godavari, Bhimarathi,[388] Tungabhadra, Venika,[389] Tapi[390] and Payoshni.[391] Bhagirathi, Narmada, Yamuna, Sarasvati, Vishoka and Vitasta have a refuge on the slopes of the Himalayas. These rivers are most sacred and are spoken of as the *tirtha*s of the gods. The *tirtha*s where Gaya, Kolasura, Vritra, Tripura, Andhaka, Hayamurdha, Lavana, Namuchi, Shringaka, Yama, Patalaketu, Madhu and Pushkara performed rites are known as auspicious *asura tirtha*s. O Narada! *Tirtha*s frequented by sages like Prabhasa, Bhargava, Agasti, Nara, Narayana, Vasishtha, Bharadvaja, Goutama, Kashyapa, Manu and others are *tirtha*s of the *rishi*s. The auspicious *tirtha*s created by Ambarisha, Harishchandra, Nahusha, Rama, Kuru, Kanakhala, Bharata, Sagara, Ashvayupa,Nachiketa

---

[386] Meaning *asura tirtha*s.

[387] Brahma. Dhatri can loosely be translated as Creator. Dhatri is the Creator, Vidhatri is the one who controls/ordains.

[388] The river Bhima.

[389] Venya.

[390] Tapti.

[391] Identified with Purna, or part of Tapti.

and Vrishakapi, scorcher of enemies are human *tirtha*s. O Narada! They created them for the fruits of fame and prosperity. Anywhere in the three worlds, wherever *tirtha*s have originated of their own accord, those sacred *tirtha*s are known as the *tirtha*s of the gods. I have, thus, spoken about the differences between *tirtha*s. Anything not dug up by anyone else is spoken of as something that has been dug up by the gods. O sage! I have briefly spoken to you about the differences between *tirtha*s. Even if a man merely knows about them, he is freed from all sins.'

Chapter 2(2) (Preparations for Shambhu's marriage)

Narada asked, 'Among all the *tirtha*s where the three gods[392] exist, which one is the best? Please tell me in detail about the differences in its nature.'

Brahma replied, 'Sacrifices and other rites in the other *tirtha*s give rise to good merits only as long as the three gods do not show themselves.[393] If one resorts to the Ganga, great fruits are obtained from vows, fasting and by undergoing various kinds of hardship. It is seen that those with bodies undertake hardships in all the *tirtha*s. O sage! Those with bodies thus purify themselves, their objects, fathers, mothers and others. However, in the absence of the three gods, how can sins be destroyed? Ganga is the best among rivers and grants everything that one desires. Remembering, seeing or touching Ganga bestows everything that one asks for. O best among sages! The three gods exist there. Hear about her origin. Ten thousand years ago, a task of the gods presented itself. Because of the boons bestowed by me, Taraka became extremely insolent and strong. Using his strength, he took away the great prosperity of the gods. With Indra at the forefront, the gods went and sought refuge

---

[392] Brahma, Vishnu and Shiva.
[393] The sense seems to be that once the three gods show themselves and grant boons, the good merits are exhausted.

with the divinity Vishnu, the great grandfather[394] of the universe. He was lying down on the ocean of milk and the gods had no other refuges. Joining their hands in salutation, the gods spoke to him. The gods said, "O protector! You are the saviour of the universe. You extend the deeds of the gods. You are the lord of everything. You are the origin of the universe. The three[395] are your forms. We bow down to you. You are the creator of the worlds. You are the destroyer of *asura*s. You are the lord of the universe. You are the reason behind creation, preservation and destruction. You pervade the universe. For those with bodies other than you, there is no saviour in the three worlds. When they face calamities, who else can they go to? O one with eyes like the petals of a lotus! Other than you, who can pacify the three kinds of calamity?[396] You are the mother and father of the entire universe. O divinity! Through serving you, you can easily be obtained. O lord! Be pleased and save us. We are suffering from great fear. Other than you, who can dispel our affliction? Please tell us. You are the original creator. You are the boar, the fish and the tortoise.[397] When fear arrives, you save us through such diverse forms. Large numbers of *asura*s have taken away our possessions. They have taken away our wives. They have taken away our abodes. O divinity! O Hari! Other than you, who will save us? Where will we seek refuge?" Lying down on Shesha, the illustrious one, Shri's consort, spoke to them. "Forget your anxiety. Where has this fear surfaced from? Please tell me." Therefore, they spoke to Shri's consort about Taraka's death. The gods said, "This terrible fear has arisen on account of Taraka and it makes the body hair stand up. We are incapable of destroying him through fighting, austerities or curses. He cannot come about his death except through a child who is not yet ten days old.[398] O divinity! Therefore, other than you, who can devise an appropriate

---

[394] Since the grandfather, Brahma, originated from Vishnu.

[395] Brahma, Vishnu and Shiva.

[396] Relating to *adhidaivika* (destiny), *adhibhhoutika* (nature) and *adhyatmika* (one's own nature).

[397] Vishnu's *varaha*, *matysa* and *kurma avatara*s.

[398] This was the boon Taraka received from Brahma.

method?" Narayana spoke to them again. "O gods! I am not someone who is excessively strong. His death cannot come about through me, my offspring, or the offspring of the gods. Ishvara will have an extremely strong son. Taraka, the one who scorches the worlds, will come by his death through him. O gods! Therefore, along with the mendicants and the *rishi*s, let us go to him. The first task for Vishnu and the other lords is that one should make efforts so that he accepts a wife." Thus addressed, the large number of gods went to the supreme mountain, Himalayas, full of jewels and to Mena,[399] loved by the Himalayas. All of them spoke to the snow-covered mountain and his wife. The gods said, "Dakshayani[400] is the mother of the worlds. She is Shakti, Shivaa, Buddhi, Prajna, Dhriti, Medha, Lajja, Pushti and Sarasvati.[401] Purifying the worlds, she is present in the world in many forms. To accomplish the task of the gods, she will enter your union. The mother of the universe will be born as your daughter and will become Shambhu's wife. She will protect us and you." Himalayas welcomed the words of the gods. Mena was also extremely enthusiastic and approved of these words. Thus, Gouri, the mother of the universe, was born in the home of the Himalayas. She was always devoted to meditating on Shiva. She was his beloved and was devoted to him. The large number of gods told her, "For the sake of Isha,[402] perform austerities." At this, Gouri performed great austerities on the slopes of the Himalayas. The gods consulted among themselves again. "How can Isha meditate on her? We do not know what Bhava[403] meditates on. Does he meditate on the *atman* or on something else? How can the mind of the lord of the gods be focused on Menaka's daughter? We should think about the best means of achieving this. That will be beneficial for us"' At

---

[399] The wife of the Himalayas, also referred to as Menaka.

[400] Daksha's daughter, Sati. In the course of Daksha's sacrifice, Sati immolated herself and was reborn as Parvati, the daughter of the Himalayas and Mena.

[401] The personified forms of strength, everything auspicious, intelligence, wisdom, fortitude, comprehension, modesty, nourishment and speech. Shiva is the masculine, Shivaa the feminine.

[402] Shiva.

[403] Shiva.

this, the immensely intelligent one, extensive in his wisdom, spoke. Brihaspati said, 'The intelligent Madana Kandarpa[404] is the one who wields a bow made out of flowers. Let him pierce the serene Shiva with auspicious arrows that are made out of flowers. Pierced by him, the three-eyed Isha's mind will turn towards her. There is no doubt that Hara will marry Girija[405] then. He will be vanquished by the one with the five arrows.[406] No one has been able to repulse his arrows. When the mother of the universe is married, Shambhu's son will be born. When a son is born to the three-eyed one, the son will kill Taraka. Let Vasanta,[407] the one with the beautiful lips who has a storehouse of flowers, go as Kama's aide. He delights everyone's mind.' The large number of gods, scorcher of enemies, were eager to defeat the *asuras*. They agreed and sent Madana and the storehouse of flowers to Shiva's presence. Along with Madhava, Kama swiftly departed, wielding his bow. Kama went with Rati[408] to perform this extremely difficult task. He held his bow and arrows and stood in front of Ishvara. "The lord Shambhu is the preceptor of the worlds. He cannot be pierced. Will I pierce him? My arrows can vanquish the three worlds. But will they be firm in front of Shambhu?" The fire from his eyes reduced him completely to ashes.[409] The excellent gods had also gone to witness the firm act. When they arrived, hear about the astounding event that occurred. The large number of gods looked at Shambhu and Manmatha and seeing that Kama had been reduced to ashes, they were filled with fear. The gods joined their hands in salutation and praised Ishana, the lord of the gods. The gods said, "On account of Taraka, we are suffering from fear. Please accept the daughter of the mountain as your wife." With his mind pierced, Hari immediately agreed to the words the gods had spoken. For the sake of others, great-souled ones do not think about what is good or bad for them. For the sake of the alliance between

---

[404] Madana and Kandarpa are the names of Kama, the god of love. Manmatha is also one of his names.

[405] Girija, the daughter of the mountain, is Parvati's name.

[406] Kama is the one with five arrows to his bow.

[407] Spring. Another name for Spring is Madhava.

[408] Rati is Kama's wife.

[409] Shiva's glance reduced Kama to ashes.

the Himalayas and the protector of the worlds, the immortals sent Arundhati,[410] Vasishtha, me and the wielder of the *chakra*[411] to make arrangements for the marriage.'

Chapter 2(3) (Brahma receives a water-pot)

Brahma said, 'Himalayas, best among mountains, is decorated with many wonderful jewels. It is full of diverse trees and creepers and is frequented by many kinds of birds. It is covered with female rivers, male rivers, lakes, wells, ponds and other water bodies and is frequented by gods, *gandharvas*, *yakshas*, *siddhas* and *charanas*. An auspicious breeze blows there and is sufficient reason for a great deal of joy. It is surrounded by mountains like Meru, Mandara, Kailasa and Mainaka. Vasishtha, Agastya, Poulastya, Lomasha and other sages frequent it. The marriage was organized amidst great festivities. A lofty platform, adorned with gold and embellished with jewels was erected. Vishvakarma[412] created a divine and agreeable pavilion. The pillars were encrusted with diamonds, rubies and lapis lazuli. The divinities Jaya, Lakshmi, Shubha, Kshanti, Kirti, Pushti and others surrounded it.[413] The mountains Meru, Mandara, Kailasa and Raivata adorned it. The powerful Vishnu, protector of the worlds, showed it his respect. The golden Mainaka, best among mountains, was resplendent. The *rishis*, the guardians of the worlds, the Adityas and the large number of Maruts fashioned the altar for the wedding of the wielder of the trident, the lord of the gods. Tvashta Vishvakarma himself constructed the platform, along with the gates. There were divine cows like Surabhi, Nandini, Nanda and Sunanda, who yielded every object of desire.

---

[410] Vasishtha's wife.

[411] Vishnu.

[412] The architect of the gods.

[413] The personified forms of victory, prosperity, auspiciousness, forbearance, fame and nourishment. These are intended to indicate Daksha's daughers.

As the wedding was about to take place, they too made the place beautiful and pleasant. The oceans, the rivers, the *nagas*, the *rishis*, the mothers of the worlds, the trees and all the seeds also arrived. Ila[414] performed the earth's work. The herbs undertook the task of praising. Varuna took care of tasks connected with drinking and Kubera took care of tasks connected with donating. Agni did whatever the Himalayas and the protector of the worlds desired. The eternal Vishnu undertook separate tasks of worship. The Vedas and their mysteries sang and spoke. All the *apsaras* danced and all the *gandharvas* and *kinnaras* sang. O supreme among sages! Mainaka held the parched grain. O Narada! The sacred words were spoken inside that house. The couple, supreme among the gods, sat on the platform. O son! Following the norms, the fire was ignited on the stone altar. Following the norms, the couple offered the parched grain and performed *pradakshina*. Having touched the stone on Vishnu's instructions, Shambhu touched the toe on the right foot of the goddess with his hand.'

'At that time, I was offering oblations near Hara. On seeing her toe, my mind turned perverse and my semen was ejaculated. In the three worlds, who is not distracted by Kama? I was ashamed because of this sin and the semen gathered in drops. The minute *valakhilyas*[415] were born from the drops of my semen. The gods raised loud sounds of lamentation. Overcome by shame, I stood up from my seat and started to leave. O Narada! In silence, the large number of gods looked on. Seeing that I was leaving, Mahadeva spoke to Nandi. Shiva said, "Bring Brahma here. I will free him from his sin. Even if a person commits a sin, the mind of a virtuous person is compassionate towards him. Attracted to the material senses, even the learned are confounded." Saying this, out of compassion towards me and for the welfare of the worlds, along with Uma, the illustrious Hara started. O Narada! Hear attentively what the lord of the worlds did. "The earth and water will cleanse sinners of their sins. I will take out the purifying essence from all the waters." Having said

---

[414] Being used here as a synonym for Goddess Earth.

[415] 60,000 sages who were the sizes of thumbs. They preceded the sun's chariot.

this, the illustrious one extracted the essence from the water. Having placed a *kamandalu*[416] on the ground, he placed the water inside it. He carefully recited the *pavamana sukta* and other *mantras*.[417] He remembered Shakti, who purifies the three worlds and destroys sins. The lord of the worlds told me, "Accept this *kamandalu*. The goddesses who are mothers are in the water. The earth is another mother. For the sake of creation, preservation and destruction, both of them are located here. The eternal *dharma* of sacrifices is established here. Objects of pleasure and emancipation are here and so are all mobile and immobile objects. As soon as one remembers this, all sins of thought and speech are destroyed. By using water to bathe, drink and consecrate, all physical sins are destroyed. In the worlds, there is nothing else that offers greater purification. O Brahma! I have sanctified this *kamandalu* with *mantras*. Accept it. If a person remembers the water that is inside it, or drinks it, he obtains all the objects of desire. Accept this *kamandalu*. Among the five elements, water is the greatest element. There is nothing that is superior to it. Accept this *kamandalu*. The water inside it is auspicious, sacred and purifying. O Brahma! If one touches it, remembers it or sees it, one is freed from sins." Saying this, Mahadeva gave me the *kamandalu*. When the lord of the gods said this, all the large number of gods was delighted. There were loud roars of joy and shouts of "Victory". At the time of the divine festivities, I saw the tip of the mother's foot and a sin caused my downfall. However, out of compassion towards me, the father gave me the water of the Ganga in that sacred *kamandalu*. Even if one remembers the water, one is purified.'

Chapter 2(4) (Ganga enters Shiva's hair)

Narada said, 'The goddess in the *kamandalu* enhances what is sacred. O lord! Tell me in detail how she reached the earth.'

[416] A sacred water-pot.
[417] This is a hymn for purification found in *Taittiriya Samhita* and *Taittiriya Brahman*. *Pavamana* means something that flows and purifies, that is, water.

Brahma replied, 'There was a great *daitya* named Bali and this
enemy of the gods could not be vanquished. There was no one in
the three worlds who was his equal in *dharma*, fame, protecting the
subjects, devotion to the *guru*, truth, valour, strength, renunciation
and forgiveness. Witnessing his rise, the gods were filled with
thoughts. The immortals spoke to each other. "How will we
triumph over Bali?" As long as he ruled over the kingdom, the three
worlds were bereft of thorns. There were no enemies. There were
no physical or mental ailments. There was no drought or *adharma*.
There were no non-believers or wicked people. As long as Bali ruled
over the kingdom, such things were not seen, not even in dreams.
The gods could find no peace. The arrows of his prosperity mangled
them. The sword of his fame sliced them into two. The javelin of
his commands pierced their limbs. Since envy was most important
for them, they consulted among themselves. They were extremely
anxious because his fame ignited a fire in their limbs. They went to
Vishnu. The gods said, "O lord of the universe! O one who holds
the conch shell, the *chakra* and the mace! We are afflicted. For our
sake, you have always wielded weapons. O lord of the universe!
When you are our lord, we have been reduced to such a state of
misery. Our heads have bowed down before you. How can they
bow down before a *daitya*? In our thoughts, deeds and words, we
seek refuge with you. We seek refuge at your feet. How can we bow
down before a *daitya*? We perform sacrifices to you. O Achyuta!
In great sacrifices, our words are meant for you. You are the only
one we seek refuge with. How can we bow down before a *daitya*?
With Indra at the forefront, the gods have always sought refuge in
your valour. We have obtained our status because of you. How can
we bow down before a *daitya*? Assuming the form of Brahma, you
are the one who creates. Assuming the form of Vishnu, you are the
one who preserves. In your power as Rudra, you are the one who
destroys. How can we bow down before a *daitya*? In the world,
everything is due to prosperity. Without prosperity, everything is
futile. O lord of the gods! With our prosperity taken away, how can
we bow down before a *daitya*? You are without a beginning. You are
the creator of the universe. You are infinite. You are the preceptor
of the universe. Facing destruction at the hands of an enemy, how

can we bow down before a *daitya*? With your prosperity nourishing
our limbs, we will use our energy to conquer the three worlds. O
lord of the gods! We will then attain stability. How can we bow
down before a *daitya*?" The destroyer of *daitya*s heard the words
spoken by the gods. To accomplish the task of the gods, he spoke
to all the immortals. Vasudeva replied, "The *daitya* Bali is devoted
to me. He cannot be vanquished by gods or *asura*s. Just as you
are sustained by me, Bali is also nourished by me. The kingdom of
heaven has been taken away from the gods. Without a conflict, I
will take it back and return it to you. Using *mantra*s, I will bind Bali
down." Thus addressed, the large number of gods went to heaven.

'The illustrious lord of the gods entered Aditi's womb.[418]
When he was born, there were festivities. O brahmana! The lord of
sacrifices, the being who is the sacrifice, was born as a *vamana*.[419] O
brahmana! At this time, Bali, the best among those who were strong,
summoned the best among *rishi*s and consecrated himself for a horse
sacrifice. His priest was Shukra,[420] knowledgeable about the Vedas
and the *Vedanga*s. Bali was the one who undertook this sacrifice. The
best among *rishi*s officiated at this sacrifice and Shukra was the chief
priest. Gods, *gandharva*s and *pannaga*s seated themselves to receive
their shares of the oblations. There were separate sounds of—"Let it
be given", "Let it be enjoyed", "Let the worship be undertaken", "It
has been filled" and "It has been completed". While this was going
on, he slowly approached the spot, chanting hymns from the *Sama
Veda*. Wearing earrings and holding an umbrella, Vamana reached
the sacrificial altar. Vamana praised the sacrifice. The divinity was
in the form of a brahmana. The destroyer of *daitya*s was in the form
of a dwarf. He is the one who bestows sacrifices and austerities. He
is the one who slays *rakshasa*s. Bhargava[421] saw him and recognized
who he actually was. He quickly spoke to the king, extensive in his
energy. Bali, the best among those who were strong, was a victor,

[418] Aditi, Kashyapa's wife, was the mother of the gods.
[419] A dwarf.
[420] Shukracharya, the preceptor of the demons.
[421] Shukracharya. Shukracharya was descended from Bhrigu and is
therefore known as Bhargava.

following the *dharma* of *kshatriya*s. He was generous, faithfully donating riches. Along with his wife, he had consecrated himself for the sacrifice. Meditating on the being who is the personified form of sacrifices, he was separately offering oblations. The extremely intelligent Shukra, tiger of the Bhrigu lineage, spoke to him. Shukra said, "In the form a brahmana, this dwarf has come to your sacrifice. O Bali! He is not really a brahmana. He is actually the lord of sacrifices, the creator of sacrifices. He is the being who is greater than the greatest. Having come here, he will ask you for something. O lord! Give it to him only after consulting with me." Bali, scorcher of enemies, replied to Bhargava, the chief priest. Bali said, "I did not even imagine that the lord of sacrifices would come to my house. Since he has come here, if he asks me for something, what should I think of now?" Saying this to Shukra, the chief priest along with his wife went to the place where Vamana, Indra among *brahmanas* and Aditi's son, was. He joined his hands in salutation and asked, "Why have you come? Please tell me." Vamana replied, "Give me as much of land that can be covered in three of my steps. I wish to place my feet. I do not desire anything else." There was a water-pot that was decorated with many kinds of jewels. While the best among *rishi*s and Shukra, the chief priest looked on, he poured water from this and gave Vamana the required ground. While the best among the gods looked on, he gave Vamana the required ground. As the large number of *daitya*s looked on, there were sounds of "Victory". Vamana spoke gently. "O king! May you be fortunate. May you be happy. As you have promised, grant me the land that can be measured out in three of my strides." As soon as he heard these words and as Vamana looked on, the lord of the *daitya*s agreed and replied, "Please take it." The lord of sacrifices used his valour to extend his form. As his size increased, the sun and the moon were between his breasts. The gods were near his head. This is what the divinity Ananta Achyuta, the creator of the worlds who pervades the universe, did. The king of the *daitya*s was full of humility. Along with his wife, he saw this and spoke. Bali said, "O Vishnu! O lord of the worlds! O one who pervades the universe! O lord of the gods! O one who has created the universe! Take your steps and vanquish me in every possible way." At the same time, Shukra spoke these harsh words.[422] "O Indra among kings! Thanks to my intelligence, I had warned you earlier. You have now been extinguished." At the same time, Vishnu, who is the great sacrifice, spoke to him. Vishnu said, "O lord of the *daityas*! O mighty-armed one! O king of the *daityas*! Behold my strides." Thus addressed, he repeatedly replied, "O Vishnu! Take your strides. Placing his feet on the back of the tortoise,[423] he placed one foot on Bali's sacrifice. Hari said, "O lord of the *asuras*! Give me all the worlds for my second step. There is no place left for my third step. O Bali! Give me the ground for my third step." With his wife, Bali joined his hands in salutation and smiled. Bali replied, "O lord of the gods! You have created the entire universe. I am not the creator. O one who pervades the universe! It is because of your fault that the area is limited. What can I possibly do? O Keshava! Nevertheless, I have never uttered a falsehood in the past and never will. Make my words come true. Place your foot on my back." The illustrious one, who assumes the three forms[424] and is worshipped by the gods was pleased. "O fortunate one! O king of the *daityas*! I am pleased at your devotion. Ask for a boon." He replied, "O protector of the universe! O Trivikrama![425] There is nothing I desire from you." Pleased, Vishnu himself gave him what his mind wished for—the lordship of Rasatala, the future status of Indra,[426] lordship over his *atman* and a lot of fame that would transcend that of Hari's.[427] Having granted all these boons to Bali, Hari placed Bali, the enemy of the immortals, in Rasatala along with his wife and sons. As was the case earlier, Shatakratu was given the kingdom of the gods. After this, worshipped by the gods, he returned to his own abode, where he had come from.

'O immensely wise one! The region where my father, Vishnu, had placed his second foot became my home and abode. Seeing

[422] Since Bali had not heeded his warning, Shukra was angry. In other accounts, Shukra cursed Bali.

[423] Meaning the earth, since the earth is held up on the back of a tortoise.

[424] Brahma, Vishnu and Shiva.

[425] Vishnu's name, the one with the three valiant strides.

[426] Bali will be Indra in the next *manvantara*.

[427] Hari is also one of Indra's names. That is, Bali's fame would transcend that of Indra's.

that, I thought, "I have received this position from Vishnu. What auspicious act shall I perform? I looked at everything and saw that the *kamandalu* was the best. It had been given to me by Tripura's enemy[428] and its water was the best. It confers boons and serenity and is worshipped. It bestows supreme peace. It is auspicious and bestows what is auspicious. It always confers objects of pleasure and emancipation. It is like a mother of the worlds. It is pure medication and is *amrita*. It is sacred and purifies. It should be worshipped. It is the greatest and best and brings everything that is auspicious. When it is remembered, it purifies the worlds, not to speak of when it is seen. Using that pure water, I will offer an *arghya* to my father." I thought in this way. Taking that water, I offered *arghya*. Invoked with *mantras*, the water from the *arghya* fell on Vishnu's foot. That pure water descended on Meru and flowed on earth in four different streams—east, south, west and north. O sage! The water that descended towards the south was caught in Shankara's matted hair. The water that flowed towards the west was again received by the *kamandalu*. The water that descended towards the north was again received by Vishnu. The water that flowed towards the east bestows everything auspicious and is spoken of as the best. It was received by the *rishis*, the gods, the ancestors and the guardians of the worlds. The waters that flowed towards the south are the mothers of the worlds. For the sake of *brahmanas*, these mothers of the world flowed from Vishnu's foot. They remained in Maheshvara's matted hair and give rise to everything that is auspicious. By remembering their powers, one obtains everything that one desires.'

Chapter 2(5) Interaction between Vinayaka and Goutama

Narada said, 'O god! I have heard how the goddess from the *kamandalu* entered Maheshvara's matted hair. Please tell me how she came to earth.'

---

[428] Shiva. Shiva destroyed Tripura, a city of the demons.

Brahma replied, 'O immensely intelligent one! Because there were two people who brought them down, there were two divisions of the divine water in Maheshvara's matted hair. One portion was brought by a brahmana who was devoted to vows, donations and meditation. Goutama, revered in the worlds, worshipped Shiva and brought it down. O immensely wise one! The other one was a powerful *kshatriya*. He worshipped the divinity Shankara through austerities and rituals. This was King Bhagiratha, who brought down the second portion. O supreme among sages! In this way, Ganga assumed two different flows.'

Narada asked, 'Why did Goutama bring down the water that was in Maheshvara's matted hair? Which *kshatriya* brought it down? Please tell me.'

Brahma replied, 'O son! For the sake of your pleasures, I will tell you all the details about how one part was brought down by a brahmana and how the second was brought down by another person. O immensely radiant one! At the time when Uma became the beloved wife of the lord of the gods, Ganga also became Shambhu's beloved. At that time, Shiva was thinking about a method for dispelling my taint. Though he was with Uma, the prosperous one glanced towards the goddess.[429] Immersed in creating an excellent juice for me, he was focused on her juice too. He loved her beloved juice, feminine and purifying in nature. O supreme among *brahmanas*! In particular, he loved Ganga the most. He placed Ganga on his head. Since Uma knew about it, Maheshvara was always full of thoughts. Despite being hidden in his matted hair, there some other reason for Ganga coming out. However, Shambhu hid Ganga in his matted hair. Knowing that she was hidden in his head, Uma was unable to tolerate this. She could not tolerate the idea of Ganga repeatedly emerging from the matted hair. Full of intolerance, Gouri spoke to her lord, Bhava.[430] "O Shambhu! O one who loves juices! She has excellent juices, but she should not reside here. Please send her away." Miserable, Uma addressed her lord in these words. However, she also thought about the goddess

[429] Ganga.
[430] Gouri is Uma and Bhava is Shiva.

being hidden in matted hair. Therefore, in private, she addressed Vinayaka, Jaya and Skanda in these words.[431] "Ishana, the lord of the gods, desires her and will never let Ganga go. She is loved by Shiva. How will he cast away his beloved?" Thinking about this in many ways, Gouri spoke to Vinayaka. Parvati said, "Even if gods, *asura*s, *yaksha*s, *siddha*s, kings, you, and others try, the lord will not give up Ganga. I will go to the Himalayas, supreme among mountains, and perform austerities. Or, I will leave it to sacred *brahmanas* who can cleanse sins through their austerities. Perhaps they can pray and bring down Ganga from the matted hair." Thus addressed by his mother, Vighnaraja[432] replied to his mother. "We should consult my brother, Skanda and Jaya. We will act so that my father casts Ganga away from his head.' O brahmana! At this time, there was a drought that lasted for twelve years. It caused great fear to beings in the mortal world. Everything mobile and immobile in the world was destroyed. The only exception was Goutama's sacred hermitage, which yielded every object of desire. O son! Earlier, I desired to create mobile and immobile objects. Therefore earlier, I had performed a sacrifice on Mount Devayajana. Since then, because of my name, that mountain has always been famous as Brahmagiri.[433] Goutama has always resorted to that excellent mountain. His extremely sacred hermitage was on the auspicious and excellent Brahmagiri. There were no physical or mental ailments there. There was no famine or drought. Fear, sorrow and poverty have never been heard of there. Other than his hermitage, there was no *havya* or *kavya*. O son! There was no one to donate, offer oblations or perform sacrifices. The gods in heaven were honoured only when the brahmana Goutama gave and offered oblations, not otherwise. In the world of the mortals and in the world of the gods, the sage Goutama was heard of. Learned people

[431] Vinayaka is Ganesha, Skanda is Kumara/Kartikeya and Jaya is Goutama's daughter and Uma's companion.

[432] The king of impediments, Ganesha. He creates impediments and also removes them.

[433] Brahmagiri is in the Western Ghats, bordering Kerala and Karnataka.

knew that he alone was the giver and enjoyer. There were sages who resided in many hermitages. Hearing about Goutama's hermitage, they asked where it was. Those stores of austerities went there. When all these sages arrived, Goutama faithfully nurtured them like a father, as if they were his disciples or sons. The sage served them in accordance with what was appropriate for each in due order of worth, and gave them everything that they wished for. On Goutama's command, the herbs became the mothers of the world and Brahma, Vishnu and Maheshvara were worshipped again. When the herbs were generated, they were used to enjoy. Through the strength of Goutama's austerities, it could be resolved that they should be sown. Everyone became prosperous and every mental desire was accomplished. Every day, Goutama humbly addressed the sages who had arrived like sons or disciples and asked, "What can I do for you?" For many years, he nurtured them like a father. O son! In this way, Goutama attained great fame.

'After this, Vinayaka spoke to his mother, brother and Jaya. Vinayaka said, "O mother! In the abode of the gods, the brahmana Goutama is chanted about. 'Goutama has made efforts to ensure that the tasks of the large number of gods is accomplished.' O goddess! I have heard this about the strength of the brahmana's austerities. O mother! This brahmana may be able to dislodge Ganga from the matted hair. Through austerities or other means, he can worship the three-eyed one. He can then ask for my father's beloved, who is in the matted hair. We should determine a proper method so that the brahmana asks for her. Through his powers, the best among rivers will descend from the hair." Having told his mother this, Vighnaraja, along with his brother and Jaya, went to the spot where Goutama was. The brahmana was lean and wore a sacred thread. They resided for a few days in the circle that was around Goutama's hermitage. Then Vighnaraja spoke to all the *brahmanas*. "We should not remain here. We should return to our own abodes and our own pure hermitages. We have been nourished by Goutama's food. Let us go and ask the sage Goutama." Those excellent sages consulted amongst themselves and went and took their leave from the sage. With his mind full of affection, he separately tried to restrain the sages. Goutama said, "I am humbly joining my hands in salutation and asking you to remain here. O bulls among sages! I will serve at your feet. I will always serve you, as one does towards a son. You should stay here. You are like gods on earth and it is not proper that you should go and stay in some other hermitage. It is my view that this hermitage is sacred in every possible way. O sages! Enough of this. Please do not go to any other hermitage." Hearing the words of the sage, Ganadhipa[434] remembered his duty of creating impediments. He joined his hands in salutation and spoke to the *brahmanas*. Ganadhipa said, "Simply because he has bought us over with food, how can Goutama restrain us? Using words of conciliation, we have not been allowed to go to our own respective abodes. The supreme among *brahmanas* has done us a good turn and does not deserve to be punished.[435] Therefore, I will use my intelligence to devise a means and all of you should approve of this." At this, all the best among *brahmanas* replied, "So as to do him a good turn and for the welfare of the worlds, act. Do what is best for all the *brahmanas*." Hearing the words of the *brahmanas*, Ganadhipa approved and addressed them in the following words. Vinayaka said, "I will do that which ensures special benefit to Goutama." Pervasive in his intelligence, he repeatedly entreated the *brahmanas*. Assuming the form of a brahmana, he repeatedly prostrated himself before the *brahmanas*.'

'Knowing what was in his mother's mind, Ganeshvara[436] spoke to Jaya. Vinayaka said, "O auspicious one! O one with the beautiful face! Act so that no one else gets to know. Assume the form of a cow and go to the place where Goutama is. O beautiful one! Eat the *shali* rice[437] and act perversely, as if you are destroying it. If you are beaten, or if anyone pronounces *humkara*[438] and glances towards you, scream loudly. Remain as if you are struggling between life

---

[434] Lord of *gana*s, another name for Ganesha.

[435] The traditional four means are *sama* (conciliation or negotiation), *dana* (bribery), *danda* (punishment) and *bheda* (dissension) and there is an allusion to this.

[436] Lord of *gana*s, Ganesha.

[437] A fine variety of rice.

[438] *Humkara* means to utter the sound 'hum', a sound believed to possess special powers.

and death." Following what was in Vighenshvara's[439] mind, Vijaya did exactly this. Jaya assumed the form of a cow and went to the spot where Goutama was. She went and started to eat the *shali* paddy. Goutama saw her. On seeing that the cow was destroying the paddy, the brahmana tried to restrain her with a blade of grass. As soon as he tried to restrain her, she screamed loudly and fell down on the ground. When she fell down, there were loud sounds of lamentation. Hearing the scream, the distressed *brahmanas* saw what Goutama had done. With Vighnaraja at the forefront, they spoke to him. The *brahmanas* said, "All of us will leave this place. We will not remain in your hermitage. O bull among sages! You have nurtured all of us like sons, but we will take your leave now." Hearing the words of the *brahmanas* that they were about to leave, it was as if the sage had been struck by the *vajra*. He prostrated himself before the *brahmanas*. All the *brahmanas* spoke to him, "Look at her, fallen down on the ground. She is the mother of the Rudras. She is the beloved goddess who purifies the world. All the *tirtha*s and all the gods are in her nature. Through the force of destiny, this cow has fallen down. O best among sages! We should not remain here, but should go elsewhere. If we reside in this hermitage, the fruits of our vows will be diminished and destroyed. O brahmana! We do not possess any other riches. We are rich only because of our austerities." Standing in front of the *brahmanas*, Goutama replied humbly. Goutama said, "You are my refuge. You should remain here and purify me." Surrounded by the *brahmanas*, the illustrious Vighnaraja answered. Vighnaraja said, "This is neither dead, nor alive. Therefore, we are unsure about what we should state as a proper rite of atonement." Goutama replied, "The cow is not just senseless, there is no doubt that she will die. You should tell me about how she can be made to rise up again and about my atonement. There is no doubt that I will act accordingly." The *brahmanas* responded, "This intelligent one will express our collective view. O Goutama! His words are indicative of all our views." Urged by the *brahmanas* and also strongly urged by Goutama, the creator of impediments, in the guise of

[439] Vighnaraja.

a brahmana, addressed them in the following words. Vighnaraja said, "I will accurately state everyone's views. Let the sages and Goutama follow my words. We have heard that the water from the *kamandalu* of Brahma, whose birth is not manifest, is located in Maheshvara's matted hair. Following austerities and rituals, quickly bring it. O illustrious one! Sprinkle the cow that is lying down on the ground with it. After that, all of us will reside in your house, as used to be the case earlier." In the assembly of *brahmanas*, the Indra among *brahmanas* addressed him in this way. Sounds of "victory" were uttered and flowers were showered down. Joining his hands in salutation and bowing down, Goutama spoke these words. Goutama said, "Through austerities, through Agni's favours, through the favours of the divinity Brahma and through your favours, may my resolution meet with success." Agreeing with this, the *brahmanas* took their leave of the bull among sages and returned to their own respective regions, nourished with food and water.'

'When the *brahmanas* departed, along with his brother and Jaya, Ganeshvara returned, extremely happy that he had accomplished his objective. When the group of *brahmanas* and Ganesha had left, Goutama, the best among sages performed austerities to cleanse himself of his sin. The sage meditated about the meaning of this. "Why have I been reduced to this state?" Thinking about it in many ways, the brahmana used his *jnana* to understand. He made up his mind that he had been tainted by this sin to accomplish some purpose of the gods. "This will bring welfare to the worlds and please Shambhu. Through bringing Ganga, Uma will be pleased. I think it will be best for everyone. Therefore, I have not been tainted by sin." Thinking this in his mind, the best among *brahmanas* was extremely delighted. The excellent brahmana consulted his wife and said, "I will worship the three-eyed Vrishadhvaja, the lord of the universe. I will bring the best among rivers and please the daughter of the mountain. The co-wife of the mother of the universe is in Maheshvara's matted hair." Having made up his mind, Goutama, the excellent sage, went to Brahmagiri. He wished to please Shambhu, who is fierce in his energy, who resides in Kailasa and is worshipped by the gods.'

Chapter 2(6) (Bringing of Goutami)

Narada said, 'Having gone to the summit of Kailasa, what did the illustrious *rishi* Goutama do? What austerities did he perform? What excellent praise did he use?'

Brahma replied, 'O child! Having gone to the mountain, Goutama controlled his speech. The wise one spread *kusha* grass on the excellent mountain of Kailasa. Purifying himself, he sat down on it and chanted hymns. As he praised Maheshvara, flowers were showered down. Goutama said, "To bestow objects of pleasure on those who desire objects of pleasure, along with Uma, he assumes eight great forms.[440] People always praise the god Mahadeva's qualities. He is the lord of all mobile and immobile objects and himself brings bliss in his dominions. For the sake of prosperity and its increase, Ishvara assumes the form of the earth. For the sake of creating, preserving and destroying the earth and upholding it, he assumes his own form of water. For the happiness of people and for the sake of establishing dharma in the universe, he assumes the tranquil body of Shiva. For the sake of creating, preserving and destroying beings, he is established as Kala and exudes *amrita*. He brings joy, happiness and upliftment to subjects and assumes a body that has fire, the sun and the moon. For enhancement, progress, undecaying strength, the conduct of subsistence and the manifold joy of beings, Isha assumes the form of Vayu. O illustrious one! You are indeed this. *Dharma* will not exist without differences. Nor will the directions and the firmament exist. Heaven, earth and the space between them will not exist. There will be no objects of pleasure or emancipation. O Isha! Therefore, you assume the form of space. For the sake of establishing *dharma*, you divide the branches of *Rig Veda*, *Sama Veda*, *Yajur Veda* and the sacred texts. In this world, there also exist the tales, *smriti* texts, Puranas and others that are articulated through words. There are *yajnas*,

---

[440] These eight forms are Bhava, Sharva, Rudra, Pashupati, Ugra, Mahadeva, Bhima and Ishana. However, the text doesn't quite follow this and mentions earth, water, Shiva, Kala (Time/Destiny), Sun/Moon/Fire, Vayu, space and Shambhu.

kratus[441] and other means. Depending on the fruits, the time and the place, the officiating priest is your own form. You are Shambhu, the supreme objective. You are spoken of as the one whose body has all the limbs of the sacrifice. You are the doer. You are the giver. You are the representation. You are the donation. You are the omniscient witness. You are the Supreme Being. You are the realization of the *atman.* Your form is the supreme objective. You are everything. What purpose do these words serve? The Vedas, the sacred texts and *guru*s have not instructed about you. You cannot be perceived through intelligence and other means. You are without origin. You are beyond measurement. O illustrious one! You are the truth, articulated in the words "Shiva". I bow down before you. O Shiva! Your nature is one and can sometimes be visualized as "My *atman.*"[442] Sometimes, you are perceived as different. You are many and your power is unthinkable. The universe is your form. Because of her sentiments, she[443] is pervasive in Bhava. She is the cause. But because of her own reasons, she is established in Bhava. Shivaa is eternal. She possesses all the signs. She is without signs. She is the Shakti that creates the universe. Generation, preservation and the increase and destruction of food—these are always necessary for offspring. She is the entire earth. What is impossible for Hara's beloved? For the sake of food and wealth, beings offer sacrifices to her and perform austerities of *dharma.* She is the mother of the universe. His beloved is the one who gives birth. Soma's great deeds are her manifestation. Vasava desires her glances and through those, we obtain everything that is auspicious. She pervades the universe and makes it pure. She is Somaa, her form is always like that of Soma. It is through her favours that intelligence, sight, consciousness and mental pleasures of Brahma and others, mobile and immobile, always yield fruits. She is the Ishvari of speech. She is the extremely

---

[441] A *yajna* and a *kratu* are both sacrifices. However, the former is performed with a sacrificial post and the latter without one. More specifically, the former is performed with sacrificial animals and the latter without sacrificing animals.

[442] This abrupt *shloka* is unclear and we have taken liberties in the translation.

[443] Parvati.

beautiful preceptor of the worlds. "The mind of the one with the four faces[444] has been defiled. What can be said of other beings?" Thinking this, she should devise many means for Ganga's descent and purify the entire world. Considering the *shruti* texts and all their proofs, people in the universe accepted Hara's lordship. They performed acts of *dharma* and enjoyed objects of pleasure. This is always due to Shiva's powers. He is the original agent behind tasks, rites, instruments and agents mentioned in the Vedas and popular practice. He is the best means and is spoken of as the beloved. He is the one who ensures success. For meditations, he is the supreme one. He is the supreme *brahman*. He is the foremost being. He is the unmanifest one whose essence is worshipped. Having obtained him, *yogis* are instantly emancipated and do not have to return again. Uma's consort is emancipation. O mother! For the welfare of the universe, whenever Shambhu assumes an immeasurable form full of *maya*, devoted to your husband, you also assume a corresponding form.' 'As he praised in this way, along with Uma, Vrishadhvaja appeared in front of him. The prosperous one was surrounded by Ganesha and the other *ganas*.'

'Shambhu himself appeared before him, pleased, and addressed him in these words. Shiva said, "O Goutama! I am pleased with your auspicious devotion, hymns and vows. What will I give you? Ask for something that is difficult for even the gods to obtain." Hearing the words of the one whose manifestation was the universe, Goutama, accomplished in speech, was filled with tears of delight that flowed over his limbs. He thought, "This is the divinity. How wonderful is *dharma*. How wonderful is the worship of a brahmana. How wonderful is the progress of the worlds. How wonderful is the creator. I bow down to you." Goutama said, "O lord of the gods! O one who is the refuge of the three![445] O one who is worshipped by the gods! If you are pleased with me, grant me auspicious Ganga, who is in your matted hair." Ishvara replied, "For the welfare of the three worlds, you have asked for her. Speak without any fear. Ask for something for yourself." Goutama said, "I praised you

---

[444] Brahma.
[445] The three *Veda*s.

and the goddess with a *stotram*. If people praise you devotedly
using this, let them prosper with everything that they desire. This
is the boon I ask for." Pleased, the lord of the gods agreed and
spoke these words. "Without any anxiety, ask for some other boon
from me." Thus addressed, Goutama happily spoke to Shankara.
Goutama said, "This goddess in your matted hair is the mother
of the worlds. She is the one who purifies. O lord of the universe!
She is loved by you. On the words of this brahmana, please release
her. As she flows towards the ocean, let all the *tirtha*s be along
her side. O Shankara! As soon as one bathes in her, let all sins of
thoughts, speech and deeds, the killing of a brahmana and others
be destroyed. O divinity! O Hara! There are fruits that are obtained
from bathing at other sacred *tirtha*s at the time of a solar or lunar
eclipse, the change of one *ayana* into another, *vishuva sankranti* and
conjunctions like *vaidhriti*.[446] If one only remembers this auspicious
one, let all those fruits be obtained. During *krita yuga*, austerities
are praised. In *treta yuga*, this becomes rites of sacrifices. In *dvapara
yuga*, it becomes sacrifices and donations. Donations are praised in
kali yuga. There is *dharma* of the *yuga* and different regions have
their own *dharma*s. Depending on the time and the region, different
kinds of *dharma* are praised. There are other good merits obtained
through bathing, donating and self-control. O divinity! O Hara!
If one only remembers this auspicious one, let all those fruits be
obtained. Wherever she goes as she flows towards the ocean, let
yourself also be present there. This is the excellent boon that I ask
for. O Shiva! Even if great sinners come within a distance of ten
*yojana*s of her banks and bathe in her, let them and their ancestors
be freed. Let all mortals who bathe in her be emancipated. Let all
the *tirtha*s in heaven, earth and the nether regions be on one side and
let her be on the other side, with her being superior. O Shambhu!
That will be enough. I bow down to you." Hearing Goutama's
words, Shiva replied that it would be this way. "There has been
no *tirtha* which is superior to her, nor will there ever be. This is

---

[446] *Vaidhriti* is also known as *vyatipata*, an inauspicious period that
lasts for almost 24 hours during every lunar month.

the truth. This is the truth. This is the truth.[447] This is in the Vedas. Goutami will be the most sacred of all." Saying this, he vanished. When the illustrious one who is worshipped by the worlds departed because of his command, Goutama became full of strength. He received the best of rivers from the matted hair. Surrounded by the gods, he entered Brahmagiri. O Narada! As soon as Goutama received her from the matted hair, flowers were showered down. The lords among the gods, rishis, immensely fortunate brahmanas and kshatriyas assembled there. Full of delight, they worshipped the brahmana with words of "Victory".'

Chapter 2(7) (Greatness of this tirtha)

Narada asked, 'After receiving the Ganga from Maheshvara's matted hair and going to Brahma's sacred mountain, what did Goutama do?'

Brahma replied, 'Accepting Ganga, Goutama purified and controlled his mind. He was worshipped by gods, gandharvas and the residents of the mountain. Placing the one from the matted hair on the summit of the mountain, he remembered the three-eyed divinity. The best among brahmanas joined his hands in salutation and spoke to Ganga. Goutama said, "You have originated from the three-eyed one's matted hair. You bestow everything that one wishes for. O mother! O serene one! Flow happily and do everything that is beneficial." The goddess Ganga was in a divine form. She was adorned with divine garlands and unguents. Thus addressed by Goutama, she replied to Goutama. Ganga asked, "Where will I go? Will I go to the abode of the gods, the kamandalu or to the nether regions? You have been born as someone who is truthful in speech." Goutama said, "I have asked for you for the welfare of the three worlds. O goddess! That is the reason you have been given by Shambhu. Let there be no violation of that." Hearing Goutama's words, Ganga listened to the words spoken by

---

[447] The statement is made thrice to firmly establish its veracity.

the brahmana. She divided herself into three flows—for heaven, the world of the mortals and the nether regions. She flowed in heaven in four streams. She flowed in the mortal world in seven streams. She flowed in the nether regions in seven streams. There are, thus, fifteen different streams. Everywhere, she destroys all sins committed by all living beings. She always grants every object of desire. She is chanted about in the Vedas. The mortals only perceive that part of her that flows through the mortal world, not that which flows in the nether regions. Ignorant in their intelligence, mortals do not see that part of her which flows in heaven. As long as the goddess flows towards the sea, it is said that all the gods are in her. Released by Goutama, she flowed from the west towards the eastern ocean. The auspicious mother of the universe is frequented by gods and rishis. Goutama, tiger among sages, performed pradakshina around her. Goutama first worshipped the three-eyed one, the lord of the gods. He made up his mind, "I will bathe along both her banks." As soon as he remembered him, the three-eyed, who is an ocean of compassion, appeared before him. Devotedly, he joined his hands in salutation and asked the divinity Sharva how a bath would become successful.'

Goutama said, 'O lord of the gods! O Mahesha! For the welfare of the worlds, please tell me about the proper methods for bathing in the tirthas.' Shiva replied, 'O maharshi! Hear all the norms about Godavari. Having purified the body, it is recommended that nandimukha should be performed first. Brahmanas must be fed and their permission must be obtained. As one proceeds towards the river, one must observe brahmacharya, avoiding conversing with those have fallen down.[448] If the hands, feet and mind are controlled properly and if one possesses learning, austerities and deeds, fruits are obtained from a tirtha. One must cast aside all wicked sentiments and be devoted to one's own dharma. One should massage the limbs of those who are exhausted and give them the appropriate food. Garments and blankets must be given to virtuous people who possess nothing. One must hear divine accounts about Hari and about Ganga's origin. If one follows

---

[448] In the sense of having committed sins.

these norms properly as one proceeds, one obtains the fruits from visiting a *tirtha*.' The three-eyed one again spoke to Goutama as he was surrounded by the sages. 'O Goutama! The *tirtha*s are at a distance of two hands from each other. I am present everywhere and bestow everything that one wishes for. Bhagirathi[449] bestows everything auspicious and emancipation to men—in Gangadvara,[450] Prayaga and the confluence with the ocean. Narmada, best among rivers is in the mountain of Amarkantaka. Yamuna and Sarasvati join the Ganga in Prabhasa.[451] O Narada! There are Krishna, Bhimarathi and Tungabhadra. The *tirtha* that is the confluence of the three bestows emancipation on men.[452] The river's confluence with Payoshni also bestows emancipation.[453] O son! Such is the Goutami.[454] On my instructions, she always confers emancipation on all the men who bathe in her. On some occasions, because the gods assemble there at those times, some *tirtha*s are extremely sacred. However, there is no doubt that Goutami is always the best among all these *tirtha*s. Bathing in Bhagirathi for sixty thousand years is equivalent to bathing once in Godavari when Brihaspati[455] is in Simha.[456] This *tirtha* is special because Rama's feet were placed there when he visited it. It is extremely rare for men to bathe in Goutami when Brihaspati is in Simha. When the sun is in Simha, the rivers Bhagirathi, Narmada, Yamuna, Sarasvati, Bhimarathi and others arrive to bathe in Goutami. When the two preceptors[457] are in Simha, if a foolish person avoids Goutami Ganga and

[449] Ganga's name.

[450] Gangadvara usually refers to Har ki Pauri in Haridvara/Haridwar.

[451] This means Prayaga. The word *prabhasa* should hence be interpreted as the splendid place, rather than the famous Prabhasa.

[452] This means Sangameshvara in Kurnool district, near Shrishailam.

[453] Since Payoshni is the river Purna, this must be a reference to Mudagaleshvara in Parbhani district.

[454] As should be obvious by now, Goutami Ganga is the Godavari.

[455] Jupiter.

[456] The constellation Leo.

[457] Brihaspati and the sun. Because of the position of the sun, it would be incorrect to identify this with the current *kumbha* in Tryambakeshvara/Nashik. In the current *kumbha*, Brihaspati is in Leo, but the sun is in Cancer.

frequents any other *tirtha*, he goes to hell. O tiger among sages! O Goutama! Within a distance of two hundred *yojana*s, there will be three and a half crores of *tirtha*s. This Ganga from Maheshvara is known as Goutami, Vaishnavi, Brahmi, Godavari, Nanda and Sunanda. She bestows everything desired. She has been brought through a *brahmanas*'s energy and destroys all sins. As soon as she is remembered, she destroys sins. She is always loved by me. Among the five elements, it is water which is the best. Among all kinds of water, water in the *tirtha*s is said to be the best. Among these, Bhagirathi is the best. But among the flows of Bhagirathi, Goutami is the best. You brought this Ganga from the matted hair and there is nothing more auspicious than her among all the *tirtha*s in heaven, earth and the nether regions. O sage! This bestows everything.' O son! He said this to the great-souled Goutama. Pleased, he himself granted him a boon and I have told you about it. Thus, it is held that Goutami Ganga is the best. I have spoken about her nature. What else do you wish to hear?

Chapter 2(8) (Descent of Bhagirathi)

Narada said, 'O best among gods! But you spoke about two of her forms. You have only spoken about the form that was brought by the brahmana. A *kshatriya* brought down the other part from the matted hair of Bhava, the lord of the gods. Please tell me about this.'

Brahma replied, 'O sage! There was a king who descended from Vaivasvata Manu.[458] He was born in the Ikshvaku lineage and his name was Sagara. The ocean takes his name from him.[459] He performed sacrifices and was devoted to donations. He always thought about the conduct of *dharma*. He had two wives who were extremely attached to their husband. However, since he had no sons,

---

[458] That is, born in the solar dynasty. The first king of the solar dynasty was Ikshvaku.

[459] The ocean is known as *saagara*.

he was overcome by thoughts. When Vasishtha arrived in his house, as is appropriate, he worshipped him. The king spoke to him, asking how he might obtain offspring. Hearing his words, he thought about it and spoke to the king. Vasishtha said, "O king! Along with your wives, always worship rishis." O brahmana! Uttering these words, the sage returned to wherever he had come from. On one occasion, a store of austerities came to the rajarshi's[460] house. When the rishi was worshipped, he was satisfied and addressed him in these words. "O extremely fortunate one! Ask for a boon." Thus addressed, he asked for the boon that he might have sons. The sage told the king, "One of your wives will have a son who will sustain the lineage. The other wife will have sixty thousand sons." Having granted the boon, the sage left and thousands of sons were born. He performed many horse sacrifices and gave away a lot of dakshina. On one such occasion following the norms, the king consecrated himself for a horse sacrifice. Along with the soldiers, the king entrusted his sons with the task of guarding the horse. Detecting an opportunity, Shatakratu stole the horse. The sons searched for the horse's trail, but could not find it. There were sixty thousands of them and they were skilled in many kinds of fighting. Sagara's sons had been engaged to guard the horse. But even as they looked on, the horse was abducted and taken to the nether regions. Because the maya of rakshasas had been used,[461] Sagara's sons could not see the horse. Sagara's strong sons could not see the horse. Meanwhile, the officiating priests pronounced benedictions and performed the auspicious rites for the king to be consecrated. However, unable to see the beautiful animal, the king was filled with thoughts. Searching for the horse's trail, all of Sagara's sons searched and even went to the world of the gods. But they did not see it there. Therefore, the sons of the king returned to earth and searched the mountains and forests. But they could not see the horse. At that time, a divine voice was heard. "O sons of Sagara! The horse is tethered in Rasatala, not anywhere else." Hearing these words, they wished to go to Rasatala. In every direction, Sagara's sons dug up the ground. Afflicted by hunger,

---

[460] Rajarshi means royal sage.
[461] From Indra, the rakshasas obtained the horse.

day and night, they ate the dry earth. Having dug up the earth, they swiftly went to Rasatala. The powerful sons of King Sagara reached the place. Hearing this, the *rakshasas* were terrified and approached Kapila. The immensely wise Kapila was lying down in Rasatala. Earlier, he had accomplished an excellent task for the gods. Exhausted because of the task he had accomplished for the gods, he was asleep. The prosperous Kapila had told them, "Give me a place to sleep in." When they gave him Rasatala, the sage told the gods, "If a wicked person wakes me up, he will instantly be reduced to ashes. I will sleep in the nether regions only on this condition. Otherwise, I will not sleep." Thus addressed, the large number of gods agreed and gave him Rasatala to sleep in. The *rakshasas*, full of *maya*, knew about his powers. All of them thought of a means to kill Sagara's sons. Even though there had been no fighting, the *rakshasas* were scared. Hence, they quickly went to the place where Kapila, great in his rage, was. They tied the horse near his head and swiftly withdrew some distance away, from where, they silently wished to observe what would happen. All the sons of Sagara entered Rasatala. They saw the horse tethered near a man who was asleep. They thought that this was the thief who had ruined the sacrifice. "We will kill this extremely wicked person and take the horse back to the king." Others said, "Let us take the bound animal. What do we have to do with this person?" Still others said, "We are brave kings and we are rulers. We must wake up this extremely wicked person and using the splendor of being *kshatriyas*, kill him." Uttering these words, they cruelly kicked the sage with their feet. Kapila, the excellent sage, was filled with great rage. He glanced at the sons of Sagara and this rage was used to reduce them to ashes. All the sons of Sagara were consumed in that blaze. Not knowing all this, King Sagara consecrated himself. However, Narada told the great-souled Sagara this.[462] He also told him where Kapila was, where the horse was, the perverse deed perpetrated by the *rakshasas* and about the destruction of Sagara's sons. The king was filled with thoughts and did not know what he should do.

[462] Narada would of course have known and there was no need to tell him.

'The king had another son known by the name of Asamanja. In his folly, he used to hurl children and citizens into the water. Sagara got to know this in an assembly of the citizens. When he got to know that he was a bad son, the king was angry and spoke to his own advisers. The king said, "This Asamanja has given up on the *dharma* of *kshatriya*s and has killed children. We must act so as to exile him from the kingdom." Hearing Sagara's words, the advisers swiftly abandoned the king's son and Asamanja went to the forest. "All the sons of Sagara have been destroyed in Rasatala because of a *brahmanas*'s curse. The single one has gone to the forest. What shall happen to me now?"[463] Asamanja had a son known by the name of Amshuman. The king summoned the child and told him about the task that needed to be undertaken. The child, Amshuman, went to Kapila. He gave the horse to Sagara and the sacrifice was thus completed. Amshuman had an energetic son named Dilipa who was devoted to *dharma*. Dilipa had an intelligent son known by the name of Bhagiratha. He heard about the destination obtained by his grandfathers and was extremely miserable. With humility, he asked Sagara, tiger among kings. "How can all the sons of Sagara be saved?" The king told Bhagiratha, "O son![464] Kapila knows." Hearing his words, the child went to Rasatala. He bowed down to Kapila and told him everything. The sage thought for a long time and said, "Use austerities to worship Shankara. O excellent king! Flood your ancestors with the water that is in the matted hair. In this way, you and your ancestors will become successful." He prostrated himself before the sage and spoke to him again. "I will act accordingly. O best among sages! But where should I go? You should tell me this." Kapila replied, "Go to Kailasa, best among mountains, and praise Maheshvara. According to your capacity, perform austerities and you will obtain what you desire." Hearing the sage's words, he bowed down before the sage and went to Mount Kailasa. The child, prone to activities of children, purified himself. Bhagiratha resolved to perform austerities and spoke these words. Bhagiratha said, "O lord! I am a child and my intelligence

---

[463] These were Sagara's thoughts.
[464] Son in an extended sense.

is that of a child. You are the one who holds up the young moon.
O lord! I do not know anything. Nevertheless, be pleased with me.
O lord of the immortals! O Soma![465] O one who is worshipped
by gods and others! O one who holds the crescent moon on his
head! O Shiva! Act for the benefit of those who are devoted to my
welfare, those who have done me good turns in words, thoughts
and deeds, for those who have given me birth, for those who have
reared me, for those who possess my own *gotra* and for those who
follow own *dharma*. I always prostrate myself before you. Please
act so as to ensure what they desire." Praised in this way, Shiva
appeared before him. He asked Bhagiratha to unhesitatingly ask for
the boon he wished. Shiva said, "O Bhagiratha! O immensely wise
one! Without any fear, tell me what you desire. I will certainly give
it to you, even if it cannot be given to *sadhya*s and the large number
of gods." Cheerfully, Bhagiratha prostrated himself before Isha and
spoke to Shankara. Bhagiratha said, "My ancestors can be purified
by the best among rivers, who is in the matted hair. O lord of the
gods! Please grant her to me and everything will be accomplished."
Mahesha laughed and spoke to Bhagiratha. Shiva replied, "O son!
O one who is excellent in vows! I am giving her to you. Please praise
her once again." Hearing his words, he performed great austerities
for that purpose. Controlling his mind, he devotedly praised Ganga.
Though he was still a child, acting as if he wasn't a child, he
obtained her favours too. Obtaining Ganga from Maheshvara, he
took her down to the nether regions and told the great-souled sage,
Kapila, everything. In the proper way, he carefully placed Ganga
and performed her *pradakshina*. He joined his hands in salutation
and spoke to her. Bhagiratha said, "O goddess! Because of the curse
of the great sage, Kapila, my ancestors have come to a perverse
end. O mother! You should save them from their downfall." The
divine river, who performs good deeds for everyone, agreed. For
the sake of the welfare of the worlds, for the sake of purifying his
ancestors, especially for the sake of filling up the ocean which had
been drunk up by Agastya,[466] for the sake of destroying sins as soon

---

[465] Meaning Someshvara, the lord of the moon (Soma).
[466] The sage Agastya drank up the ocean.

as she is remembered and for the sake of acting in accordance with Bhagiratha's words, the divine river remained in Rasatala. Because of the brahmana's curse, the sons of King Sagara had been reduced to ashes. She flooded the ashes of those who had been consumed and filled up the holes they had dug. She flooded Meru and remained there. The young king told her, "You must remain in this *karma bhumi*." Agreeing to this, she went to the Himalayas. From the sacred mountain of Himalayas, she came to Bharatavarsha. Through its midst, the sacred river flowed towards the eastern ocean. O great sage! Ganga is Maheshvari, Vaishnavi, the purifying Brahmi and the divine river. I have spoken about how she was brought down by a *kshatriya* and became Bhagirathi on the summit of the Himalayas. From Maheshvara's matted hair, the water divided into two parts. To the south of the Vindhyas, Ganga is known as Goutami. To the north of the Vindhyas, she is known as Bhagirathi.'

Chapter 2(9) (Varaha *tirtha*)

Narada said, 'Hearing the account spoken by you, my mind is not content. My mind wishes to hear separately about the fruits of the *tirtha*s and please tell me about them in the due order, starting first with how the brahmana brought Ganga. Then separately, please tell me about the history and the fruits of the *tirtha*s.'

Brahma replied, 'I am not capable of separately telling you about the fruits and the greatness of all the *tirtha*s, nor are you capable of hearing them. O Narada! Nevertheless, I will tell you something. Listen attentively. After bowing down to the three-eyed one, I will briefly tell you about what has been said about the *tirtha*s in the words of the sacred texts. O sage! The *tirtha* where the illustrious three-eyed one directly manifested himself is known as Tryambaka and it bestows objects of pleasure and emancipation.[467] There is

---

[467] The *jyotirlingam* of Tryambakeshvara in Nashik district, near the Godavari's origin.

another *tirtha* known as Varaha, famous in the three worlds.[468] I
will tell you about its nature and also how it came to be named after
Vishnu. It has been heard that in ancient times, a *rakshasa* named
Sindhusena defeated the gods and seizing the sacrifice, went to
Rasatala. When the sacrifice was taken to the nether regions, there
were no sacrifices on earth. When there are no sacrifices, nothing
exists in this world or in the world hereafter. That was the state then.
Following their enemy, the gods also entered Rasatala. However,
with Indra at the forefront, the gods were incapable of defeating
him. They went to Vishnu, the ancient being, and told him about the
rakshasa's deeds, especially about the destruction of the sacrifice.
The illustrious one said, "I will assume the form of a boar, holding a
conch shell, a *chakra* and a mace in my hands. I will go to Rasatala,
slay the bull among *rakshasa*s and bring back the sacred sacrifice.
O gods! Dispel all your mental anxiety and return to heaven." O
son! There was a path Ganga had followed when proceeding to
the nether regions. Using that, the wielder of the *chakra* swiftly
penetrated the earth and went to Rasatala. Assuming the form of
a boar, the prosperous one killed the *rakshasa*s and *danava*s who
were residents of Rasatala. He held the giant sacrifice in his mouth.
In his form of a boar, the illustrious enjoyer of sacrifices seized the
sacrifice. Using the path that Vishnu, the vanquisher of enemies,
had used to go to the nether regions, with the great sacrifice in his
mouth, he emerged from Rasatala. The gods were waiting for Hari
in Brahmagiri. O Narada! Along the path that Ganga had used to
flow down, he washed off the blood from his own limbs. The water
from the Ganga formed Varahakunda. Holding the great sacrifice
in his mouth, Hari presented himself before the gods. The best of
the gods gave it to them and the great sacrifice thus originated from
his mouth. Since the divinity assumed the form of a boar, the ladle
has been the first limb of the sacrifice.[469] Therefore, Varaha *tirtha* is

---

[468] There are different places named Varaha *tirtha*. Since this is in the
context of the Godavari, this Varaha *tirtha* must be the one near the temple
in Tryambakeshvara.

[469] There is an implicit pun. *Sruva* means sacrificial ladle, as well as a
spring or cascade of water.

most sacred and confers everything that is desired. Bathing, donating and all the sacrifices performed there yield fruits. If a person stands there and remembers his ancestors, he performs an auspicious act. Freed from all sins, his ancestors go to heaven.'

Chapter 2(10) (Kapota *tirtha*)

Brahma continued, 'I am not capable of telling you about the greatness of Kushavarta.[470] Even if a man remembers it, he accomplishes every objective. The place famous as Kushavarta yields all objects of desire to men. There, the great-souled Goutama stemmed the flow with *kusha* grass. When the sage brought her, he stemmed the flow with *kusha* grass. Bathing and donations there bring satisfaction to the ancestors. Nilaganga, best among rivers, emerges from Mount Nila.[471] If a man controls himself and performs a little bit of bathing and other rites there, his learning and everything else become inexhaustible and provide satisfaction to his ancestors. The excellent Kapota *tirtha* is famous in the three worlds. O sage! I will tell you about its nature. Hear about its great fruits. There was an extremely fierce hunter in Brahmagiri.[472] He made *brahmanas*, virtuous people, mendicants, cattle, birds and animals suffer. The evil-souled one was like that, prone to anger and someone who uttered falsehoods. His form was fierce. His eyes were blue. His arms were short. His teeth were decayed. He had lost his nose and eyes.[473] His feet were short, but his waist was large. His hands were small. His stomach was small. He was malformed and his voice was like that of a donkey. He had a noose in his

[470] This is a lake (*kunda*) next to Tryambakeshvara. When Godavari descended from Brahmagiri, Goutama stopped the flow in Kushavarta with a wall of *kusha* grass.

[471] Since Nilaganga is in Ujjain, this breaks the geographical continuity. This must therefore mean the Nilambika temple, atop Mount Nila, near Tryambakeshvara.

[472] This Brahmagiri hill is to the west of Tryambakeshvara.

[473] The eyes were probably sunken.

hand and his mind was evil. He was wicked and always wielded a
bow. O Narada! His wife and children were also like him. Goaded
by her, he entered the dense forest. The wicked one killed many
kinds of birds. He flung some others which were still alive inside
a cage. Suffering from hunger, distracted by thirst and hot all over
his limbs, he wandered in many regions before he headed home. It
was afternoon and the spring months were over. Clouds arrived in
an instant and there was thunder and lightning. A wind blew and
hail-stones showered down. There was an extremely terrible shower
of rain. As he proceeded, the exhausted hunter could not discern
the path. He could not distinguish water from land, the pits and the
path or the directions. The sinner was exhausted and looked for a
refuge. He thought, "Where will I go? Where will I stay? What will
I do? Like the Destroyer, I have taken away the lives of all living
beings. My destroyer, in terms of this shower of hail-stones, has
arrived. I do not see anyone who can save me. There is no boulder
or tree nearby." In this way, the hunter thought in many ways.
He then saw a tree in the forest, like a king of trees. It resembled
the moon[474] among the *nakshatra*s, the lion among animals, a
householder among the *ashrama*s and the mind among the senses.
It was like a saviour of creatures. This sparkling tree was the best,
ornamented with branches and sprouts. With his clothes wet, the
hunter sought refuge there and sat down under it. He remembered
his wife and children and wondered whether they were still alive. At
that time, the sun set.

'Along with his wife, a *kapota*[475] lived on that tree. Surrounded
by his sons and grandsons, he lived on that excellent tree. He was
happy and without any fear. He was extremely content and
delighted. The bird had resided there for many years. His wife was
devoted to her husband and was exceedingly happy with him. They
dwelt in a hollow inside that excellent tree, where there was no
water, wind or fire. The pigeon was always surrounded by his wife
and sons. On that particular day, because of destiny, the male

[474] The text uses the word Atrija, Atri's son. This means the moon, the
moon was the sage Atri's son.
[475] *Kapota* means any bird. Specifically, it means a dove or pigeon.

pigeon and the female pigeon had both gone out in search of food and the male pigeon had returned. O son! But such was destiny that the female pigeon was captured by the hunter. Though she was alive, she was inside the cage. The male pigeon looked at his children, separated from their mother. The terrible rain was showering down and the sun had set. He looked at his own empty hollow and started to lament. The king of pigeons did not know that she was bound inside the cage. The male pigeon started to sing about the qualities of his beloved. "The fortunate one, who extends my delight has not returned. She is the mother of my *dharma*. She is the mistress of my body. She is always my aide in the pursuit of *dharma*, *artha*, *kama* and *moksha*. When I am content, she laughs. When I am angry, she wipes away my misery. She is my friend and constantly counsels me. She always abides by my words. Though the sun has set, the fortunate one has not yet returned. She is devoted to her husband and does not know of any other vow, *mantra*, divinity, *dharma* or *artha*. Her husband is her life. Her husband is her *mantra*. She loves her husband. The fortunate one has not yet returned. What will I do? Who will I go to? Without you, is it not evident that my house is a desolate forest? With her, everything is full of prosperity. With her, even something terrible seems to be agreeable. My beloved has not returned to the place that is known as home. I will not remain alive without her. I will even give up my beloved body. However, what will my children do? My *dharma* will also be destroyed." From inside the cage, she heard her husband's words of lamentation and addressed her husband in these words. The female pigeon said, "O excellent bird! I am helpless and am bound here. O immensely wise one! Binding me in a noose, the hunter has brought me here. I am blessed. I am favoured that my husband has spoken about my qualities. Whether this is true or whether this is false, there is no doubt that I am content. When a woman's husband is satisfied, all the gods are satisfied. When it is the converse, a woman is certainly destroyed. You are my divinity. You are my lord. You are my well-wisher. You are my refuge. You are my vow. You are the supreme *brahman*. You are heaven. You are emancipation. O fortunate one! Do not worry. Steady your intelligence. Through your favours, I have enjoyed many kinds of

objects of pleasure. Enough of this sorrow. Immerse yourself in
dharma and steady your intelligence." Hearing the words of his
beloved, the male pigeon swiftly descended from that excellent tree
and approached the place where the female pigeon was inside the
cage. Having approached, he saw his beloved and also saw the
hunter. He said, "The hunter is motionless now. I will free you." She
replied, "O immensely fortunate one! Do not release me. Know that
all relationships are fickle. Birds provide food for hunters. A living
being feeds on another living being. He has not committed a crime.
Remember *dharma* and steady your intelligence. For *brahmanas*,
Agni is the preceptor. For *varna*s, a brahmana is the preceptor. For
women, their husbands are the preceptors. But for everyone, a guest
is the preceptor. When a guest arrives, if he is satisfied with words
of welcome, the goddess of speech is certainly satisfied. When he is
satisfied with the offering of food, Shakra is satisfied. When his feet
are washed, the ancestors are satisfied. When he is given food,
Prajapati is satisfied. When he is served in other ways, Lakshmi and
Vishnu are pleased. When he is given a bed, all the gods are satisfied.
Therefore, a guest[476] must always be worshipped. If a guest is
exhausted and scorched by the hot sun when he arrives home, one
should know that he has arrived in the form of all the gods. He
represents the fruits of all sacrifices. When a guest leaves exhausted,
all the gods, the ancestors and Agni follow him. When he is satisfied,
they are happy. When his hopes are dashed, their hopes are also
dashed. O beloved! Therefore, in every possible way cast aside your
grief. Be calm. Be steady and use your auspicious intelligence.
Follow *dharma* in your conduct. Doing a good turn to a person who
has caused injury is revered as excellent. Everyone does a good turn
towards someone who has done a good turn. Someone who exhibits
virtuous conduct towards a person who has caused injury is spoken
of as an auspicious person." The male pigeon said, "O one with the

[476] This is an unexpected guest, *atithi*. *Tithi* is a lunar day and there are
guests who are invited and arrive on specific *tithi*s, because these are festive
occasions. These are expected and invited guests, visitors. *Atithi* means
a-tithi and is therefore not any guest, but a guest who arrives uninvited and
is unexpected.

beautiful face! What you have said about us is appropriate. What you have thought is virtuous. But I have something to say. Listen. There are some who fill their stomachs with thousands, others with hundreds and consider themselves to be happy. We fill our stomachs with a great deal of difficulty. Some have pits filled with grain and riches, others obtain wealth through hardships. Some fling their wealth into pits, our wealth is in our beaks. O auspicious one! How will we worship this exhausted guest?" The female pigeon replied, "Fire, water, auspicious words, grass, wood and the like can be offered. In addition, the hunter is suffering from the cold." Hearing the words of his beloved, the king of birds climbed back onto the tree and saw a fire burning, some distance away. He went to the spot where the fire was burning and using his beak, brought back a burning splinter. The male pigeon lit a fire in front of the hunter. In the night, the king of pigeons repeatedly flung dry wood, leaves and grass into the fire. The hunter was suffering on account of the cold. Seeing the blazing fire, the hunter heated his incapacitated limbs and was happy. The female pigeon saw that the hunter was scorched by the flames of hunger. She told her husband, "O immensely fortunate one! Release me. I will use my own body to please the hunter who is suffering from grief. O one who is excellent in vows! A person who satisfies a guest obtains the desired worlds." The male pigeon replied, "As long as I am here, this is not your recommended dharma. O auspicious one! Grant me leave. I will give the guest what he wishes for." Having said this, he circumambulated the fire thrice and remembered Mahavishnu, the four-armed divinity who is the *atman* of the universe, the refuge who is affectionate towards his devotees. "Happily, eat me." Saying this, he entered the fire. On seeing that he had flung his life into the fire, the hunter spoke these words. The hunter exclaimed, "How wonderful! Shame on this life in a human body. For my sake, the king of birds has acted so bravely." When the hunter said this, the female pigeon spoke to him in these words. The female pigeon said, "O immensely fortunate one! Please release me. My husband is going a long distance away." Hearing the words of the female pigeon from inside the cage, as if he was frightened, the hunter quickly released her. She performed *pradakshina* of the fire and sung these words towards her husband.

The female pigeon said, "Serving the husband is supreme *dharma* for women. This is the path indicated in the Vedas, revered by all the worlds. A snake-catcher forcibly takes a snake far away from its hole. Like that, if a woman follows her husband, she goes to heaven with him. There are three and a half crores of body hair in a human body. A woman who follows her husband resides in heaven for that many years." Bowing down to the earth, the gods, Ganga and the large tree, she comforted her children and addressed the hunter in these words. "O immensely fortunate one! Through your favours, this opportunity has presented itself before someone like me. You should pardon my children. I am going to heaven with my husband." Saying this, the virtuous female bird entered the fire. As soon as she entered the fire, there were sounds of "Victory". An extremely beautiful *vimana* that was as resplendent as the sun appeared in the sky. The couple was seen astride this, resembling the gods. The hunter was astounded and full of joy, they spoke to him. The couple said, "O immensely intelligent one! Taking your permission, we are going to the abode of the gods. These stairs will take us to heaven. O *atithi*! We bow down before you." The hunter saw the two of them, astride that excellent *vimana*. He threw away his bow and cage. Joining his hands in salutation, the hunter said, "O immensely fortunate ones! You should not abandon me. I am ignorant. Something should be given to me. I am your revered *atithi* here. You should tell me the means for my salvation." The couple said, "O fortunate one! Go to Goutami and tell her about your crime. If you bathe there for a fortnight, you will be cleansed of all your sins. After being freed from your sins, if you bathe in the Ganga again, you will obtain the sacred fruits of a horse sacrifice and be purified. Goutami is best among rivers and is praised by Brahma and Vishnu on earth. If you bathe there again, you will cast aside this defiled body. There is no doubt that you will go to heaven then, astride a *vimana*." Hearing their words, this is what the hunter did. Astride an excellent *vimana*, he assumed a divine form. He was attired in celestial garlands and garments and was worshipped by large numbers of *apsara*s. Through the powers of Ganga, the male pigeon, the female pigeon and the hunter as the third, went to heaven. Since then, the place has been famous as *kapota tirtha*. Bathing, donating, worshipping the ancestors, *japa*, sacrifices and other rites performed there bring infinite fruits.'

Chapter 2(11) (Kumara *tirtha*)

Brahma said, 'There is another supreme *tirtha* known by the name of Kumara or Kartikeya. Merely hearing about it purifies one's lineage. When Taraka *daitya* was slain, there was relief in heaven.[477] Parvati was pleased with her eldest son, Kartikeya, and spoke to him. 'Enjoy yourself happily with all the objects of pleasure in the three worlds that delight your mind. Through my command and your father's favours, you will be happy.' Vishakha,[478] loved by the gods, was addressed by his mother in this way. As he pleased, the powerful one amused himself with the wives of the gods. O Narada! The wives of the gods also amused himself with them and the residents of heaven were unable to restrain Kartikeya. They went and told Parvati about her son's deeds. His mother, or the gods, were unable to restrain the wielder of the spear. The one with the six faces[479] was so attached to women that their words were unable to restrain him. Scared of a possible curse, Parvati thought about this. She was constrained by love for her son, but also wanted to accomplish the task of the gods. Deciding to protect the wives of the gods, she repeatedly thought for a long time. Whichever lady Skanda wished to sport with, Parvati made her assume a form that was just like Parvati's own. Whenever the one with the six faces summoned the wives of Indra or Varuna and when he looked at her, he saw a form that was just like that of his mother's. Seeing this, he bowed down and summoned someone else instead. However, seeing his mother's form in her too, he was ashamed. He saw everything outside pervaded by his mother's form. Thinking about

[477] Taraka/Tarakasura was killed by Kartikeya.
[478] Vishakha is Kartikeya's name.
[479] Kartikeya.

this, Gangeya[480] developed non-attachment. Realizing that this was his mother's doing, he refrained from *pravritti*. 'If I was supposed to withdraw from physical pleasures, why was I asked to indulge in it in the first place? Because of what my mother has done, I have become a laughing stock before everybody.' Filled with great shame, he went to Goutami. 'This also has my mother's form. Therefore, listen to my words. From now one, it will be my view that everything feminine will be like my mother.' Realizing this, Shankara, the lord of the worlds, and Parvati tried to restrain their son.' However, he replied that he had already decided this. His father, the lord of the gods, thought, 'What can I possibly give him?' Joining his hands in salutation, Skanda replied to his father. Skanda said, 'I am the commander of the gods and I am your son too. O lord of the gods! O one who is worshipped by the gods! What other boon can there be? Or perhaps, if you wish to give, give me something for the welfare of the worlds. O divinity! With your permission, I do not desire anything for myself. There are great sinners, such as those who have intercourse with the wives of their preceptors. As soon as they bathe here, let them be purged of all sins. O lord of the gods! Let inferior species also have excellent births. As soon as they bathe here, let those who are deformed become beautiful.' Shambhu agreed to the words spoken by his beloved son. Since then, that place has been famous as Kartikeya *tirtha*. Bathing and donations there yield the fruits of all sacrifices.'

Chapter 2(12) (Krittika *tirtha*)

Brahma said, 'The next, after Kartikeya *tirtha* is known as Krittika *tirtha*. Even if one hears about it, one obtains the fruits obtained from drinking *soma*. O sage! Earlier, for the destruction of Taraka, Kavi had drunk the semen.[481] On seeing that Kavi had

---

[480] Gangeya is one of Kartikeya's names.
[481] Kavi is being used as a term for Agni. Agni swallowed up Shiva's semen, produced for Kartikeya's birth.

the semen inside him, the wives of the *rishi*s desired him. With the exception of Arundhati,[482] the wives of the other *saptarshi*s had bathed after their periods. Through Agni, these six wives conceived. O sage! Having just bathed after their periods, these beautiful women were scorched. "What will we do? Where can we go? How will we perform a good deed?" Having spoken to each other in this way, they anxiously went to Ganga and massaged themselves. As a result of this, the fetuses emerged and floated in the water in the form of foam. Fanned by the wind, all these bits united in the water. Therefore, the baby who was born had one body, but six faces. When the fetuses were discharged, the wives of the *rishi*s returned home. However, seeing that their forms were distorted, the *rishi*s told them, "Leave. Quickly do. One should not follow the conduct of a *svairini*. O son! The women were, thus, refused by their husbands. Being abandoned by their own husbands, those six were miserable. Seeing them, Narada said,[483] "Kartikeya is the son of Hara. But the slayer of Taraka will also be famous as the son of Ganga and Agni. Go to him.[484] Within a short while, he will grant you objects of pleasure.' Following the words of the devarshi, they approached the one with six faces. The Krittikas[485] themselves told him exactly what had happened. Kartikeya accepted the words of the Krittikas and told them, 'All of you go to Goutami. Bathe there and worship Maheshvara. Come. I will take you there to the god's temple.' Agreeing to this, the Krittikas bathed in Goutami Ganga. Following Kartikeya's instructions, they worshipped the lord of the gods. Through the favours of the lord of the gods, they went to the god's temple. Since that time, that *tirtha* has been spoken of as Krittika *tirtha*. In the month of Kartika,[486] if one bathes there when the *nakshtra* Krittika is in the ascendant, one obtains the fruits of all the sacrifices. One becomes a king who is devoted to *dharma*. Even

---

[482] Vasishtha's wife.

[483] Since this is being told to Narada, this is superfluous.

[484] Kartikeya.

[485] The wives of the *rishi*s. The Pleiades. Kartikeya was reared by the Krittikas. They adopted him as their son. That is the reason he is known as Kartikeya.

[486] October–November.

if a person remembers the *tirtha* or hears about it, he is freed from
all sins and obtains a long lifespan."'

Chapter 2(13) (Dashashvamedha *tirtha*)

Brahma said, 'O sage! Hear about Dashashvamedha *tirtha*.
Even if a person hears about it, he obtains the fruits of a horse
sacrifice. Vishvakarma's son was the handsome and immensely
strong Vishvarupa. His son was Pramati and Pramati's son was the
lord Bhouvana. His priest was Kashyapa, accomplished in all forms
of knowledge. The mighty-armed Bhouvana, the emperor of all the
worlds, asked him the following question. "O sage! I simultaneously
wish to perform ten horse sacrifices. O preceptor! O brahmana!
Therefore, I am asking you. Who among the gods has performed such
a sacrifice?" He told him, "O best among kings! These are the various
places where the gods have performed sacrifices. These are the places
where excellent *brahmanas* have performed great sacrifices. These
are the places where large numbers of *rishi*s have performed circles
of sacrifices. These are the places where the priest simultaneously
started ten horse sacrifices, but they weren't successfully completed.
Avoiding the places where the gods performed their sacrifices, the
sacrifices can be undertaken at other spots. The other sacrifices that
were started were tainted and faced impediments." Seeing this, the
king became full of thoughts. Seeing that the sacrifices had not been
completed, the king spoke to his preceptor. The king asked, "Was
the place tainted? Was the time tainted? Is there some taint in me
or in you? Why were those ten horse sacrifices not completed?"
With his priest, Kashyapa, the miserable king went to Samvarta,
Gishpati's[487] elder brother, and spoke to him. Kashyapa and
Bhouvana said, "O illustrious one! O one who bestows honours!
We wish to simultaneously perform ten horse sacrifices. Which is
the place where we can complete them? O preceptor! Please tell us."
The best among *rishi*s meditated for some time and told Bhouvana,

---

[487] Gishpati is another name for Brihaspati.

"Go to Brahma. He will tell you about the preceptor and the spot."
The immensely wise Bhouvana and the great-souled Kashyapa came
to me and asked me about the appropriate preceptor, the spot and
other things. O son! I spoke to Bhouvana and Kashyapa. "O Indra
among kings! Go to Goutami. That is an extremely sacred spot for
performing a sacrifice. Kashyapa is the best preceptor for you. He
is accomplished in the Vedas. O king! Through the favours of your
preceptor and through Goutami's favours, if you bathe there and
perform a single horse sacrifice, you will obtain the fruits of ten
horse sacrifices." Hearing this, King Bhouvana went to the banks
of Goutami. With Kashyapa as an aide, he consecrated himself for
a horse sacrifice. The great horse sacrifice, the lord of all sacrifices,
commenced there. When it was completed, the king was ready to
donate the entire earth. The excellent king was standing there,
having worshipped the *brahmanas*, the officiating priests and the
assistant priests. A loud voice was heard from the firmament. The
voice from the firmament said, "O king! With Kashyapa as your
priest, you have evinced a desire to donate the entire earth, along
with its mountains and forests. That is as good as giving it away.
Give up this desire to donate land. Donate food. That brings great
fruits. In the three worlds, nothing yields as much of good merits as
the donation of food. O sage![488] This is especially because you have
devotedly performed a horse sacrifice on the banks of the Ganga
and have given away a lot of *dakshina*. O fortunate one! You have
already accomplished your objective. There is no need to think
about this." Nevertheless, since he wanted to give, the earth spoke
to Bhouvana. The earth said, "O Vishvakarma's descendant! Do not
repeatedly want to give me away. If a person resorts to the banks of
Goutami and gives a mouthful of food, it is as if everything has been
given. O Bhouvana! Why will you give me away? I will then sink
into this water. Therefore, you should not give me away." Bhouvana
was scared and asked, "What should be given away then?" The earth
again spoke to Bhouvana, who was surrounded by *brahmanas*. The
earth said, "On the banks of Goutami, if a person gives away a
little bit of sesamum, cattle, riches and grain, that donation is as

---

[488] Bhouvana is being addressed as a sage.

good as inexhaustible. O Bhouvana! Why will you give me away?
If a person resorts to the banks of Goutami and gives a mouthful of
food, it is as if everything has been given. O Bhouvana! Why will
you give me away?"[489] Hearing the earth's words, Bhouvana, the
universal emperor, agreed that this was indeed the case. He gave the
brahmanas a great deal of food. Ever since then, that spot has been
known as Dashashvamedha[490] *tirtha*. Bathing there yields the fruits
of ten horse sacrifices.'

Chapter 2(14) (Paishacha *tirtha*)

Brahma said, 'There is another one named Paishacha *tirtha*.
It is worshipped by those who know about the *brahman*. I
will describe its nature. It is on the southern bank of Goutami. O
Narada! Along the side of Brahmagiri, there is a mountain named
Anjana.[491] O excellent sage! On that mountain, there was a supreme
apsara who had been dislodged because of a curse. Her name was
Anjana and her face was like that of a she-monkey. Her husband's
name was Kesari and he had another wife named Adrika. This wife
of Kesari's was also a supreme *apsara* who had been dislodged
because of a curse. Her face was like that of a she-cat and she too
resided on Mount Anjana. Kesari, famous in the worlds, once went
to the southern ocean. Meanwhile, Agastya went to Mount Anjana.
Following the norms, both Anjana and Adrika happily worshipped
Agastya, supreme among *rishi*s. The illustrious one was pleased and
requested both of them to ask for boons. Both of them told Agastya,
"O lord of sages! Please give us sons. They should be stronger and
superior to everyone else. They should do good deeds to everyone."
Having agreed, the best among sages left for the southern direction.
There was an occasion when Anjana and Adrika were singing,

---

[489] This bit is repeated.

[490] *Dasha* (ten) *ashvemedha* (horse sacrifice).

[491] There are several mountains that have this name, but this is the one
near Brahmagiri.

dancing and laughing on the summit of that mountain. The gods
Vayu and Nirriti saw them and smiled. Overcome with desire,
both of them rushed forward. "We are gods. We are the ones who
bestow boons. Please be our wives." When they agreed, they amused
themselves on the summit of that mountain. Through Vayu, Anjana
gave birth to Hanuman. Through Nirriti, Adrika gave birth to the
king of the *pishacha*s. They said, "Thanks to the best among sages,
these sons have been born to us. However, our forms are disfigured
and our faces are tainted. We have been cursed by Shachi's
consort.[492] You should know about this." The illustrious Vayu and
Nirriti replied, "If you bathe in Goutami, you will be released from
your curse." Saying this, those two delighted gods disappeared. To
please them, Adri,[493] who had the form of a *pishacha* took Anjana,
his mother and his brother Hanuman and made them have their
baths there. In similar fashion, Hanuman also swiftly took Adri,
whose form was like that of a cat, to the banks of Goutami Ganga.
Since then, this *tirtha* has been named after Paishacha and Anjana.
It is auspicious and is near Brahmagiri. It yields all the objects of
desire. The region known as Marjara extends fifty-three *yojana*s to
the east. Since then, it has been named after Marjara and Hanuman
Vrishakapi.[494] The auspicious confluence of Phena[495] yields all the
objects of desire. Its form, nature and location are spoken about in
that place.'

Chapter 2(15) (Kshudha *tirtha*)

Brahma said, 'O Narada! Listen attentively about the place
known as Kshudha *tirtha*. I will describe this extremely sacred
place. For men, it yields all the objects of desire. In ancient times,
there was a *rishi* named Kanva. He was an ascetic and knew about

[492] Indra.
[493] Adrika's son.
[494] Vrishakapi is another name for Hanuman, Marjara means cat.
[495] The confluence of the river Phena with Godavari.

the Vedas. Once, he was exhausted from wandering around and was suffering from hunger. Goutama's sacred hermitage was prosperous and was full of food and water. Kanva saw that he was hungry, while Goutama was prosperous. Because of this inequity, he developed non-attachment. "Goutama is the best among *brahmanas*, but I am also devoted to austerities. One should not seek from someone who is an equal. Therefore, though I am hungry and my body is suffering, I should not eat in Goutama's home. I will go to Goutami Ganga and earn riches." Having decided this, the intelligent one went to the purifying Ganga. He bathed and with a pure mind, sat down on a mat of *kusha* grass. He praised Goutami Ganga and the great calamity of Kshudha.[496] Kanva said, "I bow down to Ganga, the remover of great afflictions. I bow down to Kshudha, who causes suffering among all beings. I bow down to the auspicious one, who emerged from the great Ishana's matted hair. I bow down to the great one who emerged from the mouth of Death.[497] O one who is serene in form to those who have pure minds! O one who is angry in form to evil-souled ones! O one who assumes the form of a river to dispel the torments and sins of everyone! O one who assumes the form of Kshudha to cause torment to everyone! I bow down before you. I bow down before the one who confers everything that is beneficial, the one who crushes sin. I bow down before the goddess who delivers peace. I bow down before the one who destroys poverty." Praised in this way, two forms appeared before him. One beautiful form was that of Ganga and the other form was terrible. The best among *brahmanas* joined his hands in salutation and prostrated himself again. Kanva said, "O auspicious one! O one who is the cause behind everything auspicious! O Brahmi! O Maheshvari! O sacred Vaishnavi! O three-eyed one! O goddess Godavari! I bow down before you. O one who emerged from the three-eyed one's matted hair! O one who destroyed Goutama's sins! O one who proceeds to the ocean in seven flows! O Godavari! I bow down before you. O one who destroys all sins! O one who destroys sins committed in the pursuit of *dharma*, *artha* and *kama*! O goddess

---

[496] *Kshudha* means hunger.
[497] That is, Kshudha.

Kshudha! O one who destroys both misery and avarice! I bow down before you." Hearing Kanva's words, they were extremely pleased and spoke to the brahmana. Ganga and Kshudha said, "O fortunate one! O one who is excellent in vows! Speak. Ask for your desired boon." In due order, Kanva prostrated himself before Ganga and Kshudha and spoke. Kanva said, "O goddess! Please grant me agreeable and desired prosperity, a long lifespan, wealth, enjoyment of objects of pleasure and emancipation. O Ganga! Please give me this." After addressing Goutami Ganga in this way, the best among *brahmanas* spoke to Kshudha. Kanva said, "O Kshudha! O thirst! O cause of penury! O wicked and harsh one! Let my lineage never suffer from these afflictions. If anyone is afflicted by hunger and praises you with this hymn, let them not suffer from either poverty or miseries. This *tirtha* is extremely sacred. If a man undertakes bathing, donations and *japa* here, let Lakshmi always serve him. If a person reads this hymn in this *tirtha* or at home, let him not suffer from poverty, misery or fear." Having told Kanva that they agreed to this, they returned to their respective abodes. Since then, this *tirtha* has been named after Kanva, Ganga and Kshudha. O son! It destroys all sins and extends the delight of the ancestors.'

Chapter 2(16) (Ahalya and Indra *tirtha*)

Brahma said, 'There is a *tirtha* named Ahalya-Sangama that purifies the three worlds. O best among sages! Listen properly to the account that transpired there. O lord of sages! Driven by curiosity, I had created many kinds of maidens earlier. They were beautiful and possessed all the qualities. Among them, I created one who was the best. She possessed the auspicious signs. That maiden was beautiful in all her limbs. On seeing her beauty and qualities, I started to wonder. 'Who has the capacity to nurture her? There is no one among the *daitya*s, gods or sages who possesses the capacity to nurture her.' This is what I thought. There was an intelligent and senior brahmana who possessed the qualities. He was devoted to austerities and possessed all the signs. He was learned in the

Vedas and the *Vedanga*s. This was the immensely wise Goutama
and to nurture her, I bestowed her on him. "O best among the
sages! Protect her, until she attains youth. When she attains youth,
bring the virtuous one back to me." Saying this, I gave Goutama
the slender-waisted maiden. The best among sages, whose sins had
been cleansed through austerities, obtained her. He nurtured her
in the proper way. Then, ornamenting her, he brought her back to
me. Indifferent towards Ahalya, the best among sages brought her.
On seeing her, all the gods, Shakra, Agni, Varuna and the others
separately said, "O lord of the gods! She should be given to me."
In a similar way, on seeing her, all the sages, *sadhya*s, *danava*s,
*yaksha*s and *rakshasa*s approached me for the sake of the maiden.
In particular, Indra had a great desire to obtain her. I remembered
Goutama's greatness, depth and fortitude and was extremely
surprised. Therefore, I had this good thought. "It is appropriate
that the one with the beautiful face should be given to Goutama and
to no one else. Therefore, I will bestow her on him." I also thought,
"This maiden has agitated the minds and patience of everyone."
The gods and the *rishi*s said, "Ahalya is mine." I looked at the gods
and the *rishi*s and loudly proclaimed the following. I repeatedly
said, "This one with the excellent eyebrows will be given to the
person who circumambulates the earth and presents himself before
me first. She will not be given to anyone else." The large number
of gods heard the words I had spoken. For Ahalya's sake, the
gods started to circumambulate the earth. When the large number
of gods had departed, Goutama, lord of sages, also made some
efforts for Ahalya's sake. O brahmana! Meanwhile, Surabhi,[498]
who yields all the objects of desire, had partly delivered her calf.
Seeing her, Goutama remembered that she represented the earth
and circumambulated her. He also performed *pradakshina* of the
lingamm of the lord of the gods. After circumambulating both of
them, Goutama, supreme among sages, said, "All the gods have not
yet completed a single circumambulation. They have left and have
not returned. I have completed two circumambulations." Having

---

[498] The divine cow, *kamadhenu*, the cow who yields all the objects of
desire.

decided this, the sage approached me. The immensely intelligent Goutama bowed down and addressed me in these words. "O one who is seated on the lotus! O one who is the *atman* of the universe! I repeatedly prostrate myself before you. O Brahma! I have circumambulated the entire earth. O lord of the gods! Under the circumstances, you yourself know what is appropriate." Through the *yoga* of meditation, I understood what Goutama had spoken. "You have performed *pradakshina*. The one with the excellent eyebrows will be given to you. O brahmana *rishi*! Know that even the *nigama* texts[499] find it difficult to comprehend *dharma*. Surabhi has partially delivered and she is identical with the earth and its seven *dvipa*s. Since you have circumambulated her, you have also circumambulated the earth. The circumambulation of the *lingamm* yields the same fruits. O sage! O Goutama! O one who is excellent in vows! I am pleased with all your efforts, fortitude, learning and austerities. O tiger among rishis! I will bestow this maiden, supreme in the worlds, on you." O sage! After saying this, I bestowed Ahalya on Goutama. After the marriage was over, the gods slowly returned, having completed the circumambulation. They saw the couple, Goutama and Ahalya, and this increased their delight. After returning, the gods saw them and were amazed. When the marriage was over, all the gods went to heaven. Shachi's consort was full of envy. He glanced towards her and went to heaven. Pleased in my mind, I gave the great-souled Goutama the auspicious Brahmagiri, which yields all the sacred objects of desire.'

'Ahalya found pleasure with Goutama, best among sages. In heaven, Shakra heard about Goutama's sacred account. Shatakratu[500] assumed the form of a brahmana and came to the hermitage to see the sage and his unblemished wife. He saw his house, his wife and his prosperity. His mind was full of wickedness and he glanced towards Ahalya. He did not think of himself, or of others. He did not think of the time and the place. He was not scared of the *rishi*'s curse. O son! Overwhelmed by desire, Shatakratu did not comprehend any of this. He was insolent

---

[499] The texts of the *Veda*s, or related to them.
[500] The one who performed 100 sacrifices, Indra's name.

because he was the king of the gods and constantly thought about
her. His limbs were heated and he thought, "What will I do? How
will I enter?" He resided there in the guise of a brahmana, but did
not find an opportunity to enter. On one occasion, the immensely
wise Goutama went out of the hermitage along with his disciples
to perform the rituals of the forenoon. He went to the hermitage
on the banks of the Goutami, full of *brahmanas* and many kinds
of grain. Indra, who was looking, saw that the excellent sage had
left. He said, "This is my opportunity." Accordingly, he did what
would bring pleasure to his mind. Desiring his beloved, Shatakratu
assumed Goutama's form. He saw Ahalya, beautiful in all her
limbs, and addressed her in these words. Indra said, "I am attracted
towards you. Remembering your qualities and your beauty, my
steps falter." Saying this, he held her by the hand and entered.
Ahalya did not realize this was a paramour. She thought he was
Goutama. Before Goutama returned with his disciples, they happily
indulged in pleasure. When he returned, Ahalya, pleasant in speech,
always went ahead to greet him. She welcomed him with pleasant
words and satisfied him with her qualities. That day, the immensely
wise one did not see her and thought this was exceedingly strange.
O Narada! Everyone saw the best among sages standing at the
door. There were those in the *agnihotra* altar. There were guards
and those engaged in household duties. Scared and astounded,
they spoke to Goutama, supreme among sages. The guards said,
"O illustrious one! What is this amazing incident! You are seen
inside and outside. With your beloved, you entered inside. But you
are outside too. How wonderful is the power of your austerities!
You can assume many different kinds of forms." Hearing this, he
was surprised and entered inside. "Who has entered inside? Who
is there? O beloved Ahalya! Why don't you reply?" Hearing the
rishi's words, Ahalya spoke to the paramour. Ahalya asked, "Who
are you in the form of the sage? You have committed a sin." Saying
this, she quickly arose from the bed, terrified. Scared of the sage,
the wicked Shakra assumed the form of a cat. The sage saw that his
beloved Ahalya had been forcibly outraged and defiled. He angrily
exclaimed, "Who has committed this rash act?" When her husband
said this, she was ashamed and did not say anything. The sage saw

the cat wandering around, anxious and scared. He asked, "Who are you? If you utter a falsehood, you will be reduced to ashes." Joining his hands in salutation, Shachi's consort replied. Indra said, "O store of austerities! I am Shachi's consort. Earlier, I was the one who has been praised as the destroyer of cities.[501] This sin has been committed by me. O unblemished one! I am telling you the truth. O sage! I have committed an extremely reprehensible act. When a person's heart is pierced by the arrows of the god of love, what does he not do? O brahmana! O ocean of compassion! You should pardon my great sin. The virtuous are never harsh, not even towards those who have committed crimes." Hearing his words, full of rage, the brahmana spoke to Hari.[502] Goutama said, "Because of your love for vaginas, you have committed a sin. Let there be one thousand vaginas in your body." Full of rage, the sage told her, "Become a river that is dry." She spoke to him about her transgression and sought to placate him. Ahalya said, "Even if women desire other men in their minds, they are wicked. They will be sent to hell for an eternity. All other men are like their brothers. O illustrious one! Be pacified and understand my words. He assumed your form and came to me. These people are witnesses." The guards confirmed this and said that Ahalya was speaking the truth.'

Through his meditation, the sage also realized this. He became calm and spoke to the one who was devoted to her husband. Goutama said, 'O fortunate one! When you come into contact with Goutami, foremost among rivers, you will become a river and again attain a form that is loved by me.' Hearing the *rishi*'s words, this is what the one who was devoted to her husband did. Ahalya, loved by Goutama, met with that goddess. She again attained the form that had been created by me earlier.[503] Joining his hands in salutation, the king of the gods addressed Goutama. Indra said, 'O tiger among sages! I am a sinner who has come to your house. Please save me.' Seeing that he was prostrate at his feet, Goutama was filled with

---

[501] Indra's name is Purandara, the destroyer of cities.

[502] Hari is one of Indra's names.

[503] In this Purana, the river Ahalya has a confluence with the Godavari. The description in other Puranas is different.

compassion and spoke to him. He was also placated by the large
number of gods. Goutama, the excellent sage, said, 'I will act so that
Indra, Shachi's husband, is freed from his curse. O Shachi's consort!
Bathe in the sacred *tirtha* that is the confluence of Ahalya. In an
instant, you will be cleansed of your sins and have one thousand
eyes.' O Narada! I witnessed both these astounding events—
Ahalya regaining her old form and Shachi's husband obtaining one
thousand eyes. Since then, the *tirtha* that is the confluence of Ahalya
has been pure. It is also famous as Indra *tirtha* and grants men every
object of desire.

Chapter 2(17) (Janasthana *tirtha*)

Brahma said, 'There is another *tirtha*, known as Janasthana. It
extends for four *yojana*s. As soon as it is remembered, it bestows
emancipation on men. In ancient times, in the solar dynasty, King
Janaka was born. He married Gunarnava, the daughter of the lord
of the waters.[504] The king was the father of many Janakas who strove
for *dharma*, *artha*, *kama* and *moksha*. His wife was similar to him
in beauty and qualities. She was an ocean of qualities. Yajnavalkya,
Indra among *brahmanas*, was the king's priest. The best among kings
asked the priest Yajnavalkya. Janaka said, "The best among sages
have determined that the enjoyment of pleasures and emancipation
are both excellent. Female servants, male servants, elephants, horses
and the others are the best means of enjoying objects of pleasure.
But these come to an end and are without substance. Compared to
enjoyment, emancipation alone is permanent. Thus, emancipation
is superior to enjoyment. While enjoying, how can one proceed
towards emancipation? The pursuit of emancipation by giving up
all attachment is extremely difficult. O tiger among *brahmanas*!
Therefore, please tell me. How can emancipation be obtained
easily?" Yajnavalkya replied, "The lord of the waters is your senior
and father-in-law. He will do what brings you pleasure. O lord

---

[504] She was Varuna's daughter. Gunarnava means ocean of qualities.

of men! Go to him and ask. He will instruct you about what is best for you." Hearing Yajnavalkya's words, King Janaka went to Varuna and asked him how one could duly proceed along the path of emancipation. Varuna said, "There are two established paths for emancipation—undertaking *karma* and refraining from *karma*. The path determined in the Vedas is that *karma* is superior to refraining from *karma*.[505] The four objectives of human existence[506] are all bound to *karma*. Those who say that refraining from *karma* is a path towards emancipation utter a falsehood. O best among kings! All the crops mature through *karma*. Therefore, men who follow the Vedas must make every effort to undertake *karma*. In this way, men obtain both objects of pleasure and emancipation. *Karma* is more sacred than lack of *karma*. *Karma* depends on the *ashrama*. O Indra among kings! O one who knows about *dharma*! It also depends on one's birth. Listen. O one who bestows honours! For the four *ashramas*, there are different kinds of *karma*. Of the four *ashramas*, that of the householder is said to be the most sacred. Hence, it is my view that enjoyment and emancipation are simultaneously possible." Hearing this, Janaka and the intelligent Yajnavalkya worshipped Varuna and again addressed him in these words. "Which region and what *tirtha* bestows enjoyment and emancipation? O best among gods! You know everything. We bow down before you. Please tell us." Varuna replied, "O son! Within earth, Bharatavarsha is the most sacred and within it, Dandaka is the best.[507] Any *karma* undertaken in that *kshetra* bestows enjoyment and emancipation on men.[508] Among *tirthas*, Goutami Ganga is the best. It bestows emancipation on men. Through sacrifices and donations there, a person obtains objects of pleasure and emancipation." Hearing the words of the lord of the waters, Yajnavalkya and Janaka took their leave of Varuna and returned to their own city. King

---

[505] This is reminiscent of Bhagavad Gita 3.8.

[506] *Dharma, artha, kama* and *moksha*.

[507] Etymologically, the forest of Dandaka, or Dandakaranya, has a sense of punishment, that is, it is a place to which one was exiled or banished. Today, Dandakaranya straddles several central Indian States.

[508] Both *tirthas* and *kshetras* are sacred places of pilgrimage. However, *tirthas* are associated with water, while *kshetras* are not.

Janaka performed a horse sacrifice and other rites. Yajnavalkya, Indra among *brahmanas*, was the officiating priest for the king. Resorting to the banks of Ganga, the king undertook a sacrifice and obtained emancipation. Many other kings known as Janaka also undertook *karma* there. Through Goutami's favours, those immensely fortunate ones obtained emancipation. Since then, that *tirtha* has been famous as Janasthana.[509] Since this was the seat of sacrifices performed by Janakas, it is spoken of as Janasthana. It extends for four *yojana*s. As soon as one remembers it, all sins are cleansed. Bathing there, donating there, offering oblations to the ancestors there, remembering that *tirtha*, faithfully going there and frequenting it—through these, a person obtains all the objects of desire and emancipation.'

Chapter 2(18) (Chakra *tirtha* and the courtesan)

Brahma said, 'O brahmana! There is a great *tirtha*, known by the name of Chakra *tirtha*. If a man bathes there faithfully, he goes to Hari's world. O lord of the earth![510] If a person fasts on *ekadashi* in *shukla paksha* and bathes in the place known as *ganika sangama*, one obtains the eternal destination. In ancient times, an event occurred there. Listen to me attentively. There was a *vaishya* named Vishvavara and he possessed a great deal of riches. O rishi! When he was advanced in age, an excellent son was born to him. He possessed qualities and beauty. He indulged in pleasures and was handsome to behold. After some time his beloved son, whom he loved more than his own life, died. Seeing that the son was dead, the couple was full of grief. They made up their minds that they would die along with him. "Alas, son! Wicked destiny is extremely evil-souled. O ocean of qualities! Though you were in the prime of youth, he has taken you away. We love you more than our own

---

[509] A part of the forest of Dandakaranya. Janasthana means place with people. The text suggests an etymological link with the name Janaka.

[510] This is an odd way of addressing Narada.

lives, which are so difficult to obtain." Hearing the couple lament in this way, Yama felt compassion towards them. With his mind overwhelmed by compassion, he swiftly abandoned his own city. He stood on the auspicious banks of Godavari and meditated on Janardana. Within a short time, everywhere, the subjects turned old. No one died and the earth was over-burdened with creatures. The earth filled with sounds of "This bit of ground is mine." O excellent sage! The goddess earth quickly went to the place where Shakra, the destroyer of enemy cities was, along with the gods. Seeing the earth, Indra prostrated himself and spoke these words. Indra said, "O earth! What is the reason for your coming here? Please tell me." The earth replied, "O Shakra! Since no one is dying, I am suffering from a heavy burden. I have come to ask the reason for this. Please tell me." Hearing what the earth said, Indra spoke these words. Indra said, "Had there been a reason, I would have known it by now. I am the unwavering lord of all the gods." Hearing these words, the earth replied to Shachi's consort. "Please command Yama that he should destroy subjects." O great sage! Hearing the earth's words, the great Indra instructed the *siddha*s and the *kinnara*s that Yama should quickly be brought before him. All of them swiftly went to Vaivasvata's[511] city. The *siddha*s and the *kinnara*s did not see Yama there. They quickly returned and reported this account to Shakra. The *siddha*s and *kinnara*s said, "O lord! We could not see Yama in Yama's city. With great care, we looked in every direction." Hearing their words, Shakra asked Savitar,[512] Yama's father, "Where is he?" Surya replied, "O Shakra! Kritanta[513] is now on the banks of Godavari. He is performing extremely fierce austerities there. I don't know the reason." Hearing Bhanu's words, Shakra was worried. Shakra said, "Alas, this is a hardship. This is a great calamity. My lordship over the gods will be destroyed. Yama is making wicked efforts, performing austerities near Godavari. O gods! It is my view that he certainly desires to seize my position." Stating this, Indra instantly summoned the large number of *apsara*s.'

[511] Yama's.
[512] Savitar, Surya and Bhanu are all names for the sun-god.
[513] The Destroyer, Yama's name.

'Indra asked, "Who amongst you is capable of standing before the austerities of Yama,[514] my enemy? Who possesses the capacity to destroy his austerities? Tell me quickly." O great sage! Hearing Shakra's words, no one spoke. In great rage, Shakra spoke to the large number of *apsara*s again. Indra said, "Not a single one has said anything. Therefore, we will ourselves go. O gods! Get ready. Without any delay, let the soldiers be brought. We will slay the enemy who desires to obtain heaven through his austerities." When this was said, the soldiers of the gods presented themselves. Hari, who holds up the worlds, got to know what was in Indra's mind. For Yama's protection, the wielder of the *chakra* sent his *chakra*. The supreme Chakra *tirtha* is the place where the *chakra* manifested itself. Menaka, who was scared, addressed Indra in these words. Menaka said, "O lord of the gods! Not a single one among us is capable of looking at Kala. O god! It is better to die at your hands rather than at the hands of Yama. O lord! You should ask this courtesan who thinks she possesses youth and beauty. She accepts your lordship and you should send her." Hearing her words, Shakra, the supreme lord of the gods, honoured the courtesan Kshama and commanded the woman. Shakra said, "O courtesan! O beautiful one! Go and perform my task without any delay. Accomplish your objective and return. I will love you, just as I love Shachi." Hearing Shakra's words, the courtesan leapt up, over the directions. In a short while, beautiful in form, she reached Yama's presence. Illuminating the ten directions, she approached Yama. The maiden sang in beautiful tones and danced and swung gracefully. Kala's fickle mind wavered. The mobile and immobile objects seemed to be agitated. Full of the fire of desire, Yama opened his eyes. O great sage! Her conduct was inimical towards what was good for him. Before his gaze, she instantly melted and attained the state of becoming a river. The extremely fortunate one merged with Goutami. As the large number of courtesans and servants sung her praise, because of the powers of the *tirtha*, she went to heaven. On seeing the courtesan astride a *vimana* proceeding towards heaven, Kala's darting eyes were filled with great wonder. The sun-god

[514] The text uses Yama's name of Kala.

approached Yama and spoke to him. Surya said, "O son! Perform your own task of destroying subjects. Behold the wind that blows, the creator creating subjects, me traversing the three worlds and the earth carrying subjects."[515] Hearing his father's words, Yama addressed him in these words. Yama replied, "I will certainly not carry out this reprehensible task. It is an extremely cruel task. You should not command me to undertake it." Hearing these words, Bhanu spoke the following words. "O Yama! How is your task tainted and condemned? Did you not see the courtesan, wet with water from Goutami, who just left for heaven with large numbers of courtesans and servants singing her praise? O son! You have undertaken extremely difficult and fierce austerities here. I do not see an end to this. Therefore, go to your own city." Saying this, the illustrious Bhanu bathed there and went to heaven. Bathing at the confluence, Yama also left for his own city. O great sage! The slayer of beings thus discarded his great doubt. Seeing that Yama had departed, the *chakra* also returned to the place where Govinda was, adorned with a garland of wild flowers. If a mortal person controls himself and reads or hears this, all his calamities are destroyed and he obtains a long lifespan.'

Chapter 2(19) (Ashvabhanu *tirtha*)

Brahma said, 'O supreme sage! The two rivers Aruna and Varuna are extremely sacred and auspicious. Their confluence with Ganga is also extremely sacred. This place is more sacred than Manasa, Prayaga and Mandakini and destroys every kind of sin. Hear about its origin. Kashyapa's eldest son, Aditya,[516] is famous in the worlds. He is the eye of the three worlds. His rays are sharp. He has seven horses and is worshipped by the worlds. His wife, Usha, is Tvashta's daughter and is the most beautiful woman in the three worlds. The extremely slender-waisted one was incapable of

---

[515] That is, each is performing the appointed task.
[516] Surya.

withstanding her husband's sharp heat. The beautiful one thought, "What will I do?" Her sons were the extremely wise Manu and Vaivasvata Yama.[517] Her daughter was the sacred river, Yamuna. Hear about the wonderful way this came about. She took great care to create her shadow, with a form that was exactly like her own. Usha told her, "Be like me. Instructed by me, nurture my husband and children. Until I return, be loved by him and my children. You should not reveal this to anyone, my beloved or the children." When Chhaya[518] agreed, Usha left the house. Having said this, she swiftly departed, desiring a serene form. She went to the house of her father, Tvashta, and told him everything. Tvashta was surprised. Since he loved his children, he spoke to his daughter. Tvashta said, "When a husband exists, a wife should not freely act in this way. How will your children manage? What will happen to your husband, Savitar? O fortunate one! I am virtuous and I am scared. Return to your husband's house again." Thus addressed by her father, she repeatedly refused. She went to the region of Uttara Kuru and performed austerities there. Assuming the form of a mare, she tormented herself through fierce austerities there. Usha unwaveringly meditated on her beloved, whose form was impossible to behold.'

'O son! Meanwhile, in Usha's form, Chhaya lived with her husband and children were born. They were Savarni[519] and Shani. There was also a wicked daughter, named Vishti. Chhaya always differentiated in her dealings with her own children and those of Usha. Yama became angry at this. Since Chhaya's conduct was partial, Yama, the lord of the southern direction, struck his mother with his foot. Agitated at her son's wickedness, Usha cursed Vaivasvata Yama. "At my command, your foot will fall down." With his foot destroyed, he wept miserably and went to his father. He told Savitar everything that had happened. Yama said, "O best among the gods! Since she has cursed me in this way, she

---

[517] Vaivasvata means the son of Vivasvat (Surya). Hence, Manu is also Vaivasvata Manu.

[518] *Chhaya* means shadow.

[519] Savarni Manu.

cannot possibly be my mother. Even if a child acts in a contrary way, a mother is never enraged. I may have said something in my childishness. I may even have committed a wicked act. But a mother never becomes angry. Therefore, she is not my mother. Irrespective of whether a child does something good or bad, a mother tolerates everything. That is the reason she is known as a mother. O father! She constantly looks at me with eyes that seem to burn me down. When she speaks to me, her words are like the fire of destruction. She is not my mother." Hearing his son's words, Savitar became thoughtful.[520] "This is Chhaya, not his mother. Usha, his mother, is elsewhere. Desiring that I become serene, she is in some other region, performing austerities. Tvashta's daughter is in the Uttara Kuru region, in the form of a mare." Knowing that she was there, Divakara[521] went to the spot where his beloved was.'

'He himself assumed the form of a horse. On seeing her in the form of a mare, in the form of a horse, he rushed towards her. Usha saw a horse, in the throes of desire. She heard the sound of the neighing. Usha was devoted to her husband. She was devoted to meditating on her husband. She did not know who it was and was scared of being ravished by the horse. When her husband approached her, she swiftly fled in a southern direction. "Who will save me now, the *rishi*s or the gods?" As his beloved fled in the form of a mare, he himself pursued her in the form of a horse. Wherever Usha went, Bhanu followed. When a person is seized and comes under the control of desire, what wicked act is he not capable of performing? Heading in the southern direction, the two of them crossed Bhagirathi and other rivers, forests, groves, Narmada and the Vindhyas. Anxious and terrified, Tvastha's daughter went to Goutami. It has been heard that there are sages in Janasthana who protect. Arriving in the region of Goutami, the mare entered a hermitage of *rishi*s. Bhanu also followed her, in the form of a horse. The residents of Janasthana tried to restrain the horse. Full of rage, the lord who was Usha's husband cursed them. Bhanu said, "Since

[520] Surya realized this through his powers of meditation.
[521] Surya's name.

you have restrained me, you will become *vata* trees."[522] Through
their insight of *jnana*, the sages knew that the horse was Usha's
husband. The sages happily praised Bhanu, the lord of the gods.
Praised by the large number of sages, Bhanu approached the mare.
In the form of the horse, his face touched the face of the mare.
Realizing that it was her husband, Tvashta's daughter released the
semen through her mouth. Through this semen, the two Ashvins[523]
were born in Ganga. The large number of gods, the *siddha*s, the
sages, the male rivers, the female rivers, the herbs, the large number
of stellar bodies, Aruna, Bhanu's charioteer, with the sacred chariot
drawn by seven horses, Yama, Manu, Varuna, Vaivasvata Shani,
the sacred river Yamuna, Tapi and Mahanadi arrived there. O sage!
The rivers were amazed at his form.'

'Full of wonder, his father-in-law also arrived, to see what has
happening. Understanding his father-in-law's intention, Bhanu
spoke. Bhanu said, "O Tvashta! Usha has performed excellent
austerities. For her sake, mount me on your machine and pare off
a lot of energy. O Prajapati! Pare off parts until she is pleased."
Near Somanatha,[524] in the place known as Prabhasa, he started
to slice off the energy. There is a place near Goutami, where she
met with her husband, in the form of a horse. That is the place
where the Ashvins originated and it is known as Ashva *tirtha*.
The hermitage where five *vata* trees exist is known as Bhanu
tirtha. Tapi[525] and Yamuna arrived to see their father. There is
an auspicious confluence of the rivers Aruna and Varuna with
Ganga. Associated with the gods who arrived, there are separate
*tirtha*s there. There are twenty-seven thousand such *tirtha*s, all
possessing qualities. Bathing and donating there, yield all the
inexhaustible good merits. O Narada! If a person remembers,
reads or hears it, he is freed from all sins. He becomes devoted to
dharma and is happy.'

---

[522] *Vata* is the holy fig tree.
[523] The physicians of the gods.
[524] In Gujarat.
[525] Tapi/Tapati is the daughter of Surya and Chhaya.

Chapter 2(20) (Garuda *tirtha*)

Brahma said, 'The *tirtha* named Garuda pacifies all kinds of impediments. I will tell you about its powers. O Narada! Listen attentively. There was a great serpent named Maninaga. He was Shesha's son. Scared of Garuda, he devotedly propitiated Shankara. The illustrious Parameshthi Maheshvara was pleased at this. He told the great *naga*, "O *pannaga*! Ask for a boon." The *naga* replied, "O lord! Grant me freedom from fear of Garuda." Shambhu agreed and said, "You will no longer suffer any fear on account of Garuda." The *naga* emerged, no longer scared of Garuda, Aruna's younger brother. He went near the ocean of milk, where the one who lies down on the ocean of milk[526] was. The *naga* wandered around here and there, in a place that was pleasant and cool. Garuda also went to that region. He saw the *pannaga* roaming around fearlessly. He seized the great *naga* and brought him to his own residence. Garuda bound that excellent *naga* in Garuda's nooses.

'Meanwhile, Nandi spoke to Isha, the lord of the universe. Nandikeshvara said, "O lord of the gods! The *naga* must certainly have been devoured or bound by Garuda. He may not be alive. He is not wandering around." Hearing Nandi's words and understanding what had happened, Shambhu said the following. Shambhu said, "The *naga* has been bound and is in Garuda's home. Quickly go and tell Vishnu Janardana, the lord of the universe. Though I have myself given him the word, the *naga* has been bound by Kashyapa's son."[527] Hearing the lord's words, Nandi went to Shri's lord and reported these words to Vishnu, the refuge of the worlds. Pleased, Narayana addressed Garuda in these words. Vishnu said, "O Vinata's son! Follow my words and hand over the *pannaga* to Nandi." Though the bird who was Vinata's son understood, he refused. In Nandi's presence, Suparna[528] addressed Vishnu in words that were full of rage.

---

[526] Vishnu.
[527] That is, Garuda.
[528] Garuda.

'Garuda said, "O Vishnu! Other masters give their servants what they like. Not only do you not do that, you take away what they have obtained. Behold! The three-eyed divinity will free the *naga* through Nandi. But you wish to give Nandi the *naga* I have captured. I always carry you along your path. Therefore, you must always give me something. I have captured the *naga* and you should not ask me to give him away. This should not be the conduct of virtuous masters who wish to ensure good conduct. The virtuous give to their servants. But you are taking away what I have obtained. O Keshava! It is through my strength that you defeat the *daitya*s in battle. In vain do you boast that you possess great strength." While the guardians of the worlds watched, in Nandi's presence, the wielder of the *chakra* and the mace heard Garuda's words and laughed. The immensely intelligent one said, "O supreme bird! Indeed, I do defeat all the *asura*s through your strength. By bearing me, you have become extremely lean." O brahmana! After saying this, the rage of Shri's lord was pacified. He continued, "In Nandi's presence, bear the little finger of my hand." He placed the finger on Garuda's head and said, "O bird! You have spoken the truth. Look towards your *dharma*." When the finger was laid on his head, it entered his stomach. From the stomach, it went to the extremities of his feet. It entered and seemed to crush him. He was distressed and suffered. Full of shame, he joined his hands in salutation and spoke. Garuda cried, "Save me! O lord of the universe! Save me! Your servant has committed a crime. You are the master of all the worlds. You are the support and you are also the one who is supported. O Vishnu! The powerful pardon thousands of offences. Even for those who are sinners, your compassion is great. All the sages say that you are a store of compassion. O mother of the universe! O one who resides in the lotus! I am suffering. Please save me. O Kamala![529] I am miserable and suffering. I am a child and you are devoted to your children." Taking pity, the goddess Shri spoke to Janardana. Kamala said, "O lord! Save your own servant, Garuda. He is facing a calamity." At this, Janardana spoke to Nandi, Shambhu's servant. Vishnu said, "Take the *naga* and Garuda to Shambhu's presence.

---

[529] The one seated on the lotus, Shri/Lakshmi.

When Maheshvara looks at Garuda, through his favours, Garuda will get back his own form again." Thus addressed, the bull,[530] the *naga* and Garuda slowly went to Shankara and told him everything. Shankara, with the moon on his forehead, spoke to Garuda. Shiva said, "O mighty-armed one! Go to Goutami Ganga, the purifier of the worlds. She is serene and grants all the objects of desire. Once you have bathed in her, you will get your form back. You will accomplish hundreds and thousands of your wishes. There are those who are tormented by all kinds of sins. There are those whose efforts are ruined by adverse destiny. Such beings obtain their desires through Goutami. O bird! Seek refuge with her." Hearing his words, Garuda prostrated himself and went there. Bathing in Ganga, Garuda bowed down to Shiva and Vishnu. The bird's body turned golden and became as firm as the *vajra*. He became immensely strong. O best among sages! The intelligent one speedily rushed to Vishnu. Since then, that place has been known as Garuda *tirtha* and yields all the objects of desire. O son! It is a place loved by Shiva and Vishnu. Anything that a man does there, bathing and other rites, bring inexhaustible benefits.'

Chapter 2(21) (Govardhana *tirtha*)

Brahma said, 'There is Govardhana *tirtha*. It destroys every kind of sin. For the ancestors, it generates everything that is auspicious. Even if it is remembered, it destroys sins. O Narada! I have witnessed its powers. There was a brahmana known as Jabali. He was a farmer. Even when the sun touched midday, he did not release his two bulls. He struck them on the back and on the sides with his whip. On seeing those two bulls with their eyes full of tears, Surabhi,[531] the mother of the universe, who yields all the objects of desire, told Nandi everything. He was also distressed and told

---

[530] Nandi.
[531] The celestial cow, the mother of all cattle.

Shambhu everything. Shambhu told the bull,[532] "Everything that you say will come true." With Shiva's permission, Nandi took away all the cattle species. All the cattle, in heaven and in the mortal world were swiftly destroyed. The large number of gods came to me and said, "Without cows, it is impossible to live." I told all the gods, "Go to Shankara and ask him." All of them praised Isha and told him what needed to be done. Isha told the gods, "My bull knows everything." The immortals spoke to the bull. "Give us the cows and the bulls. They give us benefits." The bull told the gods, "Perform the sacrifice known as *gosava*. Through this, you will get back all the cattle, divine as well as human." Thus, the sacrifice of *gosava*, devised by the gods, was started on the auspicious banks of Goutami and cattle flourished. This *tirtha* of Govardhana[533] enhanced the pleasure of the gods. O best among sages! If one bathes there, this yields the fruits of donating thousands of cows. We do not know the fruits of performing even a little bit of donations there.[534] If one sees Goutameshvara Shankara,[535] the lord of the gods, one obtains the world of heaven for as long as Meru lasts.'

Chapter 2(22) (Papapranashana *tirtha*)

Brahma said, 'There is a *tirtha* named Papapranashana.[536] It dispels fear of sins. I will tell you how it came by that name. O Narada! Listen attentively. There was a brahmana who was known in the worlds as Dhritavrata. His wife was named Mahi. She was young and was the most beautiful woman in the world. Their son was known as Sannajata and he was like the sun in complexion. O sage! Death, urged by Kala took Dhritavrata away. She became a

---

[532] Nandi.

[533] Literally, the place where cattle flourish.

[534] Meaning, they are so many that they cannot be described.

[535] There is more than one Goutameshvara temple. This must be the one in Manthani, in Telangana.

[536] Literally, the destroyer of sins.

young widow who was extremely beautiful and she had a young son. Unable to see a protector, she went to Galava's hermitage. After entrusting his son to him, the *svairini*, confounded by sin, wandered around in many countries. She followed her desires and sought out men. In Galava's house, the son became accomplished in the Vedas and the *Vedanga*s. However, because of the sins of his mother, ever since he was born, his mind turned towards courtesans. There is a place known as Janasthana and it was full of people from different classes.[537] Mahi lived there, surviving as a woman who sold herself. Her lecherous son also wandered around in many countries. Under the subjugation of destiny, he came to reside in Janasthana. Desiring women, the brahmana who was Dhritavrata's son looked for a harlot. Mahi also waited for men who would give her some wealth. She did not know her son and the son did not know his mother. As a result of destiny, there was intercourse between the mother and the son. In this way, many days passed and the son used to have intercourse with the mother. They possessed no knowledge about their mutual relationship of being a mother and a son. Though this was his conduct, he possessed sufficient knowledge to follow his father's *dharma*. O Narada! Listen to the wonderful event that occurred. Though he acted as he willed, the brahmana did not give up the rituals practiced at the time of *sandhya*. When this was done, he sought to earn wealth. Because of the strength of his learning, he earned a lot of riches and gave it to her. In the morning, he would get up and go to Ganga to perform the rituals. He purified himself, bathed and observed all the *sandhya* rites in the due order. Having done this, he would bow down before *brahmanas* and be cleansed of his sins. When he went to Goutami in the morning, he was ugly. His limbs were lax because of leprosy and pus and blood would flow. Having bathed in Goutami Ganga, he would become exceedingly handsome. He was peaceful and resembled the sun or the fire. He seemed to be the embodied form of the sun. The brahmana was himself not aware that he possessed two different forms.

'The illustrious Galava was devoted to austerities and *jnana*. At that time, surrounded by sages, he sought refuge in Goddess

---

[537] We have translated *jati* as class, to distinguish it from *varna*.

Goutami. The brahmana always came to that *tirtha*. Bowing down before Galava, he always went to his own residence. Galava always noticed both of the brahmana's forms—the form that Sannajata possessed before bathing in Ganga and the brahmana's form after bathing and the *sandhya* rites. On seeing this, he was astounded and wondered, "What is the reason for this?" Full of amazement, Galava spoke to the brahmana, just as Sannajata was leaving for his house, after bowing down before his *guru*.[538] Because of wonder and compassion, the intelligent one carefully summoned him. Galava asked, "Who are you? Where will you go? What do you do? What do you eat? What is your name? Where do you sleep? Who is your wife? Please tell me." Hearing Galava's words, the brahmana replied to the sage. The brahmana said, "I will tell you everything tomorrow. Knowing this, one should determine what needs to be done." Telling Galava this, Sannajata went home. Having eaten properly, he lay down at night with the courtesan. Suddenly remembering Galava's words, he addressed her in these words. The brahmana said, "You possess all the qualities. Though you are a courtesan, you behave like a woman who is devoted to her husband.[539] Our love is mutual and similar. We should live like this for the rest of our lives. Nevertheless, there is something I must ask you. What is your name? What is your family? Where do you come from? Who are your relatives? Tell me everything." The courtesan replied, "There was a brahmana known as Dhritavrata. He was initiated and pure. I am his wife, Mahi. My son is in Galava's hermitage. I left him there. The child is intelligent and is known as Sannajata. Because of my former sins, I abandoned my *dharma* and my family and came here. O brahmana! Though I am residing here as a *svairini*, know that I am a brahmana lady." When he heard her words, it was as if his inner organs were pierced. He suddenly fell down on the ground. The courtesan addressed him in these words. The courtesan asked, "O best among *brahmanas*! What has happened to you? Where has your love gone? Have the words I spoke led to a change in your feelings?" Comforting and reassuring

---

[538] Galava had taught Sannajata.
[539] Since they were living as man and wife.

himself, the brahmana addressed her in the following words. The brahmana replied, "The brahmana, Dhritavrata was my father. I am his son, Sannajata. Goaded by destiny, my mother, Mahi, has come here." Hearing his words, she became extremely miserable. Both of them grieved throughout the night.'

'When the sparkling sun dawned, the brahmana went to Galava, the tiger among sages and told him everything. The brahmana said, "O brahmana! I am the son of Dhritavrata. You had reared me earlier. O lord! My mother, Mahi and I have come before you. What shall I do? How will I be cleansed?" Hearing the brahmana's words, Galava became full of compassion and spoke these words. "I had earlier noticed the two forms in you every day. That is the reason I had asked you about your account. I have heard and understood everything. Everything that you did was cleansed as soon as you went to Ganga. Through the greatness of this *tirtha* and through the favours of the goddess, you were cleansed every day. O son! There is nothing to think about. Every day and every morning, your form used to be full of sin. Thereafter, I have seen your form, possessing all the qualities. When you came, you were full of sin. When you departed, you were without blemish. I have witnessed this every day. You have now been purified by the goddess. Therefore, there is nothing else that remains to be done. O brahmana! This mother of yours is known as a courtesan. However, she has repented and has refrained from sinning again. O son! For all creatures, affection is a natural attribute. But if one associates with virtuous people, great merits are reaped and through destiny, one can achieve *nivritti*. Because of her earlier good conduct, she has repented a lot. Bathing in this *tirtha*, she will become purified." O Narada! The mother and the son acted accordingly. When they bathed, there is no doubt that they were cleansed of their sins. Since that time, this *tirtha* has been known as Dhoutapapa.[540] It is also famous as Papapranashana and Galava. Whether one commits a grave sin or a trifling sin, all sins are destroyed at Dhoutapapa. It bestows extremely great merits.'

[540] *Dhoutapapa* means a place where sins are washed a away. *Papapranashana* means a place where sins are destroyed. The meanings are effectively identical.

Chapter 2(23) (Vishvamitra *tirtha*)

Brahma said, 'O brahmana! To its south,[541] there is an extremely rare *tirtha*. It is known as Pitri *tirtha*. It is sacred and destroys all sins. O brahmana! Along with Sita, Dasharatha's son, Rama, offered oblations and satisfied the ancestors[542] there. That is the reason it is known as Pitri *tirtha*. Bathing, donating and offering oblations to the ancestors there, brings everlasting benefits. There is no need to think about this. This is the place where Dasharatha's son Rama, Indra among kings, worshipped the great sage Vishvamitra and the other sages who know about the truth. This is the extremely sacred Vishvamitra *tirtha* and it bestows great benefits. I will tell you about its nature, as it has been read by those who know about the Vedas. Earlier, there was a drought that was extremely terrible for subjects. Along with his disciples, the immensely wise Vishvamitra arrived at Goutami. He saw that his disciples, sons and wife were suffering from hunger and were emaciated. Miserable, the resplendent Koushika[543] spoke to his disciples. Vishvamitra said, "Get whatever can be obtained, wherever. Without any delay, get something that can be eaten. Go and bring it back quickly." Hearing the *rishi*'s words, the hungry disciples quickly left. Wandering around here and there, they saw a dead dog. Picking this up, they quickly returned and offered it to their preceptor. Saying, "This is good," he accepted it with his hand. "Slice up the dog's meat. Wash it with water. Utter the *mantras* and cook it. Follow the norms and offer oblations into the fire. When the gods, *rishis*, ancestors, *atithis*, *gurus* and others have been satisfied, we will eat what is left." This is what Koushika said. Hearing Vishvamitra's words, the disciples acted accordingly.

'When the flesh of the dog had been cooked, Agni, the messenger of the gods, went to the abode of the gods and told the gods everything. Agni said, "Since the *rishi* has thought of

541 South of Papapranashana *tirtha*.
542 *Pitris*.
543 Vishvamitra was descended from Kusha and is, hence, known as Koushika.

this, the gods must now eat a dog's flesh." At Agni's words, Indra assumed the form of a hawk. He flew through the sky and stole the vessel that was full of the flesh.' Witnessing his deed, the disciples went and told the *rishi* about the hawk. 'O best among sages! The hawk has no sense and has stolen the vessel.' The illustrious one was enraged and desired to curse Hari.[544] Learning this, the lord of the gods filled the vessel with honey. With the speed of a meteor, Hari, in the form of a bird, placed the vessel back. On seeing that it was filled with honey, Vishvamitra became angry. Glancing at the vessel, Koushika spoke in rage. Vishvamitra said, "Please take away this excellent *amrita* and give us the dog's flesh. Otherwise, I will reduce you to ashes." Terrified, Indra replied. Indra said, "Follow the norms and offer oblations of honey. Drink it with your sons. O great sage! Why this flesh of a dog? It is not suitable for an offering." Vishvamitra said, "No. What is gained if I am the only one who gets to eat? All the subjects are suffering. O Hari! What purpose will your honey serve? If everyone gets to eat the *amrita*, then I will also eat the pure *amrita*. Otherwise, let the gods and the ancestors also eat the flesh of a dog. Thereafter, I will also eat that flesh. I do not utter a falsehood." Scared, the one with the one thousand eyes instantly summoned the clouds. They showered down *amrita* and this *amrita* satisfied the subjects. When this had been done, the brahmana, Vishvamitra, followed the rituals and used the sacred *amrita* given by Hari to first satisfy the gods and the three worlds. Along with his disciples and wife, he then ate it. Since then, that *tirtha* has been described as one that confers great merits. It is a place where the lord of the gods came and *amrita*, without meat, was offered. Because of this, that *tirtha* brings great benefit to men. Bathing and donating there bestows the fruits of all sacrifices. Since then, it has been known as Vishvamitra *tirtha*. The *tirtha* is also named after Madhu, Indra, Shyena and Parjanya.'[545]

[544] Indra.

[545] *Madhu* is honey, *shyena* is a hawk and Parjanya is the god of rain, that is, Indra.

Chapter 2(24) (Shveta and other *tirthas*)

Brahma said, 'The auspicious place known as Shveta tirtha is famous in the three worlds. Even if a person remembers it, he is freed from all sins. Earlier, there was a brahmana named Shveta and he was Goutama's beloved friend. He resided on the banks of Goutami and was always devoted to worshipping *atithis*. In his thoughts, words and deeds, he was devoted to Shiva. The best among *brahmanas* always meditated on Shiva and worshipped him. Till the end of his life, that excellent brahmana was devoted to Shiva. The messengers of the lord of the southern direction came to take him away.[546] O Narada! However, they were incapable of entering his house. When the time passed, Chitraka spoke to Mrityu.[547] Chitraka said, "O Mrityu! Why has Shveta not arrived yet? His lifespan is over. Mrityu's servants have also not returned. This is not appropriate." Mrityu became angry and himself went to Shveta's house. He saw Mrityu's messengers standing outside the house, scared. Mrityu asked the messengers, "O messengers! What is the matter?" The messengers replied, "Please pardon us. Shveta is protected by Shiva and we are incapable of looking at him. If Girisha[548] is pleased with a person, he has no reason to be afraid." With a noose in his hand, Mrityu entered the place where the brahmana was. The brahmana did not realize that Mrityu and Yama's messengers had come. He was devotedly worshipping Shiva. Nandi saw Mrityu, noose in his hand, approach Shveta and was amazed. Nandi said, "O Mrityu! What are you looking at here?" Mrityu replied to Nandi. Mrityu said, "I have come here to take Shveta away. Therefore, I am looking at the excellent brahmana." Nandi replied, "Go away." O tiger among sages! However, Mrityu hurled his noose towards Shveta and Nandi became angry. Nandi struck Mrityu with the staff given by Shiva. With the noose in his hand, Mrityu fell down on the ground. The messengers saw that Mrityu

---

[546] When he died, Yama's messengers came.

[547] Chitraka/Chitragupta maintains a record of a person's good and bad deeds. Mrityu is Death.

[548] Shiva.

had been struck down. They swiftly went to Yama and reported that Nandi had struck Mrityu down. At this, Dharma Yama was enraged. Astride his buffalo, he summoned Chitragupta, Kala, the protector in the form of Yama's staff, the buffalo, *bhutas*, *vetalas*,[549] physical ailments, mental ailments, diseases of the eyes, diseases of the stomach, diseases of the ears, the three kinds of fever,[550] and the different kinds of sins and hells. Yama asked them to hurry. Surrounded by all these, Yama went to the place where Shveta, supreme among *brahmanas*, was. Seeing Yama advance, Nandi raised his weapon and spoke to Vinayaka, Skanda and the leader of the *bhutas*, who held a staff. A clash ensued and it was fearful to all beings. Kartikeya used his spear to pierce Yama's servants. He powerfully struck the lord of the southern directions himself. Those of Yama's followers who were left went and reported this to Aditya. Along with the gods, Aditya heard of this extraordinary event. Surrounded by the guardians of the worlds, they approached me. I, the illustrious Vishnu, Indra, Agni, Varuna, Chandra, Aditya, the two Ashvins, the guardians of the world, the large number of Maruts and many others went to Yama. The powerful lord of the southern directions was lying down on the banks of Ganga, dead. The oceans, the rivers, the *nagas* and many kinds of beings gathered there to see the lord of the gods, Vaivasvata Yama. Seeing that Yama and his soldiers had been killed, the gods were afflicted by fear. All of them joined their hands in salutation and repeatedly praised Shambhu. The gods said, "You are always favourable towards your devotees and slay those who are wicked. You are the original creator. We bow down before you. O Nilakantha![551] We bow down before you. O one who loves Brahma! We bow down before you. O one who loves the gods! We bow down before you. The brahmana Shveta is devoted to you. His lifespan came to an end, but Yama and all the others were incapable of taking him away. Glance at us with great contentment. You love your devotees. You are truly the

---

[549] Ghost or goblin.

[550] Relating to *adhidaivika* (destiny), *adhibhoutika* (nature) and *adhyatmika* (one's own nature).

[551] The one with a blue throat, Shiva's name.

protector. You are the refuge of those who seek refuge with you. You are compassionate. Even Kritanta[552] is incapable of looking at you. O Shiva! Having learnt this, all of them are worshipping you with great devotion. You are the protector of the universe. You are the lord of the universe. O lord! With your exception, who is capable of ordaining anything?" Praised in this way, Shiva appeared in front of them. Cheerfully, he asked the gods, "What can I give you?" The gods replied, 'Vaivasvata controls *dharma* in all those with bodies. He is a guardian of the world and establishes the practice of *dharma* and *adharma*. He does not deserve to be killed. He has not committed a crime. He is no sinner. Without him, the task of holding up the world cannot be undertaken. O lord of the gods! Therefore, along with his soldiers and mounts, please revive him. O protector! A request made to a great person is never futile.' The illustrious one replied, 'If the gods agree to what I say, there is no doubt that Yama will come back to life.' All the gods said, 'We will certainly act in accordance with your words. Along with Hari and Brahma, the entire universe is under your control.' At this, the illustrious one told the assembled immortals, 'Let my devotee not die.' The immortals replied, 'That is not possible. Everything in the worlds, mobile and immobile, will then become immortal. O lord who pervades the universe! There will be no difference between the mortal and the immortal.' Shambhu spoke again. 'Listen to my words. Vishnu and I are the lords of those who are devoted to me and those who are devoted to Vishnu. If such devotees come to Goutami, Mrityu will have no control over them. Let Yama never act against this agreement. They should never suffer from physical ailments or mental ailments. Anyone who seeks refuge with Shiva will be instantly emancipated. Yama and all his followers should bow down before them.' All the gods told Shiva, the lord of the gods, that they agreed to this. The illustrious lord then spoke to his mount, Nandi. Shiva said, 'Sprinkle the dead Yama with water from Goutami.' Nandi sprinkled Yama and all the others. All of them were revived and arose. They left for the southern direction.'

---

[552] Yama.

'Vishnu and all the other gods remained on the northern bank of Goutami. Remaining there, they worshipped Maheshvara, the lord of the gods. There are eight thousand, fourteen thousand, six thousand and six thousand *tirtha*s there.[553] There are six thousand and three thousand *tirtha*s on the southern bank.[554] O Narada! I have described to you the sacred account of Shveta *tirtha*. The place where Mrityu fell down is known as Mrityu *tirtha*. Even if one hears about it, one lives for one thousand years. Bathing and donating there, destroy all sins. If one hears or reads about it, or remembers it, all impurities are destroyed. For everyone, it bestows objects of pleasure and emancipation.'

Chapter 2(25) (Shukra *tirtha*, Mritasanjivani *tirtha*)

Brahma said, 'The place known as Shukra *tirtha* brings every kind of success to men. It destroys every kind of sin. It destroys every kind of ailment. The two *rishi*s, Angiras and Bhrigu, were extremely devoted to *dharma*. Both of them had sons who were extremely wise. They possessed beauty and intelligence. They were known as Jiva and Kavi and they were devoted to their parents.[555] On seeing that the sons had been initiated, fathers spoke to each other. The *rishi*s said, "Our sons are always controlled. Therefore, only one of us needs to be the instructor. The other one can do as he wills." Hearing this, Angiras quickly spoke to Bhrigu.[556] "I will teach them equally. O Bhrigu! Do what you will.' Hearing the words of Angiras, Bhrigu agreed with Angiras and entrusted Shukra to Angiras. However, since he was partial in his attitude, he taught the two sons separately. After some time, Shuka spoke.

---

[553] There are thirty-four thousand *tirtha*s on the northern bank.

[554] Nine thousand on the southern bank. However, this is written in such a way that one can also obtain an aggregate of thirty-six thousand.

[555] The son of Angiras was Jiva/Brihaspati, while Bhrigu's son was Kavi/Shukracharya.

[556] The text says Bhargava, though Bhrigu is intended.

Shukra said, "O *guru*! You always discriminate in the way you teach me. It is not appropriate for a *guru* to differentiate between sons and disciples. Only foolish and ordinary teachers differentiate between disciples. If a person's intelligence causes discrimination, his sins become innumerable. O *acharya*![557] I have understood you correctly. I bow down before you repeatedly. I will go to another *guru*. Please grant me permission. O brahmana! I will go to my father. If his behaviour is also discriminatory, I will go somewhere else. O lord! Please grant me permission to leave.' He, thus, took leave of his *guru* and also took Brihaspati's leave. He thought he would go to his father after having obtained learning. Therefore, he thought, "Who will be my *guru*? Who will be the best?" Thinking in this way, he asked the immensely wise and aged Goutama. Shukra asked, "O best among sages! Please tell me. Who is a *guru*? Who, in the three worlds, can be my *guru*? I will go to that *guru*." He told him, "The divinity Shambhu, the lord of the universe, is the *guru* of the universe." Shukra asked, "How can I see the lord of the gods? How can I worship Girisha?" Thus addressed, Goutama replied to him. Goutama said, "Go to Goutami and purify yourself. Praise Shankara with hymns. When he is pleased, the lord of the universe will bestow learning on you." Hearing Goutama's words, Bhargava[558] first went to Ganga. The child bathed and purified himself and praised in the proper way. Shukra said, "O lord of the distressed! You are the only refuge. O Shambhu! I seek refuge with you. I am a child. My intelligence is that of a child. O lord who wears the young moon! I do not know anything about how one should praise you. I bow down before you. I have been abandoned by my *guru*. I do not have well-wishers or friends. You are my lord in every possible way. O lord of the universe! I bow down before you. O god! You are heavier than the heaviest.[559] You are greater

---

[557] Here, the text uses the word *acharya*. Unless used synonymously, in the hierarchy of teachers, *upadhyaya* is inferior to *acharya* and *acharya* is inferior to *guru*. There is an intended slight in this address.

[558] Bhrigu's descendant, Shukracharya.

[559] The word *guru* means heavy, as well as preceptor. There is, thus, a double meaning.

than the greatest. I am only a slight child. O one who pervades the universe! I bow down before you. O lord of the gods! I have come to you for the sake of learning. I do not know anything about your ways. Look on me with compassion. O witness to the worlds! I bow down before you." Praised in this way, the lord of the gods was pleased. Shiva said, "O fortunate one! Ask for your desired boon, even if it is extremely difficult for the gods to obtain." Joining his hands in salutation, Kavi, extensive in his intelligence, spoke to the lord of the gods. Shukra said, "There is learning that Brahma and the others, the noble *rishi*s, do not have access to. O lord! I seek that learning from you. You are my *guru*. You are my divinity." The knowledge of Mritasanjivani[560] is unknown even to the gods. When Shukra asked, the best among the gods bestowed that on him. That apart, he gave him general knowledge from the Vedas, unknown to others. When Shankara is pleased, where is the need to think about what remains? Having obtained this great knowledge, he went to his father. Kavi was worshipped because of his learning and became the *guru* of the *daityas*. On another occasion, because of a different reason, Brihaspati's son, Kacha, obtained this knowledge from Kavi. Brihaspati obtained this from Kacha and the different gods also separately obtained it. This great knowledge is known of as Mritasanjivani. This is the knowledge Kavi obtained after worshipping Maheshvara. Shukra *tirtha* is said to be on the northern bank of Goutami. This is Mritasanjivani *tirtha*. It grants a long lifespan and freedom from disease. Anything undertaken there, bathing and donating, confers inexhaustible good merits.'

Chapter 2(26) (Seven thousand *tirtha*s)

Brahma said, 'The famous Indra *tirtha* destroys the sin of killing a brahmana. Even if a person remembers it, a large number of sins and hardships are destroyed. O Narada! Earlier when Vritra was killed, the sin of killing a brahmana pursued and terrified Hari,

---

[560] The knowledge of bringing the dead (*mrita*) back to life (*sanjivani*).

Shachi's consort. Indra, Vritra's slayer, rushed around here and there, but it also followed him. Wherever he went, that sin of killing followed Indra. He entered a great lake and hid inside the stalk of a lotus. Hiding inside the fibres, Shachi's consort resided there. The sin of killing waited on the shores of the lake for one thousand divine years. O sage! During all this time, the gods were without an Indra. They anxiously consulted among themselves, "How can we possibly get an Indra?" Thinking about the place where the slaying had taken place, I told the gods, "For the sake of purifying Indra, sprinkle him with water from Goutami. When he is sprinkled in this way, Indra will again turn pure." Making up their minds to do this, they quickly went to Goutami. The gods and the *rishi*s wished to bathe the lord of the gods there. All of them desired to sprinkle Shachi's beloved there. However, as Indra was about to be sprinkled, Goutama angrily spoke to them. Goutama said, "You wish to sprinkle the great Indra. He is wicked and has violated his *guru*'s bed.[561] O noble gods! Leave swiftly. Otherwise, I will reduce all of you to ashes." Hearing the *rishi*'s words, they left Goutami. Taking Indra with them, they quickly went to Narmada. They stood on the northern bank of Narmada, ready to sprinkle him. As Indra was about to be sprinkled, the illustrious *rishi* Mandavya spoke to them. He said, "If you sprinkle him, I will reduce all of you to ashes." The immortals worshipped Mandavya and praising him, reasoned with him. The gods said, "This Indra possesses one thousand eyes. O sage! In whichever place he is sprinkled, terrible impediments present themselves. O one who bestows boons! Therefore, be pleased with us and perform a rite of pacification. Let us perform this rite of cleansing and we will give you many boons. All of us will give you a place. Therefore, you should grant us permission. The spot where the great Indra is sprinkled will give men every object of pleasure. It will be full of grains and trees laden with fruit. There will never be any drought or famine there." Mandavya, best among sages and worshipped by the worlds, agreed to this. For the sake of cleansing impurities, the sprinkling took place there. The gods and

---

[561] This is a reference to the Ahalya incident.

the sages spoke of that region as Malava.[562] When he was sprinkled, the lord of the gods became sparkling again. They brought Goutami Ganga and performed the rite of purification. The gods, the *rishi*s, I, Vishnu, Vasishtha, Goutama, Agastya, Atri, Kashyapa, other *rishi*s, gods, *yaksha*s and *pannaga*s bathed him with the pure water and sprinkled him. I also sprinkled Shachi's husband with water from my *kamamdalu*. From this, two rivers resulted—Punya and Sikta. There is a confluence of Ganga with Sikta. Since then, those two confluences are famous and are always frequented by sages. Since then, that confluence has been spoken of as Punya *tirtha*.[563] The sacred confluence of Sikta is known as Aindra *tirtha*.[564] There are seven thousand auspicious *tirtha*s there. Bathing and donating there, especially at the confluences, should be known to bestow inexhaustible benefits. There is no need to think about this. If a person reads or hears this sacred account, he is freed from all sins committed through thoughts, words and deeds.'

Chapter 2(27) (Poulastya *tirtha*)

Brahma said, 'The place known as Poulastya *tirtha* yields every kind of success for men. I will tell you about its powers. It bestows kingdoms that have been destroyed. Earlier, the lord of the northern directions[565] possessed every kind of prosperity and success. Earlier, he was the lord of Lanka and was Vishrava's eldest son. His brothers were strong and extremely resplendent. They were Ravana, Kumbhakarna and Vibhishana, and they were his step-brothers. They too were Vishrava's sons. However, since their mother was a *rakshasa* lady, they were *rakshasa*s.[566] On Pushpaka

[562] Derived from *mala* (dirt/impurity). Malava is the Malwa region.
[563] The confluence of Punya. Punya might the river Purna.
[564] Sikta might therefore be the river Indravati.
[565] Kubera.
[566] Vishrava was the son of Pulastya. Kubera was the son of Vishrava and Ilavida, while Ravana and his brothers were the sons of Vishrava and

vimana, Dhanada, along with his brothers, always used to faithfully come to me and go back. Ravana's mother became angry and spoke to her sons. Ravana's mother said, "I won't live. Because of this disparity, I would much rather die. It is said that the gods and the *danava*s are step-brothers.[567] To win over prosperity and bring it under their control, they seek to kill each other. Therefore, you are not men. You are not capable. You do not desire victory. If a person seeks permission from a rival, his life is futile." O sage! Hearing their mother's words, the three brothers went to the forest to perform austerities. They performed great austerities. The three *rakshasa*s obtained boons from me. Because of the instigation of their maternal uncle, Maricha and their maternal grandfather and because of their mother's words, he[568] asked for Lanka. Because of their *rakshasa* sentiments and because of their mother's words, there was great enmity between the brothers. There was a battle between them, like that between the gods and the *danava*s. In the clash, he defeated his elder brother, the serene Dhanada. He took away everything, Pushpaka and the city of Lanka. In the three worlds and among all mobile and immobile objects, Ravana made an announcement. "Anyone who offers refuge to my brother deserves to be killed by me." The banished brother, Vaishravana,[569] did not find shelter anywhere. He went to his grandfather Pulastya. Bowing down, he addressed him in the following words. Dhanada said, "I have been expelled by my wicked brother. Please tell me what I should do. Where will I find refuge and shelter, or a divine *tirtha*?" Hearing his grandson's words, Pulastya replied in the following words. Pulastya said, "O son! Go to Goutami and praise the divinity Maheshvara. He will not be able to enter there in the midst of Ganga's waters. You will obtain fortune and success. Act in accordance with my words." Dhaneshvara[570] agreed and

---

Kaikasi (also known as Nikasha or Keshini). Dhanada means the lord of riches and is one of Kubera's names.

[567] They were born through different wives of the sage Kashyapa.

[568] Ravana.

[569] Kubera.

[570] The same as Dhanada.

went there along with his wife, his father, his mother and the aged Pulastya.

'Having gone to Goutami Ganga, he bathed and purified himself. He controlled himself and followed the vows. He praised the lord of the gods, Shiva, who bestows objects of pleasure and emancipation. Dhanada said, "You are the lord of everything mobile and immobile in the universe. O Shambhu! There is nothing superior to you. Because of delusion, if a person brags about ignoring you, one should grieve about him. You are radiant in all your eight forms. Everything happens because of your command. Nevertheless, there are those who are ignorant about you. They do not know about your ancient glory. Something was born from your dirt and Amba[571] laughingly said, 'O divinity! This is your brave son.' You glanced at it and Vighnaraja was born. This is what happens through Isha's glance. On seeing that the couple was separated, Girija's eyes filled with tears and she spoke to Isha.[572] Bhava's mind led to Madana being born again. Because of you and Uma, he and Rati obtained complete good fortune." Praised in this way, the one with the three-eyes manifested himself before him. He asked him to choose a boon. However, because of his delight, he did not say anything. Dhanada and Pulastya were both silent. Maheshvara repeatedly asked him to choose a boon. Shiva was delighted. Meanwhile, an invisible voice was heard to speak to Maheshvara. "He should become the protector of riches. It was only after ascertaining the minds of Pulastya and Vaishravana's father that the invisible voice uttered these auspicious words. The future should be like the past. What is received should be what was received earlier. What is given should be what was given earlier.[573] He has many enemies. He has suffered a great deal of grief. He has worshipped Someshvara *lingam*.[574] He deserves to be a lord of the directions and a lord of riches. He should become generous with many wives and sons." These were

---

[571] Parvati, Shiva's wife.

[572] Shiva burnt down Kama and Kama and Rati (Kama's wife) were thus separated. Girjia means daughter of the mountain, that is, Parvati.

[573] That is, Kubera should regain his earlier status.

[574] This must be the one in Nashik.

the auspicious words of the divine voice. Hearing these words, Dhanada told the lord of the gods, the one who wields a trident, "Let it be this way." Telling Dhanada that it would be that way, the lord of the gods approved of the divine words. Shiva, the lord of the gods, honoured Pulastya, the sage Vishrava and the protector of riches with these boons and departed. Since then, the spot has been known as Poulastya[575] *tirtha*, Dhanada *tirtha* and Vaishravasa *tirtha*. It is sacred and auspicious and yields every object of desire. Bathing and all the other rites undertaken there yield many good merits.'

Chapter 2(28) (Agni *tirtha*)

Brahma said, 'The place known as Agni *tirtha* yields the fruits of all sacrifices. It destroys every kind of impediment. Hear about the fruits of this *tirtha*. Agni's brother is known as Jataveda. He is Havyavat.[576] In a sacrifice that took place in the abode of the *rishi*s, along the banks of Goutami, Agni's excellent brother was bearing *havya* for the gods. He was accomplished and was loved by his brother. While the foremost *rishi*s and the gods looked on, Madhu, Diti's powerful son, slew him. With Jataveda dead, no one carried *havya* to the gods. Agni's beloved brother, Jataveda, was killed. Filled with great rage, he entered Ganga's waters. When Agni entered Ganga's waters, gods and men gave up their lives because it is held that they owe their lives to Agni. All the gods, *rishi*s and ancestors went to the place where Agni had entered the waters. They especially praised Agni. "We cannot live without Agni." Seeing their beloved Agni inside the water, the residents of heaven spoke. The gods said, "The gods survive through *havya* and the ancestors survive through *kavya*. Men survive through cooking food and seeds survive when they are moistened." Agni told the

---

[575] Meaning descendant of Pulastya.

[576] Jataveda and Havyavat/Havyavahana (the bearer of oblations) are usually given as Agni's names.

gods, "Since my younger brother has gone, I am incapacitated.
Your task will not be accomplished. However, since Jataveda has
gone, I will also follow him. O gods! I am not interested in carrying
out your task. Your task was always carried out by Jataveda. Since
he has been reduced to this state, I do not know what will become
of me. I will no longer possess the strength to pervade this world
and the next world. Even if I try to carry out the task, I will not
possess the speed." Full of emotions, all the gods and the *rishi*s
spoke. "You will be given a lifespan, love for work and pervasive
strength. O Havyavahana! We will give you the oblations offered
before the sacrifice and the oblations offered after the sacrifice.[577]
You are the excellent mouth of the gods. The first oblations will be
for you. O supreme god! We will enjoy the objects that are offered
to you." At the words of the gods, Vahni[578] was pleased and in
due order, pervaded this world and the next world and bore *havya*
and *kavya*. Because of the command of the gods, Vahni became
fearless and capable everywhere. He is spoken of as Jataveda,
Brihadbhanu, Saptarchi, Nilalohita, Jalagarbha, Shamigarbha and
Yajnagarbha.[579] The gods took Vibhavasu out of the water and
consecrated him. Agni goes everywhere and obtained two places
to reside in.[580] The gods returned to wherever they had come from.
That place is known as Agni *tirtha*. There are seven hundred *tirtha*s
in the spot, possessing all the qualities. If one goes there, controls
oneself and bathes and donates, one obtains the auspicious fruits
of a successful horse sacrifice, performed with the use of fire. It is
known as Deva *tirtha*, Agni *tirtha* or Jataveda *tirtha*. There is a
lingam of many complexions there, established by Agni. If a person
beholds the divinity there, he obtains the fruits of all sacrifices.'

[577] Respectively, *prayaja* and *anuyaja*. These will be Agni's share.

[578] Agni.

[579] All of these are Agni's names. They respectively mean: the origin of
the *Veda*s, the extremely radiant one, the one with seven rays, the blue-red
one, the one hidden in water, the one hidden inside a *shami* tree and the one
inside a sacrifice. Vibhavasu is also one of Agni's names, meaning the one
with a wealth of light.

[580] Heaven and earth.

Chapter 2(29) (Rinamochana *tirtha*)

Brahma said, 'Those who know the Vedas know the name of Rinapramochana *tirtha*.[581] I will tell you about its nature. O Narada! Listen attentively. Kakshivan had a favourite son named Prithushrava. Because of his non-attachment, he did not marry. Nor did he worship the fire. O sage! Though his younger brother was capable, he was scared of becoming a *parivetta*.[582] He did not perform the rites for ascending to heaven. Nor did he worship the fire. The large number of ancestors spoke these auspicious words separately to the elder brother, Kakshivan and to the younger brother. The ancestors said, "For the sake of repaying the three types of debts, let the marriages be performed."[583] The elder responded, "That will not happen. Who has incurred a debt?" The younger told the ancestors, "It is not appropriate that I should marry. O immensely wise ones! While I have an elder brother, I am scared of becoming a *parivetta*." The grandfathers spoke to both of them again. The ancestors said, "O sons of Kakshivan! Both of you go to the sacred Goutami. Bathing in Goutami yields everything one wishes for. Go to Goutami Ganga. She purifies everything in the three worlds. Full of devotion, bathe and perform the water-rites. When one sees her, bathes in her and meditates on her, Goutami bestows everything that is desired. The rules of place, time and *jati* do not apply for bathing there. The elder brother will be freed from the debt and the younger brother will not become a *parivetta*." At this, the elder brother, Prithushrava bathed and performed the water-rites. Kakshivan's son was freed from the three types of debt he owed to the worlds. Since then, that place has been spoken of as Rinamochana *tirtha*.[584] O Narada! By bathing and donating there,

---

[581] Rinamochana is the same as Rinapramochana.

[582] A *parivetta* is someone who marries or accepts a share in a sacrifice before his elder brother. By not worshipping the fire, what is meant is that Prithushrava did not worship the householder's fire.

[583] The debt to gods is repaid through sacrifices, that to ancestors is repaid by obtaining sons and that to the sages is repaid through studying.

[584] Release (*mochana*) from debt (*rina*).

a person becomes happy and is freed from debts mentioned in the *shruti* and *smriti* texts and also from all other debts.'

Chapter 2(30) (Kadru and Suparna *tirtha*)

Brahma said, 'There are two confluences named after Kadru and Suparna.[585] On the banks of Ganga, the divinity Maheshvara resides there. There are sacrificial altars for fire there, named after Rudra, Vishnu, Surya, Soma, Brahma, Kumara and Varuna. There is the confluence of the river Apsara with Ganga. Even if a man remembers that *tirtha*, he becomes successful in every venture. It destroys every kind of sin. O Narada! Hear about it attentively. Earlier, the *valakhilya maharshi*s were harmed by Indra. Having given up half of their stores of austerities, they spoke to the sage Kashyapa. The *valakhilya*s said, "Use this to have an auspicious son who will rob Indra of his insolence. We are giving you half of our stores of austerities." The sage agreed to this. The Prajapati impregnated Suparna's womb. The brahmana also slowly impregnated Kadru, the mother of snakes, with snakes. When both of them conceived, Prajapati wished to leave and spoke to them. "You must not commit an offence and you must not go anywhere. If you go elsewhere, there is no doubt that you will be cursed." Having spoken to his two wives in this way, he left. When their husband departed, both of them went to a sacrifice performed by *rishi*s who had cleansed their souls. The place was populated by large numbers of *brahmanas* and was on the banks of Ganga. Since both of them were proud of their youth and prosperity, they behaved in this mad way. They were repeatedly restrained by sages who possessed the insight of truth. Nevertheless, they spoilt the hymns and oblations of the sacrifice.[586] Who is master enough to control the dark and fickle minds of women? On seeing that both of them had traversed along this perverse path, the *brahmanas* were agitated. "Since you

---

[585] Elsewhere, Suparna is called Vinata.
[586] Presumably because pregnant women shouldn't have gone there.

have followed this perverse path, both of you will become rivers with contrary flows." Thus, Suparna and Kadru became rivers.'

'After some time, Kashyapa Prajapati returned home. From the *rishi*s, he heard in detail about what they had done and how they had been cursed. Hearing this, he was amazed and became immersed in thoughts. "What will I do?" He spoke to the *rishi*s known as *valakhilya*s. They told the brahmana Kashyapa, "Go to Goutami Ganga and worship Mahesha. They will then again become your wives. Scared of the sin of having killed a brahmana,[587] the divinity Maheshvara always resides in the middle of Ganga and is known as Madhyameshvara."[588] Addressed in this way, Kashyapa, who was observant in his vows, bathed in Ganga. He praised Maheshvara, the lord of the gods, through sacred hymns. Kashyapa said, "He alone is the lord of the three worlds. He does not possess the slightest bit of pride about where he resides. He is Siddhanatha,[589] the creator of the entire universe. He is Shivaa's[590] consort. Let him be pleased. Embodied creatures and mobile and immobile objects are extremely scorched from the heat of the three kinds of hardships[591] and are running around here and there. You are the one who is competent to dispel their miseries. You possess the three kinds of yoga related to *sattva* and the others,[592] and Shakra and the others are incapable of describing this. You are the one who should be worshipped. Thinking about Soma's wonderful behaviour,[593] a man is always happy and becomes devoted to donating." Shiva, loved by Gouri was praised in these and other ways. Shambhu was pleased and gave Kashyapa many kinds of boons. He was looking for his wives and he told him, "Your two wives will have the forms of rivers. In

[587] A reference to Shiva having sliced off one of Brahma's heads. The sin pursued him.

[588] This is Nandur Madhmeshwar in Nashik district, along the banks of Godavari.

[589] The lord of success.

[590] Parvati's.

[591] Relating to *adhidaivika* (destiny), *adhibhoutika* (nature) and *adhyatmika* (one's own nature).

[592] Relating to *sattva*, *rajas* and *tamas*.

[593] A reference to the moon on Shiva's head.

that form, your two wives will reach Ganga, best among rivers. As soon as they unite with her, they will regain their own forms once again. Through Ganga's favours, they will become pregnant once again." In this way, the great-minded Prajapati got his two wives back and was delighted. He invited the *brahmanas* who had sought refuge on Goutami's banks. Pleased, Prajapati performed their *simantonnayana* rite.[594] In accordance with the prescribed norms, he fed the *brahmanas*. The *brahmanas* had their food in Kashyapa's house. Standing near her husband, Kadru looked at the *brahmanas*. Kadru glanced at the *rishi*s with slanted eyes and laughed at them. They were disturbed and said, "O wicked one! You have laughed at us with evil eyes. Your eyes have committed a sin. Let them be slanted." At this, Kadru became blind in one eye and is known as the mother of snakes. Kashyapa pacified the illustrious *rishi*s. Pleased, they continued, "Goutami is supreme among rivers. If one frequents her, she protects against one thousand sins." Along with his wives, Kashyapa, supreme among sages, did this. Since then, their confluences have been known as *tirtha*s. Kadru is in all directions and River Souparnika[595] is to the east. The *tirtha* of Jatadhara[596] is more sacred than Varanasi. It destroys every kind of sin and yields the fruits of every kind of sacrifice.'

Chapter 2(31) (Confluence of Sarasvati)

Brahma said, 'Those who know about the Vedas speak about the *tirtha* of Pururava. Even if one remembers it, all sins are destroyed, not to speak of when one sees it. Pururava went to Brahma's assembly. He saw the divine river, Sarasvati. In Brahma's

[594] The *simantonnayana samskara* means parting the hair and is performed in the 4th month of pregnancy.

[595] Named after Suparna. There is a Souparnika river in Andhra Pradesh, but this should be near Nashik. Kadru is probably the river named Kadva.

[596] There is a Jatadhari river in Odisha, but this may not be the same one.

presence, she was laughing as she willed. Seeing her store of
beauty, the lord of the earth spoke to Urvashi. The king asked,
"Who is this virtuous and beautiful lady who is standing next
to Brahma? She is best among all the women and is illuminating
this place." Urvashi replied, "She is the auspicious river of the
gods, Sarasvati. She is Brahma's daughter. She always comes to
this place and returns." Hearing this, the amazed king said, "Bring
her to my presence." Urvashi again replied to the king, who was
copious in his donations. Urvashi replied, "O great king! I will tell
her everything and bring her." Delighted, the king sent Urvashi
to her. Having gone there, Urvashi reported the king's words.
Sarasvati agreed to what Urvashi had said. She pledged to do that
and went to the place where Pururava was. He found pleasure
on the banks of Sarasvati for many years. She had a son named
Sarasvan and Sarasvan's son was Brihadratha. I saw that Sarasvati
was going to the king's house every day. I got to know about
Sarasvan and about everything else that she had done. Therefore, I
cursed her, "Become a great river." Scared of my curse, Vagisha[597]
went to the goddess Goutami, the sacred mother who originated
from the *kamandalu* and purifies the worlds. She is the one who
dispels the three kinds of hardships and bestows what is desired
in this world and in the next world. Having gone to the goddess
Goutami, she reported everything about the curse, starting at the
beginning. Ganga told me, "You should free her from this curse.
It is not appropriate that you should impose a curse on Sarasvati.
Her nature is feminine and women desire men. O Brahma! All
women are naturally fickle. O one who is seated on a lotus! O
one who created the universe! How is it that you don't know this?
Whose nature does Kama not cause a disturbance in?" I freed her
from the curse and said, "Sarasvati will also be visible." Because
of the curse in the world of the mortals, Sarasvati is both visible
and invisible. Distracted by her curse, there is a spot where she
united with the divine Ganga. Pururva, supreme among kings and
devoted to *dharma*, went there. He tormented himself through

---

[597] Meaning, goddess of speech, that is, Sarasvati.

austerities and worshipped the divinity, Hara Siddheshvara.[598] Through Ganga's favours, he obtained everything that he desired. Since then, that has been spoken of as Pururava *tirtha*. It is also known as Sarasvati's confluence and Brahma *tirtha*. The divinity Siddheshvara is there and he grants everything that one desires.'

Chapter 2(32) (Five *tirtha*s)

Brahma said, 'The sages know that there are five sacred *tirtha*s— Savitri, Gayatri, Shraddha, Medha and Sarasvati. If one bathes there and drinks the water, one is freed from all sins. Savitri, Gayatri, Shraddha, Medha and Sarasvati were my daughters, created for the sake of establishing *dharma*. Among them, the eldest[599] was the most beautiful. I had created her as the most beautiful woman in the world. O supreme sage! On seeing her, my intelligence turned perverse. Full of desire, I tried to seize her. On seeing me, the maiden fled. The maiden assumed the form of a doe and I assumed the form of a stag. For the sake of preserving *dharma*, Shambhu assumed the form of a hunter who killed deer.[600] Scared of me, the five daughters went to Ganga, the great river. Maheshvara also went there and for the sake of preserving *dharma*, picked up his bow and arrow. Isha spoke to me, as I was in the form of a stag. Hara, as a hunter of deer, told me, "I will kill you." Therefore, I refrained from the act and bestowed the maiden on Vivasvat. The five daughters, Savitri and the others, assumed the form of rivers. They returned to the world of heaven again and approached me. O Narada! There are five *tirtha*s where the goddesses united.[601] The confluences of the five rivers, Sarasvati and the others, are sacred. If a man bathes, donates,

---

[598] This should be the one in Kaygaon Toka in Ahmednagar. In that case, Pravara would be the river Sarasvati.

[599] Sarasvati is usually the daughter Brahma pursues. But here, the eldest daughter seems to be Usha, distinct from Sarasvati.

[600] Shiva assumed this form and pursued Brahma.

[601] With Godavari.

or does anything else there, all the objects of desire are obtained. It is said to confer emancipation and freedom from *karma*. The *tirtha* of Mrigavyadha[602] is also there and it bestows everything that men want. It is said to bestow the fruits of heaven and emancipation. It is also said to bestow the fruits of Brahma *tirtha*.'

Chapter 2(33) (Shami *tirtha*)

Brahma said, 'The place known as Shami *tirtha* pacifies every kind of sin. I will tell you about its account. O Narada! Listen attentively. There was a *kshatriya* named Priyavrata and he was supreme among victorious ones. On the southern banks of Goutami, his priest initiated him for a horse sacrifice and he was surrounded by officiating priests and *rishi*s. Vasishtha was the mighty-armed king's chief priest. A *danava* named Hiranyaka arrived at the sacrificial arena. On seeing the *danava*, the gods, with Indra at the forefront, were terrified. Some went to heaven and Havyavat entered a *shami* tree. Vishnu entered an *ashvattha* tree, Bhanu entered an *arka* tree and Shiva entered a *vata* tree. Soma went to a *palasha* tree.[603] Havyavahana entered the waters of Ganga. The two Ashvins seized the horse and Yama became a crow. Meanwhile, the illustrious *rishi*, Vasishtha, grasped a staff and commanded the *daitya* to stop. Though the *daitya* possessed his own strength, he went away and the sacrifice commenced again. These spots became auspicious *tirtha*s and bestowed the fruits of ten horse sacrifices. The first *tirtha* is known as Shami, the second is named after Vishnu. The other *tirtha*s are named after Arka, Shiva, Soma and Vasishtha. They yield every object of desire. When the extensive sacrifice was completed, all the gods and *rishi*s were satisfied. Delighted, they repeatedly spoke to Vasishtha, Priyavrata, who had performed the sacrifice and the trees and Ganga. "People have gone here and there

---

[602] Hunter (*vyadha*) of deer (*mriga*).

[603] *Asvattha* and *vata* are holy fig trees, *palasha* is a tree with red blossoms and *arka* is the sun-plant.

to undertake horse sacrifices. But these *tirtha*s will yield the fruits of horse sacrifices." This is what the gods said. Thereafter, bathing and donations at those *tirtha*s have yielded the fruits of a sacred horse sacrifice. Those words were not false.'

Chapter 2(34) (Twenty-two thousand *tirtha*s)

Brahma said, 'There are sacred *tirtha*s named after Vishvamitra, Harishchandra, Shunahshepa, Rohita, Varuna, Brahma, Agni, Indra, Indava, Ishvara, Mitra, Vishnu, Yama, the Ashvins and Ushanas. Hear from me about them. In the Ikshvaku lineage, there was a king named Harishchandra. Narada and Parvata came to his house. Having offered them hospitality in the proper way, Harishchandra spoke to the two *rishi*s. Harishchandra said, "For the sake of a son, people undertake hardships. What is obtained through a son? A son may be learned or ignorant, excellent or middling. O *rishi*s! I have always had a doubt about this. Please tell me." Parvata and Narada replied to Harishchandra. Narada and Parvata said, "O king! There can be one, ten, one hundred, or one thousand different answers. However, the proper answer is said to be the following. O supreme among kings! For a person without a son, the world hereafter does not exist. For such an evil-doer, this world does not exist either. O lord of men! A father who bathes after a son has been born, obtains the fruits of consecrating himself for ten horse sacrifices. When a son is born, a person is established and becomes like a best among immortals. The gods become immortals through *amrita*, *brahmana*s and others through sons. A son releases his father and grandfather from the three kinds of debts. Without a son, what does one get from roots? What does one get from water?[604] What does one get from growing a beard? What does one get through austerities? O Indra among kings! A son is said to lead to heaven and emancipation. The son is the world hereafter, the son is success in the pursuit of *dharma*, *artha* and

---

[604] Respectively, surviving on roots, or on water.

kama. The son is emancipation. The son is the supreme light. The son enables all embodied beings to cross over.[605] O Indra among kings! Anything given without a son, any oblations offered without a son, indeed without a son, birth itself is futile. That is the way it appears to me.[606] A son frees from the debt. Sons make a person free from blemish. If a father lives to see the birth and behold the face of a son who remains alive, he enjoys all the objects of pleasure obtained in the world of mortals or in the firmament. When a father sees a son, he obtains everything. Therefore, there is nothing in the three worlds that is desired as much as a son." Hearing this, the king's mind was amazed and he asked again. Harishchandra asked, "How can I obtain a son? Please tell me accurately. I will endeavor to make every kind of effort and practice every kind of manliness. So that I can get a son, I will use *mantra*s, sacrifices and donations." They heard what Harishchandra, the best among kings said, desiring a son. They meditated properly for a while and said, "O one who bestows honours! Go to Goutami. There, the lord of the waters bestows any excellent object that is in one's mind. The sages have said that Varuna bestows everything. If he is pleased, over a period of time, you will have a son." Hearing the words of the sages, the best among kings acted accordingly.'

'He resorted to the banks of Goutami and satisfied Varuna. Varuna was content and spoke to Harishchandra. Varuna said, "O king! You do not possess sons and have tried to follow vows. I will give you a son, provided that you certainly offer that son in a sacrifice." Harishchandra promised Varuna that he would offer him in a sacrifice. Leaving the place, Harishchandra prepared a *charu*[607] that was offered to Varuna. The king offered this to his wife and a son was born to the king. When the son was born, the lord of the waters, supreme among those who bestow boons, spoke. Varuna said, "Remember the words you spoke earlier. Offer the son today." When Varuna appeared in front of him, Harishchandra replied, "An

---

[605] Cross the ocean of *samsara*.

[606] Though both sages are speaking, the word 'me' is used.

[607] *Charu* is an oblation of rice, barley and pulses, cooked in butter and milk.

animal is fit for a sacrifice only after ten days have passed. I will perform the sacrifice thereafter." Hearing the king's words, Varuna returned to his own abode. When ten days had passed, he appeared again and asked the king to undertake the sacrifice. The king told Varuna, "Unless an animal has teeth, the sacrifice is futile. O lord of the waters! Go now and return when the animal has teeth." Hearing the king's words, the lord of the waters went away again. O Narada! When the son was seven years old, the teeth appeared. He again asked the king to undertake the sacrifice. The king replied, "O lord of the waters! These teeth will fall off. I will perform the sacrifice when other teeth grow. Please go away now." O Narada! When the permanent teeth appeared, Varuna appeared again and said, "O king! Perform the sacrifice." But the king replied to the lord of the waters. The king said, "O lord of the waters! If it is a *kshatriya*, he becomes an excellent animal for a sacrifice only when he has learnt *dhanurveda*."[608] Hearing the king's words, Varuna went away to his own abode. Rohita,[609] scorcher of enemies, became accomplished in the use of *astra*s and *shastra*s, all the Vedas and all the sacred texts. Having attained the age of sixteen years, Rohita became the heir apparent. The delighted Varuna went to the place where the king and Rohita were and said, "Sacrifice your son now." The best among kings agreed. While Varuna heard, the lord of the earth spoke to the officiating priest and to Rohita, his eldest son. Harishchandra said, "O extremely brave son! Come. I will offer you in a sacrifice to Varuna." Rohita asked his father, "What is this?" Thereupon, his father told him in detail what had transpired. While Varuna heard, Rohita spoke to his father. Rohita said, "O great king! I will first purify himself and along with the officiating priests and the chief priest, quickly offer a sacrifice to Vishnu, the lord of the worlds. Varuna will be the sacrificial animal. O lord! Please grant me permission." Hearing Rohita's words, the lord of the waters was

---

[608] The art of fighting.

[609] The son's name. The text uses both *astra* and *shastra*. These are both weapons and the words are often used synonymously. However, an *astra* is a weapon that is hurled or released, while a *shastra* is held in the hand.

overwhelmed with great rage. Astride his chariot, wielding a divine bow and arrow, he departed.'

'Rohita, King Harishchandra's son, went to the forest where Harishchandra, lord of men, had worshipped Varuna. Rohita went to the place along the Ganga where he[610] had obtained a son. Five years had passed and the sixth year had started. The king's son remained there. He heard the king was suffering from the ailment of dropsy.[611] "Through the birth of a son like me, my father is being made to suffer from this hardship. What fruit has he obtained? What will I do now?" This is what he thought. On those sacred banks, the king's son saw some *rishi*s. He saw an excellent *rishi* wandering around along the banks of Ganga. The aged rishi was named Ajigarta and he was followed by his three sons and his wife. Lacking a means of subsistence, they were emaciated. On seeing him, the king's son bowed down and addressed him in these words. Rohita asked, "You seem to be distressed in your mind and are emaciated, lacking a means of subsistence. Why is this?" Ajigarta replied to Rohita, the king's son. Ajigarta said, "I have no means of sustaining my body. I have many who need to be fed. Without food, we will die. Tell me. What can we possibly do?" Hearing this, the king's son spoke to the *rishi* again. Rohita said, "O supreme among eloquent ones! Please tell me what is on your mind." Ajigarta replied, "I do not possess gold, silver, cattle, grain or garments. O tiger among kings! It is evident that I do not possess a means of subsistence. I have three sons and a wife and I am the fifth. O supreme among kings! There is no one who will purchase one of us for food." Rohita asked, "O immensely intelligent one! O Ajigarta! Who will you offer for purchase? Tell me truthfully. There is nothing else that you need to say. *Brahmanas* are truthful in speech." Ajigarta said, "Take one of the three sons or me or their mother, my wife. If you purchase one of us, we will remain alive." Rohita replied, "O immensely intelligent one! What will I do with your wife? Since you are aged in form, what will I do with you? Give me one of your young sons, whichever son you wish to give." Ajigarta said, "O Rohita! I will

---

[610] Harishchandra.
[611] Varuna had inflicted Harishchandra with this.

not sell my eldest son, Shunahpuccha. The mother will not sell the youngest one. I will sell the son in the middle, Shunahshepa. Tell me about the riches you will give." Rohita replied, "A man must be thought of as a sacrificial animal to Varuna. He must possess the qualities. O great sage! If you are willing to sell him, tell me the price truthfully." Thus addressed, Ajigarta told him about the price he expected for his son. "O prince! One thousand cows, grains, gold coins and garments—give me this excellent price and I will give you my son." Agreeing to this, Rohita gave him garments and riches. Having given this to him, Rohita went to his father with the *rishi*'s son. He told his father about the purchase of the *rishi*'s son. Rohita said, "With this as an animal, perform the sacrifice to Varuna and be freed of your ailment." When his son had spoken, Harishchandra replied. Harishchandra said, "It has been said that a king must protect *brahmanas*, *kshatriyas* and *vaishyas*. In particular, supreme *brahmanas* are best among the *varnas*. They are worshipped by Vishnu, not to speak of people like me. If kings show them disrespect, they destroy their own lineages. All the *tirtha*s exist in *brahmanas* and all the gods are also in them. They are the ones who save men who descend into hell. If I make such a person suffer by making him a sacrificial animal, how can I say I protect them? It is not proper that I should make a brahmana a sacrificial animal. It is better that I die as a result of this ailment. How can I make a brahmana a sacrificial animal? O son! That is the way I will act. Along with the brahmana, leave happily." At this time, an invisible voice was heard.'

'The voice spoke from the sky, "O Indra among kings! Along with the officiating priests and the chief priest, go to Goutami. Take the brahmana's son as a sacrificial animal and take Rohita, your son. Your task is to perform the sacrifice without Shunahshepa getting killed. O immensely intelligent one! The sacrifice will be completed there." Hearing these words, the excellent king swiftly went to Ganga along with *rishi* Vishvamitra, the chief priest Vasishtha, the *rishi* Vamadeva and other sages. Having reached Goutami Ganga, he consecrated himself for a *naramedha* sacrifice.[612] He arranged

---

[612] A sacrifice at which a human being (*nara*) is sacrificed.

for the altar, pavilion, sacred pit, sacrificial stake and other
things. When everything had been arranged in the proper way, the
sacrifice commenced. With *mantras* being chanted, Shunahshepa
was tied to the sacrificial stake as a sacrificial animal. Seeing
that water was being sprinkled over him, Vishvamitra spoke the
following words, especially to the gods, the *rishis*, Harishchandra
and Rohita. Vishvamitra said, "I seek leave from all of you about
Shunahshepa, the excellent brahmana. Oblations are going to be
separately offered to the gods. In particular, I seek leave from all of
you about Shunahshepa. With *mantras*, oblations of fat, body hair,
skin and flesh will be offered into the fire, along with Shunahshepa,
the excellent brahmana. I entreat you. Let all the Indras among
brahmanas be sprinkled with water. Let the Indras among *brahmanas*
go to Goutami and bathe separately. Let them praise the gods with
mantras and hymns. Let everything be auspicious and let them leave
happily. O sages and gods! Please save him and enjoy the oblations."
The sages agreed to this and so did the excellent king. Shunahshepa
also went to Ganga, the purifier of the three worlds. He bathed and
praised the gods, the ones who partake of oblations. O sage! The
large number of gods were satisfied. While Vishvamitra heard, all
the gods spoke to Shunahshepa. The gods said, "Let the sacrifice be
completed without Shunahshepa being killed." In particular, Varuna
also spoke to the excellent king. The king's *naramedha* sacrifice,
famous in the worlds, was completed. Through the favours of the
gods, through the favours of the sages and through the favours of
that *tirtha*, the king's sacrifice was completed. In that assembly,
Vishvamitra honoured Shunahshepa. In the presence of the gods, he
honoured him and adopted him as his son. Koushika[613] made him
the eldest of his sons. The other sons of the intelligent Vishvamitra
did not accept Shunahshepa as the eldest son and Koushika cursed
them. He honoured only those of his sons who accepted him as
the eldest son. The tiger among sages bestowed boons on them. I
have thus told you everything that happened on the southern bank
of Goutami. There are sacred *tirthas* there, famous even among
the gods. O immensely intelligent one! There are many names.

---

[613] Vishvamitra.

Hear about them from me. They are named after Harishchandra, Shunahshepa, Vishvamitra, Rohita and others. There are twenty-two thousand such *tirtha*s. Bathing and donating there yield the fruits of a *naramedha* sacrifice. O supreme sage! I have described the greatness of the *tirtha* to you. If a person hears, reads or makes heard this account faithfully, he obtains everything that pleases his mind. A man without sons gets a son.'

Chapter 2(35) (Confluences of twenty-five rivers)

Brahma said, 'There is a place known as Soma *tirtha*. It enhances the delight of the ancestors. An extremely sacred event transpired there. O Narada! Listen attentively. Earlier, King Soma, full of *amrita*, was the king of the *gandharva*s and not of the gods. The gods came and spoke to me. The gods said, "Earlier, Soma used to bestow life on the gods. But he has been taken away by the *gandharva*s. Unable to meditate on him, the large number of gods and *rishi*s are extremely miserable. You should think of a policy so that Soma belongs to us again." At this, Sarasvati[614] spoke to the gods. "The *gandharva*s are extremely attached to women. O gods! Give me to them and take back Soma." The immortals replied to Sarasvati, "Please pardon us. We are incapable of giving you away. We are incapable of existing without him, or without you." Sarasvati spoke to the gods again. "I will come to you again. We must use our intelligence to think of a means to undertake an excellent sacrifice. Let it be performed on the southern bank of Goutami. If the gods are prepared to come, let a place be found for the sacrifice. Let the best among gods come. The *gandharva*s are always attached to women. Using me as a price, get him[615] back." The gods agreed to the words Sarasvati had spoken. Messengers of the gods were separately sent to gods, *yaksha*s, *gandharva*s and *pannaga*s. They

---

[614] The text uses the word Vak, meaning Sarasvati, the goddess of speech.

[615] Soma.

were invited to that sacred and divine mountain. O sage! Since then, that mountain has been known as Devagiri. Large number of gods, *gandharvas*, *yakshas*, *rakshasas*, *siddhas*, *rishis* and the eight species[616] of inferior gods arrived there. On the banks of Goutami, the *rishis* performed a great sacrifice. Surrounded by the gods, the one with one thousand eyes spoke. In Sarasvati's presence, Indra honoured the *gandharvas* and said, "Take Sarasvati as a price and give us *amrita*." The *gandharvas* were attached to women. Hearing Shakra's words, they accepted Sarasvati and gave the gods Soma. The immortals got Soma and the *gandharvas* got Sarasvati. While residing there, the goddess of speech always came to see the gods secretly and spoke to them in a low voice. O Narada! That is the reason why one must always speak in a low voice when purchasing *soma*.[617] The purchase of Soma took place in that way. Thus, the gods possessed both Soma and Sarasvati. The *gandharvas* had neither Soma, nor Sarasvati.'

'For the sake of Soma, all of them came to the banks of Goutami—cows, gods, mountains, *yakshas*, *rakshasas*, *siddhas*, *sadhyas*, sages, *guhyakas*, *gandharvas*, Maruts, *pannagas*, all the herbs, the mothers of the worlds, the guardians of the worlds, Rudras, Adityas, Vasus, the two Ashvins and all the other gods who were entitled to shares of the sacrifice. O sage! Twenty-five rivers merged into Ganga. The place where complete oblations were offered is spoken of as Purna.[618] I have spoken about the confluences all of them had with Ganga. *Tirthas* were named after them. O Narada! I will tell you about them briefly. There were Soma *tirtha*, Gandharva *tirtha*, Deva *tirtha*, Purna *tirtha*, Shala, the confluence of Shriparna, the confluence of Ila, the sacred confluence of Kusuma, the place known as the confluence of Pushti, the auspicious confluence of Karnika, the confluence of Vainavi, the

---

[616] This probably means *apsaras*, *kinnaras*, *vidyadharas*, *guhyakas* and the like. The number eight is difficult to pin down, since *gandharvas*, *yakshas*, *rakshasas* and *siddhas* have already been separately mentioned. It is also possible that the eight Vasus are meant.

[617] There should not be any confusion between Soma, the moon-god, and *soma*, the drink.

[618] The word *purna* means complete.

confluence of Krisharasa, the confluence of Vasavi, Shiva, Sharya, Shikhi, Kusumbhika, Uparathya, Shantija, Devaja, Aja, Vriddha, Sura and Bhadra.[619] All of them merged into Goutami. There were many other male and female rivers from earth that went along as companions to that *tirtha* of Devaparvata.[620] For the sake of Soma, there were others who went to the sacrificial pavilion. In due order, their confluences with Ganga became *tirtha*s. There were some in the form of female rivers, there were others in the form of male rivers. There were some in the form of lakes, there were others that were in the form of streams. All of these separate *tirtha*s are famous. Bathing, *japa*, oblations and water-rites performed for the ancestors there yield all the objects of desire. A man obtains objects of pleasure and emancipation. If a person remembers it or reads about it, he is freed from all sins and goes to Vishnu's city. There are twenty rivers between Purna and Pravara. They are the daughters of divine rivers. Taken together, twenty-five have been spoken about.'

Chapter 2(36) (Amrita and other confluences)

Brahma said, 'At the confluence of Pravara, the great river is the best.[621] The divinity Siddheshvara, who brings welfare to all beings is there. There was an extremely terrible clash between gods and *danava*s. O great sage! However, they became affectionate towards each other. The gods and the *danava*s consulted each other. Desiring to do what would be good for each other, they went to Mount Meru. The gods and *daitya*s said, "*Amrita* ensures immortality. Therefore, let us generate the excellent *amrita*. When we drink it, all of us will become immortal. Uniting ourselves, we will happily rule over the worlds. Giving up all conflict, we will get

[619] There are actually twenty-four names. So perhaps Shriparna is meant to be two separate rivers, Shri and Parna. Or it is possible that Pravara should be added to the list.

[620] The same as Devagiri.

[621] The confluence of Pravara and Godavari is in Ahmednagar district.

it. Conflict is the cause of miseries. We will obtain riches through affection and abandoning jealousy, enjoy it. Affectionate conduct has always brought happiness to us. We must never remember our perverse conduct. The happiness one obtains through lack of enmity alone is not obtained through lordship over the three worlds or through an elevated status." In this way, the gods and *danava*s became affectionate towards each other. Having united and become extremely happy, they churned Varuna's abode.[622] They made Mandara the churning rod and made Vasuki the rope used for churning. All the gods and *danava*s churned Varuna's abode. As a result, the sacred *amrita*, loved by the gods, was generated. When the sacred *amrita* had been produced, they spoke to each other. "Having accomplished the intended task, we are exhausted. Let us go to our respective abodes. As is appropriate, let this be distributed equally. O excellent gods! At an auspicious moment, when all of us have assembled, let this sacred *amrita* be divided among us." Saying this, all the *daitya*s, *danava*s and *rakshasa*s departed. When the large number of *daitya*s left, all the gods consulted amongst themselves. The gods said, "Our enemies, the scorchers of enemies, have left, trusting us. This *amrita* must never be given to the enemies." Brihaspati agreed with this and spoke to the gods. Brihaspati said, "Drink the *amrita* in such a way that the wicked ones do not get to know. So that the enemies are defeated, this is the apt advice. Those who are conversant with good policy know that those who cause hate must be hated in every possible way. One must not trust or be friendly with enemies. They should not be consulted. They should not be given *amrita*. Otherwise, they will become immortal. When those who are naturally our enemies, the *daitya*s, become immortal, we will be unable to defeat them. Therefore, they must not be given *amrita*." The gods consulted among themselves and spoke to Vachaspati.'[623]

'The gods asked, "Where will we go? Where will we consult with each other? Where will we drink? Where will we base ourselves? O lord! O Vachaspati! We must first do that. Please tell us." Brihaspati

[622] The ocean.
[623] Vachaspati means Brihaspati.

replied, "O immortals! Go to Brahma and ask him about this supreme objective. The grandfather is the one who knows, speaks and gives." Hearing Brihasapati's words, they came before me. All the gods bowed down before me and told me what had happened. O son! Hearing their words, along with the gods, I went to Hari. Vishnu was told everything and so was Shambhu, the one who destroys poison. I, Vishnu, Shambhu, the gods, the *gandharvas* and the *kinnaras* went to a cave in Meru. The *asuras* did not know. Having decided to drink *soma* there,[624] Hari was appointed as the guard. Aditya was to keep track of who had partaken of the *soma*. Soma[625] was given the task of apportioning out the *amrita*. The wielder of the *chakra* was the guard. The *daityas*, *danavas* and *rakshasas* did not know of this. The only exception was the immensely wise Rahu, Simhika's son. He drank *soma*. He could assume any form at will. Assuming the form of a Marut, Rahu sat down amidst them. In the form of a Marut, he held up the drinking-vessel. Soma gave the *daitya amrita*. However, Divakara[626] got to know that this was a *daitya* in the form of a god. He went and told Vishnu that Soma had given him *soma*. While the *daitya* was drinking *amrita*, Vishnu severed his head with his *chakra*. O son! Though the head was quickly severed, it became immortal. Without the head, the body fell down on the ground. O tiger among sages! When the body which had touched *amrita*, fell down on the southern bank of Goutami, the earth trembled. O son! This was extraordinary, but the body also became immortal. The body needed the head and the head needed the body. Both became immortal and therefore, the *daitya* became extremely strong.'

'All the gods were scared. "If the body gets united with the head, he will devour all the gods. Therefore, we must first destroy the body, which has fallen down on the ground." The gods spoke to Shankara. The gods said, "O excellent god! Please destroy the body that has fallen down on the ground. O divinity! You are an ocean of compassion. You protect those who seek refuge with you. Please

---

[624] *Soma* is being used as a synonym for *amrita* here.

[625] The moon-god, not to be confused with *soma*.

[626] A name for the sun-god.

act so that the *daitya*'s head does not unite with his body." Isha sent
the excellent Shakti, part of his own being. She is the mother who
protects the worlds. The goddess went, along with the other mother
goddesses. The goddess wielded Isha's weapon. She possessed Isha's
powers. She went to the place where the body had fallen down on
the ground, wishing to devour it. All the gods pacified the head by
placing it on Meru. The goddess and the body fought for many
years. Rahu told the gods, "Pierce my body first. There are excellent
juices inside. Take them out from the body. The excellent juices
inside the body are the excellent *amrita*. When they are taken out,
the body will be reduced to ashes in an instant. Therefore, take
them out first." Hearing Rahu's words, all the enemies of the *asura*s
were delighted. They happily consecrated him as a planet and said,
"You will become a planet." Hearing the words of the gods and
strength of the gods, Shakti, also spoken of as Ishvari, pierced the
body of the lord of the *daitya*s. She swiftly extracted the excellent
amrita outside. Thereafter, having placed the body there, Ambika
devoured it. Extremely strong, she is spoken of as Kalaratri and
Bhadrakali. The juice that had been extracted was an excellent juice.
It oozed out from the place where it had been kept and became the
river Pravara.[627] Once the *amrita* had been extracted, the body was
placed there and devoured. After this, the excellent river Pravara
originated. She is auspicious and is full of *amrita*. She emerged from
Rudra's body and possesses Rudra's powers. She is beautiful and is
the best among rivers. She originated from *amrita*. There are five
thousand *tirtha*s there and they possess all the qualities. Shambhu,
worshipped by the gods, is himself always present there. Satisfied,
all the gods happily bestowed separate boons on the divine river.
"As long as Shambhu, the lord of the gods is worshipped, you will
also be worshipped by the worlds. O goddess! For the welfare of
the worlds, reside here. May Isha's juices always remain with you.
May you bring every kind of success to everyone. When you are
praised, eulogized and meditated upon, you will bestow every kind
of desire. Those who desire anything will always devotedly bow
down before you. Through the command of the gods, all their tasks

---

[627] The word *pravara* means excellent.

will be accomplished. Both Shiva and Shakti will always reside here." Therefore, the sages speak of this place as Nivasapura.[628] In ancient times, extremely happily, the gods bestowed these boons on Pravara. Her confluence with Ganga is famous and is loved by the gods. Those who bathe there obtain objects of pleasure and emancipation. They satisfy the wishes that are in their minds, even those that are extremely difficult for the gods to obtain. Having granted her everything, the gods departed. Since then, that *tirtha* has been known as the confluence of Pravara. She originated from Shakti, who in turn was sent by the lord of the gods. The great river of Pravara is known by the name of Amrita. Bathing, donations and other rites undertaken at the confluence of Pravara bring eternal benefits and learning. They bring delight to the ancestors.'

Chapter 2(37) (Vriddha Sangama)

Brahma said, 'There is a place known as Vriddha Sangama. Vriddheshvara Shiva is present there.[629] I will tell you about the account, which destroys sins. Listen. There was a sage in Goutama's lineage. He was a great ascetic and was known as Vriddha. In earlier times, the brahmana, descended from Goutama's lineage, did not have a nose. Therefore, he was originally disfigured in form. Full of non-attachment, he wandered around in various regions and *tirtha*s. Since he was ashamed, he did not approach any preceptor. Since he was ashamed, he could not study with fellow disciples either. He somehow managed to go to his father, Goutama. After teaching him, Goutama went out on his travels. For a long period of time, the brahmana was nurtured by his brahmana mother. Though he had descended from Goutama, he did not study. Nor did Goutama's son study the sacred texts. However, he was always firm in his vows and performed the fire rites. He also practiced the chanting of *gayatri mantra*. He was a brahmana only in name,

[628] Meaning the city of residence.
[629] The temple in Parthardi Taluka in Ahmednagar.

though he performed the fire rites and chanted the *gayatri mantra*. O sage! This was all there in terms of Goutama's son being a brahmana. The great-souled one worshipped the fire and chanted *gayatri mantra*. Goutama's son possessed a long lifespan and his age increased. He could not obtain a wife because no one would bestow his daughter on him. Therefore, he roamed around in many regions and *tirtha*s and many kinds of forests. Goutama's son wandered around in sacred hermitages. While wandering around, Goutama's son arrived in the cold mountains. He found a beautiful cave there, covered with creepers and trees.'

'Making up his mind to reside there, the Indra among *brahmanas* entered it. When he entered, he saw an excellent woman there. Her limbs were flaccid and she was emaciated. She was aged, engaged in austerities. Practising *brahmacharya*, she was still a maiden and lived in isolation. Seeing her, the best among sages stood there, ready to bow down. However, as Goutama's son, the best among sages, was about to bow down, she restrained him. The aged woman said, "You will become my *guru*. You should not worship me. If a *guru* bows down, the disciple's lifespan, learning, riches, fame, *dharma*, heaven and everything else are destroyed." Goutama's son was amazed. He joined his hands in salutation and spoke. Goutama's son replied, "You are an ascetic lady. You are aged. You are superior to me in qualities and are beautiful. Relatively, I possess little learning. I am also younger in age. How can I possibly be your *guru*?" The aged woman said, "O one who is excellent in vows! In this connection, there is an ancient account. I will tell you about it. Arshtishena had a son who was known as Ritadhvaja. He possessed the qualities and was intelligent. He was brave and followed the *dharma* of *kshatriyas*. On one occasion, his mind was attracted to the idea of hunting and he came to his forest. To rest, Ritadhvaja entered this cave. He was young and intelligent. He was accomplished and was surrounded by a large army. While the best among kings was resting, he saw an *apsara*. She was the daughter of the king of *gandharva*s and was known as Sushyama. The king saw and desired her and she saw and desired the king. O immensely intelligent one! There was an act of sexual intercourse between her and the king. When the desire was satisfied, the Indra among kings sought her permission to leave for his own home. O immensely wise one! I was born as Sushyama's daughter. O store of austerities! As she was leaving, my mother spoke to me. Sushyama said, 'O fortunate one! Whoever enters this cave will become your husband.' O immensely wise one! Saying this, my mother departed. Since then, no man other than you has entered. After ruling over the kingdom for eighty thousand years, my father tormented himself through austerities and has now gone to heaven. O tiger among sages! After my father went to heaven, my brother ruled over the kingdom for ten thousand years. However, he has also gone to heaven and I alone am left. O brahmana I have not had relationships with anyone. I possess neither a mother, nor a father. O brahmana! I alone decide what I will do. I am the daughter of a *kshatriya* and I am attracted to you. O brahmana! Therefore, accept me. I have been observing the vows and have been in search of a man." Goutama's son replied, "O fortunate one! I am one thousand years old and you are senior to me in age. In relative terms, I am but a child and you are aged. Hence, our union is not possible." The aged woman said, "You have formerly been ordained as my husband. In my view, there is no one else who can be my husband. You have been given to me by the ordainer himself. Therefore, you should not refuse me. I have not been defiled and am ready to follow you. Nevertheless, if you do not desire me, while you look on, I will now give up my life. For all embodied creatures, death is superior to not getting what one has been waiting for. If one gives up one's life for someone one is attached to, no sin results from that." Hearing the aged lady's words, Goutama's son replied in the following words. Goutama's son said, "I do not possess austerities. I do not possess learning. I possess nothing. I am not an appropriate groom for you. I am disfigured and do not have any objects of pleasure. I do not possess a nose. I do not possess either austerities, or learning. What will I do? O auspicious one! Therefore, I must first become handsome and possess learning. After that, I will act in accordance with your words." The aged lady spoke to the brahmana. The aged lady said, "O brahmana! Through my austerities, I have satisfied the goddess Sarasvati. In that way, I have also satisfied the beautiful water and Agni, who grants form. Therefore, the goddess of speech will bestow learning on you. Agni, the god of beauty will bestow a handsome form on you." Having told Goutama's son this, the aged lady spoke to Vibhavasu.[630] She desired excellent learning and supreme beauty for the sage. He became extremely learned and extremely fortunate. He became exceedingly handsome and happily made the aged lady his wife. Together, they found pleasure for many agreeable years. They were delighted and lived happily in the cave.'

'O tiger among sages! While the couple resided happily in the cave in the mountain, there was an occasion when the unblemished sages arrived there. There were Vasishtha, Vamadeva and other *maharshi*s. While roaming around the sacred *tirtha*s, they arrived at that cave. Learning that the *rishi*s had come, Goutama's son, along with his wife, offered them hospitality. However, there were some who laughed at them. Some of them were young and were proud of their youth. Some were middle-aged. Some saw Goutama's son and the aged lady and laughed at them. She was huge and emaciated. Her lips hung down. She possessed body hair and her ears were like winnowing baskets. Her teeth jutted out and her nose was long. The tips of her hair were long and she was aged. In contrast, Goutama's son possessed beauty, charm, good fortune and learning. Some young sons of *rishi*s saw them and laughed. There were also disciples who possessed limited intelligence. They saw them, smiled and spoke. The *rishi*s said, "O aged lady! Who is Goutama's son? Is he your son or your grandson? O fortunate one! Tell us truthfully." In this way, the *brahmana*s laughed. "O ascetic lady! It has truly been said that the fruits of austerities are extremely powerful. One obtains serenity through austerities. However, if one doesn't possess the requisite strength, one is exhausted. O extremely beautiful one! Behold. The equanimity and poise that has been cultivated through many births must be protected. That indeed, has been spoken of as the truth. What is the need to speak a lot in this connection? That will now prove to be futile speech. You alone are blessed in this world. Please tell us about the good fortune you possess. Your sins have been burnt down by your austerities. Your exertions in pursuit of austerities are spoken about a lot. In

[630] Meaning Agni.

this world, you have become emaciated through your austerities and self-control. You have worshipped guests and have nurtured your son. In this world, let this body which is a store of sins, not be nurtured. Compassion, donations, austerities, truth, control of the senses, honouring guests, serenity, protecting sons and others—you have followed all of these and practiced your own *dharma*. If a person only acts so as to fill his own stomach, it is evident that he is destined for hell. He is only interested in his body. That is the view. O beautiful one! In this world, where is there such a woman who has undergone every kind of misery? Please tell us. O one who possesses excellent eyebrows! Though you have always honoured guests, you are like a dog. Without a husband or a son, you should be known as impure. However, you have indeed fed *brahmanas*. O beautiful one! Therefore, there is no doubt that you do possess *dharma*, though you are extremely aged and do not have a husband. Hence, though you are disfigured, you must be regarded as beautiful. Though lacking riches, you must be regarded as possessing riches. You have tormented yourself through fierce austerities, like standing on one toe. These are extremely difficult to undertake. You must have faithfully worshipped Lakshmi's consort in your earlier births. You must have given away copious donations. You must have undertaken sacrifices, with large amounts of *dakshina*. You must have properly visited the *tirtha*s and offered a lot of oblations. That is the reason you have obtained a son like Goutama's son, who knows the Vedas. He is accomplished in the Vedas and the *Vedanga*s and knows the truth. He is learned in all the sacred texts. For those in the three worlds who perform good deeds, someone like Goutama's son is extremely difficult to obtain. Is he your son, your son's son, your daughter's son or your great grandson? A son's son is like grain that gives satisfaction, but a daughter's son is like sesamum kept in a leather bag.[631] However, because of him, your lineage will obtain a sparkling and pure destination with Vishnu. O one who is aged in austerities! There is no need to think about this." Extremely surprised, some disciples of the *rishi*s said, "A young woman is like poison to an old man,

---

[631] There is a problem with this *shloka*, which doesn't make sense.

but a young man is like *amrita* to an old woman. After a long time, we have seen the desirable and the undesirable together." While the couple heard, some of them spoke in this way. Saying this, when the hospitality was over, all the *maharshi*s left.'

'Hearing the words of the *rishi*s, both of them were extremely sad. Goutama's immensely wise son was ashamed along with his wife. O tiger among sages! They asked Agastya, supreme among *rishi*s. Goutama's son asked, "In what region and in which *tirtha* can one obtain the greatest benefit? O immensely wise one! What bestows objects of pleasure and emancipation quickly?" Agastya replied, "O brahmana! I have heard these words when the sages spoke about it. There is no doubt that all the wishes are met in Goutami. O immensely intelligent one! Therefore, go to Goutami. She destroys all sins. I will follow you. Do what you want." Hearing Agastya's words, the aged lady and Goutama's son went there. Along with his wife, the illustrious *rishi* tormented himself there with fierce austerities. They praised the divinity Shambhu and Vishnu. For the sake of his wife, the illustrious *rishi* satisfied Ganga. Goutama's son said, "O Bhava! Our minds are distressed. O Shiva! You are the refuge. You are like a tree to travelers in the desert. You are the one who dispels every kind of sin committed by superior and inferior beings. O Krishna! When the planets dry everything up, you are like a cloud for crops. O river that is full of nectar! You are like a flight of stairs leading to Vaikuntha[632], which is so very difficult to reach. O Goutami! You are the refuge for the seven generations that will follow." Goutami was pleased at the words spoken by Goutama's son and the aged lady. She is the refuge for those who are afflicted and they had sought refuge with her. Goutami said, "After pronouncing *mantra*s over my water, sprinkle your wife with that. Like that, pour water from the pots over your beloved wife. She will become beautiful and lovely in all her limbs. She will become extremely fortunate, with beautiful eyes. She will possess all the auspicious signs and obtain a handsome appearance. When she is sprinkled in this way, your wife will become beautiful once more. She will then sprinkle water over you and you will possess all

---

[632] Vishnu's abode.

the auspicious signs and become beautiful in form." They agreed with the words spoken by Ganga and acted accordingly. Through Goutami's favours, both of them became extremely handsome. O supreme among sages! Because the sprinkling was performed with water from that river, the river became famous by the name of Vriddha.[633] This river became known as Vriddha and Goutama's son also came to be known after her. The *rishi*s who dwelt with them addressed him by the name of Vriddha-Goutama. The aged lady spoke to Goutami Ganga when she manifested herself before her. The aged lady said, "O goddess! After my name, let this river be known as Vriddha. Let the confluence of the river with you become an excellent *tirtha*. Let bathing, donating, oblations and the performance of water-rites to ancestors become extremely pure there, bestowing youth, good fortune and prosperity and enhancing the number of sons and grandsons. Let these lead to a long lifespan, freedom from disease and fortune and enhance victory and joy." Ganga agreed to what the extremely aged lady, beloved by Goutama's son had said. Goutama's son established a *lingam* there and it is spoken of by the name of Vriddha. Along with the aged lady, the supreme among sages enjoyed himself there. Bathing and donations there yield everything that is wished for. Since then, that *tirtha* has been known as Vriddha Sangama.'[634]

Chapter 2(38) (Sixteen thousand *tirtha*s)

Brahma said, 'The place known as Ila *tirtha* bestows every kind of success on men. It cleanses sins like that of killing a brahmana and yields everything that is desired. A lord of men, named Ila was born in Vivasvat's lineage.[635] With a large army, he went to the forest to hunt. He wandered around in a dense forest, frequented by many predatory creatures. The trees were adorned

[633] *Vriddha* means aged woman.
[634] Confluence of Vriddha.
[635] Ila was the son of Vaivasvata Manu.

with many types of birds. Making up his mind to hunt, the best
of kings wandered around in that forest. Ila made up his mind to
reside there and spoke to his advisers. Ila said, "All of you return
to the city which is protected by my son. Protect him, the country,
the treasury, the army and the kingdom. Taking our lord, Agni,
let Vasishtha also go.[636] Let the intelligent one leave, along with
my wives. I will reside here in the forest. I will subsist on forest
fare along with some horses, elephants and men who are skilled in
hunting. Let everyone else leave this place and go to the city." They
agreed and left. King Ila himself went to the Himalaya mountains,
which were full of jewels, and started to live there.'

'He saw a cave there, decorated with many kinds of wonderful
gems. A lord of the yakshas, known by the name of Samanyu,
resided on that beautiful and excellent mountain. The yaksha was
accompanied by his wife, named Sama, who was devoted to serving
her husband. Along with his wife, the immensely wise one roamed
around in the form of a deer. In his own forest, the yaksha sported
as he willed, singing and dancing. Though he was in the form of a
deer, the yaksha knew everything about the place. However, Ila did
not know that the cave was protected by the yaksha. The yaksha's
home was huge, decorated with many kinds of wonderful jewels.
Surrounded by many soldiers, the king sat down there. He started to
live in the home of the intelligent yaksha. In the form of a deer, the
yaksha was with his wife and he was enraged at this act of adharma.
"I am incapable of defeating Ila. He has taken away my home. Even
if I ask for it, he will not give it back to me. What will I do?" He
thought in this way. The king of yakshas made up his mind. "I will
fight with him. But how can I kill him?" He sent his own relatives,
brave yakshas who wielded bows. The yaksha said, "In a battle,
defeat King Ila. He is insolent because he possesses tuskers. You
should act so that he leaves my home and goes somewhere else."
The yakshas were indomitable in battle and heard the words spoken
by the lord of the yakshas. All of them went to Ila and said, "Leave
this home, inside the cave. Otherwise, you will be routed in a battle
and be forced to run away." Hearing the words of the yakshas, the

---

[636] The householder's fire was always carried everywhere.

king of kings became angry and started to fight. After defeating many types of *yaksha*s, he dwelt there for ten nights.'

'In the form of a deer, the lord of *yaksha*s resided in the forest with his wife. With his home taken away and his servants killed, he lived there with the *yakshini*.[637] He was overcome by thoughts and spoke to his beloved who was in the form of a doe. The *yaksha* said, "He is powerful and impossible to assail. He possesses prosperity and is proud of his valour. He is addicted to hunting those like me. O beloved! How will I defeat the king?" The *yakshini* replied, "O beloved! Please tell me. Is there any way to destroy his insolence? Tell me if my words will help. I will do whatever you ask me to do." The *yaksha* said, "O beautiful one! A method to destroy the king's insolence exists. Through this excellent means, the king's pride can be destroyed. O immensely fortunate one! Do what is auspicious and extremely agreeable according to me. O fortunate one! Go to the place where that foolish king lives. O auspicious one! There, show yourself in front of Ila. Attract King Ila to the place known as Umavana.[638] O immensely fortunate one! Assume the form of a doe in front of the one who is living in my home. The evil-minded one's mind is addicted to the flesh of deer and he will become a woman.[639] O beloved! This king is evil-minded and his mind is addicted to pleasure. I have thought of this means, whereby he can be made to face a calamity. Because of wicked intelligence, entire kingdoms of kings come to an end. O one with the excellent eyebrows! Assume the form of a beautiful doe and entice him to Umavana. There is no doubt that once the king enters that place, he will become a woman. O fortunate one! You should do what I am urging you to do. I am male. But you are female and a *yakshini*." The *yakshini* asked, "Why can't you go to the excellent Umavana? What will be the sin if you go there? Please tell me the truth." The *yaksha* replied, "Surrounded by the gods, Shiva is happily roaming around with Uma on the slopes of the Himalayas. On an earlier occasion, in secret, Parvati spoke to Shankara. Parvati said, 'The nature of women is such that

[637] Female *yaksha*.
[638] Uma's forest.
[639] This will be explained a little later.

they want to indulge themselves in secret. Therefore, give me a controlled place that is protected in accordance with your words. O Ishana! O lord of the gods! Give me a place known as Umavana. Barring you, Ganesha, Kartikeya and Nandi, any male who enters there will become a woman.' Thus addressed, the one who wears the moon on his crest was pleased and gave her Umavana. When a beloved lovingly asks for something, what will a man not do? Therefore, I should not go to the excellent Umavana." The *yakshini* could assume any form at will. Hearing her husband's words, the large-eyed one assumed the form of a doe and appeared in front of Ila. The *yaksha* remained where he was. Ila saw the doe. His mind was addicted to hunting and moreover, this was a doe. Alone, he jumped onto a horse and followed the doe. She slowly enticed the king who was addicted to hunting, away. Slowly, she went to the spot that was spoken of as Umavana. Sometimes, the doe showed herself. Sometimes, she disappeared. Sometimes, she stood there. Sometimes, she walked. Sometimes, she seemed to be frightened and ran away. The doe, with darting eyes, enticed him to Umavana. Astride the horse, he reached Umavana. As soon as she realized that he entered Umavana, the *yakshini* gave up her form as a doe. The *yakshini* could assume any form at will. She assumed a divine form and stood near an *ashoka* tree with branches that bent down. She was smeared with divine unguents. She was slender and celestial in appearance. Sama had accomplished her objective. She looked at the exhausted king, astride the horse, and laughed. Ila had been searching for the doe with darting eyes. Remembering everything that her husband had said, she spoke to the lord of men. Sama said, "O slender-limbed woman! Where are you going alone, astride a horse? O Ilaa![640] Attired in the form of a man, who are you following?" Hearing himself addressed as "Ilaa", the king became senseless with rage and censured the *yakshini*, who had earlier been in the form of a doe. However, the *yakshini* continued, "O Ilaa! What are you looking at?" Hearing the word "Ilaa", astride the horse, he seized his bow. He angrily showed her the bow that had vanquished the three worlds. However, she again spoke to the great-souled king. "O

[640] We will use Ila for the masculine and Ilaa for the feminine.

Ilaa! Look at yourself. After that, tell me whether I am speaking the truth or am lying." At this, the king looked and saw a pair of peaked breasts between his arms. He was bewildered at what had happened to him. Ilaa said, "What has happened to me? You evidently know the answer. Please tell me everything accurately. O one who is excellent in vows! Who are you? Please tell me." The *yakshini* replied, "My husband, Samanyu, used to reside in an excellent cave in the Himalayas. He is a prosperous lord of the *yaksha*s. I am his wife, a *yakshini*. O king! That is the extremely cool cave you sat down in. It is his *yaksha*s you killed in your delusion, though there never was a proper battle. Therefore, to make you emerge, I assumed the form of a doe and came to Umavana. I entered and so did you. Earlier, Maheshvara had said, "Any evil-minded male who enters this place will become a female." Therefore, you have become a woman and you should not grieve about this. Even an aged person does not know the wonderful course that destiny will take." Hearing the *yakshini*'s words, he fell down from the horse. The *yakshini* comforted him and again addressed him in the following words. The *yakshini* said, "You have become a woman. You should not behave like a man. Accept the skills that are appropriate for a woman—dancing, singing, decorating, feminine grace, feminine charm and everything else that a woman does." When Ilaa had learnt everything,[641] she addressed the *yakshini* in the following words.'

'Ilaa asked, "Who will be my husband? What should I do now? How will I become a man again? O fortunate one! Tell me this, especially since I am suffering from a great deal of grief. There is nothing that brings greater benefit than the act of pacifying the grief of those who are miserable." The *yakshini* replied, "Soma's son is named Budha. O extremely fortunate one! He possesses beauty and youth and his hermitage is to the east of this forest. The planet Budha follows this path every day to go and see his father, Soma, and pay him his respects. When the serene Budha goes, show yourself to him. O extremely fortunate one! When you see him, you will get everything that you wish for." Having reassured him, the *yakshini*, with the excellent eyebrows, vanished.

[641] From the *yakshini*.

The *yakshini* went and told the *yaksha*, who was delighted. Ila's soldiers, who had been there went away, as they willed. Ilaa remained in Umavana and danced and sang. She followed feminine activities and thought about the path of *karma*. On one occasion, Ilaa was dancing. While the intelligent Budha was going to visit his father, he saw her. Seeing Ilaa, he moved away from his path. Budha approached and spoke to her. Budha said, "Be my wife. Be my beloved and be comfortable in every possible way." Ilaa faithfully accepted the words Budha had spoken and acted accordingly. O sage! Remembering the *yakshini*'s words, she was satisfied at this. Having taken her to his excellent place, Budha happily found pleasure with her. In every possible way, she also satisfied her husband. After a long period of time had passed, the satisfied Budha spoke to his beloved. Budha asked, 'O fortunate one! What shall I give you? What is the agreeable wish that exists in your mind?' Budha, Soma's son, loved her and was delighted with her. As soon as he spoke these words, Ilaa replied, "Give me a son." Budha said, "My semen is infallible and will bring delight. There will be a *kshatriya* son who will be famous in the worlds. He will be handsome and will be like the sun in his energy. He will establish the Soma lineage.[642] He will be like Brihaspati in intelligence and like the earth in forgiveness. He will be like Hari in valour and energy and like the fire-god in rage." When Budha's great-souled son was born, there were sounds of "victory" everywhere in the abode of the gods. As soon as Budha's son was born, all the lords among the gods arrived there. O immensely wise one! Full of joy, I also went there. As soon as the son was born, he cried in a loud voice. Therefore, all the assembled *rishi*s and gods said, "Since he cried loudly, he will be Pururava."[643] Delighted in their minds, all of them gave him this name. Budha taught his son all the auspicious knowledge meant for a *kshatriya*. Budha taught his son about the application of *dhanurveda*. He grew up fast, like the moon during *shukla paksha*.'

---

[642] The lunar dynasty, *chandra vamsha*.
[643] *Puru* (loud) and *rava* (sound).

'The immensely intelligent one noticed that his mother, Ilaa, grieved. Aila[644] humbly bowed down before Ilaa and addressed her in these words. Aila said, "O mother! My father is Budha. He is your husband and you love him. I am your son and am capable of undertaking tasks. Why do you have this mental anxiety?" Ilaa replied, "O son! It is true that Budha is my husband. It is also true that you, my son, are a reservoir of qualities. I never have any worries on account of my husband or son. However, I remember what had happened earlier and am repeatedly miserable. O immensely intelligent one! I think about that." He replied to his mother. Aila said, "O mother! First tell me what it is." Ilaa answered, "It is a secret. How can I speak about it? However, since you are my son, I will tell you. A son is the ultimate refuge of the parents. When one is submerged in an ocean of grief, a son is the best ship." Hearing his mother's words, he humbly placed her feet on his head. With his eyes overflowing with tears, he spoke to her in a faltering voice. "If a son does not remove the hardships of the parents in every possible way, then his birth and life are useless. Even if he is alive, he is as good as dead. Frequenting *tirtha*s, donations, sacrifices, austerities and other sacred tasks are undertaken so that the parents are satisfied. O mother! Therefore, tell me truthfully everything that there is in your mind." She spoke to her son with quivering lips. With hot breaths, she was distracted and submerged in an ocean of grief, as she told him everything—the birth in the Ikshvaku lineage of the solar dynasty; her birth and name; her obtaining the kingdom and her beloved sons; the chief priest Vasishtha; his beloved wife and his own status; his departure for the forest; the sending back of the advisers and the chief priest to the city; the addiction to hunting; the entry into the home of the lord of the *yaksha*s in the cave in the Himalayas; the entry into Umavana and the complete transformation into a woman; Maheshvara's command about a man who entered the place; the words of the *yakshini* and the obtaining of a boon; getting Budha; and the delight at having given birth to a son. She told him all this. Hearing all this, Pururava asked, "What will I do? In the form of a good deed, what shall I do? O mother!

---

[644] Ilaa's son, Pururava.

What will bring you sufficient pleasure? Tell me everything else that
is in your mind. Command me." Aila answered, "I wish to become
a man again and get back my excellent kingdom. I wish to crown
my sons, especially you. I wish to donate and sacrifice and look
towards the path of emancipation. Through your favours, I desire
to accomplish all this." The son said, "I am asking you about the
method whereby you can become a man again. Will that be through
austerities or through some other means? Please tell me the truth."
Ilaa answered, "O son! Go and ask your father, Budha, about the
truth. He knows everything and he will instruct you about what is
the best." Following his mother's words, Aila went to his upright
father. He prostrated himself and asked what he and his mother
should do.'

'Budha said, "O immensely wise one! I know how Ila turned
into Ilaa. I know about his entry into Umavana and Shambhu's
command. O son! Hence, it is only through the favours of Shambhu
and the favours of Uma that the curse can be countered. There is
no means other than that of worshipping him." Purarava asked,
"How can I see the divinity? How can I see the mother, Shivaa?
Will that be through *tirtha*s or through austerities? O father! Please
tell me that first." Budha replied, "O son! Go to Goutami. Shiva is
always present there, along with Uma. The prosperous one dispels
curses and grants boons." Hearing his father's words, Pururava
became happy. To perform austerities, he went to Goutami Ganga,
the purifier of the three worlds. Desiring to ensure that his mother
would become a man, he quickly performed austerities. He bowed
down before the Himalaya mountains, his mother, his father and
his *guru*. As he proceeded, Ilaa and Soma's son followed him. From
the excellent Himalaya mountains, all of them reached Goutami.
They bathed there and performed some austerities. They then used
supreme hymns to progressively praise Bhava, the lord of the gods.
Budha praised him first, followed by Ilaa. Then the son, Pururava,
praised the goddess Gouri and Shankara. Budha said, "Those two
take pleasure from the sound of the girdle. Their complexion is
like that of natural gold. They are extremely beautiful. They are
worshipped by Skanda and Ganeshvara. They are the ones in
whom one should seek refuge. Let them be my refuge." Ilaa said,

"Embodied creatures are scorched by the forest conflagration of *samsara* and are overcome by worries. However, one instantly obtains *nivritti* through Shankara and Shankari.[645] Let them be my refuge. I am afflicted and my mind is suffering. Against hardships, there is no protector who is superior. O divinity! Your feet are extremely auspicious. They are the ones in whom one should seek refuge. Let them be my refuge." Pururava said, "Let Gouri and Hara be my refuge. They are the ones from which everything visible originates and prospers and they are the ones into which everything is merged. They are the refuges of the entire universe. They are the *atman*s of the universe. In a great festival of the gods, it was said, 'O Isha! Clasp the feet of the daughter of the lord of the mountains.' As soon as this was said, Shiva lovingly did this. They are the ones with whom one should seek refuge." The illustrious goddess asked, "What is it that you desire? What will I give you? Please tell me. O fortunate ones! You have accomplished that which is extremely difficult for even the gods to accomplish." Pururava replied, "O Ambika! In his ignorance, King Ila entered your forest. O goddess of the gods! Please forgive him and give him his manliness back." She always abided by Bhava's views and agreed to all this. The illustrious one, who always abided by the words of the goddess, spoke. Shiva said, "As soon as he is sprinkled with water from here, the king kill get his manliness back." When Budha's wife bathed, water flowed out from her body. She had obtained knowledge of singing and dancing and feminine grace from the *yakshini*. Along with this water, all of this entered Ganga's waters. The rivers Nritya, Gita and Soubhagya[646] emerged from this flow. They merged into Ganga and these three confluences are sacred. Bathing and donations there yield the fruits of obtaining the kingdom of the gods. Through the favours of Gouri and Shambhu, Ilaa became a man.'

'To accomplish the objective of great upliftment, he undertook a *vajapeya* sacrifice. The supreme among kings brought the chief priest, Vasishtha, his wife and sons, his advisers, arm and treasury.

---

[645] Uma.

[646] Respectively, dancing, singing and good fortune.

With an army consisting of the four divisions,[647] he established a kingdom in Dandaka. The city there became famous under the name of Ila. This is located in the valley of the Sahya mountains and is superior to the great Indra's city. In that excellent and supreme city, he became detached from the enjoyment of earthly pleasures. In due order, he instated his former sons as heirs to the *surya vamsha*. After this, he lovingly instated Aila in the kingdom. This handsome king was the one who established *chandra vamsha*. O sage! He was the most intelligent and respected among all the sons and was the eldest. O Narada! Sixteen thousand auspicious *tirtha*s resulted in the auspicious places where King Ila performed sacrifices, where he got back his manliness, where he met his sons, where the auspicious rivers originated from the dancing, singing and good fortune bestowed by the *yakshini* and at their confluences with Ganga. O son! They were on both sides of the river and Shambhurileshvara[648] is there. Bathing and donations there, yield the fruits of all sacrifices.'

Chapter 2(39) (Chakra *tirtha*)

Brahma said, 'The place known as Chakra *tirtha* destroys the sin of killing a brahmana and other sins. This is the place where Hari obtained his divine *chakra* from Chakreshvara.[649] For the sake of obtaining the *chakra* from Lord Shankara, Vishnu himself remained there and worshipped him. That *tirtha* is known as Chakra *tirtha*. Even if a person hears about it, he is freed from all sins. Daksha's sacrifice was being conducted. At an assembly of the gods, Daksha abused the divinity, Shiva Sharva Maheshvara. Daksha's mind was so polluted that he did not invite the lord of the gods. When Ahalya spoke about it, from her words, Dakshayani got to know the reason

[647] Chariots, elephants, cavalry and infantry.

[648] Shambhu, Ila's lord.

[649] There is more than one Chakreshvara temple. This is probably the one in Chakan, near Pune.

about the invitation not being used. Sureshvari was enraged.[650] On hearing the abusive words her father had spoken about her husband, she said, "I will not forgive my father, the sinner. I will destroy him. There is no limit to the sins of women who hear their husbands being censured. Whatever be the nature of the husband, he is the ultimate refuge for a woman. What need be said about Mahadeva, who is a lord for everyone and the preceptor of the universe? Since I have heard him being censured, I will not bear this body any longer. Therefore, I will give up this body." This is what the great Sati said. Overwhelmed by great rage, Sureshvari blazed up. With her mind fixed only on Shiva, she used the power of *yoga* to give up her body. From Narada, Maheshvara heard everything that had transpired. He angrily looked towards Jaya and Vijaya and asked them.[651] Both of them told the divinity what they had heard from Dakshayani about Daksha's sacrifice being destroyed. Hearing this, Maheshvara left for the sacrifice. He was surrounded by terrible *gana*s and the lords of the *bhuta*s went with him. They surrounded the sacrifice, which had been organized by the gods, with Brahma at the forefront. With pure sentiments, it had been guarded by Daksha, who was performing the sacrifice. It was surrounded by Vasishtha and other fierce sages. It was protected in every possible direction by Indra, the Adityas, the Vasus and others. It was embellished by the sounds of chants from *Rig Veda*, *Yajur Veda* and *Sama Veda* and there were sounds of *svaha*. It was ornamented from every direction by Shraddha, Pushti, Tushti, Shanti, Lajja, Sarasvati, Bhumi, Dyou, Sharvari, Kshanti, Usha, Asha, Jaya, Mati and others.[652] The great-souled Tvashta and Vishvakarma had constructed it.[653] There were the cows Surabhi, Nandini, Kamadhuk and Kamadohini. There were many others that showered down every kind of desire. It was prosperous, with every kind of wish being met. There were

---

[650] Sureshvari and Dakshayani (Daksha's daughter) are Sati's names.

[651] Jaya and Vijaya were Sati's companions.

[652] Respectively, the personified forms of faith, nourishment, satisfaction, peace, bashfulness, speech, earth, heaven, night, forbearance, dawn, hope, victory and intellect.

[653] Here, Tvashta and Vishvakarma are not being used synonymously.

*kalpavriksha*s like Parijata. There were creepers that yielded everything one desired. Everything that was wished for was present in that sacrifice. It was protected by Maghavan, Pusha and Hari himself. There were cheerful sounds of "Give", "Eat", "Do" and "Stay". In this way, Daksha's sacrifice was revered through many words. At first, Virabhadra and Bhadrakali went on ahead. Overwhelmed by sorrow and anger, the wielder of Pinaka followed, holding a trident. As Mahadeva advanced, many great *bhuta*s ornamented him. Those *bhuta*s surrounded Maheshvara and the sacrifice. They destroyed the sacrifice and there was great agitation. Some fled, others sought refuge with Shiva. Some praised the lord of the gods, others were angry with Shankara. Seeing that the sacrifice was being destroyed in this way, Pusha advanced. O brahmana! In an instant, Virabhadra knocked out Pusha's teeth, routed Indra and plucked out Bhaga's eyes. Using both his arms, he whirled Divakara around and flung him away.'

'At this, all the large number of gods sought refuge with Vishnu. The gods said, "Please save us. O one with the mace in your hand! Save us from the fear on account of Bhutanatha. There is a leader of the *pramatha*s[654] amidst Maheshvara's *gana*s. While Hara looked on, he has burnt down the entire sacrifice that was undertaken in Vishnu's honour." To slay Bhutanatha, Hari hurled his *chakra*. However, as the *chakra* descended, Bhutanatha devoured it. When Vishnu's *chakra* was devoured, all the guardians of the worlds fled in fear. Standing there, Daksha looked at the sacrifice and at the gods. Full of devotion, Prajapati Daksha praised the divinity Shankara. Daksha said, "Victory to Shankara Somesha.[655] Victory to Shambhu, who knows everything. Victory to the fortunate Shambhu. Victory to the one who is the *atman* of destiny. I bow down before you. I bow down before the one who is the original creator. O Nilakantha! I bow down before you. O one who is fond of Brahma! I bow down before you. O one who assumes the form of Brahma! I bow down before you. O one who assumes

---

[654] *Pramatha*s are Shiva's companions, who strike.
[655] The lord of the moon.

the three forms![656] O divinity! O refuge of the three worlds! O Parameshvara! I bow down before you. O one who has every kind of form! I bow down before you. O one who is the support of the three worlds! O one who grants desires! I bow down before you. O one who can be known through *Vedanta*! O *paramatman*! I bow down before you. O one who has the sacrifice as your form! I bow down before you. O refuge of the sacrifice! I bow down before you. O one who is the donations of the sacrifice! I bow down before you. O one who bears the oblations of a sacrifice! I bow down before you. O one who is the destroyer of a sacrifice! I bow down before you. O one who bestows the fruits! I bow down before you. Save me. O lord of the universe! Please save me. O one who is affectionate towards those who seek refuge! O lord! You are the refuge of everyone, whether they are devotees or non-devotees.' Praised in this way, Maheshvara was pleased. He asked, 'What will I give you?" The reply was, "O lord! Please allow my sacrifice to be completed." The illustrious Mahadeva, the lord of all the gods, agreed. He is Shankara, who is in the *atman*s of all living beings. He is an ocean of compassion. O sage! In this way, Daksha's sacrifice was successfully completed. Having said that it would be, the illustrious one vanished along with the *bhuta*s. All the gods returned to their own respective abodes.'

'Once, there was a great battle between the gods and the *daitya*s. The terrified gods praised Shri's consort in every possible way and spoke to Janardana. The gods said, "Shakra and the other gods perform austerities so that Lakshmi may cast favourable sidelong glances at them. However, she seeks refuge at your feet and the *brahman* is in you. In the three worlds, there is no one who is superior to Nrisimha, whose mount is Tarkshya.[657] Let the lord of the gods protect us from every kind of great fear. Let him show compassion towards those who have sought refuge." The illustrious one, who holds the conch shell, *chakra* and mace, was pleased. He asked, "Why have all of you come? I will do that for you." The gods continued, "O Madhusudana! On account of the

---

*daitya*s, we are suffering from a terrible fear. O Janardana! Please
turn your mind towards saving us from them." Hari told the ones
who had come, "My *chakra* has been devoured by Hara. You are
suffering and have come to me. But what I will I do without the
chakra? O large number of gods! Leave. I will do what is necessary
to protect you." When the gods had left, Vishnu prepared to get
the *chakra* back. He went to Godavari and started to worship
Shambhu. Using one thousand divine and fragrant golden lotuses,
every day, Vishnu worshipped Uma's lord. "I bow down to the
one who destroys the great fear from this forest of *samsara*. O
wielder of Pinaka! O Mahesha! O one bestows everything that is
desired." Using this *mantra* and with his mind filled with devotion,
he worshipped Shiva, loved by Bhavani,[658] in the proper way. As
the worship continued, listen to what happened between them.
The number of lotuses was less than one thousand by one. When
the enemy of *asuras*[659] noticed this, he plucked out one of his eyes
and offered that as *arghya*. He took those one thousand lotuses
and held the vessel full of *arghya* in his hand. Hari, who had no
other refuge, meditated on Shambhu and offered this *arghya*.
Vishnu said, "O divinity! You know all the innermost desires of
men. You alone are the refuge and the lord. There is no doubt
about this." He said this with tears in his eyes and merged himself
completely into Ishvara. Along with Bhavani, Shambhu appeared
before him. He embraced Hari firmly and bestowed many kinds
of boons on him. He got back his *chakra* and regained his eye, as
was the case earlier. At this, all the large number of gods praised
Hari and Shankara. They praised Ganga, best among rivers, and
Vrishadhvaja. Since then, that *tirtha* has been known as Chakra
tirtha. Even if one hears about it, one is freed from all sins. If a
person bathes or donates there and performs the water-rites for
the ancestors, he is freed from all sins. Along with his ancestors,
he goes to heaven. Even now, that *tirtha* can be seen to be marked
with the sign of a *chakra*.'

[658] Bhavani is Parvati/Uma.
[659] Vishnu.

Chapter 2(40) (Various *tirthas*)

Brahma said, 'After Chakra *tirtha*, there is the place named Pippala *tirtha*. It is known as Chakra *tirtha* because the divinity Chakreshvara is present there and because Hari got back his *chakra* there. For the sake of obtaining the *chakra* from Lord Shankara, Vishnu himself remained there and worshipped him. That is the reason that *tirtha* is known as Chakra *tirtha*. The place where Shambhu was pleased with Vishnu is known as Pippala.[660] Even the great lord of serpents[661] is incapable of describing the greatness of this spot. That is the reason Chakreshvara is also known as Pippalesha. O Narada! Listen devotedly to what I say. This has also been mentioned in the Vedas.'

'There was a sage, famous by the name of Dadhichi. He possessed all the qualities. His immensely wise wife was born in a noble lineage and was devoted to her husband. She was Lopamudra's[662] sister and was known as Gabhastini. She was known by this name but was also spoken of as Vadava. Dadhichi loved her. Along with her, he always tormented himself through great austerities. Dadhichi was devoted to the *dharma* of being a householder and always had a fire burning in his house. He lived along the banks of Bhagirathi and worshipped gods and guests. He loved his own wife and was as serene as Kumbhayoni.[663] Because of his powers, there were no enemies like *daitya*s and *danava*s in that region. The tiger among the sages went to the place where Agastya's hermitage was. Having defeated the *daitya*s, all the gods, Rudras, Adityas, the two Ashvins, Indra, Vishnu, Yama and Agni also arrived there. There were delighted sounds of "victory" and the large number of Maruts praised them. On seeing Dadhichi, tiger among sages, the lords of the gods bowed down before him. Dadhichi was also delighted and separately honoured the gods. Along with his wife, he

---

[660] *Pippala* is the holy fig tree.
[661] Shesha.
[662] Lopamudra was the wife of the sage Agastya.
[663] Kumbhayoni is Agastya's name.

exhibited a householder's hospitality towards the gods.[664] He asked
the gods about their welfare and the gods also asked Dadhichi and
his wife about their welfare. They sat down with joyous minds and
repeatedly bowed down before the *rishi*. The gods said, "O *rishi*!
Since we have obtained the compassion of someone like you, we
have now got something that is extremely rare in this world. O sage!
You are like a tree that bestows every object of desire. O excellent
sage! This is the kind of fruit that a man who is alive should get—
bathing in the *tirtha*s, compassion towards creatures and meeting a
person like you. O sage! Listen to what we are affectionately telling
you. We have come here after defeating the *daitya*s and slaying the
bulls among *rakshasa*s. O brahmana! We are happy, especially after
seeing you. Our weapons have not given us such fruits. Indeed, we
are incapable of bearing them. O lord among sages! We do not see
a place where we can lay down our weapons. If we keep them in
heaven, the enemies of the gods will get to know and will steal them.
That is also what will happen if we place the weapons in Rasatala.
O one who shows honours! Therefore, let us keep our weapons in
your sacred hermitage. O brahmana! There is no fear here from
the *danava*s and the terrible *rakshasa*s. There is no one who is
equal to you in austerities and your commands protect this sacred
place. O supreme among those who know about the *brahman*! We
have already defeated the enemy and have killed large numbers of
*daitya*s. Enough of these weapons. They are a heavy load to bear
and they have served their purpose. O lord of sages! Let us keep
them in this place near you. We will enjoy divine objects of pleasure
along with the women in celestial gardens like Nandana. Having
accomplished our task, along with Indra, we will leave for our
own respective abodes. The weapons will be protected here. Your
commands are capable of holding and protecting them." Hearing
their words, Dadhichi agreed to the words spoken by the gods,
though his beloved wife tried to restrain him. "What do we have to
do with the tasks of the gods? For those who know the sacred texts,
for those who are devoted to the ultimate objective, for those who
have lost attachment for worldly objectives and for those who have

---

[664] The hermitages of Agastya and Dadhichi were next to each other.

nothing to do with the activities of others, these can have perverse effects. O sage! They will not bring happiness in this world, or in the next world. O noble brahmana! Listen. If you grant a place here for the weapons, those who hate the gods will hate us. O lord of sages! If the weapons are lost or stolen, the gods will be angry and will become our enemies. O supreme among those who know about the Vedas! In addition, there can be a sense of ownership towards something that belongs to others. As long as the object remains with one's own self, there is friendship. But the moment it is lost or taken away, enmity results. If one has the capacity to donate objects, one should donate them to those who are in need. There is no need to think about that. If a person does not have possessions, he should try to help others through thoughts, words and deeds. However, the virtuous do not approve the idea of keeping other people's possessions. O loved one! Therefore, instantly get rid of them.' Hearing the words of his beloved, the brahmana spoke to his wife, the one who possessed excellent eyebrows. Dadhichi said, 'O fortunate one! I have already given my word to the gods. Therefore, saying no will not bring me pleasure.'' Hearing the words of her husband, the beloved wife remained silent. She thought, "Other than destiny, no one is capable of doing anything to men." The gods placed their radiant weapons there. Having accomplished their objective, the enemies of the *daitya*s bowed down to the Indra among sages, placed their weapons there and went to their own world. When the gods had departed, the noble sage happily lived there with his wife, following *dharma*.'

'After they left, one thousand divine years passed. O lord among sages! The gods did not say anything about their weapons. They did not even seem to think about them. Dadhichi told Gabhastini, "O fortunate one! The enemies of the gods are now full of energy. They will hate me. Having deposited their weapons here, the gods do not seem to want them back. Please tell me what is appropriate." Full of humility, she spoke to her husband in these words. "O lord! I told you and you know what is appropriate under the circumstances. The strength of the *daitya*s has increased a lot because of their austerities. They will use their own weapons to take these away." To protect the weapons, he pronounced *mantra*s and washed them with sacred water. The extremely sacred water sucked up the energy from all those weapons and Dadhichi drank up the water. The weapons were robbed of their energy and form. In the course of time, they gradually decayed. The gods returned and told Dadhichi, "On account of our enemies, we now suffer a great fear. O supreme sage! Please give us the weapons the gods deposited with you." Dadhichi replied, "I was scared of the enemies of the gods and you did not return for a long time. I have drunk up the weapons and they are inside my body now. Please tell me what is appropriate under the circumstances." Hearing his words, the gods spoke to him humbly. "O Indra among sages! Please give us our weapons. Are you capable of giving them to us or are you refusing? O lord among sages! Without our weapons, we will always be defeated and our enemies are well-nourished. Where will we go? O father![665] The gods will now find it impossible to reside in heaven, in the mortal world, or in the nether regions. You are a noble brahmana who is full of austerities. In your presence, it is not proper for us to say anything else." The brahmana replied, "Accept the weapons that are in my bones. There is no need to think about it." The gods replied, "What will we do with this? Without weapons, the Indras among gods are reduced to the state of being women." The excellent sage responded again, "Using yoga, I will give up my body. You can then construct excellent weapons, supreme in forms, out of my bones." The gods asked him to do this. Dadhichi was never distressed in spirit and was like Agni in form. O lord of sages! At that time, his beloved was not near him and couldn't address him in agreeable words. The gods were also scared of her. Not seeing her, they told the brahmana, "Please hurry." Life is very difficult to give up. However, he cheerfully gave it up and said, "O gods! As you wish, accept this body. May all of you be pleased with my bones. What purpose does a body serve?" Saying this, he sat down in *padmasana*.[666] He fixed his eyes on the tip of his nose and was as pure as light. Using *yoga*, he slowly conveyed the fiery wind inside

[665] The word used is *tata*.
[666] The lotus posture.

him up to the narrow cavity inside the heart.[667] The great-souled one fixed his intelligence in the immeasurable and supreme destination of the *brahman*, which is what should be meditated on. He united himself with the *brahman*. The gods saw that his body had become completely lifeless. The gods swiftly told Tvashta, "Make many weapons immediately." He told them, "How can I do this? O gods! This is the body of a brahmana. I am terribly scared and incapable of doing this. If the body is split apart, I can immediately make excellent bones out of the weapons." The gods quickly spoke to cattle. The gods said, "O cattle! We will make your mouths as firm as the *vajra*. For welfare and for the sake of weapons, instantly tear apart Dadhichi's bones. Give us the pure bones now." They followed the words of the gods. They licked the bones clean and gave them to the gods. Not distressed at all, the gods quickly went to their own abodes and the cattle also left. Making the weapons for the gods, Tvashta also departed in great haste.'

'After some time, the extremely fortunate one, who was loved by her husband, returned. She possessed good conduct and there was a son in her womb. She hurried there with a pot full of water in her hand. She had gone to worship Uma. She returned swiftly wishing to see the household fire, her husband and the hermitage. She carried some fruits and flowers. Her mind was tormented, because along the path, the necklace had got dislodged from around her neck and had fallen down on the ground. The bangles had also fallen down from her hand. Her right eye throbbed.[668] She thought, "This is a great misery. Alas! What calamity will visit me soon?" As she was returning, a meteor fell down and checked Pratitheyi.[669] Scared, she arrived in the hermitage, but did not see her husband in front of her. "Where could he have gone?" Amazed, Pratitheyi asked Agni.[670] Agni told her everything in detail—the arrival of the gods, the

---

[667] *Daharakasha* is the narrow cavity inside the heart, an image of the expansive sky. What is described is a *hatha yoga* principle of driving up the breath of life into the *anahata chakra*.

[668] A bad omen.

[669] Pratitheyi is one of Gabhastini's names.

[670] Agni in the household fire.

request for the body, the collection of the bones and their departure. Hearing everything, she was miserable. Full of misery and anxiety, she fell down on the ground. Pratitheyi said, "I am incapable of cursing the immortals. What should I do? I will enter the fire." The virtuous lady controlled the rage and sorrow on account of her husband and spoke the following words, full of *dharma*. Pratitheyi said, "Everything generated in the world of humans is subject to destruction. Therefore, one should not grieve. For the sake of cattle, *brahmanas* and gods, men who earn good merits give up their own lives. Having obtained a capable body in this whirling wheel of *samsara*, beings who give up their beloved lives for the sake of gods and *brahmanas* are blessed. For all embodied beings, the breath of life is certain to go away. There is not the slightest bit of doubt about this. Knowing this, lords give it up for the sake of *brahmanas*, cattle, gods and the distressed. I tried to restrain him, but he kept the weapons of the gods who sought refuge. What can those in the mortal world do to know the mind of the one who ordains?" Having said this, taking the body hair and skin of her husband, she worshipped the fire and entered it.[671] Splitting aside her stomach, Pratitheyi took out the son in her womb and took him in her hand. She bowed down before Ganga, the earth, the hermitage, the trees and the herbs and patiently entered the hermitage. Praitheyi said, "This boy does not have a son. He is without relatives and those from his own *gotra*. He is without a mother. Let the large number of beings, the herbs and the guardians of the world protect this child. Those who look after and protect this child, who is bereft of his parents, will be praised and certainly deserve to be worshipped by Brahma and the others." Saying this, with her mind fixed on her husband, she cast aside her son. She bowed down to the *pippala* trees and placed her son near them. With the sacrificial vessel in her hand, Praitheyi performed *pradakshina* of the fire and entered it. Along with her husband, she went to heaven.'

'All the trees and residents of the forest wept, since *rishi* Dadhichi had nurtured them like a son. Remaining alive without him was like remaining alive without a mother. All the birds, animals and trees

---

[671] She entered the fire a little later.

spoke to each other. The trees said, "Our parents, who naturally
looked after us children, have gone to reside in heaven. They are
the successful humans, having constantly showered affection on us.
Before this, Dadhichi and Pratitheyi looked after us in a way that
even a mother and a father don't do. We are wicked. Shame on us.
For all of us, it is certain from now on that this child is Dadhichi.
This child is Pratitheyi. That is the eternal *dharma*." Saying this, the
trees and the herbs approached King Soma and asked him for the
excellent *amrita*. Soma gave them the excellent *amrita* and they gave
the child the *amrita*, which is loved by the gods. He was satisfied
with this and grew, like the moon during *shukla paksha*. Since he
was reared by *pippala* trees, the child became Pippalada. When he
grew up, he was surprised and spoke to the *pippala* trees. Pippalada
said, "Humans are born from humans. Birds are born from birds.
Herbs and plants grow from seeds. In this world, nothing contrary
is ever seen. With hands, feet and the breath of life, how could I
have been born from trees like you?" Hearing his words, the trees
told him everything in the due order—Dadhichi's death, the entry
into the fire by the virtuous lady and the collection of bones by the
gods. They told him everything in detail. Hearing this, he became
full of misery and fell down on the ground. The trees comforted
him and again addressed him in words that were full of deep
meaning. When he was comforted, he again spoke to the herbs and
the trees. Pippalada said, "I will slay the one who killed my father.
Otherwise, it is impossible for me to live. However, a real son is
one who pardons the foes and enemies of his father. He is the true
son. Others are said to be enemies in the form of sons. It is said
that a true son saves and does good even to his father's enemies."
The trees took the child with them and went to Soma's presence.
The trees reported the child's words to Soma. Hearing this, Soma
addressed the child Pippalada in these words. Soma said, "In the
proper kind of way, accept every kind of learning. O son! Through
my command, you will obtain austerities, prosperity, auspicious
speech, bravery, beauty, strength and intelligence." Pippalada
humbly replied to the lord of the herbs.[672] Pippalada said, "I think

---

[672] The moon-god.

all of these will be futile unless I rebuff those who killed my father. Therefore, I won't do that. Instead, please tell me what I should do first. O supreme among gods! In which region, at what time, praying to which divinity, using what *mantra* and in what *tirtha* will my resolution be successful?' Chandra meditated for a long time and said, 'There is no doubt that all objects of pleasure and emancipation originate from the divinity Maheshvara." He asked Soma again, "How can I possibly see Maheshvara? I am a child and my intelligence is childish. I do not possess the capacity, or the austerities." Chandra replied, "O fortunate one! Go to Goutami and praise Chakreshvara Hara. O child! Ishana is pleased with very little effort. Mahadeva will be pleased. Shiva is compassion himself. The powerful Vishnu saw Shambhu himself and he bestowed boons on Vishnu. He gave Vishnu the *chakra* that is worshipped by the gods. O immensely intelligent one! Go to the river Goutami, in the region of Dandaka. The herbs know about Chakreshvara *tirtha*. Having gone there, with a concentrated mind, praise Shankara, the lord of the gods. O son! When he is pleased, he will grant you everything you wish for." O brahmana! Hearing the king's words, Pippalada, the great sage, went to the place where Rudra, the lord of the universe and the one who bestowed the *chakra*, was.'

'Full of compassion for the child, the *pippala*s took him to their own hermitage. He bathed in Godavari and bowed down before the lord of the three worlds. Having purified himself, with a concentrated mind, Pippalada praised Shiva. Pippalada said, "Giving up every kind of *karma* and every kind of desire, those who are persevering conquer this mind and their breath of life. For the sake of emancipation, they make efforts to seek refuge with the original divinity. I bow down before Shambhu. He is witness to everything. He is inside everyone's *atman*. He is the lord of everything. He is a reservoir of every kind of art. Knowing everything that there is in my mind, let Smara's enemy take compassion on me.[673] In earlier times, Dashanana conquered the lords of the directions and agitated Kailasa, worshipped by the gods. With the pressure of the toe, he was

---

[673] Smara is Kama, the god of love. Shiva is Smara's enemy because he burnt down Smara.

dispatched to Rasatala.[674] Hearing the shriek when the mountain made him suffer, along with the goddess, he laughed and gave him what he wished for. Though he was angry, he became pleased. O Maheshvara! You give even to those who are undeserving. With *soutramani* sacrifices, Bana always worshipped and praised Hara.[675] In beautiful and agreeable ways, he worshipped the one who wears a slice of the moon on his crest and obtained prosperity. Having defeated the enemies of the gods, Vishakha[676] worshipped and bowed down to his senior. But he became angry when he saw that Gananatha was seated astride his lap.[677] Soma laughed. Though he was seated on Isha's lap, because of his childish nature, the child did not let go of his mother's lap either. Unable to pacify his angry son, Soma assumed the Ardhanarishvara form."[678] At this, Svayambhu[679] was extremely pleased and spoke to Pippalada. Shiva said, "O fortunate one! O Pippalada! Ask for the boon you desire." Pippalada replied, "O Mahadeva! My extremely illustrious father has been slain by the gods. He wasn't proud. He was truthful in speech. My mother was also devoted to her husband. O lord! After having heard in detail about how the gods caused their destruction, I am filled with grief and rage. I am no longer interested in remaining alive. Therefore, please grant me strength, so that I can destroy the gods. O one with the moon on your crest! With your exception, they cannot be slain by anyone in the three worlds." Ishvara replied, "O unblemished one! If you are capable of glancing at my third eye,

---

[674] Dashanana is Ravana. In his insolence, Ravana tried to raise up Kailasa. Shiva pressed down on Kailasa, with Ravana trapped under it, with his toe and Ravana was crushed.

[675] A *soutramani* sacrifice is an animal sacrifice in which liquor is also offered. Bana means Banasura.

[676] Kartikeya.

[677] Gananatha is Ganesha. Soma, in this context, means Shiva. Soma is one of Shiva's names, though rarely used. Kartikeya became angry, seeing that Ganesha was seated on Shiva's lap. But Ganesha was also half-seated on his mother's lap.

[678] *Ardha* (half) *nari* (female) *ishvara* (lord), the half male, half female form.

[679] In this case, meaning Shiva.

only then will you possess the capacity to destroy the gods." The lord made up his mind to see the third eye, but he was incapable of seeing it. He said, "O Shankara! I am incapable of seeing it." Ishvara said, "O child! If you wish to see the eye, undertake some austerities. When you see the third eye, there is no doubt that you will accomplish your wishes." Hearing Ishana's words, he made up his mind to undertake austerities. Dadhichi's son had *dharma* in his soul and he remained there for many years. Like a strong person, the child was devoted to meditating on Shiva. Every day, he got up in the morning. Having bathed, in the proper way, he bowed down to his seniors. Seated comfortably, he fixed his mind on the *sushumna*, thinking about nothing else.[680] Crossing his hands over his navel, he made the *svastika* sign. He forgot everything about the world. He was indifferent towards a superior place or an inferior place and fixed his mind on the great Shambhu. Pippalashana[681] saw the divinity's third eye. He joined his hands in salutation and humbly spoke these words. Pippalada said, "Earlier, Shambhu, the lord of the gods, granted me a boon. If I managed to see the light of the third eye, at that very instant, all that I wish for would come true. This is what the lord of the gods had said. Therefore, please grant me an instrument that will destroy the enemy." At this, the tops of the *pippala* trees said, "O immensely radiant one! Before your mother, Pratitheyi went to heaven, she said the following. 'Men who are always engaged in harming others and forget about what is good for them, have minds that wander around here and there and descend into the noose of hell.' Hearing what his mother had said, Pippalashana became angry. When a person blazes in pride, all virtuous words are pointless.'

'The brahmana had remembered *vadava* and Kritya assumed the form of *vadava*.[682] Kritya emerged from his eyes[683] and exclaimed,

---

[680] *Sushumna* is the central artery in the body. Those who pass through this reach the *brahman*.

[681] The same as Pippalada.

[682] *Vadava* is the subterranean fire and Kritya is a demoness. The subterranean fire is in the form of a mare (*vadava*).

[683] Out of Shiva's eyes.

"Give! Give!" For the sake of destroying all creatures, she had emerged from the womb of the fire. Pippalashana was meditating on his mother, Gabhastini, in the form when she still had the child in her womb. Because of that *yoga* of meditation, she[684] emerged from the fire inside the womb. She originated in an extremely fierce form, her tongue was as terrible as death. She asked Pippalada, "What is my duty towards you? Please tell me." Pippalada told her, "Devour the gods. They are my enemies." Pippalada was standing in front of her. Addressed in this way, she seized him. He asked, "O Kritya! What is this?" She replied, "I am doing what you asked me. This body has been created by the gods." Terrified, the sage went to Shiva and praised the divinity. At this, Shiva spoke to Kritya. Shiva said, "Following my command, do not seize any living being who is within a distance of one *yojana*. O Kritya! Therefore, go far away and do what you have to do there." Kritya, created by the rishi, stood at a distance of one *yojana* to the east of Pippala tirtha, assuming the form of *vadava*. A great blaze emerged from her, capable of destroying the worlds. On seeing this, all the gods were terrified and approached Shambhu. Scared in their minds, they went to Chakreshvara Pippaleshva, satisfied by Pippalada. The residents of heaven spoke to Shambhu. The gods said, "O Shambhu! Please save us. Kritya and the fire that originated from her is making us suffer. O Bhava! You are the refuge. You are the lord of everything. For those who are scared, you grant freedom from fear. There are creatures who are afflicted from all sides. They suffer and their minds are exhausted. O Shiva! For all such beings, you are the refuge. Requested by the rishi, Kritya emerged from the fire in the eyes. She wishes to destroy the worlds. There is no saviour other than you." The lord of the universe told them, "Kritya will not oppress anyone who resides within a distance of one *yojana*. Therefore, night and day, you must always reside within this space. O immortals! Within this region, you will have nothing to fear." The gods spoke to the lord of the gods again. "O one who is worshipped by the gods! You have given us heaven. O protector! Having given that up, how will we survive?" Hearing

[684] Kritya.

the words of the gods, Shiva addressed them in these words. Shiva said, "The god who has his eyes in every direction is here. The god who has his faces in every direction is here. The one who melts with his rays is here. It has always been held that he is the father. Surya himself will always be here, alone. His remaining here is the same as everyone remaining here, in his form." Agreeing with Shambhu's words, the gods created Divakara[685] from the *parijata* tree. Tvashta told Bhaskara, "O lord of the universe! By remaining here, you are yourself capable of protecting the gods. In our own portions, we will also remain here, in Shambhu's presence." Everywhere around Chakreshvara, within a distance of one *yojana*, on both banks of Ganga, the excellent gods remained there. Along the banks of Ganga, each occupied an area of one-fourth of an *angula*.[686] O supreme sage! There are three crores and five hundred *tirtha*s. Who is capable of hearing about or speaking about their praise? After this, the large number of gods humbly spoke to Shiva. The gods said, "O lord of the gods! O one who pervades the universe! Please grant peace to Pippalada." Approving of these words, the lord of the universe spoke to Pippalada.'

'Shiva said, "If the gods are destroyed, your father will not return. Your father gave up his life to accomplish the task of the gods. For those who are afflicted and suffering, is there any relative who can be as compassionate as him? O son! Therefore, he has gone to heaven and so has your mother, who was devoted to her husband. No one is held to be her equal, not Lopamudra, nor Arundhati.[687] Thanks to his bones, all the gods have been victorious and are always happy. Therefore, he has obtained extensive fame and your mother has obtained inexhaustible good merits. O son! Everywhere, you have obtained even great fame and deeds. You should save those who have been dislodged from heaven, scared of your strength. Out of fear of you, some immortals have fled. You should save them. There is nothing on earth that earns more good merits than saving those who are afflicted. For as many days as a

---

[685] Surya. Bhaskara is another name for Surya.

[686] An *angula* is a finger.

[687] The respective wives of Agastya and Vasishtha.

man's sparkling fame exists in this world, when he goes to heaven, he resides in the world hereafter for that many years, without any ailment. In this world, those who possess no fame are like those who are dead. Those who are devoid of learning are like those who are blind. Those who are not devoted to donations are eunuchs. Those who are not devoted to *dharma* should be grieved about." Hearing the words that the lord of the gods spoke, the sage was pacified. He joined his hands in salutation before the protector. Bowing down, he spoke these words. Pippalada said, "I will engage myself in ensuring the welfare of those who have done me a good turn in thoughts, words and deeds. I will always be engaged in their welfare and that of others. I prostrate myself before Soma,[688] who is worshipped by gods and others. There are those who have protected me, those who have reared me. I possess the same *gotra* as they do. I follow the same *dharma* as they do. May Shiva do what they desire. I will always bow down before the one who wears the young moon on his crest. O lord! O lord of the gods! There are those who have always reared me, like a mother and a father. In the three worlds, let this *tirtha* be known by their names. If they become famous, I will be freed from the debt I owe them. If the gods grant that this place is superior to all the *kshetra*s and *tirtha*s of the gods on the surface of the earth, I will always pardon the gods for the crime they have committed." In the presence of the gods, with the one with one thousand eyes at the forefront, he softly spoke these words to the gods in clearly articulated syllables. The gods agreed with the generous words spoken by Dadhichi's son. Knowing about the child's intelligence, humility, learning, bravery, strength, courage, truthfulness in speech, devotion towards his parents and purity of sentiments, Shankara spoke to Pippalada. Shankara said, "O son! You will obtain whatever is your cherished desire and whatever is loved by the gods. Please tell me. You will get whatever is good for you. Do not hesitate to say what is in your mind." Pippalada replied, "O Mahesha! Those who are devoted to *dharma*, bathe in Ganga and see your lotus feet—let them obtain everything that they wish for. After death, let them obtain a destination with Shiva.

---

[688] Shiva.

O lord! My father, my mother, the *pippala*s and the immortals obtained a destination with you. O lord of lords! After they have obtained happiness, let them go to your destination and see you." Maheshvara, the lord of the gods, agreed to what Pippalada had said. He addressed him, along with the gods, and honoured them.'

'The gods were happy at being freed from fear on account of him. In Shiva's presence, all of them spoke to Dadhichi's son. The gods said, "There is no doubt that you have done what is desired by the gods. The commands of the lord of the gods ornament the three worlds and you have carried them out. O brahmana! What you asked for earlier, is for others and not for your own self. Therefore, tell us about something else. We wish to give you something." The large number of gods repeatedly said this to the excellent brahmana. Pippalada joined his hands in salutation and bowed down to Shambhu, the original god, Uma and the *pippala*s and then spoke. Pippalada said, "I have always heard about my parents through words. I wish to see them. Blessed are creatures in this world who are under the control of their mother and father. They are the ones who always serve them and wait for their commands. Having obtained senses, a body, a lineage, capacity, intelligence and a form, a person should devote himself to serving those two.[689] He then accomplishes his objective. Even for animals and birds, it is very easy to see the mother. But that has been extremely difficult for me. Is that because of a sin I have committed? Had this been something that was difficult for everyone, it wouldn't have mattered. However, this is very easy for some to obtain. Therefore, there is no sinner like me. O excellent gods! Even if I can see the two of them, that will be fruits obtained through my thoughts, words and deeds. If a person is born and cannot see his parents, which lord is capable of enumerating his sins?" Hearing his words, the gods consulted among themselves and spoke. "Today, you will certainly see your parents, the auspicious couple, seated astride an excellent *vimana*. They wish to see you. Abandon your sorrow, avarice and delusion. Make your mind serene." The excellent gods told Dadhichi's son, "Look. Behold. The two of them are in heaven, adorned with golden

---

[689] The parents.

ornaments. They are astride an excellent *vimana*. The auspicious couple is there. Your parents are anxious to see you. They are being fanned by celestial women. They are being praised by *kinnara*s." He saw his parents in Shiva's presence, and bowed down before them. His eyes were filled with tears of delight. But somehow, he managed to speak to them. The son said, "Sons who make their parents cross over are those who extend the lineage. However, I am one who has only been able to split aside my mother's stomach. Such am I, an extremely evil-minded person. Nevertheless, in my confusion, I am looking at them." Looking at them, he could not say anything more because of his misery. The gods spoke to Pippalada and his parents. The gods said, "O son! You are blessed. Your fame is known in this world and has reached heaven. You have directly seen the three-eyed one, you have reassured the gods. For you, the virtuous worlds will never be exhausted." From heaven, flowers showered down on his head. O great sage! The gods pronounced words of "Victory". Dadhichi, along with his wife, pronounced benedictions over their son. After bowing down to Shambhu, Ganga and the gods, he addressed his son in these words. Dadhichi said, "Get a wife. Be devoted to Shiva. Serve Ganga. Have sons. Perform sacrifices in the proper way and donate *dakshina*. O son! You will then accomplish your objective and reside in heaven for a long time." Pippalashana told Dadhichi that he would act accordingly. Dadhichi and his wife repeatedly comforted their son. Taking the permission of the large number of gods, they then returned to heaven.'

'With trepidation, all the gods spoke to Pippalada. The gods said, "O fortunate one! Pacify Kritya and the large fire that has originated from her." Pippalada replied, "I don't have the capacity to restrain her. I have never uttered a falsehood. You speak to Kritya. If she sees me, that extremely terrible one will do exactly the opposite." To pacify her, the gods went and spoke to her and the fire. But both of them refused. "The brahmana has created me for devouring everything. In that way, the fire has been created from me. How can it be otherwise? Everything must be in our mouths, the five great elements and mobile and immobile objects. There must be nothing that remains." Having consulted me, the gods spoke to them again. "In due order, both of you devour everything."

O Narada! Listen to what Vadava told the gods. Vadava said, "O excellent gods! As you have desired, everything should be devoured by me." O sage! Vadava became a river and merged with Ganga. There was an extremely terrible fire that originated from her. The immortals speak of this fire as the first among the elements. The gods said, "Water is known as the first among the elements, but you are also the first. Though you have originated from water, you are the first. Hence, devour the ocean. As we have told you, go and devour it, as you please." Anala[690] told the gods, "There is water there. How can I go? I can go only if you convey me to that great water." They asked, "O Agni! What will your progress be like?' Agni told the gods, "There must be a maiden who possesses all the qualities. She must place me in a golden pot and take me there. That will be my progress." Hearing his words, they spoke to the maiden Sarasvati. The gods said, "Bearing Anala on your head, quickly convey him to Varuna's abode." Sarasvati told the gods, "I don't have the capacity to bear him alone. If I am helped by four others, I will quickly convey him to Varuna's abode." Hearing Sarasvati's words, the gods separately spoke to Ganga, Yamuna, Narmada and Tapati. Placing Anala in a golden pot, they placed him on their heads and went to Varuna's abode. They placed him in Prabhasa, where Somanatha, the lord of the gods and the lord of the universe, with the moon as his ornament, resides, along with the gods. The five rivers, including Sarasvati, took him there. The great fire resides there and slowly drinks the water.'

'After this, the large number of gods spoke to Shiva, supreme among the gods. The gods said, "Please tell us how the bones, the gods and the cattle can be purified." Shiva told them, "All of you carefully bathe in Ganga. There is no doubt that the gods and the cattle will then be freed from sins. Also wash the bones that have been obtained from the *rishi*'s body. When they are washed, they will become pure." The place where the gods were freed from their sins is a *tirtha* that destroys all sins.[691] Bathing and donating there cleans the sin of killing a brahmana. The place where the cows were

---

[690] Another name for Agni.
[691] Known as Papanashana *tirtha*.

purified is known as *Go-tirtha*. An immensely intelligent one who bathes there obtains the fruit of the sacrifice of a cow. O Narada! The place where the brahmana's bones were purified is known as Pitri *tirtha*. It enhances the delight of the ancestors. If the ashes, bones, nails and body hair of any living being fall into this *tirtha*, even if he is extremely evil in his deeds, he resides in heaven for as long as the moon, the sun and the stars circle. O Narada! Thus, three *tirtha*s originated from Chakra *tirtha*. Having been purified, the large number of gods and cattle spoke to Shambhu. The cattle and the gods said, "We will leave for our own abodes. Surya is established here. As long as the one who makes the day is established here, all the gods are also established here. O lord of the universe! You should now grant us permission to leave. Surya is the eternal *atman* of everything in the universe. We have established Divakara here and all the gods are in him. Ganga, the mother of the universe and Tryambaka are also here. All the gods exist when Tryambaka is present." Taking their leave of Pippalada, the gods left for their own abodes. In the course of time, the *pippala*s obtained an eternal place in heaven. The powerful brahmana, Pippalada, obtained a position for the trees. Having worshipped Shankara, he made them the master of a *kshetra*. Dadhichi's son was a sage who was fierce in his energy. He obtained Goutama's daughter as a wife. Having obtained sons, prosperity and fame, along with his well-wishers, the persevering one went to heaven. Since then, that *tirtha* has been spoken of as Pippaleshvara. It is sacred and yields the fruits of all sacrifices. Even if one remembers it, sins are destroyed. What need be said about bathing or donating there, or seeing it? Chakreshvara and Pippaleshvara are the names of the lord of the gods. If one knows about this mystery, one will obtain everything that one desires. The place where Surya is established and the gods are also established is known as the *kshetra* of Pratishthana.[692] It is loved by the gods. This is an extremely sacred account. If one reads it, hears it, or remembers it, one lives for a long time and obtains riches and

[692] The word *pratishthana* means foundation/position. There is more than one place known as Pratishthana. This is Paithan, in Aurangabad district.

dharma. If one remembers Shambhu at the time of death, one will always obtain him.'

Chapter 2(41) (Naga *tirtha*)

Brahma said, 'The place known as Naga *tirtha* is auspicious and yields everything that one desires. The divinity known as Nageshvara exist there.[693] Hear about it in detail. In the city of Pratishthana, there was a king known as Shurasena. He was born in the lunar dynasty. He was handsome and intelligent and was an ocean of qualities. Along with his beloved, he made great efforts for the sake of a son. After a long time, a son was born to him. But he was a snake, who was terrible in form. Surasena, lord of the earth, reared his son. Other than the king, no one knew that his son was a snake. Except his mother and his father, no one in the inner quarters also knew. The nurse-maid did not know, nor did the adviser, or the priest. On seeing that terrible snake, the supreme among kings and his wife were always tormented. However, they thought that having a snake was better than having no son. There was something special about this great snake. He always spoke like a human. The snake spoke to his father. 'Please perform the rites of *chudakarma* and *upanayana*.[694] Please arrange for me to study the Vedas. Until he studies the Vedas, a *dvija* is as good as a shudra.'[695] Hearing his son's words, Shurasena became extremely miserable.

[693] This must, therefore, be the one in Gujarat.

[694] There are thirteen *samskara*s or sacraments. The list varies a bit. But one list is *vivaha* (marriage), *garbhalambhana* (conception), *pumshavana* (engendering a male child), *simantonnayana* (parting the hair, performed in the 4th month of pregnancy), *jatakarma* (birth rites), *namakarana* (naming), *chudakarma* (tonsure), *annaprashana* (first solid food), *keshanta* (first shaving of the head), *upanayana* (sacred thread), *vidyarambha* (commencement of studies), *samavartana* (graduation) and *antyeshti* (funeral rites).

[695] Here, the word *dvija* is meant to be taken as twice-born, not as a *brahmana*. Thus, it means any of the first three *varna*s.

He summoned a brahmana and had the *samskaras* performed. When he had studied the Vedas, the snake spoke to his father. The snake said, "O king! O supreme among kings! Please perform my marriage. I desire a woman. It is my view that otherwise, the requisite tasks will not be completed. The father must perform all the *samskaras* recommended in the Vedas for his son. A father who does not do this cannot escape from hell." Amazed, the father spoke to his son who was in the form of a snake. Shurasena said, "Even brave men are scared when they hear his voice. O son! Who will bestow a maiden on such a person? What will I do?" Hearing his father's words, the discriminating snake replied. The snake said, "O king! O lord of men! There are many kinds of marriages. Forcible abduction and marriage with weapons is also praised.[696] When a son gets married, a father accomplishes all his tasks. If this is not done, there is no doubt that I will die in Ganga." The supreme among kings got to know about his son's intention. Lacking a human son, he summoned his advisers for the sake of the marriage and addressed them in the following words. Shurasena said, "My son Nageshvara is the heir apparent and he is an ocean of qualities. He possesses qualities and is intelligent. He is brave and impossible to defeat. He scorches his enemies. When the *naga* is seated on a chariot with his bow, there is no one on earth who is his equal. His marriage must be undertaken. I am old. Passing on the burden of the kingdom to my son, I will be reassured. Until my beloved son has a wife, he will not give up his childish sentiments. Therefore, all of you should agree to this. Engaged in ensuring my welfare, please make efforts for the marriage. When my son is married, I will no longer have any worries. I will pass on the burden to my son and leave for the forest to perform austerities." Hearing the king's words, all the advisers humbly joined their hands in salutation. Full of delight, they spoke to the immensely energetic king. The advisers said, "Your son is superior in qualities and is famous everywhere. About your son's marriage, there is nothing to be consulted. There is nothing to be thought about." When the advisers said this, the

[696] When the groom is not physically present, marriage can take with the groom's weapons, the weapons acting as a stand-in for the groom.

excellent king turned somber. He did not tell his advisers that his son was a snake and they did not know. The king again said, "Who is a maiden who is superior in qualities? Who is the prosperous king born in a great lineage who is a reservoir of qualities? Who is best for a matrimonial alliance? With which brave one will a matrimonial alliance be praised?" Amongst the advisers, there was an extremely intelligent one. He had been born in a noble lineage and was exceedingly virtuous. He was engaged in the king's tasks. Hearing the king's words and knowing the king's mind, he read the signs and spoke. The adviser said, "O great king! In the eastern region, there is a king named Vijaya. His horses, elephants and jewels cannot be enumerated. The intelligent king has eight sons who are great archers. Their sister, Bhogavati, is like another Lakshmi herself. O king! I think she will be an appropriate wife for your son." Hearing the aged adviser's words, the king replied. The king asked, "How can his daughter become my son's wife? Please tell me that." The aged adviser answered, "O great king! I have noticed what is in your mind. Please grant me permission to carry out Shurasena's task." Hearing the words of the aged adviser, he honoured him with ornaments, garments and words. He sent him, along with a large army.'

'He went to the eastern region and met the great king. In the proper way, he honoured him with words and other modes sanctioned by good policy. The intelligent one arranged for a marriage between the great king's daughter, Bhogavati and King Shurasena's intelligent son, who was a *naga*. In the matrimonial alliance, both true and false words were used. He honoured the king with ornaments, garments and other things. Having obtained these honours, the king said that he would bestow his daughter. After this, the immensely intelligent aged adviser returned to King Shurasena and told him that arrangements for the marriage had been made. After many days passed, the immensely intelligent aged adviser again went with a large army, garments and ornaments. He went quickly, surrounded by many other advisers. The intelligent chief adviser spoke to the great king[697] about the marriage. Surrounded

697 Vijaya.

by the other advisers, the aged adviser spoke about everything. The aged adviser said, "King Shurasena's son is known as Naga. He is intelligent and is an ocean of qualities. He does not wish to come here. O king! There are many kinds of marriages for a *kshatriya*. O immensely intelligent one! Therefore, let the marriage be with the weapons and ornaments. *Kshatriya*s and *brahmanas* speak the truth. Hence, allow this marriage to take place with weapons and ornaments." Hearing the aged adviser's words, Vijaya, the excellent king, took the words spoken the adviser and the king[698] to be the truth. Therefore, the king arranged for a complete marriage of Bhogavati with the weapons, as is recommended in the sacred texts. He then sent her. Full of joy, Vijaya sent his own advisers and many cows and horses and a lot of gold along with her. Taking these with them, the advisers, with the aged adviser leading the way, went to Pratishthana and presented Shurasena with his daughter-in-law. They presented her and reported the many words that Vijaya had spoken. They presented the wonderful ornaments, female servants and garments to Shurasena. The king welcomed and honoured Vijaya's advisers, who had come along with Bhogavati. He showed them a great deal of respect and having expressed his affection for Vijaya, allowed them to leave.'

'Vijaya's daughter was a maiden who was young and beautiful. The slender-waisted one always served her father-in-law and mother-in-law. Bhogavati's husband was an extremely large and terrible snake. He lived alone, in a deserted house that was beautifully adorned with jewels. It was strewn with fragrant flowers and was cool and pleasant. The snake repeatedly spoke to his mother and father. "Why doesn't my wife, the princess, approach me?" Hearing her son's words, the snake's mother replied. The king's wife said, "O nurse-maid! O extremely fortunate one! Quickly go to Bhogavati and tell her that her husband is a snake. Tell me what she says." The nurse-maid agreed and went to Bhogavati. In private, she humbly told her everything, from the beginning. The nurse-maid said, "O extremely fortunate one! O fortunate one! I know that your husband is a divinity. You should never reveal

[698] Shurasena.

that he is a snake and not a man." Hearing her words, Bhogavati
replied. Bhogavati said, "In general, a human woman obtains a
human man as a husband. But a husband who is divine in form is
only obtained through good merits." In due order, she went and
reported all of Bhogavati's words to the snake, the snake's mother
and the king. Hearing her words and remembering the course of
karma, the king wept. Bhogavati spoke to the friend she had spoken
to earlier.[699] Bhogavati said, "O fortunate one! Show me my beloved
husband. My age is passing in vain." At this, she showed her the
extremely terrible snake. In secret, she went to the place that was
strewn with fragrant flowers and saw her husband, the extremely
terrible snake, lying down, ornamented with jewels. She joined her
hands in salutation and addressed her beloved in energetic words.
Bhogavati said, "I am blessed that I have been favoured in this way.
My husband is a divinity." Saying this, she remained on the bed,
following the inclinations of snakes and playing with the snake.
The slender-limbed one embraced his limbs and sang songs. She
satisfied her husband with fragrant flowers and drinks. O sage!
Through her favours, the snake remembered what had happened.
He remembered everything that had happened because of destiny.'

'In the night, the snake spoke to his beloved. The snake asked,
"O princess! O beloved! When you see me, why are you not
scared?" She replied, "O lord! Who is capable of transgressing what
destiny has determined? The husband is the refuge for women. In
particular, all the gods are in him." Pleased at this, the immensely
intelligent Indra among *naga*s spoke to his wife. The snake replied,
"I am satisfied with your devotion. What will I give you? What do
you desire? O slender-limbed one! Through your favours, I have
remembered everything. The wielder of Pinaka, the lord of the gods,
was angry with me and cursed me. I am a *naga* and am the immensely
strong son of Shesha. I was coiled around Maheshvara's arm. I was
your husband earlier too. You were my wife, named Bhogavati. In
private, Shambhu was once delighted at Uma's words and laughed
loudly. O fortunate one! In the divinity's presence, I too laughed. At
this, Shambhu became angry and cursed me that I would be reduced

---

[699] That is, the nurse-maid.

to this state. Shiva said, 'Though you will possess learning, you will be born as a snake in a human womb.' O fortunate one! Along with me, you also sought Shambhu's favours. O fortunate one! He again said, 'I will give you knowledge. In the form of a snake, you will worship me in Goutami. Through Bhogavati's favours, you will then be freed from your curse.' O one with the beautiful face! That is the reason I have obtained you, despite being reduced to this state. Please take me to Goutami and worship him, along with me. Freed from the curse, both of us will then go to Shiva. For everyone, in every possible situation, Shiva is the ultimate refuge." Hearing her husband's words, along with her husband, she went to Goutami. They bathed in Goutami and worshipped Shiva. O sage! Pleased, the illustrious one gave them divine forms. Along with his wife, the snake got ready to leave for Shiva's world and sought the permission from his parents. Knowing this, the immensely intelligent father replied. The father said, 'You are my only son. You are the eldest and the heir apparent. Therefore, rule over this entire kingdom and have many sons. When I leave for the supreme destination, go to Shiva's city.' Hearing his father's words, the king of *naga*s agreed. Along with his wife, the one who was excellent in his vows could assume any form at will. Along with his father, mother and sons, he ruled over the extremely extensive kingdom. When his parents went to the world of heaven, he instated his sons in his own place. With his wife, advisers and others, he went to Shiva's city. Since then, that *tirtha* has been known as Naga *tirtha*. The divinity Nageshvara was established there by Bhogavati. Bathing and donating there yield the fruits of all sacrifices.'

Chapter 2(42) (Matri *tirtha*)

Brahma said, 'The place known as Matri *tirtha* brings every kind of success to men. Even if a being remembers that *tirtha*, he is freed from all mental ailments. There was a terrible battle between the gods and the *asura*s. In the battle, the gods were unable to vanquish the *danava*s. With the gods, I went to the place where the wielder of the trident was standing. I joined my hands in salutation and praised him with many kinds of gentle words. "Having consulted among themselves, all the gods and *asura*s decided that they would churn the ocean. O Mahesha! The poison known as *kalakuta* resulted from this. Other than you, who is capable of swallowing it up? There is the one who is capable of robbing the three worlds of their dependence by striking them with flowers.[700] He deserves to be worshipped by all the gods. However, when he sought to strike Hara, he headed towards his own destruction. O Ananga's enemy! O Shambhu! When the lord of waters was churned, you gave the residents of heaven the excellent object[701] and withdrew the poison into your own self. That certainly established your greatness." The illustrious original creator, Trilochana,[702] was pleased with this. Shiva said, "O excellent gods! Speak. I will give you what you want." The gods replied, "O Vrishadhvaja! On account of the *danava*s, we are suffering from a terrible fear. O lord! You are our protector. Slaughter the enemies of the gods. O Shambhu! You are a well-wisher without any motive. Had you not been there, what would have become of us? What would afflicted creatures, suffering from grief, have done?" Addressed in this way, he immediately went to the place where the enemies of the gods were. There was a battle between Shankara and the enemies of the gods. When Trilochana Shiva was exhausted, he assumed a form that was full of *tamas*. As he fought, drops of sweat fell down from his forehead. Resorting to his *tamasa* form, he slaughtered large numbers of *daitya*s. Seeing this form, the *asura*s fled to the slopes of Meru. Slaying all the *daitya*s, Hara went to earth. Terrified, all of them rushed around here and there, on earth. Angry, Rudra also followed the enemy. Wherever Shambhu fought, drops of sweat fell down. O sage! Wherever Maheshvara's sweat fell down on the ground, Matrikas[703] were generated and they were like Shiva in form. All of them told Maheshvara, "We will eat the *asura*s." Surrounded by large numbers of gods, the

---

[700] Meaning Kama, the god of love. Ananga is one of Kama's names.
[701] *Amrita*.
[702] One with three eyes, Shiva.
[703] Mother goddesses.

illustrious one spoke to all of them. Shiva said, "From heaven, the *rakshasas* came to earth and have now reached Rasatala. Listen to the words I speak. Let the Matrikas go wherever the enemies are. Scared of me, the enemies have now reached Rasatala. Follow the enemies to Rasatala." Following his words, they shattered the earth and went to the place where the *daitya*s and *danava*s were. The Matrikas killed all the extremely terrible enemies of the gods. The Matrikas followed the same path and returned to the gods. Once the Matrikas left and until they returned, the gods went to the banks of Goutami and remained there. The place the Matrikas left from, and the place where the gods remained, is the extremely sacred *kshetra* of Pratishthana. It extends victory. The places where the Matrikas originated are separate Matri *tirtha*s. There are holes there, for going to Rasatala. The gods spoke and granted them boons. "As long as Shiva is worshipped in this world, let the Matrikas also always be worshipped, in the same way." Saying this, the gods vanished, but the Matrikas remained there. The places where the goddesses remained are known as Matri *tirtha*s. The gods also frequent them. What need be said about humans and others? Following Shiva's words, bathing, donations and water-rites performed for the ancestors there, are known to yield all the inexhaustible benefits. If a person constantly hears, reads or remembers this account of Matri *tirtha*, he obtains a long lifespan and is happy.'

Chapter 2(43) (Brahma *tirtha* and other *tirtha*s)

Brahma said, 'After this, there is another *tirtha*. Even the gods find it extremely difficult to reach this. This is known as Brahma *tirtha*. It bestows objects of pleasure and emancipation on men. O best among sages! When the *daitya*s entered Rasatala and the Matrikas followed them, the soldiers of the gods remained there. My fifth face had assumed the terrible form of a donkey. With that face, I remained amidst the soldiers of the gods and said, "O *daitya*s! Why are you running away? Do not be scared. I will come and quickly devour all the gods in an instant." On seeing that

I was about to devour them, all the gods restrained me. Scared, they told Vishnu, "O Vishnu! O lord of the universe! Please save us and cut off Brahma's face." The one who wields the *chakra* spoke to the gods. "I will sever his head with this *chakra*. But the moment it is destroyed, all mobile and immobile objects will also be destroyed. O gods! Therefore, I will tell all of you a *mantra*. Listen to me. There is no doubt that the one with the three eyes is the right person to sever the head, since he will hold it." Thereupon, as suggested by me, I and all of them, praised Shambhu. "Sacrifices are seen to yield fruits for a short while. It is therefore held that they don't yield fruits to those who undertake them. Hence, those who wanted fruits from donations have determined that the rites must be performed for the one with the matted hair." At this, the lord of the gods was pleased. To accomplish the task of the gods and for the welfare of the worlds, he told the gods that he agreed. That face was evil in form and was extremely terrible. It made the body hair stand up. Using his nails as a weapon, he severed it and asked, "Where will it be placed?" Ila[704] told the gods, "I am incapable of bearing the head. I will go to Rasatala.' The ocean said, "I can't hold it. I will be dried up in an instant." The gods spoke to Shiva. "Out of compassion for the worlds, you must hold Brahma's head. If it is not severed, the world will be destroyed. However, if it is severed, because of the taint, that is exactly what will happen." While thinking about it, Somesha[705] held the head. Witnessing this extremely difficult task on the banks of Goutami, the gods devotedly prostrated themselves and praised the lord of the universe. The extremely terrible head would have harmed the gods. For the sake of devouring them, it had approached. However, using his needle-like nails as weapons, the one with the moon on his crest severed it. Out of compassion, because of the taint it would cause if it was released, he held onto that fragment. All the gods were standing near Brahma. On witnessing this deed, which surpassed the deeds of the gods, the gods praised Ishana. Since then, that *tirtha* has been known as Brahma *tirtha*. Even today, Brahma is present

---

[704] A name for the earth.
[705] Shiva's name.

there with his four faces. If a person sees only the head, he obtains a destination with Brahma. Rudra himself remained there to cut off Brahma's head. That place is known as Rudra *tirtha*. The extremely wonderful place where Divakara himself remains in the form of the gods is known as Sourya *tirtha*. It yields the fruits of all sacrifices. If a person bathes there and sees the sun, he doesn't have to be born again. Ensuring what would bring benefit to the gods, Mahadeva severed Brahma's fifth head and placed it in a *kshetra* known as Avimukta. Along the banks of Goutami, in Brahma *tirtha*, this is the place where the head alone can be seen. This is the *kshetra* of Avimukta, where the head was placed. If a person sees Brahma's sacred head, he is purified even if he has killed a brahmana.'

Chapter 2(44) (Avighna *tirtha*)

Brahma said, 'The *tirtha* known as Avighna is said to remove all kinds of impediments.[706] In this connection, I will recount an incident. O Narada! Listen devotedly. The gods organized a sacrifice on the northern bank of Goutami. However, because of the taint of some impediments, the sacrifice could not be completed. At this, all the gods spoke to me and Hari. I meditated on what they had said and ascertained the reason. "The sacrifice has not been completed because of impediments created by Vinayaka.[707] Therefore, all of you should praise Vinayaka, the original god." Agreeing to this, the large number of gods bathed along Goutami's banks. They devotedly praised Ganeshvara, the divinity who is the original god. The gods said, "In every undertaking, Vighnaraja must always be worshipped by the gods, Isha and the one who originated from the lotus.[708] He should be bowed down to and thought about.

---

[706] *Vighna* means impediment. Thus, *avighna* means without impediment.

[707] Vinayaka, Ganeshvara and Vighnaraja are names for Ganesha. So is Ambikeya (Ambika's son).

[708] Brahma.

We seek refuge in him. In bestowing desires of the mind, there is
no other divinity who is Vighnaraja's equal. Having determined
this, before destroying the cities,[709] the destroyer of Tripura also
worshipped him. Let Ambikeya quickly removed the impediments
that exist in our great sacrifice. When he is meditated upon, all the
mental wishes of those with bodies come to complete fruition. As
soon as the goddess thought about him, a son was born and there
were great festivities everywhere. Therefore, large number of gods
who have accomplished their objectives speak of Vighnaraja as
Sadyojata[710] and bow down before him. When he was lying down
on his mother's lap and his mother tried to restrain him, he used
his force to hide the moon in his father's matted hair. This is how
Ganadinatha found delight. Having drunk milk from his mother's
breast, he was content. Nevertheless, his mind was full of envy
towards his brother. Therefore, Shambhu said, 'Be Lamodara'.[711]
Thus, Vighnaraja is known as Lambodara. Surrounded by a
large number of gods, Mahesha said, 'Start dancing'. Ganeshvara
delighted him merely by the sound of the tinkling of his anklets.
His father consecrated him.[712] He holds the noose of impediments
in one hand. With the other hand, he holds an axe on his shoulder.
If he is not worshipped, he causes impediments, even to his mother.
Who is Vighnapati's[713] equal? In the pursuit of *dharma*, *artha*, *kama*
and other things, he must be worshipped first. The gods and *asura*s
always worship him. If he is worshipped, there is no destruction. He
must be worshipped first. I bow down before the first one. When he
is worshipped and prayed to, all the fruits and success are seen to be
appropriately obtained. He is extremely proud of his independent
capability. He loves his brother. He rides on a mouse. I worship
him. He satisfies his mother exceedingly well with delightful singing
and dancing and all the desired kinds of amusement. I seek refuge
with the illustrious Ganesha. Because of his father's favours,

---

[709] The three cities of Tripura.
[710] Meaning, instantly born.
[711] Someone with an elongated stomach, pot-bellied.
[712] As lord of the *gana*s.
[713] Vighnapati means lord of impediments, as does Vighnesha.

he is always prosperous. For the benefit of the gods, I am using
*stotram*s, bowing down and other *mantra*s to seek refuge with
the illustrious Ganesha. In ensuring victory against the cities, his
father did something unparalleled. Instead of being worshipped by
him, he cheerfully worshipped him.[714] Hence, he removed all the
impediments. I prostrate myself before Ganesha." When the large
number of gods praised him, Vighnesha spoke to them. Ganesha
said, "Through my favours, from now on, all sacrifices performed
by the enemies of the *asura*s will be without impediments." When
the sacrifice of the gods was over, Ganesha spoke to the gods again.
Ganesha said, "Those who are firm in their vows and devotedly
satisfy me with this *stotram*, will never suffer from poverty and
misery. Let this be known. Those who attentively and devotedly
bathe and undertake donations here will always be successful in
all their objectives." Simultaneously, the gods also agreed with this
statement. When the sacrifice was over, the gods left for the abode
of the gods. Since then, that place has been known as Avighna
tirtha. It yields every kind of desire to men and destroys every kind
of impediment.'

Chapter 2(45) (Shesha *tirtha* and other *tirtha*s)

Brahma said, 'The place known as Shesha *tirtha* bestows every
object of desire. I have already spoken about it and I will
describe its nature. There was a giant *naga* named Shesha and this
lord was the king of Rasatala. Surrounded by all the *naga*s, he went
to Rasatala. But the *rakshasa*s, *daitya*s and Danu's offspring[715]
entered Rasatala and exiled Bhogipati.[716] He was agitated and
spoke to me. Shesha said, "You gave Rasatala to me and also to the
*rakshasa*s. However, they are not giving me a place. Therefore, I
have sought refuge with you." At this, I told the *naga*, "O *pannaga*!

[714] Shiva (the father) worshipped Ganesha (the son).
[715] *Danava*s.
[716] Meaning, the lord of the *naga*s.

Go to Goutami. When you praise Mahadeva there, you will obtain
what you wish for. In the three worlds, there is no one else who can
give you what you desire." Urged by my words, the *naga* carefully
bathed in Ganga. He joined his hands in salutation and praised the
lord of the gods. Shesha said, "O lord of the three worlds! O one
who destroyed Daksha's sacrifice! I bow down to you. O original
creator! I bow down to you. O one whose form is the three worlds!
I bow down to you. O one with one thousand heads! I bow down
to you. O one who brings about destruction! I bow down to you.
O one with forms as Soma, Surya and Agni! I bow down to you. O
one with the form as water! I bow down to you. O one who always
has every kind of form! I bow down before you. O one with a form
as Kala! I bow down before you. O Shankara! Save me. O lord
of everything! O Somesha![717] O one who goes everywhere! Save
me. O lord of the universe! I bow down before you. Please grant
me what my mind wishes for." At this, Maheshvara was pleased
and gave the *naga* the desired boon. For the destruction of the
enemies of the gods—the *daityas*, *danavas* and *rakshasas*, he gave
Shesha a trident and said, "Slay the bulls among the enemies with
this." When Shiva said this, with the other *naga*s, Shesha went to
Rasatala and used the trident to slay the enemies in a battle. When
he had killed the *daityas*, *danavas* and *rakshasas* with the trident,
the *naga* returned to the place where the divinity, Shesheshvara[718]
Hara was. A hole was created, along the path the king of *naga*s
used to come to the place where the divinity was, that is, when he
returned from Rasatala to see the divinity. Even now, the waters of
Ganga flow through that hole and it is sacred. That water merges
with Ganga and the flow has a confluence with Ganga. In front
of the divinity, the *naga* created an extremely large sacrificial pit
and offered oblations to him. Agni is always present there. At the
confluence with Ganga, the water is hot. After having worshipped
the lord of the gods, the immensely illustrious *naga* was delighted
at having got what he wanted. Obtaining this from Shiva, he went
to the nether regions of Rasatala. Since then, that *tirtha* has been

[717] Lord of Soma.
[718] Meaning Shesha's lord.

known as Naga *tirtha*. It is sacred and yields everything that is
desired. It destroys disease and poverty. It bestows a long lifespan
and prosperity. It is auspicious. Bathing and donating there, bestow
emancipation. This also happens if one devotedly hears about it,
reads about it, or remembers it. The place where Shiva gave the
trident is Shesheshvara *tirtha*.[719] O tiger among sages! Along both
banks, there are two thousand and one hundred *tirtha*s. They
bestow every kind of prosperity.'

Chapter 2(46) (Vadava and other *tirtha*s)

Brahma said, 'The place known as Mahanala is also known
as Vadavanala.[720] The divinity is Mahanala and the river is
Vadava. O son! I will tell you about that *tirtha*. It destroys death,
old age and other taints. In earlier times, the *rishi*s performed a
sacrifice in Naimisha forest. The ascetic *rishi*s made Mrityu the
shamitri.[721] While the sacrifice was going on, Mrityu stood there
as the *shamitri*. Therefore, no mobile or immobile objects died. O
best among sages! Barring the sacrificial animals, mortals became
immortal. As a result of this, heaven became empty and the mortal
world was crowded because Mrityu was ignoring it. At this, the
gods told the *rakshasa*s, "Go to the sacrifice of the *rishi*s. Go and
destroy that great sacrifice." Hearing the words of the gods, the
*rakshasa*s spoke to the gods. "We will destroy the sacrifice. But
what fruits will we get from this? Nowhere does anyone engage in
an undertaking without a motive." The gods told the *asura*s, "The
sacrifice is also for you. Therefore, you should go to the excellent
sacrifice of the *rishi*s." Hearing this, they quickly went to the place
where the sacrifice was taking place. They went there to destroy it,
especially because the gods had asked them to. Getting to know,

---

[719] This is the same as Shesha *tirtha* or Naga *tirtha*.

[720] Respectively, the great fire and the Vadava fire.

[721] In the course of a sacrifice, a *shamitri* is the one who undertakes the
slaughtering. Thus, Death was made the slaughterer.

the *rishi*s asked Mrityu, "What will we do? Urged by the words of
the gods, the *rakshasa*s have come here to destroy the sacrifice."
The residents of Naimisha forest consulted with Mrityu. O Narada!
Along with the *shamitri*, all of them left their own hermitages.
They only took the sacrificial fire with them and left vessels and
other things behind. To complete the sacrifice, they quickly went
to Goutami. They bathed there. For the sake of their protection,
they joined their hands in salutation and praised Mahesha, the
lord of the gods. The *rishi*s said, "In his pastimes, he created this
entire universe. He is the creator of the three worlds and he is the
one who ordains. The universe is his form. He is beyond cause
and effect. We seek refuge with that Someshvara." Mrityu said,
"Merely through his will, he destroys everything. He is the one
who creates and preserves. He is the lord of the gods. I seek refuge
with Shankara. He is immense in size. He is gigantic in strength.
He is adorned with a great serpent. He is the divinity who has a
huge form. I seek refuge with that Shankara." Thus addressed, the
illustrious one asked Mrityu, "What is it that you want?" Mrityu
replied, "O lord of the gods! There is a terrible fear on account
of the *rakshasa*s. Please protect our sacrifice, so that the sacrifice
can be completed." The illustrious three-eyed Vrishadhvaja did
this. With Mrityu as the *shamitri*, the sacrifice of the *rishi*s was
completed. To take their shares of the oblations, the immortals
arrived there, in the due order. Along with Mrityu, the large
number of agitated sages spoke to them. The *rishi*s said, "You sent
the *rakshasa*s to destroy our sacrifice. Therefore, from now on,
the wicked *rakshasa*s will be your enemies." Since then, the gods
and the *rakshasa*s have been enemies. Along with the unblemished
*rishi*s, the gods told the Kritya Vadava to be Mrityu's wife and
consecrated her accordingly. The water used for the consecration
led to the creator of the river Vadava. The *lingam* established by
Mrityu is known as Mahanala. Since then, that *tirtha* has been
known as the confluence of Vadava. The divinity Mahanala exists
in that *tirtha* and bestows objects of pleasure and emancipation.
Along both banks, there are one thousand *tirtha*s there and they
give everything that one wishes for. Even if one remembers these,
all sins are destroyed.'

Chapter 2(47) (Atma *tirtha*)

Brahma said, 'Atma *tirtha* is famous and bestows objects of pleasure and emancipation on men. I will describe its powers to you. Jnaneshvara Shiva is present there. Atri's son was known as Datta[722] and he was loved by Hara. His beloved brother, Durvasa, was accomplished in all kinds of *jnana*. He went to his father. Prostrating himself, he spoke humbly. Datta asked, "How can I obtain *jnana* about the *brahman*? Who shall I ask? Who will I go to?" Hearing his son's words, Atri meditated and addressed him in these words. Atri replied, "O son! Go to Goutami and praise Maheshvara there. If he is pleased with you, you can obtain *jnana* from him." Thus addressed, Atri's son went to Ganga. He purified and controlled himself. Joining his hands in salutation, he devotedly praised Shankara. Datta said, "I have fallen into this pit of *samsara*. Because of destiny and delusion, I am hidden in this mire of misery in the world. I am enveloped in the darkness of ignorance. O lord of the gods! I do not know the supreme. I have been mangled by the strong trident of sin. The razor of worries has shattered me. I am scorched by the fierce heat of the five senses. I am exhausted. O Somanatha! Please help me to cross over. I am bound in the bondage of poverty. I have been struck by the fierce heat of disease. I have been attacked by the serpent of death. I am extremely scared. O Shambhu! What shall I do? I am suffering a great deal from birth and death, hunger and thirst, *rajas* and *tamas*. I have been overwhelmed by such old age. O protector! Behold my state and show compassion on me now. I am suffering many hardships on account of desire, anger, envy, insolence, pride and many other things. They have pierced me. O protector! Strike these enemies away. O protector! It is true that when a man is suffering from hardships and has fallen down, someone or the other will save him. O Somanatha! However, with the exception of you, there is no one who has a word of pity for me. Until I utter the words 'I bow down to Shiva', I will have to suffer anger, fear, delusion,

[722] That is, Dattatreya.

sorrow, ignorance, poverty, ailments, desire and other things and
death. I do not possess *dharma*. I do not possess devotion. I do not
possess discrimination. Where is there compassion in me? You are
the one who bestows. You are the refuge. Therefore, let the word
'Soma' be fixed in my mind. O Somanatha! I do not wish to be a
god or a king. But you should be in the lotus in my heart. I wish to
be near the illustrious Soma's lotus feet. Reflect on this and please
do it. Though you know that I am a sinner, please listen to what
I am saying. Let me be in a place where the word 'Shiva' is heard.
Let Soma always be with me. O Gouri's consort! O Shankara! O
Somanatha! O lord of the universe! O ocean of compassion! O one
who is the *atman* of everything! If such praises are heard in a place,
surely a successful person resides there." Hearing Dattatreya's
praise, the illustrious Hara was satisfied. Bhava, the creator of
the universe, told the *yogi*, "I am the one who bestows boons."
Atri's son replied, "O one who is worshipped by the gods! I seek
the boon of knowledge about the *atman*, emancipation, extensive
devotion[723] towards you and the greatness of this *tirtha*." Shambhu
said he agreed with this and vanished. Since then, learned ones
have known that *tirtha* as Atma *tirtha*. O Narada! Bathing and
donations there, yield emancipation.'

Chapter 2(48) (Ashvattha Pippala and other *tirtha*s)

Brahma said, 'To the north, there are Ashvattha *tirtha*, Pippala
tirtha and Manda *tirtha*. Hear about their greatness. Earlier,
the Lord Agastya, the illustrious lord of the southern direction, was
sent by the gods to request Vindhya. Surrounded by one thousand
sages, he slowly approached Vindhya. He went to the best among
mountains, full of many trees. Vindhya, with one hundred summits,
was challenging Meru and the sun. The mountain was exceedingly

---

[723] We have corrected an obvious typo in the text. It says *bhukti* (object
of pleasure), but should be *bhakti* (devotion).

lofty. When Lopamudra's patient husband, the sage, approached, he and other *brahmanas* were treated with hospitality. To accomplish the task of the gods, the best among sages praised the mountain and spoke to him. Agastya said, "O best among mountains! Along with these sages, who know the truth, I am going on a visit to the *tirtha*s. I will go to the southern direction. O lord of the mountains! Please show me hospitality. Please grant me passage. Until I return, please remain in your present position.[724] Let it not be otherwise." The excellent mountain agreed. Surrounded by the sages, the sage reached the southern direction. He slowly went to Goutami and consecrated himself for a sacrifice there. Surrounded by the *rishi*s, he performed that sacrifice for an entire year.'

'Kaitabha had two wicked sons. These two *rakshasa*s were thorns in the path of *dharma*. In the residence of the gods, they were known as Ashvattha and Pippala. Ashvattha assumed the form of an *ashvattha* tree and Pippala assumed the form of a brahmana. They entered inside, wishing to destroy the sacrifice. Desiring to do this, those two evil-minded *danava*s assumed these forms. Ashvattha was in the form of a tree and Pippala was in the form of a brahmana. O store of austerities! Those two always oppressed the *brahmanas*. Whoever touched the *ashvattha* tree, was eaten by it. The *rakshasa* Pippala assumed the form of a chanter of Sama hymns and devoured the disciples. Even now, *brahmanas* who chant Sama hymns are completely devoid of compassion. Because the number of *brahmanas* was declining, the sages got to know that this was because of the two *rakshasa*s. Realizing this, the immensely wise ones resorted to the southern bank. They approached Shanaishchara, Surya's evil son.[725] Firm in his vows, he was performing austerities. All the large number of sages went and told him about the deeds of the rakshasas. Surya's son told the large number of sages, "O *brahmanas*! When my austerities are completed, I will kill the two *rakshasa*s. As long as my austerities are incomplete, I am incapable." The large number of sages replied,

---

[724] Before Agastya, Vindhya had bent down.

[725] Shanaishchara (Shani) is evil because he has an evil eye. The word Shanaishchara means slow-moving. Saturn is a planet that moves slowly.

"We will give you our great stores of austerities." Addressed by
the *brahmanas* in this way, Surya's son said that it would be done.
Surya's son assumed the form of a brahmana and approached the
rakshasa who was in the form of an *ashvattha* tree. As a brahmana,
he performed *pradakshina*. While he was performing *pradakshina*,
the wicked *rakshasa* took him to be a brahmana. As was always
the case, he used his *maya* to devour him. When he was inside, he
looked at his entrails with his eye. As soon as Ravi's evil son looked
at him, the wicked *rakshasa* was reduced to ashes in an instant,
like a mountain that has been struck by the *vajra*. After reducing
Ashvattha to ashes, he went to the other one, who was in the form
of a brahmana. He approached the *rakshasa*, who was a store of
sin. He humbly approached, just as a disciple would approach a
brahmana to study. As earlier, Pippala devoured Bhanu's son. One
he had been devoured, as was the case earlier, he looked at his entrails
with his eye. Through that glance alone, the *rakshasa* was reduced
to ashes. Having slain both of them, Bhanu's son asked, "What else
remains to be done? Let the sages tell me." With Agastya at the
forefront, all the ascetic sages were filled with delight. Pleased, the
*rishi*s wished to bestow boons on Surya's slow-moving son. Pleased,
Shani, Surya's powerful son, spoke to the *brahmanas*. Surya's son
said, "On my day,[726] if people control themselves and touch an
ashvattha tree, let all their tasks be successful and let them not
suffer hardships on account of me. Let this be known as Ashvattha
tirtha. If men bathe here, let all their tasks be successful. There is
another boon too. 'Throbbing of the eyes, throbbing of the arms,
nightmares, worrying thoughts and the uprising of enemies. Let all
these be quickly pacified for me.' O *devarshi*![727] On my day, if men
rise in the morning, devote themselves to meditating on Shiva and
touch an *ashvattha* tree while reciting this *mantra*, let the adverse
effects of evil planets be dispersed for them." Since then, that place
has been known as Ashvattha Pippala *tirtha*. Shanaishchara *tirtha*
is there and the one where Agastya performed his sacrifice. Other
than the *tirtha* where the sacrifice was performed, there is the *tirtha*

---

[726] Shani's day, Saturday.
[727] This is specifically addressed to Agastya.

where the Sama hymns were recited. In this way, there are sixteen thousand and eight *tirtha*s. Bathing and donating there, yield the fruits of all sacrifices.'

Chapter 2(49) (Soma *tirtha*)

Brahma said, 'Great-souled ones have spoken about the place named Soma *tirtha*. Bathing and donations there yield the fruits obtained from drinking *soma*. Earlier, herbs were the mothers of the universe and were honoured by living beings. Those goddesses are also my mothers. They originated before the earliest who originated. *Dharma*, studying and the rites of sacrifices are established in them. They hold up everything in the three worlds, mobile and immobile objects. There is no doubt that they cure every kind of ailment. They provide food and save every kind of life. These herbs deserve to be worshipped by the universe. Without any ego, they spoke to me in these words. The herbs said, "O supreme among gods! Give us a king and a husband." Hearing their words, I spoke to the herbs. "All of you will obtain a husband and a king who will enhance your delight. O sage! Hearing the word "king", they spoke to me again. "Where will we go?" I replied, "O mothers! Go to Goutami. If she is satisfied, you will get a king who is worshipped by the worlds." O best among sages! They went and praised the river Goutami. The herbs said, "O Goutami! O one who is loved by Shambhu! O one with the auspicious waters! People on earth are miserable because of their association with many kinds of sins. If you had not descended on earth, what would have happened to them? O queen of rivers! What would have been the fate of those who have come to earth with human bodies? O Ganga! You are the one who destroys the aggregate of great sins. O mother! You can easily be reached. O mother of the universe! O Ganga! O one who deserves to be worshipped by the three worlds! Who is capable of knowing about your powers? Though his body is embraced by Gouri, Smara's enemy[728] holds you on his head. O

---

[728] Shiva.

mother! I bow down before you. O one who bestows what is desired!
I bow down before you. O one who is full of the *brahman*! O one
who destroys sins! I bow down before you. O one who flows from
Vishnu's lotus feet! I bow down before you. O one who flows from
Shambhu's matted hair!" Thus praised, the goddess asked, "What
will I give you?" The herbs replied, "O mother of the universe! Please
give us a husband, a king who will be extremely energetic." Addressed
by the herbs, the river Ganga answered in these words. Ganga said,
"My form is made out of *amrita* and the herbs are the mothers of
amrita. I will give you Soma as a husband. He has *amrita* in his *atman*
and he is like you." The gods, the *rishi*s and Soma agreed with these
words. The herbs also agreed with these words and returned to their
own abodes. The great herbs obtained Soma, who has *amrita* in his
atman, as their king. He is the one who counters every kind of torment
and sin. The place where this occurred is known as Soma *tirtha* and it
confers the fruits of drinking *soma*. Bathing and donations there lead
to the ancestors going to heaven. If a person constantly hears this,
reads it, or remembers it with devotion, he obtains a long lifespan,
daughters and riches.'

Chapter 2(50) (Dhanya *tirtha*)

Brahma said, 'The place known as Dhanya *tirtha* bestows
everything desired on men. It gives men what has not been
asked for and peace. It counters every kind of calamity. Having
obtained King Soma as a husband, the herbs were delighted. They
spoke these words, agreeable to all the worlds and to Ganga. The
herbs said, "There is an auspicious chant in the Vedas. Those who
know the Vedas know about it. "The land near Ganga is as revered
as his mother, indeed, it is his mother.[729] From that region, if a
man donates some land that yields crops, he obtains everything that
he desires. This land has the form of Vishnu, Brahma and Isha.

---

[729] The text does not indicate where the chant begins and where it ends.
What we have placed within quotes seems to be right.

If a man cheerfully and devotedly donates such land with crops, cattle and herbs, his learning becomes inexhaustible and he obtains everything that he desires. The king of the herbs is Soma. Soma is the lord of the herbs. Knowing this, if a person donates herbs to a person who knows about the *brahman*, he obtains everything that he desires and attains greatness in Brahma's world." Pleased with Soma as their king, the herbs repeatedly said this. The herbs said, "O king! Near the Ganga, if someone donates us, you make him cross over. You are the lord of the excellent herbs. Everything mobile and immobile is under your control." The herbs spoke to King Soma in this way. "O king! If a person gives us to *brahmanas*, you make him cross over. Our form is that of the *brahman*. Our form is that of the breath of life. O king! If a person gives us to *brahmanas*, you make him cross over. O king! If a person controls himself, observes the vows, worships us and always gives us to *brahmanas*, you make him cross over. We pervade everything in the universe, mobile and immobile. O king! If a person gives us to *brahmanas*, you make him cross over. O king! If a person gives *havya*, *kavya*, *amrita*, anything that is consumed or anything that is superior to that, you make him cross over. This is a chant in the Vedas. O king! If a person hears this, remembers it or reads it devotedly, you make him cross over." The place on the banks of Ganga where the herbs recited this chant along with King Soma, is spoken of as Dhanya *tirtha*.[730] Since then, that *tirtha* has also been named after herbs, Soma, amrita, the chant of the Vedas and Matri *tirtha*. A person who bathes, meditates, offers oblations, donates, performs water-rites for the ancestors and donates food there deserves infinite benefits. Along both banks, there are one thousand and six hundred *tirtha*s. They destroy every kind of sin and enhance every kind of prosperity.'

Chapter 2(51) (Confluences of Vidarbha and Revati)

---

[730] *Dhanya* means grain.

Brahma said, 'The confluence of Vidarbha and the confluence of Revati are auspicious. I will tell you what happened there. Those who know about the ancient accounts know about this. There was a *rishi* named Bharadvaja and he was superior to others in austerities. Revati was his sister. She was ugly in form and her voice was loathsome. On seeing that she was disfigured, her brother, the powerful Bharadvaja, who lived on the southern bank of Ganga, was filled with great worries. "Who will I bestow this maiden, my sister, on? She is terrible in form. No one will accept her. However, my sister has to be given away. Alas! No one should have a daughter who becomes the cause of miseries. For any living being, even if he is alive, this is like death at every step." In his extremely beautiful hermitage, he thought in this way. An excellent sage came there, to see Bharadvaja, who was generally firm in his vows. He was sixteen years of age and his form was handsome. He was serene and controlled. He was a reservoir of qualities. He was known by the name of Katha. He bowed down to Bharadvaja. Bharadvaja also honoured the brahmana Katha in the proper way. Standing in front of him, he asked him about the reason why he had come. Katha told Bharadvaja, "I have come to you for the sake of learning. That is the reason I wished to see you. What is appropriate should now be done." Bharadvaja told Katha, "Study what you wish—the Puranas, the *smriti* texts, the Vedas and the many sacred texts on *dharma*. O immensely wise one! I know them all. Without any delay, tell me what appeals to you. You have been born in a noble lineage. You are devoted to *dharma*. You are devoted to serving your *guru*. You are proud and possess a sharp memory.[731] Such a disciple is only obtained through a lot of good merits." Katha replied, "O brahmana! I am your disciple and I am without any sins. Please instruct me. I am devoted to serving. I am faithful. I have been born in a noble lineage. I am truthful in speech." Bharadvaja agreed and bestowed every kind of learning on him. Having obtained this learning, Katha was pleased and spoke to Bharadvaja. Katha said, "O *guru*! I wish to give you

---

[731] *Shrutadhara*. Literally, someone who remembers something as soon as he has heard it.

the *dakshina* that your mind desires.[732] Please tell me, even if it is something extremely difficult to get. You are my *guru* and I prostrate myself before you. Having obtained the knowledge, out of delusion, if a person does not give the *guru* the fee, he descends into hell for as long as the moon and the stars exist." Bharadvaja answered, "Accept this maiden. Following the norms, make her your wife. She is my sister. I ask for the *dakshina* that you make her happy." Katha said, "A disciple is always like a *guru*'s son. Since the *guru* is like a father, I am like her brother. How can there be a relationship with her?" Bharadvaja answered, "Act in accordance with my words. Make your pledge come true. I command you that this is your *dakshina*. O Katha! You have learnt everything. Now turn your mind towards supporting Revati." Katha agreed with his *guru*'s words and accepted her hand. When Revati was bestowed in the proper way, Katha looked at her. For the sake of Revati's beauty and his prosperity, he worshipped Shankara, the lord of the gods, there itself. Since Shiva was pleased, Revati became extremely beautiful, lovely in all her limbs. There was no one who was superior to her in beauty. The water with which Revati was sprinkled flowed into the Ganga as river. After her name, the river was known as Revati. It bestows every kind of beauty and good fortune. For the sake of an auspicious form and success, he again used *darbha* grass to perform many kinds of sprinkling. This became the river Vidarbha.[733] Full of faith, if a man bathes at the confluence of Ganga and Revati, he is freed from every kind of sin and obtains greatness in Vishnu's world. O sage! In that way, if a person faithfully bathes at the confluence of Vidarbha and Goutami, he instantly obtains objects of pleasure and emancipation. Along both banks there, one hundred excellent *tirtha*s exist. They destroy every kind of sin and bestow every kind of success.'

Chapter 2(52) (Purna *tirtha* and other *tirtha*s)

[732] Here, *dakshina* is the fee that is given to a *guru* after the successful completion of studies.
[733] From *darbha*.

Brahma said, 'On Ganga's northern bank is the place known as Purna *tirtha*. Even if a man bathes there inadvertently, he obtains what is auspicious. Which living being is capable of describing the greatness of Purna *tirtha*? The wielder of the *chakra* and the wielder of Pinaka, both reside there. In ancient times at the beginning of the *kalpa*, Ayush had a son named Dhanvantari. He performed many kinds of sacrifices, a horse sacrifice being the most important. He donated many kinds of objects and enjoyed all the objects of pleasure. He understood the perversity associated with objects of pleasure and became supremely non-attached. Dhanvantari thought, "If one undertakes austerities, offers oblations and performs *japa* on the summit of a mountain, on the far side of the ocean along the banks of the river Ganga, in the temples of Shiva and Vishnu and particularly in sacred confluences, one obtains eternal benefits. Understanding this, he tormented himself through great austerities there. Resorting to the feet of Bhimesha,[734] he was filled with *jnana* and non-attachment. At the confluence of Ganga with the ocean, he undertook extensive austerities. Earlier, in a battle, a great *asura* had been repulsed by this king. He fled and scared, hid in the ocean for one thousand years. When Dhanvantari left for the forest, his son obtained the kingdom. When the king[735] developed non-attachment, Tamas[736] emerged from the ocean. O sage! On the banks of Ganga, King Dhanvantari was engaged in austerities and the powerful *asura*, named Tamas, went there. Devoted to knowledge about the *brahman*, the king was constantly engaged in *japa* and offering oblations. To destroy his enemy, Tamas emerged from the ocean. 'This powerful king has repulsed me several times. I will now destroy this enemy.' That is the reason Tamas emerged from the ocean. He used his *maya* to assume the form of a beautiful woman and appeared before the king. She possessed excellent eyebrows and was beautiful to behold. Singing, dancing and laughing, she arrived there. For a long time, he looked at her beautiful limbs. She was serene and devotedly followed him. Taking pity, he spoke to her.

[734] Shiva.
[735] Dhanvantari.
[736] The *asura*.

The king asked, 'Who are you? Who do you belong to? Why are you residing in this desolate forest? O fortunate one! Who are you laughing at? I am asking you. Please tell me.' Hearing his words, the lady replied to the king. The lady said, 'When you are here, who else can be the reason for my joy? I am Indra's prosperity. On seeing you, I have been smitten with desire. That is the reason, full of delight, I am repeatedly roaming around in front of you. Unless a person possesses innumerable good merits, I am impossible for him to obtain." Hearing her words, the king instantly abandoned the austerities, which were very difficult to perform. He thought about her. He was devoted to her. He was attached to her. She became the king's only refuge. O brahmana! When his extensive austerities had been destroyed, Tamas vanished.'

'Meanwhile, I arrived there, to bestow a boon on him. I saw that he was distracted, having deviated from his austerities. It was as if he was dead. Using many different kinds of arguments, I comforted the excellent king. "Your enemy, named Tamas, has caused this deviation from austerities. O king! With the objective accomplished, he has departed. You should not grieve. Women not only give men delight, they also torment them. This is true of all of them. Why should it not be true of one who was created out of *maya*?" Forgetting his distraction, the king joined his hands in salutation and spoke to me. The king asked, "O Brahma! How will I obtain what is beneficial for me? What will I do? O Brahma! How will I obtain what is beyond austerities?" I answered, "Make every effort to praise Janardana, the lord of the gods. He will give you what is the best. That is the way you will obtain success. He is the creator of everything in the universe. He is the ancient being who can be known through the Vedas. He is the one who bestows every kind of success on men. In the three worlds, there is no one else." The excellent king went to the Himalayas, supreme among mountains. He joined his hands in salutation and devotedly praised Vishnu. Dhanvantari said, "Victory to Vishnu. Victory to the one who cannot be thought of. Victory to Jishnu.[737] Victory to Achyuta. Victory to Gopala, Lakshmi's lord. Victory to Krishna, who pervades the universe. Victory to the lord and master

---

[737] Jishnu is Vishnu's name, meaning the one who is victorious.

of all living beings. Victory to the one who lies down on a *pannaga*. Victory to Govinda, who goes everywhere. Victory to the creator of the universe. I bow down before you. Victory to the divinity who enjoys the universe. Victory to the one who holds up the universe. I bow down before you. Victory to the lord who is existence and non-existence. Victory to Madhava, the one who is full of *dharma*. Victory to the one who is desired, the one who bestows objects of desire. Victory to Rama, the ocean of qualities. Victory to the one who bestows victory and nourishment, the one who is the lord of nourishment. Victory to the one who bestows welfare. Victory to the lord and master of living beings. Victory to the one who arranges for honour. Victory to the one who bestows *karma*, the one who is *karma*. Victory to the one who is attired in yellow garments. Victory to the lord of everything, the one who is everything. Victory to the one whose form is auspicious. Victory to the supreme lord of living beings. Victory to the one who can be known through the Vedas. I bow down before you. Victory to the one who bestows birth, the one who is all those who are born, the *paramatman*. I bow down before you. Victory to the one who bestows emancipation, the one who is emancipation. O Keshava! Victory to the one who bestows objects of pleasure. Victory to the one who bestows worlds, the lord of the worlds. Victory to the one who destroys sin. Victory to the one who is devoted to devotees. Victory to the one who holds the *chakra*. I bow down before you. Victory to the one who bestows honour, the one who is honour. Victory to the one who is revered by the worlds. Victory to the one who bestows *dharma*, the one who is *dharma*. Victory to the one who enables the crossing over of *samsara*. Victory to the one who bestows food, the one who is food. Victory to the lord of speech. I bow down before you. Victory to the one who bestows strength, the one who is strength. Victory to the victorious one who bestows boons. Victory to the one who bestows sacrifices, the one who is sacrifices. Victory to the one with eyes like the petals of a lotus. Victory to the one who bestows donations, the one who is donations. Victory to the one who slew Kaitabha. Victory to the one who bestows deeds, the one who is deeds. Victory to the one who bestows forms, the one who assumes forms. Victory to the one who bestows happiness, the one whose *atman* is happiness. Victory to the one who purifies those who purify. Victory to the one who bestows peace, the one who is peace. Victory to the one who originated from Shankara. Victory to the one who bestows drinks, the one who is drinks. Victory to the one whose form is light. Victory to Vamana, the lord of riches. Victory to the one who has smoke on his flag.[738] Victory to the one who is everywhere in the universe, in the form of a donor. I bow down before you. For those who live and subsist in the three worlds, you alone are the one who is accomplished in destroying hardships. O glorious Pundarikaksha![739] O ocean of compassion! O Vishnu! Place your hand on my head." Praised in this way, the illustrious one, the one who holds the conch shell, the *chakra* and the mace, the one who bestows every kind of desire and prosperity, asked him to choose a boon. Dhanvantari's mind was pleased that the one who holds a *chakra* was ready to bestow a boon on him. Govinda, the lord of the gods, was standing in front of him, ready to bestow a boon. The king told him, "I desire to obtain the kingdom of the gods. O Vishnu! If you grant me that, I will accomplish everything that I wish for." Praised and worshipped properly in this way, Vishnu vanished from the spot. Progressively, the king became the lord of the gods.'

'The one with the one thousand eyes came under the subjugation of a lot of his earlier *karma* becoming fructified. Therefore, he was dislodged from his own position thrice—by Nahusha when Vritra was killed, in connection with the killing of Sindhusena and because he had intercourse with Ahalya.[740] These were the reasons. Remembering these incidents, Indra was tormented by thoughts and distress in his mind. Therefore, the lord of the gods addressed Vachaspati[741] in these words. Indra asked, "O lord of speech! Once in a while, why am I dislodged from my kingdom and prosperity by men, even though I am superior? The progress of *karma* in living

---

[738] That is, fire.

[739] Vishnu's name, the one with eyes like a lotus.

[740] Indra (the one with one thousand eyes) committed the crimes of killing Vritra and violating Ahalya. Sindhusena was a demon who ousted Indra. But Sindhusena was killed by Vishnu.

[741] Brihaspati.

beings is mysterious. Who knows the truth? O one who is eloquent in speech! Other than you, no one knows this mystery in all creatures." Brihaspati told Hari, "Go and ask Brahma. He is the one who knows about the past, the present and the future. O immensely wise one! He is the one who will tell you how this happens." Those two immensely wise ones came to my presence and bowed down. They joined their hands in salutation and addressed me in these words. Indra and Brihaspati said, "O illustrious one! Shachi's consort is pervasive in his intelligence. O protector! What fault causes him to be dislodged from his kingdom? You should clear up this doubt." O brahmana! I thought about it for a long time and spoke to Brihaspati. "The sin of violating *dharma* causes him to be dislodged from his kingdom. Among those with bodies, the violation of *dharma* occurs in different ways—taints in the time and the place; transgression of faith and *mantra*s; not donating appropriate *dakshina*; donating objects that should not be given; and in particular, showing disrespect to gods and *brahmanas*. The effects of these are impossible to give up and cause mental torment and loss of status. If one causes injury to *dharma*, the mind is agitated. Since one is anxious, the tasks are not successfully completed. When one's own *dharma* is left incomplete, why should injury not result?" O unblemished one! I told the two of them about the earlier account. Ayush had a prosperous son named Dhanvantari, who was extensive in his intelligence. Tamas created an impediment for him and this was destroyed by Vishnu. I properly described the incidents from the earlier births. Hearing this, the two of them were surprised and spoke to me again. Indra and Brihaspati asked, "O supreme divinity! How can the taint be countered?" I thought about it again and told them, "Listen to how the taint can be countered. Hear about the reason behind every kind of success and how one can cross the ocean of *samsara*. Hear about the refuge for those whose senses are tormented and about how living beings can obtain emancipation. Go to the goddess Goutami and praise Hari and Shankara. In the three worlds, barring those two and her, there is no other means for purification." O excellent sage! At this, both of them went to Goutami.'

'They happily bathed there and simultaneously praised the two divinities. Indra said, "I bow down to Matsya, Kurma and Varaha.

I prostrate myself before you. I bow down to you. I bow down to the divinity Narasimha. I bow down to Vamana. I prostrate myself before you. I bow down to Hayarupa. I bow down to Trivikrama. I bow down to the one who has the form of Buddha, the one who has the form of Rama and Kalki. I bow down to the lord who is Ananta and Achyuta. I bow down to Jamadagni's son. I bow down to the one who has the form of Varuna and Indra, the one who has the form of Yama. I bow down to the divinity who is the supreme lord. The three worlds are his form. Your radiant form has Sarasvati in your mouth. You are omniscient. I bow down to you. O unblemished one! You are the one with Lakshmi. Your radiant form has Lakshmi on your chest. You possess many arms, thighs and feet. You possess many ears, eyes and heads. It is from you that happiness is obtained. In many ways, you are the one who is bliss. O Hari! When men seek refuge with you, their adversity, jadedness and misery end. You are an ocean of compassion."[742] Brihaspati said, "O Isha! You are the subtle and infinite light. You are infinite in form. You are Omkara[743] and you are beyond Prakriti. You are the form of consciousness and bliss. You are everything. O Isha! Those who desire emancipation praise you. O Isha! Even those who possess no desire worship you through the five great sacrifices.[744] They cross the ocean of *samsara* and obtain their supreme desire of entering your divine world and form. They are impartial in their intelligence in the way they look at all creatures. Against the six waves, their sentiments are serene.[745] They use their *jnana* to cast aside the fruits of *karma*. O Shambhu! They meditate and enter you. This is not

[742] In this eulogy, several of Vishnu's *avatara*s are named—Matsya (fish), Kurma (tortoise), Varaha (boar), Narasimha (man-lion), Vamana (dwarf), Hayarupa (Hayagrive/Hayashira), Trivikrama (as Vamana), Buddha, Rama, Kalki and Jamadagni's son (Parashurama).

[743] The sound of Oum.

[744] Every householder has to undertake the five great sacrifices—studying, worshipping gods, worshipping ancestors, honouring humans through hospitality, and offerings to animals and birds.

[745] The six waves are the six vices of *kama* (desire), *krodha* (anger), *lobha* (avarice), *moha* (delusion), *mada* (arrogance) and *matsarya* (jealousy). Alternatively, this could be the five senses and the mind.

obtained through the *dharma* of *jati*s, the sacred texts of the Vedas, *dhyana*, *yoga* or the *dharma* of *samadhi*. Rudra Shiva Shankara is obtained through devotion and a serene mind. O divinity! O Soma! I bow down before you. O Shambhu! Though I am foolish, your feet are the manifest form of emancipation. Through devotion towards them, I will obtain your body. *Jnana*, sacrifices, austerities, *dhyana* and oblations yield great fruits. However, those excellent fruits are also obtained through constant devotion to Someshvara. O one in whom the universe resides! O one who is always loved by all living beings! Devotion towards you represents the flight of stairs through which one obtains the fruits that are seen and heard of, heaven and emancipation. Those fruits are obtained through your feet. However, persevering ones do not speak about that flight of stairs. O compassionate one! Hence, let me be devoted towards you. I do not know the means whereby one should serve your form. O Isha! Use your greatness to glance towards us, as if towards a relative. We are sinners, but show us your favours. You are the gross and the subtle. You are without beginning. You are eternal. You are the father and the mother. You are the existent and the non-existent. You are praised in this way in the *shruti* texts and in the Puranas. I bow down to Someshvara Isha, who is praised in this way." At this, Hari and Hara, the two lords of the gods, were pleased.'

'Hari and Hara said, "Ask for the boon that is in your mind, even if it is extremely difficult to obtain. Indra told the lords of the gods, 'My kingdom is repeatedly lost and regained. Let that sin be pacified. Let me be stable in my kingdom. Let everything that belongs to me be steady. If the two lords of the gods are extremely pleased, let everything always remain stable for me.' They honoured Hari's[746] words and said that they approved of them. Extremely pleased, the two of them glanced towards them with smiling faces. They never leave. They are without support. They are without transformations. They have their own respective forms. They are refuges for all the worlds. They are the ones who bestow objects of pleasure and emancipation. Hari and Hara said, 'This great *tirtha* has three divinities. Goutami bestows whatever is wished for. Using

---

[746] Indra's.

the following *mantra*, one should lovingly bathe in her. For the great Indra's consecration, let Brihaspati pronounce the auspicious benediction. Let the two of us be remembered for prosperity, stability and success. "Let all the good deeds I have performed in this and earlier lives achieve fruition. O Godavari! I bow down before you." Remembering this, if a person bathes in Goutami through our favours, all his acts of *dharma* will become complete. He will be freed from all the sins committed in earlier lives and become pure.' Pleased, Indra of the gods and Dhishana[747] acted in that way. The divine *guru* performed Indra's great consecration. The sacred river that originated from the water is known as Mangala. It bestows everything that is auspicious and its confluence with Ganga is sacred. Vishnu pervades the universe. Indra praised him. Thus, Shakra obtained an image of the lord of the universe that is revered by the three worlds. There, it is known by the name of Govinda. The wielder of the *vajra* obtained a cow that is revered by the three worlds. Hari gave it and Hari became Govinda.[748] O sage! There is a place where Brihaspati, the preceptor of the gods satisfied Maheshvara. Because of this, the kingdom of the great-souled Indra of the gods became stable. There, the divinity's *lingam* is Siddhesvhara and it is worshipped by the gods. Since then, that *tirtha* has been known as Govinda. The confluence of Mangala is the supreme Purna *tirtha*. It is also famous as Indra *tirtha* and is also known after Brihaspati. The divinities there are Siddheshvara, Vishnu and Govinda. Any good deeds that are performed there, like bathing and donations, bring inexhaustible benefits and one obtains learning. The place is extremely dear to the ancestors. If a person constantly hears about the greatness of this *tirtha*, reads about it and remembers it, he gets back the kingdom he has lost. Along both banks, there are thirty-seven thousand *tirtha*s. O tiger among sages! Along both banks, they yield every kind of success. There is no

---

[747] Brihaspati's name.

[748] There is a play on words. Hari and Govinda are Vishnu's names. Hari is also Indra's name. Govinda means someone who has obtained a cow (*gou*). Thus, Indra became Govinda.

other *tirtha* that yields great fruits like Purna *tirtha*. If a man does not frequent it, his birth is futile.'

Chapter 2(53) (Rama *tirtha*)

Brahma said, 'The place known as Rama *tirtha* destroys the sin of killing a brahmana. Even if one remembers it, one is freed from all sins. In the Ikshvaku lineage, there was a powerful *kshatriya* who was famous in the worlds. He was strong, intelligent and brave. He was like Shakra Purandara. Like Bali, he ruled over the kingdom of his father and grandfather. O immensely wise one! He was King Dasharatha and he had three queens—Koushalya, Sumitra and Kaikeyi. They were extremely fortunate and had been born in noble lineages. They possessed beauty and qualities. O sage! The king was the lord of the kingdom of Ayodhya. His chief priest was Vasishtha, supreme among those who knew about the *brahman*. There was no physical ailment in the kingdom, no famine. There was no drought, nor any mental ailment. All the *brahmanas*, *kshatriyas*, *vaishyas* and shudras happily subsisted in their own separate *ashrama*s. That Indra among kings, the extender of the Ikshvaku lineage, ruled in this way. For the sake of the kingdom,[749] there was a battle between the gods and the *danava*s. Sometimes, the gods triumphed. Sometimes, the others did. While this continued, the three worlds suffered excessively. O Narada! At this, I spoke to the gods, *daityas* and *danava*s. However, they did not act in accordance with what I said. An extremely great battle took place between them again. The gods went and spoke to Vishnu and to Ishana, who pervades the universe. Both of them spoke to the gods, *daityas* and *danava*s. "Become strong through austerities. Fight after that." They agreed to this. All of them engaged in austerities, observing rituals and vows. However, full of envy, the gods attacked the *rakshasa*s again. There was an extremely terrible battle between the gods and the *danava*s.

---

[749] The kingdom of the gods.

The gods did not win. Nor did the *daitya*s and *danava*s.[750] While the battle was going on, an invisible voice was heard. The voice from heaven said, "The side aided by King Dasharatha will win, not the other." Hearing this, for the sake of victory, both the gods and the *danava*s went to him. Vayu rushed to the king and spoke to him. Vayu said, "O king! Come to the battle between the gods and the *danava*s. It has been heard that the side aided by King Dasharatha will be victorious. Therefore, you must side with the gods, so that the gods are victorious." Hearing Vayu's words, King Dasharatha replied, "O Vayu! I will come. This is my pledge. Return happily." When Vayu had left, the *daitya*s arrived before the lord of the earth. They said, "O illustrious one! You should help us. O prosperous King Dasharatha! If you are with us, we will be victorious. Hence, you should help the lord of the *daitya*s." The lord of men answered, "Vayu asked me earlier and I have promised him. O *daitya*s and *danava*s! Please leave." Thus, the king went to heaven and fought against the *daitya*s, *danava*s and *rakshasa*s. Namuchi's brother was watching the battle with the gods. Using many kinds of sharp arrows, he shattered the axle of the king's chariot. Because he was preoccupied, the king did not realize that the axle of his chariot had been shattered. O Narada! Kaikeyi, the one with the excellent eyebrows, was standing near the king and noticed. Though the one who was good in her vows saw this, she did not inform the king. Instead, noticing that the axle had got shattered, she placed her own hand there instead. O tiger among sages! She used her hand like an axle and this was exceedingly wonderful. On the chariot where she had placed her hand, the best among charioteers defeated the *daitya*s and sons of Danu. He obtained many boons from the gods. Taking the permission of the gods, he returned to Ayodhya. Halfway along the path, the great king noticed his beloved. Witnessing what Kaikeyi had done, he was filled with great wonder. O Narada! Therefore, he granted her three boons. Accepting what the king had said, Kaikeyi replied to him in these words. Kaikeyi said, "O Indra among kings! For the moment, let the boons granted by you remain

[750] The text says *manava*s. It should read *danava*s and we have corrected it.

with you." The Indra among kings gave his beloved ornaments.
Victorious on his chariot, the king happily returned to his own city.
When the appropriate time comes, what does one not give to one's
beloved wife?'

'On one occasion, Dasharatha was wandering around in the
forest, surrounded by those who were addicted to hunting. In the
night, he stopped the flow of water.[751] A lord of the earth should
be free from the seven vices.[752] But this was destiny. Though he
knew because he was under the subjugation of destiny, he did not
act accordingly. The mighty-armed one used his sharp arrows to
kill the animals that entered the watering-hole to drink. Listen to
the catastrophe that destiny brought about. The king entered that
watering-hole in the excellent mountain. There was an aged man
named Shravana. He could neither see, nor hear. His wife was
also like him. They spoke to their son. The mother and the father
said, "We are thirsty and the dark night has set in. O son! For the
aged like us, though you are a child, you are the only means for us
to remain alive. Shame on the lives of aged people who are blind
and deaf. O son! Our bodies are suffering from old age. Shame on
our lives. Men should remain alive for only as long as they possess
prosperity and firm bodies and as long as their commands are not
ignored. After that, in *tirtha*s or in other places, they should die."
Hearing the words of the aged couple, the son, who was devoted
to his seniors, replied in sweet words, so that he could dispel their
unhappiness. The son said, "As long as I am alive, why should you
suffer from this kind of misery? If a son's conduct is such that he
does not do what brings delight to his parents, what is the point
of his possessing a body? He only increases his family's anxiety."
Saying this, the great-minded one bowed down to his parents. He
placed his aged parents on the branch of a tree. Taking a water-pot

---

[751] The flow of water in a river, so that he could kill the animals which
came to drink water.

[752] The number of vices is not usually listed as seven. Ten vices are
usually listed as resulting from desire and eight vices resulting from anger.
One can't deduce which seven are being singled out.

in his hand, the *rishi*'s son left. The *rishi*[753] did not know about the king and the king did not know about the brahmana. Both of them were in a hurry. With his water-pot, the brahmana bent down near the water, so as to quickly fill it with water. Taking the brahmana to be an elephant, the king pierced him with sharp arrows. A wild elephant should not be killed by a lord of the earth. Nevertheless, the king pierced him. What can one do if one is deceived by destiny? Pierced in his inner organs, he miserably addressed him in these words. The brahmana said, "I am a brahmana. Why have you perpetrated this wretched act against me? O father![754] I have never committed a crime against you." Hearing the words spoken by the afflicted sage, the king was unable to move. He lost all enterprise. However, slowly, he approached the place. He saw the excellent brahmana, blazing in his energy. As if he had been struck by a stake, he fell down unconsciousness. After comforting and steadying himself, the king spoke. The king asked, "O tiger among *brahmanas*! Who are you? Why have you come here? Please tell me. I have committed a sin. Please tell me about the best means for atonement. O immensely intelligent one! A person who has killed a brahmana should not be touched or seen by the *varnas*,[755] not even by one who has been born as a *shvapaka*." Hearing the king's words, the sage's son addressed him in these words. The sage's son replied, "My breath of life is about to leave, but I do wish to tell you something. Know that your willful and ignorant conduct has led to your *karma* being cooked. I am not grieving for my own sake. But my parents are aged. Who will tend to them? They are blind and I was their only son. Without me, how will they survive in this great forest? Alas! This is my misfortune. My serving my parents will suffer. I have been alive so far, but will lose my life now. Because of destiny, what have you done? Nevertheless, take this water-pot and go there quickly. So that they do not die, give them this water." Saying this, he gave up his life in that great forest. Casting aside his bow and arrows, the king grasped the water-pot. He quickly

---

[753] Meaning the son.

[754] The word used is *tata*.

[755] That is, the first three *varnas*.

went to the spot in the great forest where the two aged ones were.
Though they were aged and it was night, they were conversing with
each other. The aged ones said, "We are anxious. Is he angry with
us? Has he been devoured? He is like our staff[756] and he has not
yet returned. What will we do? What will happen to us? Among all
mobile and immobile objects, a son like him is not to be found. Even
when he is reprimanded, he does not act against the words of his
parents. If we are unable to see him, our life is hard as the *vajra*. But
the breath of our lives does not quickly emerge from our bodies." In
the forest, the aged couple spoke to each other in many similar ways.
At that time, King Dasharatha slowly approached the spot. Hearing
his footsteps,[757] they thought that the son had come. The aged ones
said, "O son! Where have you come from? Why has it taken you
such a long time? You are like our sight. Why aren't you saying
anything? Are you angry that you are the son of a blind couple?"
He was afflicted by grief, as if he had been struck by a stake. He was
miserable because of his evil act. He was scared. O Narada! The
Indra among kings spoke. "Please drink the water." They heard the
king's words and remarked, "These aren't words spoken by our son.
Who are you? First tell us that. We will drink the water later." The
king spoke to them. The king said, "Your son is where the watering-
hole is." Hearing this, the miserable couple replied, "Please tell us
the truth and not what is false." At this, the king told them everything
that had happened. The aged couple fell down. They said, "Take us
there. But do not touch us. The sin of touching someone who has
killed a brahmana is never destroyed." The excellent king took the
aged Shravana and his wife there, to the spot where their son had
fallen down. They touched him and lamented. The aged couple said,
"The separation from our son will bring about our death. O wicked
one! You will also come by your death through separation from
your son." O brahmana! As they were saying this, their breath of life
departed. The king lit the funeral pyre for the aged couple and the
rishi's son. O sage! Miserable, the king returned to his city. He told

[756] For support.

[757] There is an obvious inconsistency. In other accounts, they are only
blind.

Vasishtha everything, in detail. For kings who belonged to *surya vamsha*, Vasishtha was the ultimate refuge. Vasishtha consulted with other excellent *brahmanas* about the means for atonement. Vasishtha said, "Summon Galava, Vamadeva, Jabali, Kashyapa and others here and make efforts for a horse sacrifice. Undertake a horse sacrifice, with copious amounts of *dakshina*." Along with the *brahmanas*, King Dasharatha performed the horse sacrifice.'

'Meanwhile, an invisible voice was heard. The voice from the sky said, "King Dasharatha's body has been rendered pure. One can now have an association with him. He will have sons. Through the favours of his eldest son, the king will be freed from his sin." After many days had passed, through Rishyashringa, lord among sages, sons were born. They were like gods and were born to accomplish the tasks of the gods. Koushalya's son was Rama, while Sumitra's son was Lakshmana. Kaikeyi's sons were Shatrughna and Bharata, who was supremely intelligent. All of them were intelligent. They were loved by the king and were obedient to him. The *rishi*, Prajapati Vishvamitra, came before the king. O immensely intelligent one! He asked for Rama and Lakshmana for the sake of protecting sacrifices. The sage knew about their greatness. The aged king had obtained sons after a very long time. He refused. The king said, "O sage! In my old age, through the great working of destiny, they have somehow been born to me. These two sons bring me a great deal of joy. I will give you my body and this kingdom, but not these two sons." At this, Vasishtha told King Dasharatha to do what was asked. Vasishtha said, "O king! Those born in Raghu's lineage[758] have not been taught to refuse anything that is asked for." With some effort, the king spoke to Rama and Lakshmana. The king said, "Please protect the sacrifice of *brahmarshi* Vishvamitra." Telling his sons this, the king let out warm sighs. He acted in accordance with the sacred texts and handed over his two sons to Vishvamitra. They agreed with what Dasharatha had said and repeatedly prostrated themselves before him. For the sake of protecting, they cheerfully went along with Vishvamitra. Pleased with them, the sage happily bestowed on them the great knowledge known as Maheshvari,

---

[758] Raghu was Dasharatha's grandfather.

the science of *dhanurveda*, the sacred texts, human and divine weapons, the knowledge of fighting with chariots, the knowledge of fighting with elephants, the knowledge of fighting with horses, the knowledge of fighting with maces and *mantra*s for summoning and withdrawal.[759] Rama and Lakshmana imbibed all these different kinds of knowledge. For the welfare of the residents of the forest, in the forest, they killed Tataka. By touching Ahalya with the foot, they freed her from the curse. They killed the *rakshasa*s who arrived to destroy the sacrifice. Having obtained all the knowledge, with bows in their hands, they protected the sacrifice. Vishvamitra, lord of sages, completed his great sacrifice. With both the sons, he went to see King Janaka. Taking the permission of his *guru*, along with Soumitri,[760] in the midst of the kings, Prince Rama exhibited his wonderful skill with the bow.[761] Pleased at this, Janaka bestowed Sita, born from Lakshmi's portion, on him. O sage! Listening to what Vasishtha said, the prosperous King Dasharatha arranged for the marriages of Bharata, Shatrughna and the others.'

'Many days passed. With everyone's permission and with the permission of his *guru*, the king decided to hand over the kingdom to him.[762] Manthara was sent by evil destiny. Urged by her and overcome by jealousy, Kaikeyi created an impediment by asking that the king not bestow the kingdom on him, that he be sent to the forest and that Bharata be given the kingdom instead.[763] To make his father's words of pledge come true, with Soumitri and with Sita, he entered the great forest. The minds of the virtuous are pure. In addition, because of his own qualities, Rama emerged, readying himself for a period of exile in the forest, with Lakshmana and Sita. He was devoid of any hankering for the kingdom. He thought of the curse imposed by the brahmana and about the qualities possessed by Rama, Soumitri and Sita. Overwhelmed by great sorrow, King

---

[759] There were *mantra*s for invoking, releasing and withdrawing divine weapons.

[760] Lakshmana.

[761] Sita's *svayamvara* was taking place.

[762] To Rama.

[763] These were the three boons Kaikeyi asked for.

Dasharatha miserably gave up his life. O immensely wise one! Like
all mobile and immobile objects, because of the wicked deed he
had committed, the king was taken away by Yama's followers. O
Narada! In Yama's abode, the king was conveyed to many terrible
and fierce hells, Tamisra and others. The king was flung there, in
different types of hells. O immensely wise one! There, the king
was cooked, sliced, crushed, pulverized, dried, stung and burnt
many times. In this way, he was cooked in terrible hells. In the
forest, Rama reached Chitrakuta. O immensely wise one! He spent
three years there. He then proceeded to the southern direction and
reached Dandaka forest. This region is famous in the three worlds
and bestows everything auspicious. He entered that great and fierce
forest frequented by *daitya*s. The *rishi*s had abandoned it because of
fear, but he killed the *daitya*s and *rakshasa*s. Serving the *rishi*s, he
roamed around in Dandakaranya.'

'O Narada! Listen attentively to what occurred there. While
the king was in hell, Rama slowly reached within five *yojana*s of
Goutami. Yama spoke to his own servants. "Rama, Dasharatha's
intelligent son, is proceeding towards Goutami. There is no doubt
that you should take the king, his father, out from hell. As long
as Rama is within a distance of five *yojana*s from Goutami, his
father should not be cooked in hell. If you messengers do not act in
accordance with my sacred words, then all of you will be immersed
in terrible hell. The virtuous say that Goutami's waters are
supreme. They unite with Shiva's Shakti. Therefore, those waters
are honoured and worshipped by Hari, Brahma and Mahesha. If
anyone crosses her, that sin can never be countered. If a sinner's
son remembers Ganga on any occasion, even if the sinner has been
submerged in many impenetrable hells, he obtains emancipation.
What need be said of a son like this, who is stationed near Goutami?
No one is capable of cooking him in hell now." Yama's servants
heard the words spoken by the lord of the southern direction. The
king, the lord of Ayodhya, was being cooked in hell. Listening to
his words, they took him out of that terrible hell and spoke these
words. Yama's servants said, "O tiger among kings! Since you have
a son like this, you are blessed. Who obtains a good son like this,
so that one can obtain rest in this world and in the next world?"

Having rested, the king slowly spoke to the servants in these words. The king said, "I was repeatedly cooked in terrible hells. Why have I been taken out from there? You should tell me quickly." One of them was tranquil in his mind and he replied to the king. Yama's messenger said, "This secret of the Vedas, the sacred texts and the Puranas are carefully preserved. But it is being revealed. This is because of the powers of both your son and the *tirtha*. Your prosperous son, Rama, has come to Goutami. O supreme among men! That is the reason you have been taken out from the terrible hell. O supreme among kings If Rama and Lakshmana bathe in Goutami, remember you and offer you *pinda*, you will be freed from all your sins and go to heaven." The king answered, "I will go there and tell my two sons about your words. You are my refuge and you should grant me permission." Hearing the king's words, Yama's servants took pity on him. They gave him permission and the king went to his two sons. Because of the terrible pain his body had been through, he sighed repeatedly. He looked at himself. Full of shame, he remembered what he had done. As he wished, Raghava[764] roamed around and reached Ganga. Rama and Lakshmana were near Goutami's banks. Along with Vaidehi Sita, they followed the norms and bathed. Along the banks of Goutami, there was nothing to eat. At that time, there were those who resided along the banks of Goutami. Seeing them, Lakshmana was unhappy[765] and spoke to his brother, Rama. Lakshmana said, "We are the sons of Dashartha and you possess such strength. Nevertheless, there is nothing for us and the residents along the banks of Ganga to eat." Rama replied, "Nothing can counter the *karma* that has been ordained. The earth is full of food and we desire food. O Soumitri! However, it is also true that we have not offered oblations through the mouth of a brahmana. We have neglected the earth. We have not offered oblations to the gods and worshipped them. O Lakshmana! That is the reason those who are born are always hungry. We must bathe and worship the gods. We must offer oblations into the fire. Then, at the right time, the divinity will arrange for us to get food." O

---

[764] That is, Dasharatha.
[765] Since the residents had nothing to eat.

brahmana! Having witnessed the progress of *karma*, the brothers conversed in this way. At that time, King Dasharatha slowly arrived at the spot. On seeing him, Lakshmana pulled the string of his bow and quickly said, "Wait! Are you a *rakshasa* or a *danava*? Wait!" On seeing that he continued to approach, he added, "Go away. Behold. King Rama, the son of Dashartha, who always does what is auspicious and in accordance with *dharma*, is here. He is devoted to his seniors and is firm in adherence to the truth. He serves gods and *brahmanas*. Raghava, who possesses the capacity to protect the three worlds is here. Evil-doers like you are not allowed to enter this place. O sinner! If you enter, you will be killed." Hearing his son's words, he reflected for a while on the consequences of wicked deeds. With a downcast face, he joined his hands in salutation and softly addressed his two sons and daughter-in-law in these words. The king said, "I am King Dasharatha. O sons! Listen to my words. I am surrounded by the sin of having killed three *brahmanas*. That is the reason I face this misery. Look at my body. It has been sliced and cooked in hell." Rama, Lakshmana and Sita joined their hands in salutation.'

'All of them prostrated themselves on the ground and addressed him in these words. Sita, Rama and Lakshmana asked, "O father! O supreme among kings! What deed has led to such fruits?" He told them what had happened and about the slaying of the three *brahmanas*. The king said, "O sons! Having killed a brahmana, no one can escape." Filled with great misery, all of them sank down on the ground. The king's son[766] remembered everything—the exile of the king, the mother and the father, the onset of misery, the progress of *karma* and the descent into hell and was filled with confusion. Seeing that the king was unconscious, Sita addressed him in these words.[767] Sita said, "Great-souled ones like you do not grieve because of a hardship. They think of how human destiny can be countered. Even if one grieves for one thousand *yuga*, a calamity cannot be averted. When a calamity arises, discriminating people never behave in that way. O lord of men! What is the point of

---

[766] This seems to mean Rama.
[767] Sita is clearly speaking to Rama.

this futile misery? The sin of that first death was extremely terrible. Please let it be given to me. That brahmana was innocent and was accomplished in the Vedas and *Vedanga*s. He was devoted to his parents and his conduct was auspicious. I will follow the sacred texts and undertake the atonement for that sin. The two of you[768] should not grieve. After that, Lakshmana will take up the sin of the second death and you accept the one that is left." Sita firmly uttered these words, which were full of *dharma*. When both of them[769] agreed with this, Dasharatha spoke. Dasharatha said, "You are the daughter of Janaka, who knows about the *brahman*. But you have not been born from a womb.[770] You are Rama's wife. It is no wonder that you should speak in this way. But there is no need for you to go through the least bit of exertion. Through bathing in Goutami, donations and the offering of *pinda*, I will be freed from the three sins of killing *brahmanas* and will go to heaven. O one born through Janaka! You have said what is appropriate for your own lineage. Such women convey the lineage to the other side of the ocean of *samsara*. Through Godavari's favours, nothing is extremely difficult to obtain." They prepared to offer *pinda*. However, the slayer of enemies[771] did not see anything that could be offered as food and spoke to Lakshmana. Lakshmana humbly told him, "Here are *inguda* fruits.[772] These will suffice." He instantly brought those oilseeds. Rama's mind was a trifle unhappy at the disagreeable prospect of offering a *pinda* to his father in Ganga, using oilcakes. However, a divine voice said, "O son of a king! Give up this sorrow. You have been dislodged from the kingdom and have come to the forest. You possess nothing. You are not deceitful. You follow *dharma*. You should not grieve. If a person uses deceit to obtain wealth and uses that to undertake rites of *dharma*, he is a sinner. Listen to what the sacred texts say. O Rama! Listen attentively. O king! 'The gods should be offered the food that a

---

[768] Dasharatha and Rama.
[769] Rama and Lakshmana.
[770] Janaka found Sita while tilling the ground.
[771] Rama.
[772] A medicinal tree.

man himself partakes.' As soon as the *pinda* was placed on the ground, he could no longer see his father. The place where the dead body fell down is known as the excellent Shava *tirtha*.[773] Even if a person remembers it, a large number of major sins are destroyed. Astride their own respective *vimana*s, the guardians of the worlds, the Rudras, the Adityas and the two Ashvins came there. His father was in their midst, astride an extremely radiant *vimana*, praised by *kinnara*s. His form was like that of an Aditya. However, though he saw the gods on their *vimana*s, he could not see his own father. Therefore, Rama joined his hands in salutation and asked, 'Where is my father?' At this, there was a divine voice that addressed Rama and Sita. 'King Dasharatha has been freed from the three sins of killing *brahmana*s. O son! Look at him, surrounded by the gods.' The gods said, 'O Rama! You are blessed. You have accomplished your objective. Your father has gone to heaven. Blessed is the person who saves his forefathers from the many kinds of hell. He ornaments the three worlds. O mighty-armed one! Look at him, freed from sins and as resplendent as the sun. Even if he possesses prosperity, a sinner is like a tree that has been burnt down. Even if a person possesses nothing, a person with good deeds is seen to be like the one with the moon on his head.'[774] On seeing his son, the king showered benedictions on him. He honoured him and spoke. The king said, 'O fortunate one! O unblemished one! You have succeeded in your objective. I have crossed over. In this world, a son who makes his ancestors cross over is blessed.' To accomplish the tasks of the gods, the large number of gods spoke to Rama, best among men. 'O son! Go, as you please.' Hearing their words, Rama spoke to the gods. Rama asked, 'O gods! What else needs to be done for my father, my *guru*?' The gods replied, 'There is no river that is Ganga's equal. There is no son who is your equal. There is no divinity who is Shiva's equal. There is no *mantra* that is equal to Omkara. O Rama! You have done everything that needs to be done for your *guru*. O Rama! O one who bestows honours! Because of his son, your father has crossed over. We will leave for our own

---

[773] *Shava* means dead body/corpse.
[774] That is, Shiva, a person who possesses nothing.

abodes. You can also go wherever you wish.' At these words of the gods, Lakshmana's elder brother and Sita were delighted. Amazed at witnessing Ganga's greatness, he spoke the following words. Rama said, 'How wonderful are Ganga's powers. Nothing in the three worlds is comparable. We are blessed that we have seen Ganga, who purifies the three worlds.'

'Full of great joy, he instated the divinity Maheshvara there and attentively worshipped Ishana with the sixteen kinds of service.[775] The excellent divinity possessed thirty-six *kalas*.[776] Joining his hands in salutation, Rama praised Shankara. Rama said, "I bow down to you. O Shambhu! O Purusha! O ancient being! I bow down to you. O omniscient one! O one who is beyond all sentiments! I bow down to you. O Rudra! O lord without decay! I bow down to you. O Sharva! With my head lowered, I bow down to you. I bow down to the supreme divinity, who is without transformation. O Umapati! O preceptor of the worlds! I bow down to you. I bow down to you! O one who destroys poverty! I bow down to you. O one who destroys disease! I bow down to you. I bow down to the one who is welfare. O one whose form cannot be thought of! I bow down to you. O one whose form is the seed of the origin of the universe! I bow down to you. O one who is the cause behind the preservation of the

[775] There are sixteen kinds of service (*upachara*)—*dhyana*, *avahana* (invoking the deity), *asana* (offering a seat), *padya* (offering water to wash the feet), *arghya*, *achamana* (offering water to rinse the mouth), *snana* (bathing the deity), *vastra* (dressing the deity), *upavita* (offering a sacred thread), *gandha* (offering fragrances), *pushpa* (offering flowers), *dhupa* (offering incense), *dipa* (offering a lamp), *naivedya* (offerings of food), *tambula* (offering betel leaf) and *pradakshina* (combined with bowing down).

[776] Shiva has 36 principles, known as *tattvas*—(1) creation; (2) preservation; (3) destruction; (4) concealment; (5) grace; (6) *maya*; (7) *kaala* (sheath of time); (8) *vidya* (sheath of imperfect knowledge; (9) *raga* (sheath of desire); (10) *niyati* (sheath of causality); (11) *kalaa* (sheath of being limited); (12) Purusha; (13) nose; (14) tongue; (15) eyes; (16) skin; (17) ears; (18) anus; (19) genital organs; (20) legs; (21) hands; (22) mouth; (23) smell; (24) taste; (25) form; (26) touch; (27) sound; (28) earth; (29) air; (30) water; (31) fire; (32) space; (33) *manas* (mind); (34) *buddhi* (intellect); (35) *ahamkara* (ego); and (36) *chitta* (consciousness). These *tattvas* of Shaivite philosophy are similar to those of *samkhya*.

universe! I bow down to you. O one who is the destroyer! I bow
down to you. O one who loves Gouri! O one without decay! I bow
down to you. O one who is eternal! O one who is the destructible
and the indestructible! I bow down to you. O one whose form is
consciousness! O one whose existence is incomprehensible! O
three-eyed one! I bow my head down to you. I bow down to you. O
one who brings compassion to the world! O one who is terrifying! I
always bow down to you. I bow down to you. O one who bestows
everything wished for! I first bow down to you. O Somesha! O
Umesha![777] I bow down to the one whose eyes are the three Vedas.
I bow down to the one who is devoid of the three forms.[778] I bow
down to the auspicious one. You are beyond existence and non-
existence. I bow down to you. O one who destroys sins! I bow
down to you. I bow down to the one who is engaged in the welfare
of the universe. I bow down to the one who assumes many kinds
of forms. You are the protector of the universe. You are behind
cause and effect. I bow down to you. O lord of the universe! I bow
down to you. O lord of sacrifices! O one towards whom *havya* and
kavya are offered! O one who is always auspicious for the worlds!
He is the one to whom all worship is rendered. I bow down to
you. O one who loves donations! O desired divinity! I bow down
to Someshvara. O independent one! O Umapati! O Vijaya! I bow
down to you. O lord of Vighneshvara and Nandi! O one who loves
his sons! I bow my head down to you. I bow down to the divinity
who destroys the grief and misery of the world. O one who bears
the moon! I bow down to you. I bow down to the one who holds
up Ganga. O Isha! O one who deserves to be worshipped! O Uma's
consort! O supreme divinity! I bow down to you. O one whose
feet are worshipped by Aja,[779] the original lord,[780] Purandara and
the other gods and the *asura*s! I bow down to the one who wished
to have three eyes so that he could see the beautiful face of the
goddess. I bow down to Soma, who is worshipped through the five

---

[777] Uma's lord.
[778] Made out of *sattva*, *rajas* and *tamas*.
[779] Here, Aja means Vishnu.
[780] Meaning Brahma.

kinds of *amrita*,[781] fragrances, incense, lamps, wonderful flowers, many kinds of *mantra*s, many kinds of food and other articles." At this, the illustrious Shambhu spoke to Rama and Lakshmana. "O fortunate one! Ask for a boon." Rama spoke to Vrishadhvaja. Rama said, "O supreme divinity! O Shankara! If a person devotedly uses this *stotram* to satisfy you, let all his intended tasks become extremely successful. O Shambhu! There are those whose ancestors have descended into the ocean of hell. Let them be purified through *pinda*s and other things and go to heaven. Since birth, if anyone has committed a sin in thoughts, words and deeds, as soon as he bathes here, let those sins be instantly destroyed. O Shambhu! If a person faithfully gives even a trifle to some who wants it in this place, let the good merits be inexhaustible. Let such donors obtain such fruits." Delighted, Shankara told Rama that it would be that way. When the best among the gods had departed, Rama and his followers slowly went to the place where Goutami originated. Since then, that *tirtha* has been known as Rama *tirtha*. When Lakshmana was filled with compassion, the place where the arrow fell down from his hand is known as Bana *tirtha*.[782] It destroys every kind of impediment. The place where Soumitri bathed and worshipped Shankara came to be known as Lakshmana *tirtha*. This is how Sita *tirtha* also came about. It is capable of completely destroying the aggregate of many types of sins. If a person bathes in the place where Ganga who purifies the three worlds, touched the feet of the one from whose feet she originated,[783] the specialty of that place cannot be described. There is no *tirtha* that is equal to Rama *tirtha*.'

Chapter 2(54) (Putra *tirtha* and other *tirtha*s)

Brahma said, 'The place known as Putra *tirtha* is spoken of as a sacred *tirtha*. It yields everything one desires, even if one

---

[781] Meaning milk, *ghee*, curds, honey and molasses.
[782] *Bana* means arrow.
[783] Ganga originated from the feet of Vishnu (Rama).

hears about its greatness. O Narada! I will tell you about its nature. Listen attentively. The sons of Diti and the sons of Danu started to dwindle.[784] O Narada! The sons of Aditi were superior in every kind of way. From a sense of rivalry, Diti was miserable at being separated from her sons. She went to Danu. Diti said, "O fortunate one! Our sons are dwindling. What will be do? In this world, *karma* is powerful. Look at Aditi's lineage. They are excellent and possess a great kingdom. They possess fame, victory and prosperity. They have defeated their enemies and their deeds and *dharma* are increasing. This is enough to destroy the happiness in my heart. We have the same husband. Our *dharma* is the same. Our *gotra* is the same. Our beauty is the same. On witnessing the prosperity and rise of Aditi's offspring, I have been shattered and will no longer live. That will be the desired state after beholding my miserable state and the excessive prosperity of Aditi's offspring. Entering a forest conflagration will yield greater happiness than seeing the prosperity of a rival, even in a dream." She sighed and said this in an extremely miserable voice. Parameshthi's son was honoured.[785] When his exhaustion was gone, he comforted the beautiful lady. Parameshthi's son said, "O fortunate one! You should not lament. What is desired can only be obtained through good deeds. The great-minded Prajapati will tell you about the means for obtaining success. O virtuous one! When you present yourself humbly before him, he will tell you everything you need to do to become successful." O Narada! While this was being said, Danu spoke to Diti. Danu said, "O fortunate one! Use your own qualities to satisfy your husband, Kashyapa. If your husband is satisfied, you will obtain what you desire." Thus addressed, she satisfied Kashyapa in every possible way. The illustrious Kashyapa Prajapati spoke to Diti. Kashyapa asked, "O Diti! O one who is excellent in vows! What will I give

---

[784] The sons of Diti are *daitya*s, the sons of Danu are *danava*s and the sons of Aditi are *aditya*s. Diti, Danu and Aditi were married to Kashyapa and all three were Daksha's daughters.

[785] The word Parameshthi is usually used for Brahma. It is not clear who Diti went to (Parameshthi's son). It could have been either Narada or Marichi, both of whom were Brahma's sons. Kashyapa was Marichi's son.

you? What do you wish for? Ask." Diti asked her husband for a
son who would possess many qualities. He would conquer all the
worlds and be revered by all the worlds. She humbly said, "O father
of the gods! In this world, let me have such a brave son. That is the
boon I ask for." Kashyapa replied, "I will tell you about an excellent
vow that must be observed for twelve years. It will yield the fruits.
When it has been completed, I will impregnate you and you will
obtain what you wish for. Desires are met only when only when
one has been cleansed of sins." The large-eyed Diti was pleased at
the words her husband had spoken and bowed down before him. As
instructed by her husband, she properly observed the vow. If a living
being does not frequent *tirtha*s and donate to deserving people, and
if he does not observe vows, how can he possibly accomplish his
wishes?' After this vow was over, Diti was impregnated. In private,
Kashyapa again spoke to his beloved Diti. Kashyapa said, 'O one
with the beautiful smiles! Even those who practice austerities do
not obtain what they desire if they ignore the recommended tasks.
During the two *sandhya*s, the prohibited tasks must be avoided.
One should not sleep or go anywhere. The hair must not be worn
loose. O extremely fortunate one! At the time of *sandhya*, when
*bhuta*s congregate, one should not eat, sneeze or yawn. If these have
to be done, and especially if one has to laugh, these must always be
done behind a cover. At the time of *sandhya*, one must never remain
near the threshold of a house. O beloved one! During night or day,
one must never step over a pestle, a mortar, a winnowing basket, a
stool, a scabbard, or similar objects. One should never sleep with
one's head facing the north, especially at the time of *sandhya*. One
should not utter a falsehood, or go to someone else's house. One
should try to never look at a man other than one's own beloved. If
you follow these and other *niyama*s that I have mentioned, you will
have a son who will enjoy all the prosperity of the three worlds.'
She promised her husband, who was revered by the worlds, that
she would do this. O brahmana! Kashyapa left and roamed around,
here and there, and then went to the gods.'

'The pure and strong fetus in Diti's womb increased in size.
Through his *maya*, the *daitya* Maya got to know the truth about
all this. Maya had a friendly and affectionate relationship with

Indra. In secret, out of his affection towards Indra, Maya went and humbly told Indra about Diti and Danu's intention, the vow, the growth and energy of the fetus and various other things. If one accepts a single trustworthy friend, it is possible to avoid all kinds of fear. One can obtain many kinds of good merits, even if those have not been earned.'

Narada asked, 'The immensely strong *daitya*, Maya, was Namuchi's beloved brother. O lord of the gods! How did Maya become friendly with the person who killed his brother?'

Brahma continued, 'In ancient times, there was a powerful lord of the *daitya*s, named Namuchi. He had an extremely fierce enmity with Indra and it made the body hair stand up. Once, the brave Namuchi, lord of the *daitya*s saw that Shatakratu was leaving the field of battle. He pursued him. On seeing him advance, Shachi's consort was filled with fear. Abandoning the elephant, Airavata, Indra entered some foam. Riding on the foam, the one who has a *vajra* in his hand, quickly slew his enemy, Namuchi. To destroy his brother's slayer, Maya, Namuchi's younger brother, tormented himself through great austerities. Maya obtained many kinds of *maya*, which the gods found to be terrifying. Through his austerities, he obtained boons from Vishnu, the refuge of the worlds. Maya was generous in donating and pleasant in speech. He worshipped the fire and *brahmanas*. He waited for an opportunity to defeat Indra. He donated to those who desired. He was praised by the *bandi*s.[786] Through Vayu, Maghavan[787] got to know about his enemy Maya, who possessed powers of *maya*. Assuming the form of a brahmana, he approached the one who was preparing himself for an excellent fight. Shachi's consort repeatedly spoke to the *daitya* Maya. Indra said, "O lord of the *daitya*s! I am someone who seeks. Give me my desired boon. I have heard that you are the best among donors. I, an excellent brahmana, have come before you." Maya took him to be a brahmana and replied, "I have given it to you. When a supplicant is

---

[786] The *suta*s were charioteers, as well as raconteurs of tales. *Magadha*s were minstrels and bards. So were *bandi*s. But *magadha*s seem to have also composed, while *bandi*s sung the compositions of others.

[787] Vayu is the wind-god, Maghavan is Indra's name.

in front, accomplished people do not ponder a lot." Thus addressed, Hari responded, "I ask for a friendly relationship with you." Maya again replied to Indra, "O excellent brahmana! Why do you ask for this? There is no enmity between you and me." Hari told Maya, "May you be fortunate." When the *daitya* asked Hari to tell him the truth, he revealed his own true form, which is spoken of as thousand-eyed, to the *daitya*. The *daitya* Maya was astounded and spoke to Hari. Maya asked, "O one who has the *vajra* in his hand! What is this? O friend! This is not deserving of you." Hari laughed and embraced him. "I have achieved my objective. The learned achieve their objectives through whatever means that are possible." O tiger among sages! Since then, there was great friendship between Shakra and Maya and Maya was always engaged in ensuring Hari's welfare. He went to Indra's residence and told him everything. Hari asked Maya, who possessed knowledge of *maya*, "What will I do?" Out of affection towards Hari, Maya gave him knowledge of *maya*. Having obtained it, Hari was extremely pleased and asked, "O Maya! What will I do? Please tell me." Maya replied, "Go to Agastya's hermitage. The expectant Diti is there. Remain there and tend to her for many days. O Maghavan! Holding the *vajra*, enter her womb. Using that, sever the fetus that is growing. Because of the *vajra*, it will either come under your subjugation or be dead. In either case, your enemy will cease to exist." Maghavan agreed and worshipped Maya.'

'He went and humbly presented himself before his mother, Diti.[788] Shakra served the goddess, the mother of *daitya*s. Diti did not know that Shakra harboured enmity in his heart. But the fetus inside the womb knew, because of the invincible and unassailable energy of the sage Kashyapa, what Indra of the gods intended to do. The thousand-eyed Purandara seized his *vajra*. Desiring to enter inside, he waited for a long period of time. On one occasion, the one with the *vajra* as his weapon saw that at the time of *sandhya*, she was sleeping with her head facing the north.[789] "This is my opportunity." Saying this, he entered Diti's stomach. The fetus that was inside saw Indra with the weapon desiring to kill it. Not

---

[788] That is, step-mother.

[789] Until there was a violation in *niyama*s, Indra couldn't enter.

frightened at all, it repeatedly spoke. The fetus asked, "O one with the *vajra*! I am your brother. Why don't you protect me? Why do you wish to kill me? There is no sin greater than killing someone without a fight. O mighty-armed Shakra! That should only be done in the course of battle. Let me emerge and let there be a fight with you. Otherwise, this does not suit you. You are Shatakratu, the one with one thousand eyes. You are Purandara, Shachi's consort. You are Indra of the gods with the *vajra* in your hand. O lord! This is not worthy of you. O mighty-armed one! If you wish to fight with me, arrange for me to emerge. Withdraw from this course of action. Even if there is a calamity, great ones do not tread along a wicked path. I do not possess learning, nor knowledge of weapons. I do not have a complement of weapons I can fight with. You possess learning and you hold a *vajra* in your hand. Are you not ashamed that you are trying to kill me? A person born in a noble lineage never commits a condemned act. Having killed me, what fame or good merits will you get? If you wish to kill a brother who is still in the womb, what act of manliness is this? On the other hand, perhaps you are indeed eager to fight with your brother." He clenched his fists and stood in front of the one with the *vajra*. "You are the killer of a child. You are the killer of a brother. You are guilty of committing a breach of trust. O Shakra! Ready to kill me, these are the fruits you will obtain. Everything, mobile and immobile, follows his commands. However, he now wishes to kill me, a child. What is the fame here? Where is the manliness?" While the fetus was saying this, he used his *vajra* to slice it. A person who is greedy and blind in rage never displays any compassion. The fetus did not waver. Instead, it sorrowfully said, "We are your brothers." He sliced those fragments again, which said, "O Shatakratu! Do not kill us. We were assured, in our mother's womb. We are your own brothers." The minds of those who are overwhelmed with hatred do not exhibit the slightest bit of pity. He sliced those fragments again. They possessed hands and feet and it was as if they were alive. They seemed to be[790] indifferent. On seeing those, seven times,

---

[790] Indra first cut the fetus into seven pieces. He again sliced each of the seven into seven pieces. Thus, there were forty-nine altogether. The Maruts

seven fragments, he was extremely surprised. Those auspicious
fragments in the womb were one, but had many different forms.
They wept in many different ways and Hari said, 'Ma ruda.'[791] Thus,
the extremely powerful and energetic Maruts were born. While they
were still in the womb, they were not scared of Shakra and spoke
to each other. They spoke to Agastya, the tiger among sages. Their
mother was staying in his hermitage. Our father, your brother is
your friend and respects you a lot.[792] O sage! We know that there
is affection towards us in your mind. The wielder of the *vajra* has
done something that even a *shvapaka* will not do." Hearing these
words, Agastya was extremely worried. Diti was suffering from the
pain inside his womb and he roused her. Agastya went there and
filled with rage, cursed Shachi's beloved. Agastya said, "O Hari! In
a battle, the enemies will always see your back. When the back of a
proud person is seen, as he is running away from the field of battle,
even if he remains alive, he is as good as dead." Angry, Diti cursed
Indra, who was still inside her womb. Diti said, "O Hari! Since you
have not exhibited an act of manliness, you will be cursed. You will
be vanquished by women and will be ousted from your kingdom."
At that time, Prajapati Kashyapa arrived there and was distressed
when he heard from Agastya what Shakra had done. Scared, Shakra
spoke to his father from inside the womb. Shakra said, "Because of
Agastya and Diti, I am scared to come out." Approaching his wife,
Prajapati Kashyapa saw what his son had done, while he was still
inside the womb. He heard about the curses of Agastya and Diti
and grieved. Kashyapa said, "O Shakra! O son! Emerge. Why did
you commit this sin? The minds of those who are born in sparkling
lineages do not turn towards such sins." The one with the *vajra* in
his hand emerged. He was ashamed and stood there silently, with
his face cast downwards. The forms of men reveal the good and bad
deeds they have committed.'

are sometimes described as seven and sometimes as forty-nine.

[791] 'Do not cry.'

[792] The father of the Maruts is Kashyapa and Kashyapa wasn't
Agastya's brother. So the expression 'brother' shouldn't be taken in a literal
sense.

'Shakra said, "I will undoubtedly do what ensures welfare."
Kashyapa and all the guardians of the worlds approached me. They
told me everything. The gods again asked me in due order, how Diti's
womb could be pacified, how the one with one thousand eyes could
be freed from his curse, how there could be friendliness between all
those inside the womb and Indra, how the taint caused by Shachi's
husband could be healed and how there could be release from the
curse imposed by Agastya. I addressed Kashyapa, who was full of
humility, in these words. "O Kashyapa! O Prajapati! O one who
bestows honours! Along with the Vasus, Indra and the guardians of
the worlds, go to Goutami. Bathe there. All of you praise Mahesha.
Through Shiva's favours, everything will be beneficial." Accepting
this, Kashyapa went to Goutami. Bathing there, he used these words
to duly praise the divinity, Isha. Two entities are spoken of as the
destroyers of every kind of misery—the sacred river, Goutami, and
Shiva, the ocean of compassion. Kashyapa said, "O Shankara! O
lord of the gods! Save me. O one worshipped by the worlds! Protect
me. O one who purifies! Save me. O lord of speech! O one with a
pannaga as an ornament! Protect me. O Dharma! O one astride
a bull! Save me. O one with the three Vedas as eyes! Protect me.
O one who holds up the earth! O lord of prosperity! Save me. O
Sharva! O one who wears an elephant's hide as garment! Protect
me. O lord who destroyed Tripura! Save me. O one with the moon
as an ornament on your head! Protect me. O lord of sacrifices! O
Somesha! Save me. O one who bestows what is desired! Protect me.
O abode of compassion! Save me. O one who bestows everything
auspicious! Protect me. O origin of everything! Save me. O protector
and lord of riches! Protect me. O radiant one! O lord of wealth!
Save me. O one worshipped by Brahma! Protect me. O lord of the
universe! O lord of success! Save me. O complete one! Protect me. I
bow down before you. O Shiva! O ocean of compassion! You alone
are the refuge of embodied beings who are wandering around in
this terrible and desolate *samsara*, anxious in their minds." Praised
in this way, Vrishdhvaja appeared before him. He asked Prajapati
Kashyapa to ask for a boon. Kashyapa addressed Shiva in humble
words and told him in detail about what Indra had done, the curse,
the destruction of the sons, the mutual enmity, the perpetration

of the sin and the curse invoked on Shakra. At this, Vrishakapi[793]
spoke to Diti and Agastya. Shiva said, "The forty-nine Maruts are
your sons. All of them will be extremely fortunate and will obtain
their shares in sacrifices. Full of joy, they will always be with Indra.
Wherever Indra has a share of the oblations in sacrifices, the Maruts
will first have their shares. There is no doubt about this. When
Shakra is with the Maruts, no one will be able to ever defeat him.
He will always be victorious. O Prajapati! All of you remain happy.
From now on, if anyone slays a brother, his lineage will be destroyed
and he will always face calamities." Shambhu carefully spoke
to Agastya, the tiger among rishis. Shambhu said, "O sage! You
should not be angry with Shachi's husband. O immensely wise one!
Go in peace. The Maruts will be immortal." Pleased, Vrishadhvaja
Shiva also spoke to Diti. Shiva said, "You desired to have a son
who would have the prosperity of the three worlds. Thinking that,
you controlled yourself and engaged in austerities. Your efforts
have now become successful. You have many auspicious sons who
possess the qualities. They will be strong and brave. Therefore,
cast aside your mental grief. O one with the excellent eyebrows!
Without any anxiety, please ask for other boons." Diti heard the
words uttered by the lord of the gods. She joined her hands in
salutation, bowed down and addressed Shambhu in these words.
Diti said, "O one worshipped by the gods! In this world, the sight
of a son brings delight to the parents. In particular, a son is loved
by the mother. This is even more so if the son possesses beauty,
prosperity, valour and bravey, even if it happens to be a single
son. What need be said if there are many? Through your powers,
my sons will certainly be victorious and strong. They are Indra's
brothers and the true sons of Prajapati. This has happened through
the favours of Agastya and through Ganga's favours. O divinity!
O Shambhu! Through your favours, where is the doubt about any
of this? I have been successful in my objective. Nevertheless, please
listen to what I devotedly tell you. Please act for the welfare of the
worlds." Thus addressed, the creator of the universe spoke to Diti
who was bowing down, "Speak out." Diti said, "O one worshipped

---

[793] Being used here for Shiva.

by the gods! In this world, the obtaining of an offspring is extremely rare. An offspring is especially loved by the mother. What need be said if the offspring happens to be a son? If the son possesses qualities and happens to be handsome with a long lifespan, where is the need for heaven, emancipation or Parameshthi's status? In this world and in the world hereafter, to obtain the fruits, all beings always desire a son who possesses the qualities. Therefore, please bestow that favour on anyone who bathes here." Shankara replied, "If a person does not possess offspring, that is the consequence of great sins. If a woman is born barren or if a man is born impotent, as soon as the person bathes here, that sin will be destroyed. If a person bathes here and reads this *stotram*, bathing and donating for three months, that person will obtain the fruits of having a son. If a barren woman bathes here, she will have a son. After the period, if a woman bathes here, she will have a son. Three months after conception, if a woman uses this *stotram* and fruits to devotedly praise me and see me, there is no doubt that she will have a son who is Shakra's equal. O Diti! Hear about the supreme atonement for those who do not have sons because of the father's sins or because of the sin of stealing wealth. They should please the ancestors by offering *pinda* there and donate a little bit of gold. They will then have sons. Those who steal what has been kept with them in trust, those who steal or hide jewels and those who do not perform *shraddha* ceremonies are those whose lineages do not increase. For the world hereafter, this will be the refuge of such sinners. Those who frequent this *tirtha* will give birth to praiseworthy offspring. The lord Siddheshvara is without beginning and without end. He is without decay. He is consciousness, truth and bliss. His image is there and is frequented by gods, *rishis*, siddhas, *gandharvas* and lords among *yogis*. Mahadeva is himself present in that *lingam*, which is full of light and is without any blemish. At the place where Diti met Ganga, a person must use the various articles of worship to worship the *lingam*. He must always be devoted and controlled in his vows. Using this *stotram*, he must praise him on the eighth and fourteenth lunar days. According to his capacity, he must donate gold and feed *brahmanas*. If a person does this near Ganga, he will obtain one hundred sons. He will accomplish all his desires and at the end, go to Shiva's city. If a person uses this *stotram* to praise me, regardless of who that person is, will certainly obtain a son within six months, even if the woman is barren." Since then, that *tirtha* has been known as Putra *tirtha*.[794] Bathing, donating and other rites performed there yield everything that is desired. Because of friendship with the Maruts, it is also known as Mitra *tirtha*.[795] Since that cleansed Indra of his sin, it is also spoken of as Shakra *tirtha*. The place where Indra regained his prosperity is known as Kamala *tirtha*.[796] All these *tirtha*s yield everything that is wished for. Saying that everything would be as she wished, Shiva vanished. Successful in their objectives, all of them returned to wherever they had come from. One hundred thousand sacred *tirtha*s exist there and are spoken about.'

Chapter 2(55) (Yama, Agni and other *tirtha*s)

Brahma said, 'The place known as Yama *tirtha* enhances the delight of the ancestors. It is frequented by those who visit all other *tirtha*s. It is sacred and bestows everything that is seen and not seen. It destroys every kind of sin. I will describe its powers. There was a powerful pigeon, known by the name of Anuhrada. His wife was a bird named Heti and she could assume any form at will. Anuhrada was the son of Mrityu's son and Heti was the daughter of Mrityu's daughter. In the course of time, the couple had sons and grandsons. Their enemy was a powerful king of birds, named Uluka.[797] His sons and grandsons were the Agneyas and they were powerful. For a very long period of time, there was enmity between these two types of birds. The pigeons resided on the northern banks of Ganga. Uluka, the king of birds, resided on the southern bank. O supreme among *brahmana*s! He lived there, along with his sons and

---

[794] *Putra* means son.
[795] *Mitra* means friend.
[796] Because Kamala is one of Lakshmi's names.
[797] *Uluka* means owl.

grandsons. They were opposed to each other and for a very long period of time, there were clashes between them. Both of them had strong sons and stronger grandsons. Neither the owl, nor the pigeon were victorious or defeated. The pigeon worshipped his grandfather Mrityu and obtained *yamya* weapons.[798] Using these, he became superior to everyone else. In that way, the owl worshipped Agni and became extremely strong. Intoxicated because of their boons, there was an extremely terrible battle between them. Uluka hurled an *agneya* weapon towards Kapota.[799] Kapota hurled Yama's noose towards his enemy. He released Mrityu's noose and staff towards Uluka. The battle continued between them, like the ancient clash between Adi and Baka.[800] In that great battle, Heti, the female pigeon who was devoted to her husband, saw that the fire was approaching her husband and was overwhelmed with grief. In particular, she saw that her sons were surrounded by the fire. Heti went to the fire-god and praised him, using many kinds of appropriate words. Heti said, "His form and gifts are not directly seen. All material objects originate in his *atman*. It is through him that the gods partake of oblations. I bow down to Svaha's husband, the one who enjoys sacrifices. You are the mouth of the gods. You are omniscient. You are the bearer of oblations. For the gods, you are the *hotri*.[801] You are the messenger of the gods. I seek refuge with that god. O Vibhavasu! You are the original god. You exist inside and outside, in the form of the breath of life. Outside, you are the one who bestows food. He is the wealth of the sacrifice. I seek refuge with the one who conquers wealth." Agni replied, "O female pigeon! My weapon has been released in this battle and it is infallible. O one devoted to your husband! Where will the weapon find its resting place? Please tell me that." The female pigeon said, "Let the weapon

[798] Weapons named after Yama. In this section, Mrityu and Yama are used synonymously.

[799] *Agneya* weapons are named after Agni, *kapota* is a pigeon.

[800] The clash between Adi/Ati (*turdus ginginianus*) and Baka (Indian crane) is a famous story, recounted in many Puranas, such as the Markandeya Purana. The sages Vishvamitra and Vasishtha assumed the forms of these two birds and fought.

[801] *Hotri* is the chief priest at a sacrifice.

rest in me, not on my sons or my husband. O lord of oblations! O Jataveda! Be truthful in speech. I bow down before you." Jataveda replied, "O one devoted to your husband! I am satisfied with your words and at your devotion towards your husband. O Heti! I will bestow peace on you, your sons and your husband. My Agneya weapon will not burn down your husband, your sons, or you. O female pigeon! Go in peace." Meanwhile, the female owl noticed her husband. He was enveloped in Yama's noose and was being struck by his staff. The female owl was miserable. Suffering from fear, she approached Yama. The female pigeon said, "Because they fear you, people follow you. Because they fear you, they observe *brahmacharya*. Because they fear you, they perform virtuous deeds. Because they fear you, they are persevering and devoted to their tasks. Because they fear you, when they roam around in villages or forests, they do not cause any harm. Because they fear you, they are amiable. Because they fear you, they drink *soma*. Because they fear you, they donate food and cattle. Because they fear you, they speak about the *brahman*." When she spoke in this way, the lord of the southern direction spoke to her. Yama replied, "O fortunate one! Ask for a boon. I will give you whatever brings pleasure to your mind." Hearing Yama's words, the one who was devoted to her husband spoke to him. The female owl said, "My husband has been enveloped in your noose and is being struck with your staff. O best among the gods! Please save my sons and my husband." Hearing these words, Yama was filled with compassion and spoke repeatedly. Yama replied, "O one with a beautiful face! Tell me about a resting place for the noose and the staff." She said, "O Yama! O god! Let your noose enter and rest in me. O lord of the universe! Let your staff also rest inside me." The illustrious Yama was filled with compassion and spoke again. Yama said, "Your husband and all your sons will live, free of anxiety." Yama restrained his noose and the bearer of oblations restrained the Agneya weapon.'

'The two gods ensured friendship between the pigeon and the owl. They told the two birds, "Ask for the boon that you desire." The birds replied, "Because of our enmity, we have been able to see you, an objective that is extremely difficult to attain. O best among gods! We are birds. What will sinners do with a boon? Or, if the two of you wish to affectionately bestow a boon on us, we do not want anything for ourselves. Do not bestow the auspicious boon on us. O lords of the gods! Anyone who asks for himself should be grieved over. If a person is always engaged in ensuring welfare for others, his birth is truly successful. Fire, water, the sun, the earth and many kinds of grain only exist for the sake of others. In particular, this is true of those who are virtuous. O lords of gods! Brahma and others also have to confront death. Knowing this, it is futile to strive for one's own sake. For any man, Parameshthi has ordained everything from the time of birth. This can never be countered. Therefore, creatures strive in vain. Therefore, we ask for something auspicious that will benefit the world, something that has qualities for everyone. Please approve of this." For the sake of *dharma*, fame and the welfare of the worlds, the two birds, famous in the worlds, spoke in this way to the two gods. The birds continued, "Let our hermitages be *tirtha*s on both sides of Ganga. You are the lords of the universe. This is the first boon for us. Bathing, donating, *japa*, oblations and worshipping of the ancestors, whether undertaken by those with good deeds or bad deeds—let these bring inexhaustible good merits to anyone who undertakes these there. This is the second boon for us." Extremely pleased, the gods replied, "It shall be that way. But we have something else to say." Yama said, "If a person reads the *stotram* to Yama on the northern bank of Goutami, seven generations of his family will never suffer from untimely deaths. If a man recites this, he will always possess every kind of prosperity. If a person controls himself and always reads the *stotram* to Mrityu, he will not suffer from the eighty-eight thousand different kinds of ailments. O best among birds! If a lady who is expecting bathes in this *tirtha* every day for three months, or if a lady who is barren bathes in this *tirtha* every day for six months, that lady will give birth to a brave son who will live for one hundred years. He will be prosperous, intelligent and brave and his sons and grandsons will extend the lineage. If *pinda* is offered there, the ancestors will be liberated. If a man bathes there, he will be freed from sins committed in thoughts, words and deeds." After Yama spoke these words, the bearer of oblations spoke to the two birds. Agni said, "If a man is controlled, follows vows and reads my *stotram* on the southern

bank, I will bestow freedom from ailment, prosperity, wealth and
beauty on him. If a man reads this *stotram* anywhere, or if he writes
it down and keeps it in his house, he will never suffer any fear from
fire. If a man purifies himself and bathes and offer donations in
Agni *tirtha*, there is no doubt that he will obtain the fruits of an
agnishtoma sacrifice." Since then, learned people know of that
tirtha as Yama *tirtha*, Agni *tirtha*, Kapota *tirtha*, Uluka *tirtha* and
Heti-Uluka *tirtha*. There are three thousand, three hundred and
ninety *tirtha*s there. Each of them yields objects of pleasure and
emancipation. If men bathe and offer donations there, they are
purified after death. They possess sons and excellent wealth. They
attain auspicious and divine worlds.'

Chapter 2(56) (Tapa *tirtha* and other *tirtha*s)

Brahma said, 'The place known as Tapa *tirtha* greatly enhances
asceticism. It is sacred and bestows every object of desire. It
enhances the delight of the ancestors. Hear about what occurred
in that *tirtha*. This destroys all sins. There was a conversation
among *rishi*s about water and fire. Some thought water was
superior, others thought fire was superior. About the comparison
between water and fire, the sages spoke in the following way.
"How can there be life without fire? Life exists because fire
exists. Agni is the *atman*. Agni represents oblations. Everything
originates from Agni. Agni holds up the worlds. Agni provides the
universe with light. Therefore, there is nothing superior to Agni.
He is the great purifying divinity. He is the fire that is inside. He
is the fire that is outside. Nothing exists without fire. The three
worlds are his abode. Fire is the best among the elements. Just as
a man impregnates the womb of a woman with semen, he is the
strength inside the body. There is nothing other than Krishanu.[802]
Vahni is the mouth of the gods. Hence, it is known that there is
nothing superior." Others, who spoke about the Vedas, thought

---

[802] Krishanu is Agni's name, as is Vahni.

that water was superior. "Food results from water. The purifying one[803] originates from water. Water holds up everything. Water is remembered as the mother. Those who know about the ancient accounts say that water is the life of the three worlds. *Amrita* is produced from water. The herbs originate from water." Some said that fire was superior, others said that water was superior. The *rishi*s, who knew about the Vedas, could not come to a conclusion. Speaking in opposite ways, they approached me and spoke to me. The *rishi*s said, "You are the lord of the three worlds. Please tell us whether fire or water is superior." I replied to the *rishi*s, controlled in their vows, who had come there. "Both of them should be worshipped by the worlds. The universe originates in both of them. *Havya*, *kavya* and *amrita* result from both of them. In this world, life and sustenance of the body are due to both. Between the two, neither is superior. Both are held to be equal. My view is that neither of the two is superior." However, those excellent *rishi*s decided that one or the other must be superior. They were not satisfied with my words. Hence, those ascetics went to Vayu. The sages asked, "O Vayu! You are the breath of life and truth is established in you. Which of the two is superior?" Vayu answered, "Anala[804] is superior. Everything is established in Agni." "That is not true." Telling each other that, the *rishi*s went to Vasundhara.[805] The sages asked, "O earth! You are the one who holds up mobile and immobile objects. Speak truthfully. Who is superior?" The earth humbly spoke to the *rishi*s who had come. The earth answered, "The waters are eternal goddesses and the waters are my foundation. Everything originates in water. Therefore, it is evident that water is superior." "That is not true." Telling each other that, the rishis went to the one who lies down on the milky ocean, the one who holds the conch shell, the *chakra* and the mace. Using many kinds of *stotram*s, they praised him.

The *rishi*s said, 'You are the one who knows all the worlds. You are the reservoir in which the past, the present and the future

---

[803] Agni is the purifying one.
[804] Agni.
[805] The earth.

are hidden. At the end, all the varied and wonderful three worlds
merge into you. You are the imperishable and eternal one. You
are immeasurable. The *rishi*s speak of you as one who cannot be
known through the Vedas. By resorting to you, they obtain what
they wish for. You are the truth and we seek refuge in you. You
are the greatest of the great elements. You are the most important
entity in the universe. *Yogi*s do not get to know of Vishnu's form.
O refuge of the universe! Speak to the *rishi*s who have come here.
Please tell us the truth. You are in the *atman*s of all those with
bodies. You alone are everything. O lord! Everything is in you.
Because of Prakriti, no one anywhere gets to know about your
powers. You are inside and outside everything. Your *atman* is in
the ever-changing universe.' The creator of the universe spoke
through a divine and invisible voice. The divine voice said, 'Let
both of them be worshipped through austerities, devotion and
rituals. Whichever one bestows success first will be spoken of as
superior.' Agreeing to this, all the *rishi*s, worshipped by the worlds,
departed. They were exhausted and their minds were distressed.
They were full of supreme non-attachment. All of them went to
Goutami, the mother of all the worlds and the one who purifies
the three worlds. Controlling themselves through vows, they
performed austerities there. They got ready to worship fire and
water. Some were worshippers of fire, others were worshippers
of water. The divine voice, Sarasvati, the mother of the Vedas,
spoke to them. The divine voice said, 'Water is the origin of fire.
Purification is obtained through water. For those of you who are
worshippers of fire, how will you complete the worship without
water? One obtains the right to undertake rites only after water
has been prepared. As long as a man is impure and dirty, he is not
entitled to undertake rites. Even if he knows about the Vedas, he
must purify himself by faithfully immersing himself in cool water.
Therefore, since water is spoken of as the mother of everything,
water must be superior. Hence, water is superior, especially
because it is the mother of fire.' Hearing those words, the *rishi*s,
who knew about the Vedas, came to the conclusion that water
must be superior. O Narada! This occurred at the *tirtha* where
the *rishi*s were undertaking a sacrifice. That place is spoken of as

Tapa *tirtha* and Satra *tirtha*.[806] The learned also speak of it as Agni *tirtha* and Sarasvata *tirtha*.[807] Bathing and donations there yield every object of desire and everything auspicious. There are another fourteen hundred *tirtha*s there. These bestow good merits. Bathing and donations there confer heaven and emancipation. The place where the voice dispelled the doubt of the *rishi*s is the place where the river Sarasvati originated and merged into Ganga. Which man is capable of speaking about the greatness of that confluence?'

Chapter 2(57) (Arshtishena *tirtha*)

Brahma said, 'The place known as Deva *tirtha* is on the northern banks of Ganga. I will tell you about its greatness. It destroys all sins. There was a king named Arshtishena. He possessed all the qualities. His wife was named Jaya and she was just like another Lakshmi. Their son was named Bhara. He was intelligent and devoted to his father. He was accomplished and skilled in *dhanurveda* and the Vedas. His beautiful wife was known by the name of Suprabha. King Arshtishena entrusted the kingdom to his son. With his chief priest, the lord of men consecrated himself and made efforts for undertaking a horse sacrifice on the banks of Sarasvati. With officiating priests and foremost *rishi*s, accomplished in the Vedas and the sacred texts, the best among kings consecrated himself. There was a brave king of *danava*s, named Mithu. In the presence of the fire and the *brahmana*s, the powerful and evil-minded one destroyed the sacrifice and abducted the king, his wife and his priest. O sage! He swiftly took them to the nether regions of Rasatala. When the excellent king was taken away, the sacrifice was destroyed. Leaving the place where the sacrifice was being held, all immortals and officiating priests returned to their own respective abodes. The son of the royal priest was known as Devapi. He was a child. He could see his mother, but could not see his father. He

---

[806] *Satra* means sacrifice.
[807] Because of Sarasvati.

was amazed at this and was exceedingly miserable. He asked his mother, "O mother! Where has my father gone? Without my father, I do not wish to remain alive. O mother! Please tell me the truth. Shame on the lives of those who do not have fathers. They are those who have committed wicked deeds. O mother! If you do not tell me, I will enter the water or the fire." The mother told her son, "Along with the king, a *danava* has taken the king's wife and the priest, your father, to the nether regions." Devapi asked, "Who has taken him away and why? Where was he taken? How was he taken? Who committed this deed? Who were watching? What is the place? Where does the *danava* live? Please tell me." The mother answered, "In an assembly, the king consecrated himself for a sacrifice. The *daitya* Mithu took him to Rasatala, along with his wife and priest. In the presence of the fire and the *brahmanas*, the large number of gods looked on." Hearing his mother's words, Devapi remembered what he should do. "Irrespective of whether the gods, the fire, the officiating priests and the *asuras* looked on, it is my view that I must search for my father. There is nothing else to do." Having decided this, Devapi spoke to Bhara, the king's son. Devapi said, "Using austerities, *brahmacharya*, vows and *niyama*, I will bring back all those who have been taken to Rasatala. When something terrible has been done, if a person does not counter it, his birth is in vain and he is the worst among men. How does it matter whether such a person is dead or alive? Please rule over the entire earth, just as your father, Arshtishena, did. O king! Until I return, after achieving success, you should protect my mother. O Bhara! Please grant me permission." After carefully thinking about everything, Bhara replied to Devapi. Bhara said, "Go happily and achieve success. You need not have the slightest bit of worry."

'Devapi meditated on the feet of the king of the immortals. He carefully searched out the officiating priests. He bowed down separately before each of the officiating priests. The child, Devapi, joined his hands in salutation and addressed them in these words. Devapi said, "When the person undertaking the sacrifice had consecrated himself, you should have saved him, the sacrifice, the priest and the wife of the person who had been consecrated. O officiating priests! While you looked on, the sacrifice was destroyed and the king was abducted. This is not worthy of you. I think you should return them, free of ailments. O foremost *brahmanas*! Otherwise, you deserve to be cursed." The officiating priests replied, "In a sacrifice, Agni must be worshipped first. Agni is the divinity. Therefore, as servants of Agni, we do not know.[808] He is the lord of oblations. He is the one who bestows and he is the one who enjoys. He is the one who acts. He is the one who takes away." Turning his back on the officiating priests, Devapi followed the procedures and worshipped Jataveda. He told Agni everything. Agni replied, "Like the officiating priests, I am also the servant of the gods. I only bear the oblations for the gods. They are the ones who enjoy. They are the ones who protect." Devapi said, "I will invoke the gods and give them their separate and complete shares of the oblations. Therefore, quickly take them to the gods." Devapi went to the gods and bowed down separately before each of them. He told them about the words of the officiating priest, the words of Agni and the curse.[809] The gods replied, "O supreme among *brahmanas*! When the officiating priests used *mantra*s from the Vedas to summon us, in due order, we enjoy our shares of the oblations. We aren't independent. Thus, we always follow the Vedas. We are urged by the Vedas. O brahmana! Since we are dependent, you should go and report this to the Vedas." Devapi purified himself and carefully invoked the Vedas, using meditation and austerities. The Vedas appeared before him. Devapi bowed down repeatedly and spoke to the Vedas, informing them about the words of the officiating priests, the words of Agni and the words of the gods. The Vedas replied, "O son! We are dependent. We are under Ishvara's subjugation. He is the one who holds up the entire universe. He is himself without a support and without blemish. He is a reservoir of every kind of power. He is the abode of every kind of prosperity. He is Mahadeva, the creator. He is Maheshvara, the destroyer. O brahmana! Though we speak and we know, we are only in the form of sounds. But we must do this much, tell you what you ask—who took them away, his name, his city and his strength and whether they have been eaten. We know that they have not been

---

[808] That is, the responsibility is being passed on to Agni.
[809] His threatened curse.

destroyed. We know your capacity, who you should worship and
where so that you can get them back." Hearing what the Vedas said,
for a long time, he thought about this in his mind. Devapi answered,
"O Vedas! Please tell me everything quickly and truthfully. I bow
down to you. I bow down to all those who have been taken down
to the nether regions. I shall get them back." The Vedas said, "O
Devapi! Go to Goutami and praise Maheshvara there. When he is
extremely pleased, the compassionate one will give you what you
wish for. O immensely wise one! If Shiva is praised and pleased, this
is indeed what will happen. King Arshtishena, his faithful wife, Jaya,
and Upamanyu, your father, are in the nether regions. They do not
suffer from any ailments. Through a boon bestowed by Mahesha,
you will slay the *rakshasa* Mithu and attain fame and *dharma*. This
is possible and the opposite will not happen." Hearing their words,
the child, Devapi, went to Goutami.'

'The brahmana bathed, and at the right time, praised
Maheshvara. Devapi said, "O lord of the gods! I am a child. You
are the *guru* of my preceptors. I do not possess the capacity to praise
you properly. O Shambhu! I bow down before you. The *nigama*
texts do not know you, nor do the gods or the sages. Nor do Brahma
and Vaikuntha.[810] You are who you are. I prostrate myself before
you. O Maheshvara! In the world, there are those who are without
protectors, miserable, distressed, diseased and evil-souled. You save
them. O lord of the universe! When they are worshipped through
austerities, rituals and *mantra*s, you are the one who bestows fruits
on the residents of heaven. Those who seek cannot be donors.[811]
What they wish for is with you. It is not extraordinary that you
should be the cause of this perversity. O preceptor of the universe! O
protector! When the word 'Shiva' is uttered, you save the ignorant,
sinners and those who are submerged in the ocean of hell.' Praised
in this way, the three-eyed one appeared in front of him and spoke
to him. Shiva said, 'O Devapi! O child! Tell me the boon you want.
Enough of this misery.' Devapi replied, 'O lord of the universe! I
wish to get back the king, the king's wife and my father and *guru*.

---

[810] That is, Vishnu.
[811] The gods cannot give.

I wish that my enemy should be killed.' Hearing Devapi's words, the lord of everything signified his consent. Through Shankara's command, Devapi obtained everything. O Narada! Shambhu, the ocean of compassion, summoned his own *ganas*. Shambhu sent Nandi, with his trident. In Rasatala, Nandi killed Mithu, bull among the *asuras*. He brought his father and the others and handed them over. The intelligent Arshtishena's horse sacrifice was performed there. Agni, the officiating priests, the gods, the Vedas and the *rishis* spoke. Agni and the others said, 'O Devapi! The place where Shambhu, the lord of the gods and the lord of the universe, himself appeared will be Deva *tirtha*. It will destroy every kind of sin and bestow every kind of success on men. This *tirtha* will be sacred and your deeds will be eternal.' When the horse sacrifice was over, the gods bestowed boons on them. After bathing in Ganga and having accomplished their objective, they[812] went to heaven. Since then, along both banks, fifteen thousand and one hundred and eight *tirthas* developed. It is known that bathing and donations there confer great fruits.'

Chapter 2(58) (Tapovana and other *tirthas*)

Brahma said, 'There is a place known as Tapovana, the confluence of Nandini and Siddheshvara *tirtha*. This is on Goutami's southern bank. It is also known as Shardula. Hear about their accounts. Even if one hears about this, one is freed from all sins. Earlier, Agni was the *hotri*[813] and bore the oblations for the gods. As a wife, he obtained the extremely beautiful Svaha, Daksha's daughter. Initially, she didn't have any sons and performed

---

[812] Arshtishena and the others.

[813] There were four classes of priests, though the classification varied over time. The *hotri* is the chief priest and is accomplished in the *Rig Veda*. The *adhvaryu* is the assistant priest and is accomplished in the *Yajur Veda*, though later, the *udgatri* came to be identified with the *Sama Veda*. In addition, there was the *brahmana* or *purohita*.

austerities for the sake of a son. Through extensive austerities, she satisfied Hutashana.[814] Her husband, the enjoyer of oblations, spoke to his wife, the unblemished Svaha. Agni said, "O beautiful one! There will be offspring. Do not engage in austerities." Hearing her husband's words, she refrained from austerities. Except the words of a husband, nothing ever fulfils the wishes of a woman. After some time passed, a fear arose on account of Taraka. Kartikeya had not been born. Maheshvara and Bhavani were in private for a very long period of time. To accomplish the task of the gods, the scared gods appeared before Agni. The residents of heaven spoke to him. The gods said, "O immensely fortunate one! Go to the divinity Shambhu, worshipped by the three worlds. Inform Shambhu about the fear that has risen on account of Taraka." Agni replied, "I will not go to a spot where a couple remains in privacy. This is the norm for an ordinary person, not to speak of a person who holds the trident in his hand. As they wish, they are alone and are conversing lovingly. If a person hears a couple's words, he cannot be saved from hell. He is the lord of all the worlds. He is Mahakala who wields the trident. When he is in a private place with Bhavani, who is capable of looking at him?" The gods said, "When a great fear presents itself, this is good policy. What else are you describing? When there is a fear on account of Taraka, you are the Taraka.[815] When others are submerged in an ocean of great fear, the lives of the virtuous are meant for those others. Or assume some other form and go. Go and speak the words. After making Shambhu listen to the words of the gods, return quickly. O wise one! In both the worlds, we will then worship you." Following the words of the gods, Hutashana assumed the form of a parrot and went quickly. He went to the place where the lord of the universe was sporting with Uma. Scared, Anala approached in the form of a parrot. However, the bearer of oblations was incapable of entering through the doorway. He went and sat on a window sill. He was trembling and his face was cast downwards. On seeing him, Shambhu laughed and in private, spoke to Uma. Shambhu said, "O goddess! Look. Following the words of

---

[814] Agni's name.
[815] There is a pun on words. Taraka means rescuer/deliverer.

the gods, Hutashana has come in the form of a parrot." Ashamed, Parvati told the divinity, "Enough!" The lord of the gods saw Agni roaming around in front of him, in the form of a bird. He said, "O Agni! In many different ways, you have been recognized. Do not speak anything. Open your mouth, accept it and take it away." Saying this, he released a lot of semen into Agni's mouth. With that semen inside him, Agni was incapable of leaving. Exhausted, Agni sat down on the banks of the celestial river.[816] He flung the semen into the Krittikas and Kartika resulted.'

'Some of Shambhu's semen was still left inside Agni's body. Vahni divided this semen into two parts and deposited it inside his own beloved wife, Svaha, especially because she was keen to have a son. Earlier, he had assured her that she would have offspring. Remembering this, Vahni deposited Shambhu's semen. Through this semen, an excellent pair of twins was born to Agni. They were Suvarna and Suvarnaa and in their beauty, they were unmatched on earth. They pleased Agni, who was always engaged in ensuring pleasure to the worlds. Delighted, Agni bestowed Suvarnaa on the intelligent Dharma. He made up his mind that Samkalpa would become the beloved wife of his son, Suvarna. In this way, the wise one arranged for the marriages of his son and daughter. However, because of their associations with others, both of Agni's offspring suffered from taints. His son, Suvarna, could assume many different forms. He assumed the forms of excellent gods, Indra, Vayu, Dhanada,[817] the lord of the waters,[818] and lords among the sages, and had intercourse with their wives. Whichever lord a wife loved, was a form Suvarna assumed. Sometimes, the wise one's son assumed the form and had intercourse even if the wife was faithful to her husband. In this way, he pleased Madana[819] and with that extensive dalliance, thought that he was successful in his objective. This is what Suvarna did. As for Suvarnaa, Svaha's daughter, though she was Dharma's wife, she was a *svairini* and

---

[816] Ganga.
[817] Kubera.
[818] Varuna.
[819] The god of love.

went to whoever appealed to her. If any human, *asura*, god, *rishi* or ancestor possessed a beautiful wife, she assumed her form and had intercourse with her husband. She indulged in intercourse with those who were handsome, generous, stable and profound. Whichever divinity she desired, she assumed the form of his wife and had intercourse with him. Through many different kinds of means and diverse techniques, she attracted his heart and accomplished her desire. All the gods and *asura*s witnessed the activities Agni's son, Suvarna, and Agni's daughter were engaged in. They became angry and cursed Agni's son and daughter. The gods and *asura*s said, "This is in the nature of adulterous behaviour. This is deceitful and wicked conduct. O bearer of oblations! Therefore, your son will become a transgressor and will go everywhere. O Agni! Similarly, Suvarnaa will never be satisfied with a single person. She will be satisfied not with one, but with many. She will enjoy the bodies of many who belong to condemned species. Because of her own sins, your daughter will enjoy them." Hearing the words of their curse, Agni was extremely frightened. He came to me and asked, "How can my son and daughter be saved?" I told Vahni, "Go to Goutami. O mighty-armed one! Praise Shankara and tell the lord of the universe everything. O Vahni! Such offspring have been born to you because Maheshvara's semen was deposited in your body. Tell the divinity that the gods have imposed such a curse. Shambhu will do what is best for his own offspring. If you devotedly praise the divinity and the goddess, Shiva will be pleased. Concerning your offspring, you will then obtain your cherished objective." Following my words, Agni went to Ganga. He controlled himself and praised Maheshvara, using words and hymns that are revered by the Vedas. Agni said, "He is the creator of the universe. He is the one who sustains. The universe is his form. He is without blemish. He is the original creator. He is the one who created himself. I bow down to the lord of the universe. Assuming the form of fire, he destroys. Assuming the form of water, he creates. Assuming the form of the sun, he preserves. I bow down to the three-eyed one. In the form of a person who performs a sacrifice, he is the cause behind the contentment of the gods. In the form of Vayu, he makes arrangements for living beings. He saves in the form of Shiva. In

the form of Hari, he brings eternal bliss. To create spaces inside
living beings, he assumes the form of space." The illustrious, infinite
and undecaying Shambhu was pleased at this. The one who is
worshipped by the gods asked Pavaka to choose a boon. He humbly
told Shiva, "Your semen was inside me. Because of that, a handsome
son, Suvarna, famous in the worlds was born. O divinity! O lord
of the universe! In that way, a daughter, Suvarnaa, was also born.
Because of this association with someone else's semen, both of them
suffer from a sin. O Shiva! My offspring have committed the sin of
adulterous behaviour. O lord! All the gods have imposed a curse
on them. Please arrange for its pacification." At this, Shambhu
addressed Agni in words that would ensure what was auspicious.
Shambhu said, "It is because of my semen that Suvarna, extensive in
valour, was born to you. For his benefit, I will bestow every kind of
complete prosperity on Suvarna. O Vahni! You should not have any
doubt on this account. Listen to my words. He will purify the three
worlds. He will be like *amrita* in this world and will be loved by the
gods. He will represent objects of pleasure and emancipation. He
will be the *dakshina* at sacrifices. He will have all these forms and
be the preceptor of all preceptors. It should be known that he will
be supreme in valour. My semen is excellent. This is all the more
because it has been deposited in you. What is the need to think about
this? Without him, no kind of prosperity will be complete. Without
Suvarna, men who are alive will be as good as dead. Even if he
possesses no qualities, a rich man is respected. Even if he possesses
qualities, a man without riches is not respected. Therefore, there
will be nothing that is superior to Suvarna.[820] In that way, though
she is fickle, Suvarnaa will be excellent. If she glances at anything,
everything will become complete. In the three worlds, she will be
obtained through austerities, *japa* and oblations. Her powers will
be extensive. O Agni! A little has been described. She will be present
everywhere. She will come, but will wander around. Suvarnaa will
be like Kamala herself and will be pure. From today, though your
offspring will roam around as they please, they will be pure. There
has been no one like them nor will there ever be." Shambhu said

---

[820] *Suvarna* means gold. It is also one of Shiva's names.

this. Then, for the welfare of all the worlds, Shiva himself assumed the form of a *lingam* there.'

'Having obtained the boons for his son and daughter, Vahni was satisfied. Suvarnaa, Agni's daughter was henceforth content with her own husband, Dharma. Vahni's son was also happy with Samkalpa. O sage! Meanwhile, Shardula, lord of the *danava*s, defeated Dharma and deceitfully abducted Swarnaa,[821] Agni's daughter. She was the abode of good fortune and pleasure. He took Suvarnaa, famous in the worlds to Rasatala. Dharma, Agni's son-in-law, and Agni, the lord of oblations, repeatedly praised Vishnu, the protector of the worlds. Both of them informed the powerful Vishnu about what had happened. Hari used his *chakra* to sever Shardula's head. Vishnu brought back the goddess Suvarnaa, the supreme beauty in the worlds. She was the beloved daughter of both Maheshvara and Agni. O Narada! Vishnu showed her to Maheshvara. Maheshvara was delighted and repeatedly embraced her. The place where the blazing *chakra* was washed after severing Shardula's head is famous by the name of Chakra *tirtha*. It is also known as Shardula *tirtha*. The place where Vishnu brought Suvarnaa to Shankara's presence is known as Shankara *tirtha*, Vishnu *tirtha* and Siddha *tirtha*. O supreme among sages! In the place where Agni and Dharma obtained eternal bliss and tears of joy fell down from Agni's eyes, the river Ananda or Nandini started to flow.[822] The confluence of the river with Ganga is sacred. Shiva is himself present there and Suvarnaa is also there. She is also known as Dakshayani, Shivaa, Agneyi Ambika, Jagadadhara, Katyayani and Ishvari. Both of her banks are ornamented and she always grants devotees what they want. The place where Agni tormented himself through austerities is known as Tapovana *tirtha*. O sage! There are such *tirtha*s on both banks. Bathing and donating there

---

[821] The same as Suvarnaa.

[822] The tears created the river, perhaps also from Dharma's eyes, although that is not specifically mentioned. *Ananda* means joy/bliss, while *Nandini* means one who delights. *Nandini* also means daughter. Perhaps two separate rivers were created, Ananda from Agni's tears and Nandini from Dharma's tears. However, the subsequent *shloka* suggests that both rivers were the same.

yield every kind of auspicious desire. There are fourteen thousand *tirtha*s on the northern bank and sixteen thousand on the southern bank. In each of these *tirtha*s, there are signs to identify them. They have separate names, but I have spoken about it briefly. If a man listens to this, reads it or remembers it, all his desires are fulfilled. Knowing this account, if a person bathes and performs the other rites there, Lakshmi is always present with him. Specifically, so is Dharma. The place that is to the west of Abjaka[823] is known as Shardula *tirtha*. It is superior to all other *tirtha*s, such as Varanasi. If a person bathes there, worships the gods and the ancestors and performs water-rites, he is freed from all sins and attains greatness in Vishnu's world. There are many *tirtha*s between Tapovana *tirtha* and Shardula *tirtha*. No one is capable of describing the greatness of each one of them.'

Chapter 2(59) (Indra *tirtha* and other *tirtha*s)

Brahma said, 'The place known as Indra tirtha is also known as Vrishakapi. The confluence of Phena is where Hanumanta is.[824] It is also known as Abjaka, where the divinity Trivikrama exists. If one bathes or donates there, it is extremely rare for that person to return.[825] I will tell you what transpired on the southern banks of Ganga. Indreshvara is to the north. Listen attentively, with devotion. Indra's enemy, Namuchi, was strong and extremely insolent. When he fought with Indra, Indra used foam to sever his head.[826] The foam from the water assumed the form of the *vajra* and severed the head of the enemy, Namuchi. Thereafter, the foam fell down on the southern bank of Ganga. It penetrated the earth and entered

---

[823] *Abjaka* means lotus. But it is not clear which place is intended. Perhaps it means Vishnu *tirtha*. Alternatively, Abjaka might be a typo for Ambika. However, Abjaka has also been identified as the confluence of Phena/Sindhuphena with Godavari.

[824] The river Phena/Sindhuphena is probably Penganga/Painganga.

[825] To be reborn.

[826] The word used is *phena*, which means foam.

Rasatala. The purifying water of Ganga from the nether regions followed the path laid down by the *vajra* and came to the surface of the earth. The water, made out of foam, constituted the river named Phena. Its confluence with Ganga is sacred and is famous in the worlds. Like the confluence of Ganga and Yamuna, it destroys every kind of sin. Through the favours of Vishnu and Ganga, Hanuman's stepmother was freed from the curse of being a cat as soon as she bathed in the water. This is Marjara *tirtha* and I have told you about it earlier.[827] That place is known as Hanumanta and I have described the account earlier. It is also known as Vrishakapi and Abjaka. Listen attentively.'

'There was a powerful ancestor of the *daitya*s, famous by the name of Hiranya. He tormented himself through austerities and none of the gods could defeat him. He was extremely terrible. He had a powerful son, who could never be defeated by the gods. He was known as Mahashani and his wife was Parajita.[828] For a very long period of time, there was an incessant battle between him and Indra. Mahashani was extremely energetic. In the field of battle, he always vanquished Shakra, along with his elephant and handed him over to his father. Once he and his elephant had been bound and were devoid of substance, he would glance at them and giving up his cruelty, would hand them as offerings to the *daitya* Hiranya. His father, the *daitya* Mahashani, was superior to all those who had come before him. He would place Shachi's beloved in the nether regions and guard him there. After defeating Hari,[829] Mahashani advanced against Varuna, wishing to vanquish him. The immensely intelligent Varuna bestowed his daughter on Mahashani. Varuna offered his own abode in the ocean to Mahashani. Thus, there was friendship between Varuna and Mahashani. Mahashani also loved the daughter, Varuni. Mahashani was a great *daitya*. He possessed valour, fame, bravery and strength. In the three worlds, there was no one who has his equal. When there was no longer an Indra in the worlds, the gods consulted among themselves. The gods said,

[827] In Chapter 2(14).
[828] This should probably read Aparajita.
[829] Indra.

"Vishnu is the only one who can give Indra back to us. He is the one who slays *daitya*s. He is the one who knows the *mantra*s and he will create another Indra." Having consulted in this way, the gods went and told Vishnu the import of their consultations. He said, "The great *daitya*, Mahashani, cannot be killed by me." Therefore, Vishnu went to the father-in-law, Varuna, the lord of the waters. Keshava went to Varuna and told him about Indra's defeat. "You must do something, so that Purandara returns." O sage! Hearing Vishnu's words, the lord of the waters quickly went to the brave Mahashani, his daughter's husband and Hiranya's son. The son-in-law showed the lord Varuna a great deal of respect. Humbly, he asked his father-in-law why he had come. Varuna told the *daitya* the reason why he had come. Varuna said, "O mighty-armed one! Give me Indra, whom you have defeated earlier. O friend! The lord of the gods has been bound in Rasatala. He is always respected by us. O slayer of enemies! Please give him to me. If an enemy who has been bound is freed, that brings great fame to the virtuous." When he was addressed in this way, the lord of the *daitya*s thought about it for some time. He then returned Shachi's beloved to Varuna, along with his elephant. In the midst of the *daitya*s, Hari was extremely resplendent. In the presence of the lord of the waters, Mahashani worshipped him with many great objects and spoke to him. Mahashani said, "O Indra! Who has created you? Though you boast a lot, where is your valour? In a battle, you have been defeated by an enemy. Nevertheless, you remain as Indra. This is amazing. If a woman is imprisoned by a man, it is appropriate that her husband should free her. Women are not independent. It is men who are important. O Shakra! If you become a man, that will be praiseworthy. In a battle, I have bound you, along with your mount. Where is your weapon, the *vajra*, which is said to possess powers? As the king of the gods, you possessed everything that deserves to be enjoyed—the jewel Chintamani, Nandana, women, fame and strength. However, you have been freed by the lord of the waters. Shame on you! You wish to remain alive. Anything that is a store of fame is life. Anything that is contrary to fame is death. O Shakra! Knowing this, why aren't you ashamed at having been freed by the lord of the waters? You were in heaven, surrounded by all the gods. You were fanned by your beloved. You were praised by the *apsara*s. But on seeing you, I think shame itself will be scared. 'You are the slayer of Vritra. You are the slayer of Namuchi. You are the destroyer of cities. With the *vajra* in your hand, you have shattered mountains.' The gods have worshipped you in this way. O victorious one! Therefore, give all this up. Creating such transgressions and causing such harm, you roam around in the worlds. How did the one who was born from the undecaying lotus create a person like you? Why does your heart not shatter?" Speaking in this way, the lord of *daitya*s handed Indra over to the great-souled Varuna. He then again addressed him in these words. Mahashani said, "From now on, Varuna will be the *guru* and Indra will be the disciple. O Vasava! You have been freed through my father-in-law. Therefore, you should behave like a servant towards Varuna. Otherwise, I will bind you again and fling you into Rasatala." Reprimanding Shakra in this way, he repeatedly laughed at him. He told him, "leave" and took his leave of Varuna.'

'He returned to his own abode, tainted by shame. He went and told Poulami everything about how he had been defeated by the enemy.[830] Indra said, "O one with the beautiful face! This is the way the enemy has treated me and spoken to me. O fortunate one! Please tell me how I can pacify my soul." Indrani replied, "O Shakra! O slayer of Bala! I know about the origin, *maya*, defeat, boons and death of *danava*s. Therefore, hear from me everything about his birth, defeat and death. For the sake of your pleasure, I will tell you. He is Hiranya's brave son. He is the powerful son of my paternal uncle. Therefore, he is my brother.[831] He is insolent because of the boon he received. Through austerities and *niyama*, he satisfied Brahma. He, thus, obtained strength like this. What cannot be achieved through austerities? Therefore, your mind should not be surprised or disheartened. Listen to the task that must progressively be undertaken." Telling Indra this, Poulami humbly continued. Indrani said, "There is nothing that cannot be achieved

---

[830] Poulami is Shachi. She was Puloma's daughter. Shachi is also known as Indrani.

[831] That is, cousin.

through austerities. There is nothing that cannot be achieved through sacrificial rites. There is nothing that cannot be achieved through devotion to Hara and Vishnu, the lord of the worlds. O beloved one! I have also heard this extremely wonderful account. O lord of gods! Only women can know about feminine nature. O lord! Therefore, there is nothing that cannot be achieved by the earth or the water.[832] Austerities and sacrificial rites are undertaken through them. Hence, go to a land that has become a *tirtha*. If you worship Vishnu and Shiva there, you will get everything that you wish for. I have also heard this. Only women who are devoted to their husbands know everything. They hold up all mobile and immobile objects. The forest of Dandaka is in the middle of the earth and is its essence. O lord! Ganga, the mother of the world, is there. Worship Isha there. Or worship Vishnu, the lord of the universe. The protector is the one who dispels the miseries of the afflicted. Without a protector, men are immersed in an ocean of grief. For such people, there is no refuge other than Hari, Hara and Ganga. Therefore, make every effort to control yourself and satisfy them. Along with me, use devotion, *stotram*s and austerities. Through the favours of Isha and Vishnu, you will then obtain what is good for you. If a man performs a task unknowingly, the fruits obtained are only of one portion. However, when performed knowingly, the fruits obtained are one hundred times. When performed with the wife, the fruits are infinite. In every task undertaken by a man, the wife is an aide. Without her, there is no success in even the slightest of tasks. If he undertakes a task alone, he gets only half the fruits. O lord! If a man undertakes the task along with his wife, he obtains the entire fruit. This has been said about the wife in the sacred texts and those who are familiar with *dharma* know this well. It has been heard that Goutami, best among rivers, is in Dandakaranya. She destroys every kind of sin. She bestows everything desired. Therefore, along with me, go there and undertake meritorious deeds that yield great fruits. Thereby, you will slay your enemy and obtain great joy." Addressed in this way, Shatakratu agreed. Along with his *guru* and his wife, he went to Ganga, the mother of the universe, known as Goutami.

---

[832] The earth and water are feminine in nature.

Delighted, Hari went there, in the middle of Dandakaranya. He made up his mind to perform austerities to Shambhu, the lord of the gods.'

'He first bowed down and bathed in Ganga. Joining his hands in salutation, he sought refuge with Shiva alone. He recited the following *stotram*. Indra said, "Using your own *maya*, you create, preserve and destroy all mobile and immobile objects. But you do not get entangled in this. You are alone and independent. You are the consciousness that has no duality. Your *atman* is bliss. May the one with the Pinaka in his hand be pleased with us. Sanaka and the others, who know about Vedanta, do not know the truth about him. They are ignorant about his mysteries. Parvati's lord is the one who satisfies every kind of wish. Let the slayer of Andhaka be pleased with me.[833] He is the one who created himself. The illustrious one created Virinchi and saw his fearful head.[834] He severed it with the tips of his nails. When it stuck to his nails, he flung it away and the three *varga*s were created from it.[835] Sin, poverty, avarice, begging, delusion and calamities were born from this and obtained their powers. There were others and all these assumed the form of the misery of *samsara*. Everything is pervaded by them. Seeing all this, the lord of the gods was bewildered and spoke to the goddess. 'Please save the universe. O goddess of the worlds! O mother of the universe! O Uma! O one who is the refuge! O extremely gentle one! O extremely fortunate one! O one in whom the universe is established! O one who bestows boons! Victory of you. You are the enjoyment of objects of pleasure. You are *samadhi*. You are supreme emancipation. You are Svaha. You are Svadha. You are Svasti.[836] You are without origin. You are success. You are speech. You are intellect. You are without old age. You are without death. You are in the form of learning and other things. Following my instruction, you are the one who protects the three worlds. You

---

[833] Andhaka was a demon killed by Shiva.

[834] Virinchi is Brahma. Shiva severed one of Brahma's heads.

[835] The three *varga*s are the three objectives of existence—*dharma*, *artha* and *kama*.

[836] Benediction for welfare/prosperity.

are the one who creates the wonderful three worlds, in your form as Prakriti.' Addressed in this way, Hara's beloved was eager to embrace him and converse with him. When she was exhausted, she clung to the upper half of Bhava's body and used her fingers to fling away the drops of sweat. From these drops, Dharma was born first. He was followed by Lakshmi, donations, excellent rain, prosperous living beings, lakes, grain, flowers, fruits, objects that bring good fortune, handsomeness of form and attire, objects used for *shringara*,[837] dancing, singing, *amrita*, Puranas, *shruti* texts, *smriti* texts, *niti* texts, food, drinks, weapons,[838] sacred texts, appropriate equipment and weapons for houses, *tirtha*s, forests, sacrifices, civic works, auspicious vehicles, sparkling ornaments and seats. 'You embraced Bhava's limbs and laughed and conversed with him.[839] Mobile and immobile objects were generated from the beads of your perspiration. O goddess! Everything that was thus born became cleansed of sin. There is abundance of joy. There is eternal auspiciousness that is radiant. This is because of your sentiments. O goddess! O mother of the universe! Therefore, save me. O supreme one in the universe! I am scared of *samsara*. There are some who are confused because of debates. There are others who are drowned. I bow down to the beautiful Shiva and Shakti, who are one.' While he was praising in this way, Shiva appeared in front of him. Shiva asked, 'O Hari! O one who is devoted! What is the boon you desire? Tell me.' Indra replied, 'My enemy is strong. He is like the *vajra* to behold. There are many occasions when I have been defeated by him, bound and taken down to the nether regions. I have been pierced by his words, which are like arrows. I have done this so that he can be killed. O lord of the universe! O lord! So that I can defeat my enemy, please give me energy and everything else needed to destroy my enemy. He is the one who is responsible for my defeat. If I can destroy him, I will think that I have been born again. Fame, victory and prosperity are the best.' Shiva told Shakra,

---

[837] Amorous passion.

[838] These weapons, as compared to the subsequent mention, are divine in nature.

[839] As will become evident, this is being said by Indra.

'Your enemy cannot be killed by me alone. Along with Poulami, you must worship the undecaying Vishnu Hari, the divinity Janardana. He is the refuge of the three worlds. Single-mindedly fix your intelligence on Narayana. O Hari! From him and from me, you will then obtain what you love.' The illustrious Maheshvara, the original creator, spoke again. 'The sages know that *mantras*, practice of austerities and practice of *yoga* at any confluence ensure success. O brahmana![840] What need be said about the confluence of Goutami and the river Phena? What need be said about a confluence of that river in a cave within the mountain? On the southern banks of Ganga, there is a brahmana named Apastamba. He is a lord among sages. His intelligence is fixed on Mukunda's feet. O slayer of Bala! I am also pleased with him. With your wife, satisfy him and Gadadhara.'[841] He bathed at the sacred confluence of Phena with Ganga. He controlled himself and on Ganga's southern bank, along with Apastamba, he praised the divinity Janardana. With many kinds of *mantras* from the Vedas, he performed austerities and satisfied him. Content, Vishnu appeared and asked, 'What should be given to you?' The illustrious Hari replied, 'Please give me someone who will kill my enemy.' Janardana answered, 'Know that it has already been given.' Through the favours of Shiva, Ganga and Vishnu, a man arose from the waters. He was born in the form of both Shiva and Vishnu. He held a *chakra* in his hand and wielded a trident. He went to Rasatala and killed the *daitya* Mahashani, Indra's enemy. He became Indra's friend. He is Abjaka Vrishakapi. Though he resided in heaven, Indra always followed Vrishakapi.'

'On seeing that he was affectionate towards another, Shachi became angry. But Shatakratu laughed and reassured her. Indra said, "O Indrani! O beautiful one! I am not seeking refuge with anyone other than you. O beloved one! I pledge on water, on oblations, on the fire that always brings pleasure and on your limbs that I do not go anywhere else. Therefore, you should not speak about any suspicion regarding anyone else. You are devoted

---

[840] Since this is being spoken to Indra and not to Narada, this is an anomaly.

[841] Gadadhara is one who holds the mace, Vishnu.

to your husband and you are my beloved. You are my aide in
dharma and *mantra*s. You have offspring and you have been born
in a noble lineage. Other than you, how can anyone else be my
beloved? Thus, because of your instructions, I went to the great
river, Mahanadi.[842] Through the favours of Vishnu, the lord of the
gods who holds a *chakra* in his hand, and through the favours of
the divinity Shiva, Vrishakapi arose from the water. He is my friend
Abjaka, famous in the worlds. O extremely fortunate one! I have
overcome my grief. I am the Indra who cannot be dislodged. When
the wife follows the husband's wishes, what cannot be achieved? O
auspicious one! Though emancipation may be extremely difficult
for us to obtain, the three[843] can be obtained. A wife is the greatest
friend. She brings welfare in this world and in the next world. If
she is born in a noble lineage, is pleasant in speech, is devoted to
her husband, is beautiful, possesses the qualities and is indifferent
towards prosperity and adversity, there is nothing in the three
worlds that cannot be achieved by her. O beloved one! It is because
of your intelligence that everything auspicious has happened to
me. From now on, I will only do what you tell me and nothing
else. For *dharma* in the world hereafter, there is nothing to match a
virtuous son. But for a man who is afflicted, there is no medication
like a wife. For obtaining what is beneficial and for cleansing sins,
there is nothing like Ganga. O one with a beautiful face! Now listen
to something else. For *dharma*, *artha*, *kama* and *moksha* and for
destroying sins, there is nothing other than realization that there is
no difference between Shiva and Vishnu. There is no other means
for emancipation. O virtuous one! It is because of your intelligence
that I have obtained what was in my mind. I have obtained it
because of the favours of Shiva, Vishnu and Ganga. I think that
my position as Indra is now stable, thanks to the strength of my
friend. O beautiful one! Vrishakapi, who originated from the water,
is my friend. You are my eternal beloved friend. There is no one
whom I love more. Goutami Ganga is best among *tirtha*s, Hari and
Shankara are best among gods. It is through their favours that I

---

[842] Poulami should have known all this, since she went with Indra.
[843] *Dharma*, *artha* and *kama*.

have obtained everything that I desired. This *tirtha*, famous in the three worlds, brings me pleasure. Therefore, in due order, I will ask the gods for something. Let the *rishi*s, Ganga, Hari and Shankara sanction this. In Abjaka Indreshvara, let the gods be on both banks. Let the divinity Shankara be on one bank and Janardana on the other. Let Vishnu Trivikrama himself purify Dandakaranya. Let all the *tirtha*s that are inside bestow every kind of good merit. As soon as they bathe here, let everyone obtain emancipation. Even if they are wicked and sinners, let them obtain emancipation. If they follow *dharma*, let them obtain supreme emancipation, along with five generations of their ancestors and five generations of their descendants. If something is given to supplicants here, even if that happens to be a sesamum seed, let it bestow on the donor infinite merit, everything that is desired and emancipation. Let such a person be blessed and famous. Let him have a long lifespan and freedom from disease. Let it enhance his good merits. Knowing about this account of Vishnu and Shambhu, if a person bathes here, let him obtain emancipation. Let those who hear, or read about this *tirtha*'s greatness obtain good merits. Let them remember Shiva and Vishnu. They are the ones who sever the aggregate of every kind of sin. They are the ones for their whom sages have controlled their senses and minds seek." The gods and the *rishi*s said that it would be this way. There are seven thousand *tirtha*s on the northern banks of Goutami that yield emancipation. These are frequented by gods, *rishi*s and *siddha*s. Similarly, there are eleven thousand *tirtha*s on the southern bank. Lords among sages have said that Abjaka is the heart of Godavari. It is the place where Isha, Vishnu and Brahma rest.'

Chapter 2(60) (Apastamba Someshvara *tirtha*)

Brahma said, 'The *tirtha* known as Apastamba is famous in the three worlds. Even if one remembers it, this is capable of destroying an aggregate of every kind of sin. Apastamba was an immensely wise and extremely famous sage. His wife Akshasutra was devoted to following her husband's *dharma*. His son was the immensely wise and was named Karki. He knew about the truth. Agastya, supreme among sages, came to his hermitage. Apastamba, lord among sages, worshipped Agastya. Along with his disciples and followers, the intelligent one started to ask him. Apastamba asked, "O supreme among sages! Who among the three divinities[844] should be worshipped? Who is the one who bestows objects of pleasure and emancipation? Who is the one who provides food? O brahmana! Who is the infinite one? Who is the god of the gods? Who does one worship through sacrifices? Who is the divinity that the Vedas sing about? O great sage! Please dispel my doubt about this. Please tell me." Agastya replied, "For the sake of *dharma*, *artha*, *kama* and *moksha*, the sacred texts are said to be the authority. Among sacred texts, it is held that the Vedas represent the supreme authority. The Vedas speak about a Purusha who is greater than Para.[845] The one who dies is known as Apara, the one who is immortal is spoken of as Para. The one without a manifest form is known as Para and the one with a manifest form is spoken of as Apara. Anything with a manifest form is pervaded by differences in the three kinds of *guna*s.[846] Brahma, Vishnu and Shiva are the same, though they are spoken of as three. The single one, who is superior to the three gods, is the one to be known. Depending on attributes and actions, the single one pervades in many different forms. The three forms result for the welfare of the worlds. A person who knows this supreme truth is learned, not someone else. A person who speaks of differences is described as someone who differentiates the sign.[847] There is no atonement for a person who speaks of a difference in this way. The difference between the three gods is in the three different forms they assume. Every proof in the Vedas is about these separate manifested forms. It is held that the single one who has no manifest form is superior to them." Apastamba said, "From this, I

---

[844] Brahma, Vishnu and Shiva.

[845] Para means something that is higher than everything else, beyond everything else. Apara means something that is not Para.

[846] *Sattva*, *rajas* and *tamas*.

[847] The word used is *lingambhedi*.

have not come to a firm determination. Therefore, quickly explain this mystery to me. Let there be no doubt and no alternative, so that the worship can bestow every kind of prosperity." Hearing this, the illustrious Agastya spoke these words. Agastya replied, "There is no mutual difference between the gods. Nevertheless, every kind of success and bliss in the soul is obtained through Shiva. Shiva, the supreme brilliance, is the cause behind Prapancha.[848] O sage! With supreme devotion, worship Hara. The one who destroys all sins is in Dandaka forest, near Goutami." Hearing the sage's words, he was filled with great delight. He asked, "Which form bestows objects of pleasure and emancipation on men, the one that is manifest or the one that is not manifest? Which form undertakes creation? Who preserves? Who is the donor? Who destroys everything? Into which form is everything withdrawn?" Agastya replied, "The form of Brahma is the one who is the creator, the form of Vishnu is the one who is the preserver. The form of Rudra is the destroyer. This is what can be read in all the Vedas." Thereupon, Apastamba went to Ganga. He controlled himself and bathed. O Narada! Using this *stotram*, he praised the divinity Shankara. Apastamba said, "O Somanatha! You are present in all living beings, like fire in wood, fragrance in flowers, trees in seeds and gold in stones. I seek refuge with you. In his pastimes, he is the creator of the three worlds and the one who ordains them. The universe is his form. He is beyond existence and non-existence. I seek refuge with that Someshvara. When one remembers him, one is not affected by the great curse of poverty and the body is not touched by different kinds of ailments. On resorting to him, one obtains everything that one desires. I seek refuge with that Someshvara. Earlier, because of him, Brahma and the others considered the *dharma* of the three[849] and desired to divide the body into two.[850] I seek refuge with that Someshvara. Sanctified by *mantras*, it is into him that oblations proceed. It is he who is worshipped through oblations. He renders the oblations

---

[848] Prapancha means the visible universe.

[849] This probably means Brahma, Vishnu and Shiva.

[850] What this means is not clear. Since Shiva is being eulogized, perhaps two means Brahma and Vishnu.

that gods subsist on. There is nothing superior to him. There is no one who is more praiseworthy. He is subtler than the most subtle. No one is greater. He is greater than the greatest. I seek refuge with that Someshvara. This wonderful universe, varied and great, becomes unified in action and follows his command. His form is unthinkable. I seek refuge with that Someshvara. The power is his. All the lordship is his. The states of creator and donor and greatness are his. Delight, fame, friendship and the original *dharma* are his. I seek refuge with that Someshvara. He is the one who should always be worshipped by everyone. He always loves those who seek refuge with him. He is always auspicious. He has every kind of form. I seek refuge with that Someshvara." O Narada! At this, the illustrious one was pleased with the sage and asked him to seek something for himself or for others. Apastamba told Shiva, "Let those who bathe here and see the divinity Ishvara, the lord of the universe, obtain all that they wish for." Shiva agreed to what the sage said. Since then, that place has been known as Apastamba *tirtha*. It is capable of destroying the darkness of ignorance, which is without beginning.'

Chapter 2(61) (Several *tirtha*s)

Brahma said, 'The place famous as Yama *tirtha* enhances the delight of the ancestors. It completely destroys every kind of sin. Hear about what transpired there. This account is ancient history.[851] O sage! There was a dog of the gods, famous by the name of Sarama. She had two excellent and extremely great sons. Those two dogs always followed people. They could move, even though they subsisted on air. They possessed four eyes and were loved by Yama. She protected the cows of the gods and the animals earmarked for sacrifices. As she protected, the *rakshasa*s, *daitya*s and *danava*s followed her. The immensely wise female dog, the mother of the two dogs, protected them. They made efforts to tempt her with many kinds of words and gifts. The wicked *rakshasa*s

[851] The word used is *itihasa*.

abducted the cattle and the auspicious animals earmarked for sacrifices. Gradually, the female dog approached the gods and spoke to them. Sarama said, "The *rakshasa*s bound me with nooses and struck me with rods. O gods! They abducted the cows and the animals earmarked for the success of the sacrifice." Hearing her words, Brihaspati quickly spoke to the gods. Brihaspati said, "Her figure is malformed. Her sin can be discerned. The cows have been abducted with her sanction. There can be no other reason. Through the movements of her body, it is evident that though she pretends to perform good deeds, she is wicked." Hearing his *guru*'s words, Indra struck the female dog with his foot. Struck by the foot, milk began to flow out of her mouth. Shachi's husband said, "O female dog! You have drunk milk. The *rakshasa*s have given it to you. That is how they have taken away my cattle." Sarama replied, "O lord! I have not committed a crime. I have not acted in any perverse way. O lord of the gods! There has been no crime or negligence on my part. Despite your arrival, the cattle were taken away by the *rakshasa*s. Are you tainted because of that? O lord! Your enemies are strong." At this, the *guru* of the gods meditated and understood what she had done.[852] "O Shakra! It is true that she is wicked and has taken the side of the enemy." Therefore, Shakra cursed her. "O evil one! Become a bitch in the world of the mortals. Even if you committed this crime in your ignorance, you have become full of sin." Because of Indra's curse, she was born among humans. Just as Maghavan had cursed her, the evil one became extremely terrible. The lord of the gods sought to bring back the cattle that had been taken away by the *rakshasa*s. He went and informed Vishnu.'

'Vishnu got ready to kill the *daitya*s, *danava*s and *rakshasa*s who had taken the cattle away. He seized his great bow, Sharnga, famous in the worlds, used to destroy *daitya*s. Janardana, who conquers his enemies and is worshipped by the gods, stationed himself in Dandakaranya. The lord held Sharnga in his hand. The powerful *daitya*s, *danava*s and *rakshasa*s were there. Vishnu killed the *rakshasa*s who had abducted the cattle. In Dandakaranya, he is

---

[852] She had helped the *rakshasa*s.

therefore famous as Sharngapani.[853] Vishnu fought with the *daityas* and *rakshasas*. O great sage! Scared of Vishnu, they fled towards the southern direction. Parameshvara[854] pursued and caught up with them on Garuda. With arrows as swift as thought released from Sharnga, Vishnu killed them on the northern bank of Ganga. Vishnu destroyed the enemies of the gods. From Sharnga, the powerful Vishnu shot arrows that were extremely swift. *Mantras* were invoked over them and they made a loud noise. Because of Vishnu's arrows, the enemies of the gods were exterminated. The place where the divine cows were got back is known as Bana *tirtha*.[855] It is also known in the worlds as Vishnu *tirtha* and is famous as Gou *tirtha*. Earmarked as sacrificial animals, the cattle were kept on the southern bank of Ganga. The gods gathered all those who had fled and brought them together, in Ganga. They constructed an island in the middle as a pen for the cattle. With those cattle, the sacrifice of the gods was completed in Ganga. The island where the cattle were kept in the middle of Ganga is known as Yajna *tirtha*. That auspicious spot is the place where the gods held their sacrifice and it yields every object of desire. O immensely radiant one! Ganga's powers assume a manifested form there. *Samsara* is like an ocean without substance that cannot be crossed, but it is like a boat that takes one across. She[856] is Vishveshvari Yogamaya, who always bestows freedom from fear on devotees. On Ganga's southern bank, this is the *tirtha* of Goraksha.'[857]

'Sarama's two sons, the dogs with four eyes, were loved by Yama. They went to him and reported in detail everything about their mother's crime and the curse. Having reported it properly, both of them asked Yama what task would now ensure happiness and freedom from the curse. Along with them, Surya's son[858] went to Surya and told him all this. Hearing this, Surya told his son,

---

[853] The one with Sharnga in his hand (*pani*).
[854] The supreme lord.
[855] *Bana* means arrow.
[856] Ganga's powers in manifest form.
[857] Literally, protection of cattle.
[858] That is, Yama.

"O supreme god! In Dandaka forest, there is Goutami Ganga, who purifies the three worlds. O child! Control yourself and full of great faith, bathe there. In due order, with every kind of sentiment, praise Brahma, Vishnu and Isha. Your two servants will then find delight." Hearing his father's words, Yama was pleased in his mind. To please them, Yama went there, so as to satisfy the gods. Goutami destroys every kind of sin. Extremely controlled in his mind, he satisfied Ganga and the excellent gods. Along with the dogs, the lord who is the prosperous lord of the southern direction, satisfied Bhanu[859] and Brahma on the southern bank. The powerful Dharma[860] himself satisfied Ishana and Vishnu on the northern bank. He sought many boons that would bring benefit to the worlds and they granted him excellent boons, so that Sarama would be freed from her curse. Yama said, "O Brahma! O Vishnu! O Maheshvara! If a person bathes here, for his own sake or for the sake of others, let him obtain the auspicious objects of desire. If a person bathes in Bana *tirtha* and remembers Sharngapani, from one *yuga* to another *yuga*, let him not suffer from penury or misery. If a person controls himself, bathes in Gou *tirtha* or Brahma *tirtha*, bows down to Brahma and performs *pradakshina* of the island, let that be the same as performing *pradakshina* of the entire earth, with its riches and seven *dvipa*s. If he goes to the place where the gods held their sacrifice and gives a little bit of wealth to a brahmana, or offers some oblations to the fire, let that bestow all the fruits of horse and other sacrifices. If a person reads the *gayatri mantra*, the mother of the Vedas, even once, let it be as if he has read all the Vedas. Let him have no desire and let him be deserving of emancipation. If a person bathes on the southern bank and devotedly and properly worships the goddess Shakti, let him obtain everything that he wishes for. Shakti is the mother of all three—Brahma, Vishnu and Mahesha. Let that person obtain everything that he wishes for. Let him have sons and riches. If a man controls himself and bathes on the southern bank, devotedly seeing Aditya, let him obtain everything desired that is got through sacrifices with many kinds of *dakshina*. If a person bathes

---

[859] Surya.
[860] Yama.

on Ganga's northern bank and bows down and sees the destroyer of
daityas,[861] let him obtain Vishnu's supreme destination. If a person
controls his *atman*, bathes in Yama *tirtha* and immediately sees and
worships the lord Yama, let him obtain infinite good fruits for his
ancestors and extend his fame. Through bathing, donations, *japa*
and praise there, let even evil-doers ensure emancipation for their
ancestors." O Narada! There are eight thousand and three *tirtha*s
like these. Bathing and donating there yield every kind of infinite
good merit. Remembering them is sacred and destroys the sins of
many births. Because of my command, hearing or reading about
them destroys grave sins for the person, his own family and his
ancestors. A person should control his *atman*, bathe and donate
a little. He should offer *pinda* to the ancestors and bow down
before the gods. He will then obtain wealth, grain, fame, valour, a
long lifespan, freedom from disease, prosperity, sons, grandsons, a
beloved wife and everything else that he wishes for. He will not be
separated from those he loves and will be respected by his relatives.
He will save his ancestors and family members, even if they happen
to be in hell. He will be purified and at the time of his death, he will
remember Vishnu and Shiva and be surrounded by his loved ones.
Following the words of the gods, he will obtain emancipation.'

Chapter 2(62) (Yakshini confluence)

Brahma said, 'The *tirtha* known as the confluence of Yakshini
yields every kind of fruit. Bathing and donating there, bestow
everything that one wishes for. The divinity Yakeshvara is there.
If one sees him, one obtains objects of pleasure and emancipation.
As soon as one bathes there, one obtains the fruits of *satrayaga*.[862]
Vishvavasu[863] had a sister named Pippala. Her laughter was loud.

---

[861] That is, Vishnu.

[862] *Satrayaga* is a *soma* sacrifice that extends over a long period of
time.

[863] King of the *gandharva*s.

The rishis held a sacrifice along the banks of Goutami. On seeing that the *rishi*s were emaciated, the extremely proud one laughed. Having gone, she remained there and heard "Voushad" and "Shroushad".[864] She pronounced these in distorted tones and they cursed her, "Become a river." She became a river, extremely well known as Yakshini. After this, Vishvavasu worshipped the *rishi*s and the three-eyed divinity. She was made to merge with Goutami and was hence freed of her curse. As soon as one bathes at this confluence, one obtains the fruits of *satrayaga*. Since then, that *tirtha* has been known as the confluence of Yakshini. Bathing and other rites performed there, yield every object of desire. The place where Shambhu was pleased by Vishvasu and bestowed this auspiciousness is the supreme Shiva *tirtha*. It is also known as Durga *tirtha*. It destroys the aggregate of every kind of sin. It destroys all calamities.[865] O great sage! It represents the essence of all the best *tirtha*s. All the excellent sages have described this *tirtha* as famous and it bestows every kind of success on men.'

Chapter 2(63) (Shukla *tirtha* and other *tirtha*s)

Brahma said, 'The place known as Shukla *tirtha* bestows every kind of success on men. As soon as one remembers it, one obtains everything that one desires. Bharadvaja was a well-known sage and he was extremely devoted to *dharma*. His wife was named Paithinasi and she was the ornament of a noble lineage. She resided along the banks of Goutami and was devoted to her husband's vows. She was engaged in preparing *purodasha*[866] for Agni, Soma and Indra. While the *purodasha* was being boiled, a being was born from the smoke.   He was terrible for the three worlds and wished to eat up the *purodasha*. The sage angrily asked him, "Why

---

[864] These are exclamations made when oblations are offered to gods and ancestors. Pippala deliberately mispronounced these.

[865] Since *durgati* is calamity, it is known as Durga *tirtha*.

[866] Sacrificial oblation made out of ground rice.

are you destroying my sacrifice?" Bharadvaja, supreme among
brahmanas, was full of rage and quickly spoke to him. Hearing
the *rishi*'s words, the *rakshasa* replied to him. The *rakshasa* said,
"O Bharadvaja! Know that I am famous as Havyaghna.[867] I am the
son of Sandhya and the eldest son of Prachinabarhi. Brahma has
granted me the boon that I can happily devour any sacrifice. Kali
is my younger brother. He is strong and extremely terrible. I am
dark. My father is dark. My mother is dark, and so is my younger
brother. I will destroy the sacrifice. I will sever the sacrificial post.
I am the destroyer." Bharadvaja replied, "You should protect my
beloved sacrifice. This is eternal *dharma*. I know that you are
the destroyer of sacrifices. However, protect my sacrifice and the
brahmana."[868] Yajnaghna[869] said, "O Bharadvaja! Hear my brief
words. Earlier, I used to be a brahmana. In the presence of the
gods and the *danava*s, Brahma cursed me. Thereafter, I pacified
the divinity who is the grandfather of the worlds. He said, 'O
Havyaghna! When the excellent sages sprinkle you with *amrita*,
you will be freed from your curse, not otherwise.' O brahmana! If
you act in accordance with these words, everything that you desire
will happen. This will never be a falsehood." Bharadvaja again
replied, "O immensely intelligent one! You are my friend. Please
tell me how my sacrifice can be saved and I will act accordingly. The
gods and the *daitya*s got together and churned the ocean of milk,
obtaining *amrita* with a great deal of effort. How can we obtain
that easily? If you are pleased and delighted, please tell me how that
can be easily obtained." Hearing the *rishi*'s words, the *rakshasa*
was happy and spoke. The *rakshasa* said, "Goutami's water is
amrita. Gold is spoken of as *amrita*. The *ghee* that is obtained
from cows is *amrita*. *Soma* juice is *amrita*. Sprinkle me with these
three—Ganga's water, *ghee* and gold. However, among all of these,
Goutami's water is the best and is divine *amrita*." Hearing this, the
rishi was filled with great contentment. He lovingly took Ganga's
water, the *amrita*, in his hand and sprinkled the *rakshasa* with this.

---

[867] Literally, destroyer of oblations.

[868] The priest.

[869] Literally, destroyer of a sacrifice. Therefore, the same as Havyaghna.

In the sacrifice, he also sprinkled the sacrificial post, the sacrificial animal and the entire circular area around the sacrifice. As soon as the great-souled one sprinkled, all of these turned white. The immensely strong *rakshasa* also turned white. His form had been dark earlier. However, in an instant, it turned white. The powerful Bharadvaja completed everything connected with the sacrifice. He granted leave to the officiating priests and flung the sacrificial post into the waters of Ganga. O immensely intelligent one! That sacrificial post is still in the middle of Ganga. It was sprinkled with *amrita* and is an indication of the great event that transpired at this *tirtha*. The *rakshasa* again spoke to Bharadvaja. The *rakshasa* said, "O Bharadvaja! I am leaving. You have made me white again. From now on, anyone who undertakes bathing, donating, worship and other rites at this *tirtha* will obtain everything that he desires and also obtain the fruits of this sacrifice. O sage! As soon as it is remembered, all sins will be destroyed." Since then, that *tirtha* has been known as Shukla *tirtha*.[870] This door to heaven is open along the Goutami in Dandakaranya. O tiger among sages! Along both banks, there are seven thousand *tirtha*s. They yield every kind of success.'

Chapter 2(64) (Chakra *tirtha*)

Brahma said, 'As soon as one remembers the place known as Chakra *tirtha*, all sins are destroyed. O Narada! I will describe its powers. Listen attentively. O sage! There were seven famous *rishi*s.[871] Vasishtha was the foremost. Resorting to the banks of Goutami, they started to perform a *satrayajna*.[872] Extremely terrible *rakshasa*s started to create impediments. The sages came to me and told me about the deeds of the *rakshasa*s. O Narada! Using my *maya*, I created the form of a woman. I told them, "As soon

---

[870] *Shukla* means white.
[871] The *saptarshi*s.
[872] The same as *satrayaga*.

as they see her, the *rakshasa*s will be destroyed." O sage! Saying this, I handed over the woman to the *rishi*s. Following my words, the *rishi*s took Maya[873] and returned. She is known as Ajaika and her form is black and red. Even today, she exists in her own form and is known as Muktakeshi. She can assume any form at will and causes delusion in the three worlds. Because of her powers, all the excellent sages were assured in their minds. Along the banks of Goutami, best among rivers, they consecrated themselves for the sacrifice again. To destroy the sacrifice, the *rakshasa*s arrived again. Near the sacrificial arena, those bulls among *rakshasa*s saw Maya. They danced, sang, laughed and wept. Because of the powers of Maheshvari Mahamaya, they were extremely insolent. Shambara, the lord of the *daitya*s, was among them. O Narada! The valiant one devoured the woman who was in the form of Maya. Those who had witnessed Maya's powers were extremely surprised at this. When the sacrifice was being destroyed, they sought refuge with Vishnu.[874] To protect the sages, Vishnu gave them his *chakra*. That *chakra* sliced off the *rakshasa*s, *daitya*s and *danava*s. Scared of it, the bulls among *danava*s died. The great sacrifice of the *rishi*s was completed. Vishnu's Sudarshana *chakra* was washed in Ganga's waters. Since then, that *tirtha* has been described as Chakra *tirtha*. By bathing and donating there, one obtains the fruits of a *satrayaga*. There are five hundred other *tirtha*s that destroy sins. Bathing and donating in any of them bestows emancipation.'

Chapter 2(65) Confluence of Vani

Brahma said, 'Hara Vagishvara exists in the place famous as the confluence of Vani. That *tirtha* frees from every kind of sin and bestows everything that is desired. Bathing and donating there, destroys sins like killing a brahmana. There was a dispute between

---

[873] The woman created with the use of *maya*.
[874] The sages sought refuge with Vishnu. Since Maya had been devoured, the *rakshasa*s could destroy the sacrifice.

Brahma and Vishnu, about who was superior. In their middle,
Mahadeva appeared in the form of a column of light. O son! While
they were arguing, "I am great," an auspicious and divine voice
spoke to them. The divine voice spoke to both of them. "You should
not argue. Between the two of you, whoever can see the end of this
column is superior." At her words, Vishnu proceeded downwards
and I proceeded upwards. Vishnu quickly returned and sat down
near the column of light. O sage! I went further and further, but
could not find the end. When I was exhausted, I returned and saw
the lord Isha. At this, a terrible thought entered my mind. "I have
seen the end of this divinity. Therefore, my superiority over Vishnu
has been established." O immensely intelligent one! Nevertheless,
I thought again. "The mouth must speak the truth. Even though
I am suffering, how can I utter false words? Among many kinds
of sins, uttering a falsehood is the greatest sin. Since my mouths
utter the truth, how can I utter a falsehood?" Therefore, I created
a fifth mouth. It had the form of a donkey and was exceedingly
terrible. Having created it, I thought for a long time about uttering
a falsehood. Hari, the lord of the universe, was seated there and
I spoke to him. "O Janardana! I have seen his end. Hence, I am
superior to you." As I said this, on my sides, Hari and Shankara
assumed a single form, like the sun and the moon. Seeing them, I
was amazed. Scared, I praised them. Angry, those two lords of the
universe spoke to that voice. Hari and Hara said, "O wicked one!
Become a river. There is no sin like uttering a lie." Agitated, she
assumed the form of a river. Seeing this, I was amazed. Frightened, I
spoke to her. "Stationed in Brahma's mouth, you uttered a falsehood.
Therefore, you will become invisible. There is no doubt that your
form is sinful." Getting to know about the curse, she prostrated
herself before those two divinities. She repeatedly praised them and
sought to be freed from the curse.'

'She beseeched those two lords of the gods, who were
worshipped by the gods. Hari and Hara were satisfied. Pleased, they
spoke to the voice. Hari and Hara said, "O fortunate one! When
you merge into Ganga, the purifier of the worlds, you will regain
your form. O extremely beautiful one! You will become pure."
Addressed in this way, the goddess merged into Ganga. When she

merged into Bhagirathi Goutami, she regained her own form. O brahmana! The goddess achieved what is extremely difficult for the gods. Merging into Goutami, the one who bestows auspiciousness became famous under the name of Vani. Where she merged into Bhagirathi, the goddess is also known as Sarasvati. She is famous in both the confluences[875] and is worshipped by the worlds. There is the confluence with Sarasvati and there is the confluence with Vani. The goddess, the divine voice, merged into Goutami as Vani and Sarasvati. The place where the voice worshipped the lord Shiva, the lord of the gods, and was freed from her curse is a *tirtha* that is worshipped everywhere. Brahma was cleansed of his wicked speech and returned to his own abode again. Therefore, if a person purifies himself, bathes at that confluence and sees Vagishvara, he immediately obtains emancipation. If a person undertakes some donations, oblations, fasting and other rites at that confluence, he does not return to *samsara* again. There are one thousand and nine hundred *tirtha*s along both banks. They destroy all the sins that have been accumulated across many births.'

Chapter 2(66) (Moudgalya, Vishnu and other *tirtha*s)

Brahma said, 'The place known as Vishnu *tirtha* is famous. Hear about its account. Mudgala's son was the *rishi* Moudgalya and he was well known. His wife was known by the name of Jabala and she was famous because she had excellent sons. The father, the *rishi* Mudgala, was famous in the world and was aged. His auspicious wife was famous under the name of Bhagirathi. Every morning, Moudgalya would control himself and bathe in Ganga. O supreme sage! He always followed a certain rite. He used a path taught to him by his *guru*. On the banks of Ganga, he used *kusha* grass, clay and *shami* flowers to invoke Vishnu in his heart, night

---

[875] With Goutami and with Bhagirathi.

and day. Moudgalya always performed this invocation. Invoked by him, Lakshmi's consort and the lord of the universe swiftly arrived. He would be astride Vinata's son[876] and would hold the conch shell, *chakra* and mace. He would be attentively worshipped by *rishi* Moudgalya. The lord of the universe would tell Moudgalya wonderful accounts. In the afternoon, Vishnu would repeatedly tell Moudgalya, "O child! You are exhausted. Return to your own abode." Addressed in this way by the divinity Vishnu, the brahmana would leave. Along with the gods, the lord of the universe would also leave for his own residence. Moudgalya's beloved wife was devoted to her husband. She carefully brought vegetables, roots and fruits for her husband. She served guests, her sons and her husband excellent food. Devoted to her vows, she ate only after she had served them food. Every night, after he had eaten, Moudgalya would always happily tell them the wonderful accounts he had heard from Vishnu.'

'In this way, a long period of time elapsed. Extremely surprised,[877] in private, Moudgalya's wife addressed her husband in these words. Jabala said, "When Vishnu, worshipped by the gods, appears before you, you should ask the lord of the universe why we suffer from this kind of hardship. O immensely wise one! You should ask Vishnu this. As soon as he is remembered, old age, birth, death and ailments are destroyed. What need be said when he is seen? Please ask the lord of the universe." Addressed by his beloved in these words, Moudgalya worshipped Hari, as he always did. He joined his hands in salutation and humbly asked him. Moudgalya said, "O lord of the universe! When you are remembered, sorrow, poverty and wicked deeds are destroyed. But even you are seen, how is it that I am faced with adversity?" Shri Vishnu replied, "Everywhere, living beings always enjoy the consequences of their own deeds. No one else does any good deed or bad deed towards anyone. The fruit is exactly like the seed that has been sown. How can a mango be produced from a *nimba*[878] seed? How can those

---

[876] Garuda.
[877] Because of the condition they were in.
[878] Tree with bitter fruit.

who have not served Goutami, not worshipped Hari and Shankara and not given to *brahmanas* be recipients of prosperity? You have not given anything to *brahmanas*, or to me. Only something that has been given reaches the supreme. Through clay, water, *kusha* grass, *mantras* and other acts of purification, one can always cleanse one's *atman*. One can dry up one's body too. However, without donating, men never obtain objects of pleasure. One is purified by following virtuous conduct. After this, a man becomes non-attached. Thereafter, his acquisition of *jnana* is unconstrained. Even if he is alive, he becomes emancipated. By first being devoted towards me, everyone can become emancipated. Objects of pleasure and emancipation can be obtained through donations and dispelling the misery of living beings. However, only through devotion, objects of pleasure cannot be obtained." Moudgalya asked, "How can there be emancipation through devotion? Compared to worldly pleasures, emancipation is more difficult to obtain. If emancipation has been achieved, what else does an embodied being need? O one who pervades the universe! Everyone should worship the emancipation that is brought about through devotion." Vishnu said, "O brahmana! There is a difference. After remembering me, if anything is given to *brahmanas* or other supplicants, that brings infinite benefits. However, if anything is given without meditating on me, that only brings fruits to the extent that it has been given. It does not yield any objects of pleasure in this world. O immensely intelligent one! Hence, after resorting to the banks of Goutami, you should give me or a foremost brahmana something to eat." Moudgalya told Vishnu, "I have nothing to give you. Everything, including this body, has been offered to you." At this, Vishnu, lord of the universe, quickly told Garuda, "Bring a fragment of grain to me. He will give me that. Thereby, he will obtain the objects of pleasure that are in his mind." Hearing his master's words, the king of the birds did that. Controlled in his vows, Moudgalya placed that fragment of grain in Vishnu's hand. Meanwhile, Vishnu spoke to Vishvakarma. Vishnu said, "O immensely intelligent one! For seven generations, everyone in his family will obtain whatever their minds desire. They will possess cattle, gold, grain, garments and ornaments." Through the powers of Vishnu and Ganga, Moudgalya obtained every kind of ornament that brings mental pleasure in this world. Vishnu told Moudgalya, "Go home." He returned to his hermitage and saw all this prosperity. The *rishi* said, "The powers of donations and remembering Vishnu are wonderful. The powers of Ganga are wonderful. Who could have thought of these great things?" Along with his wife, sons, grandsons and relatives, Moudgalya enjoyed the objects of pleasure. Along with his ancestors, he obtained emancipation. Since then, that place has been known as Moudgalya *tirtha* and Vishnu *tirtha*. Bathing and donating there, yield objects of pleasure and emancipation. If a person hears about this *tirtha* or remembers it, Vishnu is pleased with him. He is freed from all sins and becomes happy. Along both banks, there are eleven thousand *tirthas*. Bathing, donations and *japa* performed there, bestow every objective.'

Chapter 2(67) (Lakshmi *tirtha*)

Brahma said, 'The place known as Lakshmi *tirtha* directly enhances prosperity. O Narada! It destroys Alakshmi.[879] Hear about its sacred account. O son! Earlier, there was a dispute between Lakshmi and Daridra.[880] Acting against each other, they approached the universe. There is nothing in the three worlds that cannot be pervaded by them. They told each other, "I am superior", "I am superior". Alakshmi energetically told Shri, 'I am the one who was born first.' Shri Lakshmi replied, "I represent good lineage, good conduct and life in living beings. Without me, even if they are alive, those with bodies are as good as dead." She spoke to Daridra in this way. Daridra told her, "I am superior to everything else. Emancipation is always dependent on me. Wherever I am present, desire, anger, avarice, insolence and malice never exist. There is no cause for fear. Madness, envy and arrogant conduct do not exist wherever I am present." Hearing Daridra's words, Lakshmi replied

[879] The negation of Lakshmi, adversity/penury. Lakshmi is also referred to as Shri.

[880] *Daridra* means poverty.

to her. Lakshmi replied, "Every being who is ornamented by me is worshipped. Even if a person without riches is Shiva's equal, he is reviled by everyone. The five divinities who are present in the body utter the words 'Give' and instantly leave—Dhi, Shri, Hri, Shanti and Kirti.[881] Qualities and superiority only exist in a person as long as he does not seek riches from another. As soon as a person seeks riches, where are his qualities? Where is his pride? A living being is regarded as the best and the store of all the qualities, he is worshipped by all the worlds, only as long as he does not seek riches from others. For those with bodies, the lack of riches represents hardship and the commission of great sins. A person without riches is never respected. People don't speak to him, or touch him. O Daridra! Listen to my words. Therefore, I am the best." Hearing Lakshmi's words, Daridra addressed her in these words. Daridra said, "O Lakshmi! Do not speak in this way. Aren't you ashamed of repeatedly saying, 'I am superior'? Giving up Purushottama, you always find pleasure in wickedness. You always deceive the world? How can you boast? Having obtained you, there is no happiness. Repentance is vastly superior. Even if a man happens to be a learned person, as soon as he comes into contact with you, he becomes intoxicated, much more than through liquor. O Lakshmi! In general, you always find pleasure in those who are wicked in conduct. I always reside with deserving people, those who follow *dharma* and good conduct, those who are devoted to Shiva and Vishnu, those who are grateful and great, those who exhibit virtuous behaviour and are serene, those who serve their seniors, those who are righteous and learned, those who are brave and good and those who are accomplished in their intelligence. O Lakshmi! I always reside with them. Therefore, there is superiority in me. I reside with pure *brahmanas*, those who follow their vows, mendicants and those who are without fear. O Lakshmi! Hear about where you reside—those who follow kings, the wicked, the cruel, the deceitful, those who indulge in calumny, the avaricious, those who are wicked in deeds, those who indulge in fraud, those who are ignoble, those who are ungrateful, those who

---

[881] Respectively, the personified forms of intellect, prosperity, modesty, peace and fame. They leave in the absence of riches.

are always against *dharma*, those who harm and injure their friends
and those who are of unsound minds." Arguing in this way, both of
them came before me.'

'Hearing their words, I spoke to both of them. "The earth
originated before me and the water originated even before that. In
an argument between women, only women know the answer, not
others.[882] Among them, the one who originated from a *kamandalu*
is superior. Therefore, go to the goddess Goutami. She will tell you
about the firm determination. She is the one who destroys every
kind of affliction. She is the one who dispels every kind of doubt."
Following my words, they went to the earth. Along with the earth,
they went to water and along with both earth and water, they went
to Goutami. Bowing down before Goutami, the earth and water
clearly stated everything that had happened and the statements of
Daridra and Lakshmi, asking her to mediate. O Narada! While the
guardians of the world heard, while the earth heard and while the
water heard, Ganga addressed Daridra in these words. Praising
Lakshmi, Goutami spoke these words. Goutami said, "Lakshmi
pervades every mobile and immobile object in the world—Brahma's
prosperity, the prosperity of austerities, the prosperity of sacrifices,
the signs of deeds, the prosperity of wealth, the prosperity of fame,
learning, wisdom, the goddess of speech, the prosperity associated
with objects of pleasure, emancipation, memory, shame, fortitude,
forgiveness, success, satisfaction, nourishment, peace, the water, the
earth, ego, the strength of herbs, sacred texts, purification, the night,
heaven, moonlight, benedictions, auspicious pronouncements,
pervasiveness, the dawn, everything auspicious and everything
radiant. The patience of *brahmanas*, forgiveness of the virtuous,
those who possess learning, objects of pleasure, emancipation and
everything that is beautiful and pleasant - all of these are characterized
by Lakshmi. What is the need to speak a lot? Everything in the
universe is full of Lakshmi. Everything, everywhere, that exhibits
excellence is pervaded by Lakshmi. There is nothing without her.
Hence, aren't you ashamed of challenging that beautiful goddess?
Go. Leave." Ganga addressed Daridra in these words. Since then,
the waters of Ganga have driven away poverty. One suffers from

---

[882] The earth and water are both feminine.

Daridra only as long as one does not resort to Ganga's waters. Since then, that auspicious *tirtha* has been one that destroys Alakshmi. Through bathing and donating there, one obtains Lakshmi and everything auspicious. O immensely intelligent one! In that tirtha, there are another six thousand *tirtha*s. They are frequented by gods, *rishi*s and sages and bestow every kind of success.'

Chapter 2(68) (Bhanu *tirtha*)

Brahma said, 'The place known as Bhanu tirtha bestows every kind of success on men. I will tell you what happened there. This destroys great sins. There was a famous king known as Sharyati and he was extremely devoted to *dharma*. His wife was Sthavishtha and in her beauty, she was unmatched in the world. The king's priest was a lord among brahmana *rishi*s. He was born in Vishvamitra's lineage and was known as Madhuchhanda. Along with his priest, the king, supreme among kings, departed, to conquer the directions. Having conquered the directions, on the road back to where they had camped, he spoke to the extremely great priest. He asked, "O extremely great one! Why are you full of dejection? Please tell me the reason. In my kingdom, you are the one who is respected by everyone. You are the one who has comprehended every kind of learning. You have cleansed your sins. Why can it be discerned that your mind lacks contentment? The earth has been conquered. Lords of men have been defeated. There is cause for great delight. Why are you emaciated? O noble one among *brahmanas*! O great one! Please tell me the truth." So as to make Sharyati understand, the brahmana Madhuchhanda affectionately spoke these loving words. Madhuchhanda said, "O lord of the earth! Listen to the words spoken to me by my wife. 'We are leaving while there is a *yama* still left.'[883] 'Half of the night is over.'[884] She is the owner of

---

[883] These are words spoken by Madhuchhanda to his wife. A *yama* is a period of three hours. Since *yama* also means 'we are leaving', there is a pun on words.

[884] These are words spoken by Madhuchhanda's wife. Since *yamini* means night, there is another pun on words.

this body and that beloved one is waiting for me. Remembering
the words of the beloved one, my body is drying up. When love
causes distraction, it is only the beloved who can restore life." The
king, the scorcher of enemies, laughed and spoke to his priest.
The king said, "You are my *guru*. You are my friend. Why are
you deceiving yourself? O immensely wise one! O one who confers
honours! What purpose will my words serve? What use do great-
souled ones have for happiness that will be destroyed in a short
while?" Hearing this, the intelligent Madhucchanda replied in these
words. Madhuchhanda said, "When a couple is favourably disposed
towards each other, the three objectives of life prosper.[885] O king!
Therefore, something regarded as a taint is actually an ornament."
Surrounded by the great army, he returned to his own kingdom. To
test the efficacy of love, he had the following news circulated in the
city. "When King Sharyati was proceeding to conquer the directions,
a bull among *rakshasa*s killed the king and his priest and went away
to Rasatala." O supreme among sages! The king's wives sought to
find out if this was true. However, on hearing the news from the
messenger's mouth, Madhuchhanda's beloved instantly gave up her
life. It was extraordinary. Witnessing what happened in the city, the
messengers went and reported to the king what the king's wives and
the priest's beloved had done. The king was astounded and grieved.
He spoke to the messengers again. The king said, "O messengers!
Go quickly and preserve the brahmana lady's body. Have the news
conveyed that the king is arriving, along with his priest." While the
king was thinking in this way, and invisible voice spoke.'

'The invisible voice said, "O king! Give up everything and
resort to Ganga. Goutami is the one who purifies and pacifies every
kind of hardship on earth." Hearing this, Sharyati resorted to the
banks of Ganga. He donated riches to *brahmanas* and satisfied the
gods and the ancestors. With a lot of riches, he sent the priest, best
among *brahmanas*, to another *tirtha*. He told him, "Make efforts
to give these riches to travelers." The king intended that the priest
should not get to know about what he was doing. The great-souled
guru, born in Vishvamitra's lineage, departed. The king also sent his

---

[885] The three objectives of life are *dharma*, *artha* and *kama*.

entire army away. On the banks of Ganga, the king entered the fire. The Indra among king spoke to Ganga, Bhanu and the gods. He said, "If I have donated, if I have offered oblations and if I have saved my subjects, through that truth, let the virtuous lady use my lifespan to come back to life." Having said this, Sharyati, supreme among kings, entered the fire. Immediately, the wife of the king's preceptor came back to life. The king's *guru* heard what had happened—the reason for the king entering the fire; his wife, devoted to her husband, dying and coming back to life; and the specific reason why the king had given up his life. He was amazed and was reminded of his own duty. "Should I enter the fire, or should I go to my beloved? Should I torment myself through austerities?" The brahmana arrived at a decision. "I think that this is the good deed I should perform. I will bring the king back to life. After that, I will go to my beloved. This is what is auspicious." Therefore, he praised Bhaskara. Other than Ravi,[886] there is no other god who can bestow all that is wished for. Madhucchanda said, "I bow down to Surya, the infinitely energetic one, the one who is emancipation. He is the divinity who is full of the Vedas. You are the meaning of Omkara. I prostrate myself before you. You are the one without a form. You possess an excellent form. You possess three *guna*s. You possess three forms. You are Vishnu's power. You are the cause behind creation, preservation and destruction." Pleased at this, Surya appeared and asked him to choose a boon. Madhuchhanda said, "O lord of the gods! Give me the king and my beloved, who is pleasant in speech. Give me auspicious sons and give the king auspicious boons." The lord of the universe gave him Sharyati, adorned with jewels. He also gave him his wife and other boons. Everything was auspicious. Pleased and delighted, the king returned to his own kingdom, along with the priest. He was happy. Since then, that *tirtha* has been remembered as an auspicious place. There are another three thousand *tirtha*s, full of qualities, there. Since then, that *tirtha* has been known as Bhanu *tirtha*. It is also famous as Mritasanjivana[887] and Sharyati. It is also famous as Madhuchhanda. O sage! When it is remembered,

---

[886] Bhaskara and Ravi are Surya's names.
[887] Literally, the place where the dead are brought back to life.

sins are destroyed. Bathing and donating there, yields the fruits of all sacrifices. The dead come back to life. The lifespan and freedom from disease are enhanced.'

Chapter 2(69) (Khadga *tirtha*)

Brahma said, 'The place known as Khadga *tirtha* is on the northern banks of Goutami. If a man bathes and donates there, he obtains objects of pleasure and emancipation. O Narada! I will tell you what happened there. Listen attentively. There was a brahmana known as Pailusha and he was the son of Kavasha.[888] He suffered from the burden of a large family and ran around here and there, in search of wealth. Since he did not get anything, he became full of non-attachment. When destiny is extremely adverse and when manliness becomes futile, nothing gives a learned person as much of strength as non-attachment. He sighed repeatedly and thought, "I do not possess any wealth that has come down to me and I have many to maintain. My soul is proud and I do not deserve this hardship. Shame on what destiny has brought about." He did find occupations, but those occupations were temporary. Those occupations did not give him sufficient wealth and he became full of non-attachment. "Serving anyone is prohibited for me. Everything is difficult to undertake. Austerities are extremely difficult to perform. The thirst attracts me with great force, but everything is extremely difficult to accomplish. O Trishna![889] Out of ignorance, you have afflicted me in this way. I bow down to you." Thinking about this, the intelligent one thought about the means to sever this bondage. Pailusha addressed his father in these words. Pailusha said, "O father! O lord! Anger, avarice and the ocean of *samsara* are extremely difficult to cross. Please tell me about the sword of *jnana* that can be used to sever these." Kavasha replied, "It has

---

[888] The text says Kavaya here, but Kavasha later. We have made it consistent.

[889] Thirst.

been said in the Vedas that one should seek out *jnana* from Ishvara. Therefore, worship Ishana. That is the way you will obtain *jnana*." Addressed in this way, for the sake of *jnana*, Pailusha worshipped Ishvara. Pleased, Mahesha bestowed this *jnana* on the brahmana. Having obtained the *jnana*, the immensely intelligent one recited this chant. It confers emancipation. Pailusha said, "The first enemy is anger. Even if it is ineffective, it destroys the body. If one uses the sword of *jnana* to sever it, one obtains supreme happiness. Trishna has many kinds of *maya*. It creates bondage and wickedness of conduct. If a man uses the sword of *jnana* to sever it, he establishes himself in happiness. Supreme *dharma* is the sword. The gods and others have said this in the sacred texts. The *atman* is not attached, but attachment is the great enemy. Using the sword of *jnana* to sever it, one obtains the state of being unified with Shiva. Doubt is responsible for great destruction. For the sake of *dharma* and *artha*, it must be destroyed. Having severed doubt, a living creature obtains what is supremely desired. Hope enters, like a demoness. Having burnt it down, one obtains every kind of happiness. Having used the sword to destroy it completely, a living being obtains emancipation." Having obtained *jnana*, he resorted to the banks of Ganga. He used the sword of *jnana* to rid himself of delusion and obtained emancipation. Since then, that *tirtha* has been known as Khadga *tirtha*.[890] It is also known as Jnana *tirtha*, Kavasha *tirtha* and Pailusha *tirtha*. It bestows everything that is desired. The *maharshi*s speak about another six thousand *tirtha*s there. These completely destroy the aggregate of every kind of sin and bestow everything that is desired.'

Chapter 2(70) (Anvindra *tirtha*)

Brahma said, 'There is the excellent place known as Anvindra *tirtha*, also famous as Atreya *tirtha*. I will describe its powers. It is capable of getting back a kingdom that has been lost. On the

---

[890] *Khadga* means sword.

northern banks of Goutami, surrounded by officiating priests and
sages, the illustrious *rishi* Atreya started to perform sacrifices. Agni,
the bearer of oblations, was the *hotri*. After this, he completed the
sacrifice known as the Maheshvari sacrifice. The brahmana obtained
prosperity and the power to go anywhere. The brahmana could go, as
he pleased, to Indra's beautiful residence in the world of heaven and
also Rasatala. This happened because of the power of his auspicious
austerities. On one occasion, he went to Indra's world. There, he
saw the one with one thousand eyes, surrounded by the auspicious
gods. He was being praised by the *siddha*s and the *sadhya*s. He
was watching the excellent dancing and hearing the sweet melodies,
while being fanned by the *apsara*s. He was seated on a grand throne
and was being worshipped by the leaders of the gods, who were also
seated. He was with Shachi and his son, Jayanta, was on his lap.
Thus, he obtained the greatest satisfaction. The great-souled lord of
brahmanas saw the great Indra, the granter of boons and the refuge
of the virtuous. Witnessing the prosperity of Indra's kingdom, the
Indra among sages was confused and deluded. Honoured by the
large number of gods in the proper way, he returned to his own
hermitage. He had seen Shakra's city, extremely beautiful, adorned
with jewels and complete with every kind of auspicious quality. In
contrast, the brahmana saw that his own hermitage was bereft of
gold and was depressed. Desiring to quickly obtain the kingdom of
the gods, the great Atri's son[891] spoke to his beloved.

'Atreya said, "Though the roots and fruits have been prepared
well, they are not excellent and I am incapable of having them. I
remember *amrita*, which is most auspicious, the various kinds of
food that can be eaten, the excellent seats, the praise, the donations,
the auspicious assembly-hall, the weapons, the garments, the city
and the groves." Through the powers of his austerities, the great-
souled one invoked Tvashta and addressed him in these words.
Atreya said, "O great-souled one! I wish to obtain Indra's status.
Quickly, please replicate Indra's region here. If you say that you
refuse to do what I have said, there is no doubt that I will reduce

---

[891] Atreya means Atri's son.

you to ashes." The lord who created subjects, Vishvakarma,[892] swiftly acted in accordance with Atreya's words. He constructed Meru, the city of the gods, *kalpadruma*, *kalpalata* and the cow.[893] He fashioned houses that were adorned with diamonds and other things. They were wonderful and sparkled. He fashioned another Shachi, beautiful in all her limbs. She was like a chamber for love to find pleasure in. It was amazing. In an instant, he constructed the assembly-hall Sudharma and also charming *apsara*s. He created Ucchaihshrava and the elephant,[894] the *vajra* and other weapons and all the gods. Though his beloved tried to restrain him, Atri's son made Shachi his bride. Along with the others, Atri being the foremost, Atri's son fashioned weapons that were like the *vajra* and others. He devised singing and dancing, just as he had witnessed in Shakra's city. On obtaining all these, the Indra among sages was content and happy in his mind. These objects are only apparently pleasurable. But in their presence, who can ignore them? Hearing about this, the *daitya*s, *danava*s and *rakshasa*s were filled with instant rage. "Why has Hari abandoned heaven and come to earth? It must be for happiness. Therefore, we will leave this place and go and fight with Vritra's slayer. His sacrifice will not last long." Just as they surrounded the gods, the *asura*s came and surrounded Atri's son. They surrounded the city created by Atri's son, known by the name of Indrapura. He was struck by the large shower of weapons. Scared, he spoke these words. Atreya said, "He was born first. The spirited god ornamented the gods with his sacrifices. Heaven and earth are raised up through Indra's powers. He is the one who protects men." After using this *sukta* to praise Hari, Atri's son spoke to his enemies. Atri said, "I am not Hari. Shachi is not mine. This is not Indra's city. This is not Indra's grove. He is Indra, Vritra's

---

[892] That is, Tvashta.

[893] *Kalpadruma* is a divine tree (*druma*) in Indra's world, *kalpalata* is a divine creeper (*lata*), also in Indra's world. The cow means the celestial cow, Surabhi. All these possess the attribute of bestowing whatever one desires.

[894] Airavata.

slayer. He is the one with one thousand eyes, the wielder of *vajra*.
He is the one who shatters mountains. He is the one who holds
the *vajra* in his hand. I am a brahmana who knows the Vedas. I
am surrounded by *brahmanas*. I reside on the banks of Goutami.
Urged by evil destiny, I have committed an act that will not bring
happiness, today or tomorrow." The *asuras* replied, "Withdraw
these imitations of Indra. You will then truly obtain peace. There
is no need to think about this." Atreya replied in these words.
"O immensely fortunate ones! I will do what you have asked me
to do. As proof of my pledge, I am touching the fire." Having
told the *daityas* this, he again spoke to Tvashta. Atreya said, "O
Tvashta! Out of affection towards me, you created this status
of Indra. Please save a brahmana and take it back again. Give
me back my own hermitage, with its animals and birds, trees
and water, all that existed earlier. There is no need for anything
divine. For learned people, anything that does not come naturally
does not bring happiness." Agreeing to this, Tvashta, lord of
subjects, withdrew everything. Making the place free of thorns,
the *daityas* returned to their own regions. Tvashta also seemed
to laugh, as he returned to his own abode. Surrounded by his
disciples and along with his wife, Atreya withdrew and resorted
to austerities along the banks of Goutami. While a great sacrifice
was going on, ashamed, he spoke these words. Atreya said, "The
strength of delusion is amazing and caused my mind to be in a
whirl. What did the status of the great Indra get for me? Earlier,
what did I do?" While the embarrassed Atreya was saying this,
the gods arrived. The gods said, "O mighty-armed one! Give up
this shame. You will have excellent fame. If a living being bathes
in Atreya *tirtha*, he will easily obtain the status of being Indra.
If he remembers it, he will obtain happiness." The learned say
there are five thousand *tirthas* there. They are described under the
names of Anvindra,[895] Atreya and Daitya. Bathing and donating
there, yield all the infinite merits. After saying this, the gods
departed and the sage was satisfied.'

---

[895] Literally, Anvindra means following Indra, or after Indra.

Chapter 2(71) (Confluence of Kapila)

Brahma said, 'The tirtha known as the confluence of Kapila is famous in the three worlds. O Narada! Listen. I will tell you the sacred and excellent account. There was a sage named Kapila. He was immensely illustrious and knew the truth. He was devoted to the vow of austerities. Though he was cruel, he was also gracious. Resorting to the banks of Goutami, the best among sages performed austerities. Vamadeva and the others came to the great-souled one and spoke to him. Because of the curse of the *brahmanas*, Vena had been killed. Without a king, *dharma* was being destroyed. Kapila was an *acharya* who had obtained success. The large number of sages arrived and spoke to him. The large number of sages said, "The Vedas have left. *Dharma* has departed. O lord among sages! What should be done?" The sage Kapila meditated and then spoke to the sages who had arrived. Kapila said, "Vena's thigh must be kneaded and something will happen." The sages acted accordingly and kneaded Vena's thigh. A being arose. He was extremely wicked and dark, terrible in his valour. On seeing him, the sages were scared and said, "Sit down." He became Nishada and all the *nishada*s originated from him.[896] In conformity with *dharma*, they kneaded Vena's right arm. Prithu, whose voice was loud, originated.[897] He was marked with all the auspicious signs. Prithu became a prosperous king. He possessed Brahma's capacity. All the gods arrived. They congratulated him and bestowed auspicious boons on him. They gave him weapons with all the qualities and their *mantra*s. Along with Kapila, the large number of sages spoke to Prithu. The sages said, "Provide food to living beings. The herbs have been swallowed by the earth." The best among kings seized his bow and spoke to the earth. Prithu said, "For the welfare

---

[896] The *nishada*s were hunters who dwelt in mountainous regions. The word '*nishida*' means 'sit down', explaining the name Nishada.

[897] The word *prithu* means large/great. An alternative explanation for the name Prithu is that Vena's arm was large. Here, the explanation is the loud voice.

of subjects, give the herbs that have been swallowed by you."
Scared, the earth spoke to the large-eyed Prithu. The earth said,
"I have digested the great herbs. Please pardon me. How can I
yield them up?" Full of rage, the king again addressed the earth.
Prithu said, "If you do not give up the great herbs now, I will kill
you and seize them." The earth asked, "O king! How can you
cause violence to a woman? O supreme among kings! Though
you possess learning, how will you sustain these subjects without
me?" Prithu replied, "There is no crime when one is destroyed for
the sake of many. O earth! There is no sin and I will sustain the
subjects through austerities. I do not see a sin. Nor are my words
spoken in vain. When a single one's destruction brings happiness
to many, the sages say that this is superior to one hundred horse
sacrifices." At this, the gods and the *rishi*s pacified the excellent
king. The large number of gods spoke to the earth, the goddess
who is the mother. The gods said, "O earth! Assume the form
of a cow and let the great herbs assume the form of milk. Give
them to King Prithu and the king will be pleased. The subjects
will be saved through this and there will be welfare." In Kapila's
presence, she assumed the form of a *kapila* cow.[898] The king who
originated from Vena's arm milked the great herbs. O great sage!
All the gods, the *gandharva*s, the *rishi*s and the sage Kapila were
present at the place where the earth assumed the form of a cow.
Specifically, this was near Narmada, Bhagirathi, Sarasvati and
Godavari and all the great rivers. The great milking took place.
Milked by Prithu, the sacred waters became a river. This was
extraordinary and it merged into Goutami. Since then, that *tirtha*
has been known as the confluence of Kapila.[899] O immensely
intelligent one! The large number of sages say that are eighty-
eight thousand *tirtha*s there, which deserve to be worshipped. O
Narada! As soon as they are remembered, in the due order, they
purify the universe.'

---

[898] Specifically, a *kapila* is a brown cow. As is obvious, there is a play
on words.
[899] That is, the river was also known as Kapila.

Chapter 2(72) (Devasthana)

Brahma said, 'The *tirtha* known as Devasthana is famous in the three worlds. O Narada! I will describe its powers. Listen attentively. Earlier, at the beginning of *krita yuga*, there was a battle between the gods and the *danava*s. There was a beautiful *daitya* lady, known as Simhika. Her son was the great *daitya* known as Rahu. He was immensely strong. When *amrita* was generated, Simhika's son was cut into two. His son was the great *daitya* known by the name of Meghahasa. Hearing that his father had been killed, he was extremely miserable and tormented himself through austerities. Rahu's son resorted to the banks of Goutami and performed austerities. All the gods and *rishi*s were scared and spoke to him. The gods and *rishi*s said, "O mighty-armed one! Give up these austerities. Through the favours of Shiva and Ganga, everything that there is in your mind will come true. Through the favours of Shiva and Ganga, there is nothing that is impossible to obtain." Meghahasa replied, "My father is my divinity and deserve to be worshipped. He has been overcome by you. If you do something that pleases him and me exceedingly, I will refrain from these austerities and my enmity towards you. The task of a son who loves his father is to harass the enemy. Therefore, I ask all of you to fulfil my wishes." At this, the large number of gods made Rahu an entity who would follow the planets. They made Meghahasa a person who would be worshipped by the *rakshasa*s. Thus, Rahu's son became a lord and a ruler of *nairrita*s.[900] The *daitya* again spoke to the gods. "It is my view that the powers of this *tirtha* should be given to me, so that my fame lasts." The gods agreed and granted him everything that was in his mind. O *devarshi*! That *tirtha* is described as being named after that lord of *daitya*s. O immensely intelligent one! That is the place where all the gods were present. Therefore, that *tirtha* is Devasthana,[901] a place that is extremely difficult for even the gods to reach. The place is known as Deva *tirtha* and the divinity there is Deveshvara.

[900] *Nairrita*s are a specific class of demons.
[901] Literally, the place of the gods.

O Narada! There are eighteen *tirtha*s there, worshipped by the *daitya*s. Bathing and donating there destroy great sins.'

Chapter 2(73) (Siddha *tirtha*)

Brahma said, 'Siddheshvara Hara is present in the place famous as Siddha *tirtha*. I will describe its powers. It bestows every kind of success on men. Ravana, who made the world shriek, was born in Pulastya's lineage.[902] He conquered all the directions and went to Soma's world. When the one with the ten heads was about to fight with Soma, I spoke to him. "O Dashanana! Please withdraw from this fight with Soma. I will give you a *mantra*." O Narada! Having said this, to pacify the Indra among the *rakshasas*, I gave him the one hundred and eight names of Shiva. In this *samsara*, for men who are without prosperity and are distressed, for those who suffer from many kinds of hardship, there is no refuge other than Shiva. With his ministers, the *rakshasa* withdrew from the attempt to conquer Soma's world. Astride Pushpaka and swift in his speed and full of pride, the one with ten heads travelled around the worlds. He saw heaven, the firmament, the earth, *naga*s, elephants and *brahmanas*. He then saw the great mountain, Kailasa, the abode of Uma's consort. On seeing this, Ravana was delighted in his mind. The persevering one approached and spoke. Ravana asked, "Which great-souled one resides on this mountain? I will uproot this mountain from the ground and take it away. Swiftly taken to Lanka, the mountain will become beautiful. Truly, Lanka will also become prosperous." Hearing the words spoken by the lord of the *rakshasas* and understanding his sentiments, the *rakshasa*'s ministers, clever in their intelligence, said, "That won't be appropriate." However, the roamer in the night didn't listen to their words. The *rakshasa* quickly set Pushpaka down and jumped onto the base of Mount Kailasa. The one with ten heads shook the

---

[902] *Ravana* means screaming/wailing. Ravana got his name because he made the worlds scream. Dashanana means one with ten faces/heads.

mountain. Bhava got to know what he was doing. Having defeated the lords of the directions, the enemy of the gods became extremely insolent and was shaking Kailasa. He pressed down with his toe and Dashanana was sent down to the world of Rasatala. He suffered and screamed. Hearing this, along with the goddess, he[903] laughed and gave him what he wished. Though he was angry, Shambhu was also pleased. There is no doubt that through Bhava's favours, even undeserving and brave people obtain excellent boons. As he proceeded to Lanka, for the sake of worshipping Bhava, he went to Ganga, who flows out of Shambhu's matted hair. Not depressed in spirit, he used many kinds of *mantras* and water from Ganga to worship Shambhu. He obtained a sword that was marked with the sign of the crescent moon, every kind of *siddhi* and all that is wished for. To save the moon, I had given him a *mantra* and he used this to successfully worship Bhava. Using this *mantra*, the lord of the *rakshasas* obtained success. Satisfied, he returned to Lanka. Since then, this extremely powerful *tirtha* has bestowed all the great *siddhi*s and everything desired. It destroys all the floods of sins and is frequented by all the *siddha*s.'

Chapter 2(74) (Confluence of Parushni)

Brahma said, 'The *tirtha* known as the confluence of Parushni is famous in the three worlds. It destroys every kind of sin. I will describe its nature. Atri worshipped Brahma, Vishnu and Maheshvara. When they were pleased, he said, "The three of you should be my sons. O divinities! Let a beautiful daughter also be born to me." Thus, he got Brahma, Vishnu and Maheshvara as his sons. An auspicious daughter named Atreyi was also born. The great-souled one's sons were Datta,[904] Soma and Durvasa. Along with burning charcoal, Angiras was born through Agni.

---

[903] Shiva.

[904] Dattatreya.

That is the reason he was known as Angiras.[905] Atri bestowed
the radiant Atreyi on him. Because of Agni's powers, he always
addressed Atreyi in harsh words. However, Atreyi always tended
to him. Through her, extremely song and powerful sons were born
to Angiras. Though Angiras always addressed Atreyi in harsh
words, the sons, the Angirases, always pacified their father. On one
occasion, because of her husband's harsh tone and words, she was
extremely miserable. Dejected, she joined her hands in salutation
and spoke to her senior, her father-in-law. Atreyi said, "O bearer
of oblations! I am Atri's daughter. I am your son's wife. I always
serve my husband and my sons. My husband addresses me in harsh
words. Without any reason, he looks at him angrily. O best among
the gods! Please instruct me. My husband is my divinity." The fire
replied, "Your husband, *rishi* Angiras, has originated from burning
charcoal. O fortunate one! So that he remains pacified, some policy
must be thought of. O one with the beautiful face! Let your fiery
husband approach Agni. Obeying my instructions, you must flow
in the form of water." Atreyi said, "I will tolerate harsh words. Let
my husband not enter the fire. If women act against their husbands,
what is the point of their remaining alive? I desire amiable words
and I also want my husband." The fire replied, "Agni is present in
water, in bodies and in mobile and immobile objects. I am always
your husband's refuge. I am thought of as his father. I am what I
am. Knowing this, you should not worry. The waters are divine
mothers and Agni is your father-in-law. O daughter-in-law! Use
your intelligence to comprehend this and do not be miserable."
Atreyi said, "You said that the waters are mothers. O Agni! I am
your son's wife. O protector! Since I am his wife, how can I act
in a perverse way, assuming the form of water and becoming his
mother?" The fire replied, "At first, you were a *patni*. Then, for
sustaining, you became a *bharya*. To give birth, you became *jaya*.
Through your own qualities, you became *kalatra*.[906] O fortunate

---

[905] Burning charcoal is *angara*.

[906] These are synonyms for a wife, with slightly different nuances.
Along with the husband (*pati*), a *patni* takes part in rites. *Bharya* is one
who sustains and maintains. *Jaya* is one in whom the husband is reborn as

one! You were radiant in all these different forms. Therefore, act in accordance with my words. If he is born through her, he becomes a son. Therefore, there is no doubt that you become his mother. Hence, those who know the truth about the sacred texts say that once a son has been born, you are no longer a *yoshit*." Hearing the words spoken by her father-in-law, Atreyi acted accordingly. Her husband was in the form of fire and she flooded him in the form of water. O brahmana! The couple merged into the waters of Ganga. Thereby, the couple assumed a peaceful form. It was like Lakshmi being united with Vishnu, Uma being united with Shiva and Rohini being united with the moon. The couple resembled that. To flood her husband, she assumed a form made out of water. This river is famous as Parushni and it merged into Ganga. Bathing in Parushni yields the benefits that are obtained from donating one hundred cows. The Angirasas performed sacrifices there and donated a lot of *dakshina*. O son! Those who know about the ancient accounts say that there are three thousand *tirtha*s there, on both banks of the river. Sacrifices performed there are known to yield separate fruits. It is held that bathing and donating there, yield benefits superior to those obtained from a *vajapeya* sacrifice. This is particularly true of the place where there is a confluence of Parushni with Ganga. It is impossible to describe the merits obtained from bathing and donating there.'

Chapter 2(75) (Markandeya *tirtha*)

Brahma said, 'The place known as Markandeya *tirtha* frees from sins. It yields the fruits of every kind of sacrifice and is auspicious. It counters sins. I will describe its powers. O Narada! Listen attentively. O Narada! Markandeya, Bharadvaja, Vasishtha, Atri, Goutama, Yajnavalkya, Jabali and other sages are those who composed sacred texts. There were accomplished in the Vedas and

---

a son. *Kalatra* has the sense of being a citadel. *Yoshit* is woman in general, applied to wife.

*Vedanga*s. They knew about Puranas, *nyaya*, *mimasa* and other accounts. Depending on their intelligence, they conversed with each other about emancipation. Some praised *jnana*, some praised *karma* and some praised both. Debating in this way, they asked me about my views on these two paths. Ascertaining my views, they went to the one who holds the *chakra* and the mace. Ascertaining his views, those immensely energetic *rishi*s again debated amongst themselves and sought to ask Shankara. To that end, along the banks of Ganga, they worshipped Bhava and asked him. The destroyer of Tripura replied, "*Karma* is most important. *Jnana* adopts the form of rites." This is what he said. "All living beings obtain success only through *karma*. *Karma* pervades the universe. There is nothing else. The practice of learning, the performance of sacrifices, the practice of *yoga* and the worship of Shiva—all this is *karma*. Nowhere does a living being exist without *karma*. Thus, *karma* is the cause. Everything else is the utterance of a mad person." There is a place where the debate between the *rishi*s took place and where the divinity Maheshvara arrived at the determination that men obtain everything through *karma*. Since Markandeya was the chief, that place is known as Markandeya. On the northern banks of Ganga, that *tirtha* is full of a large number of *rishi*s. It purifies the ancestors. Even when it is remembered, it always yields good merits. O son! The one who pervades the universe said that there are ninety eight *tirtha*s there. This has been spoken about in the Vedas and the *rishi*s accepted this.'

Chapter 2(76) (Kalanjara *tirtha*)

Brahma said, 'The next *tirtha* is named after Yayati and Kalanjara Shiva is there. It destroys every kind of sin. I will describe its greatness. King Yayati, the son of Nahusha, was like another Indra himself. He had two wives. Both were from noble lineages and possessed the auspicious signs. The elder was Shukra's auspicious daughter, named Devayani. The second was Sharmishtha and she was Vrishaparva's daughter. Although born from a brahmana lineage, the slender-waisted Devayani was immensely wise. Through Shukra's favours, she became Yayati's wife. Sharmishtha, Vrishvaparva's daughter, was also his wife. Devayani, Shukra's daughter, had two sons. They were Yadu and Turvasu and they were like the sons of the gods. Through Sharmishtha, the king obtained three sons who were like gods. King Yayati's excellent sons were Druhyu, Anu and Puru. O brahmana! Devayani's two sons were like Shukra in form. Sharmishtha's sons had the resplendence of Shakra, Agni and Varuna.'

'On one occasion, miserable, Devayani spoke to her father. Devayani said, "O descendant of the Bhrigu lineage! I am unfortunate. I only have two sons. O father! My servant-maid has good fortune. She possesses three sons. Thinking about this, I am suffering from great grief. O preceptor of *danavas*! Because Yayati has acted disagreeably, I will die. O father! For a spirited person, death is superior to being dishonoured." Hearing his daughter's words, the powerful Shukra became angry. He quickly went to Yayati and spoke to him. Shukra said, "O Indra among kings! You are intoxicated because of your beauty. Therefore, you have acted in this disagreeable and have neglected my daughter. You will immediately become old. You will hanker after material objects. But you won't be able to enjoy them. Nor will you be able to give them up. With your intelligence confounded, you will desire them and sigh. Even if an embodied being remains alive, old age is like death. O lord of the earth! Therefore, quickly leave. You will find old age impossible to bear." The intelligent Yayati heard the curse imposed on him by Shukra. King Yayati joined his hands in salutation and spoke to Shukra. Yayati replied, "I have not committed a crime. I have not been angry. I have not committed an act of *adharma*. Great-souled ones punish sinners, those who have committed acts of *adharma*. I follow *dharma*. Why have you cursed me? O best among *brahmanas*! Devayani has unnecessarily said something about me. O Indra among *brahmanas*! It is not appropriate for you to curse me like this. If learned people are confounded and curse the innocent in their rage, there is no sin when the minds of the foolish are heated by the fire of hatred." Hearing Yayati's words, Shukra remembered what she had done, how she had done evil and disagreeable things and how she was fierce, day and night. Kavya[907] told the king, "My rage has gone." Shukra said, "Knowingly or unknowingly, I never intentionally utter a falsehood. O king! Listen. I will convert this curse into a favour. O one who bestows honours! O king! Whichever son you wish to give this old age to, through my favour, this old age will pass on to that son." Yayati again humbly spoke to this father-in-law, Shukra. Yayati said, "O *guru* of the *daitya*s! Please let it be such that whichever of my sons faithfully accepts the old age given by me, will be the king. O *guru*! If any of my sons does not welcome my words, I seek your permission to firmly curse him. O *guru*! Let this be granted." The descendant of the Bhrigu lineage told the king that it would be that way.'

'Yayati summoned his son and addressed him in these words. Yayati said, "O Yadu! You are my son. Accept the old age that the curse has inflicted on me. You are the oldest and mature. You know the purport of everything and amongst my sons, you are the one who can bear the burden. A father truly has a son when the son follows the instructions of the father." Yadu refused his father Yayati, who used to give away a lot of *dakshina*. Thereupon, Yayati cursed Yadu and told Turvasu what he desired. Turvasu also refused to accept the old age given by his father. He cursed him and told Druhyu, "Accept my old age." Druhyu did not wish to accept the old age that would be given, destroying his beauty. The king told Anu, "Accept my old age." When Anu refused, he cursed him and spoke to Puru. Puru welcomed the idea and accepted his father's old age for one thousand years. The father was delighted. There are many kinds of objects of pleasure that can be enjoyed in youth. Satisfied with his son's youth, Yayati happily enjoyed these. The king, Nahusha's son, was satisfied with all these objects of pleasure. Happy, he summoned his son, Puru, and spoke to him. Yayati said, "O unblemished one! Through your youth, I have satisfied myself with all the objects of pleasure. O son! Take back your youth and return the evil old age back to me." Puru refused and said, "O father! For those with bodies, thoughts of aberrations are extremely difficult to counter. But I have used old age to extinguish them. For all those with

---

[907] Shukracharya.

bodies, the strength of old age that comes prematurely can be used to counter them. Since I have accepted this benefit from my senior, how can I cast it aside? For all those with bodies, death is superior to giving up something that has been accepted. O king! Or, I will austerities to destroy this old age." Telling his father this, he went to the supreme Ganga. On Goutami's southern bank, he tormented himself through great austerities. After a long period of time, the divinity Shiva was pleased. Puru was ornamented in the jewel of pervasive qualities, superior to any in this world. The supreme god asked him, "What will I give you?" Puru replied, "O protector! O lord of the gods! My father obtained this old age through a curse. O lord of the gods! Please destroy this. O one worshipped by the gods! Angry, my father cursed my brothers. Please free them from their curses." The lord of the universe agreed and destroyed the old age that had resulted from the curse. The lord of the universe also freed his brothers from their curses. Since then, that *tirtha* has destroyed old age and ailments. Even if one remembers it, untimely old age and other things are destroyed. Therefore, it is famous under the name of Kalanjara.[908] It is also named after Yayati, Nahusha's son, Shukra and Sharmishtha. O immensely intelligent one! There are another one hundred and eight *tirtha*s there and they yield every kind of success. Bathing and donating there, or reading and hearing about them, destroy all sins and bestow objects of pleasure and emancipation.'

Chapter 2(77) (The pair of *apsaras*)

Brahma said, 'I will tell you about the pair of *apsaras* and the confluence of the *apsaras*. This auspicious place is on the southern bank. Even if one remembers it, one obtains good fortune. If a man undertakes bathing and other rites there, there is no doubt that he is emancipated. O Narada! If a faithful woman bathes there after her period, she will give birth to a son. For three months, along

---

[908] The etymology seems to be destroyer (*kala*) of old age (*jara*).

with her husband, if she bathes and donates there, she will give birth
to a son, even if she happens to be barren. My words are always true.
This *tirtha* is famous after the pair of *apsara*s. I will tell you about
the reason for this. O Narada! Listen attentively. O brahmana!
There was great rivalry between Vishvamitra and Vasishtha. For
the sake of becoming a brahmana, Gadhi's son[909] was controlled in
his vows and tormented himself through austerities. He was seated
in Gangadvara. Indra sent Menaka. "O fortunate one! Follow
my instructions. Go and make him deviate from his austerities."
Addressed by Indra, Menaka[910] went and made Vishvamitra deviate
from his austerities. She gave him the daughter she delivered and
returned to Indra's city. When she left, Gadhi's son remembered
everything that he had done. He gave up that region and *tirtha*,
loved by the gods. He went south to Ganga where Kalanjara
Hara is. Indra, the one with one thousand eyes, asked Urvashi,
Mena, Rambha and Tilottama to bring an end to his austerities.
But scared, they refused. Thereupon, Shachi's consort asked
Gambhira and Atigambhira, both of whom were extremely proud.
They replied to the thousand-eyed god, Purandara. Gambhira and
Atigambhira said, "We will go and end the austerities of Gadhi's
immensely radiant son. We will use our dancing, singing, beauty,
youth and charms. We will use our sidelong glances, smiles, words
and enticement. The one with the five arrows[911] always resides with
us. Who cannot be defeated?" When the one with one thousand
eyes agreed, they went to the great river. They saw the great sage,
Vishvamitra, engaged in austerities. He was like Death, impossible
to assail. He was like Dhurjati[912] on earth. For one thousand and
one years, they were incapable of glancing at him. They remained
some distance away, singing, dancing and praising him. On seeing
them, the tiger among sages was filled with rage. When a contrary
act is witnessed, who does not become angry? Free from desire, the
mighty-armed one seemed to laugh when he spoke to the one with

---

[909] Vishvamitra.
[910] The text says Mena, the same as Menaka.
[911] The god of love has five arrows.
[912] Shiva.

one thousand eyes. "O one with one thousand eyes! I have been
freed from all this." Gadhi's son then spoke to the two *apsara*s
and cursed them. "Assume the form of rivers. You tried to melt
me. Therefore, assume this light form." When they pacified him, he
freed them from the curse. "When you merge with Ganga, you will
regain your divine forms." As a result of the curse, they instantly
assumed the forms of rivers. Those two rivers are famous as a pair
of *apsara*s. Their mutual confluence and their confluence with
Ganga is famous in all the worlds. Shiva is present there. He is the
one who bestows objects of pleasure and emancipation. When he is
seen, every kind of success is obtained. If one bathes there and sees
him, one is freed from every kind of bondage.'

Chapter 2(78) (Kanva *tirtha*)

Brahma said, 'The place known as Koti *tirtha* is on the southern
banks of Ganga. As soon as one remembers it, one is freed from
every kind of sin. The divinity Kotishvara is there and the place
possesses all the one crore qualities. There are a total of two crore
*tirtha*s there and they bestow all that is auspicious. O Narada! I will
describe its greatness. Listen with an attentive mind. Kanva's eldest
son was known by the name of Bahlika. People addressed him as
Kaanva[913] and he was accomplished in the Vedas and the *Vedanga*s.
On the banks of Goutami, along with his wife, the one who knew
about the Vedas and was worshipped by the worlds, performed
parvayana[914] and other sacrifices. In the morning, along with his
wife, he always offered oblations into the fire. On one occasion, he
was about to offer the oblations. He offered one round of oblations
into the fire that had been kindled. Ready to offer another round
of oblations, he took up the oblations in his hand. Meanwhile,
the fire was pacified. Kaanva became full of thoughts. Debating

[913] The father is Kanva, the son is Kaanva.
[914] Sacrifices performed on special occasions (*parva*), or at the time of
ayana.

this internally, he became greatly despondent. "What should be done? In between the two rounds of oblations, the fire has become pacified. Should one use another fire? What do the Vedas say? What is customary practice? Where should one offer the second round of oblations?" While he was trying to decide this, a divine and invisible voice spoke. "O lord of *brahmanas*! There is no need to arrange for another fire. Here or nearby, there may still be some sparks left. Offer the oblations into the half-burnt wood." Kaanva refused. The voice spoke again. "Agni's son is gold.[915] The father is like the sun. What is given to bring pleasure to the son also brings pleasure to the father. When something that should be given to the father is given to the son, the qualities and pleasure that result are one crore times more." When the divine voice said this, all the *maharshi*s decided that this was all there was to *dharma* and acted accordingly. They understood that in this world, what is given to the son is also given to the father. If something is given to the offspring, there is nothing else that pleases the father more. This is famous in the world. This is extremely well-known in the world and is honoured in all the worlds. O son! When something is given in this way, the qualities become one crore times more. Mental dejection goes away and great happiness results. The voice spoke again. "O sage! This Kaanva *tirtha* will become excellent. Because of the auspicious powers of Kaanva, it will be a great *tirtha*. In all the three worlds, no other *tirtha* will bestow such great fruits. If a person controls himself and faithfully undertakes bathing, donating and some other rites there, he will obtain all the fruits that are one crore times more in qualities. If a man undertakes anything here, bathing, donations and other rites—it should be known that the qualities will be one crore times more. Hence, it will be known as Koti *tirtha*." The place where all this occurred is also known as Agni *tirtha*, Kaanva *tirtha*, Poutra *tirtha*, Hiranyaka *tirtha* and Vanisamjna *tirtha*. It is known as Koti *tirtha* because the fruits are one crore times more. Vachaspati and the other gods are incapable of describing the greatness of Koti *tirtha*. If any rite is undertaken there, regardless of how it is

---

[915] We have translated *hiranya* as gold. The succeeding *shloka*s do not make it clear where the second oblation was to be offered.

performed, because of Godavari's favours, the qualities become one crore times more. If one gives an excellent brahmana a single cow in Koti *tirtha*, because of the *tirtha*'s greatness, the fruits obtained are identical to the fruits obtained from donating one crore cows. If one purifies oneself and with devotion in the mind, donates land there, the benefits obtained are one crore times more. Everywhere along the Godavari, donations in the name of the ancestors are excellent. In particular, in Koti *tirtha*, the fruits obtained are infinite. The sages say that there are forty-nine *tirtha*s there.'

Chapter 2(79) (Narasimha *tirtha*)

Brahma said, 'The place named after Narasimha is on Ganga's northern bank. I will describe its greatness. It is capable of protecting against all impediments. Earlier, there was Hiranyakashipu and he was supreme among strong ones. Because of his austerities and valour, he could not be defeated, not even by the gods. His mind was polluted and he hated his own son,[916] who was devoted to Hari. The one whose *atman* is in the universe appeared from within a pillar and showed himself. Narasimha killed him and drove away his soldiers. One by one, the immensely energetic and great animal defeated all the great *daitya*s. Having defeated the enemies in Rasatala, he went to the world of heaven. Having defeated the ones who were there, he went to the earth and killed the *daitya*s who were in the mountains. There were other *daitya*s in many other forms, residing in oceans, villages and forests. In the form of the animal, he slew them. He killed those who were in the sky and in the air, those who had gone to the worlds of the stellar bodies. He shook his large mane. His nails were more forceful than the strike of the *vajra*. His roar caused all the *daitya* women to miscarry. He defeated all the *rakshasa*s. He roared and when he looked around, his glances were like the fire of destruction. With blows from his paws, he plucked out the entrails of other

[916] Prahlada.

*asura*s and crushed them. In this way, after having killed many, Hari went to Goutami. She had emerged from his own lotus feet and brought delight to the mind and to the eyes. The enemy of the lord of Dandaka was there, known as Ambarya. In a battle, even the gods found him impossible to defeat. He was surrounded by a large army. There was an extremely terrible and fierce battle between them[917] and it made the body hair stand up. In the battle between Hari and the son of the *daitya*, *astra*s and *shastra*s were showered down. The prosperous Hari killed the enemy on the northern bank. Along the Ganga, Narasimha *tirtha* is famous in the three worlds. Bathing, donating and other rites performed there, destroy every kind of sin and evil planet. It always protects against everything. It counters old age and death. Among all the gods, there is no one who is Hari's equal. Like that, among all the *tirtha*s, this *tirtha* is the best. If a man bathes in this *tirtha* and worships Narasimha, there is nothing from heaven, the mortal world and the nether regions that he cannot obtain. O Narada! O sage! There are eight such great *tirtha*s there. Learned people have separately spoken about the fruits of crores of *tirtha*s. Even if one lacks faith and remembers them, all impediments are destroyed. Narasimha himself is always present there. Hence, who is capable of describing the fruits of frequenting such a *tirtha*? Just as there is no god who is superior to Hari, there is no *tirtha* which is the equal of Narasimha *tirtha*.'

Chapter 2(80) (Paishacha *tirtha*)

Brahma said, 'The place known as Paishacha *tirtha* is on the northern banks of Ganga. O immensely wise one! This is the place where a brahmana was freed from his state as a *pishacha*. Suyava's son was known in this world as Ajigarti.[918] He suffered

---

[917] Hari and Ambarya.
[918] Ajigarti sold his son Shunahshepa. The *kshatriya* was King Harishchandra. Among other places, this story is told in Markandeya Purana and is also briefly referred to in Chapter 1(8).

from the burden of supporting his family. He also suffered from famine. The son in the middle was Shunahshepa and he was supreme among those who knew about the *brahman*. In exchange for a great deal of riches, he sold him to a *kshatriya* to be sacrificed. Even if a person is learned, when he faces a calamity, what sin is he incapable of committing? The sage also accepted a great deal of riches to be the slaughterer. The worst among *brahmanas* accepted wealth for cutting him up. As a result, he suffered from a great disease, for which, there was no cure. In the course of time, he died and descended into hell. The many kinds of violence a person has committed cannot be exhausted without enjoying the fruits. Following Yama's commands, his servants moved him from one womb to another womb. He thus became a terrible *pishacha*, terrible in form. Yama's servants flung him into places littered with dry wood, forests, places without water, desolate regions and forest conflagrations during the summer. Until all beings are destroyed in the deluge, those who sell their daughters, sons, land, horses and cows, do not return from hell. As a result of the sin he had himself committed, Yama's terrible servants struck him and cooked him. Remembering what he had done, he wept loudly.'

'On one occasion, as he was proceeding along the road, Ajigarti's[919] middle son heard the voice of a *pishacha* lamenting repeatedly. O brahmana! This was the voice of his father, Ajigarti, who had sold his son for a sacrifice. "I am a wicked brahmana who has sold his son. I am the father who has killed him." Shunahshepa responded, "You are extremely miserable. Who are you?" The miserable Ajigarti said, "I am Shunahshepa's father. Having committed a wicked deed, I have been born as this terrible species. Having been cooked repeatedly in hell, I am now in this midway state. This is the destination obtained by all those who commit wicked deeds." Full of sadness, Ajigarti's son told him, "O father! I am your son. You sold me because of my sin and went to hell. I will now ensure that you go to heaven." Having said this, the

---

[919] The text switches to Jigarti. For the sake of consistency, we have retained Ajigarti.

excellent sage, who had become the son of Gadhi's son,[920] went to
Ganga, desiring to obtain excellent worlds for his father. There are
those who suffer and are purified by the fire of a large number of
miseries and are submerged in the great ocean of delusion. For such
embodied beings, there is no support in the three worlds other than
Vishnu's feet. The great-souled sage made up his mind to free his
father from the hardship. Therefore, he quickly went to Goutami
and bathing there, purified himself. He remembered Shambhu and
Vishnu. He performed water-rites for his dead father, who was
extremely miserable in the form of a *pishacha*. As soon as he did
this, Ajigarti was purified and assumed an extremely auspicious
form. Through the powers of his son and the powers of Ganga,
Hari and Shambhu, he obtained Vishnu's feet, worshipped by large
numbers of gods, astride a *vimana*. His energy was like that of the
creator. Since then, that place became extremely famous as a place
where *pishacha*s are destroyed. Even if men remember it, extremely
grave sins are quickly destroyed. I have described the greatness of
that *tirtha*. There are another three hundred *tirtha*s there. They
bestow objects of pleasure and emancipation, not to speak of other
things. These three hundred *tirtha*s have been described as those
which bestow every kind of success. They are frequented by sages.
Even when they are remembered, they grant what is desired.'

Chapter 2(81) (Nimnabheda)

Brahma said, 'The place known as Nimnabheda destroys every
kind of sin. This *tirtha*, on the northern bank of Ganga, is
famous in the three worlds. Even if one remembers it, all sins are
destroyed. Vedadvipa is also there. If one sees it, one becomes
learned in the Vedas. King Aila,[921] extremely devoted to *dharma*,
desired Urvashi. When one sees the one with intoxicating eyes, who
is not deluded? She came to him and only ate a little bit of *ghee*. The

---

[920] Vishvamitra adopted Shunahshepa.
[921] That is, Pururava.

king also accepted her condition that she would remain with him for only as long as she didn't see him naked. She was a beautiful woman and always seemed newer than the newest. When she was sleeping on the bed, Pururava got up. On seeing that he was without any clothes, she instantly left. The minds of women are as fickle as the lightning. Who can steady them?'[922]

'Meanwhile, the king went out to fight with the enemy. Having defeated them, he again[923] went to the world of the gods, where he was greatly honoured. Returning from there, the great king heard from the priest Vasishtha that Urvashi had left. He was filled with grief. He did not offer oblations. He did not eat. He did not hear. He did not see. The excellent king almost reached a state of death. Meanwhile, the priest used words full of reason to make him understand. Vasishtha said, "O great king! O immensely intelligent one! She is dead now. Do not grieve. If you remain in this state, inauspicious arrows will touch you.[924] O immensely wise one! No one knows what is in the minds of women. They are like wolves and jackals. O lord of the earth! Therefore, do not grieve. O Indra among kings! In this world, who has not been deceived by women? They are deceitful. They are cruel. They are fickle. They are evil in conduct. Since they are naturally like that, how can they lead to happiness? Who has not been slain by time? Which supplicant has been honoured? Whose prosperity has not been whirled around? Who has not been betrayed by women? O king! They are like dreams and *maya*. Their hearts are full of pride. Who has obtained happiness through women? Knowing this, steady yourself. O immensely intelligent one! With the exception of Shankara, Vishnu and Goutami, the miserable have no other refuge in the three worlds." Hearing this, the king made a great deal of effort and controlled his grief. He stood in the middle of Goutami. Extremely

---

[922] The text has a *shloka* that it states is inconsistent and interpolated. Therefore, we have not included this in the translation. It says that the king was greatly surprised in the night and the one who subsisted only on *ghee* saw him without his clothes on.

[923] Pururava had been there earlier.

[924] Probably referring to the arrows of Kama, the god of love.

devoted to *dharma*, Aila attentively worshipped the divinity Shiva,
Janardana, Brahma, Bhaskara, Ganga and the other gods there.
When a living being comes under the subjugation of destiny, faces
a calamity and does not serve *tirtha*s or the gods, what state will he
be reduced to? He sought Ishvara as his only refuge and was keen
to serve Goutami. Full of great faith, he turned away from the state
of *samsara*. With officiating priests, he performed many sacrifices
and gave away copious quantities of *dakshina*. That place came to
be known as Vedadvipa and Yajnadvipa.[925] On the night of the full
moon, Urvashi always goes there. If a man performs *pradakshina* of
that *dvipa*, it is as if he performs *pradakshina* of the earth, girdled
by the ocean. If a person remembers the *Veda*s there, or remembers
sacrifices there, he obtains fruits that are the same as the fruits of a
sacrifice performed in conformity with the Vedas. It is also known
as Aila *tirtha*, Pururava *tirtha* and Vasishtha *tirtha*. It is spoken
of as Nimnabheda. When Aila was the king, there was nothing
inferior in any of the rites. He did have inferior sentiments regarding
Urvashi. However, because of Vasishtha and Ganga, those inferior
sentiments were dissipated.[926] Hence, it became Nimnabheda and it
brings success in everything that is seen and not seen. It is said that
there are seven hundred *tirtha*s there, possessing all the qualities.
Bathing and donating there, yield the fruits of all sacrifices. If a
person bathes in Nimnabheda and sees the gods, in this world and
in the next world, there is nothing inferior for him. Having obtained
every kind of upliftment, like Shakra, he rejoices in heaven.'

Chapter 2(82) (Nanditata)

Brahma said, 'There is a *tirtha* famous as Nanditata. Those who
know the Vedas know about it. I will describe its powers. O
Narada! Listen attentively. Atri had an extremely energetic son,

[925] A *dvipa* (island) in the middle of the river.
[926] *Nimna* (inferior, baser, lower) and *bheda* (cleared away). Thus,
Nimnabheda.

known as Chandrama.[927] O immensely intelligent one. In the proper
way, he learnt all the Vedas, *dhanurveda* and all the other kinds of
knowledge from Jiva.[928] Chandrama told Jiva, "I will worship my
guru." Brihaspati was delighted and spoke to his disciple, Chandra.
Brihaspati said, "You know that my beloved is Tara. Her radiance
is like Rati's."[929] Chandrama went inside the house to ask her.[930]
Tara's face was like a star. Seeing her, he grasped her by the hand.
Greedy, he forcibly dragged her towards his own house. As long
as he is not bound in the snares of a beautiful lady's eyes, a man
possesses valour, intellect, learning and intelligence and manages to
conquer his senses. This is especially the case if one sees a large-eyed
and beautiful lady in private. Therefore, a lady from a noble lineage
must never see another man in private. If one sees him, whose mind
does not come under the subjugation of desire? The lady must be
scared that her good conduct is not tainted. Brihaspati, extensive
in his intelligence, got to know about this from his relatives. He
suddenly arose and left. He went and witnessed the wicked deeds.
Condemning that disagreeable deed in eloquent words, he angrily
cursed. Witnessing his beloved being molested, which lord can
tolerate it? Assisted by the gods, Jiva fought with Chandrama.
But Chandra was not affected by the curse or by the weapons
invoked with *mantra*s, unleashed by the gods. The *mantra*s used by
Brihaspati did not harm the moon-god. Thus, Chandra took Tara
and instated her in his house. Without any fear, he enjoyed her and
Rohini[931] for many years. The rage of the gods could not defeat him,
nor could the curse and the *mantra*s. The kings or the *rishi*s couldn't
do anything. *Sama*, *bheda* and *danda* served no purpose. Though
he tried every possible means, the *guru* could not get his wife back.
When all the means were exhausted, Jiva remembered his own
policy.[932] "A wise person must place honour behind him and place

[927] The moon-god. Chandra is the same as Chandrama.

[928] Jiva is Brihaspati's name.

[929] Rati is the wife of the god of love, Kama.

[930] To ask what she wanted, so that he could offer his *guru* the *dakshina*.

[931] Rohini is a *nakshatra*. All the *nakshatra*s were married to the moon-
god, but Chandra loved Rohini the most.

[932] Brihaspati's *niti* has maxims on good policy.

dishonour at the forefront. That is the way to enhance one's self-interest. Diminishing the self-interest is folly. Learned men must use every means possible to accomplish the objective. Those deluded by false pride quickly bring about a calamity." Having decided this, the intelligent one went to Shukra and told him everything.[933] Knowing that he had come, Kavi[934] respectfully welcomed him. When he was seated and rested, he followed the norms and worshipped him. The *guru* of the *daityas* asked him about the reason for his arrival. Those who are superior do not refuse even enemies, when they come to their houses.'

'Starting at the beginning, he told him about the abduction of his wife. Hearing Brihaspati's words, Kavi was filled with rage. O Narada! He agreed that the disciple, Chandra, had committed a crime. Hearing about his transgression, Kavi spoke in anger. Shukra said, "O lord of the planets! O brother! Your wife has been molested by another person. O mighty-armed one! Listen to my words. I will eat only after I have brought your wife back, worshipped Bhava and cursed Chandra." Saying this, the preceptor of the *daityas* left, along with Jiva. He worshipped Shiva with great care and obtained supreme capability. He worshipped Shankara with deep sentiments and obtained many boons. Through Shiva's favours, what is difficult for an embodied being to obtain? Along with Jiva, Shukra went to the place where Chandrama was, with Tara. He cursed loudly. "O Chandra! Listen to my words. O sinner! Intoxicated by insolence, you have committed an extremely grave sin. You will be overcome by leprosy." Kavi angrily cursed Chandra. He was burnt down by Kavi's curse. What kind of destruction is not faced by those who deceive and betray their *guru*, their master, or their friend? Chandra gave up Tara and Shukra took her away.'

'Shukra summoned the gods, the *rishis*, the large numbers of ancestors, the female rives, the male rivers, many kinds of herbs

---

[933] Brihaspati and Shukra were rivals. Thus, Brihaspati swallowed his pride in going to Shukracharya. In accounts of the battle over Tara, the *asuras* sided with Chandra.

[934] Shukra.

and women who were faithful to their husbands. He told them about the Tara episode and asked them how one could be freed.[935] The *shruti* texts told the gods, "Along with Jiva, let Tara go to Goutami and devotedly bathe there. She will then be purified." This is a deep secret and must never be spoken about to anyone. In every kind of hardship, Goutami is the only refuge for men. As is done, Tara bathed there, along with her husband. Flowers were showered down and there were exclamations of "Victory". The gods bestowed her again.[936] Men bestowed her again. Kings, truthful in deeds, bestowed the wife on the brahmana. Having bestowed the wife on the brahmana again, the gods cleansed her of the taint. O great sage! Everything was well in that *tirtha*. It became a place that destroys all sins and grants everything that is desired. There was peace and happiness among the gods, the enemies of the *asura*s. In particular, Brihaspati, Shukra and Tara were filled with great joy. The *guru*[937] spoke to Ganga. The *guru* said, "O Goutami! You will always deserve to be worshipped by everyone. You will bestow emancipation. O one who purifies the three worlds! O best among rivers! In particular, when I am in Simha,[938] all the *tirtha*s will assemble within you and all the *tirtha*s in heaven, the mortal world and the nether regions will go to you to bathe there. O mother! They will go there when I am in Simha." This *tirtha*, named Ananda,[939] is blessed. It enhances fame, a long lifespan, freedom from disease and prosperity. It generates good fortune and wealth. Goutama said that there are five thousand *tirtha*s there. If one remembers them, or reads about them, one obtains all that one desires. Shiva's Nandi is always there, along the banks of Ganga, performing rites of *dharma*. Therefore, it is spoken of as Nanditata.[940] The *tirtha* known as Ananda enhances every kind of happiness.'

[935] From the taint.
[936] After being purified, Tara was married again to Brihaspati.
[937] Brihaspati.
[938] When Jupiter is in Leo.
[939] *Ananda* means joy/bliss.
[940] Literally, Nandi's bank.

Chapter 2(83) (Bhava *tirtha*)

Brahma said, 'Bhava is himself present in the place known as Bhava *tirtha*. He is in the *atman* of all beings and the entire universe is in him. He is the form of truth and consciousness. In this connection, I will relate a sacred and auspicious account. Listen. There was a prosperous person who extended *surya vamsha*. He could bear the burden of *kshatriyas*. He was known as Prachinabarhi and he was accomplished in every kind of *dharma*. He was instated in the kingdom for three and a half crore years. He had taken a pledge. "When I lose my youth, when I am separated from my wife, my sons and my cherished objects, I will give up my kingdom. There is no doubt about this." This is appropriate action for discriminating men who are born in noble lineages. When everything decays, they become non-attached and remain in solitude. However, while he ruled the earth, there was no separation from anything he loved. There were no physical or mental ailments. There was no famine. Among men, there were no conflicts between relatives. He ruled the kingdom in this way and there was no separation. For the sake of a son, the immensely intelligent king performed a sacrifice. The illustrious one, the divinity Maheshvara, was pleased and granted him the boon he desired. The king was on the banks of Goutami. Along with his wife, the king told Bhava, "Please grant me a son." Delighted, Bhava told the king, "Look at my third eye." O one who bestows honours! The Indra among kings looked at Bhava's eye. A son was born from the resplendence in the eye and he was known by the name of Mahiman. It was he who composed the auspicious hymn famous as Mahimna.[941] When the illustrious destroyer of Tripura is pleased, what cannot be obtained? Hari, Brahma and the other gods always follow him. Having obtained a son, the king asked for an excellent *tirtha* that would destroy the great sins of suffering men, who are afflicted by many kinds of

---

[941] This is a *stotram* about Shiva's greatness (*mahiman*) and is known as *Shiva-mahimna stotram*. It is usually ascribed to Pushpadanta, the king of the *gandharvas*.

calamities, and give them everything that they wished for. Bhava granted him a superior place, known as Bhava *tirtha*. Bathing and donating there, yield everything that is desired. Through Bhava's favours, Prachinabarhi obtained a son, Mahiman. The place known as Bhava *tirtha* is along the banks of Goutami. There are seventy sacred *tirtha*s there and they grant everything.'

Chapter 2(84) (Sahasra kunda)

Brahma said, 'Those who are conversant with the Vedas know of the *tirtha* famous as Sahasra kunda. Even if a man remembers it, he becomes happy. Earlier, Dasharatha's son, Rama, constructed a bridge across the great ocean. He burnt Lanka down and in a battle, used arrows to kill Ravana and other enemies. Having got Vaidehi[942] back, while the guardians of the worlds looked on and his *acharya* was standing in front of him, Rama spoke these words. Sita had been purified by the fire and Lakshmana was near him. Rama said, "O Vaidehi! You are pure. You should come and be seated on my lap." However, the prosperous Angada and Hanuman said, "No. O Vaidehi! Along with the well-wishers, we will go to Ayodhya. While the brothers, the mothers and the ordinary people are watching, you must be purified. O daughter of a king! After you have been purified in Ayodhya, on an extremely auspicious day, you should sit on the lap. Who can have any doubt about her conduct? However, any condemnation by people must be warded off amidst one's own people." Lakshmana and Vibhishana ignored their words. Rama and Jambavan summoned the daughter of a king. As the gods pronounced benedictions, she sat on the king's lap. All of them were delighted. Astride the radiant Pushpaka, they quickly reached the city of Ayodhya, which was his own kingdom. All of them were happy and always followed Rama.

'After some days had passed, he heard adverse comments made by ignoble people. Hearing this, he cast away the one who was

[942] Sita.

not born from a womb.[943] She was expecting at the time. How
can those who are born in noble lineages tolerate slander, even
if it is false? The innocent Sita was weeping and Lakshmana was
also weeping. He left her near the hermitage of Valmiki, foremost
among sages. He was afraid of doing this, but he did not wish to
transgress his senior's command. After some days passed, along
with Soumitri,[944] the son of a king[945] consecrated himself for a horse
sacrifice. Rama's two illustrious sons arrived there. They were Lava
and Kusha. As singers, they were Narada's equal. They arrived at
the sacrificial arena, singing the entire Ramayana and everything
about Rama's conduct in extremely melodious voices that were
like those of the *gandharva*s. From these signs, it was discerned
that they were the sons of a king and that the two of them were
Rama's brave sons and Vaidehi's sons. Having had them brought
there, he[946] consecrated his sons, one by one. He took them up on
his lap and repeatedly embraced them. For embodied beings who
are suffering from the misery of *samsara*, embracing the son is a
supreme source of solace. He repeatedly embraced his two sons and
kissed them. Then, thinking about something, he sighed repeatedly.
Meanwhile, the *rakshasa*s, the residents of Lanka, arrived there.
Sugriva, Hanuman, Angada, Jambavan and all the other *vanara*s
also arrived. Vibhishana was at the forefront. Having arrived there,
they approached the king, who was seated on his throne. Unable
to see Sita, Hanuman and Angada, who wore golden armlets,
asked, "Where is the mother, who was not born from a womb?
Rama alone is seen." The gate-keepers replied, 'She has been cast
away by Rama." They[947] responded, "The guardians of the world
watched and said that she was noble. Having entered the fire, Sita
was purified. Nevertheless, the king behaved in this unrestrained
way. Because people uttered certain things, Rama has abandoned

[943] Sita.
[944] Lakshmana.
[945] Rama.
[946] Rama.
[947] This seems to mean Hanuman, Angada and the others, not the gate-
keepers.

his beloved. We will die." Saying this, they went to Goutami. Along with the residents of Ayodhya, Rama followed them at the rear. Having arrived at Goutami, they performed supreme austerities. Remembering Sita, the mother of the worlds, they repeatedly sighed. They no longer hankered after the state of *samsara* and were eager to serve Goutami. Rama, the lord of the three worlds, himself came there, along with his younger brothers. Having arrived and bathed in Goutami, he devoted himself to worshipping Shiva. Surrounded by thousands, he gave up all his torment. The place where this occurred is spoken of as Sahasra kunda.[948] There are another ten *tirtha*s there, which yield every kind of objective. Bathing and donating there, bestow one thousand times the usual fruit. Assisted by Vasishtha and other lords among sages, he offered oblations there, to counter all calamities and destroy all sins. With flows of wealth, he did this in one thousand different pools. Through the favours of Goutami, mother among rivers, the great ascetic, the destroyer of *rakshasa*s, obtained everything that he wished for and desired. That *tirtha*, known as Sahasra kunda, bestows great fruits.'

Chapter 2(85) (Confluence of Kapila)

Brahma said, 'Kapila *tirtha* is also known as Angiras *tirtha*. It is also known as Aditya *tirtha* and Simhika *tirtha*. O supreme among sages! On the southern bank of Goutami, the Angirases performed a sacrifice for the Adityas. As *dakshina*, the Adityas gave the Angirases the earth. The Angirases went away to undertake austerities. The earth adopted the form of Simhika[949] and devoured all the people. All the people were afraid. They went and reported this to the Angirases. Learning that they were frightened and that the earth had assumed the form of Simhika, the Angirases went to the Adityas and addressed them in these words. "Please take back the earth which you gave us." The Adityas replied, "No. Learned

---

[948] Literally, the pool of one thousand, or one thousand pools.
[949] A female lion.

people never take back what they have given as *dakshina*. If anyone
takes away the earth, given by him or given by someone else, he is
born as a worm and survives on excrement for sixty thousand years.
There is no sin greater than taking away the earth, whether given
by the one who takes away or by someone else. This is terrible and
we will not accept her back again. What will happen if we take
back what we ourselves have given? However, we can take back
the earth, given as *dakshina*, if we purchase her back." When they
agreed to this, on the southern bank of Ganga the gods gave a *kapila*
cow, possessing auspicious qualities, in place of the earth. Vishnu
himself exists in that place, which bestows objects of pleasure and
emancipation. This is the confluence of Kapila and it destroys
all sins. As a result of the donation, water flowed in the form of
the river Kapila. The donation of an excellent cow is superior to
donating land that is fertile with crops. As a consequence of this
exchange, the sage[950] saved the world. The *tirtha* where this event
occurred is known as Gou *tirtha*. The learned say that there are one
hundred *tirtha*s there. These bestow everything auspicious. Bathing
and donating there, yield the fruits of donating land. The place
where the river joined Ganga is known as the confluence of Kapila.'

Chapter 2(86) (Shankha *tirtha*)

Brahma said, 'There is the *tirtha* known as Shankha-hrada.[951]
The one who holds the conch shell and the mace is there. If a
person bathes there and sees him, he is freed from the bondage of
samsara. I will tell you what happened there. It grants objects of
pleasure and emancipation. Earlier, at the beginning of *kritya yuga*,
Brahma was chanting Sama hymns. *Rakshasa*s were born from the
store that was the cosmic egg and they could assume any form. They
were intoxicated because of their strength. They held weapons and

---

[950] This is in the singular. However, since there were Angirases, this
should be in the plural.
[951] Literally, conch shell (*shankha*) lake (*hrada*).

rushed towards Brahma, wishing to devour him. I spoke to Vishnu, the preceptor of the universe and asked him for protection. Raising his *chakra*, Vishnu was ready to slay the *rakshasa*s. He sliced down the *rakshasa*s with his *chakra* and blew on his conch shell. He removed thorns from the flat ground and made heaven free of enemies. After this, filled with delight, Hari blew on his conch shell. At this, all the remaining *rakshasa*s were completely destroyed. The place where all of this happened, because of the strength of Vishnu's conch shell, is known as Shankha *tirtha*. It confers every kind of peace on men. It is sacred and bestows all that is desired. Even if it is remembered, it bestows auspiciousness. It generates a long lifespan and freedom from disease. It enhances prosperity and sons. Even if one remembers this or reads about it, one obtains everything that one desires. O sage! There are ten thousand *tirtha*s there and they dispel every kind of sin. Even Maheshvara is incapable of knowing about their powers. In terms of destroying sins, there is nothing that can substitute for them. There is nothing that is superior.'

Chapter 2(87) (Kishkindha *tirtha*)

Brahma said, 'The place known as Kishkindha *tirtha* yields everything that men desire. It destroys every kind of sin and Bhava resides there. I will tell you about its nature. O Narada! Listen carefully. Earlier, Ravana caused the worlds to shriek. With the assistance of the residents of Kishkindha, in the field of battle, Rama, Dasharatha's son, killed him. The slayer of enemies killed him, along with his sons and soldiers and got Sita back. The king returned, along with his brother Soumitri, the extremely strong *vanara*s, the powerful Vibhishana and the gods. After the benedictions were pronounced, he was prosperous and radiant astride Pushpaka, which used to belong to the lord of riches earlier.[952] It was swift in speed and could go wherever it wishes.

---

[952] Before Ravana seized it, Pushpaka *vimana* belonged to Kubera, the lord of riches.

Astride this, all of them went to Ayodhya. Rama was the refuge of all those who sought refuge. He was the one who caused discomfort to his enemies. Along the way, he saw Ganga. Goutami is the one who purifies the universe. She fulfils every kind of desire. She is pleasant to see and removes the torments of those who seek refuge with her. The prosperous king saw her and entered the region along the banks of Ganga. On seeing her, the king was filled with joy and his voice choked because of his delight. O sage! He spoke to all the apes with Hanuman as the chief and invited them. Rama said, "It is because of her powers and favour that my lord and father was freed from all his sins and went to heaven. She is everyone's mother. She is the one who bestows objects of pleasure on beings. She is the one who grants emancipation. She destroys terrible sins. Where is there a river who is her equal? Every difficulty, hard to cross, has been eternally destroyed. Through her favours, enemies have become friends. Vibhishana became my friend. I got Sita back. Hanuman became my relative. Lanka was shattered. It is through serving her that the *rakshasa* was destroyed, along with his followers. Goutama worshipped Shiva, supreme among gods, the one with matted hair, the worthy refuge and obtained her. She is everyone's mother. She bestows everything that is desired. She destroys everything that is inauspicious. She is the one who purifies the universe. I have directly seen her today, the river who is the mother. In deeds, words and thought, I always seek refuge with Ganga. She is the one who is worthy of being a refuge. With all my sentiments, I worship the mother of the virtuous. She is the one who resides in Shambhu's matted hair." Hearing the king's words, all the apes leapt into the water. Following the norms, they separately worshipped her, using many flowers and other objects of worship found in the worlds. Worshipping Sharva, using every kind of sentiment, the king used words to praise him. All the *vanara*s were delighted and sang and danced. Along with his beloved, the great-souled one happily spent the night there. He was surrounded by those who loved him. He cast aside all the miseries caused by his enemies. If one serves Goutami, what is not possible?'

'Full of amazement, he looked at his several servants. He rejoiced and praised Godavari. Rama honoured all the large number of servants and was happy. In the morning, when the sparkling sun rose, Vibhishana spoke to Dasharatha's son. Vibhishana said, "We are still not satisfied with this *tirtha*. We will remain here for some more time. We will reside here for four more nights and leave for Ayodhya in a group." The apes agreed with his words. They stayed there for four nights and worshipped the divinity Sakaleshvara. He[953] then went to the *tirtha* named Siddheshvara, famous in the world and loved by his brother. It was through its favours that the one with the ten heads became extremely strong. They stayed there for five days. They established their own *lingam*s and worshipped them. Hanuman, Vayu's son who was the king's follower, started to serve there. As he left, the Indra among kings told Hanuman, "Immerse all these *lingam*s. Performing invocation with excellent *mantra*s, I have established a *lingam* here and so have others who are Shankara's servants. No other form of Shankara should be worshipped and other *lingam*s should not be joined to the great Bhava. If anyone still remains standing after disrespect,[954] it is as if he is standing on the edge of a sword's blade. Those who worship Shiva's *lingam* with disrespect, those who do not act in accordance with what is recommended and those who do not do what is appropriate, suffer from all kinds of hardships and are cooked by Yama's servants." Following Rama's command, Vayu's son went and used both his arms. But he couldn't uproot the *lingam*.[955] He then desired to seize the *lingam* with his own tail, by encircling it. However, he couldn't and gave up the attempt. The lords among the apes and the king found this to be a great wonder. Which immensely powerful and spirited man is capable of making Mahesha's *lingam* budge? On seeing that it could not be moved, the immensely powerful and supreme king quickly went out. Ramachandra invited *brahmana*s and performed *pradakshina* and worship in the proper way. Purifying himself, with no blemish in his heart, Rama bowed down before all those *lingam*s. All the excellent residents of Kishkindha served that *tirtha*. If one bathes at the spot, there is no doubt that all major sins are destroyed.

[953] Vibhishana.
[954] Showing disrespect to Bhava's great *lingam*.
[955] This seems to refer to the main *lingam*.

He[956] devotedly prostrated himself before Ganga again and said, "O mother Goutami! Be pleased." Full of surprise, he controlled himself and repeatedly said this. He looked at Goutami and bowed down before her. Since then, the gods have said that Kishkindha *tirtha* is sacred. If one reads this, remembers it or hears it devotedly, sins are destroyed. What need be said about bathing and donating there?'

Chapter 2(88) (Vyasa *tirtha*)

Brahma said, 'The famous Vyasa *tirtha* is also known as Prachetas *tirtha*. There is nothing that is more purifying than this. It bestows every kind of success. I had ten sons through my mental powers and they are the creators of the world.[957] Those energetic ones had an inner desire to determine the ends of the earth. Some more were created but they too had a similar urge. They did not return. Neither did those who had departed before them. They were gone. O sage! After this, the immensely wise and divine Angirases were born. They knew the purport of the Vedas and the *Vedanga*s. They were accomplished in all the sacred texts. Those stores of austerities bowed down before their *guru*, Angiras, and sought his permission. Without asking their mother, they made up their minds to perform austerities. In terms of those who deserve honour, the mother is superior to all *guru*s. O Narada! Therefore, in rage, she cursed her own sons. The mother said, "O sons! Disregarding me, you have sought to engage in austerities. Hence, you will never truly attain success of any kind." They roamed around in many regions, but could not obtain success in their austerities. There were impediments in every place they went to. Sometimes, impediments were caused by *rakshasa*s. Sometimes, they were caused by humans. Sometimes, they were caused by women. Sometimes, there were

[956] Rama.

[957] The list of sons born through Brahma's mental powers varies. Here, it probably means the seven *saptarshi*s, Narada, Daksha and Svayambhuva Manu.

taints in the body. All those stores of austerities roamed around in this way. Agastya Kumbhayoni is supreme among those who performed austerities.[958] He is the preceptor of the universe. The Angirases, who were born in Agni's lineage, bowed down before him. Humbly, they prepared to ask the lord of the southern direction.[959] The Angirases said, "O illustrious one! What sin is responsible for our austerities not being successful? We have used many different methods and used them repeatedly. What will we do? What method will we use? How will we accomplish our austerities? O Indra among *brahmanas*! Please tell us. In austerities, you are certainly our senior. O brahmana! Among those who know, you are the one who knows best. Among those who are serene, you are the most serene. You are compassionate and always do what is agreeable. You are never angry. You do not hate. Therefore, please tell us what we wish for. Those who possess ego, those who are devoid of compassion, those who have given up serving their *guru*, those who are untruthful in speech and those who are cruel do not know the truth." After thinking for a while, Agastya gradually told them. Agastya replied, "Your *atman*s are tranquil. Brahma has created you as creators. Your austerities have not been adequate. Remember the cause—your arrogance. There were those whom Brahma created earlier. They left and obtained happiness. There were those who went later, searching for them. They are the ones who became Angirases. You are they. When it was time to go, you did go. But you proceeded very gradually. There is no doubt that you will be superior to Prajapati.[960] Leave this place. Torment yourself through austerities near Ganga, the one who purifies the three worlds. In this *samsara*, there is no means other than Ganga, loved by Shiva. There is a sacred spot in the hermitage there. Worship the one who bestows *jnana* there. He is the immensely intelligent one and he will sever all your doubts. Without a good *guru*, no one has obtained success anywhere." They asked, "O supreme among sages! Who is

[958] Agastya is known as Kumbhayoni because his origin (*yoni*) was in a pot (*kumbha*).

[959] Meaning Agastya.

[960] Meaning Brahma.

spoken of as the one who bestows *jnana*? O supreme among sages! Is
it Brahma, Vishnu, Mahesha, Aditya, Chandrama, Agni or Varuna?
Who bestows *jnana*?" Agastya replied again. "Hear about the one
who confers *jnana*. That which is water is Agni. That which is Agni
is said to be Surya. That which is Surya is Vishnu. That which is
Vishnu is Bhaskara. The one who is Brahma is Rudra. Rudra is
everything. He is the one who possesses all *jnana*. Therefore, he is
the one who is described as the one who bestows *jnana*. There are
many kinds of *gurus*—the one who indicates a direction, the one
who urges, the one who explains, the *upadhyaya* and the one who
gives birth in this body. But the one who bestows *jnana* is the best.
Jnana is said to be only that which destroys differences. Shambhu
alone is known by the names of Indra, Mitra and Agni. For the sake
of helping those who are confused, *brahmanas* speak of them in
different ways." Hearing the sage's words, five of them went to the
northern bank of Ganga and five went to the southern bank. They
recited chants as they proceeded.'

'They followed the norms and worshipped the gods, as Agastya
had asked them to. Thinking about the truth, they sat on special seats.
O sage! All the large number of gods were pleased with them. At the
beginning of the *yuga*, the origin of the universe[961] had thought of
them as creators. This was for restraining *adharma*, establishing the
Vedas, ensuring the welfare of the worlds, accomplishing *dharma*,
kama and *artha* and interpreting the true meaning of the Puranas,
smriti texts, the Vedas and the *dharmashastra*s. "You have been
created in these forms for the welfare of the universe. In due order,
you will gradually become Prajapatis, whenever there is *adharma*
and the Vedas suffer."[962] Whenever the Vedas suffer from dangers,
they are born as Vyases. Whenever *dharma* suffers and the decay of
the Vedas is seen, they are born as Vyases to revive them.[963] Ganga's
excellent bank became the place where they performed austerities.
Shiva, Vishnu, I, Aditya, Agni and water are always present there.

[961] Brahma.
[962] The Angirases were told this. The place where the quote ends is
unclear. But this seems to be just about right.
[963] The first part of this is reminiscent of Bhagavad Gita 4.7.

There is nothing that is more purifying than these. This is the supreme *brahman* alone, which assumes many different kinds of forms. Shiva is in all *atman*s and pervades everything. In his own form, he assumes every kind of form. To exhibit compassion to all living beings, he is especially present in this *tirtha*. He is surrounded by all the gods and shows them every kind of favour. They are known as Dharmavyasas and Vedavyasas. In the three worlds, their *tirtha* is named after them. Vyasa *tirtha* is excellent. The waters there wash off the mire of sins. The darkness of delusion and insolence is dispelled. Men obtain every kind of success there.'

Chapter 2(89) (Confluence of Vanjara)

Brahma said, 'The place known as Vanjara *tirtha* is famous in the three worlds. *Rishi*s, *siddha*s and *rajarshi*s[964] always frequent it. Earlier, the bird Garuda had become a servant of the *naga*s. Since his mother had become a servant, he was miserable and his mind was tormented. On one occasion, he was alone. He thought about it and sighed. Garuda said, "In this world, people who have performed good deeds are blessed. They do not have to serve others and do not face any hardship. Full of happiness, they sing, sleep and laugh. They are masters of their own bodies and are blessed. Shame on those who are under the control of others." Thinking in this way, he was miserable and went to his mother. The one whose *atman* is immeasurable asked his mother, Vinata. Garuda asked, "O mother! Whose sin has led to your becoming a servant? Did my father do something? Was it I? Was it someone else? I am asking you about the reason. Please tell me." She spoke to her beloved son, Aruna's younger brother.[965] Vinata replied, "No one else committed the sin.

---

[964] Royal sages.

[965] Vinata's sons were Aruna and Garuda. Kadru and Vinata were married to the sage Kashyapa. The *naga*s were Kadru's children. Kadru and Vinata had an argument about the colour of Ucchaihshrava's tail. Vinata said it was white. Kadru said it was black. Kadru asked her children, the

It is my own fault. It is I who said, 'The person whose words are false will become a servant.' Kadru and I went there together. Kadru and I had an argument and I was deceitfully defeated by her. O son! Destiny is powerful. What does it not do? O Kashyapa's son! In this way, I became Kadru's servant. I gave birth to you when I was a servant. O son of a brahmana! Thus, you also became a servant." Extremely sad, Garuda was silent. He didn't speak to his mother. He thought about what was inevitable.'

'On one occasion, thinking about the welfare of her sons and her own prosperity, Kadru spoke to Vinata, the mother of birds. Kadru said, "Without being restrained, your son goes to Surya and bows down to him. Even though you are a servant, in the three worlds, you are blessed." She was extremely surprised at this. But hiding her own misery, she spoke to Kadru. Vinata replied, "Why don't your sons go and see Ravi?"[966] Kadru replied, 'O extremely fortunate one! Please take my sons to the abode of the nagas. That extremely cool lake is near the ocean." Suparna[967] carried the nagas, Kadru and Vinata. Delighted, she spoke to his mother, Vinata. "Let Garuda take my sons to the abode of the gods." Humbly, the mother of the snakes again spoke to Garuda. The mother of the snakes said, "My sons desire to see Hamsa,[968] the preceptor of the three worlds. After bowing down to him, they should be returned to my residence. O Vinata! Let my sons be taken to Surya's circle every day." Trembling, the miserable Vinata spoke to Kadru. Vinata said, "O mother of the snakes! I am incapable of doing this. My son will take your sons. After seeing the god who creates the day, let them return." Vinata spoke to her own son, the lord of the birds. "Through deceit, the nagas have become masters. The mother of the snakes has told me that they wish to bow down to the radiant one." Agreeing to this, Garuda replied, "Let the pannagas climb atop me." Thereupon, the snake soldiers climbed onto Garuda, the lord

---

nagas, to coil around the tail, so that it seemed black. Thus, Vinata lost the bet.

[966] Ravi is one of Surya's names.

[967] Garuda.

[968] In this context, the word Hamsa is being used to mean Surya.

of the birds. Very slowly, they approached the place where the god Divakara[969] was. They were scorched by Bhanu's fierce heat and were distressed. The snakes said, "O immensely wise one! O bird! We bow down to you. Return. Enough of bowing down to Surya in his abode. We are being burnt down by Surya's energy. O Garuda! We will leave, with or without you." When the *naga*s said this, he replied, "I will show you Aditya." Saying this, he swiftly sped through the sky, in Aditya's direction. The serpents were burnt and fell down on the island of Virana. Several hundreds of thousands suffered. Their bodies were scorched. Kadru heard the screams of her sons, falling down on the surface of the earth. Extremely anxious, she arrived there, so as to comfort them. Kadru told Vinata, "Your son has committed a very wicked deed. His intelligence is evil and they are unable to find peace. One should never act against the words of the lord Phanishvara.[970] Had the extremely energetic Kashyapa been here, he would have found a means to free them of this suffering. O beautiful one! How can my sons find peace?" Hearing Kadru's words, Vinata was extremely scared. She spoke to her great-souled son Garuda, the lord of the birds. Vinata said, "O son! This is not worthy of you. It has been said that humility is an ornament. Its opposite is not appropriate. A virtuous person must never be treacherous, not even towards enemies. The moon shines equally over learned *brahmana*s and *antyaja*s. O son! The worst among men are incapable of using force to do anything directly. Therefore, they cause harm through deceit." Vinata then asked the mother of the snakes how this could be countered. Vinata asked, "How can I ensure peace for your sons? I will do that. Old age has seized them. Please tell me. How can I ensure peace for them?" Kadru told Vinata, "There is water in Rasatala. If my sons are sprinkled with that, they will find peace." Hearing her words, he[971] immediately brought water from Rasatala and sprinkled the *naga*s with this. After this, Garuda spoke to Maghavan Shatakratu.

---

[969] The creator of the day, Surya's name. Bhanu is also Surya's name.

[970] What his means is unclear. Literally, Phanishvara means lord of the serpents (hooded ones). It is possible that Phanishvara means Shiva.

[971] Garuda.

Garuda said, "The clouds do good deeds to the three worlds. Let them shower down here." To ensure auspiciousness for the *naga*s, the clouds showered down. Ganga's water was brought from Rasatala and brought life to the *naga*s. Garuda brought it, for the purpose of destroying misery and old age. The place where the *naga*s were sprinkled is known as the abode of the *naga*s. Garuda brought water from Rasatala there. For everyone, that water from Ganga destroys every kind of sin. With old age countered, everything was auspicious for the *naga*s. Brought from Rasatala, Ganga's water revived life for the *naga*s. The place is on Ganga's southern bank and destroys misery and old age. The river Vanjara flowed from this and it is like a flow of *amrita* itself. It destroys old age, poverty, torment and hardships. This is a confluence between Ganga from Rasatala and the Ganga who is in the mortal world. How can anyone describe it? Even if one remembers it, the store of sins is destroyed. Which lord is capable of describing the fruits that result from bathing and donating there? Learned men say that there is an aggregate of one hundred and twenty-five thousand *tirtha*s there. They bestow every kind of prosperity and destroy every kind of sin. There is no *tirtha* that can match the confluence of Vanjara. Even if one remembers it, calamities and adversities are destroyed.'

Chapter 2(90) (Devagama *tirtha*)

Brahma said, 'The *tirtha* known as Devagama is auspicious and bestows everything that is desired. It bestows objects of pleasure and emancipation on men. It provides satisfaction to the ancestors. I will describe what happened there. O Narada! Listen attentively. For the sake of wealth, there was rivalry between the gods and the *asura*s. The gods obtained heaven and the *asura*s obtained the earth. Having obtained *karma bhumi*, the *asura*s spread everywhere. The *asura*s killed those who offered shares in sacrifices to the gods. All the categories of gods were deprived of their shares in sacrifices. Distressed, they came to me and asked, "What should be done?" I told the large number of gods, "Use your strength to defeat the *asura*s in a battle. When you obtain the earth, you will also get the rites, the oblations and fame." Addressed in this way, the gods went to earth, desiring to fight. The *daitya*s, *danava*s and *rakshasa*s were proud of their strength. They united and fought. They wished to fight and be victorious. Ahi, Vritra, Tvashta's son,[972] Namuchi, Shambara, Maya—there were these and many other warriors, proud of their strength. There were Agni, Indra, Varuna, Tvashta, Pusha, the two Ashvins, the Maruts and the guardians of the worlds—accomplished in fighting in diverse ways. In the battle, all the *danava*s stationed themselves in the southern direction. Resorting to the shores of the southern ocean, they made great efforts. Earlier, Trikuta, best among mountains, belonged to the *rakshasa*s. Together, all of them went southwards, to the forest. All of them gathered together at the place where Mount Malaya is. This region around Malaya also belonged to the enemies of the gods. The gods gathered along the banks of Goutami, because Shiva is present there. Since they gathered there, that place is named after *deva*s. Astride their own chariots, *deva*s arrived there. They came to the banks of Goutami, mother of rivers, whose waters are sparkling. When she is pleased, she grants everything that is desired, to the ancestors and to everyone else. After this, the large number of gods praised the divinity Maheshvara. They thought, and discussed with each other, how they might obtain freedom from fear. The gods said, "What method will we use? Will we be defeated by the enemy? This alone is best for us—victory or defeat. Shame on spirited people who still remain alive after being overcome by their enemies." O son! At this time, an invisible voice was heard. The voice from the sky said, "O large number of gods! Enough of this hardship. Quickly go to Goutami. Devotedly, worship the two lords there, Hari and Hara. If Godavari and those two are pleased, what is extremely difficult to obtain?" Hari and Isha were pleased and because of them, the gods obtained victory. Having obtained everything, the residents of heaven departed, protecting everything. The place where the gods arrived is famous as a *tirtha*.[973] The sages

---

[972] That is, Trishira.

[973] *Devagama* means the arrival (*agama*) of the gods (*deva*).

who know about the truth praise Devagama. O Narada! There are
eighty thousand Shiva *lingam*s there. The mountain of Devagama
is known as Priya.[974] Since then, that *tirtha* has also been known as
Devapriya.'

Chapter 2(91) (Kushatarpana *tirtha*)

Brahma said, 'The place known as Kushatarpana is also known
as the confluence of Pranita. Among all the *tirtha*s in the worlds,
this is the one that bestows objects of pleasure and emancipation.
I will describe its nature. Listen to the auspicious account that
destroys all sins. On the southern flank of Vindhya, there is the great
mountain known as Sahya. Rivers arise from its feet, Godavari and
Bhimarathi being the foremost.[975] The place where Ekavira arose
is Viraja. No one is capable of describing its greatness. I will tell
you about the sacred region on that mountain. O Narada! Listen
attentively. I will tell you about what is the greatest secret among all
secrets. This auspicious account is directly mentioned in the Vedas.
Even the sages, gods, ancestors and *asura*s do not know about
this. To please you, I will tell you about it. As soon as one hears
this, everything desired is obtained. The supreme one is known
as Purusha and it is without decay. The inferior one is subject to
decay and is with Prakriti.[976] The Purusha with form originated
from the Purusha who was without form. Water was born from
him and Purusha originated from water.[977] O sage! From both of

[974] *Priya* means loved.

[975] The Godavari's origin is in Tryambakeshvara. The Bhimarathi's
(Bhima) origin is in Bhimashankara. The Ekavira temple is in Virar, where
the river is known as Vaitarani. *Viraja* means without dust. Sahyadri
(literally Sahya mountain) means the Western Ghats.

[976] There is thus the notion, as in the Bhagavad Gita, of Akshara
Purusha (without decay) and Kshara Purusha (with decay).

[977] This sounds inconsistent. It probably means that water originated
from the Purusha who was without form and the Purusha with form
originated from water.

them,[978] a lotus was born and I originate from that. O sage! Earth, wind, space, water and fire were created before me and originated simultaneously. I saw only these. There was nothing else, mobile or immobile. The Vedas did not exist then. I could see nothing. I could not even see what I had originated from.[979] When I remained silent, I heard these excellent words. The voice from the sky said, "O Brahma! Create the universe and the mobile and immobile objects." O Narada! At this, I replied to Purusha's voice. "How will I create? What will I create? With what will I create the universe?" The voice replied, "The goddess known as Prakriti has been sent by Vishnu. She is the mother of the universe and she pervades the universe." The voice from the sky continued, "There is no doubt that you will have the capacity if you undertake a sacrifice. O Brahma! The eternal shruti texts say that Yajna[980] is Vishnu. Through a sacrifice, what cannot be accomplished in this world or in the next world?" I again asked the goddess, "Where will I undertake it and with what? Please tell me. O immensely fortunate one! How will the rites of the sacrifice be undertaken?" The voice from the sky replied to me. She is the goddess who assumes the form of Omkara. She is thought of as the mother. She pervades the universe. "In *karma bhumi*, perform a sacrifice to the lord of sacrifices. He is the being personified in sacrifices. He is the means and instrument. O one excellent in vows! Undertake a sacrifice to him. He is the sacrifice, *svaha, svadha, mantra*s, the chief priest, oblations and other things. Hari alone is everything. Everything is obtained through Vishnu." I again asked the goddess, "What is described as *karma bhumi*?" O Narada! At that time, there was no Bhagirathi or Narmada. There was no Yamuna, Tapi, Sarasvati or Goutami. There were no oceans, male rivers, lakes, or sparkling female rivers. Shakti repeatedly spoke to me again. The divine voice said, "The region beyond the southern slope of Sumeru, to the south of Mount Himalaya, to the south of Vindhya and to the south of Sahya is *karma bhumi*. It always brings everything auspicious to everyone, all the time." Having heard her words, I abandoned Meru, the great mountain.'

[978] Water and the Purusha with form.
[979] That is, the lotus.
[980] Sacrifice.

'I went to that region and wondered, "Where will I stay?" At this, Vishnu's invisible voice spoke to me. The voice from the sky said, "Leave this place. Stay there. Sit down here. Take the resolution to undertake a sacrifice. The sacrifice will be completed. O supreme among gods! For the sake of the sacrifice, take the resolution. Do everything else that is recommended in all the Vedas." On their own, *itihasa*, Puranas and everything else that is articulated through sound surfaced in my memory and issued through my mouth. In an instant, I got to know all the meanings of the Vedas. I remembered *Purusha sukta*,[981] famous in the worlds. I devised everything that is spoken about as a component of a sacrifice. Following the recommended means, I devised the vessels for the sacrifice. I purified myself, controlled my *atman* and remained in a certain place. I consecrated myself in that region. That spot is known as a region of *brahmanas*. It is named after me. O great sage! I undertook a sacrifice in that sacred place. After my name, it is remembered as Brahmagiri. It extends for twenty-four *yojana*s. Brahmagiri is to the east of the sacred place where I performed the sacrifice. The sacrificial altar was in the middle. I devised the *garhapatya*, *dakshinatya* and *ahavaniya* fires. The indications in the *shruti* texts are that a sacrifice is not successful without a wife. O sage! Therefore, I divided my body into two. For the success of the sacrifice, the part to the left became my wife. I remained the part to right. The *shruti* texts speak of her as Jaya. O Narada! As the best form of oblations of *ghee*, I devised the period of Vasanta.[982] I thought of Grishma as kindling and Sharad as oblations. O son! I thought of the season of Varsha as the *barhi* grass. The seven *chandas*[983] were thought of as the sticks laid around the sacrifice.

---

[981] *Purusha sukta*, also found in *Shukla Yajur Veda* and *Atharva Veda*, is hymn 10.90 of *Rig Veda*.

[982] The six seasons (*ritus*) are *vasanta* or spring (Chaitra and Vaishakha), *grishma* or summer (Jyeshtha and Ashadha), *varsha* or monsoon (Shravana and Bhadrapada), *sharad* or early autumn (Ashvina and Kartika), *hemanta* or late autumn (Margashirsha/Agrahayana and Pousha) and *shishira* or winter (Magha and Phalguna).

[983] The seven metres (*chandas*) used in the Vedas—Gayatri, Ushnih, Anushtubh, Brihati, Pankti, Trishtubh and Jagati.

Kala, *kashtha* and *nimesha*[984] were thought of as kindling, vessels and *kusha* grass. O *devarshi*! Kala[985] is without a beginning and without an end. He himself assumed the form of the sacrificial altar, to which, the sacrificial animal would be tied. The three *guna*s, *sattva* and the others, became the ropes. But there was no sacrificial animal. Therefore, I spoke to Vishnu's invisible voice. "Without a sacrificial animal, the sacrifice cannot be completed." The eternal goddess, the disembodied voice, replied. The voice from the sky said, "Use Purusha *sukta* to praise the supreme Purusha." Thus addressed, I praised Janardana, the lord of the gods, the one who was my origin. I devotedly used Purusha *sukta*. The goddess then told me, "O Brahma! Make me your sacrificial animal." I then got to know that the undecaying Purusha was my father. I tied him next to the sacrificial post, which was in the form of time, and tethered him with the noose of the *guna*s. I stood outside. Inside, Purusha stood in front of me, as the consecrated sacrificial animal. Meanwhile, everything in the universe originated from him. *Brahmana*s originated from his mouth and *kshatriya*s from his arms. Indra and Agni originated from his mouth, *prana* from his breath. The directions were born from his ears, heaven was born from his head. Everything originated in this way. The moon was born from his mind, the sun was born from his eyes, the firmament was born from his navel and the *vaishya*s were born from his thighs. The shudras were born from his feet. The earth was also born from his feet. The *rishi*s were born from his body hair, the herbs from his hair. All the wild and domestic animals were born from his nails. Worms, insects and flying insects were born from his anus and genital organs. All the mobile and immobile objects are everything seen and unseen were thus born from him. The gods were born through me. Meanwhile, Vishnu's divine voice spoke to me. The voice from the sky said, "Everything has been completed. The desired creation has taken place. Now offer all the vessels and implements into the fire. Cast aside the sacrificial post, the sacrificial cup and the *kusha*

---

[984] All three are units for measuring time. The unit for measuring time is *kalaa*. Time/destiny is Kaala.

[985] Time/destiny.

grass. O Brahma! Cast aside everything—the forms of the officiating priest and sacrificial objects you had thought of, the sacrificial ladle, Purusha and the noose." O great sage! I gradually did everything that the origin of the sacrifice had asked me to do. I progressively offered them into the *garhapatya*, *dakshinatya* and *ahavaniya* fires as oblations. I meditated on Purusha, the origin of the universe, who had been sanctified with the *mantras*. He is the lord of the sacrifice, who pervades the universe. He is the protector of the world, the creator of the universe. I saw him near the sacrificial pit. In the *ahavaniya* fire, Vishnu was white in form. In the *dakshinatya* fire, Vishnu was dark in form. In the *garhapatya* fire, the wise one was yellow in form. Vishnu was present everywhere, all the time. There is nothing without Vishnu. He is the cause of the universe. I pronounced the *mantras* over the water in the sacrificial cup, used for consecration. The water from the sacrificial cup became the auspicious river, Pranita.[986] I cleaned the sacrificial cup with *kusha* grass and cast it aside. When it was cleaned, drops of water fell from the sacrificial cup. *Tirthas*, excellent in qualities, originated at the place where those drops fell. O tiger among sages! Bathing in the river that originated, yields the fruits of all sacrifices. The wielder of the Sharnga bow, the lord of the gods, ornaments it all the time. For everyone, the flight of steps represents ascent to Vaikuntha. The auspicious *kusha* grass used for cleaning fell down on the ground. That place is known as Kushatarpana. It yields the fruits of many good merits. It is known as Kushatarpana because everyone was satisfied with *kusha* grass.[987] O immensely intelligent one! Later, for a different reason, Goutami merged with Pranita and the confluence of Pranita resulted. In the region known as Kushatarpana, the *tarpana* with *kusha* grass was performed. It is there that I devised the sacrificial post, to the north of Vindhyas. The place where I cast it aside is a spot resorted to by Vishnu and is worshipped by all the worlds. The auspicious place is without

---

[986] *Pranita* is the sacrificial cup. It also means something that has been brought forward.

[987] *Tarpana* (satisfaction) with *kusha* grass.

decay. Hence, there is an Akshaya Vata there.[988] It is in the form
of time and is eternal. The act of remembering it yields the fruits
of all sacrifices. The place where I performed the sacrifice is known
as Dandakaranya. When the sacrifice was complete, I faithfully
sought Vishnu's favours there. All pure deeds originated from
the being known as Virat in the Vedas. I was born from him and
he is the one who created this universe. I honoured the divinity
who is the lord of the gods and cast him aside. The place where I
performed the divine and auspicious sacrifice extends for twenty-
four *yojana*s. O Narada! Even today, there are three sacrificial pits
there. They are in the form of the lord of sacrifices, Vishnu, the
one who holds the *chakra* in his hand. Since then, the place where
I performed the sacrifice has been famous. Even worms and insects
obtain emancipation there. Dandakaranya is said to be the seed of
dharma and the seed of emancipation. In particular, the region that
touches Goutami is most sacred. If a person bathes and undertakes
other rites in the confluence of Pranita or in Kushatarpana, he
proceeds to the supreme destination. It should be known that if a
man remembers, reads or hears it faithfully, he obtains everything
that he desires. It is a place that bestows objects of pleasure and
emancipation. Along both banks, the learned say that there are
eighty-six thousand *tirtha*s. The sacredness of these places has
already been described. O sage! Kushatarpana is superior to even
Varanasi. Among all mobile and immobile entities, there is no other
tirtha that is its equal. Even if one remembers it, sins like the killing
of a brahmana are destroyed. O sage! On the surface of the earth,
that *tirtha* is spoken of as a gate to heaven.'

Chapter 2(92) (Manyu *tirtha*)

Brahma said, 'The place known as Manyu *tirtha* destroys every
kind of sin. It bestows everything desired on men. Even if it is
remembered, it destroys sins. I will describe its powers. O sage!

---

[988] *Vata* is the Indian fig tree and *akshaya* means without decay.

Listen attentively. Earlier, there was a battle between the gods and the *danava*s. In this, the gods were defeated and the *danava*s were victorious. Dispirited, the large number of gods withdrew from the battle. They came to me and said, "Please grant us freedom from fear." I told them, "All of you go to Ganga. On the banks of Goutami, praise the divinity Maheshvara. He is the beautiful one, the one who bestows bliss with no effort or with a little bit of effort. O gods! From Maheshvara, all of you will obtain means to ensure victory." Agreeing to this, the large number of gods praised Maheshvara. Some of them tormented themselves through austerities. Others danced. Some bathed him,[989] others worshipped him. The illustrious Maheshvara, who holds the trident in his hand, was pleased. Pleased, he told the gods, "Tell me what you desire." The gods replied to the lord of the gods, "For the sake of victory, give us a being who is greatly praiseworthy. He will stand before us in the battle. Resorting to the strength of his arms, we will be happy." The illustrious Maheshvara told the gods that he agreed to this. Through his own energy, Parameshthi created a being known as Manyu. He was fierce and he would lead the soldiers of the gods. Having obtained him, all the gods bowed down to Shiva and returned to their own abodes, along with Manyu.'

'They decided to fight again. When they stood in the field of battle, the *danava*s and the *daitya*s were extremely strong. Cladding themselves in armour, the gods stood in front of Manyu and spoke to him. The gods said, "Show us your capacity. After that, we will fight with the enemy. O Manyu! We wish to fight. But show us what you can do." Hearing the words of the gods, Manyu smiled as he spoke. Manyu replied, "The one who created me is the lord of the gods. He knows everything. He is the lord who sees everything. He knows the abodes and names of everyone and what is in their minds. He always knows everything. But there is no one who knows him. He is the creator who pervades the universe. He is without form, but knows everything that has form. He is himself the supreme and illustrious one. He is in heaven and in the firmament. Who is capable of knowing his form? He is the creator

[989] Bathed the *lingam*.

who pervades the universe. I have originated from someone like him. How are you worthy of knowing me? However, if you still wish to see me, behold." Having said this, Manyu showed them his own great form. He had originated from Parameshthi Bhava's third eye. That form was an aggregate of all the energy that is spoken about. He is manliness in men. He is ego in human beings. He is the terrible anger in everyone.[990] He is the one who causes destruction. Shankara's representative blazed in his own energy. He wielded every kind of weapon. On seeing him, all the gods prostrated themselves before him. The *daityas* and *danavas* were terrified and the gods joined their hands in salutation. They said, "O Manyu! Please be the leader of our soldiers. O Manyu! We will enjoy the kingdom that you bestow upon us. You are victorious in all your deeds. You are the one who enhances victory. Therefore, you are Indra. You are Varuna. Indeed, you are the guardians of the worlds. For the sake of victory, enter all of us gods." Manyu told all of them, "Without me, there is nothing. I enter and am inside everyone. However, no one ever knows me." Manyu was the illustrious one himself, originating in separate forms. He is the one in the form of Rudra. Rudra is Manyu and Shiva. Everything mobile and immobile is pervaded by Manyu. Having obtained him, all the gods were victorious in the battle. Victory, Manyu and valour originated from Isha's energy. In the battle, through Manyu, they obtained victory over the *daityas*. Protected by Manyu, all of them then returned to wherever they had come from. There is a place where the gods worshipped Shiva on the banks of Goutami. That is the spot where they obtained Manyu and victory and it is known as Manyu *tirtha*. If a man controls himself and remembers Manyu and his origin, he is victorious and no one can defeat him. O great sage! There is no place as purifying as Manyu *tirtha*. In the form of Manyu, Shankara himself is always present there. Bathing and donations there and remembering it, bestows everything that is wished for.'

---

[990] The word *manyu* means both anger and mettle.

Chapter 2(93) (Shveta Parvata)

Brahma said, 'The *tirtha* named Sarasvata bestows the fruits of everything that is desired. It confers objects of pleasure and emancipation on men. It destroys every kind of sin. It destroys every kind of disease. It bestows every kind of success. O Narada! Therefore, listen to its account in detail. On the eastern side of Pushpotkata, there is a mountain that is famous in the worlds. That best among mountains is named Shubhra and it is on Goutami's southern bank. Shakalya was a famous sage and he was extremely devoted. He tormented himself through excellent austerities on sacred Mount Shubhra. Resorting to the banks of Goutami, the best among *brahmanas* practiced austerities there. All the large number of beings always prostrated themselves before him and praised him. He was devoted to serving the fire and devoted to studying the Vedas. He did this on the extremely sacred mountain which gave gods and *brahmanas* freedom from fear. There was a *rakshasa* named Parashu. He hated sacrifices and killed *brahmanas*. He could assume any form at will and roamed around in the forest, assuming many different forms. In an instant, he would assume the form of a brahmana. Sometimes, he would assume the form of a tiger. Sometimes, he would assume the form of a god. Sometimes, he would assume the form of an animal. Sometimes, he would assume the form of a woman. Sometimes, he would assume the form of a deer. Sometimes, he would assume the form of a child. In this way, the evil-doer wandered around.'

'The extremely wicked Parashu, worst among *rakshasa*s, arrived at the place where Shakalya, the learned brahmana who was supreme among sages, was. Parashu always went there, intent on abducting or killing the pure and best among *brahmanas*. However, though he tried, the evil-doer was unable to do this. On one occasion, after carefully worshipping the gods, the best among *brahmanas* wished to eat. O sage! At that time, Parashu arrived there, assuming the form of a brahmana who was weak, grey-haired and feeble. He had a maiden with him. He addressed Shakalya in these words. Parashu said, "O brahmana! Know that this maiden and I wish for some food. O one who bestows honours! We have come at the time when guests should be tended to. Please do what needs to be done. In this world, those who have homes where the wishes for guests are met are blessed. When they leave, others are as good as dead, even if they are alive.[991] Having sat down to eat, if a person gives away to guests what he has earmarked for himself, it is as if he has given away the entire earth." Shakalya did not know that Parashu was only disguised as a brahmana. Hearing this, he made him sit on a seat and replied, "I will give." Shakalya followed the norms, worshipped him and gave him food. Taking water for rinsing in his hand, Parashu spoke the following words. Parashu said, "From a distance, the gods follow a tired guest. When he is satisfied, they are satisfied. If they are not satisfied, there is a calamity. The guest and the slanderer—these two are the relatives of the universe. The slanderer destroys sins and the guest bestows heaven.[992] If a person looks at a guest, who is exhausted from travelling along the road, with indifference, his *dharma*, fame and prosperity are instantly destroyed. O supreme among *brahmanas*! Therefore, as an exhausted guest, I am seeking from you. I will eat if you grant me what I desire, not otherwise." Shakalya told the *rakshasa*, "I will give you. Please eat." At this, Parashu replied, "I am Parashu, a supreme *rakshasa*. I am your enemy. I am not an aged and emaciated brahmana with grey hair. I have spent many years, looking at you. My limbs are drying up, like a small body of water during the summer. O supreme among *brahmanas*! Therefore, I will take away you and your followers and eat you." Hearing Parashu's words, Shakalya addressed him in the following words. Shakalya said, "Those born in extremely great lineages and those who know all the *agama* texts act according to their pledges, never in a contrary way. O friend! Do what is appropriate. But listen to my words. Even if a person is ready to kill you, excellent words that are good for his welfare must be stated. I am a brahmana and my body is like the *vajra*. Hari protects me in every direction. Let Vishnu protect my feet and let the divinity Janardana protect my

---

[991] If the guests leave without their wishes having been met.
[992] When the slanderer does not slander and the guest is satisfied.

head. Let Varaha protect my arms and let Dharmaraja[993] protect
my back. Let Krishna protect my heart and let the animal[994] protect
my fingers. Let the lord of speech protect my mouth and let the
one who travels on the bird[995] protect my eyes. Let the lord of
riches protect my ears and let Bhava protect me in every direction.
In many kinds of hardship, the divinity Narayana is himself the
refuge." Saying this, Shakalya continued, "As you wish, take me, or
eat me. O Indra among *rakshasa*s! O Parashu! Be attentive now."
Hearing his words, the *rakshasa* prepared to devour him. Indeed,
there is not the slightest bit of compassion in the hearts of sinners.'

'With a mouth that had terrible fangs, he approached near.
Looking at the brahmana, Parashu spoke these words. Parashu
said, "O supreme among *brahmanas*! I see you as one who holds
the conch shell, the *chakra* and the mace in your hands. You are the
lord with one thousand feet and heads. You possess one thousand
eyes and hands. You are the single refuge for all beings. Your
form is that of the Vedas. You pervade the universe. O brahmana!
When I look at you now, you no longer possess your former body.
O brahmana! Therefore, I am trying to please you. You alone are
the refuge. O immensely intelligent one! Grant me *jnana*. Tell me
about a *tirtha* that can free me of my sins. O brahmana! Visiting a
great person is never futile, even if it is done out of hatred, ignorance
or distraction. When a piece of iron touches gold, it too assumes
that form." He heard the words that the *rakshasa* had spoken. Full
of compassion, Shakalya replied, "Sarasvati is the one who bestows
boons. O lord of the *daitya*s! Therefore, without any delay, praise
Janardana. To accomplish one's wishes, there is nothing other
than the praising of Narayana. But, in this world, there is another
cause too. O *rakshasa*! Listen. If the goddess is pleased, my words
will come true." Addressed in this way, Parashu bathed in Ganga,
who purifies the three worlds. He purified and controlled his mind
and stood, facing Ganga. There, he saw Sarasvati, mother of the
universe. She was divine in form and was adorned with divine

---

[993] Yama.
[994] Meaning Narasimha.
[995] Garuda.

fragrances and unguents. He followed Shakalya's words and stood there. She is the one who removes all inactivity from the universe. She is Bhuvaneshvari, the mother of the universe. Cleansed of his sins, Parashu addressed her humbly. Parashu said, "My *guru* Shakalya told me to praise the one the one who has the bird on his standard, loved by you.[996] Through your favours, please act so that I have that capacity." The illustrious Sarasvati told Parashu that she granted him this. Through Sarasvati's favours, Parashu used many kinds of words to praise Hari. Janardana, the ocean of compassion, was pleased and granted the *rakshasa* boons. Janardana said, "O *rakshasa*! Everything that is in your mind will occur." Though the rakshasa Parashu was a sinner, through the favours of Shakalya, through the favours of Goutami, through the favours of Sarasvati and through the favours of Narasimha, he went to heaven. He went there through the favours of the one who wields the Sharnga bow, whose lotus feet represent all *tirtha*s. Since then, that place has been known as Sarasvata *tirtha*. If one bathes or donates there, one obtains greatness in Vishnu's world. Through the powers of the goddess of speech, Vishnu, Shakalya and Parashu, there are many *tirtha*s in Shveta Parvata.'[997]

Chapter 2(94) (Chinchika *tirtha*)

Brahma said, 'The place known as Chinchika *tirtha* destroys every kind of disease. It dispels every kind of worry. It bestows every kind of peace on men. I will describe its nature. That white and excellent mountain is on the northern bank of Ganga and the divinity Gadadhara[998] is present there. There was a *bherunda*[999] who was a king of birds and he was known as Chinchika. He always lived there, on Mount Shveta, and ate flesh. It was full of many kinds

---

[996] That is Vishnu, with Garuda on the standard.

[997] *Parvata* means mountain.

[998] The one who holds the mace, Vishnu.

[999] An awful species of bird.

of fruits and flowers. The mountain was covered with blossoms from every season. It was frequented by the best among birds and adorned by Goutami. It was full of *siddha*s, *charana*s, *gandharva*s, *kinnara*s and immortals. There was another mountain nearby and there were some bipeds and some quadrupeds there. They never suffered from disease, afflictions, hunger, thirst, worries and death. This mountain possessed such qualities and it was surrounded by a large number of many types of sages. There was a king of the eastern direction and he was known as Pavamana. The prosperous one was devoted to the *dharma* of *kshatriya*s and protected gods and *brahmana*s. With a large army and with his priest, he went to the forest. He happily enjoyed himself with charming women there, with dancing and the playing of musical instruments. He held a bow in his hand and was surrounded by those who loved hunting. On one occasion, wandering around in this way and exhausted, he arrived before a tree. It grew along Goutami's banks and was full of a large number of many kinds of birds. It was as if the lord of a house, who knows about *dharma*, was surrounded by those from all the *ashrama*s. Pavamana, supreme among kings, sought refuge at that excellent tree and rested. Surrounded by all these people, he looked at that excellent tree.'

'He saw a stout bird there. It was beautiful in form, but it possessed two mouths. It seemed to be worried and exhausted and the excellent king asked it. The king asked, "O bird with two mouths! Who are you? It is evident that you are full of thoughts. Here, there is no one who is miserable and afflicted. Where has this grief come upon you?" Comforted in its mind, the bird Chinchika sighed repeatedly and slowly spoke to King Pavamana. Chinchika said, "Others have no reason to fear me and I suffer no hardships on account of others. This place is full of many kinds of flowers and fruit. It is frequented by sages. Nevertheless, this mountain seems empty to me. That is the reason I am grieving. I never get any happiness. I am never satisfied. I never get any sleep. I cannot find peace. There is no end to this." Hearing what the two-mouthed bird's words, the king was amazed. The king asked, "What sin have you committed? Why is the mountain empty? On this excellent mountain, beings are satisfied with one mouth. Despite possessing two mouths, why are you not satisfied? Why have you been reduced to this state? Did you commit a sin in this birth or in an earlier one? Tell me everything truthfully. I will save you from this great fear." The bird Chinchika sighed and replied to the king. Chinchika said, "O Pavamana! I will tell you what happened earlier. Listen. I was a supreme brahmana, accomplished in the Vedas and the *Vedanga*s. I was born in a noble lineage and was known as a sage. But I loved quarrels and disturbed tasks. I would say one thing before a being and another thing when the back was turned. I was always unhappy at the prosperity of others. I used fraud to deceive the world. I was ungrateful and devoid of truth. I was accomplished in criticizing others. I caused harm to friends, masters and *guru*s. My conduct was full of insolence and I was extremely cruel. In my thoughts, words and deeds, I tormented many people. I always amused myself by causing violence to others. I always indulged in separating couples, destroying groups and breaking agreements. I acted without reflecting on it. I turned myself away from serving the learned. In the three worlds, there was no other sinner like me. Therefore, I was born with two mouths. Since I tormented others and made them miserable, I am now tormented by this grief. This mountain is empty for me. O lord of the earth! Hear some other words. They are in conformity with *dharma* and *artha*. One can suffer a sin equal to that from killing a brahmana, without having done that. During a battle, if a *kshatriya* kills someone who is fighting with another, someone who is fleeing, someone who has laid down his weapons, someone who is trusting,[1000] someone who is reluctant to fight, someone who does not know he is being attacked, someone who is seated, or someone who says he is scared—if a *kshatriya* kills any of these, that sin is like the sin of killing a brahmana. If a person forgets what he has studied, uses the word '*tvam*' for those who are superior,[1001] or shows dishonour towards *guru*s—that sin is like the sin of killing a brahmana. If a person uses pleasant words in

---

[1000] That is, someone caught unawares.

[1001] *Tvam* is to be used for equals or juniors, not for those who are superior. For them, the proper form of address is *bhavan/bhavati* (depending on the gender).

someone's presence, but harsh words behind his back; if he thinks
and says something, but always does the opposite; if he takes an oath
in the name of his *gurus* and hates them; if he criticizes *brahmanas*,
if his humility is false and if he is evil-souled—that sin is like the sin
of killing a brahmana. Out of hatred, if a person criticizes gods, the
Vedas, *adhyatma*, or an assembly of *brahmanas* devoted to *dharma*,
that sin is like the sin of killing a brahmana. O king! Because of pride
and shame,[1002] I was like that. O king! That is the reason I became a
bird. Despite being born like this, I must have performed some good
deed somewhere. O king! Because of that good deed, I remember
what I had done earlier." Hearing Chinchika's words, Pavamana
was extremely surprised. The king asked the bird, "Through what
deed can you be liberated?" Hearing these words, the king of birds
replied to the king.'

'Chinchika said, "On Goutami's northern bank, in this excellent
mountain, there is a *tirtha* named Gadadhara. It destroys every kind
of sin. O one excellent in vows! That *tirtha* is extremely sacred.
Please take me there. The great sages have said that it bestows
everything that is desired. In terms of destroying hardships, there
is nothing superior to Goutami and Vishnu. It is my view that with
every kind of sentiment, I should see that *tirtha*. Through my own
efforts, I am incapable of doing this. How else can those who have
performed evil deeds obtain what they wish for? O brave one! It
is extremely difficult to reach. Though I made efforts, I could not
see it. Through your favours, I should be able to see Gadadhara.
He is an ocean of compassion. I have told you the reason for my
misery. If men see him, they no longer suffer from the sorrows of
samsara. O one who is excellent in vows! Through your favours,
I will see him and go to heaven." The bird Chinchika thus told
the king what was in his mind and he showed the bird the divinity
and Ganga. Chinchika spoke to Ganga, the one who purifies the
three worlds. Chinchika said, "O Ganga! O Goutami! O one who
purifies the three worlds! In this world and in the next world, a man
is a sinner only as long as he has not seen you. O best among rivers!
Therefore, save me from everything. O one who has originated from

---

[1002] He hid his true nature out of shame.

Vishnu's lotus feet! For embodied beings in *samsara*, there is no refuge other than you." Thus, his *atman* purified through devotion, the bird sought refuge in Ganga. He bathed there, remembering the words, "O Ganga! Please save me." While the residents of the mountain watched, he prostrated himself before Gadadhara. Taking Pavamana's permission, he went to heaven. Along with his followers, Pavamana returned to his own city. Since then, that *tirtha* has been named after Pavamana and Chinchika. Those who know about the Vedas also know it as Gadadhara *tirtha* and Koti *tirtha*. The rites performed by men there, yield fruits that are crores and crores more in terms of qualities.'

Chapter 2(95) (Bhadra *tirtha*)

Brahma said, 'The place known as Bhadra *tirtha* counters every kind of harm. It destroys all sins and bestows great serenity. Usha, Tvashta's daughter, was Aditya's beloved wife. She was devoted to her husband. Chhaya was also Savitar's daughter and her son was Shanaihshchara.[1003] His sister was Vishti. She was extremely terrible and wicked in form. Savitar's mind turned to the question, "Who will I bestow this daughter on?" Whenever Surya, the lord and preceptor of the worlds, wished to bestow her on someone, hearing that she was terrible, said, "What will I do with such a wife?" While this was going on, extremely unhappy, she spoke to her father. Vishti said, "If a father bestows his daughter on an extremely beautiful person while she is still a child, he is successful in this world. If he doesn't do this, the father perpetrates a wicked deed. The father must undertake every effort to get his daughter married off after she is four years old, but certainly before she has completed her tenth year. The daughter must be bestowed on a groom who is prosperous, learned, young, famous and generous.

[1003] Aditya/Savitar means the sun-god. Usha is referred to as Samjna elsewhere. Shanaihshchara is Saturn. Bhaskara is one of Surya's names, as is Ravi.

He must be born in a good lineage and his father must be alive.
If a father acts contrary to this, he always descends into hell. O
Bhaskara! For the learned, a daughter is the means of accomplishing
dharma. However, for a foolish person whose mind is overwhelmed
by desire, she is also responsible for hell. In a balance, it is said that
an excellent and ornamented daughter, free from blemishes, is on
one side and the entire earth, with its mountains, forests and groves,
is on the other. If a person sells his daughter, a cow or sesamum,
nothing will be able to save him from Rourava and other hells. The
task of marrying off a daughter must never be negated. If a father
does not do this, who is capable of describing that sin? While the
daughter does not show shame and while she still plays with dust,
she should be given away. If not, the father descends downwards.
The son is the father's own form. The father is like the son. In this
world, who acts so as to not make himself happy? Donations,
rearing and worship that are done for the sake of a daughter
are good deeds. However, when she is given away, that brings
everlasting benefits. What is given to daughters at that time brings
infinite merits. O Ravi! Who does not act so as to make his sons
and grandsons happy? If a person acts for the sake of his daughters,
he becomes prosperous." Addressed by his daughter, Vishti, in this
way, Bhaskara replied to her. Surya said, "What will I do? Because
your form is terrible, no one will accept you. Whether it is for a
man or a woman, at the time of a matrimonial alliance, lineage,
beauty, youth, riches, conduct and good behaviour are considered.
O auspicious one! Except for your quality of beauty, we possess
everything. What will I do? Who will I bestow you on? Why are you
shaming me?" After saying this, Bhaskara spoke to Vishti again.
Surya continued, "O Vishti! Please grant me permission. If you allow
me, I will bestow you on whoever I can, today itself." Vishti replied
to her father, "A husband, sons, riches, happiness, a long lifespan,
beauty and joy, these are in accordance with what one has done
earlier. Whatever be a living being's *karma*, whatever good or bad
deeds the person has performed earlier, lead to fruits obtained by
the being in a subsequent birth. The father must lovingly only avoid
sins he commits. The fruits that result, depend on whatever has
been done earlier. Therefore, in bestowing through a matrimonial

alliance, a father must only consider what is appropriate for his own lineage. The rest is destiny. Whatever is going to happen, will happen." Tvashta heard the words of his daughter.'

'He bestowed his terrible daughter Vishti, who caused fear to the worlds, on Vishvarupa. Vishvarupa was also terrible and fierce in form. Thus, they were similar to each other in good, conduct, behaviour and beauty. Between the couple, on some occasions, there was love. On other occasions, there were differences. Their sons were Ganda, Atiganda, Raktaksha, Krodhana, Vyaya and Durmukha. The youngest was known as Harshana and this son was full of merits. He was good in conduct and extremely fortunate. He was serene, pure in intelligence and pure. On one occasion, he went to his maternal uncle's house, to visit him.[1004] He saw many beings, some in heaven and some miserable. He prostrated himself before his maternal uncle and asked him about eternal *dharma*. Harshana asked, "O father![1005] Who are the ones who are happy? Who are the ones who are being cooked in hell?" Asked in this way, Dharmaraja told him everything, accurately. He described everything about the course of *karma*. Yama replied, "Men who never violate what has been recommended, never see hell. Those who do not respect the sacred texts, those who do not possess good behaviour, those who are not extremely learned and those who violate what has been recommended, reside in hell." Hearing Dharmaraja's words, Harshana spoke again. Harshana said, "My father, Tvashta's son,[1006] is terrible. My mother, Vishti, is terrible. O supreme among the gods! Please tell me about the tasks I must now undertake to make them and my brothers great-souled, serene in intelligence, extremely handsome and devoid of taints. How will they bestow what is auspicious? Otherwise, I will not go back to them." Thus addressed, Dharmaraja spoke to Harshana, who was pure in his intelligence. "You are Harshana.[1007] There is no doubt

[1004] The maternal uncle is Yama.

[1005] The word used is *tata*. This means father, but is used for anyone who is senior.

[1006] That is, Vishvarupa.

[1007] Harshana means someone who causes delight.

about this. There may be many sons, but none among them may extend the lineage. But there may be a single son who holds up the lineage. The one who brings pleasure to his parents is the one who is the foundation of the lineage. A son who saves his ancestors is a true son, not one who acts otherwise. What you have asked me will also bring great joy to your maternal grandfather.[1008] Go to Goutami. Restrain your mind and bathe there. With a tranquil and happy mind, praise Vishnu, the origin of the universe. If he is pleased with you, he will grant you everything that you wish for." Hearing Dharma's words, Harshana went to Goutami. He purified himself and praised Hari, the lord of the gods. Hari was pleased and bestowed everything fortunate on Harshana's lineage. "Let everything be fortunate. Let everything unfortunate be destroyed." Therefore, Vishti is known as Bhadraa. Since the father became fortunate, the sons are known as Bhadras.[1009] Since then, that *tirtha* has been known as Bhadra *tirtha*. Bhadrapati Hari is present there and bestows everything auspicious on men. If men frequent that *tirtha*, it bestows every kind of success. The divinity Janaradana, the single ocean of everything auspicious, is himself present there.'

Chapter 2(96) (Patatri *tirtha*)

Brahma said, 'The place known as Patatri *tirtha* destroys disease and sins. As soon as a man hears about it, he becomes successful in his objective. Kashyapa had two sons—Aruna and the other was the lord of birds.[1010] Sampati was born in that lineage and Jatayu was younger to him. Tarkshya Prajapati's sons were Aruna and Garuda. Sampati, supreme among birds, was born in that lineage. The famous Jatayu was born as his younger brother. Both of them were intoxicated of their own strength and sought to rival each

---

[1008] Tvashta.

[1009] Bhadra/Bhadraa means fortunate. Bhadrapati means the lord of everything fortunate.

[1010] Garuda. Sampati and Jatayu were Aruna's sons.

other. They rose up into the sky, to bow down before the one who creates the day.[1011] Those two excellent birds approached Surya. But their wings were burnt down. Exhausted, they fell down on the summit of the mountain. Aruna saw that his relatives had fallen down. They were immobile and had lost their senses. Overwhelmed by misery, he spoke to Bhaskara. "Those born in our lineage have had their wings burnt down. They have fallen down on earth. O one with the fierce rays! Comfort them. Otherwise, they will die." Addressed in this way, the one who makes the day revived the two birds. Hearing about the state they had been reduced to, Garuda arrived there, along with Vishnu. O Narada! Having arrived, he comforted them and they were happy. To destroy the sin, all of them, Jatayu, Aruna, Sampati and Garuda, went to Ganga. To please them, Surya and Vishnu also went to the extremely sacred *tirtha*. Since then, that place has been known as Patatri *tirtha*.[1012] It destroys poison and yields everything that is desired. Surya, Vishnu, Suparna and Aruna are themselves present there, on the northern bank of Goutami. Vrishadhvaja is also present there. Since the three divinities[1013] are present there, it is an excellent *tirtha*. If one purifies oneself and bathes there, prostrating oneself before the gods, one is freed from all physical and mental ailments and obtains supreme happiness.'

Chapter 2(97) (Vipra Narayana *tirtha*)

Brahma said, 'There is a place known as Vipra *tirtha*. It is also known as Narayana *tirtha*. I will relate its account to you. It gives rise to great wonder. Listen. There was a brahmana in Antaravedi.[1014] The brahmana was accomplished in the Vedas. His

---

[1011] Surya is the one who creates the day.
[1012] *Patatri* means bird.
[1013] Vishnu, Shiva and Surya.
[1014] In East Godavari district, at the confluence of Vasishtha Godavari with the ocean.

sons were extremely wise and possessed qualities and beauty. Among
them, the youngest brother was serene and he was surrounded by
all the qualities. He was known as Asandiva. He was immensely
intelligent and possessed every kind of learning. The father made
efforts to get Asandiva married off. Meanwhile, at night, the
brahmana's son went to sleep without remembering Vishnu. He did
not control himself and his head was facing the north.[1015] There
was a terrible *rakshasa*,[1016] cruel in nature, who could assume any
form she wanted. She swiftly seized him and went to the southern
bank of Goutami. This was to the northern side of Shrigiri, a place
frequented by many *brahmanas*. This city was an abode of *dharma*.
It was Lakshmi's abode. The king there was Brihatkirti and he
possessed all the qualities of a *kshatriya*. The place was extremely
peaceful and there were many kinds of alms to be obtained. At
the end of the night, with the *brahmanas*'s son, she reached that
place. The *rakshasi* reached that city. She always assumed a radiant
and agreeable form. Assuming any form she willed, along with the
brahmana, she roamed around the entire earth. In the region that
was on the southern bank of Godavari, the terrible one assumed the
form of an aged woman and spoke to the brahmana. The *rakshasi*
said, "O best among *brahmanas*! This is Ganga and it is time for the
sandhya rites. Along with the best of *brahmanas*, undertake them.
If excellent *brahmanas* do not make efforts to perform the *sandhya*
rites at the right time, lords among sages say that when their lives
are over, they are born as the leaders of *antyajas*. Tell them that I
am your mother. If you do not do this now, you will be destroyed.
O Indra among *brahmanas*! If you act in accordance with my
words, I will do what brings you pleasure and make you happy.
You will again reach your own home and country and meet your
guru. I tell you truthfully.' The bull among *brahmanas* asked, 'Who
are you?" The *rakshasi* could assume any form at will. His senses
were in a whirl. She developed his trust and took many pledges.
She told the son of the leader among sages, "I am famous in this
world under the name of Kankalini." The brahmana replied, "I will

---

[1015] When sleeping, the head should face the south.
[1016] Female *rakshasa*.

do what you have asked me to do. There is no doubt that I will do and say what brings you pleasure." Hearing the brahmana's words, the *rakshasi*, who could assume any form at will, assumed a form that was pleasing in all its limbs. Though she was aged, she was adorned in celestial ornaments. She took the brahmana and roamed around everywhere. Everywhere, she said, "He is my son. He is an abode of qualities." This is what she did and said. The brahmana possessed beauty, good fortune and youth and was adorned with learning. They took her to be his aged mother, who possessed all the qualities.'

'There was a best among *brahmanas*. Honouring the *rakshasi*, he bestowed his daughter, adorned in ornaments, on the brahmana. Having obtained such a husband, the daughter thought that she was fortunate. However, the brahmana saw that his wife possessed all the qualities and was extremely miserable. The brahmana said, "This *rakshasi* is evil in nature. She may devour me. What will I do? Where will I go? Who will I tell this to? I confront a great calamity. Who will save me? My fortunate wife possesses beauty and qualities. This inauspicious *rakshasi* may devour her too." Meanwhile, the aged woman, impossible to assail, had gone somewhere. His wife possessed all the qualities. The maiden was devoted to her husband and was confident about his love. She got to know that her husband was miserable. In private, she humbly spoke to him. The wife asked, "O husband! Why has this sorrow come upon you? Please tell me." Gradually, he told his wife everything that had taken place earlier. To a beloved friend and a wife born in a noble lineage, what cannot be told? Hearing her husband's words, the supreme among eloquent ones spoke to him. The wife said, "If a person is not in control of himself, fear seizes him from every direction, even in his own home. If a person is in control of himself, what is there to fear, especially along the banks of Goutami? Those who are devoted to Vishnu reside here, those who are discriminating and non-attached. Purifying yourself and bathing here, praise the divinity, who bestows freedom from ailments." Hearing this, he bathed in Ganga and was freed from his sins. On Goutami's banks, the brahmana praised Narayana. The brahmana said, "You are inside the *atman* of the universe. O Mukunda! You are the

creator, the preserver and the destroyer. You are the protector. O
Narasimha! You are the protector of those who are distressed. If
you do not protect, how can there be protection?' Narayana is the
one who counters the misery of the universe. Hearing his prayer, he
used his radiant Sudarshana *chakra*, with one thousand edges, to
slay the evil *rakshasi*. The lord gave him his desired boons and he
reached his *guru* again. Since then, that *tirtha* has been known as
Vipra *tirtha* and Narayana *tirtha*.[1017] Through bathing, donations
and worship performed there, one obtains the desired success.'

Chapter 2(98) (Bhanu *tirtha*)

Brahma said, 'There is a *tirtha* named after Bhanu, Tvashta,
Maheshvara, Indra, Yama and Agni. It destroys every kind of
sin. There was a king known as Abhishtuta and he was handsome
to behold. He started to worship the gods by performing a sacred
horse sacrifice. There were sixteen officiating priests there.
Vasishtha and Atri were the foremost. "When a *kshatriya* is
performing the sacrifice, what should the sacrificial ground be
like? When a brahmana has consecrated himself for a sacrifice,
the king grants the land required for the sacrifice. However, when
a king has consecrated himself for a sacrifice, who will give it to
him? Who shall he ask? If he asks it from any of the *brahmanas*,
that will give rise to a sin. In particular, how will a *kshatriya* then
undertake the sacrifice?" In this way, the *brahmanas* discussed
this amongst themselves. The immensely wise Vasishtha, supreme
among those who knew about *dharma*, spoke. Vasishtha said,
"When a king consecrates himself for a sacrifice, the land should
be sought from Surya. 'O god! O Savitar! Please grant me the land
appropriate for undertaking a sacrifice to the gods. You are the
divine *kshatriya*. You are also the brahmana. O lord of beings! I
bow down before you.'[1018] To undertake an auspicious sacrifice for

---

[1017] *Vipra* means *brahmana*.
[1018] This should be the king's prayer.

the gods, the king should ask Savitar in this way. O king![1019] When you ask the lord Divakara in this way, he will give it to you." Abhishtuta agreed to this. Full of devotion, he praised Divakara. He asked Ravi, the lord of the gods, who has Hari, Isha and Aja in his *atman*. The king said, "O Savitar! I bow down before you. Please grant me a sacrificial ground to undertake a sacrifice to the gods." Surya is the divine *kshatriya*. He gave the lord of the earth the ground that was required. Savitar, the divinity who is the lord of the gods, said, "I will give." If a person undertakes a sacrifice in this way, he never comes to any harm. Thus, the horse sacrifice was performed by *brahmanas* who were accomplished in the Vedas. King Abhishtuta undertook the sacrifice and the place where Ravi gave the lord of the earth the land, for the sake of undertaking a sacrifice to the gods, is known as Bhanu *tirtha*. The excellent horse sacrifice was undertaken for the gods. The *daitya*s, *danava*s and others who destroyed sacrifices also arrived there, disguising themselves in the garb of *brahmanas*. All of them recite the Sama hymns. Therefore, the immensely wise ones did not bar their entry. Some of the *asura*s criticized the ladles, the vessels, the rings on the sacrificial posts, the Sama hymns, the drinking of *soma*, the oblations, the officiating priests and the king. Some flung objects away. Others laughed.'

'O sage! Other than Vishvarupa, no one got to know what they were attempting. Vishvarupa told his father, "These are *daitya*s." Hearing his son's words, Tvashta spoke to the gods. Tvashta said, "Take water and *darbha* grass and sprinkle it in every direction. 'All those who criticize the sacred sacrifice, the ladles and the *soma* are hereby removed by me.' While you do the sprinkling, say this." The large number of gods did what Tvashta had asked them to. All of them were reduced to ashes and fled. "Those extremely wicked ones have been slain by me." Saying this, he sprinkled the water. At this, the angry *daitya*s lost their lifespans and left the place where they had been stationed. The spot where Tvashta, the Prajapati of the worlds, sprinkled the water came to known as Tvashta *tirtha*. It destroys every kind of sin. Yama

[1019] Addressed to Abhishtuta.

slew the *daitya*s who were dislodged as a result of Tvashta's words. He angrily used his staff of destiny, his *chakra* and his noose of destiny. The spot where he killed the *daitya*s came to be known as Yama *tirtha*. There was the spot where the sacrifice was completed and a lot of *amrita* was offered as oblation into the fire. That is the place where the bearer of oblations[1020] was praised and pleased with the incessant flow of oblations, resembling a flight of arrows, at the great sacrifice. This came to be known as Agni *tirtha* and it yields the fruit of a horse sacrifice. Indra and the Maruts addressed the king in these auspicious words. "O king! In both the worlds, you will become a universal emperor. You will always be my beloved friend. There is no doubt about this." If a person performs water-rites at this Indra *tirtha*, in the mortal world, he is the one who is successful. In particular, to please the ancestors, water-rites must be performed in Yama *tirtha*. There is the spot where *brahmanas*, accomplished in all the rites, worshipped Shiva, full of devotion. This is known as Maheshvara *tirtha*. Maheshvara, who deserves worship, was worshipped with *mantra*s from the Vedas and ordinary *mantra*s, singing, dancing, the playing of musical instruments, the five articles of worship,[1021] many other objects, prostrating oneself on the ground, *dakshina*, incense, lamps, food, flowers, fragrances and scents. With single-minded attention, Vishnu, lord of the gods, and Shambhu were worshipped. The two lords of the gods were pleased and gave him powerful boons. Both of them granted King Abhishtuta objects of pleasure and emancipation. They also bestowed greatness on that excellent *tirtha*. Since then, that *tirtha* has been known as Vishnu *tirtha* and Shiva *tirtha*. Bathing and donating there, are known to yield everything that is wished for. If one remembers or reads about all these *tirtha*s, one is freed from all sins and goes to the cities of Shiva and Vishnu. In particular, bathing in Bhanu *tirtha* yields every kind of success. In that extremely sacred *tirtha*, there are another one hundred *tirtha*s.'

[1020] Agni.
[1021] Honey, *ghee*, molasses, curds, milk.

Chapter 2(99) (Bhilla *tirtha*)

Brahma said, 'The place known as Bhilla *tirtha* destroys ailments and destroys sins. It bestows devotion towards Mahadeva's two lotus feet. O immensely intelligent one! The sacred account that transpired there is the following. Listen. Along Ganga's southern bank, to the north of Shrigiri, Mahedeva is always present in the form of the *lingam* known as Adikesha. He is worshipped by the *rishi*s and bestows everything that is desired. There was a sage known as Sindhudvipa and he was extremely devoted to *dharma*. His brother, Veda, was a supreme *rishi*. He would always faithfully worship Adikesha, the three-eyed divinity who was the enemy of Tripura. When the sun reached midday, the discriminating Veda would go to a village, in search of alms. Whenever that excellent brahmana went, a hunter, who was extremely devoted to *dharma*, would always go to that excellent mountain for a hunt. As he willed, he would wander around in different places, killing animals. Exhausted, the hunter would place a bit of meat on the tip of his bow and come to the place where the lord Adikesha Shiva was. He would place the meat outside. He would go to Ganga and take some water in his mouth. He would return to Shiva. He would devotedly take some leaves in one hand. In the other hand, he would devotedly offer the meat as *naivedya*.[1022] The energetic Veda would have already arrived and worshipped Adikesha. He[1023] would kick away his offerings with his foot. Using the water in his mouth, he would bathe Shiva and worship the divinity with the leaves. He would offer the meat and say, "May Shiva be pleased with me." He knew nothing else except this auspicious devotion to Shiva. After this, he would return to wherever he had come from, taking the remaining meat with him. He would come and go every day, going this. Nevertheless, Isha was satisfied with him. Ishvara's ways are wonderful. Until Bhilla[1024] arrived, Shiva wouldn't be happy. Who is knowledgeable enough

[1022] Offering of food given to a god.

[1023] The hunter.

[1024] The word is being used as a proper name here. *Bhilla* is a mountain-dwelling tribe.

to measure the extent of Shiva's compassion towards his devotees?
In this way, every day, he worshipped Adikesha Shiva, along with
Uma. A long period of time passed.'

'Veda angrily exclaimed, "I worship Shiva in my wonderful
way, with *mantra*s and devotion. Which sinner destroys it? He
deserves to be killed by me. If a person causes injury to a *guru*,
a god, a brahmana, or a master, he deserves to be killed, even by
a sage. That apart, if a man causes injury to Shiva, he deserves to
be killed by everyone." Having decided this, the intelligent Veda,
Sindhu's[1025] younger brother, wondered. "Whose wicked act is this?
Who is the evil-souled sinner? I perform worship with divine and
wild flowers and auspicious roots, tubers and fruits. He destroys
that and performs another worship with meat and the leaves of
trees. He deserves to be killed by me. I will hide myself and see
the sinner who worships Ishvara in this way." The intelligent one
thought in this way. Meanwhile, as happened on earlier occasions,
the hunter arrived there. When he worshipped in the usual way,
Adikesha spoke to him. Adikesha said, "O hunter! O immensely
intelligent one! Are you exhausted? You have come after a long
time. O son! I am miserable without you. O son! I cannot find
any happiness. Rest." Veda heard the divinity say this and saw.
He was full of rage and wonder, but did not say anything. As he
did every day, the hunter completed his worship and returned to
his own abode. Full of anger, Veda approached Isha and spoke to
him. Veda said, "This hunter is evil in his acts. He doesn't possess
knowledge and doesn't know the rites. He is cruel and indulges
in violence towards creatures. He is ruthless towards all beings.
He belongs to an inferior class and is ignorant. In due order, he
has not learnt from his *guru*. He always does what should not be
done. He has not conquered the aggregate of the senses. However,
you have shown yourself to him and do not say anything to me.
O Isha! I am controlled in my vows and worship you according to
the norms, using *mantra*s. You are always my only refuge. I do not
have a wife and sons. The hunter worships you with tainted meat.
O illustrious one! Yet, you are pleased with him. This is extremely

[1025] That is, Sindhudvipa's.

extraordinary. I will punish Bhilla, who acts in this injurious way. Some are pleased with mild people. Others are pleased with evil-souled people. Therefore, there is no doubt that I will bring this rock down on your head." When Veda said this, Isha laughed and spoke to him. Adikesha said, "Wait till tomorrow. After that, bring the rock down on my head.' Agreeing to this, Veda used his hand to cast aside the rock. He controlled his rage and replied, 'I will do it tomorrow." When it was morning, he bathed and performed the other rites. As was customary, Veda performed the worship. He noticed a terrible flow of blood that had covered the *lingam*'s head. Veda was amazed. "What is this on the *lingam*'s head? This is a terrible omen. What does this mean?" He worried. He wiped it clean with clay, cow dung, *kusha* grass and water from Ganga. He then performed the worship, as he always did. Meanwhile, the hunter, free of blemishes, arrived there. He entered and saw Shankara Adikesha. He saw the wound on the *lingam*'s head, covered with blood. He saw and exclaimed, "What is this strange thing?" Saying this, he used sharp arrows to cut himself, one hundred times and one thousand times. "On seeing a master disfigured, which good person is capable of tolerating it?" He repeatedly reprimanded himself. "How could this have happened while I am alive? How has this calamity come to be? Alas! What kind of evil destiny is this?" Witnessing what he did, Mahadeva was greatly surprised. The illustrious one spoke to Veda, supreme among those who knew about the Vedas. Adikesha said, "O immensely intelligent one! Look at the hunter. He is full of true devotion. You touched my head with clay, *kusha* grass and water. O brahmana! But this one has offered himself up to me. Devotion, love and strength exist when there is discrimination. O supreme among *brahmanas*! That is the reason I bestow boons on him first and on you, later." The divinity Maheshvara asked the hunter to choose whatever boon he wished for. The hunter told the lord of the gods, "Let your *nirmalya* be given to us.[1026] O protector! Let this *tirtha* be named after me. As soon as this *tirtha* is remembered, let the fruits of all

[1026] The word *nirmalya* has a double meaning—purity, as well as offerings made to a god.

sacrifices be obtained." The lord of the gods agreed. Since then, that excellent *tirtha* has been known as Bhilla *tirtha*. It destroys the cause behind every kind of sin. It generates great devotion towards the illustrious Mahadeva's feet. Bathing and donating there, yield instant objects of pleasure and emancipation. Shiva also bestowed many kinds of boons on Veda.'

Chapter 2(100) (Chakshu *tirtha*)

Brahma said, 'The place known as Chakshu *tirtha* bestows beauty and good fortune. On the southern bank of Goutami, the divinity Yogeshvara is present there. On the summit of a mountain, there was a city known as Bhouvana. The king there was named Bhouvana and he was devoted to the *dharma* of *kshatriya*s. In that excellent city, there was a brahmana named Vriddha-Koushika. His son was known as Goutama and he was supreme among those who were learned in the Vedas. However, because of his mother's mental taints, this brahmana's tendencies were contrary. His friend was a merchant, known as Manikundala. Their friendship was between unequals, between a brahmana and a *vaishya*. It was between a prosperous person and a poor one. However, they always wished each other's welfare. On one occasion, Goutama spoke to the *vaishya* Manikundala, the lord of riches. In private, he affectionately addressed him repeatedly in these words. Goutama said, "To gather riches, we should go to the mountains and the oceans. Without articles that can give rise to pleasure, youth is futile. How can we exist without riches? Shame on a man who does not possess riches." Kundala[1027] told the brahmana, "My father has earned wealth. O supreme among *brahmana*s! What will I do with this great amount of wealth?" The brahmana again strongly urged Manikundala in these words. Goutama said, "If a person is satisfied with *dharma*, *artha*, *jnana* and *kama*, he is not praised. O friend! Embodied beings are praised only if they obtain excellence

---

[1027] That is, Manikundala.

in these. Blessed creatures are those who live on the basis of their own enterprise. If one is satisfied with riches that have been given by others, it is a hard life. O Kundala! In this world, a son who does not desire what he has received from his ancestors and does not talk about it, is honoured by his parents and praised. In this world, a son who has earned wealth through the strength of his own arms is successful. He does not touch his father's wealth. A son who earns riches himself and gives it to his father and relatives, is known as a true son. The others are like worms in the womb." Hearing the words of the greedy brahmana, he accepted these words. He swiftly collected his own jewels and riches and gave them to Goutama. He said, "With this wealth, as we will, we will travel in various lands. We will collect riches and wealth and return home again." The merchant said this truthfully. But the brahmana was a deceiver. The merchant did not understand that the brahmana was evil-souled, with wicked intentions. Without their fathers and mothers knowing, the two of them got together. For the sake of wealth, the merchant and the brahmana travelled from one land to another. The brahmana wished to steal the riches the merchant possessed. The brahmana said, "Through whatever means possible, I will take that wealth away. How wonderful is this earth, with its thousands of cities. Women are divinities of love and bestow whatever is wished for. Those enchanting ones are present in different places. What will I do? After carefully gathering some riches, if it is given to women, one can always enjoy oneself with them and life becomes truly successful. One can engage in singing and dancing and always be ornamented with courtesans. I will enjoy myself. But how will the *vaishya*'s riches come into my hands?" Goutama thought in this way. He laughed and spoke to Manikundala. "There is no doubt that creatures obtain prosperity, happiness and what they desire only through *adharma*. In this world, it is seen that creatures devoted to *dharma* always obtain a share of misery. Therefore, what purpose does *dharma* serve? It only leads to the fruit of unhappiness." The *vaishya* replied, "It is not like that. Happiness is based on *dharma*. Misery, fear, grief, poverty and hardships result from sin. Emancipation is based on *dharma*. If one follows one's own *dharma*, how can one be destroyed?" As they debated amongst themselves, it became an argument and they said, "Whichever person wins the debate, will win over the other person's riches. Let us ask—which side is stronger, the one with *dharma*, or the one with *adharma*?" "Material objects of this world are superior to the Vedas." "Wherever there is *dharma*, there is happiness." Arguing in this way, they asked all the people—"Between *dharma* and *adharma*, which is more powerful on earth? Tell us what is accurate. Which is stronger?" Among them, some said, "Those who follow *dharma* experience misery. Wicked people are happy." Defeated in this way, he handed over all his wealth to the brahmana.'

'However, Maniman[1028] was supreme among those who followed *dharma* and he praised *dharma* again. The brahmana asked Maniman, "Do you still praise *dharma*?" The *vaishya* said this was indeed the case and the brahmana spoke again. The brahmana said, "O *vaishya*! I have won over your wealth. Why do you still speak, without any sense of shame? Since I was victorious, *dharma* means doing whatever you wish to do." Hearing the brahmana's words, the *vaishya* smiled and spoke. The *vaishya* replied, "O friend! I think that those who do not have *dharma* are like shriveled grain among grain and small bees among those with wings. Among the four objectives of human existence,[1029] *dharma* is mentioned first. *Artha* and *kama* are mentioned after that. Such *dharma* is present in me. O best among *brahmanas*! How can you say you have defeated me?" The *brahmanas* again told the *vaishya*, "Let our two hands be the stake." The *vaishya* agreed to this. As was the case earlier, they went to people and asked. The brahmana said, "I am victorious." He severed his two hands and asked, "What do you think of *dharma* now?" Thus reprimanded by the brahmana, the *vaishya* replied in these words. The *vaishya* said, "Even when my breath of life sticks in my throat, I will think that *dharma* is superior. For embodied beings, *dharma* is like a father, a mother and a well-wisher." As a result of this dispute, the brahmana obtained wealth. The *vaishya* lost his riches and his two hands. Roaming around in this way, they reached Ganga and Yogeshvara Hari. O best among sages!

[1028] The same as Manikundala.
[1029] *Dharma, artha, kama* and *moksha*.

Wandering around as they willed, they conversed again. The *vaishya* praised Ganga, Yogeshvara and *dharma*. Full of great rage, the brahmana again reprimanded the *vaishya* in the following words. The brahmana said, "Your riches have been lost. Your hands have been severed. All that is now left is your breath of life. If you still continue to speak in this perverse way, I will use this sword to slice off your head." The *vaishya* laughed again and spoke to Goutama emphatically. The *vaishya* said, "I think that *dharma* is supreme. Do what you want. A person who criticizes *brahmanas*, *gurus*, gods, the Vedas, *dharma* and Janardana is a sinner and should not be touched. He is an evil-doer and should be ignored. Such a person who abuses *dharma* is evil-souled and wicked in conduct." At this, he angrily replied, "Since you still praise *dharma*, let our lives be the stake." O sage! Addressed by Goutama in this way, the merchant agreed. As was the case earlier, they asked people and people said what they had said earlier. On Goutami's southern bank, in front of Yogeshvara, the brahmana brought the *vaishya* down and plucked out his eyes. The brahmana said, "O *vaishya*! Since you have always praised *dharma*, you have been reduced to this state. You have lost your riches. You have lost your eyes. Your hands have been severed. O friend! I seek your permission to leave. Do not speak to me about this again." When he had left, the *vaishya* thought about this in his mind. "Alas! O Hari! I have been single-mindedly devoted to *dharma*. What is this hardship that has befallen me?" Kundala, best among merchants, was without any wealth. He had lost his hands. He had lost his eyes. Full of grief, he remembered *dharma*. Seated on the ground, he thought about this in many kinds of ways. He made no attempt to move. He was without any enterprise. He had descended into an ocean of grief.'

'On the eleventh lunar day in *shukla paksha*, when the day was over and the lunar disc had risen in the sky, Vibhishana arrived there. He followed the norms and worshipped the divinity Yogeshvara. Along with his son and surrounded by *rakshasas*, he bathed in Goutami Ganga. Vibhishana's son was like a second Vibhishana. He was known as Vaibhishani. On seeing him, he spoke to him. The one who knew about *dharma* heard the *vaishya*'s words and got to know exactly what had happened. He reported this to his great-souled father, the lord of Lanka. The lord of Lanka spoke affectionately to his son, who was an ocean of qualities. Vibhishana said, "The illustrious Rama is my *guru*. His friend is known as Hanuman and is revered by me. Earlier, on a certain occasion, he brought a large mountain. That mountain was a store of all the herbs. When the task was over, he took it back to the Himalayas, to the place he had brought it from. The immensely intelligent one brought vishalyakarani and *mritasanjivani*[1030] and gave them to Rama, whose deeds are unsullied. When the occasion arose, he told him what could be achieved through those. When the task was over, he returned the mountain to the divine range.[1031] Remembering and establishing Hari in his heart, he brought it. That is how the extremely generous one brought what everyone wished for. When he speedily took *vishalyakarani* back again, a bit fell down on the banks of Goutami, at the place where Yogeshvara Hari is." Vaibhishani answered, "O father! Without any delay, please show me where that herb is. In the three worlds, there is nothing better than alleviating the afflictions of someone else." Vibhishana agreed to this and showed his son where it was. Out of love for the *vaishya*, the son said, "*ishetva*"[1032] and cut off the tree's branch. The virtuous are always engaged in the welfare of others. Vibhishana said, "The powerful tree fell down on this mountain. Take its branch and place it on his heart. As soon as he is touched by it, he will regain his original form." Hearing his father's words, Vaibhishani, pervasive in his intelligence, did that and placed that piece of wood properly on the *vaishya*'s heart. Maniman got back his hands and eyes. Who is capable of understanding the power of *mantra*s and herbs?'

'He[1033] took that piece of wood and remembered *dharma*. The *vaishya* bathed in Goutami Ganga and prostrated himself before Yogeshvara Hari. He again picked up that piece of wood and

---

[1030] Two herbs which respectively heal wounds/stakes and revive the dead.

[1031] The Himalayas.

[1032] Literally, 'You are the one who contains/possesses.' More than the literal meaning, this implies taking the tree's permission.

[1033] Manikundala.

wandered around. He reached a king's city, known as Mahapura. The extremely strong king was known as Maharaja. He did not have a son. He did have a *putrika*,[1034] but she had lost her eyesight. He brought his daughter up like a son and took the following vow. "If a person restores my daughter's sight, I will bestow my daughter and this kingdom on him—irrespective of whether that person is a god, a *danava*, a brahmana, a *kshatriya*, a *vaishya*, or one born as a shudra, and irrespective of whether he possesses qualities, or does not possess qualities." This is the announcement the king made. Night and day, the *vaishya* heard this announcement and spoke. The *vaishya* said, "There is no doubt that I will restore the sight of the princess." They quickly seized the *vaishya* and presented him before Maharaja. As soon as she was touched by that piece of wood, the princess got back her eyesight. The king was astounded and asked, "Who are you?" The *vaishya* accurately reported to the king all that had happened. The *vaishya* said, "I possess this kind of power because of the favours of *brahmanas*, *dharma* and austerities, the strength of donating many and various kinds of *dakshina* and the energy of this divine herb." Hearing the *vaishya*'s words, the lord of the earth was amazed. The king exclaimed, "Such a great person is almost like a god. Otherwise, how can he display such kinds of powers? I will bestow my daughter and this kingdom on him." Having made up his mind, he gave him his daughter and the kingdom.'

'On one occasion, he[1035] went out to amuse himself and was filled with great distress. "Without a friend, what does this kingdom mean? Without a friend, how can there be happiness?" The *vaishya*'s son started to constantly think about the brahmana. Among those with bodies, this is a sign of nobility of birth. Their minds are always moist with compassion, even towards those who cause injury. When Maharaja left for the forest, Manikundala became the king. On one occasion, while he was ruling over the kingdom, he saw the brahmana Goutama. Manikundala saw him. All his

---

[1034] In the absence of a son, a daughter who is brought up as a son and heir.

[1035] Manikundala.

wealth had been taken away by evil gamblers. Since he knew about
dharma, he took his brahmana friend with him and honoured him.
He told him everything about *dharma*'s powers. For the removal of
all the sins, he made him bathe in Ganga. Along with all those who
were born in their own *gotra*s, and all the *brahmanas* and relatives
who were born in their own country, with Vriddha-Koushika as
the chief, the *vaishya* and the *brahmanas* performed a sacrifice
near Yogeshvara. They worshipped the gods and went to heaven.
Since then, that tirtha has been known as Mritasanjivani *tirtha*,
Chakshu[1036] *tirtha* and Yogeshvara *tirtha*. Even if one remembers it,
everything auspicious is obtained. It brings delight to the mind and
destroys every kind of misery.'

Chapter 2(101) (Urvashi *tirtha*)

Brahma said, 'The place known as Urvashi *tirtha* yields the fruits
of a horse sacrifice, if bathing, donations and the worship of
Mahadeva and Vasudeva are performed there. The divinity there
is Maheshvara and Hari is in the form of Sharngadhara.[1037] There
was a king named Pramati. He was powerful and a universal
emperor. He defeated his enemies and quickly went to Indra's
world, surrounded by the gods. O Narada! He saw the lord of the
gods there, along with the Maruts. Pramati, bull among *kshatriya*s,
laughed at Indra, who held dice in his hand. On noticing that he
was laughing, Hari[1038] spoke to Pramati. Indra said, "O immensely
intelligent one! This is the abode of the gods, where the Maruts
play. Having conquered the directions, you have reached heaven.
Come and play with me." King Pramati heard Hari's biting words.
He agreed and replied, "O Indra of the gods! What do you think
should be the stake?" Hearing Pramati's words, the lords of the
gods spoke to the king. Indra replied, "Urvashi is our stake. She

---

[1036] Chakshu means eye.
[1037] The one who holds the Sharnga bow.
[1038] Indra.

can only be obtained through all kinds of sacrifices. I think that
Urvashi should be my stake. O king! What do you think should be
yours?" Hearing Indra's words, Pramati proudly replied, "O lord
of the gods! O Shatakratu! I will offer as a stake whatever you
think is appropriate." Indra told Pramati, "Your right hand will be
your stake, along with your armour, arrows and *dharma*. Give me
that as stake and let us play." Pledging these stakes, they started
to gamble. Pramati won Urvashi, the celestial lady. Having won
her, Pramati arrogantly spoke to Shatakratu. Pramati said, "O lord!
Offer something else as stake and I will play with you again." Indra
replied, "This *vajra* is worthy of the gods. I will offer this and the
excellent chariot, Jaitra,[1039] as a stake. O king! Without thinking
about it, I will play with you, with your hand as a stake." Pramati
laughed. He seized the unmatched dice, decorated with jewels, and
said, "O Shakra! I have won." Meanwhile, the great lord of the
*gandharva*s arrived there. He was known as Vishvavasu and he was
skilled in playing with the dice. Vishvavasu said, "O king! Using
the knowledge of the *gandharva*s, I will play with you." The king
agreed and replied, "I have won." After defeating both of them,
the foolish king addressed Indra of the gods in these sinful words.
Pramati said, "O Mahendra! Whether it is in a battle, or whether
it is in gambling, you will never be victorious. Therefore, worship
me. Tell me. How did you become Indra of the gods?" He proudly
told Urvashi, "Go and become a servant-maid." Urvashi replied,
"I will behave towards you just as I behave towards the gods. In
none of your sentiments, should you try to shame me." Pramati
told her, "I have servant-maids like you. O fortunate one! Why
are you ashamed? Go and become a servant-maid." There was a
lord of the *gandharva*s, known as Chitrasena. He was the powerful
son of Vishvavasu and he heard the king's words. Chitrasena said,
"O king! O lord of the earth! I will play with you with all these as
stake, the kingdom and life, both yours and mine." Chitrasena and
the excellent king agreed to this and played, full of great anger.
Chitrasena won. He bound the king up in the great noose of the
*gandharva*s. Chitrasena won back everything, Urvashi, the kingdom,

---

[1039] The name of Indra's chariot.

the treasury, the army and everything else. All of Pramati's riches now became Chitrasena's.'

'His son was a child and spoke to the immensely wise and energetic priest Madhucchanda, descended from Vishvamitra's lineage. Pramati's son asked, "What sin has my immensely intelligent father committed? Why has he been bound? How can he regain his own status? How can he be freed from the bondage?" Hearing Sumati's[1040] words, the excellent sage meditated. Madhuchhanda told him about where Pramati was. Maduchhanda said, "O immensely intelligent one! Your father has been bound in the world of the gods. There are many taints associated with gambling. He has been dislodged from his kingdom. Anyone who goes to an assembly of gamblers suffers from hardships. O son of a king! There are taints associated with gambling, drinking and eating flesh. Evil-souled people always develop sins from these. Each one of these leads to what is undesirable, sin and hell. Desiring vehicles, seats and other things, gamblers indulge in such things, even if they have been born in noble lineages. They love the resultant quarrels. What need be said about ordinary people who are gamblers? The wife of a gambler is always tormented. The sinful gambler looks at his wife and is also tormented. Bereft of all pleasure, the evil-doer looks at her and always says, 'Alas! In this wheel of samsara, there is no sinner who is my equal. In this world, I do not obtain the slightest bit of pleasure from material objects. In the two worlds, no gambler is ever seen to be happy. It is evident that he is always ashamed and his mind is scorched. He loses his dharma. He is devoid of happiness. He wanders around, with all his pride gone. For those who are brahmanas, any profession other than gambling is praised. Even agriculture, animal husbandry and trade are permissible, but no gambling. Anyone who wishes to lose his riches should resort to gambling as a profession.' People who strive for dharma, artha and kama are deprived of all manliness. It is an activity that is condemned in the Vedas, but your father has accepted it. O son! Therefore, what shall we do? We will do what you say. Which learned person can deviate from the path determined by the one

---

[1040] Sumati was Pramati's son.

who ordains?" Hearing the priest's words, Sumati replied. Sumati said, "What must my father, Pramati, do to get back his kingdom again?" Madhuchhanda meditated again and addressed Sumati in these words. "O child! Go to Goutami and worship Shankara, Aditi, Varuna and Vishnu. He will then be freed from his bondage." Agreeing to this, he quickly went to Ganga and prostrated himself before Janardana. He worshipped Shambhu. He was controlled in his vows and tormented himself through austerities. His father was in bondage for one thousand years. After this, he was released from the gods and got his kingdom back again. Because of Shiva and Isha[1041] and because of what his own son had done, he was freed from his bondage. He obtained the knowledge of the *gandharvas* and was loved by Shatakratu. Since then, that *tirtha* has been known as Shambhu *tirtha*, Vishnu *tirtha*, Urvashi *tirtha* and the *tirtha* of gamblers. What cannot be obtained through the favours of Shiva, Vishnu and the mother of the rivers? Bathing and donating there, yield many kinds of auspicious fruits. One is freed from the bondage of sins and all kinds of calamities are destroyed.'

Chapter 2(102) (Godavari reaches the ocean)

Brahma said, 'There is a place known as Samudra *tirtha*.[1042] It yields the fruits of all the *tirtha*s. I will tell you about its nature. O Narada! Listen attentively. Released by Goutama, Ganga, the destroyer of sins, flowed towards the ocean, for the sake of ensuring the welfare of the worlds. When she was proceeding, the divine river was held in a *kamandalu* by me. Shambhu, the *paramatman*, held the goddess in his matted hair. She originated from Vishnu's feet and was brought down to the world of the mortals by the great-souled brahmana. When she is remembered, she destroys sins. She is greater than the greatest. On seeing her, the ocean wondered. "She deserves to be worshipped. She is the goddess of the universe. She

---

[1041] Meaning Vishnu.
[1042] Samudra is the ocean.

is worshipped by Brahma, Isha and others. If I do not advance and
welcome her, I will be tainted by *adharma*. When a great-souled one
arrives, if a person is deluded and does not advance to welcome,
he becomes a sinner in both the worlds and no one can save him."
Thinking this, the lord of jewels assumed an embodied form. The
lord of the rivers joined his hands in salutation and spoke to Ganga.
The ocean said, "I will not say anything. Let the water that is in
the nether regions, on earth and in the firmament enter me. There
are jewels, *amrita*, mountains, *rakshasas* and gods inside me. I hold
many other terrible things too. Along with Kamala,[1043] Vishnu
always sleeps in me. In the world of mobile and immobile objects,
there is nothing that is impossible for me. When a great person
arrives, out of insolence, if a person does not rise up in welcome, he
is dislodged from *dharma* and other things and goes to hell. Except
for being subdued by Agastya,[1044] I do not have any fear or regret.
What need be said about someone like you, more glorious than
all of them? O goddess Ganga! I am speaking to you. Peacefully,
merge into me. But if you come in a single form, I cannot bear it.
There can be a confluence if you merge into me in many different
forms. O goddess! That is the way a confluence can take place, not
otherwise. O Ganga! Therefore, one should consider the confluence
in many different forms." Addressed in this way, Ganga replied to
the ocean, the lord of the waters. The goddess Goutami said, "Act
in accordance with my words. Bring the wives of the *saptarshis*,
with Arundhati[1045] at the forefront, here, along with their husbands.
Bring them here and I will assume a small form. The confluence
with you can then take place." Agreeing to this, he brought the
saptarshis and their wives. Surrounded by the *rishis*, the goddess
divided herself into seven streams. In seven flows, Goutami Ganga
merged into the ocean. Those seven flows of Ganga were named
after the seven *rishis*. Bathing and donating there, donations,
devotedly reading and hearing about it and remembering it, bring
all the desired auspicious fruits. In the three worlds, there is no place

---

[1043] Lakshmi.
[1044] Agastya drank up the ocean.
[1045] Vasishtha's wife.

superior to Samudra *tirtha*. It destroys sins and bestows objects of pleasure and emancipation. It brings delight to the mind.'

Chapter 2(103) (Bhimeshvara *tirtha*)

Brahma said, 'O Narada! There is a place named after the sacrifice of the *rishi*s. The seven *rishi*s sat down to perform austerities there, in the place where Bhimeshvara Shiva exists.[1046] In this connection, I will tell you the account about the gods, the *rishi*s and the ancestors. Listen attentively. I will tell you about an auspicious account that bestows everything that is desired. After the seven *rishi*s, Ganga divided herself into seven flows. O Narada! Vasishthi was to the south. Vishvamitri was to its north. The next one is known as Vamadevi. The auspicious Goutami is in the middle. Another one is known as Bharadvaji. Atreyi was next. Jamadagni was the last. These were the seven flows. All those great-souled *rishi*s performed a sacrifice together. Those accomplished *rishi*s undertook a great sacrifice.'

'The gods had a powerful enemy, known as Vishvarupa. While this was going on, he arrived at the sacrifice undertaken by the sages. Following the norms, he observed *brahmacharya*, austerities and worship. Humbly, and in due order, he spoke to all the *rishi*s. Vishvarupa said, "For the sake of my welfare, all of you must certainly do what I wish. Let me have a powerful son, whom even the gods will find to be invincible. O sages! Please tell me whether this can be accomplished through sacrifices or austerities." The immensely intelligent and great-minded Vishvamitra spoke to him. Vishvamitra said, "O son! Many kinds of fruits are obtained through *karma*.[1047] There are three causes. The first cause is the *karma* itself. The second cause is the agent who undertakes the *karma*. The motive is said to be the third cause. The learned know that *karma* alone is not the

---

[1046] This is probably the one in Nilagunda, Karnataka.
[1047] There is some interpretation in translating what Vishvamitra said. The meanings are not self-evident.

seed. While *karma* is a cause, there are other causes too. The fruits depend on their presence or absence. But fruits are dependent on *karma*. Know that there are two types of *karma*—that which is being done and that which has already been done. When one does what should be done, that has been spoken of as a means. However, *karma* becomes successful because of the motive. Hence, both these are causes. Therefore, a discriminating being undertakes *karma* according to the motive. The fruits are said to be according to the motive. If one undertakes *karma* in the proper way, but the motive is absent, the fruits are perverse. Everything depends on the motive. Therefore, the fruits that austerities, vows, donations, *japa*, sacrifices and other rites bestow, depends on the motive. *Karma* yields fruits according to the motive. Know that there are three kinds of motive—based on *sattva*, *rajas* and *tamas*. Accordingly, the fruits follow *karma*. Depending on the quality of the motive, *karma* has wonderful forms. Therefore, an accomplished person will decide on his motive according to his wishes. Thereafter, when the required *karma* is undertaken, it yields the appropriate fruits. If fruits are meant to be given, the one who bestows fruits grants the corresponding fruits. There is nothing for the agent to do, except undertake the *karma* naturally. The motive varies, according to *sattva* and the other *guna*s. Motive initiates it and fruits are dependent on the motive. *Karma* is the cause behind *dharma*, *artha*, *kama* and *moksha*. *Karma*, determined by motive, is responsible for both emancipation and bondage. In this world and in the next world, *karma* follows a person's natural qualities. Accordingly, many different kinds of fruits swiftly manifest themselves. Because of differences in motives, an object can appear differently. What is enjoyed and what is done is distinguished according to the motive. If you undertake *karma* according to the right motive, you will obtain what you wish for."
Hearing the worlds of the intelligent *rishi*, Vishvamitra, for a long period of time, he tormented himself through austerities. However, his motive was that of *tamas*. Vishvarupa undertook terrible *karma*, terrifying even to the gods. The best among the *rishi*s saw him and constantly tried to restrain him. However, he followed his own internal rage and undertook that terrible *karma*. He dug up a terrible pit and ignited a terrible fire. In the cavity of his heart, he meditated on a terrible and fierce being. On witnessing that he was tormenting

himself, an invisible voice spoke. "O Vishvarupa! Leaving aside your matted hair, offer yourself as an oblation into the fire. You will have a son who will be just like you. He will be Indra. He will be Varuna. He will be everything. Leaving aside your matted hair, offer yourself as an oblation. From that sin, he will be born as a sinner. He is the one mentioned in the Vedas as Vritra. Who knows about the ferocity and greatness of the lord of the universe? He creates everything, but is not touched by anything." The voice recited this and stopped. The lords among sages bowed down to Bhimeshvara and returned to their own hermitages. Vishvarupa was extremely terrible. His form was as terrible as his deeds. His motive was terrible. His body was terrible. He meditated and offered himself as an oblation. Therefore, in the Puranas, one reads about the divinity as Bhimeshvara.[1048] There is no doubt that bathing and donating there, bestows emancipation. A person should read and hear it devotedly. He should prostrate himself before Shiva, the lord of the gods, who has a terrible form there. He is known as the one who destroys every kind of sin as soon as the refuge of his feet are remembered. He is the one who bestows emancipation. Godavari is the one who destroys all sins. She bestows the supreme objective. This is true everywhere, but is especially true at the place where she merges into the ocean. If an embodied being bathes at the confluence of Godavari with the ocean, he become a performer of good deeds. He saves his ancestors from all the terrible hells and goes to the city of Tripura's enemy. Bhimanatha[1049] is indeed the *brahman* itself, worshipped and known through *Vedanta*. If one sees him, an embodied being is never submerged in the misery of *samsara* again.'

Chapter 2(104) (Confluence of Ganga and the ocean)

Brahma said, 'Ganga deserves to be worshipped by the gods. She merged into the eastern ocean. She was followed by all the gods

[1048] Literally, the terrible lord.
[1049] That is, Bhimeshvara.

and praised by all the sages—Vasishtha, Jabali, Yajnavalkya, Kratu, Angiras, Daksha, Marichi, Vaishnavas,[1050] Shatatapa, Shounaka, Devarata, Bhrigu, Agniveshya, Atri, Marichi,[1051] Daksha,[1052] Manu, Goutama, Koushika, Tumbaru, Parvata and others who had cleansed their sins. There were Agastya, Markanda, Pippala, Galava and others who were devoted to yoga. There were Vamadeva, Angirasa and Bhargavas, who were wise in their knowledge of the pleasant *shruti* and *smriti* texts. All of them knew the meanings of the Puranas. They knew a lot and followed Goutami, the divine river. They praised her, with many *mantra*s from the *shruti* texts. As they praised her, they were cheerful in their minds. On seeing that she had merged, Shiva and Hari showed themselves to the sages. While the immortals and ancestors watched, those two gods, who dispelled the afflictions of everyone, were praised. The Adityas, the Vasus, the Rudras, the Maruts and the guardians of the worlds—all of them joined their hands in salutation and praised Hari and Shankara. O Narada! Those two gods are always present in the seven confluences. They are always established in the confluence of Ganga with the ocean. The divinity Maheshvara is known as Goutameshvara there.[1053] Along with Rama,[1054] Madhava is always present there. For the welfare of the worlds and for my own reason, I established Shiva in the place known as Brahmeshvara. Along with the gods, I praised the one known as Chakrapani.[1055] Vishnu is present there, along with the gods and large numbers of Maruts. In the place known as Aindra *tirtha*, the divinity is present as Hayamurdha.[1056] The gods are also present where Vishnu has the form of Hayamurdha. Someshvara Shiva is present in the place known as Soma *tirtha*. For the sake of Indra, who is famous for *soma*, the gods and the *rishi*s prayed to Soma—*indrayendo pari*

[1050] Vishnu's devotees.

[1051] Marichi is repeated.

[1052] Daksha is repeated.

[1053] The one in Manthani.

[1054] Lakshmi.

[1055] The one with a *chakra* in the hand (*pani*), Vishnu.

[1056] Horse-headed, the same as Hayashira/Hayagriva.

srava.[1057] "There are many suns in the seven directions. There are seven *hotri*s and officiating priests. There are seven gods, the Adityas. O Soma! Protect us. Flow Indu[1058], for the sake of Indra. O King Soma! Protect us with this oblation. It has been prepared for you. Let enemies not be able to destroy us, nor anything that belongs to us. Flow Indu, for the sake of Indra. O sage Kashyapa! Raise up your voice, with the *mantra*s in the *sukta*s composed by the *rishi*s. In the sacrifice, bow down to Soma, the lord of the herbs. Flow Indu, for the sake of Indra. I am the artisan.[1059] I am the physician. I am the one who lays down the measure. With many kinds of intelligence, we are like cows for the earth. Flow Indu, for the sake of Indra." The *rishi*s spoke in this way and obtained some for the wielder of the *vajra*. When they gave it to him, Shatakratu's sacrifice was completed.'

'Since then, that place has been known as Soma *tirtha* and Agni *tirtha* is in front of it. Agni performed great sacrifices and worshipped me, obtaining what his mind wished for. Through my favours, he obtained it. I am always present there. For the welfare of the worlds, Vishnu and Shiva are also present there. Therefore, it is named after Agni. Aditya *tirtha* is beyond this. The one who is the form of the Vedas is always worshipped there. Assuming a different form, he arrives there at midday, to see me, Shankara and Hari. Therefore, at midday, everyone should always be bowed down to. That is because one doesn't know what form Savitar will assume when he arrives. Therefore, it is named after Aditya. Brihaspati *tirtha* is after that. Brihaspati was worshipped by the gods there. That is the reason it has this name. He also performed many sacrifices there. That is the reason it is named after Brihaspati. As soon as one remembers that *tirtha*, the adverse planets are pacified. There is another *tirtha* on the excellent mountain of Indragopa.

[1057] This is a *mantra* from *Rig Veda* 9.113. This bit means, 'Flow Indu (Soma) for the sake of Indra.'

[1058] These are now *mantra*s from *Rig Veda* 9.114. We have skipped the Sanskrit and only given the English translation.

[1059] This bit is from *Rig Veda* 9.112. The artisan means Vishvakarma, the physician means the two Ashvins.

For a different reason, a great *lingam* was established there by the Himalayas. That *tirtha* is known as Adri *tirtha*.[1060] Bathing and donating there, yield all the auspicious desires. In this way, Goutami Ganga originated from Brahmagiri. As she proceeded towards the ocean, I have briefly mentioned a few of the *tirtha*s. They are auspicious and possess many secrets. Goutami is famous in the Vedas and the Puranas and the worlds and the *rishi*s bow down to her. O Narada! Who is capable of describing her powers completely? Who has that strength? If one devotedly tries and something is left out, there is no offence in that. There is no doubt about this. For the welfare of the worlds, I have sought to give some indications. Which lord is capable of describing her powers in every *tirtha*? Perhaps Vishnu, Lakshmi's consort, or Someshvara Shiva might be able to. O immensely wise one! Over the course of time, some *tirtha*s, sometimes, come to possess qualities for men. But Goutami always has these. She is always sacred, everywhere. Who is capable of describing and recounting her qualities? Therefore, it is appropriate that one should prostrate oneself before her.'

Chapter 2(105) (Benefits of listening to Ganga *mahatmya*)

Narada said, 'O lord of the gods! O master of the gods! You have said that Ganga has three presiding divinities. The auspicious one was brought down by a brahmana. The sacred one purifies the universe. O supreme among the gods! In the beginning, in the middle and in the end, along both banks of the river, she is pervaded by Vishnu, Isha and you. I have still not obtained satisfaction. Please tell me again, briefly.'

Brahma replied, 'She was originally in the *kamandalu*. She then flowed from Vishnu's feet. She was next stationed in Maheshvara's matted hair and is bowed down to. Because of the energy and power

---

[1060] *Adri* means mountain.

of the brahmana and because Shiva was carefully worshipped, she reached the sacred mountain and flowed towards the eastern ocean, where the goddess reached and merged. She has all the *tirtha*s and bestows what men desire. Her powers are special. In the three worlds, I do not think that there is any superior *tirtha*. Through her powers, any wish of the mind can be satisfied. Till today, no one has been able to describe her greatness. She is the supreme *brahman* that one devotedly speaks about. It is my view that there is no *tirtha* superior to her. If one mentions her in conjunction with any other *tirtha*, that won't be *dharma*. My words, which describe her qualities, are like *amrita*. After hearing those words, why doesn't everyone's intelligence turn towards what is beneficial? O sage! In the three worlds, this is indeed a great wonder.'

Narada said, 'You know about *dharma*, *artha*, *kama* and *moksha* are the one who can instruct. The Vedas and their mysteries, the smriti texts, the *dharma shastra* texts and everything eles has a foundation in your words. O lord! Among *tirtha*s, donations, sacrifices, austerities, divinities, *mantra*s and service, what is best? Please tell me. O illustrious one! Whatever you faithfully say must be true. It cannot but be otherwise. O Brahma! I have a doubt and you should use your words to sever it.'

Hearing what was in his mind, Brahma was surprised.

Brahma replied, 'O Narada! Listen. I will tell you about the supreme mystery of *dharma*. There are four kinds of *tirtha*s. There are also four *yuga*. There are three *guna*s. There are three beings who are the eternal divinities. It is said that the Vedas and the *smriti* texts are four. The objectives of human existence are four. There are four kinds of speech.[1061] O Narada! Along with *samatva*,[1062] the *guna*s are also four. Because *dharma* is eternal, *dharma* generally exists everywhere. There are many kinds of views about what one should try to achieve and about how those can be achieved. These always depend on two kinds of things, the time and the place.

[1061] Probably meaning *vadin* (sonant), *samvadin* (consonant), *anuvadin* (assonant) and *vivadin* (dissonant), the four classes mentioned in *natya shastra*.

[1062] Meaning equilibrium.

Depending on the time and the place, *dharma* is always enhanced, or diminished. Depending on the nature of the *yuga*, it diminishes by one quarter.[1063] O immensely wise one! *Dharma* depends on both, the time and the place. Even when *dharma* is a function of time, it can be firmly established in the place. Thus, though it is diminished with the *yuga*, it does not decay because of the place. If both are absent, *dharma* becomes non-existent. When *dharma* is firmly established in the place, it possesses all its four quarters. That is the reason *dharma* exists in places that assume the form of *tirtha*s. When it is *krita yuga*, *dharma* has the foundation of both time and place. In *treta yuga*, *dharma* loses one of its quarters, but can find it in a specific place. In *dvapara*, only half of what is due to time is left, but *dharma* can find that in the place. With a single quarter left in *kali*, *dharma* wavers and faces a difficulty. However, even when this happens, for those who know, *dharma* does not diminish. Depending on the nature of the *yuga*, there are differences in how it is established. The qualities and the qualities of the agents differ. Therefore, the way *dharma* is established is wonderful. *Tirtha*s, *varna*s, Vedas, heaven and *moksha* have increased or diminished powers, depending on the qualities. Depending on their nature and inclination, *dharma* is distinguished. Time is spoken of as the one who causes the manifestation. The place is what is manifested. O brahmana! When time is the one who causes the manifestation, its foundation is accordingly established. There is no doubt about this. The forms of the gods and the Vedas are appropriate to the *yuga*. This is also true of *karma*, *tirtha*, *jati* and *ashrama*. In *satya yuga*, people worship a *tirtha* where all three divinities are present. In *treta yuga*, a *tirtha* with two of the divinities present is worshipped. In *dvapara yuga*, a *tirtha* with one divinity present is worshipped. It should be known that there is nothing like this in *kali yuga*. However, listen to something else. In *krita yuga*, a *tirtha* is known to belong to the gods. In *treta yuga*, it is known to belong to the *asura*s. In *dvapara yuga*, it is said to belong to the *rishi*s. In *kali yuga*, it is said to belong to humans. O Narada! I will tell you about

---

[1063] *Dharma* has four parts in *krita yuga*, three in *treta yuga*, two in *dvapara yuga* and one in *kali yuga*.

another reason for this. Listen. You have asked me about Goutami and I will describe it to you in detail.'

'O great sage! Ever since Ganga reached Hara's head, Shambhu started to love Ganga the most. Uma is the goddess of the three worlds. She is the mother who is engaged in the welfare of the universe. She is spoken of as the serene *shruti* texts. She is the one who bestows objects of pleasure and emancipation. She got to know what was in the god's mind and spoke to Gajavaktra.[1064] Hearing his mother's words, Gajavaktra spoke to her. Gajavaktra asked, "O mother! What needs to be done? Please instruct me and there is no doubt that I will do it." Uma told her son, "Ganga is established in Maheshvara's matted hair and Isha has truly come to love her a lot. She needs to be brought down. O son! It is strange that Isha is also always present there. The gods, the eternal Vedas, all the *rishi*s, men and ancestors also reside wherever Shiva is. Therefore, Ishana Mahadeva, the lord of the gods, must be made to return. When the divinity withdraws from Ganga, everyone else will also withdraw. Listen to my words. In every possible way, Shankara must be made to withdraw from her." Hearing his mother's words, Ganeshvara spoke again. Ganeshvara replied, "I am not capable of making the divinity Shiva withdraw. As long as Shiva does not withdraw, the gods are also incapable of withdrawing. O mother of the universe! There is another reason too. Earlier, the great-souled Goutama *rishi* made Ganga descend, to ensure the welfare of the three worlds. She was worshipped by the worlds. Following your words, I suggested the means. Full of energy, the brahmana worshipped the lord of the gods, using austerities. He praised Bhava. Pleased, Shankara spoke to Goutama. Shankara said, 'O immensely intelligent one! Choose a sacred boon. Ask for whatever is loved and desired by your mind. Today, I will give you everything that you wish for.' When Shiva said this, while I listened, Goutama replied. 'O Shankara! Give me the one who is in your matted hair. I ask for the auspicious Ganga. What will I do with any other boon?' Shambhu, who ensures the welfare of all the worlds, spoke again. Shambhu said, 'You have not asked anything for yourself. Ask for something that is extremely difficult to obtain.' Indomitable in spirit, Goutama

---

[1064] The one with a face like an elephant, Ganeshvara.

joined his hands in salutation and spoke to Bhava.[1065] Goutama said,
'Amongst everything, the most difficult thing is to see you. O Shankara!
Through your favours, I have been able to achieve that today. As soon
as they remember your feet, learned people become successful in their
objectives. O Maheshvara! What need be said when you have been
directly seen?' Addressed by Goutama in this way, Bhava was filled
with delight. 'O immensely intelligent one! You asked for this for the
welfare of the three worlds. Ask something for your own self.' Shiva
told the brahmana this. Addressed again in this way, the brahmana
thought and spoke to Shiva. He was not depressed in spirit. He spoke
humbly full of devotion towards Shiva. He again asked for the welfare
of all the worlds. While the guardians of the worlds heard, Goutama
spoke. Goutama said, 'O Vrishadvaja! The goddess has been released
from Brahmagiri. As she proceeds towards the ocean, you must always
be present everywhere. O lord of the universe! For those who desire
fruits, you alone are the one who bestows fruits. O lord of the gods!
The other *tirtha*s are only auspicious in certain places. But the places
where you exist are known to always bestow what is auspicious.
You have handed over Ganga, who was located in the crown of your
matted hair. O Shankara! You are always present with her and every
such place is a *tirtha*.' Hearing Goutama's words, Shiva happily spoke
to him again. Shiva said, 'O Goutama! Any person can give anything
anywhere, as long as he is full of devotion. He may go on pilgrimages,
bathe, donate and offer water-rites to the ancestors. He may hear,
read and remember. As long as a man is controlled in his vows and
faithfully does this along the Godavari, he obtains *dharma* equivalent
to the *dharma* obtained by donating the entire earth, with its seven
*dvipa*s, mountains, groves, forests, jewels, herbs and beautiful oceans.
He is adorned with equivalent *dharma*. This is said to be the *dharma*
associated with Goutami. O brahmana! Near the river Godavari, the
ground is like that. At the time of a solar or lunar eclipse, a learned
man may be controlled in his vows, in my presence. He may devoutly

---

[1065] The text suggests that all this is being reported by Brahma. While
Brahma is indeed telling Narada everything, this bit is still part of the
Ganeshvara quote. Ganeshvara is still speaking to his mother.

donate a beautiful cow, along with her calf, to a brahmana[1066] or to
Vishnu, at a confluence that is famous in the world. O best among
brahmanas! A person who donates in this way obtains good merits.
However, Goutami is a great river, worshipped by the universe. If a
man bathes and donates along her, he obtains superior good merits.
Therefore, brought by you, Godavari Ganga will destroy every kind
of sin and bestow everything that is desired.' O mother! I heard
Shiva tell Goutama this. This is the reason why Shambhu is always
present near Ganga. O mother! Who is capable of making that ocean
of compassion return? O mother! However, it can still be achieved.
Because of the noose of impediments, men may be bound. They will
not go to Godavari, even though she is nearby. They will not prostrate
themselves before the divinity Shiva. They will not remember and
praise him. O mother! So as to satisfy you, that is what I will do.
Please pardon my words. But if one doesn't do what you say, there is
hardship.' Since then, Vighnesha creates some impediments for men.
However, ignoring the impediments, if a person devotedly goes to
Goutami and performs the worship, he is successful in this world and
nothing else remains for him to do. If a worst among men desires
to leave his house, many kinds of impediments present themselves.
However, if he places them on his head and firmly steps towards going
to Ganga, what fruits cannot be achieved? Baring Shiva himself, who
is capable of describing her powers?"'

'Following the steps indicated in *itihasa*, I have briefly described
them. In this world of mobile and immobile objects, there are methods
for achieving *dharma*, *artha*, *kama* and *moksha*. All of them have
been described in detail in *itihasa*. It has brought together everything
stated in the Vedas and in the *smriti* texts. The mysteries and the
reasons are always described. For the welfare of the universe, this
has been properly stated and described in this Purana, who is full of
many kinds of *dharma*. If a person faithfully reads or hears one of
its *shloka*s or one of its lines and pronounces the words "O Ganga!
O Ganga!" he obtains everything auspicious. It has the capacity to
destroy the impurities of *kali yuga*. It brings every kind of success. It

[1066] Here, we have translated 'lord of the earth' as *brahmana*, instead
of king, as that seems to be more appropriate.

is sacred and auspicious. If one utters the excellent word, "Ganga", worshipped by the universe, one obtains every fruit that is desired. O Goutama! O fortunate one! You have done well. Who else is your equal? You are the one who lovingly brought Ganga to Dandaka forest. Even if a person utters the words "O Ganga! O Ganga!" from a distance that is one hundred *yojana*s away, he is freed from all sins and goes to Vishnu's world. In the three worlds, the number of *tirtha*s is three and a half crores. When Brihaspati is in Simha, all these come to Ganga to have a bath. When Brihaspati is in Simha, bathing once in Godavari is equal to bathing in Bhagirathi for sixty thousand years. O son! Because of Shiva's command, such is Goutami. Bathing in her bestows emancipation on all men, all the time. Hearing about this yields the fruits that are obtained from undertaking thousands of horse sacrifices and one hundred *vajapeya* sacrifices. O Narada! If a person keeps the Purana narrated by Brahma in his house, he faces no fear on account of *kali yuga*. This excellent Purana must not be narrated to anyone. It must only be narrated to those who are faithful and tranquil, great-souled ones who are devoted to Vishnu. It bestows objects of pleasure and emancipation. As soon as a man hears it, he accomplishes his objective. If a person writes it down in the form of a book and gives it to a brahmana, he is freed from all sins and does not have to enter a womb again.'

This ends Part II of Brahma Purana, the Goutami Mahatmya section.

This ends Brahma Purana.